School and Community Partnerships

SCHOOL, FAMILY, AND COMMUNITY PARTNERSHIPS

Preparing Educators and Improving Schools

JOYCE L. EPSTEIN

Center on School, Family, and Community Partnerships
Johns Hopkins University

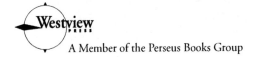

Westview
PRESS

A Member of the Perseus Books Group

Copyright © 2001 by Westview Press, A Member of the Perseus Books Group

Published in 2001 in the United States of America by Westview Press, 5500 Central Avenue, Boulder, Colorado 80301-2877, and in the United Kingdom by Westview Press, 12 Hid's Copse Road, Cumnor Hill, Oxford OX2 9JJ

Text design by Heather Hutchison

Find us on the World Wide Web at www.westviewpress.com

Library of Congress Cataloging-in-Publication Data
Epstein, Joyce Levy.
   School, family, and community partnerships : preparing educators and improving schools / by Joyce L. Epstein.
      p.   cm.
   Includes bibliographical references.
   ISBN 0-8133-8755-8 (pb)
   1. Community and school—United States.   2. Home and school—United States.   3. School improvement programs—United States.   I. Title.
LC221.E68   2001
371.19'0973—dc21   2001022040

The paper used in this publication meets the requirements of the American National Standard for Permanence of Paper for Printed Library Materials Z39.48-1984.

This book is dedicated to Molly and Ed Levy, whose love and support helped three sisters set and reach their goals; and to Paul Jerrold Epstein, who turned research on school, family, and community partnerships into treasured real-life experiences.

Contents

Part Two
Applying Research on School,
Family, and Community Partnerships

Tables and Figures

Tables

Figures

Preface and Acknowledgments

TWENTY YEARS SOUNDS like a long time to work on a topic, but it is not very long to build new knowledge about school, family, and community partnerships. My colleagues and I began our research on parent involvement in elementary schools in 1981. We initiated studies of involvement in the middle grades in 1987 and in high schools in 1990. Since 1987 we also have explored state and district policies and conducted fieldwork with schools at all levels. All of this information led in 1996 to the establishment of the National Network of Partnership Schools at Johns Hopkins University. The Network now guides schools, districts, and states to use research-based approaches to build better partnership programs and to study new questions that arise. All of my proposals, projects, publications, presentations, and interactions with many wonderful researchers, educators, and parents have been a true delight, making 20 years seem like a very short time indeed.

My work, conducted in various education research centers at Johns Hopkins University, was primarily supported by the U.S. Department of Education's Office of Educational Research and Improvement (OERI) and its predecessor, the National Institute of Education (NIE). The centers at Johns Hopkins were renamed with each new major grant and included the Center for Social Organization of Schools (CSOS); Center for Research on Elementary and Middle Schools (CREMS); Center for Research on Effective Schooling for Disadvantaged Students (CDS); Center on Families, Communities, Schools and Children's Learning; and, currently, Center for Research on the Education of Students Placed at Risk (CRESPAR).

Grants from the Lilly Endowment, Edna McConnell Clark Foundation, Leon Lowenstein Foundation, and the National Endowment of the Arts also supported my research and development projects. To give this work a permanent home, I established the Center on School, Family, and Community Partnerships in 1995. That center presently is supported by grants from Disney Learning Partnership and the Wallace–Reader's Digest Funds.

Over the years, many funders became colleagues in helping me think about needed directions for school, family, and community partnerships. They include Oliver Moles and Ron Pedone at OERI; Joan Lipsitz, Gayle Dorman, and Kent McGuire, then at Lilly; John Van Gorder at Lowenstein; Hayes Mizell at the Clark Foundation; Jane Quinn and Catherine Pino at Wallace–Reader's Digest

Funds; and Laurie Lang, Tony Jackson, and Pamela Rubin at Disney Learning Partnership. I value their ideas and support.

Special thanks are due to many educational leaders in Baltimore who have supported, assisted, and inspired me for many years. These include Jerry Baum, who directed the Fund for Educational Excellence and who was a partner in fieldwork for nearly 10 years; Lucretia Coates, the first facilitator for School, Family, and Community Partnerships, whose deep knowledge about schools and families continues to influence our work; and Vivian Jackson, who assisted middle schools for several years in implementing interactive homework. Other talented facilitators for School, Family, and Community Partnerships worked with more than 160 elementary, middle, and high schools in Baltimore City to help teams of educators and parents learn how to organize and maintain programs of school, family, and community partnerships. They include (by history of participation) Marsha Powell-Johnson, Paula Williams, Brenda G. Thomas, Joyce Bowyer, Marsha Greenfeld, Patricia Kidd-Ryce, Joann E. Brown, Sandra E. Morgan, and Anjali Patel. Their knowledge and talents have helped many schools turn research into action.

Many other district leaders in Baltimore supported the work of their facilitators and their schools in developing programs of partnership. They include (by history of participation) Gary L. Thrift, Clifton Ball, Cynthia Janssen, Christolyne Buie, Charlene Cooper Boston, Sandra L. Wighton, Ellen D. Gonzales, Anne Carusi, Jeffrey Grotsky, Barry Williams, Patricia E. Abernathy, Cecil Ramsey, Irby Miller, and Carole Seubert. The area superintendents and other administrators taught me valuable lessons about how different district leadership styles may contribute to improving schools' connections with families and communities.

Many local foundations supported the fieldwork that was conducted with my community-based partner, the Fund for Educational Excellence. I owe a great debt to the Fund for making it possible to systematically gather ideas from countless teachers, principals, parents, and students in the Baltimore City Public School System (BCPSS). BCPSS was a "learning laboratory" for school, family, and community partnerships for more than a decade and helped identify the challenges and possibilities for organizing districtwide programs of school, family, and community partnerships in elementary, middle, and high schools. The knowledge gained with the help of so many in BCPSS now is being applied and adapted across the country.

At this writing, the National Network of Partnership Schools at Johns Hopkins has grown to include over 1,200 schools and 1,400 school districts located in more than 30 states, as well as 18 state departments of education. Educators and families from across the country have added their expertise and activities to this field of study. Their trials, tribulations, and triumphs have led to questions for new research, and their hard work on partnerships contributed to the repertoire of practical approaches that are included in this volume. I am convinced that researchers learn most about schools by collaborating with educators, parents, students, and others who implement programs and report their results. All that we know or ever will learn about school, family, and community partnerships—or any aspect of school improvement—depends on researchers, educators, families, students, and others sharing the role of expert.

Many colleagues and students at Johns Hopkins University have worked with me over the years on the studies that are reported in this volume. I am grateful to all of them, especially Henry Jay Becker, who met the challenge in 1981 to start our research program with a survey of educators and parents. His creative work and collaborative spirit helped generate many questions for the studies that followed. Other valued partners at Hopkins included Susan L. Dauber, Susan C. Herrick, Seyong Lee, Lori Connors-Tadros, and many helpful graduate and undergraduate students.

Colleagues who worked with me from 1990 to 1995 in the Center on Families, Communities, Schools and Children's Learning included codirector Don Davies and researchers Carole Ames, Josephine Bright, Melvin Delgado, Larry Dolan, Charles Glenn, Nitza Hidalgo, Vivian Johnson, Sharon Lynn Kagan, Colleen Morisset, Saundra Nettles, Diane Scott Jones, Sau-Fong Siu, and the late Susan M. Swap. These researchers conducted many studies that contributed important ideas for understanding partnerships. Their work, and that of many other researchers cited throughout this volume, deepened my thinking about the course content that is needed to prepare teachers, administrators, social workers, school psychologists, sociologists of education, and others to understand and conduct school, family, and community partnerships.

Special thanks are due to my colleagues at the Center on School, Family, and Community Partnerships: Mavis G. Sanders, Natalie Rodriguez Jansorn, Jameel Nolan, Mary G. Nesbitt, Karen Clark Salinas, Steven B. Sheldon, Beth S. Simon, Frances Van Voorhis, and Kenyatta Williams. Many were helpful readers of earlier versions of this volume, and all influenced the topics, discussions, and activities that appear in various chapters. This uniquely talented team is dedicated to conducting important research and to making research useful in practice. Other longtime colleagues and valued friends at Johns Hopkins University have supported and encouraged my work, including James M. McPartland, Edward L. McDill, and the late John H. Hollifield. All of my colleagues at CSOS and our research partners at CRESPAR/Howard University are working to show that social and educational research can help educators improve schools for all students and benefit families and communities.

My family's interest in this work has been most appreciated, including my late mom's unconditional support, my dad's continuing attention and active "clipping service" on education, and my sisters' endless encouragement. My son Paul's experiences in school literally brought my theories and research to life. He showed how important it was for his mom and dad to be positively involved in his education, and how crucial it is for the child—the student—to be the focus of school, family, and community partnerships.

In 1998, over 160 deans of education and other leaders from colleges and universities around the country participated in a survey of how well their institutions prepared educators to involve families and communities in children's education. Their responses revealed a dramatic gap between the high importance they placed on the topic of school, family, and community partnerships and the low preparedness of their graduating teachers and administrators to successfully involve parents and community partners in children's learning. The data guided the expansion and completion of this volume as one way to help new teachers and administrators begin their professional lives with a better understanding of and more useful approaches to family and community involvement.

The field of school, family, and community partnerships is young, vibrant, and rapidly improving. Each year, more and better studies are completed, including master's theses and doctoral dissertations, and more innovative and effective approaches to partnerships are implemented in practice. I expect attention to partnerships to become as important a topic in research, policy, and practice as other components of school organization and school improvement. This book aims to encourage new research by young scholars, inform the development of effective policies on partnerships, and guide teachers and administrators on a clearer path to partnerships with all families and communities.

Joyce Levy Epstein
Baltimore, February 2001

PART ONE

Understanding School, Family, and Community Partnerships

Introduction

WHOSE DREAMS ARE THESE? Children will like school; work hard; do the best they can; graduate from high school; continue their education; gain employment; and become good citizens, friends, and members of their families. Countless surveys and projects with thousands of educators, families, and students reveal that these are common goals and dreams. Too often, though, these ideals are unattained by this nation's children. How can more students be helped to meet these goals?

To answer questions about *goals*, we must ask questions about *roles:* What should families do, what should schools and communities do, and what should students do to reach their common objectives for children's futures? These questions are the reasons for studying, implementing, and improving school, family, and community partnerships.

MATCHING RHETORIC WITH PRACTICE

No topic about school improvement has created more rhetoric than "parent involvement." Everyone says that it is important. In study after study, teachers, parents, administrators, and even students from elementary through high school say that involvement benefits students, improves schools, assists teachers, and strengthens families. There are basic beliefs and agreements about the importance of families and the benefits of parent involvement.

There also are some clearly expressed hopes or wishes for parent involvement. Teachers would like families to assist, guide, and influence their children to do their schoolwork. Families wish teachers would let them know how to help their children at home. Students wish their families were knowledgeable about their schools and helpful to them on school matters at home. These desires are expressed in numerous studies with diverse samples, in varied communities, and at all grade levels.

There is some confusion and disagreement, however, about *which* practices of involvement are important and *how* to obtain high participation from all families.

Some educators expect parents to become involved in their children's education on their own. If they do, they are "good" parents. If not, they are irresponsible, uninterested, or "bad" parents. Some educators and parents expect the school to "tell parents what to do" and that parents will simply respond. Neither of these approaches—waiting for involvement or dictating it—is effective for informing or involving all families.

Research suggests that "partnership" is a better approach. In partnership, educators, families, and community members work together to share information, guide students, solve problems, and celebrate successes. Partnerships recognize the shared responsibilities of home, school, and community for children's learning and development. Students are central to successful partnerships. They are present in all three contexts, and they link members of these groups to each other. Students are actors and contributors, not bystanders or recipients, in the communications, activities, investments, decisions, and other connections that schools, families, and communities conduct to promote children's learning.

What should programs of partnership look like? How can they be developed? How can teachers, administrators, parents, and others in communities be prepared to initiate and maintain productive relationships in their work to benefit students? How can teachers, administrators, and others who work with children and families put the best knowledge and practices to work? How must practices change over time as students proceed through the grades? How can research address these questions to increase knowledge and improve practices?

THE NEED

All teachers and administrators have one thing in common, whether they are in Maine or California; work with students in grade 1 or grade 12; teach Anglo, Latino, African American, Asian American, Native American, or other students; or have students succeeding or having trouble in school: *All teachers' students have families.* All schools serve children and families.

Students' families, however, are not all the same. Some students live with two parents, and others have only one parent at home; some parents are working and some unemployed; some speak English and some speak other languages. Indeed, there is an endless variety of characteristics and situations of students, families, schools, and communities.

However configured, however constrained, families come with their children to school. Even when they do not come in person, families come in children's minds and hearts and in their hopes and dreams. They come with the children's problems and promise. Without exception, teachers and administrators have explicit or implicit contact with their students' families every day.

Also, all students and their families live in communities, whether close to or distant from schools, that are diverse in geography and history and in economic and social characteristics. Wherever they are located, all communities have individuals, groups, and organizations that care about children; share responsibility for children's futures; and are potentially valuable resources for children, families, and schools. Children, families, and schools also are potentially valuable resources for their communities as well.

Educators need to understand the contexts in which students live, work, and play. Without that understanding, educators work alone, not in partnership with other important people in students' lives. Without partnerships, educators segment students into the school child and the home child, ignoring the whole child. This parceling reduces or eliminates guidance, support, and encouragement for children's learning from parents, relatives, neighbors, peers, religious leaders, and other adults.

THE GAP

Teachers learn to teach reading, math, science, or other specialties. They learn to teach kindergarten or other grade levels. Administrators learn how to manage whole organizations, create schedules, and supervise many tasks and people. Most teachers and administrators, however, are presently unprepared to work positively and productively with one of the constants of life in school: their students' families.

Consequently, many educators enter schools without adequately understanding the backgrounds, languages, religions, cultures, histories, structures, races, social classes, or other characteristics of their students or families. Without such information, it is impossible for educators to communicate effectively with the people who matter most in their schools, classrooms, and communities. Far too many educators initially do not have a clear understanding of the part they must play in developing and maintaining *programs* of partnership that inform and involve all families every year that the children are in school. Without such programs, it is impossible for all families to initiate and maintain active roles in their children's education and development. Even fewer educators understand and are prepared to work with businesses, agencies, and institutions in their students' communities to promote their success in school and beyond.

A Southwest regional survey in 1980 found that only 4 to 15 percent of teacher educators taught a full course or part of a course on parent involvement, and only 37 percent of teacher educators surveyed included even one class period on the topic. Just about all of the practicing teachers and administrators who were surveyed agreed that better preparation was needed to understand and work with families. Over 70 percent thought that there should be a required course on the topic in undergraduate education (Chavkin and Williams, 1988).

At about the same time, Becker and Epstein's (1982) survey (see Reading 3.1) of elementary school teachers in the state of Maryland indicated that few attributed their practices of partnership to their formal education. Most teachers who had even one class on the topic of parent involvement specialized in early childhood or special education or took administrative or other courses as part of an advanced degree. Sometimes the topic was limited to families' legal rights and responsibilities to make specific decisions about children with special needs.

Little change occurred during the 1980s and 1990s in the preparation of educators to understand and work with families and communities to support their children's education, despite considerable progress in research, policy, and practice. An informal survey of six campuses of the University of California that prepare teachers found that few courses or even classes within courses were offered on family and school partnerships (Ammon, 1990). In Minnesota, more than half of the 27 colleges and universities with degree-granting undergraduate education programs offered no course related to parent involvement for prospective teachers of grades K–12, and only one had a required course on the topic (Hinz, Clarke, and Nathan, 1992). Most courses that were offered were in early childhood and special education; only 6 of 1,300 course listings focused on comprehensive programs of school, family, and community partnerships.

A companion (to the Hinz et al. work) study of the 50 states indicated that *no* state required an entire course in family involvement for the certification or licensing of teachers. Nine states required coverage of the topic in some course, with a few more specifying that requirement for teachers of early childhood (11 states) and special education (15 states). Approximately one-quarter of the states identified the need for elementary educators to show competence (however attained) in school, family, and community partnerships. Even fewer states expected middle or high school educators to have competence in family involvement. Only seven states required principals or central office administrators to study parent involvement or demonstrate proficiency in promoting parent involvement in their schools. No state includes this competency in recertification or renewal of certification, thereby reducing the likelihood that practicing educators will update their family and community involvement skills (Radcliffe, Malone, and Nathan, 1994).

Another study of official certification materials from all states in 1992 found very similar patterns, concluding that parent involvement is not yet a high priority in state certification (Shartrand, Weiss, Kreider, and Lopez, 1997). The researchers conducted follow-up inquiries with approximately 60 teacher education programs in 22 states that mentioned family involvement in their certification requirements. The results indicated that teacher education programs respond to state policies by offering the topic in some courses. Only nine of the universities in this sample reported having a required course on family involvement, usually for teachers of young children.

The picture is still bleak. Most teachers and administrators are not prepared to understand—much less design, implement, and evaluate—productive connections with the families of their students. Administrators are not prepared to guide and lead their staffs to develop strong school programs and classroom practices that inform and involve all families about their children's learning, development, and educational plans for the future. The problem is serious for all educators, particularly for those who will teach in economically distressed or disadvantaged communities (Mac Iver and Epstein, 1990). Little attention has yet been paid to the need to prepare teachers or administrators to work with communities or to link community resources to the goals of students, families, and schools.

There are some signs of change, however. Deans of education and other curriculum leaders at California campuses attended a conference in 1989 on the need to add school, family, and community partnerships to teacher education. They had many good ideas about how to better integrate the topic in their required and elective courses for prospective teachers and administrators. Some took action quickly. Within one year, five of the eight campuses represented at the conference reported making a few changes in the content of courses and assignments. The changes included adding readings about parent involvement to existing courses, professional development, or supervised teaching seminars. Also, on one campus discussions on the topic of partnerships were added to a support program for first-year teachers who had graduated from the university the prior year (Ammon, 1990). These examples show that small changes, such as adding readings or discussions about school, family, and community partnerships to existing courses, can be made quickly. Other changes may take longer if they require formal university approval, such as creating a required or elective course on school, family, and community partnerships.

Positive actions have been taken by individual professors at various colleges and universities who have designed courses on school, family, and community partnerships and added readings to existing courses in education, sociology, psychology, and social work (deAcosta, 1996; Kaplan, 1992; Katz and Bauch, 1999; Van Wyk, 1998). Bermudez and Padron (1988) designed a graduate-level course that includes classwork and fieldwork to help educators learn to communicate better with language minority families. Evans-Shilling (1996) initiated a responsive field-based course that provides educators with experiences in family-school relations. Allexsaht-Snider and others designed a required course for educators preparing for early childhood education that includes understanding family-school relations, and teachers work with families in school, at home, and in the community (Allexsaht-Snider, Phtiaka, and Gonzalez, 1996). She and her colleagues at the University of Georgia also infuse these topics into elementary education, field experiences, and other programs to prepare educators.

Morris and her colleagues at the University of Memphis found positive effects of a four-semester school and community relations course on students' understanding of and attitudes about partnership, confidence to work with families, and feelings of comfort and competence in planning family involvement activities and programs (Morris, Taylor, and Knight, 1998). The contents of their course increased prospective teachers' knowledge, skills, and attitudes about parent-teacher collaboration. Other individual professors also are beginning to increase their undergraduate and graduate students' understanding of partnerships as one essential component of school and classroom organization as well as an important influence on student learning and development (see descriptions of other courses and projects in Shartrand, Weiss, Kreider, and Lopez, 1997). Follow-up studies are needed to see if and how such courses affect practice.

These examples suggest that colleges and universities are now more ready than previously to add the topic of school, family, and community partnerships to their curricula. More are aware of federal policies (such as Head Start, Title I, Even Start, and Goals 2000) that emphasize connections with families and that include mandates for school administrators and teachers to develop partnership programs. More college and university professors have read the research on school, family, and community partnerships that accumulated during the 1990s, and more have graduate students at the master's and doctoral degree levels who, based on their own reading or experiences, are choosing the topic of partnerships for their studies (Epstein, Sanders, and Clark, 1999).

The new initiatives on school, family, and community partnerships by individual professors in selected locations reach very few prospective teachers or administrators. Nevertheless, the efforts of increasing numbers of professors of teacher education, educational administration, and other courses are important indicators that more and better preparation of educators on school, family, and community partnerships is possible.

States are beginning to include or consider school, family, and community connections in their qualifications for certification of teachers, administrators, counselors, and other educators. For example, California's Education Code and Commission on Teaching Credentialing, Ohio's Standards Revisions Teacher Education and Certification, Illinois's General Supervisory Endorsement, Minnesota's Higher Education Coordination Board, Virginia's student teaching requirements, and other legislation refer to the importance of school practices to involve families and communities.

National organizations for college and university program accreditation are beginning to set standards for teacher and administrator education that explicitly include preparation and competence in working with parents (INTASC, 1992; NCATE, 1994). National teacher examinations for new teachers and national assessments for highly accomplished teachers include parent and community involvement (NBPTS, 1994).

The time is right for advancing undergraduate and graduate education with options for required and elective courses in school, family, and community partnerships, or readings in courses across disciplines that include attention to families, schools, children, and communities. Simultaneously, it is important to encourage state leaders to improve certification requirements for educators by including competencies in conducting programs of partnership.

THE GOALS

Just as teachers are prepared to teach subject matter, and administrators are prepared to direct and manage schools and programs, educators also must be prepared to draw upon all the resources that will help them with their work, including families and communities. This volume aims to:

- add an understanding of school, family, and community partnerships to the education and training of teachers, administrators, and professionals in related fields;
- include this knowledge in the definition of what it means to be professional;
- promote respect, trust, appreciation, and collaboration between and among all adults who influence children's lives and learning;

- enable educators to apply their knowledge to develop effective programs of partnership in their schools and classrooms;
- integrate school, family, and community partnerships in broader programs of school improvement, giving explicit attention to improving practices of involvement; and
- encourage research on the simultaneous influences of home, school, and community contexts on children's learning and development.

The professional preparation of educators must include the information they need to understand and maintain school, family, and community partnerships. Without this information, we restrict the resources that teachers and administrators can call upon to help students do their best. Also, we limit the influence that families have on their children's learning and development for at least 12 years of school life. In so doing, we weaken the support for learning that children receive from their families and communities. All of these restrictions make it harder for students to succeed.

If we start with what we know now, we can make real progress in helping prospective and practicing educators gain the knowledge and tools they need to understand and mobilize families and communities to assist children's learning and development from preschool through high school. If we continue to encourage and conduct research on families, schools, communities, and their connections, we will build a stronger knowledge base and develop new ideas about improving policies, practices, programs, and results.

ACHIEVING THE GOALS

To recognize the need, fill the gap, and achieve the goals stated above, we must change some of the requirements, options, and content of higher education courses. Courses must be revised and expanded to include a solid base of information to prepare teachers and administrators to understand and involve families in their children's education. Ideally, there should be at least one comprehensive *required* course on school, family, and community partnerships (or home-school relations, or something similar) in every preparatory program. This requirement should be considered as important as a course in teaching reading, math, or other subjects in the preparation of school teachers, and as important as any major required course in educational administration or other educational specialties.

A less meritorious policy decision that still improves on present preparatory programs is to organize and offer *elective* courses on the topic of partnerships. There also should be a formal plan of whether and how readings on school, family, and community partnerships are integrated in other required and elective courses to ensure that all who are preparing for professions in education have had substantial exposure to and experience with the theory, research, and application of school, family, and community partnerships.

The call for required, elective, and/or integrated courses is offered with a mix of urgency and understanding. It is urgent that educators better understand families' roles in children's education and how to implement programs of school, family, and community partnerships. It is understood that change in higher education must be discussed and planned to offer students these options. Leaders in higher education can take steps to ensure that the educational professionals who are prepared in their courses, programs, departments, colleges, and universities are, in fact, well qualified to teach children and work with families and communities as partners in education.

In colleges and universities, courses also should be enhanced to prepare researchers in sociology, psychology, education, and related disciplines to understand the questions, methods, and problems of studying multiple contexts—home, school, and community—and the interactions of individuals in these contexts. We must prepare the next generation of education researchers to study the overlapping spheres of influence on children's learning and development, just as we must prepare the next generation of teachers and administrators to work effectively with families and communities.

USING THIS VOLUME

This book is about school, family, and community partnerships: how to think about them, talk about them, study and understand them, act on them, and improve them. It includes selected readings on the theory, research, policy, and practice of school, family, and community partnerships to provide a solid base of information on the development, directions, problems, and possibilities of these connections. The readings and accompanying exercises can be used as the basis for a full course or as supplementary materials in courses such as social foundations of education, learning and instruction, education policy studies, educational administration, counseling, sociology of education, sociology of family, educational psychology, school social work, and practice teaching. Following are suggestions for using this volume as a text for a full course or for supplementary readings.

A Comprehensive Required or Elective Course

This course covers the major topics that educators need to study to proceed thoughtfully in their work with children, families, and communities. This includes *theoretical perspectives, results of research* on particular approaches and understanding, *effective policies and practices* that teachers and administrators should understand and be able to use to best serve students and families, and *organizational strategies* to help educators and families work together to design and implement programs of partnership. Other texts or readings, activities, and projects may supplement this volume in a full course.

Supplementary Readings in Other Required or Elective Courses in Education and the Social Sciences

Readings on family, school, and community connections are important for fully understanding the sociology of education, sociology of the family, social foundations of education, school administration and management, political science, political action and organizations, social policy, school psychology, human development, social work, community services, group processes, urban policy, and related fields. Individual chapters, articles, and activities in this volume may be selected to bring the topic of partnerships to courses in these specialties. Presently, many courses teach about families without paying attention to children's schools; teach about schools without attending to their connections with families and communities; or instruct about communities without considering the connections and investments of community groups and organizations with educators, families, and children. The readings in this volume will help broaden the background and understanding of undergraduate and graduate students about the important *connections* among home, school, and community for the purposes of assisting students, strengthening families, and renewing communities.

Selections from this volume also may be woven into thematic courses. For example, a course in education, sociology of education, or related fields may take a historical perspective, addressing the question: How have research, policy, and practice on school, family, and community connections changed over the past half century? Family and school connections have changed from rather superficial, peripheral activities to theory-driven and research-based frameworks that guide basic and applied research and school program development. Research on "community" has changed from using mainly demographic data that rank locations as high or low on social or economic variables to studying the people and processes within any community that can assist student learning. More and different themes would emerge in a course that covers the organization and effects of connections among children, families, schools, and communities over the past two centuries.

Another elective course might address comparisons of school, family, and community connections across nations, to explore common and distinct international themes about families, schools, and communities. A third thematic course might focus on social-psychological perspectives of the interconnections and interrelationships of major institutions and individuals. This includes two-way, three-way, or many-way connections between and among schools, families, students, peer groups, and communities.

Linkages to Courses on the Methods of Teaching Specific School Subjects and Practice Teaching

Readings on school, family, and community connections should be included in curricula that prepare educators to teach all subjects. That is, teachers of every subject and grade level need to understand, design, select, conduct, and evaluate appropriate connections with families about their children's learning in specific subjects and their effects on academic decisions such as course choices or the selection of enrichment programs. Teachers of all subjects and grade levels need to understand, design, select, conduct, and evaluate connections with individuals and groups in communities to maximize learning opportunities in reading, math, writing, science, computer skills, art, music, family life, physical education, and other subjects.

There are important theoretical issues to study and discuss, such as whether and how sharing "power" with parents *increases or decreases* teachers' power and professional standing. Also, there are specific skills to learn, such as how to design homework that enables children to share skills and ideas at home, how to inform families about what their children should know and do each year in each subject, and how to inform families about children's progress and involve families in the assessment of students' work. Teachers of all subjects also should understand the community near the school; the home communities of their students; and the connections with businesses, groups, and individuals in the surrounding community that may help enrich and extend their teaching and students' learning.

Educators who are being prepared to teach, administer, or work in the schools of the 21st century should learn about the scope and expansion of research and practice in the field of school, family, and community partnerships. This information should help them develop their own perspectives; understand the pros and cons, strengths and weaknesses of various approaches; and thoughtfully select or design strategies to communicate with and involve families and communities in children's education.

Other Information

Even if a required course covers all of the topics in this volume, undergraduate and graduate students still will need other information about families, schools, and communities to be prepared for their professions. For example, students need to read about the family as a social organization, the influence parents have on their children at various age levels, diversity in family backgrounds and cultures, and trends in family life. Similarly, professionals who work with families and children need to read about school and classroom organization to understand basic school structures, functions, staffing, and alternative curricular and instructional approaches for educating students. Educators need to build their knowledge about community structures, processes, and services. The readings in this volume address these topics only as they affect the design and conduct of school, family, and community partnerships.

Of course, no single course or class in higher education will provide all the information and examples that professionals need to make decisions about which practices to use in every school in which they work. Nevertheless, a basic course or substantial coverage in several courses should increase awareness and understanding of the topic, alert educators that collaborating with families is part of their professional responsibility, and provide many ideas and examples to help teachers and administrators "tailor" programs and practices of partnership to their particular school, family, and community settings.

Links to Inservice Education

The vast majority of practicing educators, social workers, school psychologists, and others who work with families and children have had *no* prior formal education in school, family, and community partnerships. Thus, there is and will continue to be a great need for inservice education for practitioners in pre-, elementary, middle, and high schools as states, districts, and schools elect to improve their programs to involve families and communities in children's education.

Most inservice programs are limited to a few hours' duration and simply introduce teachers and administrators to some new practices of partnerships. Several readings and activities in this volume could be used in educational workshops with practicing educators, social workers, school psychologists, parent representatives, school board members, and others. A companion volume—*School, Family, and Community Partnerships: Your Handbook for Action* (Epstein, Coates, Salinas, Sanders, and Simon, 1997)—may be a more useful inservice guide to help schools, districts, and states develop and maintain their practical programs of partnership.

SETTING A COURSE

The chapters that follow include selected readings on the theory, research, policy, practice, applications, and implications of school, family, and community partnerships based on my work with colleagues and schools for many years. Along with the readings are commentaries, discussion topics, and activities designed to encourage undergraduate and graduate students' thinking, research, action, and additional reading on school, family, and community partnerships.

Some of the readings were previously published in journals or books to introduce the topic of partnerships across disciplines to diverse audiences: educators, sociologists, school psychologists, policy leaders, and so forth. Others have been presented to limited audiences at professional meetings, hearings, and workshops, or include materials that were developed with educators for use in schools.

This volume brings together a set of basic readings under one cover, with comments on new issues; topics for class discussions; questions and activities for classwork, homework, and extended projects; and other material for use in undergraduate and graduate courses in education, psychology, sociology, and other disciplines. The contents extend traditional curricula by emphasizing the connections of child development, socialization, and education with the institutions of school, family, and community and the individuals within them. Some chapters should be particularly useful for improving the actions and activities of prospective teachers, administrators, and others who plan to work with schools and families. Other chapters aim to encourage research on new and needed questions to advance the field of school, family, and community partnerships. The readings include literature reviews, original research, policy issues, activities for practice teaching and subject specialization, and a review that integrates all these topics. The final chapter serves as a bridge to the practical, inservice education and program development that must be conducted in all schools. The chapters cover the following topics:

Chapter 2—Theory and Overview. Two readings provide a broad perspective on school, family, and community partnerships; introduce a theory of overlapping spheres of influence; and lay a foundation on which to build new studies and practices of partnership.

Chapter 3—Research. Several original research studies are presented with data collected from teachers, parents, and students on the nature and extent of involvement, relationships among partners in children's education, and effects of practices of partnership. The readings help students examine research methods, interpret results, and consider implications for school practice or for new studies to extend the field.

Chapter 4—Policy. Several readings summarize issues and advances in state, district, and school policies of partnership. These include articles and guidelines on policy development, samples of state and district policies, and studies of important issues. These readings show how research helps influence policy, how policy sparks improvements in practice, and how new policies and practice open opportunities for more and better research.

Chapter 5—Framework. The main reading in this chapter integrates the information from the previous chapters, linking research to practice. It summarizes the framework of six types of involvement, sample practices of partnerships, the challenges that must be met in excellent programs, and results that can be expected if practices for each type of involvement are well designed and well implemented. The reading and related activities provide a ready reference for educators to fully understand what it means to be prepared to conduct and improve partnerships.

Chapter 6—Practical Applications. This chapter introduces two approaches for involving families in children's learning at home and at school that grew from the results of the research reported in previous chapters. Educators may use these ideas in their practice teaching and, later, in their classrooms. The two processes were developed with educators. One illustrates and organizes interactive homework assignments; the other illustrates and organizes productive family and community volunteers. Both demonstrate ways to organize family and community involvement to increase student learning.

Chapter 7—Strategies for Action in Practice, Policy, and Research. This chapter summarizes an action-team approach for implementing comprehensive programs of school, family, and community partnerships. As a team, educators, parents, and community members work together to promote children's success in school. Leadership, teamwork, written plans, funding, internal and external support, action, evaluations, and continuous improvement must be organized to sustain partnership programs in the same way that these organizational factors support reading, math, testing, and other standard school programs. This final chapter also summarizes the volume's central themes and major conclusions about school, family, and community partnerships.

FEATURED TOPICS FOR DISCUSSION

The chapters include topics that may be singled out for special attention in class discussions and for further study. In Chapter 2, for example, theories of authority and decision making and their applications at school, district, and state levels are explored, and may be expanded. In Chapter 3, the involvement of parents in one- and two-parent homes is discussed to focus on what schools may do to involve all parents, not just those who usually become involved on their own. This chapter also introduces homework as an important school-family connection. In Chapter 4, the complex issue of funding for school, family, and community partnership programs and practices is featured, along with comments and activities about state and district leadership that may be of particular interest in educational administration courses. Chapter 5 discusses how specific activities for six types of involvement pose unique challenges and lead to different results for students, parents, and teachers. Chapter 6 illustrates how to implement viable family and community connections with the curriculum by organizing volunteers who present interdisciplinary discussions of art and social studies and by designing interactive homework for students to discuss with their families at home. This information may be helpful for all curricular specialists and student teachers. Chapter 7 shows how all of the research and development in this volume may be applied in practice by organizing school Action Teams for Partnerships. Plans for partnerships must be written as clearly as plans for lessons.

The chapters introduce provocative and useful new terms that change the way we think about school, family, and community partnerships. For example, Chapter 2 describes *school-like families* and *family-like schools* to contrast collaborative actions with previous narrow views of the different goals and missions of these institutions. This chapter also asks readers to consider how the *multiplication of labor* may describe how educators and families help students learn better than the *division of labor* that was previously emphasized in studies of organizations. Chapter 3 illustrates and emphasizes the importance of multiple reporters and multiple measures of partnerships. This chapter also identifies 10 purposes for homework and discusses the need for improving the *design* of homework to ensure higher quality, before simply assigning more homework. Chapter 4 emphasizes the need for *side-by-side* policies to balance top-down and bottom-up approaches. It also recommends *food-for-thought stamps* for talent-development programs that support extracurricular, after-school, and summer enrichment activities for economically distressed students and families. Chapter 5 suggests *re-definitions* for each of the six types of involvement that will bring school, family, and community partnerships into alignment with family factors in the 21st century. For example, a new definition states that *workshops* for parents are not only meetings at school but also the content of those meetings disseminated to all who could not come, thereby enabling parents to *attend* workshops in different ways. Chapter 6 shows that homework can be purposely *interactive*, and that volunteers in the middle grades can make real contributions to student learning. Chapter 7 explains how concepts of *trust* and *mutual respect* are central to the success of all partnerships and how seemingly contradictory concepts of *equity* and *diversity* in partnerships must coexist. The readings and discussions in several chapters contrast what *is* and what *might be* in school, family, and community partnerships to encourage fuller interpretations of research results, new directions for research, and the implications and applications of research for school improvement.

ACTIVITIES AND EXERCISES

Each chapter includes comments and key concepts that extend the readings; topics for informal classroom discussions; classroom activities; written assignments; and field activities that encourage students to reflect on the readings, debate ideas, describe related experiences, and conduct short-term and long-term projects. Activities include oral discussions; written comments; interviews with parents, teachers, administrators, community members, and students; panel presentations; role play; school visits; and other activities. Sometimes questions are provided for students to use in their interviews, and at other times students are asked to compose their own questions. Some of the interviews with educators, parents, or others may be assigned to all students to be completed individually, or interviewees may be invited to the class for group interviews. Field activities and other tasks also may be assigned to individuals, pairs, or groups.

> *Selection of assignments.* There are more questions and activities in each
> chapter than students in most classes can address in one semester. Professors are encouraged to balance assignments so that students engage
> in a mix of reflective writing, interviews, research, discussions, and
> other activities. The assignments should reflect course themes and meet
> the needs of undergraduate or graduate students in teaching, administration, research, and other fields.
>
> *Answers to questions.* Most of the discussion topics and questions have
> many correct answers, not just one right answer. Some questions first
> ask students to "identify a school level (preschool, elementary, middle,
> or high) or grade level that interests you. . . ." Thus, students will select
> different settings on which to base their answers. Students should contribute ideas and written work using information from the readings as

well as their own perspectives and experiences. They should be asked to justify their responses based on data or summaries provided in the chapter or refute ideas with specific examples. It is important for professors to encourage well-argued discussions and debates based on the content of the readings, other research, data collected by students for homework or projects, and students' experiences.

Follow-up. Some assignments may be productively followed up in class by sharing ideas, discussing issues, and pooling data to create larger and more representative samples for additional discussions. Some exemplary products may be compiled in a resource notebook or computerized idea file for research and practice.

Adaptation. Professors are encouraged to adapt or expand the exercises to match the emphases of particular courses and classes. For example, topics and questions about home-school connections at the school level can be adapted and redirected to focus on district, state, or community issues to meet the needs of students in educational administration or community studies. Professors may increase the difficulty or length of assignments by requiring students to complete additional readings, conduct and report activities marked "optional," provide more examples, or complete other related activities.

Elaboration. The questions in each chapter may spark ideas for term papers, master's or doctoral theses, or other research projects.

SUMMARY

This book offers a clear perspective on the importance of theory-driven and research-based approaches to school, family, and community partnerships. To think about, talk about, and take action to improve home, school, and community connections that support students' education and school improvement, educators must have a foundation on which to build. It is not acceptable to base ideas and future actions only on personal, limited, or selected experiences. It is necessary to understand the basic and complex aspects of a field of study to decide whether, when, why, and how to apply research in practice or to select important questions for new research.

The volume supports five facts and one urgently needed action:

- Fact: All students have families. All students and families live in communities. Families and communities are important in children's lives and, along with schools, influence students' learning.
- Fact: Teachers and administrators have direct or indirect contact with students' families every day of their professional careers.
- Fact: Few teachers or administrators are prepared to work with families and communities as *partners* in children's education.

- Fact: There is widespread agreement and accumulating evidence that well-designed programs and practices of school, family, and community partnerships benefit students, families, and schools.
- Fact: Although there is much more to learn, we know enough now to begin to implement school, family, and community partnerships that help students succeed.
- Action Needed: There must be immediate and dramatic changes in the preservice and advanced education of teachers, administrators, and others who work with schools, families, and students. Changes are needed in coursework and field experiences to prepare professionals to better understand, respect, and collaborate with parents; other family members; and individuals, groups, and organizations in communities that can help students succeed.

This book can help. The readings will provide a sense of history and a window on how the field of school, family, and community partnerships is developing. The comments, questions, and activities in each chapter introduce new topics that need to be discussed, debated, and studied. Whether used to organize a full course or to supplement other courses in education and social science, this volume introduces the field of school, family, and community partnerships, and should help to generate new ideas for research, policy, and practice.

REFERENCES

Allexsaht-Snider, M., H. Phtiaka, and R. M. Gonzalez. (1996). International perspectives: Preparing teachers for partnership. Paper presented at the Education Is Partnership conference, November, in Copenhagen, Denmark.

Ammon, M. S. (1990). University of California project on teacher preparation for parent involvement. Report I, April 1989 Conference and initial followup. Berkeley: University of California. Mimeographed.

Becker, H. J., and J. L. Epstein. (1982). Parent involvement: A study of teacher practices. *Elementary School Journal* 83: 85–102. (Reading 3.1).

Bermudez, A. B., and Y. N. Padron. (1988). University-school collaboration that increases minority parent involvement. *Educational Horizons* 66: 83–86.

Chavkin, N. F., and D. L Williams. (1988). Critical issues in teacher training for parent involvement. *Educational Horizons* 66: 87–89.

deAcosta, M. (1996). A foundational approach to preparing teachers for family and community involvement in children's education. *Journal of Teacher Education* 47: 9–15.

Epstein, J. L., L. Coates, K. C. Salinas, M. G. Sanders, and B. Simon. (1997). *School, family, and community partnerships: Your handbook for action.* Thousand Oaks, CA: Corwin.

Epstein, J. L., M. G. Sanders, and L. A. Clark. (1999). *Preparing educators for school-family-community partnerships: Results of a national survey of colleges and universities.* Report 34. Center for Research on the Education of Students Placed at Risk (CRESPAR). Baltimore: Johns Hopkins University.

Evans-Shilling, D. (1996). Preparing educators for family involvement: Reflection, research, and renewal. *Forum of Education* 51: 35–46.

Hinz, L., J. Clarke, and J. Nathan. (1992). *A survey of parent involvement course offerings in Minnesota's undergraduate preparation programs.* Minneapolis: Center for School Change, Humphrey Institute of Public Affairs, University of Minnesota.

Interstate New Teacher Assessment and Support Consortium (INTASC). (1992). *Model standards for beginning teacher licensing and development: A resource for state dialogue.* Washington, DC: Council of Chief State School Officers.

Kaplan, L. (1992). Parent education in home, school, and society: A course description. Pages 273–277 in *Education and the family,* edited by L. Kaplan. Needham Heights, MA: Allyn & Bacon.

Katz, L., and J. P. Bauch. (1999). The Peabody family involvement initiative: Preparing preservice teachers for family/school collaboration. *The School Community Journal* 9: 49–69.

Mac Iver, D. J., and J. L. Epstein. (1990). *How equal are opportunities for learning in the middle grades in disadvantaged and advantaged schools?* Report 7. Baltimore: Johns Hopkins University, Center for Research on Effective Schooling for Disadvantaged Students.

Morris, V. G., S. I. Taylor, and J. Knight. (1998). Are beginning teachers prepared to involve families in education? Paper presented at the annual meeting of the American Educational Research Association, April, in San Diego.

National Board for Professional Teaching Standards (NBPTS). (1994). *What teachers should know and be able to do.* Washington, DC: NBPTS. (See standards for specific certificates, e.g., family partnerships in early adolescence/generalist standards.)

National Council for Accreditation of Teacher Education (NCATE). (1994). *Standards for teacher education.* Washington, DC: NCATE.

Radcliffe, B., M. Malone, and J. Nathan. (1994). *Training for parent partnership: Much more should be done.* Minneapolis: University of Minnesota, Center for School Change, Hubert H. Humphrey Institute of Public Affairs.

Shartrand, A. M., H. B. Weiss, H. M. Kreider, and M. E. Lopez. (1997). *New skills for new schools: Preparing teachers in family involvement.* Cambridge, MA: Harvard Family Research Project.

Van Wyk, J. N., ed. (1998). *Home-school relations study guide.* Pretoria: University of South Africa.

Theory and Overview

THE FIRST READING in this chapter examines theories of family and school connections; discusses how data support or refute different theoretical perspectives; and presents a new theoretical model—*overlapping spheres of influence*—to explain and guide research on school, family, and community partnerships. This article should give you a good understanding of the organizational and interpersonal components of the theory of overlapping spheres of influence and how this view extends previous models.

The second reading is an overview of research on school, family, and community connections. It summarizes the theories discussed in the first reading, provides a literature review of research, introduces the framework of six types of involvement for studying partnerships and for developing comprehensive programs in schools, and discusses five topics and questions that would benefit from more research. The reading introduces topics that you can explore further in other chapters of this volume or in other journals and books and alerts you to important issues for new research and for improving school and classroom practice.

These readings provide information on how to think and talk about school, family, and community partnerships with a useful theory, a solid research base, and an overview of needed new studies.

Toward a Theory of Family-School Connections: Teacher Practices and Parent Involvement*

THREE PERSPECTIVES ON FAMILY-SCHOOL RELATIONS

Three perspectives currently guide researchers and practitioners in their thinking about family and school relations:

1. Separate responsibilities of families and schools
2. Shared responsibilities of families and schools
3. Sequential responsibilities of families and schools.

These perspectives are profoundly different. Assumptions based on the *separate* responsibilities of institutions stress the inherent incompatibility, competition, and conflict between families and schools. This perspective assumes that school bureaucracies and family organizations are directed, respectively, by educators and parents whose different goals, roles, and responsibilities are best fulfilled independently. It asserts that the distinct goals of the two institutions are achieved most efficiently and effectively when teachers maintain their professional, universalistic standards and judgments about the children in their classrooms and when parents maintain their personal attention and particularistic standards and judgments about their children at home (Parsons, 1959; Waller, 1932; Weber, 1947).

The opposing assumptions, based on shared responsibilities of institutions, emphasize the coordination, cooperation, and complementarity of schools and families and encourage communication and collaboration between the two institutions. This perspective assumes that schools and families share responsibilities for the socialization and education of the child. Teachers and parents are believed to share common goals for their children, which can be achieved most effectively when teachers and parents work together. These assumptions are based on models of inter-institutional interactions and ecological designs that emphasize the natural, nested, and necessary connections between individuals and their groups and organizations (Bronfenbrenner, 1979; Leichter, 1974; Litwak and Meyer, 1974).

The third perspective, *sequential* responsibilities of institutions, emphasizes the critical stages of parents' and teachers' contributions to child development. This approach is based on the belief that the early years of a child's life are critical for later success, and that by age five or six, when the child enters formal schooling in kindergarten or first grade, the child's personality and attitudes toward learn-

---

* By Joyce L. Epstein. Originally published in K. Hurrelmann, F. Kaufmann, and F. Losel, eds., *Social intervention: Potential and constraints* (New York/Berlin: de Gruyter, 1987), pp. 121–136. Reprinted with permission.

ing are well established. Parents teach their young children needed skills, arrange educational programs and experiences, and are guided or supported by social and educational agencies (e.g., pediatricians, preschool teachers, and the media) to prepare their children for school. At the time of children's formal entry into school, the teacher assumes the major responsibility for educating them (Bloom, 1964; Freud, 1937; Piaget and Inhelder, 1969).

Understanding the Contrasting Theories: Mechanisms Producing Family-School Relations

In addition to the three major theoretical distinctions between separate, shared, and sequential responsibilities, there are other theories that help explain the *mechanisms* for building family and school relations and the resulting variations in the connections between institutions and their members. Among the most useful are the symbolic interactionist and reference group theories. *Symbolic interactionism* (Mead, 1934) assumes that self-concept, personality, values, and beliefs are products of our interactions with others. The theory suggests that we learn how others perceive and anticipate our goals and behaviors, and that we fashion our behavior to fulfill the expectations of others and to receive their recognition. In terms of family and school connections, if teachers do not interact with parents, they cannot be informed about or understand the parents' expectations for their children and the teachers. They cannot shape their teaching behavior to be responsive to those expectations. If parents avoid teachers, they cannot be informed about or understand the schools' expectations for their children or the parents. They cannot shape their behavior to provide useful assistance to the students and teachers.

Reference group theory (Merton, 1968) makes other important connections between esteem and interaction. A reference group is a collectivity or an individual who is taken into consideration by another group or individual to influence their attitudes and behaviors. This happens when one group or individual recognizes the importance of the other or admires the positions and actions of the other. For example, if, in planning children's educational programs, a teacher considers the part parents can play, it may be because the teacher considers parents an important reference group. If, in planning their family activities, parents take the teachers' or schools' goals and actions into account, it may be because they consider teachers an important reference group. Sometimes only the higher-status group influences the behavior of the other, in an unreciprocated pattern. Teachers may take parents into account without parents reciprocating the consideration, as in some communities where parents have strong control of educational politics and policies. Or parents may consider teachers an important reference group without the teachers reciprocating, as when parents try to help their children with schoolwork even if the teacher has not given them encouragement or ideas about how to help at home.

The three main theories explain the basic differences in philosophies and approaches of teachers and parents that produce more or fewer, shallow or deep family-school connections. The supplementary theories explain the motivations to remove or reinforce boundaries between schools and families.

Understanding the Contrasting Theories: Changing Patterns in Family-School Relations

There have been important changes in the patterns of partnerships between the home and school over time. In the early 19th century, parents and the community greatly controlled the actions of the schools. The home, church, and school supported the same goals for learning and for the integration of the student into the adult community (Prentice and Houston, 1975). The community, including parents and church representatives, hired and fired the teachers, determined the school calendar, and influenced the curriculum. When the students were not in school, the families and others in the community taught their children important skills and knowledge needed for success in adulthood.

In the late 19th and early 20th centuries, a different pattern of family and school relations emerged. Increasingly, the school began to distance itself from the home by emphasizing the teachers' special knowledge of subject matter and pedagogy. Teachers began to teach subjects that were not familiar to parents, using methods and approaches that were not part of the parents' experiences. The family was asked to teach children good behavior and attitudes to prepare them for school and to take responsibility for teaching children about their ethnicity, religion, and family origins. These family responsibilities were separate from the schools' goal to teach a common curriculum to children from all ethnic, religious, social, and economic groups.

During the 1980s and 1990s, family-school relations changed again in response to increased demands from the public for better, more accountable schools. Both better-educated *and* less-educated parents want a good education for their children and are requesting or requiring schools to keep them informed about and involved in their children's education.

AN INTEGRATED THEORY OF FAMILY-SCHOOL RELATIONS

Changing times require changing theories. School and family relationships have been different at different times in history. It is not surprising, then, to see a restructuring of theories, from inter-institutional separation in the 1930s–1950s to cooperation between schools and families in the 1970s–1980s to accommodate the social changes affecting these organizations. But we do not yet have a model of family-school relations that accounts for the variation and process of change that will continue to influence the interactions of families and schools. The existing theories omit attention to history, student development, and the influence families and schools have on each other.

A life-course perspective (Elder, 1984) enables us to integrate useful strands from the different theories of family and school relations to correct the weaknesses of the separate theories. This perspective requires that we pay attention to three characteristics in family-school relationships: history, developmental patterns, and change.

History

Four recent trends help to explain why changes are needed in our theories of family and school relations:

1. More mothers with a college education and bachelor's degree. Over the past 40 years there has been a dramatic increase in the number of U.S. high school students, especially women, who attend and graduate from college. Whereas fewer than 20 percent of bachelor's degrees were earned by women prior to 1950 (mostly in the field of education), fully half of the earned bachelor's degrees were awarded to women in 1980 in many fields (Bureau of the Census, 1984). The education of mothers affects their interactions with teachers. Whereas most mothers were once less educated than the college-trained teachers, most mothers are now attending some college and have near, equal, or higher educational status than their children's teachers. There is still great variation in the education of women, but the proportion of educated mothers has made a difference in how parents view teachers, how teachers view parents, and whether and how mothers become involved in their children's education.

2. Baby and child care. Dr. Spock's (1950) influential and popular book increased the number of parents who became knowledgeable about and involved in the education of their infants and toddlers. The book offers sensible information to all parents about the importance of home environments for children's learning, information that had previously been known to only a few parents. Although Spock's book is not very useful in its discussions of older children and has little to say about school, it increased parents' awareness of and experience with their children as young learners. Spock's book, other child care books, and private and public health care programs continue to prime new generations of parents of infants and toddlers for the next phase of their children's lives: school.

3. Federal regulations and funding for parent involvement. In the 1960s, Head Start and other federally sponsored programs for disadvantaged preschoolers recognized that parents needed the help of educators to prepare their preschool children for regular school to break the cycle of school failure that threatened their children. More important, the preschools recognized that, despite the lack of advanced education of many mothers, the schools and the children needed the mothers' involvement to be successful. Mothers of children in Head Start often became involved on advisory councils, in classrooms as volunteers and paid aides, and at home as tutors.

During the same decade, Follow-Through programs required schools to recognize the continued importance of parents as educators beyond the preschool years (Gordon, Olmsted, Rubin, and True, 1979). The Education for All Handicapped

Children Act (Public Law 94-172) of 1975 brought teachers and parents together to discuss the educational program of each child. The federal programs and their official recognition of the importance of parents put parent involvement on the agendas of the local schools (Hobson, 1979; Keesling and Melaragno, 1983; Valentine and Stark, 1979). Schools could not easily limit parent involvement to the parents of children in federally sponsored programs and so more parents at all grade levels, regardless of education or economic background, became involved with their children's schools and teachers.

4. Changing family structures. In the past decade, two key changes in family structure have dramatically affected family and school relations. These are the increase in the number of single parents and in the number of mothers working outside the home. Mothers who work outside the home need to manage the care and schooling of their children with more exactitude than do mothers who work at home. They must arrange for their children's care before and after school, on school holidays, or during illness. Attention to the needs of the children has increased the concern of working mothers about the quality of day care, school, and after-school programs.

Single mothers are even more likely than other mothers to work outside the home and are especially sensitive about their responsibilities to their children. They have accentuated the need of all parents for information from teachers to help them use their limited time at home more productively in the interest of their children. Although working mothers and single parents do not volunteer to help at the school building as much as other mothers, research shows that they are just as interested as other mothers in their children's education and spend as much or more time helping their children at home (Epstein, 1984 [Reading 3.5]).

Increasingly, schools have had to replace traditional images of family life and patterns of communication with mothers at home with new images and new patterns of communication to accommodate different types of families. Some schools have made these adjustments to help all families, however structured, to interact successfully with the school. Other schools have not changed their expectations for or communications with families, despite the changes in families.

These four trends, over the last 40 to 50 years of the 20th century, changed family-school connections in the United States. These changes, singly and in combination, involved more parents in their children's education beyond preschool, officially and publicly recognized parents as "teachers," and increased the need for better communication between the home and school.

Developmental Patterns

Schools' and families' interactions need to fit the age, grade level, and level of social and cognitive development of the children. Schools are more like families for young students, with closer ties between teachers and parents of preschool and early elementary students. Schools may become increasingly impersonal in the secondary grades, with the aim of preparing students for interactions in adulthood with other formal organizations in government, work, and society. But *through high school,* schools vary in the extent to which they communicate with, inform, and involve parents in their children's education. We do not know the type, degree, or optimal mix of personal and impersonal relations across the grades that lead to maximum learning and successful preparation for adulthood. But our model of family-school relations must be based on a developmental framework to account for *the continuity* of school and family actions and interactions across the school years and *the changes* in forms and purposes of parent involvement at different student ages and stages of development.

Change

Families and schools are ever-changing. Families change as the members mature, developing new skills, knowledge, contacts, and patterns of social interaction. A family builds a changing, cumulative history of relationships with the school for each child in attendance. Interactions with one school affect the family's knowledge and attitudes in dealing with new schools that their children enter.

Schools change as the members come and go. New students enter the school each year, new combinations of students enter classes, and new teachers and administrators join the staff. The talents, perspectives, and leadership of the school change with the maturity and stability of the abilities to consider complex educational issues, practices, and goals. They may be more open to parents' requests and to parental involvement. Schools can build a changing, cumulative history of relationships with families as the students proceed through the grades.

A MODEL OF OVERLAPPING FAMILY AND SCHOOL SPHERES

Figures 2.1 and 2.2 introduce a model of family and school relations that accounts for history, development, and changing experiences of parents, teachers, and students.

External Structure

The external structure of the model consists of overlapping or nonoverlapping spheres representing the family, school, and community. The degree of overlap is controlled by three forces: time, experience in families, and experience in schools.

Force A represents a developmental time and history line for students, families, and schools. Time refers to individual and historical time: the age and grade level of the child and the social conditions of the period during which the child is in school. For example, in infancy the spheres in our model may be separate. The child first "attends" home, and the family provides the main educating environment. Parents and teachers do not initially interact directly about the child's learning. Even in infancy, however, the spheres may overlap. For example, if an infant

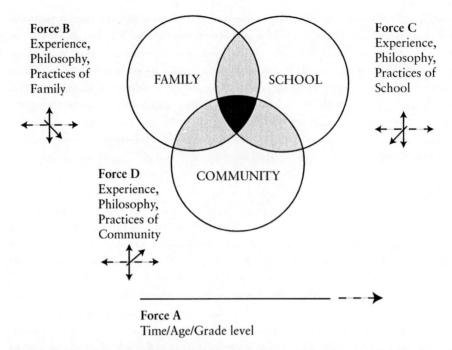

Force B
Experience,
Philosophy,
Practices of
Family

FAMILY SCHOOL

Force C
Experience,
Philosophy,
Practices of
School

COMMUNITY

Force D
Experience,
Philosophy,
Practices of
Community

Force A
Time/Age/Grade level

FIGURE 2.1   Overlapping Spheres of Influence of Family, School, and Community on Children's Learning (External Structure of Theoretical Model)

FAMILY   SCHOOL

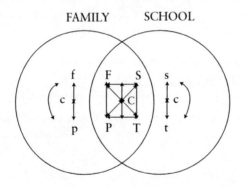

KEY: Intra-institutional interactions (lowercase)
     Inter-institutional interactions (uppercase)

f/F = Family   c/C = Child
s/S = School   p/P = Parent
                      t/T = Teacher

Note: In the full model the internal structure is
      extended, using the same KEY to include:
      co/CO = Community
      a/A   = Agent from community/business

FIGURE 2.2   Overlapping Spheres of Influence of Family, School, and Community on Children's Learning (Internal Structure of Theoretical Model)

is physically, mentally, or emotionally handicapped, parents and special teachers may begin a highly organized cooperative program to benefit the child. For all children, the family and school spheres may overlap to some extent in infancy and early childhood, as parents apply knowledge of child rearing and school readiness from books, their own school experiences, and information from pediatricians, educators, and others. Later, in a regular pattern, the spheres overlap when the child "attends" home, school, and the community.

There will be a "typical" or expected pattern of separation or overlap at different times based on the age of the child, the level of school, and the historical period when the child is in school. Up to now, the greatest overlap of family and school spheres for most children has occurred during the preschool and early elementary grades. But there has also been great overlap for some children at all grade levels because of the varying philosophies, policies, practices, and pressures of parents, teachers, or both, as represented by Forces B and C.

Force B and Force C represent the experiences of and pressures on family and school organizations and their members that need to be accounted for to study, understand, or change family-school relations. These forces push together or pull apart the spheres to produce more or less overlap of family and school actions, interactions, and influence all along the time line. When parents maintain or increase interest and involvement in their children's schooling (Force B), they create greater overlap of the family and school spheres than would be expected on the average. When teachers make parents part of their regular teaching practice (Force C), they create greater overlap than would typically be expected.

After the child enters school there will be some overlap of the two organizations at every grade level. This is true as long as there are family members (or surrogates) with whom the child and school interact. Even in seemingly separate situations such as private, elite boarding schools or state boarding schools for delinquent youngsters there are family and school contacts about contracts, payments, rules, visits, evaluations, and so forth that define the "minimum" overlap of the two spheres over the school years. The "maximum" overlap occurs when schools and families operate as true "partners," with frequent cooperative efforts and clear, close communication between parents and teachers in a comprehensive program of many important types of parent involvement (Epstein, 1986 [Reading 3.4]; Gordon, 1979; Seeley, 1981). But there is never "total" overlap because the family maintains some functions and practices that are independent of the schools' or teachers' programs, and the school maintains some functions and practices that are independent of families.

Children are connected to the same families but to different teachers over the course of their school years. Each new teacher (Force C) and each family's continuing or new involvement (Force B) create dynamic patterns of family-school relationships. There is continual adjustment in the overlap or separation of the two spheres.

Time alone (Force A), or the increasing age of the child, does not make parents more knowledgeable about how to help their children with particular school problems. Indeed, our research shows that it currently works the other way. The older the child (after grade 1), the less overlap there is in the two environments, and the less the parent feels able to help the child in school (Epstein, 1986). Thus, in Figure 2.1, if we included only Force A, we would see, for most families and schools, quite separate spheres in infancy, increasing overlap during the preschool years and grade 1, and decreasing overlap from grades 2 or 3 on.

By adding Forces B and C we recognize that the parents' and teachers' practices and the pressures they put on each other alter the typical patterns to create more or less overlap for families and schools at every grade level. For example, some teachers of older students increase their interactions with the parents of their upper elementary and secondary school students to keep the families involved in their children's education. For children in these teachers' classes, there will be greater overlap of family and school goals and interactions than for children whose teachers ignore the role of parents in their teaching practice.

Internal Structure

The internal structure of the model in Figure 2.2 shows the interpersonal relationships and influence patterns of primary importance. Two *types* of interactions and influence are shown: within organization (lowercase letters) and between organizations (capital letters). Two *levels* of interaction are also shown: standard, organizational communications (family and school) and specific, individual communications (parent and teacher). Family (f) and school (s), and parent (p) and teacher (t) interactions are those that occur separately as parents, offspring, or other relatives conduct their family life and personal relationships, or as teachers, principals, and other school staff create school policies or conduct school or individual activities. Family (F) and School (S), and Parent (P) and Teacher (T) interactions are those that occur as members of the two organizations interact in standard, organizationally directed communications (F and S), or in unique, individually directed communications (P and T).

Family (F) and School (S) connections refer to the interactions between family members and school staff that concern all families and the general school staff or school programs. These include, for example, communications to all parents about school policies; workshops available to all parents on child rearing or child development; programs for all parents to become involved at the school as parent volunteers; or family actions that may affect the schools, such as activities of parent-teacher organizations, parent advisory councils, or citizen advocacy groups in the community. These types of involvement establish common structures for communications and interactions between families and schools as organizations.

Parent (P) and Teacher (T) connections refer to specific interactions between parents and teachers about an individual child. These may include, for example, parent-teacher conferences about the child's progress; parents' notes or phone calls to teachers about the child's academic, social, or personal problems or needs; or the teacher's specific suggestions to parents about how they can help their own child with learning activities at home.

The Child (C) has the central place in all of the patterns of interaction and influence in this model. We assume that the child's welfare and interests are the parents' and teachers' reasons for interacting. For the child, the school and family policies, parent and teacher interactions, and the child's understanding and reactions to these connections influence academic learning and social development. The multidirectional arrows in the model show that children interact with, influence, and are influenced by their families and especially parents, and by changes in their families and parental behavior that result from the actions of the schools. Children interact with, influence, and are influenced by their schools and especially teachers, and by the changes in schools' and teachers' practices that result from the actions of families.

The external and internal structures of the model are, of course, intimately related. The internal organizational and individual relationships are influenced simultaneously by the age and grade level of the student and the common practices of the time period (Force A) and by the actions, attitudes, experiences, and decisions of teachers and parents (Forces B and C). The degree of overlap of family and school organizations and their goals and practices affects the social and psychological distance between the family and school members, their patterns of communication, and the results or outcomes of more or less interaction. Each of the components of the model can be translated into well-specified measures to study the effects of parent involvement (e.g., teachers' practices of parent involvement, parents' initiatives or responses to teachers' requests) on student achievement, attitudes, and other student, parent, and teacher outcomes.

The model recognizes the interlocking histories of the institutions and the individuals in each, and the continuing, causal connections between organizations and individuals. The model energizes an integrated theory of family and school relations by acknowledging the continuous change that occurs in families and schools; the accumulated knowledge and experiences of parents, teachers, and students; and the influence of these different patterns on student motivations, attitudes, and achievement.

SCHOOL-LIKE FAMILIES AND FAMILY-LIKE SCHOOLS

The proposed model of overlapping spheres assumes that there are mutual interests and influences of families and schools that can be more or less successfully promoted by the policies and programs of the organizations and the actions and attitudes of the individuals in those organizations. Although there are important differences between schools and families (Dreeben, 1968), we need to recognize also the important similarities, overlap in goals, responsibilities, and mutual influence of the two major environments that simultaneously affect children's learning and development.

Earlier theories asserted that schools treat students equally, judging them by universal standards and rewarding students for what they do (achievements) and not for who they are (ascriptions). In contrast, families are said to treat children individually, judging them by personal standards and special relationships, basing rewards and affection on the children's individual growth and improvement or on their membership in the family and not on achievements relative to other children. These "pure" images of different institutional approaches and functions are not very accurate portrayals of how schools or families actually work to motivate students toward success in school. The distinction between universalistic and particularistic treatments has been blurred in families that are more aware of the importance of schooling and its components and in schools with more personal and individualized environments. These are *school-like families* and *family-like schools*.

School-Like Families

Some parents run "school-like" homes. They know how to help their children in schoolwork and take appropriate opportunities to do so. School-like families often have persistent and consistent academic schedules of learning for their children from infancy on, with books and colors, shapes and sizes, and music and art as part of their early "school-like" curricula. Before the children enter school, these families are directed by "absentee" or remembered teachers or by contemporary educational sources and resources. During the early years the family teaches the young child, but in fact it may be that images of school or teachers in absentia influence the family in how and what to teach the child.

Some families operate very much like schools. They not only create school-like tasks for their children and reward them for success but also match tasks to each child's level of ability and involve the children in active learning rather than passive listening. These families not only translate the curriculum of the school into home tasks but also put into practice principles of organizational effectiveness (Rich and Jones, 1977) and use the same structures (i.e., the task, authority, reward, grouping, evaluation, and time or TARGET structures) that guide effective classroom instruction (Epstein, 1988, b).

Although most parents accept and love their children for their unique qualities and lineal connections, many families reward their children for real and objective accomplishments, as teachers do. Many families judge their children on standard criteria and reward their children as they learn the "basic skills" (from learning to walk to learning to read) and as they acquire social skills and advanced academic skills or other talents. School-like families place more emphasis than other families on their children's place in a status hierarchy.

Family-Like Schools

Teachers vary in their recognition and use of the overlap between family and school spheres of influence. Some schools make their students feel part of a "school family" that looks out for their interests and provides unique experiences for each child. Schools may relax and destandardize their rules, vary the students' roles, and alter the reward system to be more responsive to the student and to be more like a family.

Although schools impose some uniform standards on all students (e.g., attendance regulations, graduation requirements, formal codes for dress or conduct), these may not be as important as student-teacher relationships and personal, individual attention for influencing and improving student motivation and progress. Presently, brighter students often are given various opportunities to interact on friendly and preferential terms with teachers. Slower students often experience less personal, less family-like treatment, which may further reduce their motivation to come to school to learn.

Schools vary in how much they emphasize uniform or special standards. Some schools recognize and reward only students who are in the top groups or tracks or who get the highest grades. Other schools reward students for individual progress and improvement in achievement, as parents do. They place less emphasis on the students' place in a status hierarchy. Particularistic treatment, associated with family relations, implies a degree of favoritism or special attention to the unique and endearing qualities of individuals. This kind of treatment occurs at some schools, also, with some students receiving family-like treatment, attention, and even affection from teachers.

Time in Family and School Environments

The child is either in or out of school. Some count the hours that students spend in school (e.g., *Fifteen Thousand Hours,* by Rutter et al., 1979). Others cite the time that students are *not* in school and are under the influence of the family, community, media, churches, camps, day care programs, peer groups, or part-time employers (Csikszentmihalyi and Larson, 1984). At least 16 hours per school day plus weekends and vacations are out-of-school time. The seemingly clear dichotomy of time in or out of school is obscured by the degree of overlap in the two environments. For example, when the student is *in school,* the family's influence may still be at work. A student knows whether a parent knows what is happening in school, what the student is learning, and how he or she is expected to behave. Homework activities may affect the student's attention in class and readiness for new and more difficult work. Similarly, when the student is *at home,* the school's influence may be still at work. At home, a student may consider how a teacher wants homework to be completed and may use school skills and information to discuss ideas and solve problems.

Time in and out of school, then, is not "pure" school or family time. Time in school may be influenced by the family; time out of school may be influenced by teachers and other school programs and experiences. The degree of overlap in the two environments on matters of schoolwork and on the recognition and support of students' unique, individual talents influences the students' attention, motivation, and learning in and out of school.

EXPLORING THE THEORY:
EFFECTS OF FAMILY-SCHOOL OVERLAP ON
PARENTS, STUDENTS, AND TEACHING PRACTICE

From research completed over the past several years, we have some evidence of how teachers' practices reflect the three current theories of family and school relations and how the degree of overlap in family and school spheres influences parents' attitudes and behaviors and student attitudes and achievements.

Variation in Overlap in Teaching Practice

As stated previously, the philosophies and practices of teachers reflect the three theories of school and family relations: separate, sequential, and shared spheres of family and school responsibilities and influence. For example, some teachers believe that they can be effective only if they obtain parental cooperation and assistance on learning activities at home. In their classrooms, cooperation is high. These teachers make frequent requests for parental assistance in reinforcing or improving students' skills. They orchestrate actions to increase the overlap in family and school spheres of influence.

Other teachers believe that their professional status is in jeopardy if parents are involved in activities that are typically the teachers' responsibilities. In their classrooms, inter-institutional cooperation is low. These teachers make few overtures to parents and rarely request them to help their children with learning activities at home. They maintain more separate spheres of influence for the school and the family (Becker and Epstein, 1982 [Reading 3.1]; Epstein and Becker, 1982 [Reading 3.2]).

Teachers' present practices also illustrate assumptions of sequential patterns in family-school relations. More teachers of young children (grade 1) than of older children (grades 3 and 5) are frequent users of parent involvement techniques. In a clear, linear pattern, most teachers of young children assist parents to become involved in their children's education, but most teachers of older children ignore or discourage parental involvement. Along the time line, then, there is increasingly less overlap of family and school spheres.

Benefits from Greater Overlap

Our surveys of teachers, principals, parents, and students show that:

- Teachers control the flow of information to parents. By limiting or reducing communications and collaborative activities, teachers reinforce the boundaries that separate the two institutions. By increasing communications, teachers acknowledge and build connections between institutions to focus on the common concerns of teachers and parents: a child who is also a student (Becker and Epstein, 1982).

- Parents do not report deep conflict or incompatibility between schools and families. Rather, parents of children at all grade levels respond favorably to teachers' practices that stress the cooperation and overlap of schools and families. Frequent use by teachers of parent involvement leads parents to report that they receive more ideas about how to help their children at home and that they know more about the instructional programs than they did in the previous year (Epstein, 1986).
- Teachers who include the family in the children's education are recognized by parents for their efforts. They are rated higher by parents than are other teachers on interpersonal and teaching skills, and they are rated higher in overall teaching ability by their principals (Epstein, 1985 [Reading 4.3], 1986).
- Students' test scores suggest that schools are more effective when families and schools work together with the student on basic skills. Students whose teachers use frequent practices of parent involvement gain more than other students in reading skills from fall to spring (Epstein, 1991 [Reading 3.7]). And fifth-grade students recognize and benefit from cooperation between their teachers and parents (Epstein, 1982 [Reading 3.9]).

The results of our research show that although teaching practice reflects all three of the major theoretical positions, parents, students, and teachers benefit most from practices that increase the overlap in school and family spheres of influence all along the developmental time line.

CONCLUSION

Over the last few decades of the 20th century, ideas about family-school relations changed as other social conditions affected schools and families. Theories moved away from the separation of family and school and toward greater teacher-parent cooperation and communication. Our model of family-school relations integrates the discrete, extant theories and reflects the fact that at any time, in any school, and in any family, parent involvement is a variable that can be increased or decreased by the practices of teachers, administrators, parents, and students. Programs and practices can be designed, revised, and evaluated to learn which variations produce greater school and family effectiveness and student success. The members of the school and family organizations can act and interact with others in ways that include or exclude parents from their children's education and that include or exclude teachers as influences on the family. These actions push the spheres of family and school influence together or apart in a continuous, dynamic pattern, and influence student learning and development.

Schools and families vary on the dimensions that are supposed to distinguish family and school treatments and attention to children. There are family-like schools and school-like families, as well as schools and families that are distinct in their approaches to education and socialization. Some have suggested that schools and families have different goals for their children (Lightfoot, 1978), but our research suggests that although parents' educational backgrounds differ, both more- *and* less-educated parents have similar goals to those of the school for their children's education (Epstein, 1986).

The main differences among parents are their knowledge of how to help their children at home, their belief that teachers want them to assist their children at home, and the degree of information and guidance from their children's teachers in how to help their children at home. These factors create more or less school-like families.

The main differences among teachers are their ability to put principles of child and adolescent development and organizational effectiveness into practice in instruction and classroom management, their ability to communicate with students as individuals, their belief about the importance of parents' involvement and parents' receptivity to guidance from the school, and their ability to communicate with parents as partners in the children's education. These factors create more or less family-like schools.

The theoretical model of overlapping spheres of influence, its underlying assumptions, and research on the effects on parents and students of teachers' practices of parent involvement aim to:

- *extend studies* of *families* by intensifying attention to the interplay of family and school environments during that part of the parents' and children's lives when the children are in school or are preparing for school, from infancy through the high school grades; and
- *extend studies of school organization and effects* by intensifying attention to the total educational environment of children including the home, and by examining the implications of this extension for teachers' roles and student learning and development.

REFERENCES

Becker, H. J., and J. L. Epstein. (1982). Parent involvement: A study of teacher practices. *Elementary School Journal* 83: 85–102. (Reading 3.1).

Bloom, B. S. (1964). *Stability and change in human characteristics.* New York: Wiley.

Bronfenbrenner, U. (1979). *The ecology of human development.* Cambridge, MA: Harvard University Press.

Bureau of the Census (1984). *Statistical abstract of the United States, 1985.* Washington, DC: Government Printing Office.

Csikszentmihalyi, M., and R. Larson. (1984). *Being adolescent.* New York: Basic Books.

Dreeben, R. (1968). *On what is learned in school.* Reading, MA: Addison-Wesley.

Elder, G. H., Jr. (1984). Families, kin, and the life course: A sociological perspective. Pages 80–135 in *Review of child development research,* edited by R. Parker. Chicago: University of Chicago Press.

Epstein, J. L. (1982). Student reactions to teacher practices of parent involvement. Paper presented at the annual meeting of the American Educational Research Association, New York. (Reading 3.9).

————. (1984). *Single parents and the schools: The effect of marital status on parent and teacher evaluations.* Report 353. Baltimore: The Johns Hopkins University Center for Social Organization of Schools. (Reading 3.5).

———. (1985). A question of merit: Principals' and parents' evaluations of teachers. *Educational Researcher* 14: 3–10. (Reading 4.3).

———. (1986). Parents' reactions to teacher practices of parent involvement. *The Elementary School Journal* 86: 277–294. (Reading 3.4).

———. (1988). Effective schools or effective students? Dealing with diversity. In *Policies for America's public schools*, edited by R. Haskins and D. MacRae. Norwood, NJ: Ablex.

———. (1989). Family structures and student motivation. In *Research on motivation in education*, Vol. 3, edited by C. Ames and R. Ames. New York: Academic Press.

———. (1991). Effects on student achievement of teachers' practices of parent involvement. Pages 261–276 in *Advances in reading/language research, Vol. 5: Literacy through family, community, and school interactions*, edited by S. Silvern. Greenwich, CT: JAI Press. (Reading 3.7).

Epstein, J. L., and H. J. Becker. (1982). Teacher practices of parent involvement: Problems and possibilities. *Elementary School Journal* 83: 103–113. (Reading 3.2).

Freud, A. (1937). *The ego and mechanisms of defense*. London: Hogarth Press.

Gordon, I. J. (1979). The effects of parent involvement in schooling. Pages 4–25 in *Partners: Parents and schools*, edited by R. S. Brandt. Alexandria, VA: Association for Supervision and Curriculum Development.

Gordon, I. J., P. J. Olmsted, R. I. Rubin, and J. H. True. (1979). How has Follow-Through promoted parent involvement? *Young Children* 34: 49–53.

Hobson, P. J. (1979). The partnership with Title I parents. Pages 41–46 in *Partners: Parents and schools*, edited by R. S. Brandt. Alexandria, VA: Association for Supervision and Curriculum Development.

Keesling, J. W., and R. Melaragno. (1983). Parent participation in federal education programs: Findings from the federal programs surveys phase of the study of parent involvement. Pages 230–256 in *Parent education and public policy*, edited by R. Haskins. Norwood, NJ: Ablex.

Leichter, H. J. (1974). *The family as educator*. New York: Teachers College Press.

Lightfoot, S. L. (1978). *Worlds apart: Relationships between families and schools*. New York: Basic Books.

Litwak, E., and H. J. Meyer. (1974). *School, family and neighborhood: The theory and practice of school-community relations*. New York: Columbia University Press.

Mead, G. H. (1934). *Mind, self, and society*. Chicago: University of Chicago Press.

Merton, R. K. (1968). *Social theory and social structure*. New York: Free Press.

Parsons, T. (1959). The school class as a social system: Some of its functions in American society. *Harvard Educational Review* 29: 297–318.

Piaget, J., and B. Inhelder. (1969). *The psychology of the child*. New York: Basic Books.

Prentice, A. R., and S. E. Houston. (1975). *Family, school, and society*. Toronto: Oxford University Press.

Rich, D., and C. Jones. (1977). *A family affair: Education*. Washington, DC: Home and School Institute.

Rutter, M., B. Maughan, P. Mortimore, and J. Ouston. (1979). *Fifteen thousand hours: Secondary schools and their effects on children*. Cambridge, MA: Harvard University Press.

Seeley, D. (1981). *Education through partnership: Mediating structures and education*. Cambridge, MA: Ballinger.

Spock, B. (1950). *The pocket book of baby and child care*. New York: Pocket Books.

Valentine, J., and E. Stark. (1979). The social context of parent involvement in Head Start. In *Project Head Start: A legacy of the war on poverty*, edited by E. Zigler and J. Valentine. New York: Free Press.

Waller, W. (1932). *The sociology of teaching*. New York: Wiley.

Weber, M. (1947). *The theory of social and economic organization*. New York: Oxford University Press.

Perspectives and Previews on Research and Policy for School, Family, and Community Partnerships*

During the 1980s and 1990s, the field of school, family, and community partnerships was energized by activities in research, policy, and practice. In research, scholars from different disciplines are now applying various methodologies to study connections of schools and communities with families of various backgrounds and cultures and with students at different age and grade levels. The number of master's and doctoral dissertations is increasing as graduate students and their professors become familiar with the field and seek to make new contributions.

In policy, in 1994 Congress added a new national educational goal for school and family partnerships to the major federal legislation called Goals 2000: Educate America Act. Also, Title I regulations were revised to include mandates for specific family-school connections for states, districts, and schools to obtain and keep federal funds. Other federal, state, and local policies have been and are being developed that mandate or encourage partnership activities.

In practice, school administrators, teachers, parents, students, and others in communities are increasingly working together to meet various mandates and guidelines, and, more important, to design their own programs and practices. Along with curriculum, instruction, evaluation, and staff development, a program of school, family, and community connections is now viewed as one of the components of school organization that may help to promote student learning and success in school.

AN EMERGING FIELD OF STUDY

A selective summary may help to illustrate some of the changes that have occurred in this growing field of study. Traditionally, studies of families, or schools, or communities were conducted as if these were separate or competing contexts. For example, in the late 1960s and 1970s, researchers argued heatedly about whether schools *or* families were more important. When heads cleared, the dual contributions of schools and families were acknowledged: Students are advantaged or disadvantaged by the economic and educational resources and guidance offered by their families and are advantaged or disadvantaged by the quality of their experiences in schools. The debate changed as it became increasingly clear that neither schools nor families alone can do the job of educating and socializing children and

---

* By Joyce L. Epstein.

preparing them for life. Rather, schools, families, and communities share responsibilities for children and influence them simultaneously.

In the 1960s, the topic of parent involvement gained prominence with the implementation of federal Head Start and Follow-Through programs in preschool and early elementary grades. These programs legislated the involvement of low-income parents in the education of their young children to prepare them for successful entry into school. At the same time, other factors increased the involvement of middle- and high-income parents in their children's education. For example, more women were graduating from college and entering and staying in the workforce, more mothers were equal with teachers in education, and more parents were active in decisions about early care for their children. Thus, there were pressures and opportunities for families with both more and less formal education to increase their awareness of the importance of their participation in children's education and of continuous interactions with their children's schools (Connors and Epstein, 1995).

Other early policies changed basic connections between schools and families, based on demographic data, family demands, and goals for greater nutritional equity for all children. For example, schools began to serve lunch at school to all children, responding in part to the increasing numbers of working mothers who were not at home in the middle of the day. Schools began to provide free breakfasts as well as free and reduced-price lunches to help poor families and their children. Research on these policies progressed from studies of whether to which food should be served in breakfasts and lunches to help students and their families.

The new policy agenda about partnerships is being driven by more complex family and community conditions, but emerging policies are still responses to poverty and other demographics, family demands, and goals for equity and excellence in students' education. The problems are well known: There are more two-parent homes in which both parents are employed; more young, single parents and more of them working outside the home; more children in poverty; more migrant and homeless children and families; more family mobility during the school year; and other factors that make it imperative to redesign and improve policies and practices for linking schools, families, and communities. But programs of partnership are not only responses to problems of families facing difficult conditions. The new policy agenda about partnerships reflects the advances in the understanding that all families need better information about their children, the schools, and the part they play across the grades to influence children's well-being, learning, and development.

Some mandates and emphases in earlier federal programs (such as the parent councils required in Title I) were limited, often perfunctory activities that informed and involved only a few parents (Keesling and Melaragno, 1983). Other demonstration programs were quite comprehensive, including home visits, assistance to parents in understanding their very young children, good communications with teachers, opportunities to volunteer, and other active interactions (Gordon, 1979). The early efforts to understand parent involvement were largely unsystematic, with few measures taken of the effects of specific practices of involvement. The first frameworks focused mainly on the roles that parents needed to play and not the work that schools needed to do to organize strong programs to involve all families in their children's education.

In the 1970s, the effective schools movements—a first wave of recent school reform—captured the attention of educators of students who were at risk of failing (Edmonds, 1979). Although it was not one of the initial elements of effective schools, parent involvement was quickly added to an expanding list of components that research and practice suggested would improve schools and increase student success. By the mid-1980s, the report *A Nation at Risk* (National Commission on Excellence in Education, 1983) was directing attention to the need to improve all schools, not just those for students from economically distressed homes and communities. The *effective* schools litany evolved into lists of requirements for *restructured* schools. The school reform movement may continue to change its vocabulary: There already are discussions of *renewed, reinvented, redefined, responsive,* and *reconstituted* schools. Whatever the vocabulary, all school reform efforts recognize the need to improve the quality of education for all students. Each new initiative has sharpened the focus on curriculum, instruction, and connections with families.

In the 1980s, studies began to clarify the amorphous term *parent involvement* and recast the emphasis from parent involvement (left up to the parent) to *school and family partnerships,* or, more fully, *school, family, and community partnerships,* recognizing the shared responsibilities for children within and across contexts. The concept of "shared responsibility" removed part of the burden from parents to figure out on their own how to become or stay involved in their children's education from year to year and put part of that burden on schools to create programs to inform and involve all families. Researchers collected data to identify separable components of involvement and began to focus more rigorously on measuring results of involvement for students, parents, and educators (Epstein, 1987a [Reading 2.1], 1987b, 1992).

Growth in this field of study was assisted by the federal government's creation in 1990 of the national Center on Families, Communities, Schools and Children's Learning to conduct an active research and development program on school and family partnerships from birth through high school. The Center included over 20 researchers who conducted research, development, evaluation, and policy studies in two research programs on the early years (focusing on students and their families from birth through age 10) and on the years of early and late adolescence (focusing on students and their families from age 11 to 19). The Center's researchers were from several disciplines, used varied methods and measurement models, and often worked closely with educators and parents to design and study new approaches for productive partnerships.

In addition to its research agenda, the Center created an International Network of over 300 researchers in the United States and more than 40 nations to encourage and to share work on many topics related to school, family, and community partnerships. Some researchers in other nations have followed the Center's format to establish interdisciplinary networks in their own countries (e.g., Australia, Portugal, and Denmark) and to work with and assist educators to improve school programs of partnerships with families and communities. The discussions and debates among international colleagues and collaborative cross-national projects (Davies, 1993) have added energy to this field.

For several years, the Center on Families, Communities, Schools and Children's Learning and the Institute for Responsive Education joined forces to conduct a daylong roundtable for U.S. and international colleagues to share their research and development activities prior to the annual meeting of the American Educational Research Association (AERA). The Center also organized international symposia for several years for the formal AERA meetings. The number of countries, researchers, topics, questions, methods and measures, and quality of work at these meetings has grown each year.

There is other evidence of the growth of interest and action in this field of study. In the late 1980s, the AERA had few papers at its annual meeting on topics concerning families. Now, multiple labels are needed to index presentations on family involvement, school partnerships, parent participation, fathers, mothers, and other related terms. The Families as Educators Special Interest Group (SIG) at AERA has grown in membership for more than a decade. The annual meetings of nearly every major social science and policy-related professional association include presentations of research and often interdisciplinary panels on topics of schools, families, communities, and their connections.

As should be expected in a maturing field, new theories, studies, policies, and practices generate heat as well as light. Researchers debate assumptions, definitions, and interpretations of results (Coleman, 1987; Lareau, 1989, 1996).

Policy leaders and educators take different paths toward various goals. In short, the field of school, family, and community partnerships is growing and improving with better questions, methods, and approaches. The emerging field is strengthened by three characteristics of the participants and their work, discussed below.

Academic Disciplinary Boundaries Have Blended

Progress in research on family, school, and community connections has been made across disciplines, within and across academic specialties. Researchers in sociology, psychology, social work, anthropology, education, history, economics, and other fields are conducting studies, building on each other's work, and contributing new perspectives that are, in turn, assisting policy and practice. These investments will continue to improve the understanding of families, schools, communities, and their connections.

Professional Boundaries Have Blurred

Researchers, policy leaders, and educators are working with and learning from each other. More than for most topics in social and educational research, there has been a short time line between research and its application in practice. More than for most topics, researchers, educators, and parents have been working together to identify the goals, problems, and potential solutions to create more successful partnerships to assist more students. These cross-context connections of university researchers, educators, and policy makers have transformed how some research is designed, conducted, and interpreted (Moles, 1996).

The Main Questions Have Changed

We have moved from the question, Are families important for student success in school? to, *If* families are important for children's development and school success, how can schools help all families conduct the activities that will benefit their children? Researchers and educators have raised common questions, such as, What do we need to know and do to help all children succeed in school and to enable their families to help them do so? How can schools communicate with families and community groups to enable more families (indeed all of them) to guide their children on positive paths from birth through high school? How can these communications be family friendly, feasible for schools, and acceptable to students? What are the effects of alternative designs and implementation processes of practices of partnership?

From my viewpoint, the main goal of partnerships is *to develop and conduct better communications with families across the grades to assist students to succeed in school.* Research should question, elaborate on, or clarify all of the definable parts of that goal: (1) to develop and conduct better communications (How? Which connections, interactions, and exchanges are promoted by different types of involvement? Which supporting policies are needed?); (2) with more families (How? With which strategies to reach most or all families? With which guidance for all teachers and administrators?); (3) to assist more students (How? With which roles for students? With which interactions of students and adults to motivate students to work hard and learn to their full potential?); and (4) to succeed in school (How? With which definitions and measures of success, that is, which results or outcomes of schooling?).

Research, policies, and practices are accumulating that inform all parts of this goal, but more studies and efforts in the schools are needed to fully understand whether and how the processes work. The next sections take a look *back* at the results of earlier work to describe a knowledge base on which to build, a look *around* to discuss issues that are emerging in current research and in practice, and a look *ahead to* preview some of the questions that I believe need continued or new attention.

A LOOK BACK: A BASE ON WHICH TO BUILD

For many years, my colleagues and I have been conducting studies to identify and understand what schools need to know and do to develop and implement full or comprehensive programs of partnership. This work produced a theory, framework, and vocabulary that enable researchers and educators to communicate with, learn from, and assist each other. This is still a skeletal structure, however, that needs to grow to a full body of knowledge.

In the 1980s, I developed a theoretical perspective called "overlapping spheres of influence," based on data collected with colleagues from teachers, parents, and students in the elementary grades. The results of the data analyses could not be explained by older sociological theories that stressed that social organizations would be most effective if they set separate goals and worked efficiently and effectively on unique missions. Rather, a social organizational perspective was needed that posited that the most effective families and schools had overlapping, shared goals and missions concerning children, and conducted some work collaboratively.

The model of overlapping spheres of influence includes external and internal structures (see Figures 2.1 and 2.2, page 28). The external structure can, by conditions or design, be pushed together or pulled apart by three main forces (background and practices of families, background and practices of schools and classrooms, and time). These forces create conditions, space, and opportunities for more or fewer shared activities of schools, families, and communities. The internal structure of the model specifies institutional and interpersonal communication lines and locates where and how social interactions occur within and across the boundaries of school, home, and community. Institutional-level interactions involve all members or groups with schools, families, and communities; individual interactions involve one student's parent, one teacher, or one community member; and combinations of these interactions also may occur within the areas of overlap. This theory integrates and extends a long line of ecological, educational, psychological, and sociological perspectives on social organizations and relationships (e.g., Bronfenbrenner, 1979; Leichter, 1974; Litwak and Meyer, 1974; Seeley, 1981) and a long line of research on school, family, and community environments and their effects. (For details, references, and summaries see Epstein, 1987a, 1992.)

To study the usefulness of the theory, other researchers and practitioners and I conducted surveys of and field studies with teachers, parents, and students at the elementary, middle, and high school levels. Among other questions, we wanted to know: Which practices of partnership fall in the area of overlap or shared responsibility? What can be learned about the range and the results of the activities and interactions between families and schools and among schools, families, and communities? What can be learned about the policies and practical approaches that help schools develop and implement strong programs of partnership that engage all families?

Several studies helped to identify and improve a framework of six major types of involvement that fall within the areas of overlap in the spheres of influence model. Each type of involvement may be operationalized by hundreds of practices that schools may choose to develop their programs. There will be more or less overlap and shared responsibility depending on whether many or few practices in the six types of involvement are working, and each practice that is implemented opens opportunities for varied interactions of teachers, parents, students, and others across contexts. The six types, described briefly below, explain how schools can work with families and communities to assist them to become or stay informed and involved in children's education at home and at school (Epstein, 1992).

Type 1—Parenting. Assist families with parenting and child-rearing skills, family support, understanding child and adolescent development, and setting home conditions to support learning at each age and grade level.

Type 2—Communicating. Communicate with families about school programs and student progress with school-to-home and home-to-school communications.

Type 3—Volunteering. Improve recruitment, training, work, and schedules to involve families as volunteers and audiences at the school or in other locations to support students and school programs.

Type 4—Learning at Home. Involve families with their children in learning activities at home, including homework and other curricular-linked activities and decisions.

Type 5—Decision Making. Include families as participants in school decisions, governance, and advocacy activities through PTA, committees, councils, and other parent organizations.

Type 6—Collaborating with the Community. Coordinate the work and resources of community businesses, agencies, colleges or universities, and other groups to strengthen school programs, family practices, and student learning and development.

Each of the six types poses specific challenges for its successful design and implementation; each type leads to some different results or outcomes for students, parents, and teachers; and each benefits from investments and commitments by the various members of the school, family, and community partnership (Epstein, 1987b; Epstein and Connors, 1995).

The six-types framework also helps researchers locate measures of involvement and the results of their studies in the same scheme that is useful to educators. That is, research on family or community volunteers at school or in other locations (Type 3) could contribute results that extend knowledge about the organization and effects of volunteers, and the results and knowledge gained could be particularly useful to schools interested in improving their volunteer programs (e.g., Epstein and Dauber, 1995).

The results of the early studies raise many new questions. For example, one of the most consistent results is that teachers have very different views of parents than parents have of themselves (Dauber and Epstein, 1993 [Reading 3.6]; Epstein and Dauber, 1991 [Reading 3.3]). Most teachers do not know most parents' goals for their children, nor do they understand the information parents would like to have to be more effective at home. Most parents do not know what most teachers are trying to do each year in school or about school improvement activities. Similarly, neither parents nor teachers fully understand what students think about family-school partnerships. Indeed, most adults think students want to avoid or minimize family involvement in their education. Data from students, however, suggest the opposite. Students want their families to be knowledgeable partners with their schools in their education and available as helpful sources of information, assistance, or guidance. The studies show why it is important to measure teachers', parents', and students' views to identify gaps in knowledge that each has about the other and to identify their common interests in good communication and in children's success in school.

Although the early studies confirm that there are positive connections between family involvement and student achievement, we still know relatively little about which practices, how, when, for whom, and why particular practices produce positive student outcomes. There also is evidence of some negative connections of family involvement with student behaviors, when students are in trouble or need help, but little evidence about whether the interventions help solve the problems over time. The early studies show that school and family partnerships produce a variety of results for families, teachers, and students. Three results illustrate how broadly future questions must be cast.

School Practices Influence Family Involvement

Teachers' practices to involve families are as or more important than family background variables such as race or ethnicity, social class, marital status, or mother's work status for determining whether and how parents become involved in their children's education. Family practices of involvement are as or more important than family background variables for determining whether and how students progress and succeed in school. At the elementary, middle, and high school levels, surveys of parents, teachers, principals, and students reveal that if schools invest in practices to involve families, parents respond by conducting those practices, including many parents who might not have otherwise become involved on their own (e.g., Dauber and Epstein, 1993, Epstein, 1986a [Reading 3.4]).

Teachers Who Involve Parents Rate Them More Positively and Stereotype Families Less. Teachers who frequently involve families in their children's education rate single and married parents and more and less formally educated parents equally in helpfulness and follow-through with their children at home. By contrast, teachers who do not frequently involve families give more stereotypic ratings to single parents and to those with less formal education, marking them lower in helpfulness and follow-through than other parents (Becker and Epstein, 1982 [Reading 3.1]; Epstein, 1990 [Reading 3.5]).

There Are Subject-Specific Links Between the Involvement of Families and Increases in Achievement by Students. Practices to involve parents at home with their children in interactions about a specific subject are likely to benefit student achievement in that subject. For example, with data that connected teacher practices, parent responses, and student achievement,

- teachers' practices to involve parents in learning activities at home were mainly limited to reading, English, or related activities; also, principals encouraged teachers to involve parents in reading;
- parents reported more involvement in reading activities; and

- students improved their reading scores over one school year if parents were involved, but their math scores were not affected by frequent parent involvement in reading (Epstein, 1991 [Reading 3.7]).

These results suggest that specific practices of partnership may help boost student achievement in particular subjects. Research is needed to clarify whether family involvement with a child in one subject transfers to benefit the child in other subjects over time.

Other results from the early studies provide a basis for new questions. For example:

On the importance and extent of involvement, on average:

- Teachers, parents, and students agree that parent involvement is important.
- Teachers and parents report low contact with each other—even on traditional communications.

On the variations in patterns of partnership:

- Some teachers in urban, suburban, and rural schools are leaders in involving parents in many ways; other teachers avoid partnerships.
- Teachers and parents in the elementary grades (or self-contained classes) presently report more home-school connections than in the middle and high school grades (or in departmentalized programs).
- Teachers presently contact more parents if their children have problems in school; parents presently become involved more on their own if their children are doing well in school.
- The student is an important "transmitter" of information from school to home and from home to school.

On the types of involvement:

- Few parents are involved frequently at the school building.
- Most parents want to know how to help their own child at home.

Most of these results have been confirmed and extended by several researchers in studies of diverse populations of teachers, parents, and students (e.g., Ames, Khoju, and Watkins, 1993; Brian, 1994; Davies, 1991; Davies, Burch, and Johnson, 1992; Dornbusch and Ritter, 1988; Eccles and Harold, 1996; Epstein and Jacobsen, 1994; Epstein and Lee, 1993, 1995; Lee, 1994; Montandon and Perrenoud, 1987). But there is much more to learn. Research about school, family, and community connections needs to improve in many ways. Early research was often based on limited samples, too global or too narrow measures of involvement, and limited data on student outcomes. As research proceeds with clearer questions and better data, measurement models should be more fully specified, analyses more elegant, and results more useful for policy and practice.

A LOOK AHEAD:
PERSPECTIVES AND PREVIEWS

Studies conducted by researchers at the Center on Families, Communities, Schools and Children's Learning and by many other researchers are adding new knowledge on school, family, and community connections at various age and grade levels from birth through high school; in urban, suburban, and rural locations; on families of various backgrounds and cultures; on new ways to understand and conduct studies of community connections with families and with schools; and on new understandings of policy contexts. Studies in progress include surveys, case studies, experimental and quasi-experimental longitudinal data collections, field tests, evaluations, and program and policy development. The results of these studies will extend the field considerably, but they also raise new questions. Five topics have emerged from the ongoing research that are particularly compelling and need continued and additional study:

1. Points of transition from one grade level to the next, from one school to the next, and across the years of high school
2. Results or consequences—positive or negative—of particular types of involvement at all levels for students, families, and teaching practice
3. The components of community in school and family partnerships
4. The roles of students in school, family, and community partnerships
5. Collaborations of researchers with policy leaders and educators.

Each of these topics represents an extensive research agenda, and each has implications for policy and practice.

Transitions

Perspectives and Previews: Which Practices of Partnership Are Effective at Important Points of Transition, from One Grade Level to the Next, Across School Levels, or at Other Times That Students Change Teachers or Schools? Students and their families age and grow and change grades, classes, and teachers every year. School and classroom programs and curricula become more complex each year and across levels. Schools also change as improvement plans and new programs are implemented. Teachers change as they become more experienced and as they add new approaches to their teaching repertoire. Communities change as leaders, resources, services, and citizens come and go. All parts and participants of school, family, and community connections change constantly. Studies of partnerships, even at one point in time, must be aware of the inevitable developmental patterns of schooling.

The theory of overlapping spheres of influence encourages the measurement of concepts of change. It posits the pushing and pulling of these contexts as they are drawn together or forced apart each year by the philosophies, backgrounds, and practices of teachers, families, students, and others. Longitudinal data, case study histories, and other methods are important for learning more about the changing nature of partnerships across the grades.

Studies of change and transitions are demanding. Several studies explore the continuity and change of family and community involvement with data collected over time on various topics. The studies use various methods, including surveys, interviews, observations, journals, and other reports from educators, parents, and students. Some of these studies use mixed methods (e.g., small-sample, local case studies contrasted with large-sample surveys on the same topics) to examine how families are involved in their children's education, how involvement changes, and how the changes affect students, families, and teachers.

Regular Transitions across the Grades.   Research is accumulating on patterns of partnership across the grades. For example, longitudinal studies were conducted on how family involvement changes from kindergarten to grade 2 in families with different cultural backgrounds (Bright, 1994; Hidalgo, 1994; Siu, 1994; Swap, 1994) and on how school programs to involve families change from grades 2 to 5 (Ames, Khoju, and Watkins, 1993). Many studies are still needed, however, to learn how partnerships change or remain the same across the grades from birth through high school; what the challenges that families meet at each stage of their children's development are; and the results for students, parents, and the schools of partnerships across the grades.

New issues about grade-level changes are emerging. Students and their families change teachers every year, but little is known about these regular events that alter school and family connections. For example, the research on families in different cultural groups reveals that children's new teacher may have different definitions of success than their prior teachers. Research is needed on how families learn about new teachers' ideas of how children succeed in their classrooms. A related question of equal importance is: How do teachers collect information from families about their children each year and periodically during a school year? Programmatic studies are needed on the organization and effects of various approaches to renew partnerships each year.

Alexander and Entwisle's (1996) research raises another question about the annual transitions that students and their families make from the summer to the fall of the school year. Regardless of the school organization or length of the school year, home is a year-round resource. More information is needed on the question: What do schools need to do to help families maximize their influence year-round? Presently, except in year-round schools, the summer is treated as a time that is separate from school. Research on summer learning and forgetting shows that summer is an influential time that affects students' skills and readiness for the next school year.

One study of the effects of summer learning packets suggests that marginal students, at risk of failing, are assisted in the fall by activities they conduct to keep their skills active in the summer (Epstein, Herrick, and Coates, 1996). Another study indicates that a summer community component in a family literacy program has positive effects for the family and students (Connors, 1993). Questions abound, however, about the best designs for active, interesting summer learning opportunities for students with their families and peers at home and in the community. Research and development are needed on effective approaches to integrate the summertime into the school year. For example, should (and how should) summer activities be organized for students and their families as part of the concluding school year or as part of the oncoming school year?

Key Points of Transition to New Levels of Schooling.   Another important focus for future work is on changes in practices of partnership when children change schools. Particularly, dramatic declines in involvement are reported after each transition point from preschool to regular school, from elementary to middle school, and from middle to high school (Baker and Stevenson, 1986; Epstein and Dauber, 1991). Studies indicate, however, that these declines are not fixed. For example, a national survey of principals reports that middle grade schools that conduct strong transitional activities (such as inviting parents to visit the middle school while the children are still in the elementary grades) tend to continue more practices of partnership with families through the middle grades (Epstein and Mac Iver, 1990). Only about 40 percent of the middle grade schools in the United States, however, conduct strong transitional activities for families. Another survey shows that only 22 percent of the parents in a regional sample of six urban, rural, and suburban schools report that they visited the high school when their children were in the middle grades, and only 40 percent of the students did so (Connors and Epstein, 1994).

Research is needed on the design and effects of strategies and activities to help students and their families make successful transitions from the elementary to middle schools, middle to high schools, and high schools to post-secondary settings, and on how to maintain appropriate family involvement across school levels. Educators are providing some insights into their practices. For example, an inner-city middle school conducted a formidable "orientation day" program for families and students on the first day of school and received high ratings for the effort from teachers, parents, and students (Epstein and Herrick, 1991). Such demonstration projects are informative, but studies of well-planned interventions will be needed to learn which kinds of orientation practices help most students, families, and schools. Newburg (1991) worked with educators to better understand the contacts and interactions that teachers need to make as students move from one school to the next. Research is needed on how families can be included in these transitional processes to help students prevent failure and maximize success in their new schools. What are the responsibilities of schools to conduct activities that inform families ahead of time about the changes that their children will experience when they move to new schools, and what can families do to understand and assist the transitions? Should feeder or receiver schools, or both, conduct these activities? What are the results of alternative approaches to communications about transitions? A parallel set of questions concerns the nature of family involvement in students' decisions about their post-secondary paths.

Unscheduled Transitions Due to Family Moves.   Other questions about changing partnerships are raised by patterns of mobility, such as when families move in and out of schools and communities midyear. Special problems must be solved when migrant, homeless, or other families move often (e.g., see PRIME, 1992). Unscheduled or unplanned transitions affect children, families, and their connections with schools. These transitions also affect what schools and teachers know or need to know about the entering children and families. Research is needed on the organization and effects of various approaches to partnerships with families in highly mobile schools and communities.

Other unscheduled transitions raise good research questions about the design and effects of school, family, and community partnerships. For example, when students are suspended from school, meetings with parents are required before the students are readmitted; or, when students are expelled from school, they and their families may enter new schools in new communities; or, when students drop out of school, they and their families may elect alternative schools or other programs in communities. Neither research nor practice has paid much attention to the design and results of connections with families that could assist students at times of dramatic, unscheduled changes in schools, and how to prevent these upheavals.

Transition to and through High School.   Of all the topics of continuity and change, the field has the least information about connections with families when students are in high school. Building on a handful of studies that raise numerous questions (Bauch, 1988; Clark, 1983; Dornbusch and Ritter, 1988), researchers at the Center are conducting surveys and field studies that ask: Which practices of partnerships are important for students, families, and schools at the high school level? How should practices to inform and involve families change from the freshman to senior years in high school? What are the results of partnerships for high school students, parents, and teachers?

One study included six high schools—two city, two suburban, and two rural—that agreed to work with researchers to design and administer surveys of teachers, parents, and students on their attitudes and ideas about partnerships in high schools (Epstein, Connors, and Salinas, 1993). The surveys were linked to the theory of overlapping spheres of influence and the framework of six types of involvement with questions that helped a high school chart present practices and plan a multiyear, full program of partnership. The high schools continued to implement and improve practices such as involving families with students in goal setting, improving information systems, increasing attendance, bolstering student morale, creating stronger connections with community services for students and families, and other activities (Epstein and Connors, 1994; Connors and Epstein, 1994).

Many questions about partnerships in high schools remain to be addressed. The NELS:88 Base-Year and Follow-Up surveys offer important data from middle and high schools, from 8th-, 10th-, and 12th-grade students and teachers, from 8th- and 12th-grade parents, and from students in post-secondary settings. One Center study of partnership in high schools using the NELS data from students shows that when parents continue their involvement over time (i.e., from middle school grade 8 to high school grade 10), students report better attitudes, behaviors, report card grades, and attendance in high school (Lee, 1994). Standardized achievement test scores are harder to change in the upper grades and are not directly affected by continued involvement from grades 8 to 10.

The NELS survey data from a large sample of schools, students, and families in grades 8, 10, 12, and post-secondary years will be useful to many researchers because they offer broad coverage of many types of family involvement over time. But the NELS data also are limited, as practices of partnership are measured mainly by single item indicators. Deeper data from purposeful local or regional samples are needed to study in detail the design and effects of partnerships at the high school level.

At each higher level of schooling, questions about partnerships with families and communities become more difficult because the students, contexts, and all participants become more diverse and complex. All of the topics discussed in this chapter need further study at the high school level, including transitions, outcomes, community connections, the roles of students, and how researchers and educators work together.

Results of Partnerships

Perspectives and Previews: What Are the Results or Outcomes of Particular Types of Involvement for Families, Students, and Teaching Practice at All Levels of Schooling? One of the most persistent misperceptions of many researchers, policy leaders, and educators is that any family involvement leads to all good things for students, parents, teachers, and schools. It is important to restate that the major types of involvement in the framework for research and practice are expected to bring about different important outcomes for students, parents, and educators (Becker and Epstein, 1982; Epstein, 1982 [Reading 3.9], 1986a, 1992). That is, not all activities to involve families lead quickly or directly to student learning, better report card grades, or higher standardized test scores. Rather, practices of the different types of involvement are expected to have theoretically linked results in the short term. For example, communications and interactions about parenting should first affect parents' informal interactions with their children; communications and interactions about reading should first affect a family focus on reading. If families continue to influence or reinforce student attitudes, behavior, or motivation, then student learning may improve over time. The pathways from particular family-school interactions to results for students, parents, or schools must be studied more rigorously than in the past, particularly with longitudinal data. Such studies are needed by educators to understand and predict the likely results of selecting and implementing particular practices to involve families in the schools and in their children's education.

For example, some Type 1 activities—such as workshops with parents or information about child development—may lead first to increasing (or, if poorly designed, to decreasing) parents' confidence about their understanding, supervision, and interaction with their children. Other practices, categorized in Type 3—such as new ways to organize, recruit, and train productive volunteers—may lead first to more effective (or, if poorly designed, to less effective) supervision by adults of student activities, more willingness of teachers to communicate in other ways with all families, or more varied curricular or extracurricular programs for students. By contrast, Type 5 practices—such as opening school decisions for input from parents or others in the community—may lead first to adults feeling more (or, if poorly organized, less) attachment to or support for the school. The positive or negative results of different involvement activities depend on the effectiveness of the design, implementation, measures, and improvements that are made over time.

Studies are needed on whether and how results of particular types of involvement generalize over time. For example, a chain of events may, hypothetically, take this pathway: Involvement of families in reading at home leads students, first, to greater attention to and motivation in reading. This may help students maintain or improve their reading skills. Over time, parental involvement in reading may lead to family discussions and interactions with children about other subjects. Also, teachers who communicate clearly with families about reading may, over time, improve their information to families about other subjects. This may help children see that their teachers want their families involved in their education, and that their families are interested in what they are learning and in talking with them at home about school and school plans. This support from families may motivate students to do their work in their school subjects and activities and plan for their future education and careers.

This line of events and effects may progress at different rates and with different degrees of success, depending on how much and how well the school informs and involves families and how the families and students participate. Activities, progress, and success may vary by teacher; grade level; students' starting skill levels; and other student, family, and school characteristics. For example, some types of family involvement may affect skills or test scores more in the lower grades when achievement test scores are more changeable. Change in standardized test scores may be made more easily by students with low scores and "room to grow," particularly if the involvement of families is clearly focused on specific achievement topics (Epstein, 1991). Or, changes in new classroom skills and knowledge may be made by better students, who respond more quickly to new information (Epstein and Dauber, 1995). These variations raise researchable questions that need to be asked to more fully understand the results of particular school and family partnerships.

Improving Definitions of Achievement for Studies of Effects of Partnerships on Students. The achievement question must start with clearer definitions and measures of achievements. There are many measures of achievement besides standardized test scores that indicate students' success in school. Some of these may be more responsive to school, home, and community conditions and, therefore, easier to change in the short term.

For example, specific subject knowledge and skills may change from the pretest to posttest in units of work in science, math, social studies, or English, depending on the teachers' presentation of content, students' classwork, extra activities conducted with volunteers at school, and homework. In one evaluation, a program of parent volunteers working with teachers to introduce art appreciation to social studies classes significantly increased students' familiarity with artwork. The subject-specific knowledge gained by students was linked directly to the content of the presentations by the volunteers (Epstein and Dauber, 1995). Several studies suggest that subject-specific family involvement affects learning in the related subject in the short term (Epstein, 1991; Epstein, Herrick, and Coates, 1996).

Homework completion is another measurable achievement that influences student success in school and that may be affected by particular activities that involve families (Epstein, 1987c [Reading 3.8]; Epstein, Jackson, and Salinas, 1994; Scott-Jones, 1995). If students complete their homework, they may attain higher report card grades, particularly if homework completion is counted by teachers as one component of students' marks. Or, homework completion may help students be better prepared for a class test, gain higher test scores, and, thereby, boost report card grades. New studies can help identify the effects of explicit processes and connections that are important for researchers, educators, families, and students to understand and apply.

There are other indicators of achievement. Good school attitudes, behavior, attendance, and the development of talents, interests, and other personal qualities are important for success in school. All of these may be affected (positively or negatively) by home and school practices of partnerships. Wise course choices and plans for the future also are important achievements in the upper grades that may be influenced by school, family, and student connections. These alterable outcomes that represent and contribute to success in school stand in contrast to narrow concerns with students' relative placements on standardized achievement test scores.

Because all students gain skills over time, it is difficult for many students to change their relative placement on tests or grades. There are, of course, exceptions, such as students who dramatically find their way and become much better students than they were before or students who lose their way and fall farther and farther behind. Studies are needed on the part that family involvement plays in increasing or maintaining student motivation to learn and positive attitudes and behaviors under these different conditions, or in encouraging greater effort by students who could do better in school.

Positive and Negative Results of Involvement.   Extant studies have generated compelling questions about the results or outcomes of partnerships. Although positive results of family involvement on various student outcomes are consistent and have been given the most attention (Henderson and Berla, 1994), some studies report negative correlations of some types of involvement with student achievements and behaviors and parental attitudes. For example, one study showed that students who are lower achievers spend more time on homework and receive more help with homework (Epstein, 1987c). The link of help with homework and low achievement is provocative because it either indicates that families who help are lowering their children's skills or that students who need more help are given more help by their families.

Another negative correlation reported in several studies, even under highly controlled statistical procedures, links parent and teacher contacts (e.g., frequent phone calls, conferences, and other communications) with students' academic problems and bad behavior (Lee, 1994). Also, frequent parent-teacher communications about student behavior are linked to parents' low ratings of the school and to parents' reports that their students like school less, are poorer students, are absent more, and have other negative attitudes and behaviors (Epstein and Jacobsen, 1994). These patterns stand in contrast to positive results in the same studies that are reported for other types of school-family links. The patterns are provocative because they could be interpreted to mean that home-school communications produce academic and behavioral problems, or that, presently, schools and families make contact more often when students run into difficulties, to try to solve the problems.

There are clues that the negative correlations occur because educators reach out to many sources, including parents, to obtain extra help, attention, and resources for students who are having academic or behavioral problems. These good intentions may not pay off, however, if the only communications between school and home are about trouble. Educators who are working to develop programs of partnership recognize that they need to conduct positive communications to establish a base of good relationships to draw on if they need families to help students solve academic or behavioral problems. In some high schools, for example, educators designed activities to start the school year with a positive meeting or phone call from a "key contact person" who is available as a resource to parents all year or use "positive post cards" that send home good news about a student's work or contributions throughout the school year (Epstein and Connors, 1994).

To address this issue in practice, a school district in Seattle took a comprehensive approach in two middle schools, with full-time, school-based "parent outreach coordinators" who contacted and worked with students and families if, on their report cards, students failed two or more courses. The goal was to prevent students from failing again in the next report card period. Contacts, guidance, and follow-ups with students, families, teachers, school counselors, and others were designed to alert and involve all who had a stake in the students' success. A parent room at each school, facilitated by the parent outreach coordinators, made all parents welcome. The parent outreach coordinators received very positive evaluations for involving families, creating a welcoming school climate, and establishing positive relationships to help solve difficult academic and other problems (Earle, 1989).

Any practice can be done well or poorly. There are risks, of course, that poorly designed or badly implemented practices to involve families will be ineffective or cause problems for students, families, and schools (Scott-Jones, 1987). But studies by many researchers using many methods show that well-designed and well-implemented practices yield positive results on various outcomes for students, parents, and schools (Ames, Khoju, and Watkins, 1993; Clark, 1983; Dornbusch and Ritter, 1988; Epstein and Dauber, 1991; Scott-Jones, 1987; and many others).

Studies are needed that determine if students who are having academic or behavioral difficulties in school improve over time if their families contact or are contacted by the schools, and if the students, families, and schools work together to solve the problems. It is not enough to measure family-school contact alone—the reaching out to determine whether family involvement helps students improve their behavior or skills. The results of those efforts must also be measured. Longitudinal studies are needed to determine if, after receiving attention from home and school, students improve their attendance or behavior, pass their courses, and stay in school. We need to know which contacts and follow-up activities are most successful in helping students get back on successful paths, which students and families respond best to various interactions, or how long schools should try to get students to solve their own problems before families are involved, and how these patterns of problem-solving change across the grades.

To answer such questions about the effects of family involvement on achievements and other outcomes over time, research must statistically control for students' prior achievement, other prior outcomes, and families' prior involvement. Using a full effects model with the NELS:88 Base-Year and First Follow-Up surveys of students, Lee (1994) showed that family involvement in monitoring and interacting with students about homework and, particularly, family discussions about schoolwork, courses, grades, and the future have positive effects on high school students' report card grades and attitudes about school and teachers, even after statistically accounting for family involvement and student outcomes in the middle grades.

There are indications that effects of particular types of involvement may vary by level of schooling and by reporter or participant. For example, in the middle grades, according to principals, many types of school practices of partnership appear to boost one outcome: student attendance (Epstein and Lee, 1993). At the high school level, according to students, one type of involvement—family discussions about school, courses, and the future—appears to have positive effects on many outcomes, including attitudes, behaviors, and grades (Lee, 1994). These results reflect the strengths and weaknesses of the available data and raise many questions about effects of family involvement on students, parents, and teaching practice that must be addressed with better data and varied methods of analysis.

A detailed agenda for research on the outcomes of school, family, and community involvement can be drawn with questions about how each type of involvement is implemented in a comprehensive program. Following are examples of targeted questions on specific practices and their results that could extend research and contribute immediately useful information to teachers and administrators.

For Type 1—Parenting: How are workshop topics selected, conducted, and disseminated so that all families (not just those who can come to school) can obtain and apply information on topics that are important to parents? What are the short- and long-term effects for parents, students, and schools of parental participation in or information from workshops on parenting and child rearing across the grades? How does information from families about their children assist educators or other parents?

For Type 2—Communicating: How are report cards explained so that all families can understand them? How can families be helped to work with their children and teachers if they (and the students) believe that better grades are attainable? What are the results of these efforts on student report card grades? How can conferences be designed, scheduled, and conducted to increase the attendance of parents who work outside the home? How are students included in and affected by parent-teacher or parent-student-teacher conferences about student attendance, behavior, attitudes, achievement, goal setting, or other topics? How is information provided on school programs or course choices so that all families can understand and discuss the options and consequences of choices with their children? How do such discussions affect the patterns of choices that are made?

For Type 3—Volunteering (and Supporting School Programs): How are volunteers recruited, welcomed, trained, and evaluated? How are the skills and talents of volunteers identified and matched with needs of teachers, students, and administrators? How do various volunteer programs and activities affect student learning, attitudes, and behavior; teacher attitudes toward parents; parent attitudes and skills; and other families?

For Type 4—Learning at Home: In which forms can information about students' classwork and homework be offered to help families assist their children with their school responsibilities? How can activities be designed to enable families to use their unique "funds of knowledge" (Moll, Amanti, Neff, and Gonzalez, 1992) to motivate their youngsters to learn new things at home and to enable students to interact with their families about things they are learning? How do activities at home that promote student and family interactions affect students' attitudes, skills, and homework?

For Type 5—Decision Making: How can all families give information to and receive information from parent leaders who represent them on councils and committees? How do family or community representatives on school site councils, school improvement teams, or committees alter (1) school improvement plans and activities or (2) the knowledge and attitudes of all parents about the school?

For Type 6—Collaborating with the Community: How can schools help families obtain useful information about and access to community programs, services, and resources that may benefit them and their children? Which forms or approaches are most effective for sharing this information with all families? What effects will these approaches have on students' work in school? How can schools, families, and students contribute to their communities, and with what effects?

Evaluations focused on these and many other questions for each type of involvement should contribute to a menu of practices and their results. Information on the likely results, positive or negative, and the possibilities, difficulties, and solutions to problems of involvement would help educators make more purposeful choices among practices of partnership to reach specific school or family goals.

Community Connections

Perspectives and Previews: How Can We Better Understand Components of Community in School, Family, and Community Partnerships? *Community* is an old and sweeping term in sociology that demands new and focused attention in studies of school, family, and community partnerships. A broad definition of community encompasses all individuals and institutions—in and out of school—who have a stake in the success of children in school and in the well-being of children and families. This includes schools, families, neighborhood groups, clubs and associations, businesses, libraries, local government, religious organizations, parks and recreation departments, police and juvenile justice offices, social service and health agencies, and others who serve children and families as a matter of course or in times of trouble. Presently, there is great interest in the potential and problems of connecting schools, families, and communities in ways that will benefit student learning and development. There is widespread interest in integrating services across community agencies and in creating structures and processes that encourage interagency cooperation and collaborations to promote family support, family and student health, and student success in school. (See, for example, a report series from the National Center for Service Integration, e.g., Kinney, Strand, Hagerup, and Bruner, 1994; and Wynn, Costello, Halpern, and Richman, 1994.)

The community is one of the overlapping spheres of influence on student learning and development in the theoretical model of partnerships (Epstein, 1992). The relationships and resources of people and groups in a community are expressed in family-community, school-community, and family, school, and community interactions.

Researchers often define and represent community using aggregated data about families or citizens in an area. For example, a community is sometimes defined by the average education level of all the parents of students in a school or geographic location; by the percentage of families with particular qualities (e.g., single parents, race or ethnic minority group, poverty level, or other economic indicators in a neighborhood); by the average educational aspirations that parents have for their children or that students have for themselves; or by an average or percentage of other descriptive variables. In the same way, U.S. Census (or similar) data have been used to characterize populations in geographic areas surrounding particular schools (such as the percentage of citizens below the poverty line in a census tract around a school).

These variables represent some but not all factors that may influence children's learning. They are limited because they rate communities in terms of more or less of selected economic, intellectual, and social qualities or resources, such as high/low income, predominantly black/white, employed/unemployed, or married/single parents. One variable is too simple a descriptor of communities. That is, a high-income community may also be predominantly minority; a low-income community may be highly supportive of their schools and eager for their children to attend college. Even if several descriptive variables are considered simultaneously, the resulting combined scores set communities on a continuum that labels them as high or low. Also, such labels are limiting because of the distance they place between a rating and the actual connections and activities of families and schools with children that influence student learning, attitudes, and behavior.

There are more proximate ways to characterize and study the resources and exchanges in communities that may assist students and families. Researchers are taking some different approaches to define and study community by focusing on strengths that are available in people, programs, and organizations in all communities. The idea is to get closer to what communities *do,* in contrast to what communities *are.* The same change was important for understanding families and family-school connections—that is, focusing on what schools and families can arrange to accomplish together, rather than only on their immutable (if more easily measured) characteristics. The redirection leads to new ways to measure and to influence family, school, and community connections from infancy to adolescence.

Researchers have studied the impact of community programs on *very* young children and their families, including studies of programs to help parents read with toddlers (Morisset, 1993) and studies of the organization and effects of family literacy programs for parents of preschool, elementary, and middle school students (Connors, 1993, 1994; Dolan, 1992). Another study involved the design, development, implementation, and effects of a process to train low-income women in a community for employment in child care and to improve their own parenting and involvement activities and their children's school readiness (Kagan, Neville, and Rustici, 1993).

Other researchers studied the impact of community programs for older students and families, including studies of coaching processes and programs in which adults share their skills and talents with youth (Nettles, 1992, 1993). Other studies focused on the organization of child care programs to assist teenage mothers to continue to attend high school (Scott-Jones, 1993) and on alternative approaches and results of interagency collaborations for high school students that include health, recreation, job training, child care, and other services (Burch, Palanki, and Davies, 1995; Dolan, 1994).

The programs for younger and older children and their families may be based in community locations to provide services or in school locations to more easily contact and serve families and children. Community agencies, school districts, or community or parent volunteers may be responsible for staffing these and other programs that connect students and families with the strengths and services in their communities. Other connections may be made to enable students, families, or educators to contribute to their communities.

Even limited connections—such as when one school works with one community agency—present many challenges. For example, one community-run family literacy program conducted in a school building required collaborative activities such as cross-agency planning and sharing of time, space, staff, responsibilities, and budgets (Connors, 1993). These new relationships needed to be developed by the community and school staffs. Programs operating over the long term are working to solve these problems (Dolan, 1994, 1995; Palanki, Burch, and Davies, 1995), but the challenges and solutions and the effects of interagency or integrated services programs are mainly uncharted.

Questions about interagency connections open a formidable research agenda: What are the pros and cons, possibilities and problems, benefits and disadvantages of relatively simple connections of schools or families with one or two groups or programs in the community, or of more complex interagency collaborations? How should programs with connections to the community be organized, implemented, and monitored to benefit children and families, schools, and the community?

Exploring Strengths in Diverse Communities.   Researchers also have explored the strengths of parents and communities with various racial, ethnic, and cultural characteristics (Delgado, 1992; Hidalgo, 1992, 1994; Hidalgo, Bright, Siu, Swap, and Epstein, 1995; Perry, 1993; Siu, 1992, 1994; Swap, 1994; Swap and Krasnow, 1992). These studies identified resources and strengths in families and communities that would be labeled "poor" or "deficient" if only aggregated economic statistics or census-type data were used to define them. For example, these studies suggest that resources within families and communities include rituals, traditional values, family dreams and aspirations, cultural norms for student behavior, racial identity development, practices that involve families in their children's education and schools, and formal and informal community organizations that support families.

These studies are contributed new information that may help schools understand the complex nature of families and communities. For example, Hidalgo (1992) noted that immigrant families who aim to retain cultural identities and ties in their local communities require schools to change more than do immigrant families who aim to assimilate into the mainstream community. The former wish to be recognized and respected by their schools for their differences. Their cultures and backgrounds are potential resources for the schools. The unique needs of these families and children may require some special attention from the schools. The latter, emphasizing assimilation, wish to avoid attention by the schools to their newness or differences, even if they maintain their cultural traditions and identities in the home and community. They may work to change their own behaviors and attitudes to meet the expectations and demands of the schools.

In another study, Delgado (1992) identified the potential strengths of "natural support systems" in Puerto Rican communities. These include networks of extended families, religious groups, merchants, social clubs, and other individuals or groups that people contact for assistance instead of (or in addition to) seeking help from formal institutions such as hospitals, health centers, and schools. Community strengths are not often recognized or counted in studies that employ traditional economic, educational, or social statistics. Yet the informal networks may help families and children with many basic personal, economic, spiritual, and social needs. Delgado contended that community resources could be used in better ways by formal organizations, such as schools, to communicate with students and families.

Nettles (1992) identified coaching as one way to tap communities' strengths. By coaching, adults share their skills and talents with children, including public speaking, chess, sports, music, dance, art, science, and many other interests. She proposed a framework for how to think about, organize, and implement coaching programs. To use the framework in practice, she discussed strategies of how successful coaches teach, assess, structure environments, and offer social support to students (Nettles, 1993).

Parent rooms or parent centers aim to establish a school community by welcoming parents to the school building. In these centers, parents may help each other, help the school, and receive assistance or information from the school and from the community. As described by Johnson (1993, 1994) and Coates (1992), a parent room, parent center, or parent club is a place that draws parents, teachers, students, and community participants together and increases the frequency, duration, and types of connections that could help more children succeed in school. The first studies and descriptions of parent centers in schools and family resource centers in communities raise many questions for research on whether and how these organizational structures make it easier for schools to help families meet their responsibilities to their children and to help families help students solve academic or behavioral problems, should they arise.

The new studies of community work from the inside out, starting with the traditions and talents of families or other groups. The research asks questions about how to harness the strengths that are in all communities to assist students, engage families, and improve schools. Many questions remain, however, about the organization of community resources and patterns and effects of school, family, and community interactions. For example, How can all communities' strengths be tapped in ways that support families, children's growth and development, success in school, in infancy, childhood, and adolescence? Who will organize this work? How might schools draw on the strengths of families' language and cultural differences and other family and community skills and talents to improve the education of all children and to improve the schools' relationships with families? How should partnerships change or remain the same for families with various cultural, racial, or economic backgrounds, across the grades, to both create a sense of community among all families in a school and meet the needs of particular families? How does the community foster learning, reinforce schooling, and recognize accomplishments? Results of such studies should contribute new ideas about how to define, measure, and mobilize communities' strengths and promote school, family, and community partnerships that, ultimately, benefit students who are the future citizens, leaders, and families in communities.

Role of Students

Perspectives and Previews: How Can We Better Understand the Role of the Student in School, Family, and Community Partnerships? An important, emerging theme in new research is the role of the student in school, family, and community partnerships. The theory of overlapping spheres of influence places students at the center of the model (Epstein, 1987a). The theory assumes that families, schools, and communities share an interest in and responsibility for children all across the school years and that the main reason that educators, parents, and students interact is to assist students to succeed in school and in life. It is important to focus on how schools develop good programs of partnerships and on what parents want their schools to do to inform and involve them each year. It is more important, indeed crucial, to recognize that the student is the active learner, ultimately responsible for his or her education, and the main communicator between school and home.

Research is needed to define, design, and study students' roles in school, family, and community partnerships at different grade levels. This topic ties student development to the design and effects of family involvement in education. It promotes, even demands, interdisciplinary attention to stages of youngsters' development, interactions and relationships of many individuals, and the multiple contexts or environments in which students learn and in which family, school, and community links occur.

Most studies of family-school links have not paid attention to the students' roles in partnerships. This is true despite the fact that students have long been reporters about their schools and their families. A few examples show, however, that the student role has been hovering in research on partnerships, waiting for and deserving more attention. Bronfenbrenner (1979) advised that socialization and education should be organized so that, over time, the balance of power is given to the developing person. Also, in an earlier study, Epstein (1983) found that age-appropriate decision-making opportunities at school and at home increase students' independence and other positive outcomes. Most often, however, literature on schools or families assumes that students are "acted on" rather than actors or "done to" rather than doers. The different assumptions about the students' roles in education raise questions for research about optimal designs for schooling and for school and family partnerships.

Finding the Students' Voices. This theme is finding a voice in other areas of school reform, such as reciprocal teaching, cooperative learning, constructivist approaches, and other active learning strategies. The role of the student in partnerships is being addressed in a few studies that have asked students directly about how they view the connections of their families and schools and how they participate as partners (Ames, Khoju, and Watkins, 1993; Dornbusch and Ritter, 1988; Epstein, 1982; Montandon and Perrenoud, 1987). Students' opinions are informative and often surprising. For example, students express an overwhelming desire to be active participants in parent-teacher conferences and to be represented on school committees (Connors and Epstein, 1994).

In practice, educators are keenly aware that students play *the* key role in their own education. For example, many important activities in high school (e.g., choosing courses, finding career interests, planning for the future, understanding school policies) are presently often left up to the student alone. New approaches to partnerships with families focus on how middle and high schools design and conduct activities to enable families to provide extra support, as appropriate, on important decisions that affect the lives of students and their families (Epstein and Connors, 1994, 1995).

Importantly, students at all grade levels report that they want their families to be more involved and that they are willing to be the communicators and to conduct important exchanges with their families about schoolwork and school decisions (Connors and Epstein, 1994; Epstein and Herrick, 1991). Earlier studies show that when they know their families are involved, students report that their schools and families are more similar, that their teachers and parents know each other, that they do more homework on weekends, and that they like school better (Epstein, 1982). In high school, students who report that their families are involved in many different ways at school and who discuss school and their futures at home have more positive attitudes, better attendance, and better grades than other students, even after accounting for their scores on these outcomes in the middle grades (Lee, 1994).

If youngsters do not define themselves as "students," then they must be something else, with no need to be in school. Those who feel the support of their family, teachers, peers, and community for their work as students are more likely to maintain that view of themselves and stay in school. Thus, ironically, students' participation in school, family, and community partnerships may contribute to their increasingly independent decisions about their education.

Research is greatly needed on such questions as, How shall activities be organized to enable students to take appropriate leadership for their learning at all grade levels? How much audience and support, rules and regulations, independence and self-direction do students need across the grades and in diverse communities? There are many other questions about students' motivations, goals, and achievements. Questions about the roles that students play in partnerships are linked to all of the preceding topics. That is, studies are needed on students' roles in partnerships at points of transition from one grade or school to the next, the results or outcomes of all six types of involvement that include or exclude students, and the results of activities that involve students and their families with the community.

Students' roles and student development have not yet been well integrated into studies of school, family, and community partnerships or in policies and practices of involvement. These topics may be crucial for understanding, implementing, and succeeding with partnerships across the grades. Undoubtedly, students are key to the success of all aspects of school reform, including family and community involvement.

Connections of Research, Policy, and Practice

Perspectives and Previews: How Can Researchers, Policy Leaders, and Educators Collaborate to Develop, Study, and Improve School, Family, and Community Partnerships? Collaborative work and thoughtful give-and-take by researchers, policy leaders, and educators are largely responsible for the progress made in the 1990s in understanding and developing school, family, and community partnerships. Similar collaborations will be important for future progress in this and other topics of school reform. There are two requirements for successful collaboration: multilingualism and mutual respect. That is, researchers and educators must talk each other's languages and understand and respect each other's expertise to combine talents to improve schools. For researchers, this means learning the vocabularies and communication skills that are needed to converse with and to write for diverse audiences, including educational policy leaders, principals, teachers, and parents. For educators, this requires a readiness and capacity to use research to address topics of school improvement. Also, researchers need to gain familiarity with the challenges of teaching highly diverse students and the daily life of schools. Educators need to gain an understanding of the challenges of collecting useful data to analyze processes and effects of school and classroom programs. Collaborations increase conversations and mutual respect as researchers, educators, parents, and students learn about their common goals and complementary strengths (Epstein, 1996). The same requirements hold as families and students are included as planners, implementers, evaluators, and in other roles. Researchers and educators need to build communication skills and mutual respect with families and students and an understanding that parents are, indeed, partners in their children's continuing education and that students are the main actors in education.

Sharing the Role of Expert.   The requirements for educators and researchers to speak with and develop respect for each other are addressed in a collaborative approach called "sharing the role of expert" (Epstein, 1986b; Epstein, Herrick, and Coates, 1996). This approach recognizes that educators (policy leaders, teachers, and administrators) have particular talents and opportunities that are vital to the successful design and implementation of research-based practices. For example, administrators and teachers are responsible for implementing new strategies to involve families in their schools or classrooms as volunteers or to engage students with their families on math homework. Researchers, too, have particular talents and opportunities to design, evaluate, report, and disseminate the effects of school improvement efforts. Parents also have unique perspectives, concerns, and skills that relate to their children's success in school and that expand researchers' and educators' views. Together, educators, researchers, and parents plan new practices; collect, analyze, and interpret data; and revise and improve plans, drawing on each other's expertise. The assumption is that these collaborations should lead to better practices, better processes, and better evaluations and interpretations of results than would be accomplished if the participants worked alone.

Sharing the role of expert alters how research is conducted. For example, when working directly with schools, a two-step process of evaluation is useful. The first step is to assess whether a practice actually is implemented and how its design could be improved; the second step is to study whether a practice (as implemented and improved) has measurable effects on students, families, or teaching practice. This sequence of collaborative activities helps educators and researchers get used to working with each other and ensures that measures of results will not be made before a program is actually in place.

There are several emerging forms of collaborative work by researchers and educators, all of which require sharing the role of expert: school-university cooperation (Alliance for Learning, 1994; Harkevy and Puckett, 1990; Miller and O'Shea, 1995; Sirotnik and Goodlad, 1988); teacher research, teacher-led inquiry, reflective teaching (Cochran-Smith and Lytle, 1993; Cohn and Kottkamp, 1993; Lieberman, 1993; Maher and Alson, 1990; Newburg, 1991); parent-teacher action research (Burch and Palanki, 1994; Davies, Palanki, and Burch, 1993); and action teams for school, family, and community partnerships (Epstein and Connors, 1994; Epstein, Herrick, and Coates, 1996). The various forms have different implications for the nature and products of the work of teachers and researchers. All, however, aim to encourage education policy leaders, educators, and researchers to work together, extend and share knowledge, conduct research on actions taken to improve schools, and take actions based on the results of research to continue improvements. Several include parents, and some include students or others from the community as participants in planning programs and practices, as well as in conducting and evaluating them.

Collaborations between Researchers and Education Policy Leaders. Two examples of productive collaborations of researchers and policy leaders for increasing family-school partnerships include the development of a state policy on parent involvement in California (Solomon, 1991) and the design and work of Utah's Center on Families in Education (Lloyd, 1996). In these cases, educators read, adapted, and extended research for their locations and purposes, and researchers supported and assisted the policy leaders and educators in those locations with their work. Many other researchers and educators have worked together to produce better school, family, and community partnerships (e.g., see articles by Chrispeels, Warner, Davies, D'Angelo, and others in the special section *of Phi Delta Kappan,* 1991; see also several examples of programs based on researchers' and educators' collaborations in Fagnano and Werber, 1994; Fruchter, Galletta, and White, 1992; Rioux and Berla, 1993).

Collaborations between Researchers and School Teams. Two examples of productive collaborations of researchers, educators, and parents to increase family, school, and community partnerships include Parent-Teacher Action Research Teams and Action Teams for School, Family, and Community Partnerships.

Parent-Teacher Action Research Teams, designed by Davies and his colleagues, include teachers and parents in site-based units for school improvement and problem solving (Burch, 1993; Davies, Palanki, and Burch, 1993; Palanki, Burch, and Davies, 1995). Educators and parents work together as change agents and as researchers to improve practices of partnerships in their schools. The teams define problems or needs, identify approaches to solve the problems, design and implement interventions, examine results, and follow up their work in meetings with further plans. They may choose one problem to solve or work on several aspects of partnership. This approach aims to develop "teacher researchers" and "parent researchers" who will continue to work together on projects to improve partnerships and other aspects of school reform. In the projects using this approach, paid facilitators assisted the work of the Parent-Teacher Action Teams, and researchers focused on cross-site policy studies.

Action Teams for School, Family, and Community Partnerships, designed by Epstein and her colleagues, establish teams of teachers, administrators, parents, and where possible, students and members of the community who work for three years or more as the "action" arm of the school council or school improvement team on the topic of partnerships. The action team works with others to assess their school's present practices of partnership; parent, teacher, and student needs; and desired practices. The team members become chairs or cochairs to oversee and lead the implementation of multiyear plans of projects for the six types of involvement in our framework for partnership. They assess and share progress, problems, and new plans each year; link and report to the school improvement council; and communicate with the total school community about the school's activities to involve families. This approach is useful for developing ongoing programs of partnerships in elementary, middle, and high schools (Epstein and Connors, 1994; Epstein and Dauber, 1991; Epstein, Herrick, and Coates, 1996). It has been implemented in useful forms in Utah's and Wisconsin's state grants programs (Lloyd, 1996; Wisconsin Department of Public Instruction, 1994) and in many districts and schools. Other action teams could be arranged for other topics on the school improvement agenda.

In these projects, researchers worked with educators and parents to develop and improve this approach and to study particular practices of partnership and their effects. For example, the Teachers Involve Parents in Schoolwork (TIPS) interactive homework process (Epstein, Jackson, and Salinas, 1994) and the volunteers in social studies and art process (Epstein and Salinas, 1991) were developed collaboratively by researchers and educators, based on sharing the role of expert and the two-step evaluation process. Now, other educators may use the action team approach and the research-based TIPS interactive homework and volunteer processes. Using these strategies, other researchers may become partners with school teams in their local districts, states, or regions to assist them in assessing the effectiveness of their practices.

The Center's studies demonstrate different but related routes to increasing schools' capacities to plan, implement, and continue to build programs of partnership. The emerging collaborative approaches have different emphases, however. In Parent-Teacher Action Research, the goal is for teachers and parents to design and conduct research on specific practices that they add to their programs. In Action Teams for School, Family, and Community Partnerships, the goal is for teachers, administrators, parents, and others to plan a multiyear program including the six types of involvement, informally monitor or evaluate progress, update plans, and improve practices. The collaboration of educators, parents, and researchers on these action teams relieves some of the burden on educators who, with limited time, may not be able to transform into statistical experts, and the collaboration relieves some of the burden on researchers who cannot become instant classroom experts with knowledge of what will work in daily practice. Also, this approach preserves a role for researchers in action research and increases chances of improving the research base and of assisting many schools with their work.

Research is needed on the impact of these and other forms of collaborative work by researchers with policy leaders, educators, and parents. But more pointedly, collaborative strategies could be particularly helpful for addressing the four topics discussed previously in this chapter. The first topic, understanding changes across the grades and other important transitions, is of interest to researchers who seek better information on student development and change. Educators, in turn, need better solutions to problems of student adjustment in transitions from grade to grade, school to school, or developmental stage to stage. Researchers and educators, working collaboratively, could address common questions about how one teacher should link with the next, how information might flow from school to school at points of transition, how families should be engaged in their children's transitions, and other issues discussed previously.

The second topic, understanding the results or outcomes of programs and practices that involve families, is of major interest to researchers of school effects. Educators, in turn, pay attention to the bottom-line results of their educational programs. Researchers and educators, working collaboratively, could address common questions about the effects of programs and practices to improve the school climate; increase teachers' effectiveness; assist mothers, fathers, or other family members in their interactions with their children and the school; and increase student learning and development, all expected outcomes of productive partnerships.

The third topic, understanding connections of schools and families with community services, resources, and organizations, challenges researchers to study the organization and effects of integrated services and to better define communities' roles in supporting children as students. Educators, in turn, need feasible ways to mobilize support from and connect to the school community, the students' home communities, and various communities that surround the school with potential strengths and resources. Some innovative activities to identify and tap into school communities have been designed by educators working with researchers (e.g., Floyd, 1994; Goode, 1990), but relatively little is known about the optimal organization of school, family, and community connections. Researchers and educators, working collaboratively, could address common questions about how connections with individuals, groups, and organizations in proximate and distant communities could improve the school, strengthen students' skills, assist families, benefit the community, and address issues discussed previously.

The fourth topic, understanding roles that students play in school, family, and community partnerships, interests researchers in many disciplines who study child and adolescent development. Educators want better information about ways to develop students' responsibility, including the optimal mix of guidance from school and home and the design opportunities to develop independence. Researchers and educators, working collaboratively, could address common questions about student motivation; how students should be participants in school, family, and community partnerships; and other issues discussed previously. Linked to this topic, researchers and educators working collaboratively also might explore questions on the most productive roles in school, family, and community partnerships for principals, district and state leaders, on-site coordinators, and families in relation to the roles of students in their own education.

In the next few years there will be many opportunities for new collaborations of researchers with policy leaders and educators to study the design and effects of guidelines, mandates, and other policies about school, family, and community connections. Two 1994 federal laws (Goals 2000: Educate America Act and Title I of the Elementary and Secondary Education Act) offer directives and funding to all states to enable districts and schools to design and test ideas for productive partnerships with families. The diverse responses to these federal laws across states, districts, and schools open countless opportunities for researchers to work with policy leaders and educators to address the topics discussed in this chapter and other questions that emerge in local planning sessions. Comparative studies also will be informative on the effects on partnership programs of states' contrasting decisions about budgets, staff responsibilities, and elements of the new programs.

By sharing the role of expert with those who design and implement programs in the schools, researchers could assist educators and increase the knowledge available on alternative approaches for organizing, funding, and implementing school, family, and community partnerships. Studies will be important on such questions as: How will states identify effective practices among demonstration programs and extend options for implementing successful programs to other districts and schools? How can schools be assisted to move from very limited investments in one type of involvement (e.g., volunteers or school councils only) to more comprehensive programs? Overall, what would a supportive policy structure look like at the federal, state, district, and local school levels that would support school activities to plan, implement, and evaluate practices of partnership? On many topics, then, researchers and educators can combine talents to study the effects of the growing number of investments in partnerships, with the goal of identifying effective practices and their results that may be considered by many schools, districts, and states as they plan and improve their programs.

CONCLUSION

Over the next half dozen years or so there will be intense national attention on whether and how students succeed in school, how schools improve their instructional programs, and how families are informed and involved in schools and in their children's education. Attention also will increase on whether and how communities assist schools, families, and students. These practical concerns open important opportunities for researchers to work with educators to design and study many topics for school improvement, including school, family, and community partnerships.

Studies have accumulated indicating that (1) students do better in school if their parents are involved in various ways; (2) more parents become involved when schools establish and conduct good programs of partnership; (3) schools can be assisted by federal, state, district, and school leadership and policies to develop strong, responsive programs; (4) research and evaluation activities can identify differences between strong and weak policies, good and bad practices; and (5) results of many studies have produced a research-based framework that should enable any school to plan and implement practices for the six major types of involvement, including practices to help meet specific goals for school improvement.

Despite real progress in understanding the potential and challenges of partnerships, there are many more questions to ask. This chapter previewed topics that will benefit from the attention of researchers, policy leaders, educators, and families: partnerships at points of transition in schools and at the high school level; the effects of particular practices and full programs of partnership in the short and long term; the connections of communities with schools and families for student learning and development; the roles of students in partnerships; and forms of collaborative research and development by researchers, policy leaders, educators, and parents.

Other questions may be raised. For example, we need to know more about the nature and effects of fathers' participation in school and family partnerships across the grades; the effects on partnerships of particular federal, state, and local policies separately and in combination; the impact of contrasting forms of staff development and teacher and administrator preservice and advanced education on practices of partnership; the connections of parent education programs with broader programs of school and family partnerships; and the connections of partnerships with other topics of school reform. These important issues can be targeted within the topics discussed in this chapter.

The complex questions for research and for practice ensure that family-school links will remain a dynamic field of study.

REFERENCES

Alexander, K. L., and D. R. Entwisle. (1996). Schools and children at risk. Pages 67–88 in *Family-school links: How do they affect educational outcomes?*, edited by A. Booth and J. F. Dunn. Mahwah, NJ: Lawrence Erlbaum Associates.

Alliance for Learning. (1994, April 13). *Education Week* XIII (25, Suppl.): 1–24.

Ames, C., M. Khoju, and T. Watkins. (1993). *Parents and schools: The impact of school-to-home communications on parents' beliefs and perceptions.* Center Rep. No. 15. Baltimore: Center on Families, Communities, Schools and Children's Learning, Johns Hopkins University.

Baker, D. P., and D. L. Stevenson. (1986). Mothers' strategies for children's school achievement: Managing the transition to high school. *Sociology of Education* 59: 156–166.

Bauch, P. A. (1988). Is parent involvement different in private schools? *Educational Horizons* 66: 78–82.

Becker, H. J., and J. L. Epstein. (1982). Parent involvement: A study of teacher practices. *Elementary School Journal* 83: 85–102. (Reading 3.1).

Brian, D. (1994). *Parental involvement in high schools.* Paper presented at the annual meeting of the American Educational Research Association, April, in New Orleans.

Bright, J. A. (1994. Winter). Beliefs in action: Family contributions to African-American student success. *Equity and Choice* 10(2): 5–13.

Bronfenbrenner, U. (1979). *The ecology of human development: Experiment by nature and design.* Cambridge, MA: Harvard University Press.

Burch, P. (1993). Circles of change: Action research on family-school-community partnerships. *Equity and Choice* 10(1): 11–16.

Burch, P., and A. Palanki. (1994). Action research on family-school-community partnerships. *Journal of Emotional and Behavioral Problems* 1(4): 16–19.

Burch, P., A. Palanki, and D. Davies. (1995). *From clients to partners: Four case studies of collaboration and family involvement in the development of school-linked services.* Center Rep. No. 29. Baltimore: Center on Families, Communities, Schools and Children's Learning, Johns Hopkins University.

Clark, R. M. (1983). *Family life and school achievement: Why poor Black children succeed or fail.* Chicago: University of Chicago Press.

Coates, L. (1992). The parent club. Pages 122–125 in *The school-community cookbook,* edited by C. Hyman. Baltimore: Fund for Educational Excellence.

Cochran-Smith, M., and S. Lytle. (1993). *Inside/outside: Teacher research and knowledge.* New York: Teachers College Press.

Cohn, M. M., and R. B. Kottkamp. (1993). *Teachers: The missing voice in education.* Albany: State University of New York Press.

Coleman, J. S. (1987). Families and schools. *Educational Researcher* 16: 32–38.

Connors, L. J. (1993). *Project Self Help: A family focus on literacy.* Center Rep. No. 13. Baltimore: Center on Families, Communities, Schools and Children's Learning, Johns Hopkins University.

———. (1994). *Small wins: The promises and challenges of family literacy.* Center Rep. No. 22. Baltimore: Center on Families, Communities, Schools and Children's Learning, Johns Hopkins University.

Connors, L J., and J. L. Epstein. (1994). *Taking stock: The views of teachers, parents, and students on school, family, and community partnerships in high schools.* Center Rep. No. 25. Baltimore: Center on Families, Communities, Schools and Children's Learning. Johns Hopkins University.

———. (1995). Parents and schools. Pages 437–458 in *Handbook of parenting,* edited by M. Bornstein. Hillsdale, NJ: Lawrence Erlbaum Associates.

Dauber, S. L., and J. L. Epstein. (1993). Parents' attitudes and practices of involvement in inner-city elementary and middle schools. Pages 53–71 in *Families and schools in a pluralistic society,* edited by N. Chavkin. Albany: State University of New York Press. (Reading 3.6).

Davies, D. (1991). Schools reaching out: Family, school and community partnerships for student success. *The Phi Delta Kappan* 72: 376–382.

———. (1993). A more distant mirror: Progress report on a cross-national project to study family-school-community partnerships. *Equity and Choice* 19(1): 41–46.

Davies, D., P. Burch, and V. Johnson. (1992). A *portrait of schools reaching out: Report of a survey on practices and policies of family-community-school collaboration.* Center Rep. No. 1. Baltimore: Center on Families, Communities, Schools and Children's Learning, Johns Hopkins University.

Davies, D., A. Palanki, and P. Burch. (1993*). Getting started: Action research in family-school-community partnerships.* Center Rep. No. 17. Baltimore: Center on Families, Communities, Schools and Children's Learning, Johns Hopkins University.

Delgado, M. (1992). *The Puerto Rican community and natural support systems: Implications for the education of children.* Center Rep. No. 10. Baltimore: Center on Families, Communities. Schools and Children's Learning, Johns Hopkins University.

Dolan, L. J. (1992). *Project Self Help: A first-year evaluation of a family literacy program.* Center Rep. No. 8. Baltimore: Center on Families, Communities, Schools and Children's Learning, Johns Hopkins University.

————. (1994). Implications of New Jersey's School-Based Youth Services for community interagency and school collaborations. Baltimore: Center on Families, Communities, Schools and Children's Learning, Johns Hopkins University. Mimeographed.

————. (1995). An evaluation of family support and integrated services in six elementary schools. Pages 395–420 in *School-community connections: Exploring issues for research and practice,* edited by L. Rigsby, M. C. Reynolds, and M. Wang. San Francisco: Jossey-Bass.

Dornbusch, S. M., and P. L. Ritter. (1988). Parents of high school students: A neglected resource. *Educational Horizons* 66: 75–77.

Earle, J. (1989). *Restructuring Seattle's middle schools.* Alexandria, VA: National Association of State Boards of Education.

Eccles, J. S., and R. D. Harold. (1996). Family involvement in children's and adolescents' schooling. Pages 3–34 in *Family-school links: How do they affect educational outcomes?,* edited by A. Booth and J. F. Dunn. Mahwah, NJ: Lawrence Erlbaum Associates.

Edmonds, R. R. (1979). Effective schools for the urban poor. *Educational Leadership* 37(2): 15–24.

Epstein, J. L. (1982). *Student reactions to teacher practices of parent involvement.* Rep. No. P-21. Baltimore: Center for Research on Elementary and Middle Schools, Johns Hopkins University. (Reading 3.9).

————. (1983). Longitudinal effects of family-school-person interactions on student outcomes. Pages 101–128 in *Research in sociology of education and socialization,* Vol. 4, edited by A. Kerckhoff. Greenwich, CT: JAI.

————. (1986a). Parents' reactions to teacher practices of parent involvement. *The Elementary School Journal* 86: 277–294. (Reading 3.4).

————. (1986b). Sharing the role of expert: Cooperative researcher/teacher efforts in developing a process for teachers to involve parents in schoolwork. Paper presented at the annual meeting of the American Educational Research Association, April, in San Francisco.

————. (1987a). Toward a theory of family-school connections: Teacher practices and parent involvement. Pages 121–136 in *Social intervention: Potential and constraints,* edited by K. Hurrelmann, F. Kaufmann, and F. Losel. New York: DeGruyter. (Reading 2.1).

————. (1987b). What principals should know about parent involvement. *Principal* 66: 6–9.

————. (1987c). *Homework practices, achievements, and behaviors of elementary school students.* CREMS Rep. No. 26. Baltimore: Center for Research on Elementary and Middle Schools, Johns Hopkins University. (Reading 3.8).

————. (1990). Single parents and the schools: Effects of marital status on parent and teacher interactions. Pages 91–121 in *Change in societal institutions,* edited by M. Hallinan, D. M. Klein, and J. Glass. New York: Plenum. (Reading 3.5).

————. (1991). Effects on student achievement of teacher practices of parent involvement. Pages 261–276 in *Advances in reading/language research, Vol. 5: Literacy through family, community, and school interaction,* edited by S. Silvern. Greenwich CT: JAI. (Reading 3.7).

————. (1992). School and family partnerships. Pages 1139–1151 in *Encyclopedia of educational research,* 6th ed., edited by M. Alkin. New York: Macmillan.

————. (1996). New connections for sociology and education: Contributing to school reform. *Sociology of Education* 69(May): 6–23.

Epstein, J. L., and L. J. Connors. (1994). *Trust fund: School, family, and community partnerships in high schools.* Center Rep. No. 24. Baltimore: Center on Families, Communities, Schools and Children's Learning, Johns Hopkins University.

————. (1995). School and family partnerships in the middle grades. Pages 137–166 in *Creating family-school partnerships*, edited by B. Rutherford. Columbus, OH: National Middle School Association.

Epstein, J. L., L. J. Connors, and K. C. Salinas. (1993). *High school and family partnerships: Surveys and summaries—Questionnaires for teachers, parents, and students, and How to summarize your high school's survey data*. Baltimore: Center on Families, Communities, Schools and Children's Learning, Johns Hopkins University.

Epstein, J. L., and S. L. Dauber. (1991). School programs and teacher practices of parent involvement in inner-city elementary and middle schools. *Elementary School Journal* 91: 289–303.

————. (1995). Effects on students of an interdisciplinary program linking social studies, art, and family volunteers in the middle grades. *Journal of Early Adolescence* 15: 237–266.

Epstein, J. L., and S. C. Herrick. (1991). *Improving school and family partnerships in urban middle grade schools: Orientation days and school newsletters*. CDS Rep. No. 20. Baltimore: The Johns Hopkins University Center for Research on Effective Schooling for Disadvantaged Students.

Epstein, J. L., S. C. Herrick, and L. Coates. (1996). Effects of summer home learning packets on student achievement in language arts in the middle grades. *School Effectiveness and School Improvement* 7: 383–410.

Epstein, J. L., V. Jackson, and K. C. Salinas. (1994). *Manual for teachers: Teachers Involve Parents in Schoolwork (TIPS) language arts, science health, and math interactive homework in the middle grades*, rev. ed. Baltimore: Center on Families, Communities, Schools and Children's Learning, Johns Hopkins University.

Epstein, J. L., and J. Jacobsen. (1994). Effects of school practices to involve families in the middle grades: Parents' perspectives. Paper presented at the annual meeting of the American Sociological Association, August, in Los Angeles.

Epstein, J. L., and S. Lee. (1993). Effects of school practices to involve families on parents and students in the middle grades: A view from the schools. Paper presented at the annual meeting of the American Sociological Association, August, in Miami.

————. (1995). National patterns of school and family connections in the middle grades. In *The family-school connection: Theory, research and practice*, edited by B. Ryan, G. Adams, T. Gullotta, R. Weissberg, and R. Hampton. Thousand Oaks, CA: Sage Publications.

Epstein, J. L., and D. J. Mac Iver. (1990). *Education in the middle grades: National practices and trends*. Columbus, OH: National Middle School Association.

Epstein, J. L., and K. C. Salinas. (1991). *TIPS volunteers in social studies and art manual*. Baltimore: Center on Families, Communities, Schools and Children's Learning, Johns Hopkins University.

Fagnano, C. L., and B. Z. Werber. (1994). *School, family, and community interaction: A view from the firing lines*. Boulder, CO: Westview Press.

Floyd, S. (1994). In their own voices: A case of collaboration and innovation in the English Language Arts. Saginaw, MI: Saginaw High School. Mimeographed.

Fruchter, N., A. Galletta, and J. L. White. (1992). *New directions in parent involvement*. Washington, DC: Academy for Educational Development.

Goode, D. A. (1990). The community portrait process: School community collaboration. *Equity and Choice* 6(3): 32–37.

Gordon, I. J. (1979). The effects of parent involvement in schooling. Pages 4–25 in *Partners: Parents and schools*, edited by R. S. Brandt. Alexandria, VA: Association for Supervision and Curriculum Development.

Harkevy, I., and J. L. Puckett. (1990). *Toward effective university-public school partnerships: An analysis of three contemporary models*. Philadelphia: University of Pennsylvania Graduate School of Education. Mimeographed.

Henderson, A. T., and N. Berla. (1994). *A new generation of evidence: The family is critical to student achievement.* Washington, DC: National Committee for Citizens in Education.

Hidalgo, N. (1992). *"i saw puerto rico once": A review of the literature on Puerto Rican families and school achievement in the United States.* Center Rep. No. 12. Baltimore: Center on Families, Communities, Schools and Children's Learning, Johns Hopkins University.

Hidalgo, N. M. (1994). Profile of a Puerto Rican family's support for school achievement. *Equity and Choice* 10(2): 14–22.

Hidalgo, N., J. Bright, S. Siu, S. Swap, and J. Epstein. (1995). Research on families, schools, and communities: A multicultural perspective. Pages 498–524 in *Handbook of research on multicultural education,* edited by J. Banks. New York: Macmillan.

Johnson, V. R. (1993). *Parent family centers: Dimensions of functioning in 28 schools in 14 states.* Center Rep. No. 20. Baltimore: Center on Families, Communities, Schools and Children's Learning, Johns Hopkins University.

———. (1994). *Parent centers in urban schools: Four case studies.* Center Rep. No. 23. Baltimore: Center on Families, Communities, Schools and Children's Learning, Johns Hopkins University.

Kagan, S. L., P. Neville, and J. Rustici. (1993). *Family education and training: From research to practice-implementation plan.* Center Rep. No. 14. Baltimore: Center on Families, Communities, Schools and Children's Learning, Johns Hopkins University.

Keesling, J. W., and R. J. Melaragno. (1983). Parent participation in federal education programs: Findings from the federal programs survey phase of the study of parental involvement. Pages 230–254 in *Parent education and public policy,* edited by R. Haskins and D. Adams. Norwood, NJ: Ablex.

Kinney, I., K. Strand, M. Hagerup, and C. Bruner. (1994). *Beyond the buzzwords: Key principles in effective frontline practice.* Working paper series. Falls Church, VA: National Center for Service Integration.

Lareau, A. (1989). *Home advantage: Social class and parental intervention in elementary education.* Philadelphia: Falmer.

———. (1996). Assessing parent involvement in schooling: A critical analysis. Pages 57–66 in *Family-school links: How do they affect educational outcomes?,* edited by A. Booth and J. F. Dunn. Mahwah, NJ: Lawrence Erlbaum Associates.

Lee, S. (1994). Family-school connections and students' education: Continuity and change of family involvement from the middle grades to high school. Ph.D. diss., Johns Hopkins University, Baltimore.

Leichter, H. J. (1974). *The family as educator.* New York: Teachers College Press.

Lieberman, A. (1993). The meaning of scholarly activity and the building of community. *Equity and Choice* 10(1): 4–10.

Litwak, E., and H. J. Meyer. (1974). *School, family, and neighborhood: The theory and practice of school-community relations.* New York: Columbia University Press.

Lloyd, G. (1996). Research and practical application for school, family, and community partnerships. Pages 255–264 in *Family-school links: How do they affect educational outcomes?,* edited by A. Booth and J. F. Dunn. Mahwah, NJ: Lawrence Erlbaum Associates.

Maher, C., and A. Alson. (1990). Teacher development in mathematics in a constructivist framework. Pages 147–165 in *Constructivist views on the teaching and learning of mathematics: Journal for research in mathematics education,* edited by R. B. Davis, C. Maher, and N. Noddings. Monograph No. 4. Reston, VA: National Council of Teachers of Mathematics.

Miller, L., and C. O'Shea. (1995, Winter). Partnership: Getting broader, getting deeper. Pages 1–6 in *Resources for Restructuring.* National Center for Restructuring Education, Schools and Teaching, NCREST, Teachers College.

Moles, O. (1996). New national directions in research and policy. Pages 247–254 in *Family-school links: How do they affect educational outcomes?*, edited by A. Booth and J. F. Dunn. Mahwah, NJ: Lawrence Erlbaum Associates.

Moll, L. C., C. Arnanti, D. Neff, and N. Gonzalez. (1992). Funds of knowledge for teaching: Using qualitative approach to connect homes and classrooms. *Theory into Practice* 31(2): 132–141.

Montandon, C., and P. Perrenoud. (1987). *Entre parents et ensignants: Un dialogue impossible? [Between parents and teachers: An impossible dialogue?]* Berne: Lang.

Morisset, C. E. (1993). *Language and emotional milestones: On the road to readiness.* Center Rep. No. 18. Baltimore: Center on Families, Communities, Schools and Children's Learning, Johns Hopkins University.

National Commission on Excellence in Education. (1983). *A nation at risk: The imperative of educational reform.* Washington, DC: Government Printing Office.

Nettles, S. M. (1992). *Coaching in community settings.* Center Rep. No. 9. Baltimore: Center on Families, Communities, Schools and Children's Learning, Johns Hopkins University.

———. (1993). *Coaching in communities: A practitioner's manual.* Baltimore: Center on Families, Communities, Schools and Children's Learning, Johns Hopkins University.

Newburg, N. (1991). A systems approach to school reform. Pages 53–76 in *The reflective turn*, edited by D. A. Schon. New York: Teachers College Press.

Palanki, A., and P. Burch, with D. Davies. (1995) *In our hands: A multi-site parent-teacher action research project on family-school-community partnerships.* Center Rep. No. 30. Baltimore: Center on Families, Communities, Schools and Children's Learning, Johns Hopkins University.

Perry, T. (1993). *Toward a theory of African American school achievement.* Center Rep. No. 16. Baltimore: Center on Families, Communities, Schools and Children's Learning, Johns Hopkins University.

Phi Delta Kappan. (1991). Paths to partnership (Special section on parent involvement). 72: 344–388.

PRIME. (1992). *Parental Resources for Involvement in Migrant Education* (Newsletter series). Geneseo, NY: BCCES Geneseo Migrant Center.

Rioux, W., and N. Berla, eds. (1993). *Innovations in parent and family involvement.* Princeton Junction, NJ: Eye on Education.

Scott-Jones, D. (1987). Mother-as-teacher in the families of high- and low-achieving low-income Black first graders. *Journal of Negro Education* 56: 21–34.

———. (1995). Activities in the home that support school learning in the middle grades. Pages 161–181 in *Creating family/school partnerships*, edited by B. Rutherford. Columbus, OH: National Middle School Association.

———. (1993). Adolescent Childbearing: Whose Problem? What Can We Do? *Phi Delta Kappan.* 75-K1–K12.

Seeley, D. S. (1981). *Education through partnership: Mediating structures and education.* Cambridge, MA: Ballinger.

Sirotnik, K. A., and J. I. Goodlad, eds. (1988). *School-university partnerships in action: Concepts, cases, and concerns.* New York: Teachers College Press.

Siu, S. (1992). *Toward an understanding of Chinese-American educational achievement.* Center Rep. No. 2. Baltimore: Center on Families, Communities, Schools and Children's Learning, Johns Hopkins University.

———. (1994). Taking no chances: A profile of a Chinese-American family's support for school success. *Equity and Choice* 10(2): 23–32.

Solomon, Z. (1991). California state policy on parent involvement: Initiating a process for state leadership. *Phi Delta Kappan* 72: 359–362.

Swap, S. (1994). Irish-American identity: Does it still have meaning in supporting children's school success? *Equity and Choice* 10(2): 33–41.

Swap, S. M., and J. Krasnow. (1992). A *saga of Irish-American achievement: Constructing a positive identity.* Center Rep. No. 11. Baltimore: Center on Families, Communities, Schools and Children's Learning, Johns Hopkins University.

Wisconsin Department of Public Instruction. (1994, August/September). Sharesheet. *The DPI Family-Community School Partnership Newsletter* 3: 1–2.

Wynn, J., J. Costello, R. Halpern, and H. Richman. (1994). *Children, families, and communities.* Chicago: University of Chicago, The Chapin Hall Center for Children.

DISCUSSION AND ACTIVITIES

The comments in this section extend and update the content of the two readings in this chapter. Main concepts are listed that summarize what you should know after reading the articles. Questions and activities are provided for class discussions and homework assignments. They may suggest other exercises, field activities, or research projects.

0: COMMENT

Emerging Theory

New theories develop or emerge in several ways. One—the "out-of-the-clear-blue-sky" process—is to think about an unexplained phenomenon and devise an explanation. Then the explanation must be tested to determine whether the theory is correct. Usually, a puzzle of this sort is solved little by little, as evidence accumulates to prove or disprove a theory.

Another way that new theories emerge—the "wait-a-minute-what-was-that-again?" process—is to conduct studies based on an established theory and be forced by the results to question, challenge, and reformulate existing ideas. When results repeatedly disprove a prevailing theory or parts of it, new or integrated theories are needed.

The latter example explains why I developed the theory of *overlapping spheres of influence* to explain the effects of families, schools, and communities on students' learning and development. Early sociological theory suggested that organizations are most efficient and effective if they have separate missions and operate independently. Data from my own and many other studies revealed repeated evidence that educators who worked *in partnership* with families and communities were more effective than those who worked in isolation in improving school climate, teachers' professional behavior, parents' confidence, and students' success in school. A model of overlapping spheres of influence more completely and accurately depicts and explains the simultaneous influence of schools, families, and communities on students' learning and development and on improving school programs and family support.

A new, revised, or expanded theory encourages researchers to redraw models, recast hypotheses, reexamine patterns in data, consider alternative explanations, and decide whether the theories operate as *complementary* or *competing* perspectives. The old and new theories of school, family, and community partnerships are complementary because the overlapping spheres of influence model acknowledge that families, schools, and community organizations conduct some activities separately and others jointly. Research is needed to better understand if and how the model of overlapping spheres of influence works in practice in many different types of schools, in families with different backgrounds, with children at different grade levels, in varied communities, and under other conditions.

0: COMMENT

Connecting Literature with Theory

Reading 2.2 summarizes the field of school, family, and community partnerships about 10 years after the theoretical model was first introduced. Periodically, it is important to review how a field is growing and where it needs to go. Literature reviews document and organize the hard work completed by many researchers who conduct studies to increase knowledge. Reviews also invite researchers, graduate and undergraduate students, and practitioners to identify questions for new studies to continue to improve knowledge, understand implications, and apply results.

In this chapter, the two readings are linked because the literature review shows how components of the theoretical model are translated into measurement models and studied with various experimental or nonexperimental methods. For example:

This theoretical component:	Is explored in the literature review in studies of:
Areas of *no overlap*; separate responsibilities, activities, and independent influences of family, school, or community contexts	• Family environments • School environments • Community environments
Area of *overlap*; external structure of model; shared responsibilities, shared influence of these contexts; "forces" of philosophy and practice that increase or decrease overlap	• Prevalence or extent of school practices to involve families in their children's education • Prevalence or extent of community involvement in education
Content *within* areas of overlap	• Types of involvement

Force of time/history on the nature and extent of partnerships

- Studies of partnerships at different school and grade levels

Interpersonal relationships in the internal structure of the model; results of forces that increase or limit "overlap" and results of interactions of all partners in education

- Effects on students, teachers, and parents of family and community involvement activities

MAIN CONCEPTS

From the two readings in this chapter and the comments and activities that follow, you should have a good understanding of the following concepts and terms:

- Overlapping spheres of influence
- External and internal structures of the model of overlapping spheres of influence
- Separate versus shared responsibilities of families, schools, and communities
- Importance of history for changing theories of school, family, and community relationships
- Family-like schools and school-like families
- Central role of the child in partnerships for education
- "School, family, and community partnerships" as a term that subsumes "parent involvement"
- Progress in research on the components of the theoretical model
- A research-based framework of six types of involvement that can be studied systematically by researchers and that guides educators in developing a comprehensive program of partnerships

These concepts and terms are discussed in the following questions and activities.

⫶ COMMENT

"Overlap" in Spheres of Influence

In the model of overlapping spheres of influence, there are, by definition, areas of overlap in which shared responsibilities of home, school, and community are identified and developed. There also are areas of nonoverlap in which families, educators, and community members and organizations conduct activities independently. The boundaries of home, school, and community are flexible and permeable in this model. That is, the extent of overlap is affected by the background, philosophies, and accumulated actions and experiences of families, educators, and community members. These factors lead to more or fewer practices of school, family, and community partnership, and, thereby, more or less overlap of the spheres of influence on student learning and development.

QUESTIONS TO DISCUSS

1. A. How might overlapping spheres of influence of home, school, and community create *less efficient* but *more effective* organizations than are created by separate spheres of influence? Could overlapping spheres of influence of home, school, and community ever create *more efficient* organizations or *less effective* ones? Explain your ideas.
   B. Which organizational feature—efficiency or effectiveness—would you choose for a school attended by your child, and why? When might you trade one for the other?
   C. Discuss how boundaries between and among schools, families, and communities can be fixed and rigid or flexible and permeable. How might these qualities affect the efficiency and effectiveness of each of the spheres of influence? What different effects might penetrable and impenetrable home-school-community boundaries have on student attitudes, behavior, and learning?
2. A. What statements or actions have you heard or seen that indicate that parents sometimes operate within a model of separate spheres of influence or within a model of overlapping spheres of influence?
   B. What statements or actions have you heard or seen that indicate that teachers sometimes operate within a model of separate spheres of influence or within a model of overlapping spheres of influence?
   C. How would a student describe schoolwork and homework within these two models?
3. Suppose you wanted to know which theory—separate spheres or overlapping spheres of influence—better explains changes in students' writing skills or students' classroom behavior.
   A. Write a hypothesis to test one of these theories.
   B. Briefly describe a study that would address your hypothesis and that could be conducted in one year or less.

◈ ACTIVITY

The External Structure of the Model

Figure 2.1 (page 28) represents the external structure of the theory of overlapping spheres of influence of family, school, and community on children's learning and development.

A. Draw or photocopy the diagram. Write *two* activities that you think belong in the sections that are nonoverlapping. These activities should be exclusively or mainly the family's responsibility, *or* the school's responsibility, *or* the community's responsibility. Write a sentence or two to explain why you placed these activities in the nonoverlapping areas.

B. Write two activities that you think belong in the overlapping sections. These activities should be the *shared* responsibilities of schools and families, *or* families and communities, *or* any two institutions, *or* all three institutions. Write a sentence or two to explain why you placed these activities in the overlapping areas of the spheres of influence model.

C. Share your ideas with an educator, a parent, or a student. Identify who you are working with. Ask the interviewee:

1. Do you agree or disagree that these examples (from item A) are exclusively or mainly separate responsibilities of home, school, and community? Explain your ideas.

2. Do you agree or disagree that these examples (from item B) are shared, cooperative, or overlapping responsibilities of home, school, and community? Explain your ideas.

3. Write down the responses you receive. Do you want to revise your examples, or were they confirmed in your interview? Explain.

◇ ACTIVITY

The Internal Structure of the Model

At the core or inner structure of the model of overlapping spheres of influence are the interactions that occur between a school and all families; between and among individual parents, teachers, and children; or with a few or many community groups or members. Figure 2.2 (page 28) shows one part of the internal structure of the model of overlapping spheres of influence. It illustrates the institutional and individual interactions of individuals at school and at home, with the student as the center of the interactions.

A. Draw or photocopy the diagram. Give one *positive* and one *negative* example of an interaction at the school level that might occur for each two-way arrow shown in the internal structure of the model:

Connection (2-way arrows)	A positive interaction might be . . .	A negative interaction might be . . .
1. Parent (p) and teacher (t)		
2. All families (F) and the whole school (S)		

B. Identify one more connection of two-way arrows in the diagram that interests you. Give one example of a positive and one example of a negative interaction that might occur for the connection you selected.

C. Interactions of educators and families also may occur at the school district level and at the state level. Identify one set of two-way arrows in the diagram for interactions at the district *or* state level that interests you. For example, at the district level, there may be interactions among all families and all schools in the district at a community forum on education. At the state level, there may be interactions among families from all schools at a statewide conference on parenting. Give one positive interaction and one negative interaction that might occur for the connection at the district *or* state level that you selected.

D. Draw the same diagram showing the institutional and individual interactions for the overlapping spheres of influence of family and community or school and community contexts. Describe one positive and one negative example of an interaction for one set of two-way arrows in your diagram that interests you.

ⓘ COMMENT

Forces That Activate the Model

Four "forces" are shown in the model of school, family, and community partnerships that press for more or less overlap of the spheres of influence: (1) family background characteristics, philosophy, and practices; (2) school characteristics, philosophy/policy, and practices; (3) community characteristics, policies, and practices; and (4) time and history. These forces move the external structure, creating more or less overlap, and activate the interactions and communications in the internal structure that create new interactions and exchanges, and push or pull the spheres of influence from within. In simple terms, if there is greater overlap, there will be room for more and different kinds of communication between and among students, parents, teachers, community members, or others involved in students' learning and development at home, at school, or in the community.

QUESTIONS TO DISCUSS

1. A. Select one of the "forces" that pushes the spheres together or apart: school, family, or community background; philosophy/policy; practice; or time/history.

   B. How do you think the particular force that you selected might work to increase or decrease the shared responsibilities of families and schools? What would activate the force so that educators and parents would want to have more or less contact with each other about students' work, attitudes, behavior, health, or other indicators of student success in school?

2. List three variables representing the force you selected that could be measured to study their influences on school, family, and community partnerships. Explain why each may be a useful measure of the force that you selected. For example, grade level is one variable that represents the force of time or history. This variable can be used to study whether connections between home, school, and community increase or decrease over time.

⬛ COMMENT

School-Like Families and Family-Like Schools

When educators and families recognize their shared responsibilities and interests in children, the activities and attitudes in both environments tend to change. Teachers and administrators create more family-like schools. A family-like school recognizes each child's individuality and uniqueness, and, like a family, makes each child feel special and included. Through their attitudes and practices, families create school-like families. A school-like family recognizes each child as a student, and, like a school, reinforces the importance of school, homework, and activities that build students' skills and feelings of success. These constructions and the resulting actions at school and at home help more children define themselves as students, as well as sons or daughters.

A teacher may say, "I know when a student is having a bad day, and how to approach the situation. We're like a family here." A parent may say, "I keep after my daughter to let her know that homework comes first—before TV," or, "My son's first job at home is to finish his schoolwork." A student slips and calls a teacher "mom," and then laughs with a mixture of embarrassment and happiness about the error.

As soon as you hear these concepts you will remember examples of schools, teachers, and classes that were "like a family" to you, and activities or events at home that were "just like school" that supported your work as a student. You may think of how a teacher paid individual attention to you, recognized your uniqueness, and praised you for your own progress, just as a parent might. You may recall that parents, siblings, and other family members engaged in and enjoyed some educational activities with you and took pride in the good schoolwork or homework that you did, just as a teacher might. You begin to hear, see, and read about family-like schools and school-like families in newspapers or magazines, on television, and from children in your family.

There also are school-like and family-like community groups and organizations. A local zoo or botanical gardens may be "just like school"—a place to learn. A local library that welcomes, works with, and cares for students, families, and educators may feel "like a family, here."

QUESTIONS TO DISCUSS

1. Describe and discuss one example of a school-like family and one example of a family-like school that you have experienced, read, or heard about.
2. A. Give one example of how a school-like family and how a family-like school may be positive forces for children.
   B. Give one example of how these may be negative influences.
   C. What information might a school give to families and a family give to a school to help keep their connections positive?
3. A community also may be family-like and school-like. The statement, "We're like a family here," is often used in community groups, organizations, and businesses. Some communities, however, are more active than others in supporting the needs and goals of schools, students, and families.
   A. Give one example of an activity that you have read or heard about that illustrates a family-like community that cares for children as a family should.
   B. Give one example of an activity that you have read or heard about that illustrates a school-like community that gives children messages about the importance of school, learning, citizenship, or other issues that match the messages of home and school.

⟡ ACTIVITY

Reading for Understanding

Explore the concepts and terms that other researchers use for school-like families, or families whose actions at home help their children define themselves as "students." Various terms such as *cultural capital, social capital, funds of knowledge,* and *management skills* have focused attention on how families gather and use resources and skills to help children succeed in school.

A. Read one of the following articles or books by other researchers that contribute in important ways to the literature on school, family, and community partnerships.

CULTURAL CAPITAL

Lareau, A. (1987). Social class differences in family-school relationships: The importance of cultural capital. *Sociology of Education* 60: 73–85.
————. (1989). *Home advantage.* Philadelphia: Falmer Press.

SOCIAL CAPITAL

Coleman, J. S. (1987). Families and schools. *Educational Researcher* 16: 32–38.
Coleman, J. S. (1988). Social capital in the creation of human capital. *American Journal of Sociology* 94: 95–120.
Schneider, B., and J. S. Coleman, eds. (1993). *Parents, their children, and schools.* Boulder, CO: Westview Press.

FUNDS OF KNOWLEDGE

Moll, L. C., C. Amanti, D. Neff, and N. Gonzalez. (1992). Funds of knowledge for teaching: Using a qualitative approach to connect homes and classrooms. *Theory into Practice* 31(2): 132–141.
Moll, L. C., and J. B. Greenberg. (1990). Creating zones of possibilities: Combining social contexts for instruction. Pages 319–348 in *Vygotsky and education,* edited by L. C. Moll. Cambridge: Cambridge University Press.

MANAGEMENT SKILLS

Baker, D. P., and D. L. Stevenson. (1986). Mothers' strategies for children's school achievement: Managing the transition to high school. *Sociology of Education* 59: 156–166.
Useem, E. L. (1992). Middle schools and math groups: Parents' involvement in children's placement. *Sociology of Education* 65: 263–279.

ASSETS

Benson, P. (1997). *Creating healthy communities for children and adolescents.* San Francisco: Jossey-Bass.

INTEGRATED COMMUNITY SERVICES

Dryfoos, J. (1994). *Full-service schools.* San Francisco: Jossey-Bass.
————. (1998). The Rise of the Full-Service Community School. *High School Magazine* 6 (2): 38–42.

B. Write a short summary of the main ideas on family support for children's education presented in the article or book you read. Explain whether and how the main ideas and results of correspond to, complement, or contradict the theory of overlapping spheres of influence. Include a paragraph on how the author's concepts match, contribute to, or differ from school-like families, family-like schools, family-like communities, or school-like communities.

⊡⁝ COMMENT

Central Role of the Child in School, Family, and Community Partnerships

The theory of overlapping spheres of influence sets the child at the center of the internal structure of the model. The assumption is that students are the main actors in their education and the primary reason for communication between school and home. Students are the ones who must do the work to learn to read, write, calculate, master other skills, and develop personal talents.

Not only are students responsible for learning, they also are responsible for the success of most communications among home, school, and community. Studies show that students are often the main source (sometimes the only source) of information for parents about school or community activities. In strong programs of school, family, and community partnerships, teachers prepare and encourage students to help conduct *traditional communications* such as delivering memos or report cards, and *new communications* such as interactive homework or student-led, parent-teacher-student conferences.

The central role of students in school, family, and community partnerships is supported by research in this and other countries. For example, Swiss researchers Montandon and Perrenoud (1987) describe the child as a "go-between" who is both the messenger and the message between family and school. Students serve as messengers to transmit information from school to home and from home to school. They also communicate nonverbally. Their attitudes, facial expressions, and body language also tell a great deal about their experiences at home, at school, and in the community. At different times and in many ways students speak for themselves, for their teachers, and for their parents.

REFERENCES

Montandon, C., and P. Perrenoud. (1987). *Entre parents et ensignants: Un dialogue impossible? [Between parents and teachers: An impossible dialogue?]* Berne: Lang.

QUESTIONS TO DISCUSS

1. How do or how should students' roles in school and family partnerships change from one grade level to the next?

A. Give one example of a typical activity and one example of an ideal activity that students conduct to connect home and school at each school level:

School level	Typical Activity Students Conduct to Connect School and Home	Ideal Activity Students Could Conduct to Connect School and Home
(1) Preschool		
(2) Elementary school		
(3) Middle school		
(4) High school		

2. Students can be assisted to be more effective messengers, communicators, discussants, interactors, demonstrators, and celebrators of new skills.
   A. Select a grade level that interests you.
   B. Discuss one way in which a teacher at that grade level might inform students about the roles they play in school, family, and community partnerships.
   C. Discuss one way in which parents might encourage their children at that grade level to communicate with them about school and classroom activities.

▯ COMMENT

Understanding Authority in Theories of Partnership

Underlying contrasting theories of school, family, and community connections are questions of who has responsibility and authority for children's education. What do parents do? What do teachers do? What does the community do? Where? When? How well? With what goals? These are questions of control and the *division of labor*. By contrast, the model of overlapping spheres requires the *multiplication of labor*.

Control

Principals, teachers, and district and state leaders may fully control the school organization or share control with parents, students, and others in the community. Principals can make decisions about the school and students' education with or without allowing or encouraging teachers, parents, and students to participate. Teachers can direct student learning with or without allowing or encouraging parents to assist. On their own, some parents become and stay involved in their children's education at home, at school, and in the community, regardless of whether the school shares control with them. School policies and decisions about control make a difference, however, in whether there is broad involvement by all parents or limited involvement by a few parents who are able to obtain information and organize their own activities and participation.

Division of Labor

Teachers and administrators may stress the separate skills and contributions of teachers and parents, emphasizing the specialization in their work at school and at home. Specialization requires expertise in a few well-defined tasks. Teachers who have been advised to stick to the basics restrict their attention to teaching academic skills. They may emphasize the tests they give students to show how teachers' work differs from that of families.

Teachers who separate school from home may say, "If the family would just do its job, I could do mine. I could teach these kids." Families who separate home from school may say, "I get my child to school each day, then it's the school's job to teach him." This division of labor reflects early social organizational theory that schools, families, and other organizations are more efficient and effective if they have separate goals and responsibilities to influence different behaviors. The division of labor reflects a model of separate spheres of influence.

Multiplication of Labor

By contrast, educators and families may stress the combination of skills of teachers and parents, emphasizing the generalization of their efforts to educate students at school and at home. When they teach the whole child, teachers teach academic skills and also increase their attention to the child's self-concept, aspirations, social skills, and development of talents—some of the traditional responsibilities of parents. When involved in their children's education, parents increase their attention to their children's abilities and mastery of skills, how they get along with other children and adults, and their future plans for education and work—some of the traditional responsibilities of teachers.

Shared responsibilities multiply the messages that children receive about the importance of the work they do as students. The multiplication of labor reflects the view that schools, families, and other community organizations will be more effective, if not always as efficient, when they work together as overlapping spheres of influence.

Thus, schools can be characterized by sole or shared control with families, by a strict division or separation of labor, or by the multiplication or "overlap" of labor concerning students' learning. These are not mutually exclusive concepts, and both are pictured in the model of overlapping spheres of influence.

QUESTIONS TO DISCUSS

1. Why is it important for children to receive common messages about the importance of school from their teachers, their families, and their communities? In addition to giving common messages, what is one other way in which schools, families, and communities might multiply their resources to assist students?
2. When might it be important to maintain a division of labor between school and home? Give one example of when it would be good for children to hear a unique message from home *or* from school.
3. Which groups or organizations in a community do you think are most likely to combine resources (1) with families more than schools; (2) with schools more than families; and (3) with both families and schools to assist students' learning and development?

⌷⁝ COMMENT

Mutual Respect of Teachers and Parents

All discussions about school, family, and community partnerships begin with a call for mutual respect between teachers and parents, teachers and other family members, students and teachers, business partners and educators. A perceived lack of respect is often given as the reason for the lack of communication and interactions among the home, school, and community. Parents' and teachers' respect, appreciation, recognition, and admiration for each other and for the work they do separately and together with children are represented in the structure and processes of the model of overlapping spheres of influence.

Parents and teachers establish respect for each other in different ways when they work in separate or overlapping spheres of influence on children's learning. In organizations that maintain separate spheres of influence, parents receive respect for their home training and child rearing. Depending on one's perspective, a "good mother" may have a well-behaved or creative child, or both. Teachers are respected for their school lessons and educational programs. A "good teacher" may make tough demands on students or conduct highly engaging classes, or both.

Traditionally, teachers' expertise is based on professional training; parents' expertise is based on successful home management. When the emphasis is on the efficiency of separate organizations, respect for teachers and parents is *site specific*, based on the role of the adults in each setting and the distinct jobs they do.

In organizations that support overlapping spheres of influence, respect is extended to parents and teachers who work well together and fulfill shared responsibilities for the education and socialization of children across the school years. In overlapping spheres of influence, parents and teachers require information about each other's goals to be knowledgeable partners and responsive to student needs.

When the emphasis is on overlapping influence, respect for teachers and parents is *student specific,* based on the combined interests and efforts of teachers, parents, students, and others across settings to support and encourage learning and development.

QUESTIONS TO DISCUSS

1. Why do you think the concept of *respect* is so powerful as the basis for school, family, and community partnerships? Which do you think comes first, *respect* or *partnership*? Explain your answer.
2. Give examples from your reading or experience of:
   A. respect for the *separate work* of families and schools and
   B. respect for the *shared or overlapping work* of families and schools.
3. How do the theories of social behavior (e.g., symbolic interactionism or reference group theory) described in Reading 2.1 (or other theories of behavior that you know) help explain how respect is developed in school, family, and community partnerships?
   A. Select and identify one social or behavioral theory discussed in Reading 2.1.
   B. Describe two ways in which the assumptions of the theory you selected increase or decrease mutual respect between teachers and parents or between teachers and citizens of the community.

0: COMMENT

Shared Responsibilities: Who Teaches What?

What Families Do, but Schools Do Too

Families have the major responsibility for teaching children about their cultural background, family values, beliefs, manners, and other important qualities of life. Many families also take responsibility for developing their children's talents. They reward their children's successes and redirect failures. Increasingly, schools share these responsibilities. Programs and intergroup processes in many schools nurture students' self respect and increase their knowledge, tolerance, and appreciation of other students' cultural backgrounds and values. Some teachers and some school and community programs help students develop self-confidence, manners, sportsmanship, and talents as much as or more than some families.

Parents are expected to act as buffers, liaisons, and advocates for their children, protecting and advancing their children's rights to participate in school programs and receive needed social, health, and educational services. Some families neither understand nor perform these responsibilities. Increasingly, schools provide these protections or share information with families so that they become more knowledgeable about how to work with the school, school system, and community on behalf of their children.

What Schools Do, but Families Do Too .

Schools have a major responsibility for helping students develop independence and self-reliance because teachers cannot give all students instant individual attention. By their practices, however, some schools foster children's dependence on the teacher. For example, some teachers give students few opportunities to take responsibility for designing and conducting projects, answer questions that have more than one right answer, or develop their individual talents. Some families at all economic levels influence their children's development of independence as much as or more than some schools.

Schools have the major responsibility for helping students learn school subjects and skills. Teachers' daily, focused, challenging lessons increase students' abilities to read, write, compute, think, and apply their knowledge in useful and creative ways. In partnership with schools, some families at all economic levels boost their children's knowledge and skills with numerous learning activities at home in reading, writing, computing, thinking, and solving problems. Some schools and teachers guide all or most parents to conduct activities and interactions at home that support and enhance children's learning. In some cases, the creative and useful activities at home increase student learning as much as or more than the activities at some schools.

These and many other examples illustrate why it is hard to determine "Whose job is it?" to help students develop particular attitudes, skills, talents, and knowledge. For students, learning is not limited in time or place, but occurs in school, at home, and in the community. These complex factors underlie the concept and model of overlapping spheres of influence.

QUESTIONS TO DISCUSS

1. Describe two traditional "teachings" of families that are aided by the actions of schools.
2. Describe two traditional "teachings" of schools that are aided by the actions of families.
3. Describe two traditional "teachings" of communities that are aided by the actions of families and schools.
4. Think about how children learn. Discuss your views on these questions:
   A. Is it possible for children to separate what is learned at home from what is learned at school or in the community? Give one example to support your view.
   B. Identify one school subject that is likely to be strongly influenced (1) by school, (2) by home, and (3) by the community. Are any of your examples *solely* influenced by one context? Explain.

C. How might your ideas on items A and B affect the design of school, family, and community partnerships?

⓪ COMMENT

Partnerships Subsume Parent Involvement

When educators say *parent involvement* they often put all of the responsibility on parents to connect with schools and to become involved with their children at home. By contrast, the term *school, family, and community partnerships* assigns some responsibilities to schools, families, and communities to share information, ideas, activities, and services with each other about schools and children's education. The development of programs of school, family, and community partnerships gives all families more equal opportunities to become involved in their children's education and development, rather than just a few. The broader concept also makes room for students as key members of the partnership because they are influenced by all three contexts—home, school, and community—and recognizes that students are the main actors in their education. Swap (1992) contrasted programs that separate and isolate parents with those that build good partnerships and showed clearly that educators' philosophies about involvement affect the actions they take.

REFERENCES

Swap, S. M. (1992). *Developing home-school partnerships: From concepts to practice.* New York: Teachers College Press.

QUESTIONS TO DISCUSS

The term *partnership* for programs that involve families and communities in education has been chosen with care. It has a history of meanings, connections, and examples in other fields, particularly in business, that strengthen the meaning of partnerships in education. The term will not go out of favor as a whim or fad in education. It stands for some important interactions.

1. How many similarities *or* parallels can you think of between the concepts of partnerships in business and in home, school, and community connections? Following are two examples:

Concept:	Partners in education and in business:
• *shared responsibilities*	recognize their responsibilities to each other, to the "product," and to the public.
• *shared investments*	put in the necessary *time* to reach their goals in business.

A. Give two other examples of similarities between partnerships in business and school, family, and community partnerships in education. State the concept and explain the similarities in intent or actions.

B. Give two examples of differences between partnerships in business and school, family, and community partnerships in education. State the concept and explain the differences in intent or actions.

2. A. How might the following terms guide the actions of teachers, parents, and community members to increase children's success in school? How might each term guide partnerships?

(1) unity

(2) commitment

(3) obligation

(4) assurance

B. Add one more partnership term to the list above and explain how it might help guide actions and interactions among home, school, and community to increase students' success in school.

3. A. Do you think that *school, family, and community partnerships* is a better term than *parent involvement* for studying the connections of teachers, parents, and others in research and for developing practical programs in elementary, middle, and high schools? Why or why not?

B. List other terms that you have seen, heard, or read about that refer to family and community involvement (e.g., *home-school relations, caring community*). Select one term on your list and compare its usefulness to *school, family, and community partnerships*.

⫶ COMMENT

The Influence of History on Theory

Reading 2.1 argues that changing times require changing theories. The concept of overlapping spheres of influence reflects social changes that have affected families, schools, and communities over the past half century. Four trends were discussed that have altered relationships of schools, families, and communities, reducing their separate responsibilities and increasing shared responsibilities:

1. More mothers have higher education, and are prepared to work on an equal status with teachers.

2. `Baby and child care books and media guide families through the infant and toddler years and prepare them to seek information and advice as their children continue to grow.

3. `Federal regulations and federal, state, and local programs reinforce the importance of the involvement of economically disadvantaged families in their young children's education and prepare families to continue their interest and involvement through the school years.

4. Changes in family structure (including more mothers working, more single parents, more diverse family groups) require schools to provide families with good information so they can make productive use of limited time together and require schools and communities to provide services to assist families with the supervision of children before and after school and on vacations.

The greater number of demands on schools has increased educators' awareness that they cannot do the job of educating children alone. Educators have learned that they need families and communities as partners in children's education. Similarly, the greater complexities and demands in family life have increased parents' awareness that they need their schools and communities as partners to increase their children's chances for success.

QUESTIONS TO DISCUSS

1. Select one of the historical trends listed above that interests you.
   A. Give one example of how the trend you selected might promote successful partnerships with families.
   B. Give one example of how the trend you selected might create problems for schools or for families. Explain how that problem might be solved.
2. Parents with more formal education *and* those with less formal education are increasingly interested and involved in their children's education. Discuss why you think these simultaneous trends are important for the design and implementation of programs of school, family, and community partnerships.

⑪ COMMENT

Changing the Question

Family environments and activities influence student learning and success in school. From the 1960s to today, studies in sociology, psychology, and education have been conducted on whether and how families and home environments influence children's achievement and which family practices affect children's development, learning, and success. I call these "first generation" studies of home and school connections. The results of almost all such studies show that children do better in school in many different ways if their parents support and encourage school activities. This is a social fact in children's education and development.

There still are many questions to ask about family influences on children at all grade levels and in diverse cultural, linguistic, and community contexts. However, the confirmatory results on the importance of families in children's lives prompted me to ask a new question that changed the way that I think about and study school, family, and community partnerships: *IF* families are so important, *HOW* can schools and communities help more families become and stay involved in their children's education—especially parents who would not, typically, become involved on their own? You will read studies that ask what educators, parents, and others can do to develop effective programs to involve all families and communities in children's education and in schools. I call these "second generation" studies of home, school, and community partnerships, because they take the main result that families are important from "first generation" studies and ask how the proven benefits of family involvement can be more equitably developed and distributed. Because surveys of parents from all backgrounds and cultures show clearly that they want to be able to guide and assist their children at all grade levels, the new studies on school, family, and community partnerships are designed to understand, support, and maintain the strengths and influence of all families as their children proceed in school.

QUESTIONS TO DISCUSS

1. In your view, what is the difference between the two lines of research on (1) how families are important for student success ("first generation" studies) and (2) how schools can develop programs to involve all families in their children's education ("second generation" studies)? Discuss your ideas of what each line of research contributes to knowledge about schools, families, and children. Why is each important for understanding students' success in school?
2. Read these two sentences:
   A. *It is important for all children to be ready for school.*
   B. *It is important for all schools to be ready for children and their families.*
   1. How are the two sentences linked in meaning?
   2. How do these two sentences differ in meaning?
   3. Give one idea of how each of these sentences is informed (1) by "first generation" studies of family involvement and (2) by "second generation" studies of school, family, and community partnerships.

 ACTIVITY

Next Questions

Reading 2.2 introduces five questions and related topics that need more attention in research and in practice:

Transitions. Which practices of school, family, and community partnership are needed at important points of transitions, for example, from one grade level to the next, across school levels, or whenever students change teachers or schools?

Results. What are the results of particular types and practices of school, family, and community partnership for students, parents, teachers, and others in communities?

Community Connections. How can we better understand the community structures, processes, people, resources, and activities that contribute to comprehensive programs of school, family, and community partnerships?

Students' Roles. What active roles must students play at all grade levels in programs of school, family, and community partnerships?

Collaborations in Research. How can researchers, policy leaders, and educators most effectively collaborate in developing, maintaining, and evaluating programs of school, family, and community partnerships?

Many topics and issues are embedded in these five questions.

1. Select one of the five topics/questions listed above that interests you.
2. A. From the readings in this chapter, summarize two results from prior research that you believe are "basic" for understanding the topic you selected and for conducting new research on that topic.
   B. Write one clear, detailed follow-up question that you believe is particularly important to extend knowledge on the topic you selected. Explain in a few sentences why you think your question is important.

❏⋮ COMMENT

Does Family Involvement in a Specific Subject Generalize to Help Students Succeed in Other Subjects?

It is important to learn whether and how specific practices of involvement produce specific results in the short term and over the long term. As discussed in Reading 2.2, family involvement with children in reading at home may lead students, first, to greater attention to and motivation in reading. This may help students gain reading skills over one year.

Over time, involvement in reading may lead to family discussions and interactions with children about other subjects. Also, after learning how to involve families in reading, teachers may, over time, improve their information to families about many subjects.

This may help children see that their families are interested in all aspects of their education. Initial support from families in reading, then, may translate into more serious work by students in many school subjects and activities. This line of events and effects may progress at different rates depending on how much the school informs and involves families about their children's education.

It also is possible that the effects of family support on student success in several subjects are produced in other ways. For example, most students report that their families believe education is important. But not all of these students succeed in reading, math, and other subjects. Not all graduate from high school. Indeed, most families who believe education is important are not presently involved in school-related learning activities at home unless their children's teachers guide these interactions.

There are many unanswered questions about the paths between parents' beliefs about education, activities initiated by teachers, family-child interactions, student motivation, student achievement in specific subjects, and overall success in school.

QUESTIONS TO DISCUSS

1. Draw a diagram with paths that show how family involvement in one activity (e.g., involvement in reading aloud or listening to a child read) might lead to family involvement in other subjects and activities, to increase parental involvement overall.
2. Draw a diagram with paths that show how the effects of family involvement on student learning might "travel" from family involvement in a specific subject (e.g., reading) to improved student achievement in that subject, other subjects, and success in school overall.

FIELD EXPERIENCE

Interview to Find Out
How Theory Works in Practice

There are some things that families do on their own (nonoverlapping influence) and some things that families do with information or support from schools, other families, and the community (overlapping spheres of influence). Interview *two* parents individually who have different socioeconomic situations or who live in different neighborhoods.

A. Briefly describe the two parents that you interview and the features of their economic conditions or neighborhoods.
B. Ask each one: What is one topic, problem, or decision concerning your child's development or education that you discuss as a family with:
   1. little or no information or influence from the school, community, or other families?

Parent 1 _____

Parent 2 _____

2. some or most information or influence from the school?
Parent 1 _____
Parent 2 _____

3. some or most information or influence from the community?
Parent 1 _____
Parent 2 _____

4. some or most information or influence from other families?
Parent 1 _____
Parent 2 _____

C. Record the responses from the *two* parents interviewed.
D. How do the responses from the two parents differ? How are their responses similar? What surprised you in their responses? Summarize your views on how the two families make decisions or resolve problems about child raising, independently or with school, family, and community connections.
E. Compare summaries in class to determine how other families in different socioeconomic situations work within the nonoverlapping and overlapping spheres of influence in raising children.

3

Research

S TARTING WITH A statewide study of teachers, parents, students, and administrators in 600 elementary schools in Maryland in 1980 and 1981, my colleagues and I began to learn about practices of partnership that were used by teachers, desired by families, and responsive to students. We examined how often and in what ways teachers and their schools involved parents; whether and how parents' social class and marital status affected their involvement; and how elementary school students understood and reacted to connections between their families and teachers. We studied the results of partnerships on the attitudes and practices of teachers, the actions and behaviors of parents, and the attitudes and achievements of students.

The early studies provided systematic, quantitative analyses of the nature and extent of family involvement in the elementary grades. The data raised many questions about existing theories of effective school organizations and effective families and communities and led to the development of the theory of overlapping spheres of influence (see Chapter 2).

In 1987, we began field studies with educators, families, and students in urban elementary and middle schools. This research—a collaborative effort with the Baltimore City Public School System and a community organization, the Fund for Educational Excellence, in Baltimore—increased understanding of how involvement changes across the grades, by teachers of different subjects, for parents from various racial and cultural groups, and in schools that systematically organize their programs of partnership with families and communities.

In 1991, we started a series of field studies to learn how to define, organize, and study school, family, and community partnerships at the high school level. This research in urban, suburban, and rural settings identified how to expand the language and actions of partnership for educators, parents, and students through the 12th grade. The studies reinforced and extended our understanding of the important roles students play in school, family, and community partnerships. The early studies and those that continue today aim to improve knowledge about whether and how family, school, and community connections assist student learning and development across the grades, from preschool through high school.

DATA FROM TEACHERS

Readings 3.1 and 3.2 report results of a survey of nearly 3,700 teachers in approximately 600 elementary schools in the state of Maryland. The survey, conducted in 1980, was one of the first large-scale studies of teacher attitudes and practices of involvement that also included data from administrators, parents, and students in the same schools and classrooms. In addition to the survey data, we analyzed teachers' written comments and concerns about school and family connections. Their reports revealed that some teachers were farther along on this agenda than others. That is, some teachers had figured out how to reach parents that other teachers did not reach. We learned many things from these teacher-leaders that subsequently helped other educators develop their programs of school, family, and community partnership.

In 1987, we collected data from teachers and parents in the elementary and middle grades. With these data, we tested the theory of overlapping spheres of influence and explored and extended research on the major types of involvement. Reading 3.3 reports the attitudes and practices of teachers in urban elementary and middle schools. The data show that teachers' ideas and behaviors are more positive if they believe that their *school as a whole* is working to involve families. Some teachers communicate effectively with families regardless of parents' race, formal education, neighborhood, or school context. These teachers' efforts and successes suggest that other teachers could do the same if they were helped to use similar strategies for developing partnerships, particularly if they were supported by the administrators and other teachers in the school. Data from teachers and reports from parents in the same schools (see Reading 3.6) document changes in the practices of partnerships that typically occur from the elementary to the middle grades in schools that have not started to organize partnership programs.

DATA FROM PARENTS

Three readings present results of research on parents' reactions to and involvement in their children's education, with data from families who are in the same schools as the teachers described above. Reading 3.4 presents data from a survey of parents of students in 600 elementary schools in Maryland. Reading 3.5 takes a closer look at these data to explore patterns of participation of single and married parents in their children's education. These data help explain why earlier ideas about parental involvement were limited by their inattention to whether schools and teachers were conducting practices to involve all parents. The omission of measures of what schools and teachers do to encourage and increase the involvement of all families distorts an understanding of the involvement of single parents, those with less formal education or low income, and mothers who work outside the home. Many of these families rely on information and guidance from schools to help them organize their admittedly limited time and to enable them to remain involved in their children's education at each grade level.

Reading 3.6 reports data from parents of elementary and middle school students in urban schools that were beginning to implement practices of partnership. Conventional wisdom is that low-income families, racial minorities, single parents, and parents with less formal education are not and do not want to be involved in their children's education.

Presently, in most schools, that statement is *partly true*. These families tend *not* to be as involved as other families. But the statement also is *partly false*. These families *want* to be involved. Indeed, in all surveys that we have conducted since 1980, just about all parents reported that they try to remain involved at home in their children's schooling, but they need more and better information to know what to do that will help their child each year. *In schools that are actively working to develop partnership programs* that reach out to and involve families, the conventional wisdom is *completely false*. In these schools, just about all parents are informed and involved in their children's education in important ways each year.

DATA FROM STUDENTS

The last three readings in this chapter include data from elementary school students who were in the classrooms of teachers who varied in their practices of involving families in their children's education. Reading 3.7 reports the effects on student achievement of school programs that involve families in learning activities at home. This study reveals an important subject-specific connection. Involvement by parents in a particular subject at home—here, in reading—leads to gains in student achievement in that subject.

Reading 3.8 explores how homework creates three-way connections among student, teacher, and family. Reading 3.9 uses data from a survey of fifth-grade students to better understand their views about homework, parent involvement, and their attitudes toward school. We wanted to learn whether teachers' practices to involve families affected students' perceptions of the congruency between home and school and whether their homework habits were affected by teachers' practices to involve families. We also wanted to see if reports from teachers, principals, and students about parent involvement produced similar results on these measures.

The results of these analyses influenced another line of research and development to help teachers design new forms of interactive homework to involve families in various school subjects to boost student achievement (see Chapter 6).

SUMMARY

One of the most consistent results in the various surveys that we and other researchers have conducted in the United States and other countries is that teachers have very different views of parents than parents have of themselves. Most teachers do not know parents' hopes and wishes for their children or for their parenting, nor do they understand what parents try to do at home to help their children.

Similarly, neither parents nor teachers fully understand what *students* think about school, family, and community partnerships. Indeed, most adults believe that students want to avoid or minimize family involvement in their education. Data from students from the elementary grades through high school suggest the opposite. Students want families to be knowledgeable partners with their schools in their education and available as helpful sources of information and assistance at home.

Although there are connections between family involvement and student achievement, we still know relatively little about *which* practices produce positive results for student learning. We need to learn how, when, for whom, and why particular practices increase students' skills and scores in specific subjects. The readings in this chapter should raise new questions for research on the effects of school, family, and community partnerships on student learning and development.

Data from teachers, parents, and students can be gathered with various research methods, including surveys, experimental and quasi-experimental studies, interviews, focus or discussion groups, and other strategies. Whichever study designs and methods of inquiry are used, one group's perspective—educators, parents, or students—alone will not provide an accurate base on which to plan better programs or practices of partnerships.

The readings in this chapter illustrate why it is important to measure and account for teachers', parents', and students' views to identify gaps in knowledge that each has about the other. These studies also illuminate the common interests of teachers, parents, *and* students in developing better communications between home and school. This chapter should give you a good understanding of basic research on school, family, and community partnerships, and familiarity with results from studies of teachers, parents, and students. You can apply the results in practice or use them to raise new questions in research that you conduct.

Parent Involvement: A Survey of Teacher Practices*

Teachers approach their instructional tasks with a variety of perspectives and strategies that emphasize certain aspects of teaching and de-emphasize others. For example, some teachers teach language skills using organized games, whereas other teachers teach the same skills by direct instruction. Teachers adopt different approaches to the same subject matter partly because their teaching situations differ. Their students may have different learning problems or their classrooms may have varied resources and facilities. Even in the same teaching situation, however, teachers may vary the instructional techniques they use depending on the particular skills and talents they have for using various materials and forms of instruction or the influences of their college training, supervisors, or colleagues. In a particular situation, for a certain type of student, which is the most effective teaching strategy? That is the most difficult question in the world of education and research.

One general approach that some teachers have found useful is to involve parents in learning activities with their children at home. This type of parent involvement is distinctly different from the parent involvement that brings parents into the classroom to assist the teacher or the parent involvement that includes parents as participants in decisions on school governance. Parent involvement in learning activities is a strategy for increasing the educational effectiveness of the time that parents and children spend with one another at home.

As with most educational strategies, there are different opinions about the likely effectiveness of teacher efforts to get parents to be more active in learning-related activities at home. Some educators believe that widespread parent interest in the academic progress of their children constitutes an immensely underutilized teaching resource, requiring only general guidance and modest effort to bring results in many cases. Pointing out the major competing time commitments of parents and teachers and the highly variable instructional skills of parents, others have suggested that all teaching of academic skills should be left to the teacher in the classroom. They suggest that little if any effort should be made by educators to influence parent-child academic-related interaction patterns at home.

There is very little information to support or refute either position. Research that systematically relates teachers' efforts to stimulate parent involvement in learning activities at home to the effects of this strategy on students and their families has not been conducted. Up to now, there has been very little research even to indicate how much teachers focus their activities in this direction. However,

* By Henry Jay Becker and Joyce L. Epstein. We gratefully acknowledge the contributions of the teachers and administrators in Maryland for their time and interest in this study. The research was supported by the National Institute of Education, Grant NIE-G-80-0113. No official endorsement of the authors' opinions by the NIE should be inferred. Reprinted with permission from *Elementary School Journal* 83 (1982): 85–102.

there are several studies showing that parents can influence student achievement and social development (Leichter, 1974; Lightfoot, 1978; Marjoribanks, 1979).

To measure how elementary school teachers feel about parent involvement in home learning as a teaching strategy and to see how widespread this teaching strategy is, we conducted a formal survey of first-, third-, and fifth-grade school teachers in most of the public schools in the state of Maryland in spring 1980. This survey was the first phase of an ongoing study that will give teachers and administrators information about the effects of these parent involvement strategies on the educators who use them and on the parents and students who are affected by them.

SURVEY RESPONDENTS

The survey's results describe the teaching practices and professional attitudes of approximately 3,700 public elementary school teachers in more than 600 schools in 16 of the 24 school districts in Maryland. In the 15 districts that offered full cooperation with the project, the response rate was 73 percent of the teachers selected as participants in the study. In the remaining district, where access to teachers was limited, the response rate was only 35 percent. The study also includes information from more than 600 elementary school principals in the state who responded to a brief questionnaire on parent involvement programs in the school.

Table 3.1 describes the characteristics of the 3,698 teacher respondents. Approximately 28 percent of the survey respondents are first-grade teachers, 30 percent teach third grade, 29 percent teach fifth grade, and 13 percent are either reading or math specialists or others whom the principal designated as important contacts for a study of parent involvement (e.g., parent involvement coordinators).

Approximately 90 percent of elementary teachers are female; of the male teachers, about 70 percent teach the fifth grade. About 20 percent of the sample is black, and more than 60 percent of the black teachers are in a major central city district. The teachers range in age from their early twenties to their seventies, with most teachers (38 percent) in their thirties, born between 1940 and 1949. Approximately half of the teachers have taught for more than 10 years, and of the rest, most have taught at least 5 years. Nearly half have graduate school degrees. Although a majority of teachers teach a single class of children both reading and mathematics, team teaching and departmentalization of instruction are common. For example, among fifth-grade teachers, 75 percent report some form of nontraditional teaching arrangement.

The responding teachers are representative of their profession in the state, and they reflect the broad range of geographic and socioeconomic variation in their student populations. The state's large metropolitan population and several smaller urban and rural areas are represented in the statistics in Table 3.1, as is the range of parents that are college educated, high school educated, and less educated.

The questionnaire for teachers requested information on what teachers think about parent involvement strategies and how they practice them. The survey fo-

TABLE 3.1   Characteristics of Teachers in Survey*

Teacher Characteristics	Respondents (%)
Grade level:	
Grade 1	28
Grade 3	30
Grade 5	29
Other reading, math, parent involvement specialists	13
Sex:	
Female	91
Male	9
Race:	
White	78
Black	21
Other	1
Education:	
Bachelor's	12
B.A. or B.A. plus credits	40
Master's	26
Master's and credits or doctorate	21
Experience:	
1–5 years teaching	17
6–10 years teaching	32
Over 10 years	51
Class assignments:	
Teach single class all day	55
Teach several classes during day	45
Location of school district:	
Rural/small town/small city	32
Suburban ring of metropolitan area	49
Central city of metropolitan area	19
Students' parents' education (teachers' estimates)	
Majority did not complete high school	25
Majority are high school but not college graduates	52
Majority are college graduates	23

* N = 3,698.

cused on 14 specific techniques that teachers may employ to encourage parents' participation in learning activities with their children.

Overall, the survey results indicate a very positive view of parent-oriented teaching strategies and widespread, although not intensive, use of these 14 teaching techniques. The next sections describe teachers' attitudes about parent involvement, reported practices, and some of the differences in opinions and practices among teachers who responded to the survey.

TRADITIONAL TEACHER-PARENT COMMUNICATIONS

Some forms of communication and contact between parents and teachers are nearly universal. Virtually all teachers (over 95 percent of the respondents) report that they talk with children's parents, send notices home, and interact with parents on open-school nights. Approximately 90 percent of the teachers ask parents to check and sign students' homework. These standard parent-teacher communications have become accepted ways of bridging the information gap and the sense of distance felt by teachers and parents who may be strangers to one another but who share common interests in the same children. Based on their questionnaire responses and the comments initiated on the survey form, teachers clearly support the use of these standard patterns of interaction with parents.

However, the survey shows considerable variation in the ways that teachers conduct these standard interactions with parents and in the topics teachers emphasize in these discussions. For example, 65 percent of the teachers report that they discuss "with each parent" what they can do at home with their children; the other 35 percent discuss this topic "as the need arises," which may mean once, twice, or never. Similarly, most teachers discuss with all parents how they teach reading and math in their classrooms, but some do this only with a few parents. More significantly, many teachers who discuss their own teaching methods with parents do not talk about parents' responsibilities with homework, and many who discuss helping with homework do not discuss their own teaching methods.

Only a minority of teachers initiate interactions with parents that go beyond what is traditionally expected of them. Although nearly 80 percent of the teachers conduct more than three parent conferences in a school year, only 7 percent initiate three or more group meetings or workshops for parents apart from school-sponsored parents' nights. Generally, teachers who conduct workshops for parents are the ones who most actively emphasize the teaching role of parents at home.

Principals of the schools in which teachers were surveyed reported near-universal support of traditional parent-teacher communications. Approximately 95 percent of the principals report that they have a PTA or PTO, and about half report an active parents' advisory council associated with Title I or other programs. These standard organizations for parent participation usually have a core of active parents; approximately half of the principals report that more than 20 parents are actively involved in meetings and activities each month. Of course, even 20 parents active in developing schoolwide and school-community activities is only a small fraction of the parents who may become involved in activities that concern their own children.

Like the teachers, principals generally support the concept of parent involvement. Most of the principals have strong opinions in favor of parent volunteers in the classroom, and nearly three out of five report that they have held staff meetings or workshops during the school year that focused on methods for helping parents work with their children at home.

THE FEASIBILITY OF PARENT INVOLVEMENT

The teachers' responses to the questionnaire suggest that many teachers believe parent involvement at home could be an important contributor toward achieving the goals they have set for themselves and their students. At the same time, many teachers do not know how to initiate and accomplish the programs of parent involvement that would help them most. This dilemma is suggested by responses to six statements in the questionnaire about the value of parent involvement strategies. Figure 3.1 contains the wording of these items and graphs of the teachers' responses.

On two of the six items, there was a good deal of agreement. Most teachers feel that parent involvement is an important factor in solving the problems faced by schools and that parent involvement in the classroom is useful for increasing parent learning assistance at home. On the other four items, teacher opinion was di-

Can Parent Involvement Work?   Maryland elementary school teachers . . .

Agree

Disagree

In this country, parent involvement is not an answer to the major problems of the schools—the schools must solve their problems on their own.

Teachers can only provide parents with ideas about how to help with their children's schoolwork—teachers cannot influence parents to use these ideas.

Most parents—although they can teach their children to sew, use tools, or play a sport—do not have enough training to teach their children to read or to solve math problems.

Realistically, it is too much to ask parents to spend a full hour per day working with their children on basic skills or academic achievement.

If parents regularly spend time in the classroom, one result is that they usually make a greater effort to help their children at home.

Many parents want more information sent home about the curriculum than most teachers provide.

FIGURE 3.1   Opinions of Maryland Teachers about Parent Involvement

vided concerning whether teachers can actually influence parents to help their children at home, whether most parents have sufficient skills to teach their children to read or solve math problems, whether it is fair to ask parents to spend an hour each evening working with their children on school-related activities, and whether parents want to know more about the school curriculum than they are usually told.

Although almost three-quarters of the teachers agreed that the general idea of parent involvement is a good one, approximately half of the teachers had serious doubts about the success of practical efforts to involve parents in learning activities at home. This should not come as a surprise. Teachers have not been educated in the management of parent involvement, the teachers' and parents' time is finite, teachers and the parents have different skills and often diverse goals for the children, and teachers and parents may have many children (and other family obligations) that require a share of their time and interest. Despite these real difficulties, some teachers have developed procedures that enable them to select and manage parent involvement programs.

FOURTEEN TECHNIQUES TO INVOLVE PARENTS

Teachers were asked several questions about each of 14 specific teaching techniques that involve parents in learning activities at home with their children. These techniques, as well as others added by the teachers, can be grouped into five categories: (1) techniques that involve reading and books; (2) techniques that encourage discussions between parent and child; (3) techniques that specify certain informal activities at home to stimulate learning; (4) contracts between teacher and parents that specify a particular role for parents in connection with their children's school lessons or activities; and (5) techniques that develop parents' tutoring, helping, teaching, or evaluation skills. The graphs in Figure 3.2 summarize how often the teachers in our survey use the 14 techniques, grouped according to these five categories.

Techniques Involving Reading and Books

One of the most frequently mentioned home-learning activities for parents to conduct with preschool and elementary school children is reading. It is not surprising that the teachers in our survey reported that parent-child reading is their most used parent involvement technique. Two-thirds of the teachers said they frequently ask parents to read to their children or listen to the children read, and more than one-fifth named this activity as the most valuable parent involvement technique in their own teaching practices. Parent involvement in reading activities is a more prevalent teaching practice among teachers of younger children. For example, only one-third of the fifth-grade teachers make active use of this technique in their practice, whereas seven out of eight first-grade teachers do so. The decline in use of this technique may be because teachers of older students see less need for

Evaluation
Categories:

□ Unrealistic to expect parent cooperation   "*no* support"
□ Parents do not have sufficient skills
▨ Workable, but did not use this year   "passive support"
▨ Used a few times this year
▨ Used MANY TIMES this year   "active support"
■ The MOST SATISFYING parent involvement techniques

ACTIVITIES EMPHASIZING READING

Ask parents to read to their child regularly or to listen to the child read aloud.

Loan books, workbooks, etc., to parents to keep at home for short periods as extra learning material.

Ask parents to take their child to the library.

LEARNING THROUGH DISCUSSION

Ask parents to get their child to talk about what he or she did that day in your classroom.

Give an assignment that requires the children to ask their parents questions, for example, the children write their parents' experience.

Ask parents (one or more) to watch a specific television program with their child and to discuss the show afterwards.

INFORMAL LEARNING ACTIVITIES AT HOME

Suggest ways for parents to incorporate their child into their own activities at home that would be educationally enriching.

Send home suggestions for game or group activities related to the child's schoolwork that can be played by parent and child.

Suggest how parents might use the home environment (materials and activities of daily life) to stimulate their child's interest in reading, math, etc.

(continues)

FIGURE 3.2   Fourteen Techniques for Involving Parents in Teaching Activities at Home (Evaluations by Maryland Teachers)

FIGURE 3.2 *(continued)*

CONTRACTS BETWEEN TEACHER AND PARENT

Establish a formal agreement
where the parent supervises
and assists the child in
completing homework tasks.

Establish a formal agreement
where the child provides
rewards and/or penalties
based on the child's school
performance or behavior.

DEVELOPING TEACHING AND
EVALUATION SKILLS IN PARENTS

Ask parents to come *observe*
the classroom (not to "help")
for part of a day.

Explain to parents certain
techniques for teaching, for
making learning materials,
or for planning lessons.

Give a questionnaire to
parents so they can evaluate
their child's progress or
provide some other feedback
to you.

assigning read-aloud activities, or because they believe parents are less able to organize instruction for fifth graders.

Teachers in the survey were asked about two other parent involvement techniques directly related to reading and written material: asking parents to take their child to the public library and loaning books and teaching materials to parents on a short-term basis. The majority of teachers believed these to be useful techniques.

As a group, the three techniques involving reading and books elicited more support from teachers than any of the other categories of parent involvement. Reading-related techniques have broad support across all teaching situations but are most often chosen as the most important method by first-grade teachers and by teachers with a large proportion of children who have difficulty learning.

Learning through Discussion

Schooling is more than learning the mechanics of reading. Many teachers place importance on the development of students' ability to express themselves orally.

Even if families do not usually spend much time reading together, they can provide opportunities for students to learn from conversations and discussions.

The teachers in the survey were asked about three techniques that structure parent-child conversation in ways that might be educationally useful. One of these asks parents to view a particular television program with their child and to discuss the program afterward. When this technique is employed, it may be a mild suggestion to parents or it may include a set of discussion questions prepared by the teacher for the parents prior to the evening of a specific telecast. To use this technique intensively, the teacher would have to have advanced access to, or knowledge of, the content of the television program.

The systematic assignment of discussion about television programs was one of the least frequently used parent involvement techniques in the survey. Approximately one-third of the teachers said that parents would not cooperate with a request to participate or that they would be unable to handle such discussions in ways that would be educational. Only about 2 percent of the teachers reported that they used this technique frequently. However, there was more "passive" support for this technique than for any other on the survey. Most teachers said that this was a way of involving parents that could work in their teaching practices, even though they had not used it.

Two other methods of involving parents in discussions are (1) family exchanges about daily school activities and (2) homework assignments that require children to interview parents to obtain biographical or other information. Parent-child discussions about school were frequently mentioned by teachers as a technique they request or require of parents, but student interviews of parents were infrequently assigned. Most teachers felt that students could profit from assignments that required them to ask parents questions, but only 15 percent made active use of the method. As expected, the older the children the more likely they were to be assigned homework that involved asking parents questions. There is a large amount of "passive support" among teachers for this method of parent involvement in school activities. It may be that the procedures necessary to implement these techniques are not established well enough to permit wide adoption by teachers.

Informal Learning Activities at Home

The "parent as tutor" is one model of structuring parent-child teaching and learning activities at home. This model involves efforts to have parents read to the child, supervise and review the child's homework, or give practice tests or math drills using teacher-distributed flash cards. The parents' role is to supplement the formal school curriculum to ensure greater mastery of basic skills by their child.

The "parent as role model" is another way of structuring parent-child learning activities. This model is based on the idea that the parent is a natural teacher of varied skills and serves as a role model. The child may learn different skills at home from those taught in schools and may imitate the parents or adopt the parents' values about what kinds of skills are important, interesting, or fun. A number of those who propose more intensive parent involvement in learning activities at home suggest that parents can be most effective when they informally introduce their children to skills different from those emphasized at school (Rich, 1980). The question is whether and how teachers can motivate parents who would not normally do so to take time to provide informal learning opportunities at home.

The teachers in the survey were asked about three techniques that involve parents and their children in informal educational activities: suggesting educationally enriching ways for parents to involve their child in their own activities at home; sending home suggestions for game or group activities related to the child's schoolwork that can be played by parent and child; and suggesting how parents might use the home environment (common materials and activities of daily life) to stimulate their child's interest in reading, math, and other subjects.

Each of these three techniques, as shown in Figure 3.2, elicited a similar pattern of responses from the teachers. Approximately 30 percent of the teachers rejected these techniques either because of insufficient parent cooperation or because they felt the activities would be too difficult for parents to conduct. Another 40 percent supported the use of these methods in theory but only infrequently used the techniques in their teaching practice. Finally, about 30 percent of the teachers actively supported and used these methods in their teaching practice. Approximately 10 percent chose one of the three items in this category as the parent involvement method they found most useful and satisfactory.

Many of the parent involvement techniques presented to the teachers in our survey were employed as extensively by teachers just starting their careers as by teachers who had had many years of experience in the classroom. However, all three techniques in this category were used most extensively by experienced teachers. For example, only 16 percent of the teachers in their first or second year of teaching said they frequently sent home ideas for parent-child learning games and activities, whereas 25 percent of the teachers with more than 10 years of classroom experience said they did so. Eighteen percent of new teachers often suggested ways for parents to involve their child in their own activities, but 30 percent of the experienced teachers did so. It is interesting that many of the new teachers who used these activities reported that these were their most satisfying parent involvement techniques. These techniques tended to be preferred by reading and math specialists, teachers of low-achieving students, teachers of students from highly educated families, and teachers in rural or small-town areas.

Contracts between Teachers and Parents

The techniques presented to the teachers in the survey included two that involve the use of "contracts." This term implies a formal agreement to conduct and complete an activity or set of activities. The two techniques are distinguished by the kinds of behavior requested of the parents. In one case, the parent is asked to provide or withhold privileges or punishments to the child for school performance and behavior patterns, based on rules determined jointly by the parent, teacher, and student. The parent does not engage in any direct instructional activity in this type of contract, but assists the teacher in shaping productive school behavior.

The second "contract" technique requires parents to supervise or assist with the student's homework or other projects. This may or may not involve some instruction or clarification by the parents but always involves the structuring of the home environment to support the student's school responsibilities. This kind of activity is often informally organized by teachers and parents, but we were interested in those instances where a formal contract for parental responsibilities was arranged by the teacher, parent, and child.

Teachers expressed less consensus about the value of both types of parent-teacher contracts than about most of the other parent involvement techniques. Approximately 40 percent of the teachers felt that these techniques were not worth pursuing because they would not increase learning or because of insufficient parental cooperation or skills. On the other hand, 20 percent of the teachers felt that contracts for parental supervision of homework and projects were valuable enough to use "many times" during the year or were the most important parent involvement technique in their practices. Fewer teachers gave active support to formal contracts involving parental rewards for school behavior, but many of those who used the technique believed it was the most useful one they employed.

There were some important differences in the use of contracts by teachers at different grade levels. In contrast to many other parent involvement techniques supported mainly by teachers in the lower grades, contracts were used equally across the grades. They were preferred as the most satisfying techniques by twice as many fifth-grade teachers as first-grade teachers. Teachers used contracts with parents of students at all achievement levels but were more apt to use them with students of more educated parents. Teachers in suburban districts used contracts more frequently, and younger teachers were more likely than older teachers to classify contracts as their most satisfying parent involvement technique.

Helping Parents to Teach

The list of 14 parent involvement techniques contained three activities for teachers to use to equip parents with observational and instructional skills: (1) instruction for parents in teaching and in making learning materials that could be used at home to supplement the teacher's work at school, (2) classroom observations to see how teaching proceeds in school and how the children respond to particular lessons and methods of teaching, and (3) parent responses to teachers' questionnaires to evaluate their own child's progress or problems in school. The latter activity may assist the teacher more directly than it assists the parent. However, evaluation forms are often useful sensitizers, and thus may help parents to conduct activities at home with the child. Of these three activities, more teachers use classroom observation by parents than the other choices; very few of the teachers reported frequent use of evaluation forms from parents. Classroom observations and teaching parents about teaching and evaluation were encouraged by teachers of young children. Urban teachers and experienced teachers used these techniques more than teachers in suburban and rural areas and new teachers.

Techniques Encouraged by Principals

The reports from principals show the same selective emphasis on reading as the reports from teachers. As Table 3.2 indicates, 76 percent of the principals say they have personally encouraged many teachers to adopt the technique of asking parents to read to or listen to their children read. The principals placed least emphasis on the same two techniques that were given least emphasis by the teachers: parent-led discussion of television programs and contracts with parents to systematically reward or punish student behaviors.

Although teachers and principals, as groups, seem to make similar judgments about the usefulness of different parent involvement techniques, direct influence from the principal on the teacher's practice is difficult to measure with the data available. Only one teacher in six indicates that the source of his or her most valuable parent involvement technique is a "principal or other administrator." Teachers who actively use a particular parent technique are only slightly more likely than other teachers to have a principal who encourages teachers to adopt that same technique.

HOW MUCH EMPHASIS ON THE 14 TECHNIQUES?

Most teachers understand that parent involvement is a complex process and make only tentative requests for such involvement. Regardless of which technique they use, only 9 percent of the teachers "require" parental cooperation; the rest "suggest" the technique. This means that teachers' control over the technique and the response from parents is limited. Indeed, approximately 40 percent of the teachers report that none, fewer than half, or an unknown proportion of the parents carried out their requests to conduct certain activities. These conditions may explain why nearly 60 percent of the teachers say they can provide ideas for learning activities at home but they cannot influence the parents to use them.

Teachers estimated how many parents would attend meetings or workshops on learning activities at home. As the text table below shows, only one-third of the teachers believe they could attract a good number of parents to the meetings, and then only if they were conducted in the evening. Thus, it would require extra or voluntary effort by teachers for even a small percentage of parents to become teaching partners through workshops conducted at school.

Estimated Attendance by Parents	Few or None (%)	Many or Most (%)
At morning meeting	87	13
At evening meeting	66	34

Teachers report having the most contact with parents of children with learning and discipline problems and with parents who are already active in the school. For example, one-third as many contacts with parents are reported for "average" students as for students with problems. Most teachers report that they ask only some parents (not parents of all students in the class) to conduct particular learning activities at home.

TABLE 3.2 Correspondence of Principals' Active Encouragement and Teachers' Active Use of Selected Techniques of Parent Involvement

Techniques	Principals Who Encourage (%)	Teachers Who Use Actively (%)
Read aloud or listen to reading	76	66
Informal games at home	45	24
Contract with parents on students' projects	33	25
Loan books to parents	31	41
Teach parents techniques for tutoring and evaluation	24	21
Parent contracts to reward or punish behavior	12	13
Parent-led discussion of TV shows	12	2

Actions that are requested rather than required and carried out with little or unknown frequency, meetings attended by small groups of parents rather than all parents, and selected use of parent involvement techniques with only certain parents are all indications that, for the average teacher, parent involvement at home is not indispensable to satisfactory teaching.

DIFFERENCES IN TEACHERS' USES OF PARENT INVOLVEMENT

In this section, teachers' opinions and practices are reported for different grade levels and for various educational levels of students' parents. Results are then summarized for the pattern of home visits, the use of parent involvement with different school subjects, and the relationship between parent involvement at home and parent assistance in the classroom. Finally, we discuss the use of techniques by teachers in schools in which all teachers practice parent involvement and where few teachers do so.

Grade Level of Students

Most researchers who have studied parent involvement in learning activities, as well as those who have developed programs for parent involvement, have viewed the parents of preschoolers and early elementary-aged children as their primary targets. In the 1960s and 1970s, various Head Start and Follow-Through programs systematically incorporated specific functions for parents as part of their organizational arrangements. Many of these programs were found to increase student learning of school-readiness skills more than programs used as alternate "control" treatments. Much of the emphasis on early childhood has been due to a belief that parents of young children are more willing and more able to perform useful functions in an educational program than are parents of older children. It may be, however, that procedures and tasks for useful parent participation for older children simply have not been worked out.

Figure 3.3 shows that most of the 14 parent involvement techniques in our survey were more likely to be used by teachers of younger students. However, in only a few cases were the differences of large magnitude. Parent and child reading activities had the most pronounced decline with increasing grade level. The three "informal" learning activities included in the list also declined with increasing grade level, as did efforts to teach parents techniques for teaching their children. On the other hand, the techniques of contracts and assignments that required children to ask their parents questions and the limited use of television-based family discussions and parent-evaluation forms were as often used with older children as with younger. Some teachers at all grade levels used each of the techniques in the survey.

Educational Level of Parents

Many of the written comments of teachers reinforced common stereotypes of parents: "pushy" upper-middle-class parents, "helpful" middle-class parents, and "incapable" lower-class parents. However, the statistics on the techniques teachers use successfully with different groups of parents tell a different story. Teachers who deal with college-educated parents, those who work with parents with average schooling, and those whose students' parents have very little schooling are about equally likely to be active users of parent involvement strategies. However, teachers who do not actively use parent involvement techniques respond differently to questions about the likely success of these techniques according to the educational levels of their students' parents. Teachers who are not active users and who teach children with highly educated parents report that the parent involvement techniques would work but that they do not choose to use them. Teachers who are not active users and who teach children with less-educated parents are more apt to report that the parents would not be able or willing to carry out activities related to the child's schoolwork at home.

Figure 3.4 illustrates the differences in the pattern of use of several of the techniques with parents of different educational levels. For each technique, bar graphs are shown for three groups of teachers—those whose students' parents were mainly college graduates, those whose students' parents were mainly high school graduates, and those whose students' parents nearly all lacked a high school diploma. Each bar graph shows the proportion of teachers who make active use of the technique, the proportion who believe it could work but are not frequent users, and the proportion who do not feel that their students' parents could or would participate effectively.

To summarize Figure 3.4, let us consider two examples. The upper-right panel of the figure shows that techniques that involve parent and child reading activities are used by a majority of teachers with students whose parents are from all educational backgrounds. The solid black segments indicate that approximately 60 percent of the teachers made active use of this technique at every parent-education level. Of the remaining teachers, those whose students' parents had little education were more apt to attribute their lack of use to the absence of parental cooperation or skills, whereas teachers of students whose parents had more education

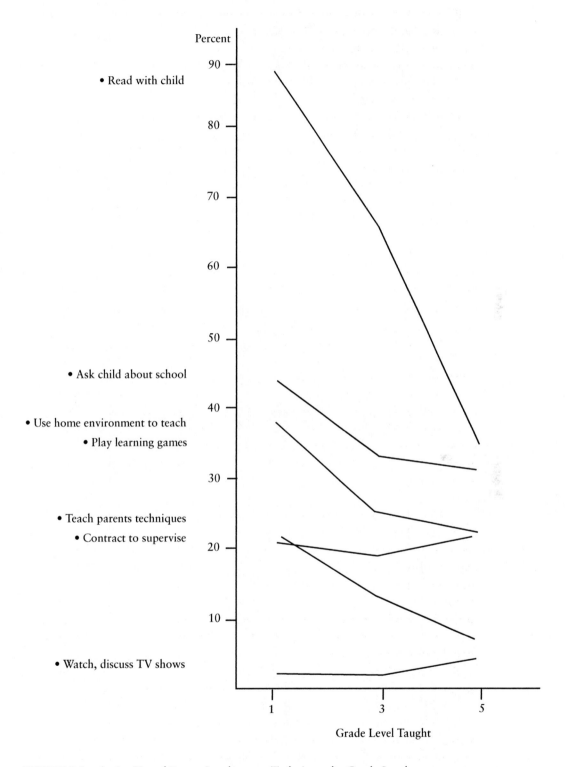

FIGURE 3.3   Active Use of Parent Involvement Techniques by Grade Level

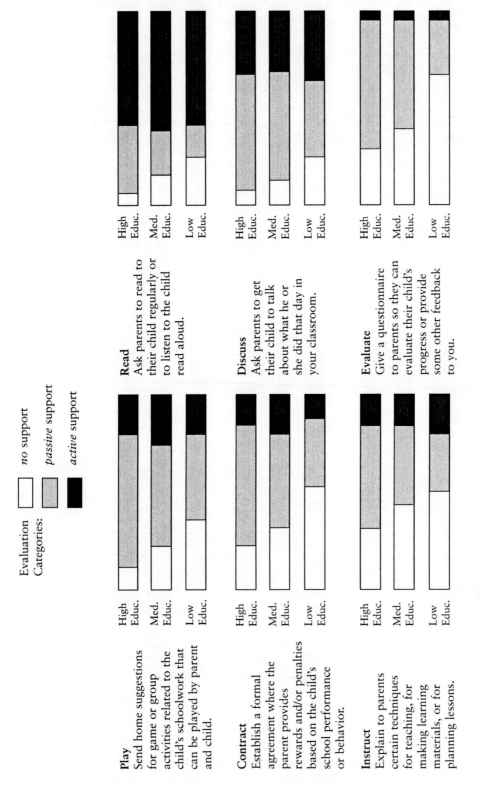

Evaluation Categories:

☐ *no* support
▨ *passive* support
■ *active* support

Play
Send home suggestions for game or group activities related to the child's schoolwork that can be played by parent and child.

Contract
Establish a formal agreement where the parent provides rewards and/or penalties based on the child's school performance or behavior.

Instruct
Explain to parents certain techniques for teaching, for making learning materials, or for planning lessons.

Read
Ask parents to read to their child regularly or to listen to the child read aloud.

Discuss
Ask parents to get their child to talk about what he or she did that day in your classroom.

Evaluate
Give a questionnaire to parents so they can evaluate their child's progress or provide some other feedback to you.

FIGURE 3.4   Levels of Support for Some Techniques by Estimated Formal Education of Parents

116

claimed the technique could work but that it was not currently part of their teaching practice. Thus, whether parents with little schooling are viewed by the teacher as "capable" of assisting their children in reading at home may depend on whether the teacher has worked out procedures and communication patterns that would enable parents with little schooling to assist.

The middle-right panel of the figure shows that approximately 30 percent of the teachers surveyed make active use of techniques that involve parent-child discussions at home with parents at all educational levels, with slightly more teachers actively using the technique with low-educated parents. Teachers who were not active users offered contradictory explanations for lack of use in relation to their students' family social class. Those who reported that their students' parents had little schooling said that using discussions could not work, whereas those whose students had better-educated parents said the techniques could work but that they were not being used.

The pattern for all of the techniques in Figure 3.4 (and the others not listed there) is fairly uniform. It seems clear that some teachers of students from families with less formal education have developed techniques that enable these parents to participate in the schooling of their children and to successfully cooperate with the school. How do they do this? Are the teachers' techniques generalizable so that other teachers with similar populations can use them? Do the efforts of the teachers and the parents benefit the students, the teachers, or the parents?

Home Visits

Most contacts between teachers and parents are in the form of notes and memos transmitted by the child. Yet personal contacts between parent and teacher may be vitally important to develop the commitment of parents to participation in a program of learning reinforcement at home. Teachers make personal contact most often by brief conversations before and after school, by parent conferences on "parent night" or by special appointment, and by telephone conversations with parents.

One infrequently used method for developing personal relationships is home visits by the teacher. Fewer than one-quarter of the teachers in the survey indicated that they had made any home visits during the school year, and only 2 percent said they had visited more than a handful of children's homes. The teachers who visited children's homes were more likely to be favorable toward parent involvement techniques. In particular, they were most likely to be active users of techniques that emphasized oral exchanges between parent and child: having parents discuss TV programs, having parents ask children about school, and having children interview parents. Also, teachers who visited several homes made more use of parent evaluations and parent classroom-observation methods than did other teachers.

School Subjects for Parent Involvement at Home

Teachers reported the academic subjects in which they used their favorite parent involvement techniques. Their responses indicate the popularity of reading as an activity parents can conduct successfully. Over 80 percent of the teachers listed one or more reading-related subjects as the focus of their most successful technique for parent involvement. In contrast, only 20 percent of the teachers emphasized parent involvement in science activities, and approximately one-half used their favorite techniques in math-related home-learning activities. Especially in the early elementary grades, teachers ask parents to supplement the teachers' emphasis on basic skills rather than enrich or extend students' experiences with other subjects such as arts, sciences, or home and hobby skills.

Parents in School

Some teachers report having many parents who are active at school and willing volunteers in their classrooms. Others report almost no parent activity in the school building and no use of classroom volunteers. Approximately half the teachers have at least some parental assistance in the classroom, ranging from a few days per month to every day. Most parents who assist are selectively recruited, although some teachers send out general requests for parental help.

Most teachers (84 percent) agree that if parents spend time at school "they usually make a greater effort to help their children learn at home." Observing a teacher's techniques for presenting material, handling questions, and analyzing mistakes may help parents to be more effective in conducting school-related learning activities at home. This helps to explain why teachers invite parents to observe their classes. If watching the class can aid the parent at home, it is a rather effortless way for teachers to help parents to assist in learning activities at home.

Not surprisingly, teachers who report more parent involvement in the school also are more favorable to using techniques that involve parents in learning activities at home. Support for each one of the 14 parent involvement techniques was positively correlated with the proportion of parents who were active at school and the frequency with which the teacher made use of parent volunteers in the classroom. Teachers who reported the most active parents in the school and in the classroom were especially supportive of the techniques that use informal activities at home and that teach parents tutoring and evaluation skills. For example, of the teachers who often suggested how parents might use materials and activities at home to stimulate their child's interest in school subjects, about 60 percent had parent help in the classroom, mostly on a weekly basis. Of those who "passively" supported this technique, fewer than 50 percent had parent classroom volunteers. Only 30 percent of the teachers who were pessimistic about this kind of at-home parent activity had parents' help during the school day.

School Support for Parent Involvement

Do teachers develop attitudes about parent involvement and related teaching practices as a consequence of their observations of, and conversations with, other teachers at the same school? This question is of interest because it is useful to know whether a "group effort" across an entire school is necessary for successful parent involvement programs or whether individual teachers develop personal programs regardless of the activities of other teachers in their schools.

For all types of parent involvement techniques except the activities involving reading and books, there was a small but positive association between an individual teacher's support for a technique and a measure of overall parent involvement orientation for all teachers in the school. It appears that some teachers are encouraged to use some techniques when their school climate supports parent involvement, but there are many examples of individual successes without support from other teachers in the school.

CONTINUING STUDIES OF PARENT INVOLVEMENT

We have documented teachers' reports of different practices in parent involvement across the state of Maryland. We discuss the teachers' comments on major issues of parent involvement in Reading 3.2. In other research we are collecting more detailed information from a small sample of teachers and principals who participated in the survey. We need to know why teachers use particular techniques, how they implement them, and why they reject other techniques. We are surveying parents and students to obtain reports of teachers', parents', and students' experiences with parent involvement and the effects of family involvement on student achievement and attitudes. (See Readings 3.3 through 3.9 and Reading 4.3.) This information will enable more teachers to make reasoned choices and decisions about implementation, adoption, or adaptations of parent involvement techniques for particular settings and students.

What do the differences in teachers' practices mean in terms of student learning, the quality of education for students, and the quality of the school environment for teachers and for parents? It may be that parent involvement helps to improve student learning or improves the process by which teachers and parents provide education. It may also be that other teaching strategies are equally or more effective and efficient. Although proponents and opponents of parent involvement in learning activities have their opinions about the answers to these questions, the facts are not yet known.

REFERENCES

Leichter, H. J. (1974). *The family as educator*. New York: Teachers College Press.
Lightfoot, S. L. (1978). *Worlds apart: Relationships between families and schools*. New York: Basic.
Marjoribanks, K. (1979). *Families and their learning environments: An empirical analysis*. London: Routledge & Kegan Paul.
Rich, D. (1980). *Families learning together*. Washington, DC: Home and School Institute.

Teachers' Reported Practices of Parent Involvement: Problems and Possibilities*

DEBATABLE ISSUES OF PARENT INVOLVEMENT

Several major issues related to parent involvement were discussed in the comments added by over 1,000 teachers to a survey of teachers' practices. Results of the survey of 3,700 teachers in approximately 600 schools in Maryland are described in Reading 3.1. The teachers' comments reflect the variation in years of experience and in the number and types of contacts individual teachers have had with parents. Each theme can be viewed from two perspectives: There are potential advantages, but there are also potential problems, with any parent involvement technique. Teachers' comments reveal their contrasting opinions on the benefits expected from parent assistance at home and on the organizational structures used to conduct parent involvement activities. Some teachers are very positive about parent involvement; others have been discouraged by their attempts to communicate and work with parents.

Teachers' Time

Many teachers commented on the amount of time needed to prepare projects, workshops, and/or directions for parents to use and supervise at home. The crucial question is whether the time required by the teacher is worth the trouble, and whether teachers should volunteer their time without knowing the likely effects of their efforts.

Some teachers telephone parents frequently to give positive messages about a child's progress in school or special skills or abilities observed as well as to discuss problems. If a teacher telephones 30 parents and talks for 10 minutes to each, the teacher spends 5 hours voluntarily on the telephone with parents. The teacher may do this in addition to preparing lessons, grading papers, preparing report cards, working with parents, and preparing parent involvement activities. How much time can teachers give to parent-related activities? How often? With what effect? These are not trivial questions.

---

* By Joyce L. Epstein and Henry Jay Becker. We gratefully acknowledge the efforts of the teachers who contributed comments to the survey. Research was conducted at the Johns Hopkins R and D Center for Social Organization of Schools and was supported by the National Institute of Education, Grant NIE-G-80-0113. No official endorsement of the authors' opinions by the NIE should be inferred. Reprinted with permission from *Elementary School Journal* (1982) 83: 103–113.

Several teachers offered positive statements that indicated that the job of teaching cannot be accomplished without programs that involve parents. For example:

I really rely on parent help. Long ago I realized that only with parent help can my job be performed adequately.

Other comments indicated that the time needed to develop learning activities for parents to use at home or in schools is just not available to teachers or not worth the trouble:

You completely omitted from your questionnaire any items regarding the additional time and effort required of the busy teacher in parent involvement activities.

I believe both parents and students *can* benefit from parent involvement. However, I also know that it takes a great deal of training and explaining and coordinating to have a good program. I've spent many hours doing just this. Frankly, I no longer feel like giving the many hours of extra time required to do this. We are not provided with time to do this type of training. It's all our own time. I no longer feel like giving my time without compensation.

Parents' Time

The teachers acknowledged that parents' time at home is limited by the responsibilities of children, spouse, and/or other family members; cooking and chores; and a general need for relaxation. Many teachers wondered whether parents should be asked to spend at least a short time with each child on academic activities, whether parents' time at home (and how much time) should be spent developing their children's nonacademic skills and responsibilities, or whether teachers have any justification in requesting or requiring parent assistance in academic or social development.

Some teachers suggested that short periods of time spent on learning activities at home can be beneficial to the students if the time is well planned:

Parents have so little "prime" time to spend with their child or children. It is essential that we give these people some very practical and meaningful tips on how to spend quality time with their children.

In my memo to parents I ask them to spend just 10 minutes a night going over the child's word cards. This way neither the child nor the parent feels overworked.

I have also experienced that parents are more than willing to help children in assignments that are short, reinforcement-type work, on which the child (and therefore the parent) can be successful. Parents love to hear their children read.

Others stressed that the "learning activities at home" should not be on school lessons but on general socialization and development:

> I find it far more profitable for the child to get "home training" at home, since today's children do not seem to display the sense of responsibility needed to do their best. . . . Self-reliance, responsibility, and a good self-concept learned at home contribute to improved academics at school. Then there would be *less* need for parental involvement in teaching the academics.

> I feel it is my job to teach and that parents may become impatient and frustrated when working on skills at home. Some reinforcement at home is quite helpful as long as it is kept to a minimum amount of time and done consistently. An hour a day is unrealistic, and unfair to parent and child. I feel that children spend a large part of their day in school (hopefully learning) and at home need to be released for relaxation, play, and pursuing interests (hopefully, not all television). Parenting is in itself a demanding job.

Students' Time and Feelings

Many teachers focused their comments on the benefits or problems for the students of parent involvement in learning activities at home. Some believed academic activities should be kept to a minimum so children could follow interests in their out-of-school time. Many stressed with deep conviction that students' time at home should be mainly the time to play, participate in activities of special interest, or relax. Others expressed concern that academic tasks at home can cause parents and children psychological stress as the pressure to perform vies with the child's need for help and the parents' desire to help. Others believe the child's time at home should reflect parents' teaching of home-related skills and responsibilities.

Several teachers expressed concern that the complex relationships between parents and children can be affected by the kinds of activities assigned for work at home by teachers:

> Most parents are very willing to assist at home and welcome ideas, but I stress working for *short* periods of time and only when both parties are not becoming upset. Some parents tell me they want to help, but they lose their patience. On the other hand, children often feel embarrassed when they don't think they are performing as well as they want to for their parents.

> Care must be taken in "home help" situations so that pressure on the child is not increased by emotional or un-enlightened parental involvement when the goal is to help the child and thereby lighten pressure placed upon him.

Teachers had varied opinions on whether they should try to maximize the potential advantages of parent assistance for some children, even if other children may not be assisted. Some teachers believe parent activities are valuable even if only some parents complete them; other teachers believe no parent-conducted learning activities should be assigned unless all parents agree to cooperate. They charge that children of parents who do not do their part are put at a disadvantage through no fault of the students. Compare the two points of view:

Although many of my students come from homes where support of schools is great, there are also a good number of students who come from homes where support is minimal and parent involvement is very low. This makes it difficult to give the class an assignment involving parents when only some of the students have parents who would bother to help.

Most parents talk a good story, but rarely follow through on any involvement. Then there are some who, given prodding, guidance, and a great deal of specific directions on what to do, will try consistently to help their child. It pays off, even if the results are minimal. It is for these few that it is worth doing what we can to get them involved—because it's ultimately for the children.

The teachers', parents', and students' time, commitment, and reactions were repeatedly discussed by the teachers. There were legitimate differences of opinion. Should some of the parents' and students' time at home be spent on lessons and school assignments, or should the time be spent on new experiences and diverse skills that build on parents' special abilities? The answers to such questions may depend on such factors as children's ages, the types of learning problems that might be involved, the parents' education, the subject matter being studied, and the existing relationship between the parents and child.

Expected Benefits

There are few rewards, other than internal ones, to encourage a teacher to spend time working toward the potential benefits of parent involvement. Some teachers lamented the lack of support from their principals or other teachers. Others recounted the psychological obstacles that prevent teachers from trying some activities or from trying more than once. In spite of some real problems, many teachers described benefits they perceived or expected for their students and for the parents from parent involvement: better basic skills, and greater retention of skills over the summer because of work conducted at home during the vacation; better behavior of students in class; greater number and variety of classroom materials developed by parents at home; enrichment in areas the teacher could not direct; and improved parental self-image because of successful cooperation with the school. The following comments reflect many of the teachers' remarks about the benefits of parent involvement:

Although my teaching career is near a close, I believe parent involvement is one of the keys to improving education, and it should be encouraged. It will not only promote better pupil performance, but it will improve the self-image of each parent, especially in a school community (Title I) such as ours.

I welcome the parents' help and their expertise that increase my children's understanding in special enrichment areas in which I may not be well-versed. For the most part, any assignment I send home is pursued and completed with parents' help.

I feel a good parent education group or program is needed to help parents enjoy and understand their children's need to try, *fail,* and *try again* on their own. Parents can guide and show their love by being there (and giving assistance) when their children need them, but not by doing the work for their children.

Subgroup Differences

Some teachers specified that benefits from parent involvement should be expected only for some children. They described some groups of parents they believed were less able to conduct learning activities successfully at home. However, other teachers pointedly commented that these same groups were successfully involved in parent involvement activities. The important question is whether benefits from parent involvement can be expected from parents of older students, parents with little education, working parents, and single parents.

For example, some teachers believed the benefits will depend on the family structure and the other activities of the parents. The following comments illustrate the debatable issue of involvement of working mothers:

I feel my experience as a working mother and as a single parent has helped tremendously in gearing my relationships and assignments involving parents.

More and more of my "parents" are single parents and sole support. Their time and energy are limited. They do want to cooperate for the most part but are too tired and overworked. I don't even help my own children very much because I am too tired when I get home.

Mother's employment—this factor has nothing to do with parental involvement. You did not ask if parents were alcoholic, drug addicts, child abusers, etc.—You did not ask if parents I work with (and for) are interested in school, impressed with my credentials, comfortable with the administrators and me. These are important facts—mother's employment activities are not.

Working parents have more demands on their time. Helping kids at home becomes a more frustrating task when a parent is tired or has many jobs to do. Other parents get carried away and ask the kids to do too much at home.

Several teachers commented on differences between parents with greater or lesser education:

> I don't feel the educational level of the parents plays too great a part because in my experience I've had tremendous parent involvement with those whose educational level did not go beyond the eighth grade.

> Parent involvement became extremely poor as the years progressed. When the emphasis of education went back to basics, the parents withdrew. This could be attributed to their own poor educational backgrounds and preparedness to help their children.

In general, teachers did not specify the benefits of parent involvement. Most teachers said, "It depends on the students and their parents," as this teacher commented:

> I have had excellent cooperation from parents this year. In many instances it has been up to 95 percent. Other years have not produced the same results. Last year, I had the cooperation of approximately 10 out of 32 parents—and it was the same school. It depends on the group of children—if I had completed this questionnaire last year my responses would have been totally different.

Many teachers thought that the school climate and the principal's support were important, as this teacher noted:

> Most of my teaching career, my principals have been *very much* against the teacher working with parents other than when discipline was involved, and have been unwilling for the teacher to have contact with parents outside of regular classroom hours. My breakthrough in working with parents has been due to working with an outstanding teacher who is excellent in home and school relations.

Use of Parent Involvement Coordinators

Many comments were offered by teachers on the Title I programs. These programs often include parent coordinators, whose job it is to get more parents involved in more aspects of school life. The Title I programs are the largest federally funded programs for parent involvement. Several teachers remarked on the benefits from excellent Title I parent programs, but just as many said the programs were poor and wasteful. The contrasting opinions suggest that some organizational strategies are necessary if the programs are to succeed from the teachers' point of view.

I teach in a Title I school where we have an organized Parent Involvement Program headed by two Parent Involvement Aides. They lead many programs and activities once conducted by the teacher, such as home visits, telephone calls, trips with children to dentist or doctor, assistance with clothing needs, recruitment of parent volunteers to operate the Reading Club, and organization of workshops for parents to learn games that can be used at home. So many of these opportunities are out of the hands of the classroom teacher. Twenty-five or 30 years ago when I taught in a rural Appalachian consolidated school, I had much more parent involvement than I do now. From my teaching point of view, I definitely had more support from parents on things I attempted to do. Although our Title I aides have very good rapport with our parents, there seems to be more of a trend to let the aides do things for the parents and less emphasis on helping parents to help themselves. We do have "star" examples of parent volunteers of more than 10 years who now are "super" paid Title I aides. That is progress, as they help not only their own families but others.

Under the Title I program, we have a home visitation aide who takes learning games into homes of our Title I students. Parents are to play these with the students. Of my eight Title I students, only two parents agreed to accept the games and neither of the two children involved ever played any of the games. I consider this a total waste of our federal money.

Many Title I programs mandate parental involvement. I've been active in helping develop and conduct parent-involvement workshops. I often have classroom workshops to bring parents up-to-date on curriculum and let them know that they are their child's primary and most important teachers.

I have found that since the school I have worked in became Title I there is less parent involvement. The conclusion that I have come to is that since there are paid assistants, parents feel that their services are not needed.

Parent volunteers require constant professional supervision and coordination. This is not done by a Title I Parent Coordinator with a high school education.

Our Title I parent coordinator has been my greatest influence in working with parents.

The reactions partly reflect the teachers' personal attitudes and partly the fact that some Title I programs are better organized, are staffed by more qualified coordinators, and communicate better with teachers. How do the successful Title I programs operate to strengthen family and school ties? What strategies from successful Title I programs can be incorporated into any school to improve home-school alliances? The teachers' opinions on Title I programs raise important questions for further study.

Problems with Parental Assistance

Many teachers who have had experience working with parents have important concerns about the likely success of parent involvement practices. Some teachers described problems often associated with volunteers: undependability, shortened schedules, low commitment, and different goals and values of volunteers and the schools. Others were concerned about the parents' lack of training in methods and approaches for teaching children who have learning problems. These concerns are related to the teachers' lack of time to provide parents with adequate training in how to teach or how to deal with learning problems. These are especially important concerns for parent volunteers in the classroom, but parents at home are also "volunteers." They are not accountable to the teacher. Some teachers commented on how parents fail to follow through in learning activities at home.

Other teachers were concerned that students might not develop responsibility if parents assume too much of the responsibility for students' assignments:

[T]he more opportunities we give our parents to be in the school and the more information given out by teachers, the more parents tend to take any work that is given to the child as *their* work rather than developing responsibility in their children.

Other teachers expressed concern that parents have many problems other than academic ones that interfere with teachers' requests for assistance with learning activities at home:

Some parents do not know how to, or will not, control their children. They expect teachers to work miracles and get their children to learn and to behave when the parents cannot make their own children behave. When contacting parents, especially for behavior problems, I hear more and more frequently, "I don't know what to do with them." No teacher can teach if time must be spent on simple discipline and manners that should be learned at home. I believe that it would help many parents to see their children work with others in the classroom.

I have found as a teacher in this transient community that the parents are too busy to bother about how their children are doing. If everything is going smoothly, the parents stay at home. Only if trouble arises does one hear from a parent. Even if you are doing a fantastic, outstanding job you do not hear from parents. Only in time of trouble.

Parent involvement *is* the problem. I have accomplished the impossible when I manage to just get some parents into the school for a conference.

The effectiveness of using these techniques depends on the community(ies) the school is serving. I have taught in a school where the parents were so involved that one did not need to use techniques. I have taught in a school where very few parents were capable of using any technique no matter how simple. I have also had a parent who could have helped her son tell me that that is my job.

Some admitted that teachers fear parents, and this fear inhibits the kinds of programs teachers attempt:

Most teachers fear parents and I, too, only use parents when I feel I have complete control.

My experience indicates that teachers are even more fearful than the parents of our interaction.

Successful Efforts

In spite of all the possible problems, some teachers with parents of all educational levels and students at all achievement levels have been able to establish programs that emphasize the link between school and home.

Reading with Children.   Many teachers described how they organize a formal program in which parents or students read on a regular basis. For example:

About 4 years ago in a school with a large minority population, most parents were contacted and agreed to see to it that their children read—either to the parent or by themselves for 10 minutes every evening. Many parents cooperated and I believe it helped the children's reading skills. Of course, the children could read longer than 10 minutes if they wished. They brought in slips signed by their parents each morning and were rewarded occasionally by small items donated by local businesses. Very few parents objected.

Signing Papers and Folders.   Many teachers have devised different systems to keep parents aware of the children's schoolwork. When teachers ask parents to sign daily work or weekly folders, they are fulfilling an obligation to keep parents informed of children's progress before or between report cards. Some teachers also send home skill-building assignments or games based on the students' problems identified in schoolwork or on tests:

By having parents sign children's graded math tests and units, I cover several problem spots. Parents always have a good idea of grade average; parents can see the child's progress or lack of it; signing math units enables parents to see all of their children's daily assignments before they are disposed of without the hassle of seeing them every night. Units get signed when the test is taken. If a child receives a poor grade, I attach a sheet telling the parents to review and study the needed skills with their child. The signing insures that the parents see the note.

I send a letter to parents each time we start a new phase of work, explaining what we will be doing and how they can help. This is signed and returned. I also send all returnable work home on blue or green paper or attached to a blue or green computer card. Parents and kids know blue papers are to be returned. I have about 95 percent respond.

Some use a system that permits the parents to communicate with the teacher with more than a signature:

A buddy-book: Each day I write a comment concerning the child's work and general behavior in a book devoted just to homework and teacher-parent comments. The parent signs and responds.

Others have devised phone conference systems to talk with working parents, evening and Saturday conferences and workshops, and other means for two-way communication with parents.

Preparation of Materials. Teachers described two ways in which parent-made materials are used for learning activities. Materials made in school are used at home:

I give parents materials to make flashcards just like mine in math or reading for use at home. Also, parents have watched "mini" lessons on skills that they could teach at home.

I like the mini-clinic: Parents of four Kindergarten and seven first-grade children were encouraged to participate. Parents alternated monthly for individual or small group meetings to discuss activities and games they could use to reinforce skills being taught by the teacher. We sent home materials to be used for a month and returned at the next meeting. Children having the most difficulty learning were selected. Of the 11 parents invited, nine participated. One grandmother and two fathers also attended. Personal contact has made a difference. The success of our parent-involvement programs appears to be closely related to teacher commitment.

Materials made at home are also used at school:

In my "read along with the family" program I send home books and a tape recorder for grandparents or parents to tape the child's favorite story or book. They can listen to it in class. I prepare an activity sheet to go with the tape.

Home Visits. Some teachers use home visits to lay the groundwork for communication with parents that will occur throughout the year. Home visits are arranged voluntarily on weekends or before the beginning of the school year by the teacher and parents or are formally organized by the school administration. Some schools give teachers release time while substitute teachers cover their classes;

other schools establish half-days for children so that the teachers' visits occur on the afternoons when no school is scheduled; other schools allocate two full days for teachers' visits when there is no school scheduled.

Our most effective technique is used in the first week of school when the first-grade children attend half days only. We make a 20-minute visit to *each* home, explain the program and needed supplies, hear concerns, etc. I feel I gain 6 weeks of knowledge about the child during that visit. Also, I feel good in being able to greet each parent by name (usually!) the next time we meet.
I visited each child's home before school opened in the fall. I took each child's photograph, chatted about the things he or she liked to do, pets, etc. On the first day of school the photos and the stories of each child were on the bulletin board. The visit also gave me an opportunity to talk with the mother (and often with both parents) about the curriculum, plans for homework, etc. I expect to resume these visits next summer because they are so useful. There are no tearful children the first week. I know the children by name before they come into the classroom. It is very easy to recruit parent volunteers. It forms the basis for continuing parent contact throughout the year—because we know each other. Telephone conversations when a child is absent or seems troubled strengthen my relationships with the parents. It seems to me that education must be a partnership between parent and teacher.

Summer Learning at Home.   Summer activities that enable parents to help their children maintain skills from the school year may be an especially important area for home-school programs. One teacher commented on the work she arranged for parents to supervise during the summer:

At the end of the year I sent home a calendar of summer activities that would involve parent-child participation and would help the child improve or retain basic skills.

Dilemmas of Parent Involvement

The teachers were aware of the dilemmas of home-school relationships:

Parents are so involved with staying alive and being able to keep up economically, there is little or no energy left to devote to children—much less spend time teaching, disciplining, etc. The time they have is spent being loving, lenient, and feeling guilty for not having time or energy to help their children. The children have no motivation to study. Many of the children I teach are too busy raising the little children in the family, cleaning house, and doing adult work at home because their parents are out trying to make ends meet. It amazes me that the children can run houses, raise siblings, and still find time to learn at all.

Many homes have no literature in them—everything comes from TV—yet the schools neglect the media. Parents want to be supportive and help, but they can't—yet without their support, schools cannot make any real difference.

If parents became actively involved and worked *with* the teachers, our students would be more successful. Our students need lots of motivation that teachers alone cannot provide.

In some ways, all of the teachers' comments are correct. There is no denying the different reactions of teachers to the parents with whom they have worked. The honest differences in teachers' opinions reflect three perspectives on parent-school relations: (1) Parents care but cannot do much to help the school or their children in actual learning; (2) parents care but should not help with school learning; (3) parents care and can be of great help if they are shown how to help. There was no disagreement, however, about the fact that successful parent involvement programs require the teachers' *and* the parents' commitment. There are usually no formal rewards for teachers or parents for the time and effort required to plan and conduct learning activities at home. However, both may have feelings of satisfaction when children make progress in learning.

Many comments stressed the parents' and students' needs for time at home that is free of academic demands; however, an equal number of teachers emphasized that many students who have trouble in school would be assisted with some structured daily work at home. Parental assistance that provides extra time for learning may be one of the few techniques that can bring a slow student up to grade level. Many teachers believe it is worth a try to develop programs for parents to conduct at home that will supplement the teachers' efforts.

Because of an absence of research on the effects of parent involvement, it is impossible to assure teachers that certain practices will lead to improved student skills, improved parent-child exchanges, or improved parent-teacher relations. It is equally impossible to assure teachers that they can be more successful if they ignore parent involvement. The differences in teachers' opinions and the lack of objective evidence on the debated topics suggest how research can contribute to this important aspect of education. From the statistical results of our survey (Reading 3.1) and from the written comments of the teachers, we have identified eight issues that may prompt new research.

1. Of all types of parent involvement, supervision of learning activities at home may be the most educationally significant. In contrast to PTA councils and classroom volunteers that involve relatively few parents, parent activities at home can involve many or all children's parents. We need to know whether and how teachers at different grade levels can successfully implement parent involvement programs to include all families.

2. Some parents work with their children at home, with or without teachers' suggestions. Most parent involvement efforts by teachers focus on parents who normally would not know what to do to assist their children with learning activities at home. We need information on the kinds of tutoring or supervisory skills all parents can learn quickly. We need to know how effective parents can be dur-

ing the relatively short, added "learning time at home" in improving their children's skills.

3. The attitudes, training, and experiences of individual teachers have a lot to do with whether they choose to develop parent involvement programs. However, the attitudes of parents and principals, the needs of the students, and the assistance the teachers receive from their colleagues at school may also contribute to the development and success of parent involvement programs.

4. The role of the parent in learning activities at home is not well defined, and the benefits or disadvantages from different kinds of parental activities and approaches are not known. For example, the parent may act as a tutor, teacher's monitor, listener, task initiator, reactor, or colearner in activities conducted at home. Which parent roles are most effective for what kinds of situations, skills, and students?

5. Differences in teachers' opinions about parent involvement techniques may depend on the skills needed by students of different abilities in the classroom. Skill building and drill for remediation or for enrichment require different kinds of learning materials and make different demands on the teachers' and parents' time and energies. Skill building requires different designs and techniques for students two years behind grade level and for students on or above grade level. How can parent involvement programs take into account the special needs of each student, so that time at home can assist each student's learning?

6. The teacher's role is changed when the teacher acts as a manager of parent involvement. The teacher shares a portion of the teaching authority when parents are given materials and instructions for supervising learning activities at home. New behaviors are required of teachers to coordinate activities for parents, and different reactions to students are required from teachers in response to activities conducted at home. What are the changes in the teacher's role that occur under different parent involvement techniques?

7. Teachers "intrude" on families' schedules and activities whenever homework is given. The older the student, the more homework and the greater the intrusion on family time. However, if homework is accepted as an important mechanism for reinforcing classroom instruction, then homework assignments that involve parents may maximize learning that can occur during the homework period. Carefully constructed assignments will not necessarily be seen negatively by parents. These assignments can be as simple as a weekly spelling drill or as complex as daily lessons in language or math. We need to know how parent involvement can be organized so that the responsibilities and goals of teachers, parents, and students are clear and attainable.

From a different perspective, we need information on how the experiences and expertise of each parent can productively be included in teachers' schedules and curricula. Parents' skills and ideas may be taught to their own children at home or introduced to whole classes in school. In either case, parent-designed lessons and activities might be used systematically by teachers to extend and enrich the schools' programs.

8. One of the reasons so many teachers and principals conduct and support visit-school nights and parents' conferences is that these activities have become

formal, accepted strategies for parent-teacher exchanges. They are school-level activities that recur in similar, predictable form in most schools. In contrast, the techniques of parent involvement in learning activities at home are classroom-level projects that are developed by individual teachers. The patterns of exchange for these activities have not been standardized and so there are no clear expectations.

It is questionable whether the familiar rituals of visit-school night and parent conferences accomplish more than a polite exchange between parents and teachers. Techniques for parent involvement in home-learning activities have greater potential for actively involving parents in important exchanges with the teacher that may assist their own children's progress in school. We need to know how teachers can organize parent involvement so the activities will become as familiar as the traditional parent-teacher events.

New research on parent involvement should take into account the natural variation in characteristics of teachers, students, families, schools, and classrooms. Important questions on the implementation and effects of parent involvement have been raised by this exploratory survey of teachers and by the variety of opinions they expressed. If the problems and possibilities of parent involvement are systematically studied, research can lead quickly and directly to useful information for teachers.

School Programs and Teacher Practices of Parent Involvement in Inner-City Elementary and Middle Schools[*]

ABSTRACT

This study uses data from 171 teachers in eight inner-city elementary and middle schools to examine the connections between school programs of parent involvement, teachers' attitudes, and the practices that teachers use to involve parents of their own students. Patterns are examined at two levels of schooling (elementary and middle), in different academic subjects, under various classroom organizations (self-contained, semi-departmentalized, departmentalized), and under different levels of shared support for parent involvement by the teachers and significant other groups. Each of these variables has important implications for the types and strengths of school programs and teachers' practices of parent involvement. The results add to the validation of Epstein's five types of school and family connections. The data used in this study were collected in a three-year action research process with the sampled schools. The process is outlined in terms that any school can follow to improve programs and practices of parent involvement.

INTRODUCTION

An extensive and growing literature documents the importance of school and family connections for increasing student success in school and for strengthening school programs. The theory of overlapping spheres of influence of families and schools on students' learning and development and on family and school effectiveness (Epstein, 1987a [Reading 2.1]) is supported by a growing number of studies. For example, when teachers make parent involvement part of their regular teaching practice, parents increase their interactions with their children at home, feel more positive about their abilities to help their children in the elementary grades, and rate the teachers as better teachers overall, and students improve

---

* By Joyce L. Epstein and Susan L. Dauber. This research was supported by a grant from the U.S. Department of Education, Office of Educational Research and Improvement (OERI), and by a National Science Foundation Graduate Fellowship to the second author. The opinions expressed do not necessarily reflect the position or policy of the OERI or the NSF, and no official endorsement should be inferred. We are very grateful to the teachers who participated in the survey and to the principals who supported the survey as the first step in a school improvement process. An earlier version of this reading was presented at the 1988 annual meeting of the American Sociological Association and in a technical report at the Center for Research on Elementary and Middle Schools, Johns Hopkins University. Reprinted with permission from *Elementary School Journal* 91 (1991): 289–303.

their attitudes and achievement (Becker & Epstein, 1982 [Reading 3.1]; Epstein, 1986 [Reading 3.4], 1991 [Reading 3.7]).

Despite increased attention to the topic of parent involvement, few studies have focused on teachers' practices of involving parents in "difficult" or "disadvantaged" inner-city schools. Indeed, a recurring theme in many studies and commentaries is that less-educated parents cannot or do not want to become involved in their children's education (Baker and Stevenson, 1986; Lareau, 1987). Other research challenges this generalization by showing that there is wide variation in the nature and quality of the involvement of less-educated parents (Clark, 1983; Scott-Jones, 1987) and that, when teachers help them, parents of all backgrounds can be involved productively (Dauber and Epstein, 1989 [see Reading 3.6]; Epstein, 1986).

Even studies that report average differences in involvement based on parent education or social class, however, recognize that *family practices* vary within any group of parents (Hoover-Dempsey, Bassler, and Brissie, 1987; Lareau, 1989; Stevenson and Baker, 1987; Useem, 1990). Part of the variation among families is due to the fact that schools vary in how much and how well they inform and involve families.

An earlier large-scale study of elementary teachers, parents, and students showed, for example, that teachers who were "leaders" in the frequent use of parent involvement did not prejudge less-educated, poor, or single parents. They rated all groups of parents higher on helpfulness and follow-through on learning activities with their children at home (Becker and Epstein, 1982; Epstein, 1986, 1990 [Reading 3.5]). In contrast, teachers who did not frequently involve parents in their children's education made more stereotypical judgments about the involvement and abilities of less-educated parents, socioeconomically disadvantaged parents, and single parents. Thus, the attitudes and practices of the teachers, not only the educational, socioeconomic status (SES), or marital status of parents, are important variables for fully understanding whether and how parents become knowledgeable and successful partners with schools in their children's education.

Studies will continue to show that better-educated families are more involved, on average, in their children's education until researchers include measures of teacher practices to involve all parents. Most parents need help to know how to be productively involved in their children's education at each grade level. School programs and teacher practices to organize family and school connections are "equalizers" to help families who would not become involved on their own.

FIVE TYPES OF INVOLVEMENT[*]

Earlier studies and reviews suggest that five major types of involvement are part of schools' comprehensive programs to share responsibilities with families for the education of their children (Epstein, 1987b).

1. *Basic obligations of families* include providing for children's health and safety, developing parenting skills and child-rearing approaches that prepare chil-

---

[*] See Reading 5.1 for discussion of advances in extending this typology to six types of involvement.

dren for school and that maintain healthy child development across the grades, and building positive home conditions that support school learning and behavior all across the school years. Schools assist families to develop the knowledge and skills needed to understand their children at each grade level through workshops at the school or in other locations, home visitors, family support programs, and in other forms of education, training, and information giving.

2. *Basic obligations of schools* include communications with families about school programs and children's progress. This includes the memos, notices, phone calls, report cards, and conferences that most schools conduct and other innovative communications with parents that some schools create. Schools vary the forms and frequency of communications and greatly affect whether the information sent home can be understood by all families.

3. *Involvement at school* includes parent and other volunteers who assist teachers, administrators, and children in classrooms or in other areas of the school. It also refers to family members who come to school to support student performances, sports, or other events. Schools can improve and vary schedules so that more families are able to participate as volunteers and as audiences. Schools can improve recruitment and training so that volunteers are more helpful to teachers, students, and school improvement efforts.

4. *Involvement in learning activities at home* includes requests and guidance from teachers for parents to assist their own children at home on learning activities that are coordinated with the children's class work. Schools assist families in helping their children at home by providing information on skills required of students to pass each grade. Schools provide information to families on how to monitor, discuss, and help with homework and when and how to make decisions about school programs, activities, and opportunities at each grade level so that all students can be more successful in school.

5. *Involvement in decision making,* governance, and advocacy includes parents and others in the community in participatory roles in the parent-teacher association/organization (PTA/PTO), advisory councils, Title I programs, or other committees or groups at the school, district, or state level. It also refers to parents as activists in independent advocacy groups in the community. Schools assist by training parent leaders and representatives in decision-making skills and in ways to communicate with all of the parents they represent and by providing information needed by community groups for school improvement activities.

A sixth type of involvement has been suggested as an important component in schools' comprehensive programs for involving families and communities in their children's education (California State Board of Education, 1988):

6. *Collaboration and exchanges with community organizations* include connections with agencies, businesses, and other groups that share responsibility for children's education and future successes. This includes school programs that provide children and families with access to community and support services, including after-school care, health services, and other resources that coordinate these arrangements and activities to support children's learning. Schools vary in how much they know and share about their communities and how much they draw on community resources to enhance and enrich the curriculum and other experiences of students.

This type of involvement was not part of the earlier research that helped to identify the five major types of involvement, nor is it included in the present study. Future research will determine whether and how this is a separate type of involvement or whether these collaborations offer strategies for strengthening the five types of school and family connections by calling on and coordinating community resources for workshops, communications, volunteers, learning activities at home, and decision making (Epstein and Scott-Jones, 1988). Other types of involvement and different typologies will be suggested by other researchers and practitioners and will require study. The typology offered in this reading is designed to be helpful to educators who are analyzing their schools' practices and developing new programs. Although the five types are not "pure" and involve some aspects that overlap, most practices that schools use to involve families in their children's education fall under one of the five types.

Schools with programs including the five types of involvement help parents build home conditions for learning, understand communications from the schools, become productive volunteers at school, share responsibilities in their children's education in learning activities related to the curriculum at home, and include parents' voices in decisions that affect the school and their children. There are, literally, hundreds of practices that can be selected to implement each type of involvement. Most practices have not yet been formally evaluated, but the available evidence indicates that the different types of involvement lead to different outcomes for parents, teachers, and students (Brandt, 1989; Epstein, 1986).

Research on the typology provides evidence of its validity, and a study of a large sample of parents using measures of the five types of involvement found moderate to high internal reliabilities ranging from .58 to .81 (Dauber and Epstein, 1989). Data from teachers in earlier studies were used to study the design and effects of types of involvement but did not provide information on whether the five types were separable. This study uses reports from teachers about the five types of involvement in school programs to further examine the typology.

Earlier studies of parent involvement have focused on one level of schooling, either elementary (Becker and Epstein, 1982; Epstein, 1986, 1990, 1991; Hoover-Dempsey, Bassler, and Brissie, 1987), the middle grades (Baker and Stevenson, 1986; Leitch and Tangri, 1988; Useem, 1990), or the high school level (Bauch, 1988; Clark, 1983; Dornbusch and Ritter, 1988; Dornbusch, Ritter, Liederman, Roberts, and Fraleigh, 1987), but studies have not included comparisons across levels of schooling. This study compares school programs and teachers' practices of parent involvement in elementary and middle schools. Dauber and Epstein (1989) present a related study on the attitudes and practices of the parents in these elementary and middle schools.

METHOD

Data were collected from 171 teachers in five elementary and three middle schools in Baltimore on the teachers' attitudes and practices of parent involvement. The eight schools were selected at random from a set of comparable Title I schools in economically and educationally disadvantaged neighborhoods to begin a three-year initiative to improve parent involvement programs and practices.

Teacher representatives for parent involvement from the eight schools were invited to attend a summer workshop. They were paid for their time, were provided with a background on the topic, helped write questionnaires, received a planning grant to administer the survey to teachers and to parents, and planned an initial activity based on the survey results. The teachers were awarded three years of support in a series of small grants to design, conduct, help to evaluate, and expand practices of parent involvement in their schools to increase the achievement and success of students.

The teacher questionnaire on which this study is based is organized into 10 questions with many subquestions that obtained 100 pieces of information on teachers' general attitudes toward parent involvement; teachers' practices of communicating with students' families; use of school and classroom volunteers (including the numbers, frequency, tasks, and training of volunteers); strength of school programs on the five types of parent involvement; importance of specific practices of five types of parent involvement to the teacher for his or her grade level and subjects taught; teachers' expectations of parents; the involvement of hard-to-reach subgroups of parents; the level of support for parent involvement of the teacher, other school staff, parents, and community; the characteristics of the student population; classroom organization; subjects taught; grade level(s); numbers of different students taught; and years of teaching experience. Open-ended comments about parent involvement practices and problems were also solicited from the teachers.

Two stages of analyses were conducted. First, descriptive statistics were provided to the teachers, principals, and parents in each school. Each school was given two profiles, or "Clinical Summaries," based on the data collected from teachers and parents. These profiles summarized the strengths and weaknesses of the school on the five types of parent involvement as perceived by the two groups of respondents and reported summary statistics for all survey questions (Epstein, 1988; Epstein and Salinas, 1988). Schools used these data to develop their initial projects to improve parent involvement programs and practices.

Second, in this study, the data from teachers in the eight schools were combined for more formal analyses of patterns and connections of teacher attitudes about parent involvement, school programs, and the actual practices that teachers use at two levels of schooling (elementary/middle); in different academic subjects; under three classroom organizations (self-contained, semi-departmentalized, departmentalized); and under high or low support by significant other groups for parent involvement. In the next sections we present correlates of strong school programs of the five types of involvement, add information to validate the typology of five major types of involvement, discuss the practices of teachers of specific academic subjects, and demonstrate the importance of a school climate that encourages parent involvement. These analyses provide new information on programs of parent involvement in inner-city elementary and middle schools. Finally, we outline the process that these schools are using and that any school could use to improve its connections with families to benefit students.

RESULTS

Teachers' General Attitudes about Parent Involvement

Overall, teachers in the inner-city elementary and middle schools in this sample have strong, positive attitudes about parent involvement. A 10-item scale, scored 1–4 for negative to positive attitudes on each item, has an average mean score of 3.07 (with a standard deviation of .32), indicating strong agreement overall and little variation in teachers' attitudes. Compared to other teachers, attitudes are more positive for teachers who teach in self-contained classrooms (correlation coefficient, $r = .234$) and for those who perceive high support for parent involvement from their colleagues and students' parents ($r = .336$). Teachers with more positive attitudes toward parent involvement place more importance than other teachers on such practices as holding conferences with all students' parents, communicating with parents about school programs, and providing parents with both good and bad reports about students' progress. More positive attitudes also are positively correlated with more success in involving hard-to-reach parents ($r = .383$), including working parents, less-educated parents, single parents, parents of older students, young parents, parents new to the school, and other adults with whom children live.

Separate Contributions of the Five Types of Parent Involvement

The items in the questionnaire were designed to measure the five types of involvement described previously. The five types are significantly interrelated, with correlations ranging from $r = .303$ to $r = .569$, as shown in Table 3.3. The modest correlations indicate, however, that the five types also make separate contributions to comprehensive programs of parent involvement.

The range of coefficients suggests a Guttman-scale-like pattern: a cumulative property such that schools with more difficult components of parent involvement have the easier ones in place. For example, a strong school program in communications from school to home (type 2) is least predictive of the other types (range of $r = .303$ to .449; range of $r^2 = 9\%$ to 20%). Because most schools communicate with families through notices, phone calls, conferences, and similar means, the power of this type of involvement to predict other types is relatively low. Knowing a school had a strong program of communication would not help much in predicting whether other types of parent involvement were also in place. By contrast, a strong school program in learning activities at home (type 4)—perhaps the most difficult type of parent involvement—is more predictive of the other types (range of $r = .449$ to .569; range of $r^2 = 20\%$ to 32%). That is, if schools are conducting programs to involve parents in learning activities at home, we could predict with up to 32 percent accuracy that one or more of the other types of involvement also were in place. The other three types of involvement—in

TABLE 3.3   Intercorrelations of Measures of Five Types of Parent Involvement*

Type of Involvement	1	2	3	4	5
1. Parenting skills, child development, and home environment for learning		.378	.482	.569	.467
2. Communications from school to home			.341	.449	.303
3. Volunteers at school				.561	.519
4. Involvement in learning activities at home					.567
5. Decision making, leadership, and governance					

* All correlations are significant beyond the .001 level. N = 171.

workshops, volunteers, and decision making—are less distinct in their intercorrelations and their predictive powers. It appears that they are usually added to school programs *after* communications practices and *before* involvement in learning activities at home.

The values show that there is considerable flexibility and unpredictability in which types of involvement are strongly implemented in schools. We found in this project, for example, that, with guidance and with small grants to enable teachers to obtain and use data from teachers and parents, schools proceed in different ways to build or strengthen parent involvement programs. For example, if schools learn that parents want this information, they initiate type 4 activities to involve parents in their children's learning at home earlier than is typical in the sequence. The data help us see typical patterns, but the actions taken by individual schools help us understand that these patterns are not fixed. Schools can take different directions in program development if they learn about the needs and interests of their families, students, and teachers.

Other cluster analyses not reported here indicate clear connections between specific school programs and teachers' practices of the same type. For example, teachers' own communication practices correlate significantly with the strength of the school communication program $(r = .154)$ but not with the strength of the school volunteer program $(r = .058)$. Teachers' own volunteer practices correlate significantly with the strength of the school volunteer program $(r = .390)$ but not as strongly with the school communication program $(r = .155)$. Teachers place more importance on their own practices in the type or types of involvement that are strong in their school as a whole.

Correlates of Strong School Programs to Involve Parents

Table 3.4 reports the zero-order correlations of the strength of the five types of parent involvement with school level: elementary versus middle schools. Teachers in elementary schools report significantly stronger programs of parent involvement than teachers in middle schools on four of the five types of involvement $(r =$

TABLE 3.4   Zero-Order Correlations of Five Types of Parent Involvement with School Level*

How Strong Is This Type of Involvement in Your School or in Teacher's Own Practice?	School Level, Elementary (0) vs. Middle (1)
1. Workshops (school)	–.403
2. Communications:	
School	–.121
Teacher	–.232
3. Volunteers (school)	–.484
4. Learning activities at home:	
School	–.343
Teacher	–.212
5. Decision making, leadership (school)	–.273

* Correlations of .14 are significant at the .05 level; .19 at the .01 level. N = 171.

–.212 to r = –.484): parenting and child development, volunteers, learning activities at home, and decision making. The exception is that elementary and middle school teachers do not report much difference in their schools' programs to communicate with parents (r = –.121, not significant). Specific communications practices, however (including informal notes, telephone calls, the actual number of children's families involved in parent-teacher conferences), are used significantly more often by elementary grade teachers than by their middle-grade counterparts (r = –.232).

Other analyses not reported here show similar, slightly weaker correlations of the types of involvement in Table 3.4 with classroom organization (Epstein and Dauber, 1989). Teachers in self-contained classrooms use significantly more parent involvement than teachers in departmentalized classes (r = –.155 to r = –.321 for the different types). School level is, however, the stronger correlate. More elementary classes are self-contained, and more middle grade classes are departmentalized (r = .631), with some overlap in semi-departmentalized arrangements. Elementary teachers in self-contained or semi-departmentalized classrooms are more likely than middle school teachers to have some school programs and some individual practices that include parents in their children's education. Still other analyses show that *within* elementary schools, the lower the grade level, the more likely the teacher is to use parent involvement, especially volunteers in the classroom. With considerably different measures, Stevenson and Baker (1987) show that parents of younger children (compared to older students through adolescence) are reported by teachers to be more involved in meetings and conferences at their children's schools.

There were no significant correlations of the types of involvement and the percentage of students below average in ability in the teachers' classrooms. All of the schools in this sample have high proportions of low-ability students: Approximately 70 percent of the teachers report that more than half of their students are below average in ability. Teachers with fewer years of experience in these schools have slightly more communications with their students' parents (r = −.178) and are in schools that use more volunteers (r = −.169). Years of teaching experience do not correlate significantly with teachers' reports of the strength of their schools' programs to involve parents in workshops, home-learning activities, or decision-making opportunities.

Effects of School Level, Student and Teacher Characteristics, and Teacher Practices on Parent Involvement Programs

Table 3.5 extends the previous discussion by showing the results of multiple regression analyses that identify the influence of four variables on the strength of three types of school programs of parent involvement. The four variables are *school level* (coded as elementary = 0 or middle = 1), years of *teaching experience*, percentage of students *below average* in ability, and the importance to the teachers of *specific practices* for their own grade levels and students. Data on teachers' practices were available for three types of parent involvement: communications from school to home, volunteers at school, and learning activities at home. Standardized regression coefficients report the independent effects of each variable, after statistically controlling the other variables in each equation.

The first column of Table 3.5 shows that strong programs of communications from school to home are not strongly influenced by school level, years of teaching experience, or percentage of students below average in ability. The strength or weakness of school programs of communications with families is explained mainly by the teachers' attitudes and practices of communicating with their own students' families (standardized regression coefficient $B = .232$).

The second column shows that, with other variables statistically taken into account, strong programs of volunteers at school are explained by school level— more volunteers are used in the elementary grades $(B = −.360)$; years of teaching experience—newer teachers are more likely to report that their schools have strong volunteer programs $(B = −.176)$; and individual teachers' practices concerning volunteers—teachers who use volunteers themselves say that their school volunteer program is strong $(B = .237)$.

The third column shows that strong school programs to involve parents in children's learning activities at home are most influenced by school level—elementary schools are more likely than middle schools to have strong programs of this type of involvement $(B = −.310)$. Regardless of level, however, reports of strong school programs to involve parents in learning activities at home are also explained by teachers' own emphases on practices that help their students' parents know how to help their children with schoolwork at home (B = .163).

The four variables explain little of the variance in the strength of communication programs ($r^2 = 07$), a moderate amount of the variance in the strength of programs for increasing involvement in learning activities at home ($r^2 = .16$), and a considerable amount of the variance in the strength of programs to involve volunteers ($r^2 = 30$).

TABLE 3.5   Summary of the Strengths of Three Types of Parent Involvement

Characteristics and Practices	How Strong Is This Type of Involvement at Your School?[a] (Standardized Regression Coefficients)		
	Communications from School to Home[b]	Volunteers at School	Learning Activities at Home
School level (elementary/middle)	−.104	−.360***	−.310***
Years of teaching experience	.003	−.176*	.016
Percentage of students below average ability	−.056	−.022	−.124
Importance to teacher of this type of practice[c]	.232**	.237**	.163*
R2	.07	.30	.16

N = 171.

a Responses range from 1 = not important, 2 = need to develop, 3 = need to strengthen, to 4 = already strong.

b *Strength of school program of communications* includes three items, *volunteers* includes two items, and *learning activities* at home includes two items.

c Teachers reported how important school and family connections were at their own grade level: *communication practices* includes five items on conducting formal conferences with all parents at least once a year, attending evening meetings, and contacts about students' report cards and progress; *use of volunteers* by the teacher includes the frequency of volunteers in teachers' classrooms in an average week; *learning activities at home* includes nine items on giving information on required skills, providing parents with ideas on how to talk with and help students on schoolwork; listen to students read and practice reading, spelling, writing, and social studies skills; and discuss television shows.

* $p < .05/.06$.

** $p < .01$.

*** $< .001$.

We know, of course, that level of schooling and associated features affect programs and practices of family involvement because the influence process cannot go the other way. However, because these data are cross-sectional—taken at one point in time—the direction of influence of school programs and teacher practices cannot be determined. It may be that the importance teachers place on specific practices of parent involvement at their own grade levels influences their perceptions of the strength of the programs at their schools. That is, the teachers' personal attitudes and practices color their reports of the school as a whole. Or the strength of particular school programs in communication, use of volunteers, or learning activities at home may influence teachers to involve students' parents in these ways. That is, the schools' programs affect the practices individual teachers use.

There is evidence from other schools that, when some teachers succeed with new activities (such as the use of volunteers), other teachers are influenced to use the same practices, thereby strengthening the school program overall (as discussed by Delia Vargas, June 1990 progress report for Schools Reaching Out project on P.S. 111 in New York). Indeed, among the schools in this study, all of these influence processes have been observed, suggesting that over time school programs and teacher practices change and improve in concert. Longitudinal data would help document and define this continuous process in which school programs and teachers' individual practices influence each other.

Parent Involvement Practices of Teachers of Different Subjects

Teachers were asked to check all of the subjects that they taught in an average week. Analyses of these data show that teachers of the major academic subjects—English/language arts, reading, math, science, and social studies—tend to stress different parent involvement practices (Epstein and Dauber, 1989). Teachers of reading (compared to teachers who did not teach reading) place more importance on involving parents in listening to their children read aloud $(r = .141)$ and on involving parents as volunteers in their classrooms $(r = .138)$.

Teachers of English/language arts (compared to teachers who did not teach the subject) emphasize the importance of helping parents become involved in several types of learning activities at home, including listening to the child read $(r = .160)$, discussing television shows $(r = .164)$, practicing skills for spelling and other tests $(r = .133)$, listening to the child's writing assignments $(r = .168)$, and assigning homework that requires parent-child interaction and discussion $(r = .143)$. These teachers also stress the importance of conferences with all parents $(r = .164)$. The specific practices of the reading and English teachers encourage parent involvement in language and reading skills and help promote students' success in these subjects. Teachers of reading and English also report stronger and more positive involvement of parents who are typically "hard to reach," including less-educated parents, single parents, young parents, and other adults (not parents) with whom some children live. In effect, they are more likely than other teachers to use practices to involve children and all families in subject-specific activities as part of their regular teaching practice.

Teachers of math, science, or social studies (compared to teachers who did not teach these subjects) do not place great importance on these parent involvement practices. Compared to other teachers, math teachers are significantly less supportive of attending evening meetings or activities $(r = -.135)$; science teachers are significantly less supportive of informing parents of the skills required to pass their subject at each grade level $(r = -.117)$; and social studies teachers are significantly less supportive of participating in student-parent-teacher clubs and activities $(r = -.148)$.

Earlier research found that elementary school teachers who frequently involve parents in learning activities at home are most likely to request involvement in reading or reading-related activities (Becker and Epstein, 1982) and that these practices have some positive influence on students' growth in reading scores (Epstein, 1991). In the present data from elementary and middle grade teachers, we see some subject-specific connections between the academic subjects taught and the teachers' use or lack of use of particular practices. Teachers of math, science, and social studies may need even more assistance than other teachers in preservice and inservice education to understand how to involve parents in their children's learning activities in those subjects.

School Climate for Parent Involvement and Program Strength

Teachers were asked about their own and others' support for parent involvement to indicate the climate at their school for supporting school and family connections. They rated their own level of support (i.e., on a four-point scale of none, weak, some, or strong) and estimated the level of support for parent involvement of their principal, other administrators, their teacher colleagues, the parents of students in the school, and others in the community. "Discrepancy scores" were derived to represent the differences between the teachers' own support and their perceptions of the support of other individuals or groups around them. We hypothesized that greater discrepancies between teachers and others in the school would be linked to weaker programs of parent involvement.

Overall, the teachers report that they are similar to their principals in their strong support for parent involvement. However, they believe that they, as individuals, are stronger supporters of parent involvement than their teacher-colleagues and much stronger supporters than the parents or others in the community.

Table 3.6 shows that greater discrepancies between teachers' beliefs about their own and parents' support for involvement occur in schools that have more students below average in ability and more departmentalized programs. Teachers in these schools believe that they are more supportive of involvement than are the parents. When teachers differ culturally and educationally from their students (as in schools with many below-average students), or when they teach greater numbers of students (as in departmentalized programs), they are less likely to know the students' parents and, therefore, more likely to believe that parents are uninterested or uninvolved.

The next section of the table shows that greater discrepancies between teachers and parents are linked to weaker programs of the five major types of parent involvement, with the exception of communications. As noted earlier, just about all schools conduct some communications with families, regardless of teachers' personal attitudes or beliefs. If the teachers believe parents are less supportive of parent involvement than they are, however, the teachers report that their schools have fewer workshops $(r = -.152)$, fewer volunteers $(r = -.140)$, fewer methods to involve parents in learning activities at home $(r = -.230)$, and fewer opportunities for decision making $(r = -.132)$.

The bottom of the table shows that greater discrepancies between teachers' reports about themselves and parents are linked to less successful connections with several groups of hard-to-reach parents. If teachers believe that parents are not interested in becoming involved in their children's schooling, teachers make fewer efforts to contact, inform, and work with them, especially with those parents who

TABLE 3.6   Discrepancy Scores: Correlates of Teachers' Reports of Differences between Their Own and Parents' Support for Parent Involvement*

	Correlation Coefficient[a]
Classroom conditions:	
Percentage of students below average	+.142[b]
Number of different students	+.172
Self-contained vs. departmentalized	+.180
Strength of school program:	
Parenting skills, home conditions	−.152
Communications from school to home	N.S.[c]
Volunteers at school	−.140
Learning activities at home	−.230
Participation in decision making	−.132
Involvement of hard-to-reach parents:	
Working parents	−.175
Less-educated parents	−.209
Single parents	N.S.
Parents of older students	−.222
Parents new to the school	−.192[b]
Other adults with whom children live	−.200[b]

* Correlations of .14 are significant at the .05 level; .19 at the .01 level; N.S. = not significant. N = 171.

a A (+) correlation suggests that a positive discrepancy score (i.e., teachers' views of own support for parent involvement are higher than their views of parents' support) is associated with a higher level of the measured variable; a (−) correlation suggests a positive discrepancy is associated with a lower level of the measured variable.

b Indicates significance when discrepancy is high between self and principal.

c Indicates significance when discrepancy is high between self and colleagues.

are hard to reach and especially on more difficult types of involvement such as involving parents in learning activities at home.

Other analyses indicate that discrepancies with principals and colleagues also reduce practices of parent involvement, as noted in the table. For example, greater discrepancy between self (teacher) and principals occurs in schools with more disadvantaged students. Also, teachers who think that they and their principal differ in supporting parent involvement make fewer contacts with hard-to-reach parents. Greater discrepancy between self and colleagues is linked to weaker school programs and fewer individual practices of traditional communication with families.

Highly discrepant environments (where teachers believe that they differ in attitudes from others at the school) are less likely to support strong, comprehensive programs of parent involvement. Less discrepant environments (where teachers see themselves as more similar to their own school administrators, colleagues, and parents) are more likely to support strong school programs and encourage strong teacher attitudes and practices.

DISCUSSION

This survey of teachers in inner-city elementary and middle schools offers new information about the strengths and weaknesses of programs and practices of parent involvement. We draw the following conclusions from the data.

School Level

Elementary school programs of parent involvement are stronger, more positive, and more comprehensive than those in the middle grades. This is especially evident for workshops for parents on parenting skills, child development, and school programs; volunteers at school; learning activities at home; and involvement in school decisions. One partial exception concerns school programs of communication. Although teachers in elementary and middle schools report their schools have about equally strong communication programs or policies, middle grade teachers use fewer specific communication practices and communicate less often than elementary teachers with fewer individual families. Parents of middle grade students receive less information or guidance at the very time they need more information and more guidance on how to be involved in larger and more complex schools and on new and more complex class schedules and subjects (Useem, 1990). This pattern is changing and will change more as middle grade schools and teachers increase their understanding of school and family connections in early adolescence and begin to develop stronger and more comprehensive programs.

Classroom Organization

Programs of parent involvement are stronger in self-contained classrooms. The organization of classrooms (e.g., self-contained, semi-departmentalized or teamed, and departmentalized programs) determines the number of students that are the teachers' responsibility and affects the frequency of and reasons for teacher contacts with students' parents. Teachers in self-contained classes (mainly in elementary schools) have fewer students to teach and are more apt to make frequent and diverse contacts with parents. They may feel more familiar with a small number of parents or more fully responsible for the students' school programs, including home-learning activities.

Students with many teachers for different subjects could benefit greatly if their parents knew how to monitor and discuss schoolwork and school decisions with their children. To adjust for the difficulties of working with large numbers of students and families, teachers in middle schools and some elementary schools will need extra information, staff development, and guidance in efficient and effective practices that can be used to involve parents of students in departmentalized or semi-departmentalized programs.

Academic Subjects

Teachers of certain academic subjects—particularly English and reading—use more practices than teachers of other subjects to involve parents in their children's education. Many of the same techniques used by English and reading teachers could be used by teachers of any subject (e.g., teachers can ask parents to listen to a child read something the child wrote or practice skills before quizzes or tests). Teachers of any subject can design and assign homework in a way that requires students to interact with a parent about something interesting that they are learning in school.

Support for Parent Involvement

Discrepancy scores show that greater differences between self (teacher) and principal, self and teacher-colleagues, and, particularly, self and parents are associated with weaker parent involvement programs and practices and less involvement with families who are typically hard to reach. Conversely, greater similarities between self and others are reported by teachers in schools with stronger parent involvement programs and practices. Teachers who believe that they share similar beliefs with parents about involvement make more contacts with parents whom other teachers find hard to reach, conduct more types of activities to involve families, and are less affected by disadvantaged characteristics of the student population and by different classroom organizations. The analyses of discrepancy scores suggest that it is important to build common understanding about shared goals and common support among teachers, parents, and principals so that teachers' feelings of isolation or separateness from others will decrease and school and family partnerships will increase.

Five Types of Involvement

The five major types of parent involvement are related but separable. In these schools, type 2 activities (communications from the school to the home) are more prevalent and, therefore, less predictive of other types of parent involvement programs or practices. In contrast, type 4 activities (involvement in learning activities at home) are difficult for many teachers to organize and so are implemented in fewer places and by fewer teachers, usually after other, more standard practices are in place. Information from parents at the schools in this study showed that parents wanted more information on how to help their own children (Dauber and Epstein, 1989). Some schools used that information to develop type 4 activities even before strengthening other types of involvement. The results support earlier studies that suggest that schools can invest in different types of involvement to address various needs and to attain different benefits.

Families in Inner-City Schools

Educators and researchers often view minority families and families of educationally disadvantaged students in terms of their deficiencies. Often, however, the deficiencies lie in the schools' programs. In this sample of eight inner-city, Title I elementary and middle schools, some schools and, within schools, some teachers have figured out how to mobilize the support of educationally and economically disadvantaged families. In the three-year action research program, all of the inner-city schools discovered that, regardless of where they started from, they could systematically improve their practices to involve the families they serve.

Linking School Programs and Teacher Practices

The study demonstrates important linkages between school programs and teachers' individual practices to involve parents. Although the direction and process of causality remain to be determined in longitudinal studies, this study provides evidence that strong school programs in particular types of involvement go hand in hand with the importance teachers place on the same types of involvement.

Other variables may also influence school programs and teacher practices. In a study of elementary schools, Hoover-Dempsey, Bassler, and Brissie (1987) found that *teacher efficacy* (feelings that one is an effective and capable teacher) is related to the strength of school programs of parent involvement, including conferences with more parents, more volunteers, and more interactive homework activities. Although their measure of teacher efficacy raises some questions because it includes estimates of students' ability to learn, the conclusion that schools with more confident teachers use more involvement strategies is provocative. The authors also found that schools with more confident teachers, on average, report more support from parents.

Another study of parent involvement in elementary schools found that parents and principals rated teachers higher in overall teaching ability and interpersonal skills if the teachers frequently used practices of parent involvement (Epstein, 1985 [Reading 4.3], 1986). Teachers' confidence may be boosted by high ratings and appreciation from parents and administrators that result from the use of more involvement practices and encourage continued and expanded use of these practices.

Studies are needed that press these questions further to increase an understanding of the links between school programs and individual teachers' practices across the grades, in different subjects, and in a variety of school communities. This study is based on a small sample of schools and teachers selected because of their initially low and infrequent family and school connections. Despite the somewhat restricted conditions in these schools, the analyses yield robust and credible results about the connections of parent involvement with the level of school, subjects, types of involvement, and climate of support. Other studies of these patterns in more varied sets of schools will help clarify the reported results.

IMPLICATIONS FOR IMPROVING
SCHOOL AND FAMILY CONNECTIONS

The schools in this study were participants in the Baltimore School and Family Connections Project—a long-term process to improve school and family connections to improve students' success in school. The process is one that may be followed or adapted by any school that is not satisfied with its present types or strengths of parent involvement. In this case, educators work with researchers and a community foundation that makes small grants to teachers to develop more responsive programs and practices of parent involvement. Small grants can come from other sources, however, such as district and school funds for school improvement and various federal, state, and local programs. Small grants that support and recognize teachers' practices of parent involvement also have been successful in other projects (Davies, 1990; Krasnow, 1990). We have learned of several steps that may maximize success.

1. **Assess present strengths and weaknesses.** Each school needs to identify its own "starting point" on practices of parent involvement to move ahead with more comprehensive and improved programs.

2. **Identify hopes, dreams, and goals.** How would parents, teachers, students, and administrators like the school to involve parents three to five years from the starting point? Rather than looking back at errors or failures in their practices and relationships, we ask the partners in education to look ahead to their goals for the future. What new goals for parents and administrator practice could be attained?

3. **Identify who will have responsibilities for reaching the goals.** Over a three-year period, progress can be made in clear steps, but some individual, team, group, or committee must be put in charge and supported in its responsibilities to conduct and supervise specific activities, revise practices, evaluate progress each year, and expand programs. Comer's (1988) process of school site management to include parents emphasizes formal committee structures; our work acknowledges and develops committees and other flexible arrangements such as large and small teams and groups to design and improve practices. In either case, responsibilities must be clear and efforts must be supported.

4. **Evaluate implementations and results.** It is important for teachers, administrators, parents, and students who invest time and energy in a new process and activities to know how well the program is implemented (e.g., are they reaching those they want to reach?). If programs are successfully implemented, one must evaluate whether and how well they promote student success or other goals. Based on each year's evaluations and reviews, programs may be revised, maintained, or extended to move toward ever more effective connections with more families.

5. **Continue to support program development activities.** Parent involvement is a process that requires teachers, administrators, parents, students, and others in the school community to plan, implement, and reflect on their efforts and goals. This takes time. We found that three years of small grants to teachers provides a minimum period in which to make a good start to improve some practices, par-

ticularly if principals exert their leadership to reinforce the concept of partnership with families and to recognize and extend specific activities. As with any aspect of school effectiveness, however, school and family connections are ongoing investments that require continuous attention and support.

WHAT QUESTIONS MUST BE ASKED?

The schools in this sample started with surveys of teachers and parents that the teachers helped design. These questionnaires are available for others' use or adaptation. There are, however, other ways in which schools can assess where they are starting from. These include gathering information from panels of teachers, parents, and students at PTA meetings, grade-level meetings, or other special convocations. Or, principals may conduct focus groups or breakfast meetings with specially invited teachers and parents to outline goals and plans for parent involvement. Questions for panels, focus groups, or discussion groups about their own schools include:

1. Which practices of each of the five types of parent involvement are presently strong at each grade level? Which are weak? What practices are particularly important at each grade level? Which practices should change from grade to grade, and which should be continued?
2. Are our parent involvement practices coherent and coordinated, or are different groups fragmented and following their own agendas? How are all families, Title I families, limited English-proficient families, special education families, and other families who seem hard to reach provided with information and included in their children's schools and education at home?
3. Which families are we reaching and which are we not yet reaching? Why are we having problems reaching some families, and what can we do to help solve problems of communication and relationships?
4. What do we expect of each other? What do teachers expect of families? What do families expect of teachers and others in the school? What do students expect their families to be able to do to help them in appropriate ways at each grade level?
5. How do we want this school to look three years from now in its practices of the five types of parent involvement? How would we like parent involvement to work here? What would teachers do? What would parents do? What would administrators do? What would students do? What are specific goals that we want to reach at the end of one year, two years, and three years?
6. How are our students succeeding on important measures of achievement, attitudes, and other indicators of success? How could parent involvement help more students reach higher standards and higher levels

of success? Which types of involvement will help students boost their achievements, accomplishments, attitudes, and behaviors?

7. What steps can we take to reach the three-year goals? Who will be responsible for developing, implementing, and evaluating each type of involvement?

8. What costs are associated with the desired improvements? Will staff development, district resources, and/or school leadership and resources be needed? Will small grants or other special funds be needed to implement the programs? How will teachers, parents, and others who design and conduct activities be supported, rewarded, and recognized?

9. How will we evaluate the implementation and results of our efforts to improve practices? What results do we think will actually be attained in one year, two years, and three years, and what indicators, measures, and observations will we use to learn how we are progressing?

10. Other questions about starting points, plans, goals, responsibilities, implementations, and evaluations.

Whether questionnaires, telephone surveys, focus groups, or other group discussions are used, each school must gather information to create a profile of present practices and a coherent plan of action to improve practices in the future.

SUMMARY

Although teachers individually express strong positive attitudes toward parent involvement, most school programs and classroom practices do not support teachers' beliefs in the importance of school and family partnerships. In this survey most teachers wanted all parents to fulfill 12 parent involvement responsibilities, ranging from teaching their children to behave, to knowing what their children are expected to learn each year, to helping them on those skills. Most schools and teachers have not yet implemented practices to help families fulfill these responsibilities at each grade level. Most teachers believe they are stronger supporters of parent involvement than are the other teachers in the school. This is, of course, logically inconsistent and indicates that the teachers do not know their colleagues' attitudes. Teachers say that parents and others in the community are not strong supporters of parent involvement, but surveys of parents in the same schools contradict the teachers' beliefs about parents (Dauber and Epstein, 1989). Thus, educators may create false or exaggerated discrepancies between themselves and others about parent involvement.

As schools in this study found when they assessed the attitudes and aims of their teachers and parents, more similarities exist than many realize. There is, then, an important (though often hidden) base of shared goals, interests, and investments in children's success on which to build more effective programs of school and family connections.

REFERENCES

Baker, D. P., and D. L. Stevenson (1986). Mothers' strategies for children's school achievement: Managing the transition to high school. *Sociology of Education* 59: 156–166.

Bauch, P. A. (1988). Is parent involvement different in private schools? *Educational Horizons* 66: 78–82.

Becker, H. J., and J. L. Epstein. (1982). Parent involvement: A study of teacher practices. *Elementary School Journal* 83: 85–102. (Reading 3.1).

Brandt, R. (1989). On parents and schools: A conversation with Joyce Epstein. *Educational Leadership* 47: 24–27.

California State Board of Education. (1988). *Parent involvement initiative: A policy and plan for action.* Sacramento: California State Board of Education.

Clark, R. (1983). *Family life and school achievement: Why poor black children succeed and fail.* Chicago: University of Chicago Press.

Comer, J. (1988). Educating poor minority children. *Scientific American* 259(5): 42–48.

Dauber, S. L., and J. L. Epstein. (1989). *Parents' attitudes and practices of involvement in inner-city elementary and middle schools.* CREMS Report 33. Baltimore: Johns Hopkins University, Center for Research on Elementary and Middle Schools. (Reading 3.6).

Davies, D. (1990). Shall we wait for the revolution? A few lessons from the Schools Reaching Out project. *Equity and Choice* 6(3): 68–73.

Dornbusch, S. M., and P. L. Ritter. (1988). Parents of high school students: A neglected resource. *Educational Horizons* 66: 75–77.

Dornbusch, S. M., P. L. Ritter, P. Liederman, D. Roberts, and M. Fraleigh. (1987). The relation of parenting style to adolescent school performance. *Child Development* 58: 1244–1257.

Epstein, J. L. (1985). A question of merit: Principals' and parents' evaluations of teachers. *Educational Researcher* 14(7): 3–10. (Reading 4.3).

_____. (1986). Parents' reactions to teacher practices of parent involvement. *Elementary School Journal* 86: 277–294. (Reading 3.4).

_____. (1987a). Toward a theory of family-school connections: Teacher practices and parent involvement across the school years. Pages 121–136 in *Social intervention: Potential and constraints,* edited by K. Hurrelmann, F. Kaufmann, and F. Losel. New York: de Gruyter. (Reading 2.1).

_____. (1987b). What principals should know about parent involvement. *Principal* 66(3): 6–9.

_____. (1988). *Sample clinical summaries: Using surveys of teachers and parents to plan projects to improve parent involvement.* Baltimore: Johns Hopkins University, Center for Research on Elementary and Middle Schools.

_____. (1990). Single parents and the schools: The effects of marital status on parent and teacher evaluations. Pages 91–121 in *Change in societal institutions,* edited by M. T. Hallinan, D. M. Klein, and J. Glass. New York: Plenum. (Reading 3.5).

_____. (1991). Effects on student achievement of teachers' practices of parent involvement. Pages 261–276 in *Advances in reading/language research, Vol. 5: Literacy through family, community, and school interaction,* edited by S. Silvern. Greenwich, CT: JAI Press. (Reading 3.7).

Epstein, J. L., and S. L. Dauber. (1989). *Teacher attitudes and practices of parent involvement in inner-city elementary and middle schools.* CREMS Report No. 32. Baltimore: Johns Hopkins University, Center for Research on Elementary and Middle Schools.

Epstein, J. L., and K. Salinas. (1988). *Evaluation report forms: Summaries of school-level data from surveys of teachers and surveys of parents.* Baltimore: Johns Hopkins University, Center for Research on Elementary and Middle Schools.

Epstein, J. L., and D. Scott-Jones. (1988). School-family-community connections for accelerating education for students at risk. *Proceedings from the Stanford University Invitational Centennial Conference* (Stanford, CA).

Hoover-Dempsey, K. V., O. C. Bassler, and J. S. Brissie. (1987). Parent involvement: Contributions of teacher efficacy, school socioeconomic status, and other school characteristics. *American Educational Research Journal* 24: 417–435.

Krasnow, J. (1990). Building new parent-teacher partnerships: Teacher-researcher teams stimulate reflection. *Equity and Choice* 6: 25–31.

Lareau, A. (1987). Social class differences in family-school relationships: The importance of cultural capital. *Sociology of Education* 60: 73–85.

———. (1989). *Home advantage*. Philadelphia: Falmer Press.

Leitch, M. L., and S. S. Tangri. (1988). Barriers to home-school collaboration. *Educational Horizons* 66: 70–74.

Scott-Jones, D. (1987). Mother-as-teacher in the families of high- and low-achieving low-income black first graders. *Journal of Negro Education* 56: 21–34.

Stevenson, D. L., and D. P. Baker. (1987). The family-school relations and the child's school performance. *Child Development* 58: 1348–1357.

Useem, E. (1990). Social class and ability group placement in mathematics in the transition to seventh grade: The role of parent involvement. Paper presented at the annual meeting of the American Educational Research Association, April, in Boston.

Parents' Reactions to Teacher Practices of Parent Involvement*

Teachers have strong opinions about parent involvement. Some believe that they can be effective only if they obtain parental assistance on learning activities at home. Others believe that their professional status is in jeopardy if parents are involved in activities that are typically the teachers' responsibilities. The different philosophies and beliefs of teachers reflect the two main, opposing theories of school and family relations.

One perspective emphasizes the inherent incompatibility, competition, and conflict between families and schools and supports the separation of the two institutions (Parsons, 1959; Waller, 1932; Weber, 1947). It assumes that school bureaucracies and family organizations are directed, respectively, by educators and parents, who can best fulfill their different goals, roles, and responsibilities independently. Thus, these distinct goals are achieved most efficiently and effectively when teachers maintain their professional, general standards and judgments about the children in their classrooms and when parents maintain their personal, particularistic standards and judgments about their children at home.

The opposing perspective emphasizes the coordination, cooperation, and complementarity of schools and families and encourages communication and collaboration between the two institutions. It assumes that schools and families share responsibilities for the socialization and education of the child. Teachers and parents are believed to share common goals for children that are achieved most effectively when teachers and parents work together. These assumptions are based on models of inter-institutional interactions and ecological designs that emphasize the natural, nested, necessary connections among individuals, groups, and organizations (Bronfenbrenner, 1979; Leichter, 1974; Litwak and Meyer, 1974).

Although teachers may combine these perspectives, they tend to emphasize the precepts of one theory or the other in organizing their teaching practice. In an earlier survey of teachers, we found that in some classrooms inter-institutional cooperation was low. These teachers made few overtures to parents, rarely requesting their help on learning activities at home. In other classrooms cooperation was high. These teachers made frequent requests for parental assistance in reinforcing or improving students' skills (Becker and Epstein, 1982 [Reading 3.1]; Epstein and Becker, 1982 [Reading 3.2]).

* By Joyce L. Epstein. Many thanks go to the teachers, principals, and families who participated in this survey. I am indebted to my colleague Henry Jay Becker, who shared responsibility for the design and data collection of the study and offered suggestions on earlier drafts of this reading. Thanks, too, go to John H. Hollifield and two anonymous reviewers for helpful suggestions. This research was supported by a grant from the National Institute of Education. The results and opinions of the author do not necessarily reflect the position or policy of the NIE, and no endorsement by the NIE should be inferred. Reprinted with permission from *Elementary School Journal* 86 (1986): 277–294.

Teachers' reports tell only one part of the story. Parents' reports are needed to verify and clarify their experiences with teachers' different practices of parent involvement. Among the most frequently mentioned expected benefits of parent involvement are the increased or sustained interest and support of parents in the school programs and in their child's progress (Gordon, 1979; Keesling and Melaragno, 1983; Mager, 1980; Morrison, 1978; Rich and Jones, 1977; Robinson, 1979; Sowers, Lang, and Gowett, 1980). Little research has been done, however, to link specific teachers' practices with the parents who experience them or to measure differences in attitudes and reactions of parents whose children are in classrooms of teachers with different philosophies and practices of parent involvement. The data collected for this study connect the teachers with the parents of their students. I examine parents' awareness of teachers' efforts, knowledge about the school program, and evaluations of teachers. The results should provide an understanding of parents' perspectives on teachers' practices that emphasize the cooperation or separation of schools and families.

METHOD

Parents of 1,269 students in 82 first-, third-, and fifth-grade classrooms in Maryland completed and returned by mail questionnaires on the parent involvement practices of their children's teachers, a response rate of 59 percent. The questionnaire, administered in the spring of 1981, contained items assessing parents' attitudes toward the schools and teachers, their experiences with different kinds of involvement and communications with the schools, and their reactions to the teachers' programs and practices. The teachers of these parents' children included 36 "case" teachers who were identified in an earlier survey as strong supporters and users of parent involvement in learning activities at home and 46 "control" teachers who, by their own report, did not emphasize parent involvement but who matched the "case" teachers in their teaching assignment by grade level, school district, years of teaching experience, estimated achievement level of the students in their classes, and average education of their students' parents. Among the "case" teachers, 17 were recognized by their principals as especially strong leaders in the use of parent involvement. In this report, "parent involvement" refers to the frequency of participation by parents in 12 types of learning activities that teachers request parents to conduct or monitor at home that support the child's instructional program at school. Overall, the 82 teachers ranged along a continuum from low to high use of parent involvement. This continuum is one measure of teachers' emphasis on the separation or cooperation of schools and families on learning activities.

Table 3.7 describes the characteristics of parents who returned questionnaires. Families were instructed that the parent most familiar with the child's school and teacher should complete the survey. Over 90 percent of the "most knowledgeable" parents were female. Other background and family characteristics showed a representative mix of the families served by Maryland's schools. Approximately one-fourth of the parents had some high school education but no diploma, almost

TABLE 3.7   Characteristics of Parents*

Characteristics	%
Grade level of children:	
K, 1, 2	45
3, 4	27
5, 6	28
Sex:	
Female	92
Male	8
Race	
White	62
Black	36
Other	2
Highest education completed:	
Some high school (or less)	25
High school diploma	28
Some college	20
Bachelor's degree	10
Some graduate school (or advanced degree)	17
Family structure:	
Two-parent home	76
One-parent home	24
Employment:	
Not working	39
Part-time work	18
Full-time work	43

* N = 1,269.

one-third had graduated from high school, about one-fifth had attended some college, and approximately one-fourth graduated from college or attended graduate school. About one-fourth of the sample comprised single parents. Two-fifths of the respondents did not work outside the home, one-fifth worked part-time, and two-fifths had full-time jobs outside the home. Approximately one-third of the respondents were black.

There were some differences between the parents who responded to the survey and those who did not. More parents whose children were above average in math and reading skills in school returned the survey than did parents of children doing average or below average work in these subjects. Regardless of how children fared academically, the response was greater from parents whose children were in the classrooms of teachers who were leaders in parent involvement. Mailing back the questionnaire may be an indicator of parental cooperation on important requests from the teacher (Becker, 1982).

The differences in return rates from parents had offsetting effects. Parents whose children were in classrooms of teachers who emphasized parent involvement tended to be more positive about school than other parents, but parents of high-achieving students tended to be more critical of school and teachers than other parents. The small differences in return rates from some parents did not seriously affect the usefulness of data from the sizable, diverse sample of parents.

Statistical methods were used to take into account the multiple characteristics of parents, teachers, and students to isolate effects on parents of teacher practices of parent involvement. The cross-sectional nature of these data prevents us from drawing conclusions about causal relationships between teacher practices and parents' reactions and evaluations. Regression techniques, however, yield information that permits informed guesses about potentially important, independent effects that should prompt new longitudinal studies.

In this article, I briefly examine parents' attitudes toward public elementary schools and their experiences with some common forms of parent involvement and then focus on parents' reactions to teacher practices of parent involvement in learning activities at home. I examine the responses of parents who have different educational backgrounds and whose children are in classrooms of teachers who differ in their leadership in the use of parent involvement practices.

RESULTS

Parents' Attitudes toward Public Elementary Schools and Teachers

Parents' attitudes toward the public elementary schools and teachers were remarkably positive. About 90 percent of the parents agreed that their elementary schools were well run. Almost as many felt comfortable at their child's school and believed that they and the teachers had the same goals for the child.

The parents' clearly positive attitudes seem to contradict recent national reports that have criticized the curricula, teachers, and standards in the public schools (National Commission on Excellence in Education, 1983; National Task Force on Education for Economic Growth, 1983). The reactions of parents in Maryland are more like the findings of a recent Gallup poll (1983), in which only 9 percent of respondents with children in public schools said that getting good teachers was a problem, only 9 percent cited parents' lack of interest, and only 1 percent reported problems with administrators. Although there are some problems in all schools, most parents were not concerned about the basic administration of the schools or with the quality of teachers. They found fewer problems with elementary than with secondary schools, and they were more positive about the public schools if they sent their children there (Gallup, 1982, 1983; Goodlad, 1983). Other studies also report generally positive attitudes of parents of public school children toward the curriculum (Klein, Tye, and Wright, 1979), parent involvement, and homework (Olmsted, Wetherby, Leler, and Rubin, 1982; Williams, 1983; Zill and Peterson, 1982).

Despite positive attitudes about schools and teachers in general, parents reported that teachers could do more to involve parents in learning activities at home. Approximately 58 percent of the parents rarely or never received requests from the teacher to become involved in learning activities at home. Fewer than 30 percent of the parents reported that teachers gave them many ideas on how to help their child in reading and math. They overwhelmingly agreed that teachers should involve parents in learning activities at home and that homework was useful for their children. More than 80 percent of the parents said they could spend more time helping their children at home if they were shown how to do specific learning activities.

Experiences with Parent Involvement

We look now at several types of parent involvement that the parents experienced. These include involvement in basic obligations at home, communication from the school to the home, assistance at the school, and assistance in learning activities at home.

Involvement in Basic Obligations. The most pervasive form of parent involvement is the parents' provision of school supplies needed by their children and general support and supervision at home. More than 97 percent of the parents in this Maryland survey said that their children had the supplies needed for school, and over 90 percent reported that their children had a regular place to do homework. These management chores are expected by the schools and are accepted as basic responsibilities by almost all parents.

Involvement in School-to-Home Communications. Communication from the school to the home is sometimes considered "parent involvement" but is usually "parent information." All schools send information home to the family about schedules, report card grades, special events, and emergency procedures. Most of these activities flow one way, from the school to the home, often with no encouragement for communication from parents. Some schools organize and require teacher-parent conferences with all parents; others hold conferences with some parents, only on request. A few schools support home visits by teachers or by aides who serve as liaisons between teachers and parents to inform parents about school procedures.

Despite the typical profusion of notices from school to home, some parents receive few communications from teachers. In the Maryland sample, approximately 16 percent of the parents said they received no memos from their child's teacher, more than 35 percent had no parent-teacher conference, and approximately 60 percent never spoke to the teacher on the phone, as shown in Table 3.8. It is not surprising that the more time required for an exchange, the less often that type of communication occurs, but it is revealing that large numbers of parents are excluded from many of the traditional forms of communication that link the school to the home.

Involvement at School. One prevalent form of involvement is parental assistance at the school: in the classroom as an aide to teachers; in other school locations such as the cafeteria, library, or playground; or at special events, such as

TABLE 3.8   Parents Who Never Received Personal Communication from Child's Teacher over One Year

Type of Communication	%
Memo from teacher	16.4
Talk to teacher before or after school	20.7
Conference with teacher	36.4
Handwritten note from teacher	36.5
Workshop at school	59.0
Called on phone by teacher	59.5
Visited at home by teacher	96.3

class parties, trips, or fund-raisers. Although some parents participate, most parents are not active at school:

- Approximately 70 percent *never* helped the teacher in the classroom or on class trips.
- Approximately 70 percent *never* participated in fund-raising activities for the school.
- Approximately 88 percent *never* assisted in the library, cafeteria, or other school areas.

Even those parents who did become active were involved infrequently. The average number of days at school per year was

- 4.1 days helping the teacher and class;
- 7.0 days helping with fund-raising activities; and
- 3.5 days helping in the school cafeteria, offices, or library.

Only about 4 percent of the respondents (51 parents distributed across 82 classrooms) were very active, spending over 25 days per year at the school. Many (42 percent) of the parents who were not active at school worked outside the home during school hours. Others had small children, family problems, or other activities that demanded their time. Others (about 12 percent) simply had not been asked to assist at school. Despite these facts, parent assistance at the school is the type of parent involvement that most teachers and administrators support (Ogbu, 1974).

Involvement with Learning Activities at Home.   A less frequently used form of parent involvement, but one that reflects the theory of cooperation between schools and families, is teacher practices that involve all or most parents in learning activities with their children at home. In this study, teachers ranged from low to high in their use of this type of parent involvement. Parents were asked about their experiences with 12 techniques that teachers use to involve parents in learning activities at home. These were grouped under five categories: (1) techniques that involve reading and books; (2) techniques that encourage discussions between parents and children; (3) techniques based on informal activities and games that use common materials at home; (4) techniques based on formal contracts and supervision among parents, teachers, and children; and (5) techniques that involve tutoring and teaching the child in skills and drills. In an earlier survey, teachers rated these techniques as their most satisfying and successful parent involvement practices (Becker and Epstein, 1982).

Most Frequent Requests to Parents by Teacher-Leaders.   Parents whose children's teachers were recognized by their principal as leaders in parent involvement reported significantly more frequent use of 9 of the 12 parent involvement practices, as shown in Table 3.9. These included reading aloud or listening to the child read, talking with the child about the events of the school day, giving spelling or math drills, giving help on worksheets or workbooks, signing the child's homework, taking the child to the library, playing learning games, using things at home to teach, and visiting the classroom to observe teaching techniques. Despite the frequent use of some activities by some teachers, from one-fourth to two-fifths of the parents never were asked to conduct the five most frequently used parent involvement activities. On the three least used practices—borrowing books, entering contracts, and using TV for learning—there were no significant differences in reports from parents of teachers who were leaders compared with other teachers.

TABLE 3.9   Parents Reporting Frequent Requests for Parent Involvement Techniques by Teacher-Leaders and Other Teachers (percent)

Activity	Parents Reporting Requests By:		χ^2 Test[a]
	Teacher-Leaders	Other Teachers	
1. Read aloud to child or listen to child read	68	51	***
2. Sign child's homework	66	52	***
3. Give spelling or math drills	61	54	*
4. Help with worksheet or work book lessons	57	47	**
5. Ask child about school day	49	42	*
6. Use things at home to teach child	44	34	**
7. Play games that help child learn	35	28	**
8. Visit classroom to watch how child is taught	34	25	**
9. Take child to library	26	17	**
10. Borrow books from teacher to give extra help	21	16	
11. Make a formal contract with teacher to supervise homework or projects	21	19	
12. Watch and discuss TV shows with child	15	15	

a χ^2 tests indicate whether parents report more frequent use of parent involvement activities by teacher-leaders than by other teachers, with frequency categorized as several times or often versus never, once, or twice.

* p < .05; **p < .01; ***p < .001

There were basic similarities between the teachers' reports in an earlier survey and the parents' accounts of their experiences with learning activities at home. The most popular techniques that teachers used (reading aloud, discussions, signing work) were the ones parents most frequently experienced. The least popular techniques for teachers (use of TV, use of formal contracts) were least frequently experienced by parents. Both teachers' and parents' responses suggested that, although infrequently used now, activities that the teacher designed to use the TV at home may be useful for structuring parent-child discussions and for building children's listening and speaking skills. The similarities in parent experiences and teacher practices lend credibility to the reports of both groups. Parents' experiences with teacher practices confirm that some parents are guided by teachers who follow the precepts of theories emphasizing the separation of school and family responsibilities, whereas others are directed toward cooperative efforts on behalf of the children.

Experiences of Parents with Different Educational Backgrounds.   Teacher-leaders whose practices supported cooperation between schools and families reported that they involved parents with many, average, or few years of formal schooling. Teachers who were not leaders in parent involvement, whose practices emphasized the separation of school and home, reported that parents with little education could not or would not help their children with learning activities at home (Becker and Epstein, 1982). We wanted to check the teachers' reports against the experiences of parents who had different educational backgrounds.

Parents' reports of their involvement in learning activities at home are shown in Table 3.10. The left half of the table presents the responses of parents with little schooling, average schooling, and advanced schooling. The right half groups the parents by the teachers' leadership in the use of parent involvement. On the left we see that, in general, parents with less education reported significantly more frequent requests from teachers than did parents with average or advanced education. The right panel shows that the differences in reports from parents with different levels of education were significant only for parents with children in classrooms of teachers who were not leaders in the use of parent involvement. In classrooms of teachers who were leaders, parents at all educational levels reported about equally frequent requests by teachers to conduct learning activities at home.

The same pattern was found in separate analyses of each type of parent involvement activity, including reading, discussions, contracts, informal games, worksheets, and signing homework. The differences in the reports from low- and high-educated parents were significant only in classrooms of teachers who were not leaders in using parent involvement practices.

The reports from parents clarify and extend the earlier information from teachers on their use of parent involvement with differently educated parents. According to parents, teachers who were leaders in the use of parent involvement practices established more equitable programs, involving parents regardless of their educational backgrounds. Teachers who were not leaders in parent involvement did not try to reach all parents. They may have seen little need to approach par-

TABLE 3.10   Parents Reporting Frequent Use by Teachers of 12 Parent Involvement Techniques, by Parents' Education and Teachers' Leadership

	% of Parents Reporting Zero, Some or Many Techniques Used Frequently		
	Zero	Some (1–4)	Many (5+)
Parent education[a]			
High	23	40	37
Average	15	39	46
Low	16	30	54
	$\chi^2 = 25.98$; $p < .34$ (N. S.)[b]		
Parent education/teacher leadership[a]			
High/leader	6	42	52
High/not leader	25	40	35
Average/leader	9	35	56
Average/not leader	17	40	43
Low/leader	18	26	56
Low/not leader	17	31	52
	χ^2 (teacher leader) = 4.55; $p < .34$ (N. S.)[b]		
	χ^2 (teacher not leader) = 18.45; $p < .001$[b]		

a Low education includes parents with some high school education (N = 240); average education includes parents with a high school diploma (N = 462); high education includes parents with at least some college education and beyond (N = 543).

b χ^2 tests were conducted to determine the independence or association of parents' education with reports of teacher requests for frequent parent involvement for all parents, parents with children in classrooms of teacher-leaders, and parents with children in classrooms of teachers who were not leaders. Parents' reports were independent of their education only in teacher-leaders' classrooms.

ents whose children were doing well in school or parents who helped their children at home without directions from the teacher. Children of parents with less education often do less well in school than other children, need more help at home, and have parents who do not know how to help without guidance from the teacher. Teachers may ask these parents to assist their children at home, even when the teachers believe that these parents will not be fully successful in their efforts (Valentine and Stark, 1979).

It could be that parents with less education agree more often with survey questions and that the patterns of parents' reports about the frequency of requests reflect response bias associated with educational level. This explanation would be plausible if we looked only at the general reports from parents by educational level. However, in the classrooms of teacher-leaders, parents of all educational levels reported about equal frequency of teachers' requests for involvement, an unbiased pattern of responses.

Effects of Involvement on Parents

Does it matter to parents whether teachers' practices emphasize separation or cooperation with families? There is little research on whether teachers' efforts have any measurable effects on the parents who are involved. It has been left up to the teacher to decide—often in the absence of information—whether to invest time in parent involvement practices.

Regression analyses were conducted to determine whether teacher leadership affected parents' reactions to teachers' efforts and parents' evaluations of teachers' merits. The analyses included other variables that have been found to influence teacher practices of parent involvement: three measures of the teaching situation: grade level, teacher quality as rated by the principal, and teacher education (highest degree); two measures of student characteristics: classroom performance in reading and math and racial composition of the class; and two characteristics of parents: educational level and extent of parent involvement at the school. Because better-educated, more active parents and parents of more capable students may pressure teachers to use more parent involvement, these variables are taken into account in the statistical analyses, and their effects on parent reactions are examined. Although these cross-sectional data do not show causality, this model is used to identify potentially important independent effects of teacher practices on parent reactions that can be reexamined in longitudinal studies.

Table 3.11 summarizes how teacher practices of parent involvement affected parents' awareness of teachers' policies, knowledge of the child's program, and evaluations of teachers' merits. We compare the effects on parents of three measures of teacher leadership: (1) teachers' reputations as leaders in parent involvement (from principals' ratings); (2) parents' consensus (at the classroom level) that the teacher is a frequent user of the 12 techniques of parent involvement; and (3) parents' consensus (at the classroom level) that the teacher frequently communicates with parents by note, phone, memo, conference, or conversation at school. On each of these measures, teacher practices fall along a continuum from low to high interaction and cooperation with families. Table 3.12 should be read in conjunction with Table 3.11 and contains corresponding statistics of the contribution of each of the three measures of teacher leadership to the explained variance of each measure of parent reactions.

Parents' Awareness of Teacher Practices

Three items measured parents' awareness of teachers' practices. Parents were asked whether the teacher worked hard at getting parents excited about helping their child at home, whether they received most ideas for home learning from the teacher, and whether the teacher made it clear that they should help their child with homework.

Efforts of Teachers. All three measures of teacher leadership had independent effects on parents' estimates of teachers' efforts, as shown in column 1 of Table

TABLE 3.11 Effects on Parents' Reactions and Evaluations of Three Measures of Teacher Leadership in Parent Involvement at Classroom Level (Standardized Regression Coefficients)*

Measure of Teacher Leadership	Parents' Reactions				Parents' Evaluations	
	Teacher Works Hard to Interest Parents	Teacher Gives Many Ideas to Parents	Parents Think They Should Help	Parents Know More about School Program	Positive Interpersonal Skills	Excellence of Teaching Skills
Reputation as a leader[a]	.243**	.268*	.081	.065	.251*	.274*
Parents' (classroom) reports of teacher's use of parent involvement	.695**	.787**	.603**	.406**	.712**	.728**
Parents' (classroom) reports of teacher's use of other communication	.356**	.216	.150	.231*	.373**	.581**
Other consistently significant variables	Grade, Race[b] Parent education	Grade[b], Parent education[b]	Grade, Race Parent education[b]	Grade, Race[b], Parent education		

*N = 82. Standardized regression coefficients are reported so that comparisons of effects across measures can be made. Effects model included these independent variables all at the classroom level: grade level, principal rating of teacher overall quality; teacher's highest degree (measures of the teaching situation); performance level of students, racial composition of students (measures of student population); parents' education composition, degree of parent activity at school (measures of parent factors).

a Reputation is the confirmation by principals of the teachers' leadership in the frequent use of parent involvement practices.

b Not a significant variable when parents' agreement with teachers is the measure of teacher's leadership.

* Significant at the .05 level.

TABLE 3.12 Contribution of Three Measures of Teacher Leadership to Explained Variance in Parents' Reactions and Evaluations*

Parents' Reactions and Evaluations	Row	R^2 [a]	Teacher's Reputation as Leader in Parent Involvement	Parents' (Classroom) Reports of Teacher Use of Parent Involvement	Parents' (Classroom) Reports of Teacher Use of Other Communication
Teacher works hard to interest and excite parents	1	R^2(a)	11	69	20
	2	R^2(b)	5	18	9
	3	R^2(c)	49	4	43
Teacher gives many ideas to parents	4	R^2(a)	8	30	10
	5	R^2(b)	6	23	3
	6	R^2(c)	18	13	13
Parents think they should help	7	R^2(a)	2	60	15
	8	R^2(b)	1	14	2
	9	R^2(c)	54	9	42
Parents know more about child's program	10	R^2(a)	2	43	17
	11	R^2(b)	0	6	3
	12	R^2(c)	42	7	30
Parents' ratings of teacher's interpersonal skills	13	R^2(a)	6	9	12
	14	R^2(b)	6	19	10
	15	R^2(c)	9	20	7
Parents' ratings of excellence of teaching skills	16	R^2(a)	10	22	28
	17	R^2(b)	7	20	24
	18	R^2(c)	14	16	13

* Equations included the following independent variables, all at the classroom level: measure of teacher leadership in parent involvement; grade level, teacher overall quality, teacher's highest degree (measures of the teaching situation); performance level of students, racial composition of students (measures of student population); parents' education composition, degree of parent activity at school (measures of parent factors).

a R^2(a) refers to the explained variance of the measure of teacher leadership before any other independent variables are entered in the equation. R^2(b) refers to the explained variance of the measure of teacher leadership after all other independent variables are entered in the equation. R^2(c) refers to the explained variance of all other independent variables after the measure of teacher leadership in parent involvement is entered in the equation. R^2(a) + (c) equals the total variance explained.

3.11. Of the three measures, teachers' frequent use of learning activities at home had the most dramatic impact (β = .695) on parents' reports that teachers work hard to interest and excite them in helping their children at home.

In Table 3.12, rows 1–3 inform us about how the measures of teacher leadership and the other variables in the regression model explain—uniquely and in combination—parents' reports that the teacher works hard to involve parents. The figures in the far right-hand column show that routine communications from the teacher to the family explained 9 percent of the variance after all other variables in the model were accounted for. The other variables—especially grade level, racial composition, and parents' education—contributed more than 40 percent of the explained variance after routine communications were accounted for.

The figures in the middle column of rows 1–3 indicate that parents' actual experiences with learning activities at home explained 18 percent of the variance in reports that the teacher works hard, after all other variables were accounted for. Other variables in the model added little information (4 percent of the explained variance) after teacher practices were taken into account.

The facts from Tables 3.11 and 3.12 reveal a strong link between parents' actual experiences with teacher practices of parent involvement and parents' awareness that the teacher works hard to interest and excite parents in their children's education.

Ideas from Teachers.   Parents received most ideas for home-learning activities from teachers who were rated by principals or by parents as leaders in parent involvement practices, as shown in column 2 of Table 3.11. Teachers' use of home learning activities (β = .787) was a more important mechanism for obtaining ideas from teachers than was the teacher's reputation for leadership in parent involvement (β = .268) or the teacher's use of other, general types of school-to-home communications (β = .216).

The corresponding rows 4–6 of Table 3.12 show how the three measures of teacher leadership explain parents' receipt of ideas for home learning activities. The variance that teacher practices of parent involvement explained (23 percent) was from four to eight times the variance explained by the other measures of teacher leadership, after all other variables were taken into account.

Encouragement from Teachers.   Parents believed they should help when teachers frequently asked them to help (β = .603). Neither the teachers' reputations as leaders (β = .081) nor routine communications (β = .150) significantly affected parents' beliefs that they should help their child on school activities at home.

In Table 3.12, rows 7–9 display the dramatic differences in the contributions of the three measures of teacher leadership to the explained variance in parents' beliefs that they should help at home. Teachers' practices explained 14 percent of the variance after all other variables were accounted for. The other variables added only 9 percent to parents' beliefs that they should help after teacher practices of parent involvement in learning activities were accounted for. In contrast, the other variables contributed 42–54 percent to the explained variance of beliefs that parents should help after routine communications or teacher reputation were accounted for.

Effects on Parents' Knowledge about School

Parents feel competent when they know what the school is doing, can help their children through the program, or can request changes to improve activities. But many parents do not understand the instructional program and cannot act in the child's interest as an advocate or mediator between the school and the family.

In this survey, parents reported whether they "understood more this year than (they) did last year about what (their) child is being taught in school." Parents increased their understanding about school most when the teacher frequently used parent involvement practices (β = .406) and when the teacher frequently communicated with the family (β = .231), as reported in Table 3.11, column 4. Principals' estimates of teacher leadership did not affect parents' knowledge about the instructional program (β = .065).

Rows 10–12 in Table 3.12 show that 6 percent of the variance in improved parent understanding about school instruction was explained uniquely by parents' experiences with teacher practices of parent involvement, after all other measures were accounted for. In contrast, little was uniquely explained by other types of school-to-home communications (3 percent) or the reputation of the teacher (0 percent).

Parents of children in lower grades, in predominantly black classes, and in classes with predominantly low-educated parents also reported that they understood more about the school program than they had in prior years. It is reasonable that parents with younger children or with less education themselves need more information than do other parents about instructional programs. The findings also reflect teachers' efforts to reach and teach parents of young students, educationally disadvantaged students, or other high-risk students. Rubin, Olmsted, Szegda, Wetherby, and Williams (1983) found that mothers in urban areas who were involved in activities at school or with a home visitor changed most in their behavior toward their children and in their opinions about themselves. Intervention programs often make special efforts to reach low-achieving children and less-educated parents to involve them in learning activities at home (Safran and Moles, 1980). What is important in our findings is that teachers' frequent use of parent involvement practices improved parents' knowledge about their child's instructional program, after the grade level, racial composition, and parent education composition of the classroom were taken into account. Also, teachers' use of these practices mitigated the disadvantages typically associated with race, social class, and grade level.

The Importance of Grade Level

The most consistently important variable in these analyses of parents' reactions to teacher practices was the grade level of the student. Parents with children in lower elementary grades reported significantly more frequent teacher use of parent involvement, more frequent communications from school to family, and more frequent participation at the school. Certain practices occurred more frequently at the lower grade levels: reading aloud or listening to the child read, giving spelling or math drills, and playing learning games. Other techniques were used more with older children: entering contracts and signing homework. Still others were used about equally with children at all grade levels: discussing school with children at home.

Parents with children in grades 1, 3, and 5 felt differently about their participation in parent involvement activities. Parents of older elementary children more frequently said that they did not have enough training to help their children in reading and math activities at home. They reported that they helped their children but that they felt less confident about their help. This expressed inadequacy was significant even after parent education was taken into account. There was, then, less use by teachers and less self-confidence of parents in helping children in the upper grades.

Compared with parents of first or third graders, fewer parents of fifth-grade students said that the teacher worked hard to involve parents or gave them many ideas for home-learning activities. It may be more difficult for teachers to involve parents of older students in learning activities because the abilities and needs of children in the upper grades are more diversified and the academic content is more complex. The data show, however, that when teachers of any grade level involve parents frequently in home-learning activities, they can positively affect the parents' awareness of the teachers' efforts and knowledge about the school program.

Effects on Parents' Evaluations of Teachers' Merits

Parents evaluated teachers on two dimensions, interpersonal skills and professional merit. Parents were asked to judge the quality of their interpersonal contacts with the teacher by rating five positive characteristics (cooperation, friendliness, respect, trust, and warmth) and five negative characteristics (conflict, misunderstanding, distance, lack of concern, and tenseness). An index was constructed of the number of positive minus the number of negative ratings. Parents were also asked to rate the teacher on overall teaching quality on a six-point scale from poor to outstanding. The last two columns of Table 3.11 indicate that all three measures of teacher leadership—teachers' reputations, parents' experiences with frequent use of teacher practices of parent involvement, and parents' reports of other school-to-home communications—had significant positive effects on parental ratings of teachers' interpersonal skills and professional merit. Most dramatically, parents gave high marks to teachers for interpersonal skills ($\beta = .712$) and overall teaching quality ($\beta = .728$) if the teachers frequently used parent involvement practices.

In Table 3.12, rows 13–15 report that teacher practices of parent involvement added 19 percent to the explained variance in parents' ratings of interpersonal skills after all other variables in the model were taken into account, more than three times the unique contribution of teachers' reputational leadership and about twice the contribution of routine school-to-home communications with parents.

The figures in rows 16–18 indicate that teachers' practices and other kinds of communication are about equally important, explaining 20–24 percent of the variance in parents' ratings of overall teaching quality.

These findings suggest that, in general, teacher practices of parent involvement maximize cooperation and minimize antagonism between teachers and parents and enhance the teachers' professional standing from the parents' perspective. Most parents (94 percent) disagreed with the statement that "it is not the teacher's business" to show parents how to help their child learn at home. When teachers frequently used home-learning activities, parents rated them as more skillful teachers. Because these analyses are based on classroom-level averages from reports of the parents of all children in the classroom, the results do not reflect personal favoritism in the relationships of a few parents and teachers.

The analyses reported in Tables 3.11 and 3.12 treated each of the three measures of teacher leadership in separate equations. In other analyses, the measures were considered simultaneously to determine whether teacher practices of parent involvement continued to affect parents' reactions and evaluations, after other school-to-home communications were taken into account. For each measure of awareness of teachers' efforts, improved parental knowledge, and ratings of teachers' merits, the positive effects of parent involvement practices continued after school-to-home communications were accounted for. In contrast, except for the ratings of overall merit, the positive effects of school-to-home communications disappeared after the teachers' actual classroom practices of parent involvement were taken into account. Although communications from school to home are important, they do not have as consistently strong links to parent reactions as practices of parent involvement in learning activities at home.

In other analyses, we found that parent activity at the school did not significantly affect parents' reactions to the school program or evaluations of the teachers' merits (Epstein, 1984). Involvement of some parents at the school requires a different investment from teachers from involvement of all parents in learning activities at home. Involvement of parents at school may help teachers or administrators fulfill their teaching and other duties, but it does not affect most parents' attitudes toward and reactions to the school or teacher.

SUMMARY AND DISCUSSION

This survey of parents revealed some important facts about parents' attitudes toward public elementary schools and reactions to teachers' practices of parent involvement.

Facts

Parents of children in Maryland's elementary schools had, in general, positive attitudes about their public elementary schools and teachers. They believed the schools were generally well run, comfortable places for parents to visit and assist and that the goals of the teachers were similar to the goals that the parents had for their children.

Despite generally positive attitudes, parents believed the schools could do more to involve them in learning activities to help their children at home.

Surprisingly large numbers of parents were excluded from some of the most basic, traditional communications from the school, such as specific memos, conversations, phone calls, or conferences with teachers about their child's progress, problems, or programs in school.

Few parents were involved at school. A few parents in a classroom sometimes assisted the teacher, but the number of active parents at school did not affect the attitudes or knowledge of all of the parents who were not—and often could not be—active at the school.

Parents' education did not explain their experiences with parent involvement unless teacher practices were taken into account. In the classrooms of teachers who were leaders in the use of parent involvement, parents at all educational levels said they were frequently involved in learning activities at home. In other teachers' classrooms, parents with less formal schooling reported more frequent requests than did other parents to help their child at home. Teacher-leaders conducted more equitable programs, reaching all or most parents as part of their teaching philosophy and instructional strategy. Other teachers did not involve better-educated parents. Their selective use of parent involvement, however, was more often built on negative expectations of a parent's and, possibly, a child's ability to succeed.

Fewer and fewer teachers helped parents become involved as the students advanced through the elementary grades. Thus, parents' repertoires of helping skills are not developed and improved over the school years, and they tend to taper off or disappear as the child progresses through school.

Parents were aware of and responded positively to teachers' efforts to involve them in learning activities at home. Parents with children in the classrooms of teachers who built parent involvement into their regular teaching practice were more aware of teachers' efforts, received more ideas from teachers, knew more about their child's instructional program, and rated the teachers higher in interpersonal skills and overall teaching quality. Teachers' practices had consistently strong and positive effects on parent reactions to the school program and on parent evaluations of teachers' merits for parents at all educational levels, net of all other variables. Teacher practices of parent involvement had more dramatic positive links to parents' reactions than general school-to-home communications or parent assistance at the school.

Implications for Parents and Teachers

What do these research findings mean to teachers' policies and practices of parent involvement? We found interesting differences in whether parents thought the teacher wanted them to help their children (i.e., that they *should* help), whether they thought they had enough training to help their children in reading and math (i.e., that they *could* help), whether they actually spent time assisting and supervising homework and learning activities at home (i.e., that they *do* help), and whether they said they could spend more time helping their children at home (i.e., that they *could* help if given directions by the teacher).

Parents think they should help if the teachers give them learning activities to do at home. Other kinds of communications, from teachers' and principals' ratings of teachers' reputations, did not make parents think that they should help with home-learning activities.

Parents' feelings that they can help (i.e., that they have adequate training to help their children with reading and math) are based primarily on their own education and their children's grade level. More parents said they could help if they had more education or if their children were in the lower elementary grades where parents needed less specialized knowledge to help the children.

Despite differences in parents' feelings about their ability to help, most parents do help. Only 8 percent of the parents reported they never helped their child with reading and math skills during the school year, whether or not they were asked to do so by the teacher. Over 85 percent of the parents spent 15 minutes or more helping their children on homework activities when asked to do so by the teacher. Most parents reported, also, that they could help more (up to 44 minutes, on the average) if the teacher showed them what to do.

The differences in whether parents believe they should help, can help, do help, and could help suggest strategies for organizing programs of parent involvement. For example, if teachers want parents to think that they should help, then they must demonstrate this with an active program of parent involvement in learning activities at home. Teachers may design or select daily or weekly activities for parents to do with their children at home. These may be skills individualized for each student's needs, general skills for review and practice, or special activities that extend learning.

If teachers want parents to feel confident that they can help, they (and the school administrators) must organize and conduct workshops for parents on *how to help* in reading, math, and other subjects. With or without workshops, teachers need materials that are clear and easy to follow to prove quickly to parents that they can help. As Ogbu (1974) points out, parents' lack of knowledge does not mean lack of interest. Workshops or special instruction may be less necessary with well-educated parents who feel confident about helping their children with reading and math and who readily ask teachers questions about how to help (Litwak and Meyer, 1974). Parents of younger children tend to feel that they can help, but the parents of older students (including many well-educated parents) may need clear and sequential guidance from teachers. Special assistance to build and maintain confidence of parents with children in the upper elementary grades is especially important.

Because many parents do help whether or not they are asked, teachers who are not already using parent involvement techniques should consider how to mobilize this available resource more effectively. Because parents say they could help more if shown how, teachers need to consider ways to organize home-learning activities to help more parents make productive use of the time they could spend helping their children.

Teachers can work as individuals, with colleagues on grade-level teams, or in other groups to develop trial programs to increase parents' involvement in learning activities at home, improve parents' understanding of the school program, and encourage home-learning activities that build on the common goals parents and teachers hold. Basic features of these programs should include clear objectives of short- or long-term activities, clear instructions for parents, and information that tells parents how the activity fits into the teacher's instructional program. Procedures should be devised that permit parents to call or contact the teacher or some other knowledgeable representative to ask questions about how to help or to comment on the child's progress or problems with the activity. Systematic follow-up of parents' efforts must occur to determine whether the activities were completed and how successfully. There should be opportunities for parents to suggest activities or changes in the parent involvement techniques.

When teachers use parent involvement activities, are they fulfilling or shirking responsibility? Grasping at brass rings or grasping at straws? Displaying strengths or displaying weakness? These findings suggest that from the parents' perspective, teachers' use of parent involvement in learning activities at home is a teaching strength. Frequent use of parent involvement results in larger collections of ideas for parents to use at home, increased understanding by parents of school programs, and higher ratings of teacher quality.

Ideas about the opposing theories of school and family relations have most often been discussed from the school's or teacher's point of view. This study contributes an interpretation of school and family relations from the parents' perspective. Parents' reports did not reflect deep conflict and incompatibility between the schools and families. On the contrary, they responded favorably to programs that stressed the cooperation of schools and families to help their children succeed in school. Teachers who included the family in the children's education were recognized by parents for their efforts and were rated higher than other teachers on interpersonal and teaching skills. Parents' reports suggest that teachers control the flow of information to parents. By limiting communications and collaborative activities, teachers reinforce the boundaries that separate the two institutions.

The message from parents is that almost all parents can be involved in learning activities at home. The message for teachers is that many parents help their children, with or without the teacher's instruction or assistance, and many would benefit from directions and ideas from the teacher that could be useful for the child's progress in school. These results from this study raise many questions for new research at the elementary and secondary levels on the benefits and disadvantages for parents, teachers, and students of cooperation or separation of families and schools.

REFERENCES

Becker, H. J. (1982). Parents' responses to teachers' parent involvement practices. Paper presented at the annual meeting of the American Educational Research Association in New York.

Becker, H. J., and J. L. Epstein. (1982). Parent involvement: A study of teacher practices. *Elementary School Journal* 83: 85–102. (Reading 3.1).

Bronfenbrenner, U. (1979). *The ecology of human development.* Cambridge, MA: Harvard University Press.

Epstein, J. L. (1984). School policy and parent involvement: Research results. *Educational Horizons* 62: 70–72.

Epstein, J. L., and H. J. Becker. (1982). Teacher practices of parent involvement: Problems and possibilities. *Elementary School Journal* 83: 103–113. (Reading 3.2).

Gallup, G. H. (1982). Gallup poll of the public's attitudes toward the public schools. *Phi Delta Kappan* 63: 37–50.

———. (1983). Gallup poll of the public's attitudes toward the public schools. *Phi Delta Kappan* 64: 33–47.

Goodlad, J. I. (1983). A study of schooling: Some findings and hypotheses. *Phi Delta Kappan* 64: 465–470.

Gordon, I. (1979). The effects of parent involvement in schooling. Pages 4–25 in *Partners: Parents and schools,* edited by R. S. Brandt. Alexandria, VA: Association for Supervision and Curriculum Development.

Keesling, J. W., and R. Melaragno. (1983). Parent participation in federal education programs: Findings from the federal programs surveys phase of the study of parent involvement. Pages 230–256 in *Parent education and public policy,* edited by R. Haskins. Norwood, NJ: Ablex.

Klein, M. F., K. A. Tye, and J. E. Wright. (1979). A study of schools: Curriculum. *Phi Delta Kappan* 60: 244–248.

Leichter, H. J. (1974). *The family as educator.* New York: Teachers College Press.

Litwak, E., and H. J. Meyer. (1974). *School, family and neighborhood: The theory and practice of school-community relations.* New York: Columbia University Press.

Mager, G. (1980). Parent relationships and home and community conditions. Pages 153–198 in *Teaching is tough,* edited by D. R. Cruickshank. Englewood Cliffs, NJ: Prentice-Hall.

Morrison, G. S. (1978). *Parent involvement in the home school and community.* Columbus, OH: Merrill.

National Commission on Excellence in Education. (1983). *A nation at risk.* Washington, DC: Government Printing Office.

National Task Force on Education for Economic Growth. (1983). *Action for excellence.* Denver: Education Commission of the States.

Ogbu, J. V. (1974). *The next generation: An ethnography of education in an urban neighborhood.* New York: Academic Press.

Olmsted, P. P., M. J. Wetherby, H. Leler, and R. I. Rubin. (1982). Parent perspectives on home-school relationships in a compensatory education program. Paper presented at the annual meeting of the American Educational Research Association in New York.

Parsons, T. (1959). The school class as a social system: Some of its functions in American society. *Harvard Educational Review* 29: 297–318.

Rich, D., and C. Jones. (1977). *A family affair: Education.* Washington, DC: Home and School Institute.

Robinson, J. L. (1979). Another perspective on program evaluation: The parents speak. Pages 467–476 in *Project Head Start: A legacy of the war on poverty,* edited by E. Zigler and J. Valentine. New York: Free Press.

Rubin, R. I., P. P. Olmsted, M. J. Szegda, M. J. Wetherby, and D. S. Williams. (1983). Long-term effects of parent education follow-through program participation. Paper presented at the annual meeting of the American Educational Research Association in Montreal.

Safran, D., and O. Moles. (1980). Home-school alliances: Approaches to increasing parent involvement in children's learning in upper elementary and junior high schools. Washington, DC: National Institute of Education. Mimeographed.

Sowers, J., C. Lang, and J. Gowett. (1980). *Parent involvement in the schools: A state of the art report.* Newton, MA: Education Development Center.

Valentine, J., and E. Stark. (1979). The social context of parent involvement in Head Start. Pages 291–313 in *Project Head Start: A legacy of the war on poverty,* edited by E. Zigler and J. Valentine. New York: Free Press.

Waller, W. (1932). *The sociology of teaching.* New York: Russell & Russell.

Weber, M. (1947). *The theory of social and economic organization.* New York: Oxford University Press.

Williams, D. L., Jr. (1983). Parent perspectives regarding parent involvement at the elementary school level. Paper presented at the annual meeting of the American Educational Research Association in Montreal.

Zill, N., and J. L. Peterson. (1982). Learning to do things without help. Pages 343–374 in *Families as learning environments for children,* edited by L. M. Laosa and I. E. Sigel. New York: Plenum.

Single Parents and the Schools: Effects of Marital Status on Parent and Teacher Interactions*

INTRODUCTION

The one-parent home is one of the major family arrangements of schoolchildren today. Over 15 million children live in one-parent homes, most in mother-only homes and most as a result of separation or divorce. From a total of about 62 million children overall, the number in one-parent homes is an important and growing subgroup of children in the country. Each year over 1 million children under the age of 18 have parents who divorce. In the United States in 1986, 25 percent of the households with children under 18—about one in four—were single-parent homes (U.S. House of Representatives, 1986).[1] Membership in one-parent homes is even greater for black children, with approximately half of all black children under 18 years old in one-parent homes (U.S. Bureau of the Census, 1982). It is estimated that more than 50 percent of all children born after 1980 will live with only one parent for at least three school years before reaching the age of 18. Most will live in poor, female-headed households (Furstenburg, Nord, Peterson, and Zill, 1983; Garbarino, 1982; Glick, 1979; Masnick and Bane, 1980).

In earlier times, single-parent homes were atypical; now they are common. This contrast raises many questions about the effects of single-parent homes on the members of the family. Much has been written about single parents, their children, their numbers, and their problems, but little research has focused on how single parents and their children fit into other social institutions that were designed to serve "traditional" families. When children are in school, the family and school are inexorably linked. Because of this linkage, changes that occur in families must be accommodated by responsive changes in schools.

---

* By Joyce L. Epstein. This research was supported by Grant NIE-G-83-0002 from the National Institute of Education (now the Office of Educational Research and Improvement) of the U.S. Department of Education. The opinions expressed by the author do not necessarily reflect the position or policy of the OERI, and no official endorsement by the agency should be inferred. An earlier version of the paper was presented at the annual meeting of the American Sociological Association in 1984. The author is grateful to Henry Jay Becker, John Hollifield, Linda Gottfredson, and Gary Natriello for their helpful comments on earlier drafts. Originally published in M. T. Hallinan, D. M. Klein, and J. Glass, eds., *Change in societal institutions* (New York: Plenum, 1990), pp. 91–121. Reprinted with permission.

[1] In 1999, the statistics were similar, with 27 percent of children in single-parent homes (Federal Interagency Forum, 2000).

THEORETICAL PERSPECTIVES

Schools and families are overlapping spheres of influence on student learning and development (Epstein, 1987 [Reading 2.1]). The model of overlapping spheres of influence recognizes that there are some practices that schools and families conduct separately but there are other practices that can best be conducted as partners. This view is in contrast to a long-standing alternative perspective that emphasizes the separateness of these institutions.

An Emphasis on Separateness

One perspective on institutions and their relationships emphasizes the importance of their *separate* contributions to society. This view assumes, for example, that school bureaucracies and family organizations are most efficient and effective when their leaders maintain independent goals, standards, and activities (Parsons, 1959; Waller, 1932; Weber, 1947). Institutions that are separate and nonoverlapping give little consideration to the ideas or histories of the other groups, or to their common or interlocking aims or goals, until there are problems or trouble. This is, in effect, a "conflict resolution" model, requiring interventions and interactions only when necessary to solve serious problems.

An Emphasis on Overlapping Spheres of Influence

A social-organizational perspective is offered as the basis for research on schools and families (Epstein, 1987) and other inter-institutional connections that influence the education of children (Epstein, 1989). In this model, the key, proximate environments that educate and socialize children are shown as spheres of influence that can, by design, overlap more or less in their goals, practices, messages, and resources for students. Major "forces" are considered in the model, including (1) time, to account for changes in the ages and grade levels of students and the influence of the historic period, and (2) the philosophies, policies, and practices of each institution. These forces affect the nature and extent of "overlap" of families and schools. The model integrates and extends the ecological approach developed by Bronfenbrenner (1979); the educational insights of Leichter (1974); the sociological studies of schools and communities of Litwak and Meyer (1974); the theory of institutions and individuals of Coleman (1974); and a long tradition of sociological research on school and family environments (Coleman et al., 1966; Epstein and McPartland, 1979; McDill and Rigsby, 1973; and others).

The model of overlapping spheres of influence recognizes the interlocking histories of institutions that educate and socialize children and the changing and accumulating skills of the individuals in them as the basis for studying connections that can benefit children's learning and development. This, in effect, is a "conflict prevention" model in which institutions invest resources in shared goals (such as student success) to prevent or reduce tensions and problems that could require later, more costly treatment.

These two theoretical perspectives are reflected in the practices of two types of teachers and may influence their interactions with single and married parents. Some teachers believe that families and schools have different responsibilities that can best be accomplished separately and independently. These teachers may make greater distinctions in their opinions about the effectiveness of single and married parents if they view single parents as lacking the resources needed to carry out family responsibilities. Other teachers believe families and schools overlap in their interests and share responsibilities for the education and socialization of their children. They may make fewer distinctions between single and married parents if they view all parents as important contributors to their children's education.

Opinions differ about whether schools and teachers should be informed about parents' marital status or changes in family structure. Some argue that teachers are biased against children from one-parent homes. They suggest that teachers negatively label children of divorced or separated parents, explain children's school problems in terms of the family living arrangement rather than in terms of their own teaching practices or the children's individual needs, or assume parental inadequacies before the facts about parents' skills are known (Hetherington, Camara, and Featherman, 1981; Laosa, 1983; Lightfoot, 1978; Ogbu, 1974; Santrock and Tracy, 1978; Zill, 1983). This view sets schools and families apart as separate spheres of influence, with families expected to cope on their own with changes and problems.

Others argue that schools should be informed about parental separation or divorce because teachers provide stability and support to children during the initial period of family disruption, can be more sensitive to children's situations when discussing families, and can organize special services such as after-school care for children that may be needed by single parents and working mothers (Bernard, 1984). This view brings schools and families together, as overlapping spheres of influence with both institutions working together to help children cope and succeed even during times of family changes and stress.

The discrepant opinions of how much families should inform schools about family circumstances are each supported by parents' accounts of experiences with teacher bias or with teacher understanding and assistance (Carew and Lightfoot, 1979; Clay, 1981; Keniston et al., 1977; National Public Radio, 1980; Snow, 1982). There are few facts from research, however, about whether and how teachers respond to students in differently structured families or about how single parents perceive, react to, and become involved with their children's schools and teachers.

Many early studies of single parents and some recent ones are based on a "deficit theory" of family functioning. One major underlying assumption of this work is that the number of parents at home is the key variable for understanding effective parenting and children's success. That is, two parents are always better than one. For example, research based on the "confluence" model argues that crucial intellectual resources are lacking when the father is absent from the home (Zajonc, 1976). This theory asserts that the father is the family member with the highest intelligence and is the educational leader of the family. This is a mechanical theory that has not been well supported in research. It establishes an unequivocal bias against one-parent homes, putting mothers in a fixed and forced subordinate position, discounting the roles most mothers play in encouraging their children's education, and ignoring the roles of schools in guiding family activities that concern school skills.

Other research on single parents based on their deficiencies assumes that one-parent homes are unstable, uncaring, and lacking in emotional and academic support or strong role models for students' school success. The number of parents at home is the measure used as a proxy for numerous alleged weaknesses of the one-parent home. Studies that include the number of parents as the only explanatory variable establish a theoretical bias against one-parent homes, without allowing for alternative explanations.

An alternative view focuses more on the strengths and potentials of families, with attention to the activities and practices of families of any size or structure. The underlying assumption of these studies is that the quality of family practices and processes explains more about parental effectiveness than marital status or the number of parents at home (Barton, 1981; Blanchard and Biller, 1971; Dokecki and Maroney, 1983; Hetherington and Camara, 1984; Marotz-Bader et al., 1979; Shinn, 1978).

The change from a "deficit model" to a "strengths model" has led to more thoughtful studies of children and parents in one- *and* two-parent homes. Models improved in small steps, from the simple, mechanistic theories of the impact of the number of parents in the home on student achievement or behavior, to only slightly more complex theories that added family socioeconomic status (SES) as another explanatory variable. Researchers recognized that because low education and low income often accompany single-parent status, it is necessary to measure these family conditions as well as marital status so that negative effects due to SES or education are not attributed falsely to single-parent status (Barton, 1981; Kelly, North, and Zingle, 1965; Milne, Myers, Rosenthal, and Ginsburg, 1986; Svanum, Bringle, and McLaughlin, 1982). For example, children from well-educated, middle-class, one-parent homes often perform as well as similar children from two-parent homes.

The improvements in knowledge gained from added measures of social class were not enough, however, to clarify the inconsistent results across studies of the effects of marital status on parent behavior and student achievement. Two relatively stable status variables—marital status and socioeconomic status—do not adequately represent the dynamics of family life that contribute to student achievement or success in school (Hanson and Ginsburg, 1986). Even studies of family contacts with the schools (Baker and Stevenson, 1986; Garfinkle and McLanahan, 1986; Kurdek and Blisk, 1983; Milne, Rosenthal, and Ginsburg, 1986; Zill, 1983) have ignored the roles of teachers in increasing or reducing differences in parent and student behavior in differently structured families. A comprehensive review by Newberger, Melnicoe, and Newberger (1986) calls for studies of the many factors that may ameliorate and explain the negative conditions of one-parent homes.

The present study looks at some potentially important variables that allow schools to change to meet the changing needs and conditions of families. We use data from teachers and parents to examine family and school connections in one- and two-parent homes. We focus on the children's living arrangements that affect the day-to-day communications and interactions between schools and families and compare single and married parents' reports of the frequency of teacher requests for parent involvement. We look next at teachers' reports of the quality of involvement of the single and married parents of their students and the teachers' reports of the quality of the homework completed by children from one- and two-parent homes. We also examine other similarities and differences among single and married parents concerning their children's education.

This study asks the following questions: Do single and married parents differ in their perceptions of teacher practices of parent involvement? Are teachers' perceptions of parents and children influenced by family living arrangements? How does marital status relate to other family and school connections? How do teachers' practices reflect the two theoretical perspectives that emphasize separateness or overlap of families and schools? To address these questions, we introduce, first, a simple model that improves upon earlier research on single parents by accounting for marital status, parent education, and teacher leadership to study parent-teacher exchanges and evaluations. We then test a more complete model that places marital status, parent education, and teachers' practices of parent involvement in a fuller social context with other characteristics of the school and family.

This exploration includes many measures of family structure and processes, student characteristics, and school and classroom structures and processes. The independent variables, introduced as they are needed in different analyses, include family size, race, and parent education; student grade level, classroom ability, and behavior in class; teacher leadership in parent involvement, teaching experience, and overall teaching quality; and specific teacher-parent interactions about the child as a student.

Unlike earlier research that often used "special problem" samples to study single-parent families (Shinn, 1978), this is a purposely stratified sample of a normal population of teachers in grades 1, 3, and 5 in public schools in the state of Maryland and the parents and students in their classes (Becker and Epstein, 1982a [Reading 3.1]). Importantly, the data from teachers, parents, and students are linked so that particular teachers' practices can be connected with the parents and students in those teachers' classrooms (Epstein, 1986 [Reading 3.4], 1991 [Reading 3.7]). Few previous studies measured the behavior and attitudes of single parents about the schools their children attend (Clay, 1981), and none link the teachers' and parents' practices and evaluations of each other.

SAMPLE, VARIABLES, AND APPROACHES

Surveys of teachers, principals, parents, and students in sixteen Maryland school districts were conducted in 1980 and 1981. Approximately 3,700 first-, third-, and fifth-grade teachers and their principals in 600 schools were surveyed (Becker and Epstein, 1982a; Epstein and Becker, 1982 [Reading 3.2]). From the original sample, 82 teachers were selected who varied in their use of parent involvement in learning activities at home. They were matched by school district, grade level, years of teaching experience, and characteristics of their student populations. Among the teachers, 17 were confirmed by their principals as strong leaders in the use of parent involvement activities. In all, the 82 teachers ranged along a useful continuum from high to low use of parent involvement, with the "confirmed leaders" making the most concerted use of parent involvement in learning activities at home.

Data were obtained on the achievements and behaviors of the students in the 82 classrooms. The parents of the children in the 82 teachers' classrooms were surveyed about their attitudes toward and experiences with parent involvement. In all, 1,269 parents responded to a questionnaire by mail, a response rate of 59 percent. Of these, 24 percent were single parents, close to the national average of 22 percent at that time (U.S. Bureau of the Census, 1982).

We requested that the parent complete the survey who was most familiar with the child's school and teacher. More than 90 percent of the respondents were female, and virtually all of the single-parent respondents were female. Thus, the research provided a sizable, useful sample of single and married mothers whose children were in the classrooms of teachers who differed in their use of practices to involve parents in their children's education.

The categories *one-parent home* and *single parent* come from the parents' reports that only one parent lives at home with the child. We prefer the terms *single-parent home, one-parent home,* or *mother-only/father-only home* to describe the living arrangements of schoolchildren, rather than the pejorative terms *broken home, broken family,* or even *single-parent family.* A single-parent home or a two-parent home may or may not be "broken" by marital, economic, or emotional conditions (Engan-Barker, 1986; Kamerman and Hayes, 1982). To determine if a family is "broken" requires clear and sensitive measures in addition to the structure of living arrangements. A child in a single-parent home may have contact with two parents, although only one parent lives at home when the child leaves for and returns from school. The data do not include information on the cause, choice, or duration of single-parent status, nor can we identify calm or troubled relations in two-parent homes. Our sample does not permit us to study one-parent homes where the father is the custodial parent or the parent most knowledgeable about the child's schooling. These are important characteristics of families that should be included in new studies of family and school effects (Bane, 1976; Eiduson, 1982; Furstenburg and Seltzer, 1983; Shinn, 1978; Zill, 1983).

Parent involvement refers to 12 techniques that teachers used to organize parental assistance at home, including reading, discussions, informal learning games, formal contracts, drill and practice of basic skills, and other monitoring or tutoring activities. For example, the most popular teachers' practices included asking parents to read to their child or listen to the child read, using books or workbooks borrowed from the school to help children learn or practice needed skills, discussing schoolwork at home, and using materials found at home to teach needed skills. Eight other activities were also used by teachers to establish parents at home as partners with the teacher to help students do better in school. The activities, patterns of teacher use, effects on parents, and effects on student achievements are discussed fully in Readings 3.1, 3.2, 3.4, and 3.7 and in other publications (Becker and Epstein, 1982a, b; Epstein and Becker, 1982; Epstein, 1986; Epstein, 1991). Parent involvement in learning activities at home is a complex, difficult type of teacher-parent partnership (Leler, 1983), but these practices include more parents and have greater positive impact than other forms of parent involvement that occur at the school building (see Epstein, 1986). Involvement in learning activities at home is the type of involvement that most parents would like the schools to increase and improve across the grades (Dauber and Epstein, 1989 [Reading 3.6]; Epstein, 1990).

Characteristics of Parents

Table 3.13 shows the characteristics of the single and married parents in the sample. There are several important differences. Significantly more single parents are black, reside in the city, have fewer years of formal schooling, work full-time, or have one child. The single and married parents are about equally represented by children in the three elementary school grades (1, 3, and 5) in the study and in the classroom of teachers who were confirmed by their principals as leaders in the use of parent involvement. These characteristics of the Maryland sample are similar to those expected from a national sample of single parents.

We use mothers' education rather than both parents' education, or either parent's occupation, to minimize missing or incomparable data for one- and two-parent homes. Mothers' education has traditionally been used as an indicator of family SES (Sewell and Hauser, 1975). As others have noted, mother's education may be more pertinent than other measures for studying family influences on children's school behaviors or as an indicator of a parent's familiarity with school organizations and procedures (Baker and Stevenson, 1986; Milne Rosenthal, and Ginsburg, 1986). In one-parent homes especially, mother's education may be a more important and accurate indicator of school-like activities at home than other occupational or economic indicators.

RESULTS: PARENTS' REPORTS OF TEACHERS' PRACTICES OF PARENT INVOLVEMENT

Parents were asked to report how often their child's teacher requested their involvement in the 12 home-learning activities described previously. Parents' reports of teachers' requests ranged from 0 to 12 frequently used activities, with a mean score of 4.1 and a standard deviation of 3.4. Table 3.14 shows how single and married parents' reports differed by the educational level of the parents and by the teachers' leadership in parent involvement. The mean scores and tests of comparisons in the first column of the table show that, compared to married parents, single parents reported significantly more requests from teachers to assist with learn-

TABLE 3.13   Characteristics of Single and Married Parents

	Single Parents (N = 273) Percentage Respondents	Married Parents (N = 862) Percentage Respondents
Race[a]		
White	35.9	73.2
Black	64.1	26.8
Residence[a]		
City	57.1	27.7
County/suburb	42.9	72.3
Parent education[a]		
Some high school (or less)	27.1	15.2
High school diploma	32.2	38.4
Some college	28.1	22.6
Bachelor's degree	4.8	10.5
Some graduate school (or more)	7.8	13.3
Employment[a]		
No work outside home	33.1	40.4
Part-time work	11.3	21.4
Full-time work	55.6	38.2
Family size[a]		
0 siblings	24.9	11.7
1–2 siblings	58.3	71.9
3–4 siblings	15.0	14.2
Over 4 siblings	1.8	2.2
Extended family (other adults)	23.8	10.2
Grade level of child		
Grade 1	41.8	38.3
Grade 3	27.8	26.9
Grade 5	30.4	34.8
Teacher leadership in parent involvement		
Confirmed leader	27.5	20.4
Not confirmed leader	72.5	79.6

a Chi-square tests yield significant differences in proportions for single and married parents beyond the .001 level.

ing activities at home (4.80 vs. 3.76). The figures in the second column indicate that among single parents, high- and low-educated single parents reported about equally frequent requests from teachers for parent involvement. Among married parents, however, less-educated married parents reported more frequent requests from teachers for parent involvement than did more-educated married parents (4.16 vs. 3.30).

TABLE 3.14 Parents' Reports of Frequency of Teachers' Use of Parent Involvement (12 Techniques) (Means, Standard Deviations, and Test Statistics from Multiple Comparisons of Mean Scores of Single vs. Married, Low- vs. High-Educated Parents and Parents of Children in Classrooms of Confirmed Leader vs. Nonleader Teacher in Parent Involvement)

Parents' reports of teachers' use of 12 parent involvement techniques

Family Structure	Parent Education[a]	Teacher Leadership in Parent Involvement	Other Significant Mean Score Comparisons
Single parent $\bar{x}$ 4.80* s.d 3.53 N (246)	Low $\bar{x}$ 4.87 s.d. 3.42 N (144)	Confirmed leader $\bar{x}$ 5.22 s.d. 3.50 N (41)	Single vs. married, low education in nonleader classroom ($\bar{x}$=4.73* vs. 3.97)
		Nonleader $\bar{x}$ 4.73 s.d. 3.39 N (103)	
	High $\bar{x}$ 4.70 s.d. 3.70 N (102)	Confirmed leader $\bar{x}$ 5.28 s.d. 3.52 N (29)	Single vs. married, high education in nonleader classroom ($\bar{x}$=4.47* vs. 3.04)
		Nonleader $\bar{x}$ 4.47 s.d. 3.77 N (73)	
Married parent $\bar{x}$ 3.76 s.d 3.23 N (801)	Low $\bar{x}$ 4.16* s.d. 3.30 N (433)	Confirmed leader $\bar{x}$ 4.76* s.d. 3.24 N (103)	Low vs. high education, married parents, in nonleader classroom ($\bar{x}$=3.97* vs. 3.04)
		Nonleader $\bar{x}$ 3.97 s.d. 3.30 N (330)	
	High $\bar{x}$ 3.30 s.d. 3.08 N (368)	Confirmed leader $\bar{x}$ 4.63* s.d. 3.04 N (60)	
		Nonleader $\bar{x}$ 3.04 s.d. 3.03 N (308)	

a Parent education is high if the respondent attended or graduated from post-secondary school; low if parent attended or graduated from high school only.

* T-test significant at or beyond the .05 level.

In the third column, the measure of teacher leadership adds important information about the experiences of parents. Single and married parents with children in the classrooms of teachers who were confirmed by their principals as leaders in parent involvement reported more requests than parents whose children's teachers were not leaders in parent involvement. The differences were especially great between married parents in teacher-leader and nonleader classrooms.

Other comparisons noted in column 4 of Table 3.14 reveal differences in single and married parents' reports about teachers who were not leaders in parent involvement. Highly educated single parents of students in these teachers' classrooms reported significantly more requests than did highly educated married parents (4.47 vs. 3.04). Less-educated single parents reported significantly more requests than less-educated married parents (4.73 vs. 3.97).

If we looked only at the differences in involvement by marital status and educational levels in columns 1 and 2 of Table 3.14, we would miss the important link between families and schools due to teachers' practices, reported in column 3. There are two important patterns of results in Table 3.14:

1. Single parents, regardless of their educational level, report more requests from teachers than do married parents to be involved in learning activities at home.
2. According to parents, teachers who are confirmed leaders in parent involvement make more equal requests of all parents, regardless of education and marital status, whereas other, nonleader teachers ask more of single and low-educated parents.

It is not enough, then, to measure only marital status or parent education to explain parents' behavior concerning their children. Research on single parents and the schools must also take into account teachers' practices concerning parents.

Table 3.15 extends the inquiry by introducing other variables that may explain the simple patterns in Table 3.14. The first line of Table 3.15 reports the independent effects of the three variables—marital status, mothers' education, and teachers' practices of parent involvement—that were introduced previously. With the other two variables statistically controlled, single parents, less-educated parents, and parents whose children are in the classrooms of teachers who were leaders report receiving more requests from teachers for their involvement with their children in learning activities at home.

The second line of the table introduces other characteristics of the family, student, and teacher that previous research suggests may also affect parents', teachers', and students' interactions and evaluations of each other. Race clearly helps to explain the effect of single-parent status on parents' reports of teachers' practices. More black parents head one-parent homes in this sample (as in the nation), and black parents report receiving more requests for parent involvement than do white parents, regardless of marital status. These results reflect the practices of the urban district in which most of the black parents in this sample reside. Teachers in the urban district reported that they used more parent involvement practices (Becker and Epstein, 1982b), and the parents' responses verify the teachers' re-

TABLE 3.15   Effects of Measures of Family, Student, and Teacher Characteristics on Parents' Reports about Teacher Practices of Parent Involvement

	FAMSTR[a]	PARED	TCHLDR	PARWORK	RACE	SEX	ACH	DISC	GRADE	YEARST	TQUAL	PARCOMF	TKNOCH	TALKHLP	R^2
Initial model	-.116*[b]	-.108*	.126*												.048
Full model	-.006	-.102*	.071*	.046	-.238*	-.029	-.055	.003	-.114*	.053	.072*	.071*	.238*	.211*	.286
	(-.138)[c]	(-.133)	(.141)	(.047)	(-.306)	(-.039)	(-.134)	(.020)	(-.195)	(-.029)	(.130)	(.114)	(.328)	(.296)	

a Variables are FAMSTR = one- or two-parent homes; PARED = schooling from less than high school (0) to graduate school (5); TCHLDR = teacher's leadership or lack of parent involvement confirmed by principal (0–4); PARWORK = no work (0) or work (1) outside home by parent; RACE = black (0) or white (1); SEX = male (0) or female (1); ACH = reading and math skills ranked by teacher (0–6); DISC = low (–1) or high (+1) discipline problems; GRADE = student's grade in school management (0–4); PARCOMF = parent feeling comfortable and welcome at school (1–4); TKNOCH = parent report that teacher knows child's individual learning needs (1–4); TALKHLP = teacher talked to parent about how to help child at home (0/1). The outcome "parents' reports" refers to the number and frequency of teacher requests for up to 12 techniques to involve parents in learning activities at home.

b Standardized regression coefficients are reported.   N = 1,135.

c Zero-order correlations are in parentheses.

* Indicates coefficient is significant at or beyond the .01 level.

ports. Teachers tend to reach out to parents when children need extra help. The results also may indicate a continuing trend for black parents to let teachers know that they want to be involved in their children's education (Lightfoot, 1978).

The regression coefficients in line 2 of Table 3.15 show that six variables in addition to race have significant independent effects on parents' reports of their experiences with teachers' practice of parent involvement. Parents report significantly more frequent requests for involvement from teachers if they have less education (PARED), have younger children (GRADE), have children whose teachers are leaders in parent involvement (TCHLDR), or whose teachers use specific strategies to build close family-school relationships. These interpersonal practices are: Parent feels comfortable and welcomed at school (PARCOMF); parent reports that teacher knows child's individual learning needs (TKNOCH); and teacher talks to parent about how to help the child at home (TALKHLP). Separate analyses show that these variables are about equally important for black and white parents.

The percentage of variance explained in parents' reports of teachers' requests for their involvement improved markedly—from 5 to 30 percent—when we added detailed information on the actual practices that bring schools and families together. It is important, too, that even with teacher-parent interpersonal practices accounted for, teacher leadership in the use of specific practices continues to significantly affect parents' reports of their experiences with learning activities at home.

In previous research, the limited focus on marital status veiled the importance of other variables that influence parents' interactions with their children and their children's schools. Single and married parents' reports about their experiences with parent involvement are influenced by many family and school factors, not simply by the categorical label of marital status.

Single and married parents' reports about what teachers ask them to do at home are one indicator of their treatment by the schools. The next two sections explore teachers' evaluations of single and married parents' abilities to conduct the requested activities and the quality of the homework that their children do.

TEACHERS' REPORTS OF SINGLE AND MARRIED PARENTS' HELPFULNESS AND FOLLOW-THROUGH

Parents' marital status is believed to influence teachers' opinions of parents and their children. Teachers were asked to rate the helpfulness and follow-through on home-learning activities of the parents of each student and the quality of homework completed by each student. In contrast to the laboratory study of Santrock and Tracy (1978), which asked teachers to rate hypothetical children from one- and two-parent homes, our questions were designed *not* to call teachers' attention to the students' living arrangements when the teachers rated parents and students. We were interested in whether, in a natural environment, teachers' evaluations were affected by parent marital status (identified by the parent) or other family characteristics and practices. It is likely that elementary school teachers are aware of family living arrangements from information provided by parents on emergency cards each year, from informal exchanges with parents or children about their families, or from discussions with other teachers. However, our method for collecting information did not ask teachers to base their evaluations on the explicit criteria of the children's living arrangements.

Table 3.16 presents teachers' evaluations of the quality of involvement of single and married parents. The ratings of parent helpfulness and follow-through on learning activities at home ranged from +1 to –1, with a mean of .18 and a standard deviation of .70, indicating that, on average, parents were perceived as neither particularly helpful nor inept, but more were helpful (35 percent) than not (17 percent). The comparisons in the first column of Table 3.16 show that teachers rated married parents significantly higher than single parents on helpfulness and follow-through on home-learning activities. The second column shows that better-educated single and married parents received higher ratings from teachers on helpfulness. The difference in ratings was significant between low- versus high-educated married parents (.267 vs. .437) and single versus married high-educated parents (.302 vs. .437).

The third column offers important information about how teachers' practices affected their evaluations of parents' helpfulness. Teachers who were leaders in the use of parent involvement practices rated single, less-educated parents significantly higher in helpfulness and follow-through at home than did teachers who were not leaders in parent involvement (.366 vs. .102). The same pattern appeared for teachers' ratings of single, high-educated parents (.483 vs. .234). Less-educated married parents were considered less responsible assistants than more-educated married parents, regardless of the teachers' leadership in the use of parent involvement.

If we had not included teachers' practices in our comparisons, we would conclude that, regardless of education, teachers rate single parents as less cooperative and less reliable than married parents in assisting their children at home. What we see instead is that teachers' own practices of parent involvement influence their ratings of the quality of parental assistance. Teachers' frequent use of parent involvement practices reduces or eliminates the teachers' differential evaluations of single and married parents.

Table 3.17 presents the results of the initial and the better specified models. The regression analyses summarized in the table show, as did the previous tables of simple mean scores, that there are significant independent effects of marital status, parents' education, and teacher leadership in parent involvement on teachers' ratings of their students' parents on helpfulness and follow-through at home. Although each variable has significant, independent effects, the three-variable model explains only 4 percent of the variance in teachers' reports of parent helpfulness.

On the second line of the table, other measures of family, student, and teacher characteristics that have been found important in other research on family-school connections are added to the basic model. These variables increase the explained variance to 23 percent. Most dramatically, student achievement levels and behav-

TABLE 3.16 Teachers' Estimates of the Quality of Parents' Responses to Requests for Involvement (Means, Standard Deviations, and Test Statistics from Multiple Comparisons of Mean Scores of Single vs. Married, Low- vs. High-Educated Parents and Parents of Children in Classrooms of Confirmed Leader vs. Nonleader Teacher in Parent Involvement)

	Family Structure		Parent Education[a]		Teacher Leadership in Parent Involvement		Other Significant Comparison of Means
Teachers' estimates of parents' helpfulness	Single parent	$\bar{x}$ = .227, s.d. = .712, N = (255)	Low	$\bar{x}$ = .174, s.d. = .733, N = (149)	Confirmed leader	$\bar{x}$ = .366*, s.d. = .733, N = (41)	Single vs. married, low education ($\bar{x}$ = .302 vs. .437*)
					Nonleader	$\bar{x}$ = .102, s.d. = .723, N = (108)	Single vs. married, low education in nonleader classroom ($\bar{x}$ = .102 vs. .260*)
			High	$\bar{x}$ = .302, s.d. = .679, N = (106)	Confirmed leader	$\bar{x}$ = .483*, s.d. = .738, N = (29)	Single vs. married, high education in nonleader classroom ($\bar{x}$ = .234 vs. .436*)
					Nonleader	$\bar{x}$ = .234, s.d. = .647, N = (77)	Low vs. high education, married, in nonleader classroom ($\bar{x}$ = .260 vs. .436*)
	Married parent	$\bar{x}$ = .346*, s.d. = .660, N = (813)	Low	$\bar{x}$ = .267*, s.d. = .693, N = (438)	Confirmed leader	$\bar{x}$ = .291, s.d. = .736, N = (103)	
					Nonleader	$\bar{x}$ = .260, s.d. = .680, N = (335)	
			High	$\bar{x}$ = .437*, s.d. = .608, N = (375)	Confirmed leader	$\bar{x}$ = .444, s.d. = .690, N = (63)	
					Nonleader	$\bar{x}$ = .436, s.d. = .591, N = (312)	

a Parent education is high if the respondent attended or graduated from post-secondary school; low if parent attended or graduated from high school only.

* T-test significant at or beyond the .05 level.

TABLE 3.17 Effects of Measures of Family, Student, and Teacher Characteristics on Teachers' Reports about Parent Helpfulness and Follow-Through on Learning Activities at Home

	FAMSTR[a,b]	PARED	TCHLDR	PARWORK	RACE	SEX	ACH	DISC	GRADE	YEARST	TQUAL	PARCOMF	TKNOCH	TALKHLP	R^2
Initial model	.072*[b]	.131*	.135*												.039
Full model	.042	.049*	.136*	.014	-.034*	-.044	-.343	.205	-.099*	.104	-.009*	.041*	.029*	.056*	.226
	(.081)[c]	(.131)	(.121)	(.027)	(.039)	(-.025)	(.365)	(-.256)	(-.079)	(.079)	(.051)	(.092)	(.069)	(.050)	

a Variables are FAMSTR = one- or two-parent homes; PARED = schooling from less than high school (0) to graduate school (5); TCHLDR = teacher's leadership or lack of parent involvement confirmed by principal (0–4); PARWORK = no work (0) or work (1) outside home by parent; RACE = black (0) or white (1); SEX = male (0) or female (1); DISC = low (–1) or high (+1) discipline problems; ACH = reading and math skills ranked by teacher (0–6); DISC = low (–1) or high (+1) discipline problems; GRADE = student's grade in school management (0–4); PARCOMF = parent feeling comfortable and welcome at school (1–4); TKNOCH = parent report that teacher knows child's individual learning needs (1–4); TALKHLP = teacher talked to parent about how to help child at home (0/1). The outcome "parents' reports" refers to the number and frequency of teacher requests for up to 12 techniques to involve parents in learning activities at home.

b Standardized regression coefficients are reported. N = 1,135.

c Zero-order correlations are in parentheses.

* Indicates coefficient is significant at or beyond the .01 level.

ior *in school* affect how teachers evaluate the students' parents. Teachers rate parents more positively if their children are high achievers or well behaved in school. Children may be successful in school because their parents help them at home, parents may give more help to children who are good students and easy to assist, or good students may be assumed by teachers to have good parents as part of a school/home "halo" effect.

Teachers of younger children and more experienced teachers tend to rate parents higher in helpfulness and follow-through than do other teachers. Teachers of the lower elementary grades tend to use more parent involvement techniques, and more experienced teachers may be more aware and appreciative of how the efforts of parents supplement the efforts of teachers (Becker and Epstein, 1982a, b). Although race was not an important variable overall for explaining teachers' ratings of parent helpfulness, separate analyses of black and white parents revealed that marital status remained a modest but significant influence on the teachers' ratings of white parents but not of black parents. White, single parents were rated lower in helpfulness and follow-through than white, married parents, with all other variables in the model statistically controlled. White, single parents may be the most distinct group in terms of their marital status because proportionately more white than black parents are married.

These analyses show that it is mainly the characteristics and needs of students—not the simple category of parental marital status—that best explain teachers' evaluations of parents. However, teachers' leadership remained an important influence on their ratings of parents, even after all other variables were statistically taken into account. Teachers who frequently use parent involvement techniques in their regular teaching practice acknowledge the help they receive and view single and married parents in a more positive light than do other teachers. When teachers involve parents in their children's schoolwork on a regular basis, creating more family and school "overlap," they tend to report that the amount and quality of help from single parents is comparable to that of married parents. When teachers use frequent activities as part of their teaching practice, they help parents build better skills to assist their children at home. At the same time, these activities may help teachers develop more positive expectations and appreciation of parents. Teachers who keep schools and families more separate and do not make parents part of their regular teaching practice tend to promote the stereotype of single parents. They rate single parents' assistance and follow-through on learning activities at home lower in quality and quantity than that provided by married parents.

TEACHERS' REPORTS OF THE QUALITY OF HOMEWORK BY CHILDREN FROM ONE- AND TWO-PARENT HOMES

Teachers were asked to rate the quality of homework completed by each of their students. Researchers identified the children from one- and two-parent homes from data provided by parents. Teachers identified the students who were homework "stars" and homework "problems." Scores on the quality of homework ranged from +1 to –1, with a mean of –.01 and a standard deviation of .64, indicating that, on average, students were neither particularly outstanding nor inferior, with about equal numbers of homework stars (20 percent) and homework problems (21 percent). Teachers' ratings of children's homework are shown in Table 3.18 according to children's living arrangements in one- or two-parent homes, parents' education, and their teachers' leadership in the use of parent involvement.

The first column of Table 3.18 shows that students from two-parent homes were more often rated as "homework stars" and were less often viewed as "homework problems" than were students from one-parent homes. The measures in the second column show that these ratings were linked to parent education. Children whose mothers had little formal education were rated lower in the quality of their homework than other children in one-parent homes (.057 vs. –.101 for more- vs. less-educated mothers) and in two-parent homes (.157 vs. .050). Family socioeconomic status in column 2 of Table 3.18 helps to explain teachers' evaluations of children in one- and two-parent homes, as has been reported before (Barton, 1981; Laosa and Sigel, 1982; Scott-Jones, 1983).

Teachers' practices of parent involvement are taken into account in column 3 of the table. Teachers who were *not leaders* in parent involvement held significantly lower opinions of the quality of homework of children from single-parent homes than of those from married-parent homes, at both levels of parent education. The results suggest that children from less-educated, single-parent families face disadvantages in school that may be exacerbated by teachers' lack of leadership in organizing parent involvement in learning activities at home.

If estimates of homework quality reflect student achievement in general, children from one- and two-parent homes in teacher-leader classrooms should have more similar grades and achievement test scores, after other important characteristics are taken into account. In classrooms of teachers who are *not leaders* in parent involvement, children from one-parent homes may do less well than children from two-parent homes in their report card grades and other school achievements.

The regression analyses in Table 3.19 show how teachers' ratings of the quality of students' homework are influenced by other parent, teacher, and student characteristics. On the first line of the table, the familiar three-variable model shows that marital status and parent education have significant independent effects on teacher ratings of student homework. Students from one-parent homes or whose parents have less education are given lower ratings on homework quality. Teacher leadership in parent involvement is not a significant independent influence on teachers' ratings of students, after the other variables are accounted for. The basic model, however, explains only 2 percent of the variance in teacher ratings of student homework.

The second line of Table 3.19 shows that 24 percent of the variance in teacher ratings of student homework is explained by other measures. The most important variables are the work students do in class and their classroom behavior. Brighter students—whatever their behavior or other characteristics—were rated higher on

TABLE 3.18 Teachers' Estimates of the Quality of Children's Homework Completion (Means, Standard Deviations, and Test Statistics from Multiple Comparisons of Mean Scores by Family Structure, Family Education, and Teacher Leadership in Parent Involvement)

Teachers' estimates of students' homework completion

Family Structure			Parent Education[a]			Teacher Leadership in Parent Involvement			Other Significant Comparison of Means
Single parent	x̄	-.035	Low	x̄	-.101	Confirmed leader	x̄	.073*	Single vs. married, low education (x̄ = .101 vs. .050*)
	s.d.	.604		s.d.	.601		s.d.	.648	
	N	(255)		N	(149)		N	(41)	
						Nonleader	x̄	-.167	Single vs. married, low education in nonleader classroom (x̄ = -.167 vs. .045*)
							s.d.	.572	
							N	(108)	
			High	x̄	.057*	Confirmed leader	x̄	.207*	
				s.d.	.599		s.d.	.620	
				N	(106)		N	(29)	
						Nonleader	x̄	.001	
							s.d.	.585	
							N	(77)	
Married parent	x̄	.346*	Low	x̄	.050*	Confirmed leader	x̄	.068	
	s.d.	.660		s.d.	.640		s.d.	.630	
	N	(813)		N	(438)		N	(103)	
						Nonleader	x̄	.045	
							s.d.	.644	
							N	(335)	
			High	x̄	.157*	Confirmed leader	x̄	.254	
				s.d.	.589		s.d.	.595	
				N	(375)		N	(63)	
						Nonleader	x̄	.138	
							s.d.	.587	
							N	(312)	

a Parent education is high if the respondent attended or graduated from post-secondary school; low if parent attended or graduated from high school only.

* T-test significant at or beyond the .05 level.

193

TABLE 3.19   Effects of Family, Student, and Teacher Characteristics on Teacher's Ratings of Children on Their Homework Completion

	FAMSTR[a]	PARED	TCHLDR	PARWORK	RACE	SEX	ACH	DISC	GRADE	YEARST	TQUAL	PARCOMF	TKNOCH	TALKHLP	R^2
Initial model	.085*[b]	.106*	.039												.021
Full model	.068*	.022	.042	-.024	-.107*	.058	.392*	.183*	-.007*	.050*	-.038	-.024	.058*	.055*	.236
	(.097)[c]	(.114)	(.026)	(-.005)	(.007)	(.132)	(.412)	(-.259)	(.001)	(.035)	(.021)	(-.005)	(.105)	(.018)	

a Variables are FAMSTR = one- or two-parent homes; PARED = schooling from less than high school (0) to graduate school (5); TCHLDR = teacher's leadership or lack of parent involvement confirmed by principal (0–4); PARWORK = no work (0) or work (1) outside home by parent; RACE = black (0) or white (1); SEX = male (0) or female (1); ACH = reading and math skills ranked by teacher (0–6); DISC = low (–1) or high (+1) discipline problems; GRADE = student's grade in school management (0–4); PARCOMF = parent feeling comfortable and welcome at school (1–4); TKNOCH = parent report that teacher knows child's individual learning needs (1–4); TALKHLP = teacher talked to parent about how to help child at home (0/1). The outcome "parents' reports" refers to the number and frequency of teacher requests for up to 12 techniques to involve parents in learning activities at home.

b Standardized regression coefficients are reported. N = 1,135.

c Zero-order correlations are in parentheses.

* Indicates coefficient is significant at or beyond the .01 level.

the quality of their homework, and well-behaved students—whatever their ability or other characteristics—were given higher ratings on homework quality. Black students were rated significantly higher in homework quality, after achievement level and behavior were taken into account. Even with these highly influential variables taken into account, the quality of homework of students from two-parent homes was still rated slightly higher by some teachers than that of students from one-parent homes.

Several researchers have questioned whether teachers base children's grades and other ratings on criteria other than performance and whether their ratings reflect bias against children from single-parent homes (Barton, 1981; Boyd and Parish, 1985; Hammond, 1979; Lightfoot, 1978). Our data show that teachers base their judgments about the quality of children's homework mainly on the performance of the children, rather than on other unrelated criteria. There is little bias evident against children in one-parent homes. When they do occur, biased reports are more likely by teachers who have less contact with parents. If teachers do not ask for and guide parent involvement, single parents and their children are assumed to be less qualified than married parents and their children.

The simple lines of inquiry in Tables 3.14, 3.16, and 3.18 suggest that there may be important statistical interactions of marital status, parent education, and teachers' leadership in parent involvement in their effects on school and family communications. For example, when we graph the mean scores in these tables (not shown here), we see that *teacher leadership* matters more in determining teachers' ratings of single parents' helpfulness and follow-through on learning activities with their children at home and on their ratings of the homework quality of children in one-parent homes. *Parent education* matters more for married parents on how teachers rate parents' helpfulness and children's homework. New research is needed on the consequences for student learning of these potentially important interactions.

The full models in Tables 3.15, 3.17, and 3.19 reveal other important patterns. Parents' reports of teachers' practices of parent involvement are influenced by several characteristics of students, teachers, parents, and family-school communications. Teachers' reports of parents are influenced especially by the teachers' interactions with the child in school. It often is said that children are reflections of their parents, but it also seems to work the other way. Parents are evaluated, in part, on the basis of their children's success and behavior in school. Teachers' reports of children are mainly determined by the children's schoolwork. However, even after achievement level is taken into account, some teachers report that children from one-parent homes have more trouble completing homework than do children from two-parent homes. The analyses show clearly that the ratings that parents and teachers give each other are significantly affected by teachers' philosophies and practices of parent involvement.

On a related theme, in the full model we also found that whether or not mothers worked outside the home had no important effect on parents' reports about teachers, teachers' reports about parents, or teachers' reports about the quality of children's homework.

PARENTS' AWARENESS, KNOWLEDGE, AND EVALUATIONS OF TEACHERS

Are single and married parents equally aware of their children's instructional program? Is marital status an important variable for explaining parental receptivity to teachers' requests to help their children? Epstein (1986) shows that teachers' practices influenced parental reactions to their children's teachers and schools. In this reading, we examine whether single and married parents react differently to teachers' efforts to involve and inform parents. The exploration of previous analyses shows that marital status had no significant effect on whether parents think the child's teacher works hard to get parents "interested and excited about helping at home." Rather, frequent experience with teachers' requests to become involved in learning activities at home had a strong effect on parent awareness of the teacher's efforts. Other variables—less formal education of parents, parents' belief that teachers know the individual needs of their children, and teachers' direct conversations with parents about helping their own child at home—also had significant, independent effects on parents' awareness of teachers' efforts to involve parents.

Similarly, teachers' frequent requests for parent involvement in learning activities at home—not marital status—had strong effects on single and married parents' reports that they get many ideas from teachers about how to help at home; the teacher thinks parents should help at home; they know more about the child's instructional program than they did in previous years; and the teacher has positive interpersonal skills and high teaching quality.

OTHER REPORTS ABOUT SCHOOL FROM SINGLE AND MARRIED PARENTS

Other data collected from parents also help explain some of the results reported in the previous tables.

Single parents reported significantly more often than married parents that they spent more time assisting their children with homework but still did not have the "time and energy" to do what they believed the teacher expected. Single parents felt more pressure from teachers to become involved in their children's learning activities. It may be that their children required or demanded more attention or needed more help to stay on grade level. Or it may be that parents who were separated, divorced, or never married felt keenly their responsibility for their children and the demands on their time. Single parents divide their time among many responsibilities for family, work, and leisure that are shared in many two-parent homes (Glasser and Navarre, 1965; Shinn, 1978).

Requests from teachers for parents to help with home-learning activities may make more of an impression on and may be more stressful for single parents (McAdoo, 1981). Our data show, however, that single parents respond successfully to teachers who involve all parents as part of their regular teaching practice. Like other parents, single parents who were frequently involved by the teacher felt that they increased their knowledge about the child's instructional program. Indeed, teachers who organize and guide home-learning activities may especially help single parents make efficient and effective use of often limited time. When teachers convey uniform expectations and guidance for involvement by all parents, single parents receive an important message about their continuing responsibility in their children's education.

Married parents spent significantly more days in the school as volunteers, as classroom helpers, and at PTA meetings than did single parents. Teachers may be more positive toward parents whom they meet and work with in the school building and classroom. These positive feelings may influence some teachers' ratings of the quality of parental assistance at home. An important fact, however, is that the teacher-leaders—whose philosophy and practices emphasized parent involvement at home—did *not* give significantly lower ratings to single parents or less-educated parents on their helpfulness or follow-through on home-learning activities, despite those parents' lower involvement at the school building. Because many single parents work full- or part-time during the school day or have other demands on their time that keep them away from school, it is important for teachers to emphasize practices that involve all parents with their children's education at home. If all involvement occurs during school hours, single parents and working parents are excluded from school activities.

There were several measures on which there were no significant differences in the reports of single and married parents. Some common beliefs about single and married parents were not supported statistically. For example, single and married parents gave similar evaluations of the overall quality of their children's teachers, the extent to which the teacher shares the parents' goals for their child, their child's eagerness to talk about school, their child's level of tenseness about homework activities, the appropriateness of the amount and kinds of homework that their children's teachers assigned, and the frequency of most communications (e.g., notes, phone calls, and memos) from the school to the home. These findings support Snow's (1982) conclusion that single and married parents had similar contacts with teachers and similar evaluations of teachers, and that socioeconomic status was more predictive than marital status of parents' contacts with teachers. We show, however, that the SES is not the most important variable. Rather, school and family communications of several types reduce or eliminate the importance of marital status and SES.

Marital status is not significantly related to the severity of discipline problems in class. The belief that children from one-parent homes tend to be disruptive in school may be one of the "myths" that has been perpetuated from earlier studies based on "special problem" populations and from studies that did not include measures of student, family, and teacher characteristics and practices—all of which are more important influences than marital status on children's classroom behavior. In our study, children's disciplinary problems in the classroom are significantly correlated negatively with gender $(r = -.262)$, academic achievement $(r = -.147)$, and whether the child likes to talk about school at home $(r = -.124)$, as might be expected. Male students, low-achieving students, and those who do not like to talk about school or homework with their parents are more likely than other students to be disciplinary problems in class. But parents' marital status is not significantly associated with behavior problems in class $(r = -.056)$.

Marital status is not correlated with parents' willingness to help at home, feeling welcome at the school, or reports that someone at home reads regularly with the child. Indeed, single *and* married parents are remarkably positive about the general quality of their children's elementary schools and teachers (see Epstein, 1986). As in earlier reports by Eiduson (1982), Keniston et al. (1977), and Sanick and Maudlin (1986), our survey shows that, like married parents, single parents are concerned about their children's education, work with their children, and are generally positive about their children's elementary schools and teachers.

SUMMARY AND DISCUSSION

Researchers have contributed three types of information on single parents. First, *descriptive reports* offer statistics about single parents and their children. Many reports have focused on the dramatic increase over the years in the prevalence of single parents; the number of children in single-parent homes; racial differences in marital patterns; and the economic disparities of single- versus two-parent homes, especially single-mother homes versus other family arrangements (Bane, 1976; Cherlin, 1981; Newberger, Melnicoe, and Newberger, 1986; Weitzman, 1985). It is important to continue to document and monitor the trends in separation and divorce, the numbers of children affected, and the emergence and increase of special cases such as teenage single parents (Mott Foundation, 1981) and never-married parents (U.S. Bureau of the Census, 1982).

Second, *analytic studies* of the effects of family structure on children or parents go beyond descriptive statistics to consider family conditions and processes that affect family members. Research of this type has measured a range of family-life variables, such as socioeconomic status, family history, family practices, and attitudes such as parental commitment to their children (Adams, 1982; Bane, 1976; Epstein, 1983; Furstenburg, Nord, Peterson, and Zill, 1983; Marjoribanks, 1979; Svanum, Bringle, and McLaughlin, 1982; Zill, 1983). These studies increase our understanding of the dynamics of family life under different social and economic conditions.

Third, *integrative, ecological studies* of the effects of family structure on children and parents go beyond the boundaries of family conditions to include other institutions that affect family members (Bronfenbrenner, 1979; Epstein, 1987; Leichter, 1974; Litwak and Meyer, 1974; Santrock and Tracy, 1978). These studies show that effects of family structure are, in large part, explained by other variables, including teachers' practices of parent involvement and other measures of family and school interaction.

The present study contributes new knowledge based on data from parents and teachers about single parents and their children's schools.

1. Single parents are not a single group. Single parents are highly diverse in their education, family size, family resources, occupational status, confidence in their ability to help their children, and other family practices that concern their children. The diversity in single-parent homes means that we cannot fully understand families by measuring only the simple category of marital status.

2. There is diversity in teachers' practices that concern families. Some teachers' philosophies and practices lead them toward more positive attitudes about single parents and about how all parents can assist the teacher as knowledgeable partners in their children's education. Some teachers' practices exemplify the theory that families and schools are overlapping spheres of influence for children, whereas other teachers' practices exemplify the belief that families and schools are better off when teachers and parents conduct separate and different activities.

Some teachers involve all or most parents successfully. Other teachers demand more but expect less of single parents and their children. Single parents' abilities to help their children may be affected by the teachers' abilities to inform and direct parents about productive activities for parent involvement at home.

Santrock and Tracy (1978) found that teachers rated hypothetical children from two-parent homes higher on positive traits and lower on negative traits than children from one-parent homes. Levine (1982) reported that teachers had lower expectations for children from one-parent homes. In actual school settings, we found that teachers differed in their evaluations of children from one- and two-parent homes. Teachers tend to rate children from one-parent homes lower on the quality of their homework, and teachers who were not leaders made even greater distinctions between children from one- and two-parent homes.

3. Teacher leadership, not parent marital status, influenced parents' knowledge about the school program and the teachers' efforts. Single and married parents whose children were in the classrooms of teachers who were leaders in parent involvement were more aware of teachers' efforts in parent involvement, improved their understanding of their children's school programs, and rated teachers' interpersonal and teaching skills higher than did parents of children in other teachers' classrooms. Evidence has been accumulating in many studies that daily practices are more important than static measures of family structure for understanding children's experiences. This has often been interpreted to refer to practices that parents might conduct on their own. However, parent involvement in school is not the parents' responsibility alone. Contexts influence practice. Kriesberg (1967) found a neighborhood effect on parents' practices. He noted that disadvantaged single mothers in middle-class neighborhoods gave more educational support to their children than similar mothers in poor neighborhoods. Our study reports a school effect on parents' practices. Teachers' practices that support and guide parents boost the involvement of all parents, including single parents—the same parents that other teachers believe cannot or will not help their children.

4. Research on single parents and their children must include measures of family and school structure and processes that affect the interactions of parents, teachers, and students. Marital status will look more important than it is unless studies include measures of teachers' practices. In this study, teachers' approaches to parent involvement; other teacher, parent, and student characteristics; and specific family-school communications were more important and more manipulable variables than marital status or mother's education for explaining parents' and teachers' evaluations of each other. Studies of school and family connections must go beyond simple structural labels such as marital status and education and include measures of the practices and attitudes of parents, teachers, and students. During the school years, it is necessary to measure the characteristics of all overlapping institutions that influence student behavior and particularly the family and the school. This is especially true for particular outcomes such as student learning and development or parental understanding and practices concerning their children as students.

5. Schools' interactions with families need to change because families are changing. Teachers must consider how they perceive and interact with single parents to minimize bias and maximize the support that all parents give their children. Family members may recover relatively rapidly from the disruption caused by divorce or separation (Bane, 1976; Hetherington, Cox, and Cox, 1978; Zill, 1983). But teachers who favor traditional families may have difficulty dealing with families who differ from their "ideal." Some administrators and teachers still consider the primary, two-parent family as the model by which other families should be judged (Bernard, 1984). The primary family—two natural parents and their children—may be an ideal type, but it is no longer the "typical" family for all school-aged children. In 1980, 63 percent of white children and 27 percent of black children lived in primary families; 14 percent of all white children and 43 percent of all black children lived in one-parent homes with their mothers.[2] Most of the others lived in "blended" families in which at least one parent had remarried (Hernandez and Meyers, 1986). Demographic trends indicate that the one-parent home will be "the new norm" because over half of all children will live in a one-parent home for some of their school years. During that time, teachers' practices to assist and involve all parents can help reduce single parents' stress about their children's well-being and help children's learning and attitudes about school and homework.

Schools need to change their understanding of single parents to better meet the parents' concerns and children's needs. Most suggestions about how the school should assist single parents and their children focus on providing psychological services, family therapy, discussion groups, or individual counseling for children who experience divorce in their families (Brown, 1980). Although discussion or therapy sessions may help children adjust to family disruptions, this study suggests that a more important general direction is to assist all parents in how to help their children at home in ways that will improve their children's success in school. This includes helping parents make productive use of small amounts of time at home for school-related skills, activities, and decisions.

School policies and practices can minimize or exaggerate the importance of family structure. Although school practices cannot solve the serious social and economic problems that single parents often face, our data show that teachers play a pivotal role in the lives of children from one-parent homes and in their parents' lives as well.

---

[2] In 1999, 77 percent of white children, 35 percent of black children, and 63 percent of Hispanic children lived in two-parent homes (Federal Interagency Forum, 2000).

REFERENCES

Adams, B. (1982). Conceptual and policy issues in the study of family socialization in the United States. Paper presented at the annual meeting of the American Educational Research Association, New York.

Baker, D. P., and D. L. Stevenson. (1986). Mothers' strategies for children's school achievement: Managing the transition to high school. *Sociology of Education* 59: 156–166.

Bane, M. J. (1976). *Here to stay: American families in the twentieth century.* New York: Basic Books.

Barton, W. A. (1981). The effects of one-parentness on student achievement. Ph.D. diss., Pennsylvania State University.

Becker, H. J., and J. L. Epstein. (1982a). Parent involvement: A study of teacher practices. *Elementary School Journal* 83: 85–102. (Reading 3.1).

———. (1982b). *Influences on teachers' use of parent involvement.* Report 324. Baltimore: Johns Hopkins University Center for Social Organization of Schools.

Bernard, J. M. (1984). Divorced families and the schools. Pages 91–101 in *Family therapy with school related problems,* edited by J. H. Cansen. Rockville, MD: Aspen Systems Corporation.

Blanchard, R. W., and H. B. Biller. (1971). Father availability and academic performance among third-grade boys. *Developmental Psychology* 4: 301–305.

Boyd, D. A., and T. S. Parish. (1985). An examination of academic achievement in light of familial configuration. Paper presented at the annual meeting of the American Educational Research Association, Chicago.

Bronfenbrenner, U. (1979). *The ecology of human development.* Cambridge, MA: Harvard University Press.

Brown, B. F. (1980). A study of the school needs of children from one-parent families. *Phi Delta Kappan* 61: 537–540.

Carew, J., and S. L. Lightfoot. (1979). *Beyond bias: Perspectives on classrooms.* Cambridge, MA: Harvard University Press.

Cherlin, A. J. (1981). *Marriage, divorce, remarriage.* Cambridge, MA: Harvard University Press.

Clay, P. L. (1981). *Single parents and the public schools: How does the partnership work?* Columbia, MD: National Committee for Citizens in Education.

Coleman, J. S. (1974). *Power and structure in society.* New York: W. W. Norton.

Coleman, J. S., E. Q. Campbell, C. J. Hobson, J. M. McPartland, A. Mood, F. D. Weinfield, and R. L. York. (1966). *Equal educational opportunity.* Washington, DC: U.S. Government Printing Office.

Dauber, S. L., and J. L. Epstein. (1989). *Parents' attitudes and practices of involvement in inner-city elementary and middle schools.* CREMS Report 33. Baltimore: Johns Hopkins University Center for Research on Elementary and Middle Schools. (Reading 3.6)

Dokecki, P. R., and R. M. Maroney. (1983). To strengthen all families: A human development and community value framework. Pages 40–64 in *Parent education and public policy,* edited by R. Haskins and D. Adams. Norwood, NJ: Ablex.

Eiduson, B. T. (1982). Contemporary single mothers. Pages 65–76 in *Current topics in early childhood education,* edited by L. G. Katz. Norwood, NJ: Ablex.

Engan-Barker, D. (1986). Family and education: The concepts of family failure and the role it plays in national educational and family policy—A review of the literature. M.A. thesis, University of Minnesota.

Epstein, J. L. (1983). Longitudinal effects of person-family-school interactions on student outcomes. Pages 101–128 in *Research in sociology of education and socialization,* Vol. 4, edited by A. Kerckhoff. Greenwich, CT: JAI Press.

———. (1986, January). Reactions of parents to teacher practices of parent involvement. *Elementary School Journal* 87: 277–294. (Reading 3.4).

————. (1987). Toward a theory of family-school connections: Teacher practices and parent involvement across the school years. Pages 121–136 in *Social intervention: Potential and constraints,* edited by K. Hurrelmann, E. Kaufmann, and F. Losel. New York: De-Gruyter. (Reading 2.1).

————. (1989). *Schools in the center: School, family, peer, and community connections for more effective middle grade schools and students.* (Paper prepared for the Carnegie Task Force for the Education of Young Adolescents). Baltimore: Johns Hopkins University Center for Research on Elementary and Middle Schools.

————. (1990). School and family connections: Theory, research and implications for integrating sociologies of education and family. *Marriage and Family Review* 15(1/2): 96–126.

————. (1991). Effects on student achievement in reading and math of teachers' practices of parent involvement. Pages 261–276 in *Advances in reading/language research, Vol. 5: Literacy through family, community, and school interaction,* edited by S. Silvern. Greenwich, CT: JAI Press. (Reading 3.7).

Epstein, J. L., and H. J. Becker. (1982, November). Teacher reported practices of parent involvement: Problems and possibilities. *Elementary School Journal* 83: 103–113. (Reading 3.2).

Epstein, J. L., and J. M. McPartland. (1979). Authority structures. Pages 293–312 in *Educational environments and effects,* edited by H. Walberg. Berkeley, CA: McCutcheon.

Furstenburg, F. F., Jr., and J. A. Seltzer. (1983). Encountering divorce: Children's responses to family dissolution and reconstitution. Paper presented at the annual meeting of the American Sociological Association in Detroit.

Furstenburg, F. F., C. W. Nord, J. L. Peterson, and N. Zill. (1983). The life course of children of divorce: Marital disruption and parental contact. *American Sociological Review* 48: 656–668.

Garbarino, J. (1982). *Children and families in the social environment.* New York: Aldine.

Garfinkle, I., and S. S. McLanahan. (1986). *Single mothers and their children: A new American dilemma.* Washington, DC: Urban Institute Press.

Glasser, P., and E. Navarre. (1965). Structural problems of the one parent family. *Journal of Social Issues* 21: 98–109.

Glick, P. C. (1979). Children of divorced parents in demographic perspectives. *Journal of Social Issues* 35: 170–182.

Guidubaldi, J., and J. D. Perry. (1984). Divorce, socioeconomic status, and children's cognitive social competence at school entry. *American Journal of Orthopsychiatry* 54: 459.

Hammond, J. M. (1979, November). A comparison of elementary children from divorced and intact families. *Phi Delta Kappan* 61: 219.

Hanson, S. L., and A. Ginsburg. (1986). *Gaining ground: Values and high school success.* Washington, DC: Decision Resources Corporation.

Hernandez, D. J., and D. E. Myers. (1986). Children and their extended families since World War II. Paper presented at the annual meeting of the Population Association of America in San Francisco.

Hetherington, E. M., and K. A. Camara. (1984). Families in transition: The process of dissolution and reconstitution. Pages 398–440 in *Review of child development research: Volume 7,* edited by R. D. Parke. Chicago: University of Chicago Press.

Hetherington, E. M., K. A. Camara, and D. L. Featherman. (1981). *Cognitive performance, school learning, and achievement of children for one parent households.* Washington, DC: National Institute of Education.

Hetherington, E. M., M. Cox, and R. Cox. (1978). The aftermath of divorce. Pages 149–176 in *Mother-child, father-child relations,* edited by J. H. Stevens Jr. and M. Matthews. Washington, DC: National Association for the Education of Young Children.

Kamerman, S. B., and C. D. Hayes. (1982). *Families that work: Children in a changing world.* Washington, DC: National Academy Press.

Kelly, F. J., J. North, and H. Zingle. (1965). The relation of the broken home to subsequent school behaviors. *Alberta Journal of Educational Research* 11: 215–219.

Keniston, K., and the Carnegie Council on Children. (1977). *All our children: The American family under pressure.* New York: Harcourt Brace Jovanovich.

Kriesberg, L. (1967). Rearing children for educational achievement in fatherless families. *Journal of Marriage and the Family* 29: 288–301.

Kurdek, L. A., and D. Blisk. (1983). Dimensions and correlates of mothers' divorce experiences. *Journal of Divorce* 6: 1–24.

Laosa, L. M. (1983). Parent education, cultural pluralism, and public policy. Pages 331–345 in *Parent education and public policy,* edited by R. Haskins and D. Adams. Norwood, NJ: Ablex.

Laosa, L. M., and I. E. Sigel. (1982). *Families as learning environments for children.* New York: Plenum Press.

Leichter, Hope Jensen, ed. (1974). *The family as educator.* New York: Teachers College Press.

Leler, H. (1983). Parent education and involvement in relation to the schools and to parents of school-aged children. Pages 114–180 in *Parent education and public policy,* edited by R. Haskins and D. Adams. Norwood, NJ: Ablex.

Levine, E. R. (1982). What teachers expect of children from single parent families. Paper presented at the annual meeting of the American Educational Research Association, April, in New York.

Lightfoot, S. L. (1978). *Worlds apart: Relationships between families and schools.* New York: Basic Books.

Litwak, E., and H. J. Meyer. (1974). *School, family, and neighborhood: The theory and practice of school-community relations.* New York: Columbia University Press.

Marjoribanks, K. (1979). *Families and their learning environments: An empirical analysis.* London: Routledge & Kegan Paul.

Marotz-Bader, R., G. R. Adams, N. Bueche, B. Munro, and G. Munro. (1979). Family form or family process? Reconsidering the deficit family model approach. *Family Coordinator* 28: 5–14.

Masnick, G., and M. J. Bane. (1980). *The nation's families: 1960–1990.* Cambridge, MA: Joint Center for Urban Studies of MIT and Harvard University.

McAdoo, H. (1981). Levels of stress in single black employed mothers of school-aged children. Washington, DC: Howard University. Mimeographed.

McDill, E. L., and L. Rigsby. (1973). *Structure and process in secondary schools: The academic impact of educational climates.* Baltimore: Johns Hopkins University Press.

Milne, A., D. Myers, A. Rosenthal, and A. Ginsburg. (1986). Working mothers and the educational achievement of school children. *Sociology of Education* 59: 125–139.

Mott Foundation. (1981). *Teenage pregnancy: A critical family issue.* Flint, MI: The Charles Stewart Mott Foundation.

National Public Radio (NPR). (1980, November). *Single parent families,* Parts 1–4, programs 272–275. Washington, DC: National Public Radio.

Newberger, C. M., L. H. Melnicoe, and E. H. Newberger. (1986). The American family in crisis: Implications for children. *Current Problems in Pediatrics, Volume 16, Number 12.* Chicago: Yearbook Medical Publishers.

Ogbu, J. V. (1974). *The next generation: An ethnology of education in an urban neighborhood.* New York: Academic Press.

Parsons, T. (1959). The school class as a social system: Some of its functions in American society. *Harvard Educational Review* 29: 297–318.

Sanick, M. M., and T. Maudlin. (1986). Single vs. 2-parent families: A comparison of mothers' time. *Family Relations* 35: 53.

Santrock, J. W., and R. L. Tracy. (1978). Effects of children's family structure on the development of stereotypes by teachers. *Journal of Educational Psychology* 20: 754–757.

Scott-Jones, D. (1983). One-parent families and their children's achievement. Pittsburgh: University of Pittsburgh. Mimeographed.

Sewell, W. H., and R. M. Hauser. (1975). *Occupation and earnings: Achievement in the early career.* New York: Academic Press.

Shinn, M. (1978). Father absence and children's cognitive development. *Psychological Bulletin* 85: 295–324.

Snow, M. B. (1982). *Characteristics of families with special needs in relation to school.* AEL Report Series. Charleston, WV: Appalachian Educational Laboratory.

Svanum, S., R. G. Bringle, and J. E. McLaughlin. (1982). Father absence and cognitive performance on a large sample of six-to-eleven-year old children. *Child Development* 53: 136–143.

U.S. Bureau of the Census. (1982). *Marital status and living arrangements: March 1982.* Current Population Report Series. Washington, DC: U.S. Government Printing Office.

U.S. House of Representatives. (1986, June 17). *Divorce: A fact sheet.* Washington, DC: Select Committee on Children, Youth, and Families.

Waller, W. (1932). *The sociology of teaching.* New York: Russell and Russell.

Weber, M. (1947). *The theory of social and economic organization.* New York: Oxford University Press.

Weitzman, L. (1985). *The divorce revolution: The unexpected social and economic consequences for women and children in America.* New York: Free Press.

Zajonc, R. (1976). Family configuration and intelligence. *Science* 192: 227–236.

Zill, N. (1983). Perspectives: Mental health of school children from single-parent families. Paper presented at the National Conference of Single Parents and the Schools, March, in Washington, DC.

Parents' Attitudes and Practices of Involvement in Inner-City Elementary and Middle Schools*

Parent involvement—or school and family connections—is a component of effective schools that deserves special consideration because it contributes to successful family environments and more successful students. Research conducted for nearly 25 years has shown convincingly that parent involvement is important for children's learning, attitudes about school, and aspirations. Children are more successful students at all grade levels if their parents participate at school and encourage education and learning at home, whatever the educational background or social class of their parents.

Most research on parent involvement has focused on parents who become involved on their own, without connecting parents' actions to the practices of their children's teachers. Some research on parent involvement conducted in the late 1980s asks more crucial questions by focusing on the actions of the schools: Can schools successfully involve all parents in their children's education, especially those parents who would not become involved on their own? How can schools involve parents whose children are at risk of failing in school? If schools involve all parents in important ways, are there measurable benefits to students, parents, and teaching practice?

From research we have learned that schools' programs and teachers' practices to involve parents have important positive effects on parents' abilities to help their children across the grades; on parents' ratings of teachers' skills and teaching quality; on teachers' opinions about parents' abilities to help their children with schoolwork at home; on students' attitudes about school, homework, and the similarity of their school and family; and on students' reading achievement (Becker and Epstein, 1982 [Reading 3.1]; Epstein, 1982 [Reading 3.9], 1986 [Reading 3.4], 1991 [Reading 3.7]; Epstein and Dauber, 1991 [Reading 3.3]).

However, few studies have focused on schools with large populations of educationally disadvantaged students or hard-to-reach parents (Epstein, 1988b). A recurring theme in some studies is that less-educated parents do not want to or cannot become involved in their children's education (Baker and Stevenson, 1986;

* By Susan L. Dauber and Joyce L. Epstein. The research was supported by grants from the U.S. Department of Education, Office of Educational Research and Improvement (OERI), and by a National Science Foundation Graduate Fellowship to the first author. The opinions expressed do not necessarily reflect the position or policy of the OERI or the NSF, and no official endorsements should be inferred. The authors, listed alphabetically, shared responsibility for this chapter. We are grateful to the parents who participated in the survey and to the teachers and principals who conducted the survey as the first step in a school improvement process. Reprinted with permission from N. Chavkin, ed., *Families and schools in a pluralistic society* (Albany: State University of New York Press, 1993), pp. 53–71.

Lareau, 1987). However, other research challenges this assumption by showing that some teachers successfully involve parents of the most disadvantaged students in important ways (Clark, 1983; Comer, 1980; Epstein, 1990 [Reading 3.5]; Epstein and Dauber, 1991; Rich, Van Dien, and Mattox, 1979; Rubin et al., 1983; Scott-Jones, 1987).

Earlier studies of teachers and parents focused on one level of schooling, either elementary schools (see Becker and Epstein, 1982; Epstein, 1986, 1990, 1991); middle or junior high schools (Baker and Stevenson, 1986; Leitch and Tangri, 1988); or high schools (Bauch, 1988; Clark, 1983; Dornbusch and Ritter, 1988). This study used comparable data from two levels of schooling: elementary and middle grades. The study asked inner-city parents in economically disadvantaged communities how they are involved or want to be involved and how family involvement differs in the elementary and middle grades.

STUDY DESIGN

Eight Title I schools in the Baltimore area were involved in an "action research" program in cooperation with a local foundation. The Fund for Educational Excellence in Baltimore made small grants directly to schools to help teachers increase and improve parent involvement. Teacher representatives for parent involvement from the eight schools attended a two-day summer workshop on school and family connections. They helped design questionnaires for teaches and parents (Epstein and Becker, 1990) for use in each school to identify where schools are starting from on five major types of parent involvement (Epstein, 1987). The teachers were provided with small planning grants to help them distribute and collect the surveys.

Each school was given nontechnical "clinical summaries" of the data from teachers and from parents to help them understand their strengths and weaknesses in parent involvement (Epstein, 1988a; Epstein and Salinas, 1988). The schools used the data to develop action plans for improving parent involvement programs and practices. The teachers who are directing the projects are supported by small grants ($1,000) each year to cover expenses to implement and evaluate the activities they designed.

Data from 171 teachers in these schools on their attitudes and practices of parent involvement were reported in a separate paper (see Epstein and Dauber, 1991). The data from teachers showed that:

- Teachers generally agreed that parent involvement is important for student success and teacher effectiveness.
- Teachers were more sure about what they wanted from parents than about what they wanted to do for parents. Almost all teachers reported that they expected all parents to fulfill 12 responsibilities, ranging from teaching their children to behave, to knowing what children are expected to learn each year, to helping their children with homework. Few teachers, however, had comprehensive programs to help parents attain these skills.

- Elementary school practices were stronger, more positive, and more comprehensive than those in the middle grades.
- The individual teacher was a key, but not the only, factor in building strong school programs. Analyses of "discrepancy scores" showed that perceived similarities between self and principal, self and teacher-colleagues, and self and parents were significantly associated with the strength of schools' parent involvement programs. Programs and practices were stronger in schools where teachers perceived that they, their colleagues, and parents all felt strongly about the importance of parent involvement.

The reports about parent involvement from teachers in inner-city elementary and middle schools are important but tell only half the story about what is happening in any school. Data from parents are needed to understand fully where schools are starting from and their potential for improving parent involvement practices. This reading combines the data from the parents in all eight schools to study the present practices and patterns of parent involvement in inner-city elementary and middle grades. We examine parents' reports of their attitudes about their children's schools, their practices at home, their perceptions of how the schools presently involve parents, and their wishes or preferences for actions and programs by the schools.

The questionnaires included more than 75 items of information on parent attitudes toward their children's school; the school subjects that parents want to know more about; how frequently the parents are involved in different ways in their children's education; how well school programs and teacher practices inform and involve them in their children's education; what workshop topics they would select; the times of day that parents prefer meetings or conferences at school to take place; how much time their children spend on homework and whether the parents help; and background information about parents' education, work, and family size.

Parents responded in large numbers to the opportunity to give their opinions about their involvement and school practices. More than 50 percent of the parents in each school returned the questionnaires (N = 2,317), a respectable rate of return given that no follow-ups were possible because of school schedules and budget constraints.

The eight Title I inner-city schools, five elementary and three middle schools, were selected at random from sets of similar Title I schools that serve children and families who live in public housing projects, rental homes and apartments, and privately owned homes in economically disadvantaged neighborhoods. Table 3.20 outlines the characteristics of the parent population. Although parents of both elementary- and middle-grade students are well represented, the sample includes almost twice as many single parents as the national average, more parents without high school diplomas, and larger family sizes than in the general population.

It is possible, of course, that the 50 percent who did not respond are among the least involved or lowest in literacy. They include parents whose children did not bring the questionnaires home or did not return them, parents who chose not to

TABLE 3.20   Characteristics of the Sample of Parents*

	Percent
Elementary school parents (N = 1,135)	49.0
Middle school parents (N = 1,182)	51.0
Single parents	43.4
Working outside home (full- or part-time)	63.7
Did not complete high school	31.0
Completed high school	40.6
Beyond high school	28.3
Average family size (adults and children)	4.4
Parent rating of student ability:	
Top student	7.6
Good student	32.4
Average/OK student	35.2
Fair student	21.8
Poor student	3.0

* N = 2,317.

answer questionnaires, or parents who cannot read well enough to answer the questions. The surveys were written, rewritten, and tested for use in Title I schools. More than 30 percent of the parents who returned the surveys did not complete high school; more than 40 percent are single parents. Thus, despite some underrepresentation of the most educationally disadvantaged families in these schools, the sample is highly diverse and highly representative of the schools.

Despite some limitations of the sample, this study offers unique comparable data from parents with children in elementary and middle schools. Indeed, because of the educational and economic disadvantages of the sample, we can put questions of parent involvement to a stringent test.

MEASURES

Parents' Reports of Their Involvement

Parents rated the frequency of their involvement in conducting 18 different practices included under five major types of parent involvement: parenting and supervising at home, communicating with the school, volunteering at the school, conducting learning activities at home, and participating in PTA or parent leadership activities. The main measures of parents' practices are:

> *Parent Involvement at the School (PINVSCH)*—a five-item measure of the frequency of helping (never, not yet, one to two times, many times) at the school building.

Parent Involvement with Homework (PINVHW)—a five-item measure of the frequency of assisting and monitoring homework.

Parent Involvement in Reading Activities at Home (PINVREAD)—a four-item measure of the frequency of parent help to students in reading.

Total Parent Involvement (PINVIOT)—an 18-item measure of the frequency of parents' use of all types of parent involvement at home and school, including the 14 items in the three scales listed previously and four other items on games, chores, and trips that involve parents and children in communication and learning activities at home.

Parents' Reports of Schools' Practices to Involve Parents

Parents rated their children's schools on whether and how well the schools conduct nine parent involvement practices. The activities include the five types of parent involvement, ranging from the school telling parents how the child is doing in school to giving parents ideas of how to help at home. The main measures of school practices as reported by parents are:

School Practices to Communicate with Parents and Involve Them at School (SCHCOMMPI)—a five-item measure of how well the school communicates with parents to provide information about school programs and activities.

School Practices to Involve Parents at Home (SCHHOMEPI)—a four-item measure of how well the school contacts and guides parents to help their own children at home.

Total School Program to Involve Parents (SCHTOTPI)—a nine-item measure of the extent to which the school contacts and guides parents to involve them in their children's education at home and at school.

Other measures are:

Parent Attitudes about the School (PATT)—a six-item measure of the quality of the child's school.

Family Background Measures—Parent Education, Marital Status, Family Size, Parent Work outside the Home, and Parent Ratings of Student Ability.

The several scales of parents' reports of their practices, the schools' practices to involve them, and their attitudes toward their children's school have modest to high reliabilities. These are reported in Table 3.21.

TABLE 3.21   Measures of Parent Involvement and Attitudes

		Mean	Reliability
Parent Involvement at the School (PINVSCH)	5 items	2.36	.69
Parent Involvement with Homework (PIVHW)	5 items	3.54	.63
Parent Involvement in Reading Activities at Home (PINVREAD)	4 items	3.00	.58
Total Parent Involvement (PINVTOT)	18 items	3.07	.81
Parent Attitudes about the School (PATT)	6 items	3.29	.75
School Practices to Communicate with Parents and Involve Them at School (SCHCOMMPI)	5 items	2.35	.71
School Practices to Involve Parents at Home (SCHHOMPI)	4 items	2.04	.81
Total School Program to Involve Parents (SCHTOTPI)	9 items	2.21	.81

EFFECTS ON PARENT INVOLVEMENT

Table 3.22 summarizes analyses of the effects of parent and student characteristics, school level, and school practices to involve families on parents' reported involvement at school and at home. The four columns of the table report the variables that significantly explain parent involvement at school (column 1); at home on homework (column 2); at home on reading in particular (column 3); and on total parent involvement at school, with homework, with reading, and in all activities (column 4).

Level of Schooling (Elementary or Middle School)

School level has strong independent effects on all measures of involvement reported by parents. Parents of children in the elementary grades are more involved than parents of children in the middle grades. According to the parents' reports, elementary school teachers do more and do better to involve parents in their children's education at school ($\beta = -.13$); at home with homework ($\beta = -.14$); with reading activities at home ($\beta = -.08$); and with all types of involvement ($\beta = -.16$).

Within middle schools, parents of sixth and seventh graders are more likely to be involved in their children's education at home. Parents of eighth graders are more involved at the school building. Because these data were collected early in the school year, parents of sixth graders were still relatively new to the school and may not have been included in the small core of parent volunteers in middle schools. Sixth-grade students may be more apt to ask for help at home if they are

TABLE 3.22   Effects on Extent of Parents' Involvement of School Level, Family Characteristics, and Reported Teacher Practices to Involve Parents

	Extent of Involvement Reported by Parents:			
	At School	At Home on Homework	At Home on Reading Skills	Total Parent Involvement
	(β = standardized beta coefficient)[a, b]			
	(β)	(β)	(β)	(β)
School level (elementary/middle)	−.13	−.14	−.08	−.16
Parents' education	.11	.08	.13	.13
Family size	NS	−.07	−.06	−.07
Parent works outside home	−.06	NS	NS	NS
Rating of student ability	.06	.10	.15	.13
Teacher practices to involve parents[c] at school	.27			
at home		.18	.16	
Overall				.30
N	1,447	1,489	1,512	1,248
R^2	.14	.09	.08	.18

a Listwise regression analyses are reported to eliminate all cases with missing data. This procedure was checked with pairwise procedures that add about 300 cases to analyses. The results were all but identical.

b All reported coefficients are significant at or beyond the .05 level; coefficients of .10 or more are particularly important.

c Each equation includes the parents' reports of teachers' practices that most directly link to the type of involvement of the parents. That is, school practices that include asking the parent to come to school are used in the equation to explain parents' involvement at school; school practices that guide parents in how to help at home are used in the equation to explain parents' involvement at home on homework and reading skills; and the sum of all school practices is used in the equation to explain parents' total involvement.

still unsure of themselves in a new school setting. Older students (eighth graders) may feel that they are more knowledgeable than their parents about schoolwork and school decisions.

Family Characteristics

In all cases, parents who are better educated are more involved at school and at home than parents who are less educated. Other family characteristics affect different types of involvement. Parents with fewer children are more involved with their children at home (β = −.07), but family size is not a significant factor for explaining parent involvement at school. Parents who work are significantly less likely to participate at the school building (β = −.06), but working outside the home is not a significant predictor of involvement at home. Marital status had no significant effects on the extent of involvement either at school or at home. These results confirm other reports at the elementary level (see Epstein, 1986) and at the middle level (Muller, 1991).

Student Characteristics

In all analyses, parents were more involved in their children's education if the children were better students. These cross-sectional data cannot be interpreted to mean that students whose parents are involved *become* better students. However, the results of earlier studies that used fall-to-spring test scores over one school year suggest that teachers' practices to involve parents in reading resulted in greater reading gains for children in those teachers' classrooms (Epstein, 1991). Parents whose children are doing well or are doing better in school are more likely to do more to ensure their children's continued success.

School Programs and Teachers' Practices

The strongest and most consistent predictors of parent involvement at school and at home are the specific school programs and teacher practices that encourage and guide parent involvement. Regardless of parent education, family size, student ability, or school level (elementary or middle school), parents are more likely to become partners in their children's education if they perceive that the schools have strong practices to involve parents at school ($\beta = .27$), at home with homework ($\beta = .18$), and at home with reading activities ($\beta = .16$). The sum of all nine school practices has the strongest effect on parents' total involvement ($\beta = .30$) after all other factors have been statistically controlled.

When parents believe the schools are doing little to involve them, they report doing little at home. When parents perceive that the school is doing many things to involve them, they are more involved in their children's education at school and at home. The schools' practices, not just family characteristics, make a difference in whether parents become involved in and feel informed about their children's education.

CLASSROOM-LEVEL REPORTS OF SCHOOL PRACTICES

Individual parents in one teacher's class may view the teacher's practices from a personal perspective. For example, one parent may receive special advice from a teacher about how to help a child at home or become involved at school. Or all parents of students in a classroom may report the teacher's practices similarly if they recognize that the teacher's regular practice is to involve all parents. We checked to see how individual parent reports compared to the reports of other parents in the same classroom. We can begin to understand whether parent involvement is a phenomenological process or a general classroom process by examining how parents of entire classrooms of students report the teacher's requests for involvement.

In this sample, only parents of children in the elementary grades could be identified by classroom for aggregated reports. The 1,135 parents of children in 86 classrooms provided assessments of school practices to inform and involve parents. An average or "consensus" score was calculated for each classroom and merged with the individual parent records.

Individual reports were significantly and positively correlated with the reports of other parents in the classroom (between $r = .28$ and $r = .44$). The highest agreement among parents came on the parents' reports about the amount of time that their children spend on homework ($r = .44$). Individual and aggregate scores were correlated slightly lower on whether the teacher guides parents on how to help with homework ($r = .32$).

Parents also were in high agreement about the overall quality of their children's school. The correlation was $+.38$ between an average parent's report that a school was good or poor and the reports of all the parents in the same classroom. The modest but significant correlations suggest that there is agreement about school and teacher practices to involve parents. The figures also show considerable variation in the interpretations of teacher practices by individual parents in the same classroom.

Classroom averages of parents' reports may be more objective measures than one parent's report of a teacher's practices. We compare the effects of the classroom-level and individual-level measures on parents' practices in Table 3.23. The first line shows the individual effects; the second line shows the effects on parent involvement of the classroom aggregate measures of teachers' practices. On all types of involvement, the individual reports have stronger effects than the aggregated reports on parents' practices at school and at home. Line 2 substitutes the average of the parents' reports for that classroom, but retains the parents' individual background variables. This analysis uses the aggregate report as an alternative "truth" about the teacher's practices as if all parents received and interpreted the same information about involvement from the teacher. The results in lines 1 and 2 can be viewed as providing a "range of effects," with the "truth" somewhere between the two coefficients. Line 3 is a classroom analysis. It uses the average reports of all parents in a classroom about teacher practices and the average family background variables. These effects are highly consistent with the individual analyses. Importantly, they show that when classroom agreement about specific teachers' practices is high, individual parents tend to respond with those practices at home.

The differences raise two questions for future studies: How accurately does any one parent report a teacher's practices? Do teachers treat all parents in a classroom similarly to involve them at school and at home? The coefficients in Table 3.23 suggest that despite some consensus about teachers' practices among parents in a class, there is considerable evidence of individual interpretation of teacher practices and the translation of those practices into parent practices. All parents of children in a classroom may not be treated the same by a teacher, and they may not interpret messages, requests, and opportunities in the same way. The strongest

TABLE 3.23 Comparison of Effects of Individual-Level and Classroom-Level Reports of Teacher Practices to Involve Parents (Elementary School Level Only)

	At School	At Home on Homework	At Home on Reading Skills	Total Parent Involvement
		Extent of Involvement Reported by Parents:		
		(β = standardized beta coefficient)[a, b]		
	(β)	(β)	(β)	(β)
Individual parent's report of teacher practices[b]	.28	.20	.16	.33
Classroom parents' consensus about teacher practices, individual parent's background with variables controlled[b, c]	.07	NS	NS	.13
Classroom parents' consensus about teacher practices, aggregate parent background with variables controlled[b, d]	.22	.24	.14	.27

a Listwise regression for these analyses include from 603 to 782 cases for elementary school parents, depending on the type of involvement measured. The same background variables are statistically controlled as shown in Table 3.15.

b Linked measures of teachers' practices (as shown in Table 3.15) are used in these analyses.

c Aggregate reports from all parents in a classroom about teachers' practices of parent involvement are used instead of an individual's report.

d Aggregate reports about teacher practices of parent involvement from all parents in a classroom, including aggregate family background variables.

effects on parent involvement at school and at home are demonstrated by parents who personally understand and act on the teacher's practices that encourage their involvement.

We believe that in strong or "improving" schools, the correspondence between one parent's report and those of all other parents in the class should increase over time. This would indicate that parents were becoming increasingly similar in how they perceived and understood the teacher's practices. There would, of course, always be some differences in individual responses to requests for involvement.

STUDENT TIME ON HOMEWORK AND PARENT INVOLVEMENT

Helping with homework is one common and important means by which parents become involved in what their children are learning in school. We asked parents several questions about their children's homework practices and their own involvement in homework activities. Table 3.24 shows comparisons of homework activities of elementary and middle school students and the help they receive from parents. According to parents:

- Middle school students spend more time doing homework on an average night than do elementary students.
- Parents of elementary school children help their children for more minutes and feel more able to help with reading and math than do parents of middle school students.
- Parents of children at both levels of school say they could help more (up to 45–50 minutes, on average) if the teacher guided them in how to help at home.
- Parents of children at both levels of school say they have time to help on weekends. Often, students are not assigned homework on weekends, when many parents have more time to interact with their children.
- More parents of elementary school students than parents of middle school students report that their children's schools and teachers have good programs that guide them in how to help at home to check their child's homework. Even at the elementary level, only 35 percent of the parents think their school "does well" on this. At the middle level, only 25 percent believe their school does well to help them know what to do.
- More parents of elementary school students than parents of middle school students report that their child likes to talk about school at home. But even at the elementary level, many parents, close to 40 percent, do not think that their children really enjoy such discussions.

Other data (not reported in Table 3.24) indicate that more-educated parents say that their children spend more time on homework. These parents may be more aware of the homework that their children have to do, the parents may make sure the children do all of their homework, or the children may be in classrooms where the teachers give more homework. Less-educated parents say they could help more if the teachers told them how to help. More-educated parents may believe they are already helping enough or that they are already receiving good information from the teacher on how to help.

Table 3.25 reports the results of multiple-regression analyses conducted to determine the factors that affect how much time parents spend monitoring, assisting, or otherwise helping their children with homework.

As noted, level of schooling affects the amount of time parents spend helping at home. With all other variables statistically controlled, parents of elementary students spend more time helping on homework (ß = −.18). Regardless of school level, parents help for more minutes if their children spend more time on homework. Alternative explanations are that when parents help, it takes students more time to do their homework, or parents help when their children have a lot of homework assigned by the teacher.

TABLE 3.24   Parents' Reports about Homework

	School Level	
	Elementary (N = 1,135)	Middle (N = 1,182)
Average time on homework	30–35 min.	35–40 min.
Average time parent helps	30–35	25–30
% Strongly agree they are able to help with reading	75.9	67.1
% Strongly agree they are able to help with math	71.8	55.4
Average time parent could help if teacher gave information	45–50 min.	45–50 min.
% Have time to help on weekends	95.3	91.9
% Report school explains how to check child's homework	35.7	25.0
% Strongly agree child should get more homework	40.0	35.6
% Strongly agree child likes to talk about school at home	62.4	45.3

TABLE 3.25   Effects on Minutes Parents Help with Homework of School Level, Family Characteristics, Students' Homework Time, and Teachers' Practices to Involve Parents in Homework

	β[a,b]
School level (elementary or middle)	–.18
Students' homework time	.51
Parent education	NS
Family size	NS
Single parent	NS
Parent works outside home	–.08
Rating of student ability	–.08
Teachers' practices to guide parent help on homework	.10
N	1,560
R²	.28

a Standardized beta coefficients for listwise regression analyses are reported.

b All reported coefficients are significant at or beyond the .05 level; coefficients of .10 are particularly important.

Parents' education, family size, and marital status—all indicators of family social class and social structure—are not significantly associated with the amount of time parents help with homework. Parents who work outside the home spend fewer minutes helping their children than do other parents. Parents whose children need the most help in schoolwork (rated by parents as "fair" or "poor" students) spend more minutes helping with homework (β = –.08). Other analyses show that this is especially true in the elementary grades. Parents of less-able elementary students may believe that if they give their children extra help on homework, the students have a chance to succeed in school. By the middle grades, parents who rate their children as "poor" students do not help their children as much as parents of "average" students. In the middle grades, parents may feel they are not able to help their academically weak children without special guidance from teachers about how to help. Parents of top students do not help for as many minutes in the middle grades, in part because the students do not need or ask for assistance and in part because teachers do not guide parents' involvement.

Other analyses show that in the middle grades, poor students spend the least amount of time on homework. Thus, there is less investment in homework time by middle-grade students who are academically weak, less investment in helping behavior by parents of these students, and less investment by middle-grade teachers in informing parents about how to help their children at this level.

Even after all family and student characteristics are statistically accounted for, there is a significant, positive, and important effect of teachers' reported practices to guide parents in how to help their children with homework ($\beta = .10$). Teachers who more often conduct practices that involve families influence parents to spend more time with their children on homework. The variables in these analyses explain about 28 percent of the variance in the amount of time parents spend helping on homework.

There is an interesting contrast between Tables 3.22 and 3.25 concerning parent involvement at home with homework. Table 3.22 shows that more-educated parents and parents of better students report that they are involved in *more and different ways* of helping at home with homework. Table 3.25 reports that parents of weaker or less-able students spend *more minutes* helping their children on an average night. Types of help and time spent helping are different indicators of involvement. It may be that over time many different ways of helping and more minutes spent helping lead to more success for students on schoolwork. The different patterns suggest that students' different needs are being addressed by parents. Students who need more help take more minutes of their parents' time. Students who are better students may require different kinds of assistance. The important similarity between the two tables is that the specific practices of teachers to guide parents in how to help at home increase the types of help parents say they give and the time they give to help their children.

DISCUSSION

Several other findings from the data regarding inner-city parents increase our understanding of parent involvement in children's education in the elementary and middle grades:

- Most parents believe that their children attend a good school and that the teachers care about their children, and the parents feel welcome at the school. However, there is considerable variation in these attitudes, with many parents unhappy or unsure about the quality of schools and teachers. Interestingly, parents' attitudes about the quality of their children's school are more highly correlated with the school's practices to involve parents (.346) than with the parents' practices of involvement (.157). Parents who become involved at home and at school say that the school has a positive climate. Even more so, parents who believe that the school is *actively working* to involve them say that the school is a good one. This connection supports earlier findings that parents give teachers higher ratings when teachers frequently involve parents in their children's education (Epstein, 1985 [Reading 4.3], 1986).

- Parents report little involvement at the school building. Many parents work full-time or part-time and cannot come to the school during the school day. Others report that they have not been asked by the school to become volunteers, but would like to be.

- Parents in all the schools in this sample are emphatic about wanting the school and teachers to advise them about *how to help their children at home* at each grade level. Parents believe that the schools need to strengthen practices such as giving parents specific information on their children's major academic subjects and what their children are expected to learn each year.

- Parents of young children and more-educated parents conduct more activities at home that support their children's schooling.

- Parents who were guided by teachers on how to help at home spent more minutes helping with homework than other parents.

- In many schools, parents are asked to come to the building for workshops. An interesting sidelight in these data is that in all eight schools, elementary and middle, parents' top request for workshop topics was "How to Help My Child Develop His/Her Special Talents." Across the schools, from 57 to 68 percent of parents checked that topic (average 61 percent). By contrast, an average of 54 percent were interested in workshops on helping children take tests, and an average of 45 percent checked interest in discipline and control of children.

- Inner-city parents need information and assistance to help develop the special qualities they see in their children. Time and resources to develop talent may be as important as time for homework for helping children's self-esteem and commitment to learning. The parents' requests for help from the schools on the topic of developing children's special talents are important calls for action, along with their requests for schools to increase information on how to help on homework.

Most important for policy and practice, parents' level of involvement is directly linked to the specific practices of the school that encourage involvement at school and guide parents in how to help at home. The data are clear that the schools' practices to inform and involve parents are more important than parent education, family size, marital status, and even grade level in determining whether inner-city parents stay involved with their children's education through the middle grades.

Although teachers in these urban Title I schools reported that most parents are not involved and do not want to be (see Epstein and Dauber, 1991), parents of students in the same schools tell a different story. They say that they are involved with their children but that they need more and better information from teachers about how to help at home. Parents and teachers have different perspectives that must be recognized and taken into account in developing activities to improve parent involvement.

Earlier research showed that some of the strongest immediate effects of teachers' practices of parent involvement are on parents' attitudes and behaviors (see Epstein, 1986). This study suggests that the same is true for inner-city parents. Parents are more involved at school and at home when they perceive that the schools have strong programs that encourage parent involvement. The implication is that all schools, including inner-city schools, can develop more comprehensive programs of parent involvement to help more families become knowledgeable partners in their children's education.

In these schools the survey data were used to help the schools plan three-year programs to improve their parent involvement practices to meet the needs and requests of the parents and the hopes of the teachers for stronger partnerships. The data served as Time 1, the starting point, for a longitudinal study of the impact of three years of work to improve practices. In this and in other research, the next questions must deal with the results of efforts to improve school and family partnerships.

REFERENCES

Baker, D. P., and D. L. Stevenson. (1986). Mothers' strategies for children's school achievement: Managing the transition to high school. *Sociology of Education* 59: 156–166.

Bauch, P. A. (1988). Is parent involvement different in private schools? *Educational Horizons* 66: 78–82.

Becker, H. J., and J. L. Epstein. (1982). Parent involvement: A study of teacher practices. *Elementary School Journal* 83: 85–102. (Reading 3.1).

Clark, R. (1983). *Family life and school achievement: Why poor black children succeed and fail*. Chicago: University of Chicago Press.

Comer, J. P. (1980). *School power*. New York: Free Press.

Dornbusch, S. M., and P. L. Ritter. (1988). Parents of high school students: A neglected resource. *Educational Horizons* 66: 75–77.

Epstein, J. L. (1982). *Student reactions to teacher practices of parent involvement*. Parent Involvement Report Series P-21. (Paper presented at the annual meeting of the American Education Research Association). Baltimore: Johns Hopkins University Center for Research on Elementary and Middle Schools. (Reading 3.9).

———. (1985). A question of merit: Principals' and parents' evaluations of teachers. *Educational Researcher* 14(7): 3–10. (Reading 4.3).

———. (1986). Parents' reactions to teacher practices of parent involvement. *Elementary School Journal* 86: 277–294. (Reading 3.4).

———. (1987). What principals should know about parent involvement. *Principal* 66(3): 6–9.

———. (1988a). *Sample clinical summaries: Using surveys of teachers and parents to plan projects to improve parent involvement*. Parent Involvement Series, Report P-83. Baltimore: Johns Hopkins University Center for Research on Elementary and Middle Schools.

———. (1988b). How do we improve programs in parent involvement? *Educational Horizons* (special issue on parents and schools) 66(2): 58–59.

————. (1990). Single parents and the schools: Effects of marital status on parent and teacher interactions. Pages 91–121 in *Change in societal institutions*, edited by M. T. Hallinan, D. M. Klein, and J. Glass. New York: Plenum. (Reading 3.5).

————. (1991). Effects of teacher practices of parent involvement on student achievement in reading and math. Pages 261–276 in *Advances in reading/language research, Vol. 5: Literacy through family, community, and school interaction*, edited by S. Silvern. Greenwich, CT: JAI Press. (Reading 3.7).

Epstein, J. L., and H. J. Becker. (1990). Hopkins Surveys of School and Family Connections: Questionnaires for teachers, parents, and students. Pages 345–346 in *Handbook of family measurement techniques*, edited by J. Touliatos, B. Perlmutter, and M. Straus. Parent Involvement Series, Report P-81. Newbury Park, CA: Sage Publications.

Epstein, J. L., and S. Dauber. (1991). School programs and teacher practices of parent involvement in inner-city elementary and middle schools. *Elementary School Journal* 91: 289–303. (Reading 3.3).

Epstein, J. L., and K. Salinas. (1988). *Evaluation report forms: Summaries of school-level data from surveys of teachers and surveys of parents*. Parent Involvement Report Series P-82. Baltimore: Johns Hopkins University Center for Research on Elementary and Middle Schools.

Lareau, A. (1987). Social class differences in family-school relationships: The importance of cultural capital. *Sociology of Education* 60: 73–85.

Leitch, M. L., and S. S. Tangri. (1988). Barriers to home-school collaboration. *Educational Horizons* 66: 70–74.

Muller, C. (1991). Maternal employment, parental involvement, and academic achievement: An analysis of family resources available to the child. Paper presented at the annual meeting of the American Sociological Association in Cincinnati.

Rich, D., J. Van Dien, and B. Mattox. (1979). Families as educators for their own children. Pages 26–40 in *Partners: Parents and schools*, edited by R. Brandt. Alexandria, VA: Association for Supervision and Curriculum Development.

Rubin, R. I., P. P. Olmsted, M. J. Szegda, M. J. Wetherby, and D. S. Williams. (1983). Long-term effects of parent education on follow-through program participation. Paper presented at the annual meeting of the American Education Research Association in Montreal.

Scott-Jones, D. (1987). Mother-as-teacher in families of high- and low-achieving low-income Black first graders. *Journal of Negro Education* 56: 21–34.

Effects on Student Achievement of Teachers' Practices of Parent Involvement*

ABSTRACT

This study uses longitudinal data from 293 third- and fifth-grade students in Baltimore City who took the California Achievement Test (CAT) in the fall and spring of the 1980–1981 school year. The students were in the classrooms of 14 teachers who varied in their use of techniques to involve parents in learning activities at home. With data from parents, students, and teachers, we examine the effects over time of teachers' practices of parent involvement on student achievement test scores.

INTRODUCTION

Social science research on school and family environments has documented the importance for student development and achievement of family conditions and practices of parent involvement in school (Clausen, 1966; Coleman et al., 1966; Epstein, 1983; Heyns, 1978; Leichter, 1974; Marjoribanks, 1979; Mayeske, 1973; McDill and Rigsby, 1973; Gordon, 1979; Henderson, 1987; Sinclair, 1980). There is consistent evidence that parents' encouragement, activities, interest at home, and participation at school affect their children's achievement, even after the students' ability and family socioeconomic status are taken into account. Students gain in personal and academic development if their families emphasize schooling, let their children know they do, and do so continually over the school years.

The earlier research considers family practices that vary naturally in the study samples. It recognizes that in any population some parents become involved in their children's education, based on their own knowledge about school and their ability to guide and encourage their children. This study examines parent involvement that results from teachers' efforts to involve more parents in their children's

* By Joyce L. Epstein. An earlier version of this paper was presented at the 1984 annual meeting of the American Educational Research Association. The author is grateful to Henry Jay Becker and Doris Entwisle for their helpful comments and suggestions and to others who reviewed or reacted to earlier drafts. Many thanks to the teachers, principals, families, and students who contributed to this study. This research was supported by grants from the Department of Education Office of Educational Research and Improvement. The results and improvements do not necessarily reflect the position or policy of the OERI. Originally published in S. Silvern, ed., *Advances in reading/language research*, Vol. 5: *Literacy through family, community, and school interaction* (Greenwich, CT: JAI Press, 1991), pp. 261–276. Reprinted with permission.

education, not just those who would become involved on their own. We want to know what happens if we change the expected variation among families to increase the number of parents who can knowledgeably assist their children to improve or maintain their academic skills. We need to know: Are there ways to increase the number of parents who become involved in their children's learning activities at home? If teachers and administrators take the responsibility to involve all parents, are there measurable effects on student achievement test scores and other important school outcomes?

Over the years there have been many programs designed to increase home-school cooperation to improve students' academic skills and attitudes or parents' attitudes (Collins, Moles, and Cross, 1982). Few programs, however, have been systematically evaluated for their effects on students. Tidwell (1980) describes positive effects on parents, although the data to evaluate Los Angeles's "Project AHEAD" were admittedly poor. Gotts (1980) reports small effects on "adaptability to school" for children in family-school preschool programs. Cochran (1986) describes a preschool program designed to "empower" parents, but the linkages in the model to the children's schools and teachers' practices are weak. Rich and Jones (1977) present important early evidence suggesting that extra learning time at home produces gains in early elementary students' reading scores equivalent to those made by students under more expensive "pull-out" programs in schools. The data, statistical controls, and methods of analysis in these studies, however, were seriously limited. Gordon (1979) reviews several studies and unpublished dissertations suggesting that there are generally positive effects of the programs on parents and on young children, but the measures of parent involvement in these studies are incomplete and the connections to schools and instructional programs are unmeasured.

Several Follow-Through models emphasized parent involvement at school and at home (Rivlin and Timpane, 1975), but in all cases the effects of the parent involvement components were poorly measured. The most reliable data and consistent results from the Follow-Through studies seem to be effects on parents' attitudes and parent-teacher relations. (See the exchange in the *Harvard Educational Review* by Anderson, St. Pierre, Proper, and Stebbins, 1978; Hodges, 1978; Wisler, Burnes, and Iwamoto, 1978.) Other studies and commentaries suggest that direct contact of parents with their own children on learning activities at home (as opposed to the contact of a few parents in the school building) *should have* important consequences for student achievement and other outcomes such as school attendance and classroom behavior (Comer, 1980; Gillum, Schooley, and Novak, 1977; Rich, Van Dien, and Mattox, 1979).

Previous studies did not link specific teachers' practices with their own students and parents, and there was little information on characteristics of the teachers, parents, or students for even cursory controls on other influences on achievement. Few studies focused on upper elementary school or older students. Overall, there is little "hard" data that address the question of whether teachers' practices of parent involvement directly influence student achievement (Olmsted, Wetherby, Leler, and Rubin, 1982). This study begins to fill some of the gaps in the earlier work by focusing on the effect of teacher practices of parent involvement on gains in reading and math achievement test scores over one school year.

DATA AND APPROACH

We use longitudinal data from 293 third- and fifth-grade students in Baltimore City who took the California Achievement Test (CAT) in the fall and spring of the 1980–1981 school year. (The full study involved many districts in the state of Maryland, but only one district administered fall and spring achievement test scores to permit analyses of change in math and reading scores over one school year.) The students were in the classrooms of 14 teachers who varied in their emphasis on parent involvement. The continuum ranged from "confirmed leaders"—teachers who reported frequent use of parent involvement in learning activities at home and who were confirmed by their principals as leaders in these practices—to infrequent users, to confirmed nonusers of parent involvement in learning activities at home—teachers who reported, and whose principals confirmed, their lack of emphasis on parent involvement (see Becker and Epstein, 1982 [Reading 3.1]). The parents of students in these teachers' classrooms were surveyed about their reactions to and experiences with teacher practices of parent involvement (see Epstein, 1986 [Reading 3.4]). The data link teacher practices to the families' responses and to the achievement of students, and enable us to analyze the consequences of teachers' uses of instructional strategies that emphasize parent involvement at home.

Several types of variables that theoretically could influence change in achievement scores are included in the analyses: *student and family background* (sex, race, and grade level of students, parent education, and students' fall achievement test scores), *teachers' characteristics and practices* (overall teaching quality as rated by the principal, years of experience, and teachers' and principals' reports of the teachers' leadership in parent involvement), *parent reactions* (parents' reports of teacher requests for involvement and parents' rating of the quality of homework assigned by the teacher), and *student effort* (teachers' rating of the quality of homework completed by the students). The variables are described in detail in Becker and Epstein (1982) and Epstein (1985 [Reading 4.3], 1986, 1990 [Reading 3.5]). Multiple regression analysis is used to identify the important independent effects of these variables on gains in reading and math achievement. We are especially interested in whether teacher practices of parent involvement affect reading and math achievement, after the other potentially influential variables are taken into account.

We use students' residual gain scores as our measure of growth or change over the school year. Because earlier family and school factors influenced prior student achievement, we must statistically control the students' initial, fall achievement test scores that reflect the earlier influences. Then we examine the effects of the ongoing teachers' practices on change in reading and math skills over the school year in our study. As Richards (1975, 1976) showed, changes in scores over a reasonable interval, such as a school year, measure school impact and individual growth as accurately as other methods (Cronbach and Furby, 1970). Changes in scores also have the conceptual advantage of giving a clear picture of growth from pretest to posttest.

Ideally, we would like to have more measures of teachers' classroom practices. It may be, for example, that teachers who frequently use parent involvement strategies also differ from infrequent users or nonusers in their other classroom activities and instructional methods. In this study we control for differences in teachers' quality and approaches by taking into account principals' ratings of the teachers' skills, including their preparation of lessons, knowledge of subject, classroom discipline, and creativity. We focus, then, on the effects of teacher practices of parent involvement, net of overall teacher quality. Although new studies of parent involvement and achievement may add other measures of specific teacher practices, our statistical controls on teacher quality and early student achievement greatly strengthen the models, measures, and methods used in previous studies.

RESULTS

Effects on Change in Reading Achievement

Table 3.26 shows the significant correlates of gains in reading achievement and the results of the regression analysis to identify the significant, independent effects of these variables on achievement gains. The variables were entered in four steps to illustrate the type, magnitude, and persistence of influence. Line 1 of the table shows the effects on change in reading scores of initial or starting characteristics of students and teachers: the students' initial, fall reading scores and the overall quality of the teacher as rated by the principal. Students with lower reading scores in the fall make greater gains by the spring than do other students ($\beta = -.259$). This effect is partly a "regression to the mean" but is also partly a consequence of the room to change and the need to change. Students who are initially low may be able to move their scores more easily than those who are at or near the "ceiling" in a range of scores, and, we assume, they and their teachers are working to improve the students' basic skills. The positive effect of teacher quality ($\beta = +.157$) shows that, independent of students' starting scores, teachers whose principals give them high ratings in classroom management, control, instructional effectiveness, and creativity help students make greater gains in reading than do teachers who receive lower ratings for teaching quality. These two variables explain 10 percent of the variance in change in reading scores.

Line 2 of the table reports that teacher leadership in parent involvement in learning activities at home positively and significantly influences change in reading achievement, adding about 4 percent to the variance explained by the initial characteristics of students and teachers.

Line 3 of the table takes into account two measures of parental resources and responses. Parents with more education and parents who report that they have learned more this year than they knew previously about their child's instructional program positively influence change in the reading achievement of their children.

TABLE 3.26 Influence on Change in Reading Achievement Test Scores from Fall to Spring*

Variables Added	Initial Reading Score (Fall)	Overall Quality of Teacher	Leadership in Parent Involvement	Parent Education	Parent Knows More This Year Than Before	Student Homework Quality	R^2
1. Student and Teacher (Starting) Characteristics	−.259	.157					.105
2. Teacher Leadership in Parent Involvement at Home	−.243	.201	.193				.141
3. Parent Resources and Response to Involvement	−.275	.164	.171	.185	.153		.185
4. Homework Completion Quality	−.330	.138	.128	.162	.122	.193	.216
5. (Zero-order Correlation)	(−.285)	(.200)	(.162)	(.092)	(.191)	(.186)	

* Achievement test scores are fall and spring scores (percentiles) on the Reading Subtest of the California Achievement Tests for 293 third- and fifth-grade students. Standardized regression coefficients are reported. In this table, all unstandardized coefficients are twice their standard errors.

Thus, we see that student gains in reading achievement are influenced by parents who usually help their children (i.e., those with more education) and, importantly, parents who are helped to help their children (i.e., those whose children's teachers involve parents in learning activities at home to increase their knowledge about the school program). An additional 4 percent of the variance is explained by these parental characteristics.

Teachers rated their students as homework stars, homework problems, or as neither stars nor problems. We see in line 4 of the table that students who complete their homework well gain more in reading achievement than do other students. When homework quality is added to the equation in Table 3.26, its effects on achievement are clearly important, and the effects of teachers' practices and parents' responses decrease slightly but remain significant. This indicates not only the generally robust importance of these variables but also the crucial contribution of students' investments in schoolwork for improving their own achievement.

Although many factors influence learning, we were especially interested in whether teachers' practices of involving parents have persistent, independent effects on student achievement. We see that teachers' leadership in parent involvement in learning activities at home contributes independently to positive change in reading achievement from fall to spring, even after teacher quality, students' initial achievement, parents' education, parents' improved understanding of the school program, and the quality of students' homework are taken into account. Indeed, the influence of teachers' practices of parent involvement may be even more important than the coefficient suggests, because improved parents' understanding and better homework quality are also influenced by these practices (Epstein, 1982 [Reading 3.9], 1986).

Effects on Change in Math Achievement

Table 3.27 tells a different story about change in math achievement scores. Again, all variables are included in this analysis that are significantly correlated with change in math achievement. We also include teachers' leadership in parent involvement, despite its low correlation, to compare its effects on math with those reported for reading.

Line 1 of Table 3.27 shows that students who start with lower math scores in the fall change more in math skills over the school year. In part this reflects regression to the mean, but also, as in reading, slower students with more room to change and greater need to change make greater gains by spring than do students who score well. Students also gain more if they have relatively new, recently trained teachers, or if they are in the younger grades (i.e., here, grade 3 rather than grade 5). It may be that making progress in math is easier for students in the lower grades, where teachers tend to help students master basic skills and do not stress the swift coverage and competitive knowledge of more advanced math topics. Younger students and their teachers may be able to improve needed math skills more easily than can older students who have, with each passing year, more skills to cover and more ground to make up if they have fallen behind. The over-

TABLE 3.27 Influence on Change in Math Achievement Test Scores from Fall to Spring*

Variables Added	Initial Math Score (Fall)	Overall Quality of Teachers	Years of Teaching Experience	Grade Level	Leadership in Parent Involvement	Homework Not Busy Work	R^2
1. Student and Teacher (Starting) Characteristics	-.349*	-.038	-.152*	-.266*			.253
2. Teacher Leadership in Parent Involvement at Home	-.348*	-.047	-.148*	-.277*	-.028		.254
3. Assigned Homework Quality	-.334*	-.047	-.146*	-.258*	-.025	.104‡	.264
4. (Zero-order Correlation)	(-.428)	(.131)	(-.151)	(.326)	(.040)	(.216)	

* Achievement test scores are fall and spring scores (percentiles) on mathematics subtest of the California Achievement Tests for 293 third- and fifth-grade students. Standardized regression coefficients are reported.

* Indicates unstandardized coefficient is at least twice its standard error.

‡ Indicates coefficient is approaching twice its standard error.

all quality of the teacher, as rated by the principal, is a significant correlate of students' growth in math but does not have an independent influence on change in math achievement after other measures of student and teacher characteristics are accounted for. The four characteristics of students and teachers shown in line 1 of the table explain approximately 25 percent of the variance in math gains.

Line 2 of the table shows that teachers' leadership in the use of parent involvement is not an important variable for understanding change in math scores. In contrast to its influence on reading achievement gains in Table 3.26, teachers' parent involvement practices are neither correlated with math gains nor significantly affected by other variables in this model.

Line 3 of the table suggests that parents' reports that teachers assign purposeful homework (not busy work) have a small, positive effect on change in math achievement, but explains only an additional 1 percent of the variance in math gains. This measure may reflect a combination of parents' awareness of their children's math work, the parents' general acceptance of their children's school programs, better quality of the teachers' decisions about homework assignments, and the students' interest and investment of time at home on their homework. New research should look into these components of homework assignments by teachers, as well as aspects of homework completion by students discussed in Table 3.26.

Comparing Effects on Change in Reading and Math Scores

Table 3.28 shows a common model consisting of variables from Tables 3.26 and 3.27 used to compare effects on changes in reading and math achievement. Two variables—student sex and race—have been added to Table 3.28 even though they lack a significant zero-order correlation with the dependent measure. We include them here to show that although sex and race are usually of interest in studies of reading and math achievement, they are not important explanatory variables for students' growth over the school year. The table presents the standardized regression coefficients and identifies the independent influences of the variables on change in reading and math over one school year. We have arranged the variables to focus on student and family background factors, teacher characteristics, and home-learning activities.

The top section of the table focuses attention on student and family background variables. As in the earlier tables, we see that initial (fall) scores influence change in both reading and math scores: Students who initially have low scores change more from fall to spring. Neither sex nor race of students influences changes in scores in either subject. Parent education and grade level are important independent influences, but for different subjects. Better-educated parents independently influence positive change in reading scores, but parents' education is not an important influence on students' math gains. Younger students (in grade 3) make greater gains in math than do students in grade 5, but grade level is not an important independent influence on change in reading achievement.

TABLE 3.28 Comparing a Common Model of Effects on Change in Reading and Math Scores

Variables	Measures	Change in Reading Achievement		Change in Math Achievement	
		β	(r)	β	(r)
Student and Family Background	Sex	.048	(.022)	.009	(.050)
	Grade Level	-.053	(-.222)	-.247*	(-.326)
	Parent Education	.170*	(.092)	.067	(-.024)
	Race	.068	(-.004)	.088	(.022)
	Fall Score ‡	-.294*	(-.285)	-.357*	(-.427)
Teacher Skills and Experience	Overall Quality of Teacher	.175*	(.200)	-.033	(.131)
	Years of Teaching Experience	-.004	(-.026)	-.152*	(-.151)
Home-Learning Activities	Teacher Leadership Involving Parents in Learning Activities at Home	.144*	(.162)	-.037	(.040)
	Homework Not Busy Work	.028	(.072)	.109*	(.216)
	R^2	.173		.274	

NOTES: ß = Standardized regression coefficients.

(r) = Zero-order correlations.

N = 293.

* Indicates unstandardized coefficient is at least twice its standard error.

‡ Fall score is the initial reading score in the analysis of change in reading achievement, and the initial math score in the analysis of change in math achievement.

The middle section of the table presents the variables in the model that concern the teachers' background and skills. The two variables have important independent effects, but on different subjects. Overall teacher quality—the reputational index based on principals' ratings of four instruction and management skills—influences change in students' reading scores but not math. More recent teacher training (reflected in fewer years of teaching) promotes greater gains in math but does not influence change in reading.

The bottom section of the table focuses attention on two types of home-learning activities. Teacher leadership in the use of parent involvement in learning activities at home has a positive influence on change in reading scores, but not in math scores. Parents' reports of pertinent homework assignments influence positive change in students' math scores, but not reading scores.

The common model explains 17 percent of the change in students' reading scores compared to 27 percent of the variance in the change in math scores. The different explanatory power of the model is due mainly to the impact of low initial scores and younger grade level on growth in math skills. Table 3.26 shows more variance explained (about 22 percent) in change in reading achievement because the equation included parents' increased understanding of their children's instructional program and the quality of students' completed homework, two measures that are, in part, explained by teachers' practices of parent involvement and that, in part, boost reading achievement.

DISCUSSION

Why do teachers' practices of parent involvement influence change in reading but not math scores? Why should changes in reading and math achievement test scores be influenced by different variables? And, what do these patterns mean for understanding parent involvement and student achievement?

We have some clues about these questions from other data collected from the teachers and parents in the study. For example, teachers report that reading activities are their most frequently used and most satisfying parent involvement practices, and principals report that they encourage teachers to involve parents in reading activities more than in other subjects (see Becker and Epstein, 1982). Parents report that they receive most requests for assistance on reading-related activities at home (see Epstein, 1986). It appears that these emphases on parent involvement in reading have real consequences for improving students' reading achievement. There is little reason to expect that these practices would have direct and immediate effects on students' math skills. This would require teachers' sequential and coordinated practices to involve parents in math activities.

More parents of fifth-grade students feel that they do not have enough training to help their children with reading and math skills at home (Epstein, 1984). Their feelings of inadequacy may be more serious about math. Teachers of older students have fewer parent volunteers in their classes and give less guidance to parents in how to help their children at home. Teachers may need to give more help to parents of older children so that they understand what to discuss about school

TABLE 3.29   Third- and Fifth-Grade City Students' Reading and Math Scores

	Fall 1980	Spring 1981
Reading achievement scores		
Mean	38.60	50.69
Standard deviation	(25.51)	(25.20)
Math achievement scores		
Mean	43.75	57.46
Standard deviation	(25.70)	(24.74)

and how to assist, guide, and monitor their children in reading, math, and other subjects at home.

Table 3.29 shows that there was dramatic improvement in reading and math scores for third- and fifth-grade city students in this sample from fall to spring. But our analyses suggest that the dramatic changes in reading and math scores are attributable to different factors. Gains in reading achievement are influenced sharply by several sources, including the teachers' leadership in parent involvement, the teachers' overall quality of instruction, the students' need to improve, the quality of the students' homework, the parents' education, and the parents' improved knowledge about the school program.

Gains in math achievement may have more to do with the grade level, methods of teaching math, and traditional homework assignments. Recently trained teachers may be more responsive to current pressures to increase attention to math and to ensure mastery of basic skills in the early grades. In present practice, few teachers ask parents to become involved in math activities at home, but most teachers assign math homework. When parents see that homework is pertinent and purposeful, the students make important math gains.

Previous research shows consistently that school effects are stronger for math achievement than for reading or language arts achievement. Here, we see one explanation for that finding. Some teachers help families help their children practice reading: listening to the child read, reading aloud to the child, borrowing books to use at home, and other reading-related practices (see Becker and Epstein, 1982).

More-educated parents independently influence their children's growth in reading skills. These would be the parents who usually are involved in their children's education. More important, after parent education is taken into account, teacher practices of parent involvement help families become informed and involved, and they influence students' reading skills.

There are many important questions raised by the findings of this study that need to be answered in new research. For example, how do teachers implement their parent involvement programs to get all or most parents involved? What happens to students' achievements and attitudes if their parents will not or cannot help their children even when the teacher requests and guides parent involvement? There are many real and difficult problems that must be solved for teachers to successfully use parent involvement in learning activities at home. These questions will be best answered by studies of the implementation and evaluation of well-designed and well-planned procedures, including the teachers' goals for parent involvement, the orientation of parents, and the management and follow-up of learning activities at home.

Teachers can take new directions to make stronger connections with the family. The Teachers Involve Parents in Schoolwork (TIPS) process helps teachers improve their own approaches to parent involvement and to improve the parents' skills with their children at all grade levels (Epstein, 1987; Epstein, Salinas, and Jackson, 1995 [see Reading 6.2]). The TIPS process includes math and science models and prototypic activities for the elementary grades and language arts and science/health models, and prototype activities for the middle grades that may enable teachers to assist parents and students in becoming involved as knowledgeable partners in learning activities at home in other subjects, as well as in reading.

For some teachers, the "bottom line" for their decisions about whether to use parent involvement practices rests with the documentation of *effects on students*. This study finds significant effects on changes in reading achievement from fall to spring for children in the classrooms of teachers who are leaders in the use of parent involvement practices. Additional studies with longitudinal achievement test scores in specific subjects, with more specific measures of teacher practices of parent involvement and with data from parents on their responses to teachers' requests, are needed to verify and support these results.

Although this study adds to an understanding of linkages between practices of parent involvement and student achievement in specific subjects, there are some serious limitations that should be addressed in new research. For example, the sample includes only urban schools and families. Future studies will want to focus on other populations or include various communities to increase the generalizability of the findings.

Another issue is the lack of specificity of the practices of involving parents. In this study, we can identify only the overall effects of multiple practices that almost exclusively involve parents in reading activities at home. Because educators need to choose among many practices, we need a more clearly defined menu of specific reading involvement practices and their associated effects on reading achievement, as well as information on specific practices to involve parents in other subjects and their effects on student achievement in those subjects.

These data do not account for prior differences in the involvement of the families in the study and the practices of earlier teachers to involve families that may cumulatively affect student achievement. A full complement of longitudinal measures would include parent involvement, teachers' practices, and student outcomes over more than one school year.

Also, teachers who use frequent practices of parent involvement may differ from other teachers in the ways in which they influence student achievement. Although this study statistically controls teacher "quality" using principals' ratings of teachers' classroom organization, management, and pedagogical approaches, this measure does not necessarily capture all of the important differences in teacher attitudes, classroom activities, teacher-student relations, and other factors that also may affect student achievement gains. More comprehensive measures of teacher practices would strengthen analyses and clarify the contribution to achievement gains of teachers' practices to involve all families.

Despite its limitations, this study contributes new information on the subject-specific connections of teacher-guided parent involvement, parent responses and interaction with their children, students' investments in the quality of their own work, and achievement gains. It supports and extends the studies of Rich and Jones (1977); Walberg, Bole, and Waxman (1980); Tizard, Schofield, and Hewison (1982); and others reviewed by Henderson (1987) that suggest that teachers' strong implementation of parent involvement and parents' responsive involvement with their children at home on schoolwork should increase student achievement, even in families with little formal education. The results of this study reveal the need for even more comprehensive and longitudinal inquiries on specific linkages of practices to involve parents and their effects on students. The study also emphasizes the importance of including school and family environments and their connections on the agenda of new research in reading and language arts.

Lightfoot (1978) and Scott-Jones (1987) caution against too great expectations of the effects of parent involvement on academic or social outcomes. Their concerns are important. It is not the parents' responsibility to teach their children new skills in the school curriculum or to take over the teachers' job. However, teachers and parents share a responsibility to their children to monitor and understand their progress in school. This includes assisting students to master the skills needed to pass each grade and to feel good about themselves as learners. Our evidence on reading achievement gains suggests that teachers can help more parents understand how to help their children when questions arise at home about schoolwork. Most parents report that they want teachers to tell them that it is all right to help their children and to explain how to use time at home productively to work toward school goals (see Epstein, 1986). Parents are one available but untapped and undirected resource that teachers can mobilize to help more children master and maintain needed skills for school, but this requires teachers' leadership in organizing, evaluating, and continually building their parent involvement practices.

REFERENCES

Anderson, R. B., R. G. St. Pierre, E. C. Proper, and L. B. Stebbins. (1978). Pardon us but what was the question again? A response to the critique of the Follow-Through evaluation. *Harvard Educational Review* 48: 161–170.

Becker, H. J., and J. L. Epstein. (1982). Parent involvement: A study of teacher practices. *Elementary School Journal* 83: 85–102. (Reading 3.1).

Clausen, J. A. (1966). Family structure, socialization and personality. Pages 1–53 in *Review of child development research*, Vol. 2, edited by L. W. Hoffman and M. L. Hoffman. New York: Russell Sage.

Cochran, M. (1986). Empowering families: An alternative to the deficit model. Paper presented at the First Bielefed Conference on Social Prevention and Intervention in Bielefeld, West Germany.

Coleman, J. S., E. Q. Campbell, C. J. Hobson, J. M. McPartland, A. Mood, F. D. Weinfeld, and R. L. York. (1966). *Equality of educational opportunity.* Washington, DC: U.S. Government Printing Office.

Collins, C., O. Moles, and M. Cross. (1982). *The home-school connection: Selected partnership programs in large cities.* Boston: Institute for Responsive Education.

Comer, J. P. (1980). *School power.* New York: Free Press.

Cronbach, L. J., and L. Furby. (1970). How should we measure change—or should we? *Psychological Bulletin* 74: 68–80.

Epstein, J. L. (1982). Student reactions to teachers' practices of parent involvement. Paper presented at the annual meeting of the American Educational Research Association in New York. (Reading 3.9).

———. (1983). Longitudinal effects of person-family-school interactions on student outcomes. Pages 101–128 in *Research in sociology of education and socialization,* Vol. 4, edited by A. Kerchkoff. Greenwich, CT: JAI Press.

———. (1984). School policy and parent involvement: Research results. *Educational Horizons* 62: 70–72.

———. (1985). A question of merit: Principals' and parents' evaluations of teachers. *Educational Researcher* 14(7): 3–10. (Reading 4.3).

———. (1986). Reactions of parents to teacher practices of parent involvement. *Elementary School Journal* 86: 277–294. (Reading 3.4).

———. (1987). *Teachers' manual: Teachers involve parents in schoolwork [TIPS].* Baltimore: Johns Hopkins University Center for Research on Elementary and Middle Schools.

———. (1990). Single parents and the schools: Effects of marital status on parent and teacher interactions. Pages 91–121 in *Change in societal institutions,* edited by M. T. Hallinan, D. M. Klein, and J. Glass. New York: Plenum. (Reading 3.5).

Epstein, J. L., K. C. Salinas, and V. E. Jackson. (1995). *Manuals for teachers and prototype activities: Teachers Involve Parents in Schoolwork (TIPS) for the elementary and middle grades.* Baltimore: Center on School, Family, and Community Partnerships, Johns Hopkins University.

Gillum, R. M., D. E. Schooley, and P. D. Novak. (1977). The effects of parental involvement on student achievement in three Michigan performance contracting programs. Paper presented at the annual meeting of the American Educational Research Association in New York.

Gordon, I. (1979). The effects of parent involvement in schooling. Pages 4–25 in *Partners: Parents and schools,* edited by R. S. Brandt. Alexandria, VA: Association for Supervision and Curriculum Development.

Gotts, E. (1980). Long-term effects of a home-oriented preschool program. *Childhood Education* 56: 228–234.

Henderson, A. (1987). *The evidence continues to grow: Parent involvement improves achievement.* Columbia, MD: National Committee for Citizens in Education.

Heyns, B. (1978). *Summer learning and the effects of schooling.* New York: Academic Press.

Hodges, W. L. (1978). The worth of the Follow-Through experience. *Harvard Educational Review* 48: 186–192.

Leichter, H. J. (1974). *The family as educator.* New York: Teachers College Press.

Lightfoot, S. L. (1978). *Worlds apart: Relationships between families and schools.* New York: Basic Books.

Marjoribanks, K. (1979). *Families and their learning environments: An empirical analysis.* London: Routledge and Kegan Paul.

Mayeske, G. W. (1973). *A study of the achievement of our nation's students.* Washington, DC: U.S. Government Printing Office.

McDill, E. L., and L. Rigsby. (1973). *Structure and process in secondary schools: The academic impact of educational climates.* Baltimore: Johns Hopkins University Press.

Olmsted, P. P., M. J. Wetherby, H. Leler, and R. I. Rubin. (1982). Parent perspectives on home-school relationships in a compensatory education program. Paper presented at the annual meeting of the American Educational Research Association in New York.

Rich, D., and C. Jones. (1977). *A family affair: Education.* Washington, DC: Home and School Institute.

Rich, D., J. Van Dien, and B. Mattox. (1979). Families as educators of their own children. Pages 26–40 in *Partners: Parents and schools,* edited by R. Brandt. Alexandria, VA: Association for Supervisors and Curriculum Development.

Richards, J. M., Jr. (1975). A simulation study of the use of change measures to compare educational programs. *American Educational Research Journal* 12: 299–311.

———. (1976). A simulation study comparing procedures for assessing individual educational growth. *Journal of Educational Psychology* 68: 603–612.

Rivlin, A. M., and P. M. Timpane. (1975). *Planned variation in education: Should we give up or try harder?* Washington, DC: The Brookings Institution.

Scott-Jones, D. (1987). Mother-as-teacher in the families of high- and low-achieving black first graders. *Journal of Negro Education* 56: 21–34.

Sinclair, R. L., ed. (1980). *A two-way street: Home-school cooperation in curriculum decision making.* Boston: Institute for Responsive Education.

Tidwell, R. (1980). *Evaluation of the accelerating home education and development (AHEAD) program, 1979–1980.* Los Angeles: University of California at Los Angeles. Mimeographed.

Tizard, J., W. N. Schofield, and J. Hewison. (1982). Collaboration between teachers and parents in assisting children's reading. *British Journal of Educational Psychology* 52: 1–15.

Walberg, H. J., R. E. Bole, and H. C. Waxman. (1980). School-based family socialization and reading achievement in the inner city. *Psychology in the Schools* 17: 509–514.

Wisler, C. E., B. P. Burnes, and D. Iwamoto. (1978). Follow-Through redux: A response to the critique by House, Glass, McLean, and Walker. *Harvard Educational Review* 48: 171–185.

Homework Practices, Achievements, and Behaviors of Elementary School Students[*]

ABSTRACT

Data from 82 teachers and 1,021 students and their parents are used to explore the correlates of homework activities and elementary school students' achievements and behaviors in school. Six groups of variables that concern homework are examined: homework time, homework appropriateness, student attitudes, teacher practices of parent involvement in learning activities at home, parent abilities and resources, and other student and family background variables.

Results suggest that at the elementary school level, students with low achievement in reading and math spend more time doing homework, have more minutes of parent help, and have parents who receive more frequent requests from teachers to help at home. Questions are raised about the design of homework, the involvement of families, and the need for research that builds on the reported correlates.

INTRODUCTION

Homework is considered one of the most important practices for establishing a successful academic environment in high school. Coleman, Hoffer, and Kilgore (1982) concluded that homework and discipline were two features of private schools that made them more successful learning environments than public schools. The implication is that if public schools assigned more homework, their students would learn more, and the schools would be more effective.

This prescription may be too simple. The notion that more is better may not be true for all students, in all subjects, at all skill levels, and at all grade levels. Indeed, if more homework is assigned than can be completed, or if inappropriate homework is assigned, then home assignments may be counterproductive for student achievement.

Most research on the effects of homework has been conducted at the secondary school level. Rutter, Maughan, Mortimore, and Ouston (1979) included three items about homework in their report on secondary school effects. They reported that the assignment of homework by teachers and the completion of homework by students were positively associated with student academic performance and

---

* By Joyce L. Epstein. This work was supported by grants from the U.S. Department of Education, Office of Educational Research and Improvement. The opinions are the author's and do not necessarily reflect the policies or positions of OERI. An earlier version of this paper is included in *ERS Information Folio: Homework* (Arlington, VA: Educational Research Service, 1987 and 1990).

school behavior. They found that schools in which teachers gave frequent, substantial homework assignments had better student outcomes than did schools in which teachers assigned little homework. It is important to note, however, that their cross-sectional data were reported only as zero-order correlations, and could mean that schools with good, hardworking students had diligent teachers who assigned more homework more often.

Similarly, a National Assessment of Educational Progress (NAEP) study of students' mathematics skills showed that among 10,000 17-year-olds, good students did about 10 hours of homework and watched about 5 hours of TV per week. Poor students often received no homework and varied in the amount of TV they watched (Yeary, 1978).

Keith (1982) conducted an important study of the effects of homework on the achievement of secondary school students. Using data collected in the High School and Beyond (HSB) survey, he found a significant, positive effect of homework on high school grades (path coefficient = .192). Race, family background, ability, and school program (i.e., track) were statistically controlled, providing a rigorous analysis of cross-sectional data. He also showed an interesting linear relationship between hours of homework per week and school grades for students at three ability levels. The grades of low-ability students who did 10 hours of homework or more per week were as good as the grades of high-ability students who did no homework. Keith's findings suggest that students' personal commitments to school and homework may have positive consequences for students at all levels of ability.

The extant studies of homework, based on limited data, leave many questions unanswered. They yield mixed results, with some showing positive results from homework and others showing no results or negative correlations (Austin, 1978; Gray and Allison, 1971). Little is known about why or how homework is associated with student achievement, behavior, attendance, or attitudes. We need to understand why homework is assigned, whether it is appropriate in quantity and quality, and how it is structured to fit into teaching and reteaching skills in the classroom. It is important to determine if there are measurable effects on students of homework time, habits, completion, and assistance or support from parents and peers.

We also need to examine homework policies and practices at the elementary school level, because the achievements of young students largely determine the ability group or curriculum track they enter in middle and high schools. Homework could be important if it were shown to help more elementary students attain skills that are needed for success in the middle grades. Also, we need to understand parental involvement as a feature of homework, including whether parental assistance helps students who need the most help and whether and how interactions affect parent-child relationships.

PURPOSES OF HOMEWORK

From the literature, I have identified 10 reasons that homework is assigned to students. Some are more defensible than others. The 10 Ps, or purposes, for homework are:

Practice: Increase speed, mastery, and maintenance of skills.

Preparation: Ensure readiness for the next class; complete activities and assignments started in class.

Participation: Increase the involvement of each student with learning tasks to increase the immediacy and enjoyment of learning.

Personal Development: Build student responsibility, perseverance, time management, self-confidence, and feelings of accomplishment; also develop and recognize students' talents in skills that may not be taught in class; extension and enrichment activities.

Parent-Child Relations: Establish communications between parent and child on the importance of schoolwork, homework, and learning; demonstrate applications of schoolwork to real-life situations and experiences; promote parental awareness of and support for students' work and progress.

Parent-Teacher Communication: Enable teachers to inform and involve families in children's curricular activities and enable parents to know what topics are being taught and how their children are progressing.

Peer Interactions: Encourage students to work together on assignments or projects, to motivate and learn from each other.

Policy: Fulfill directives from administrators at the district or school level for prescribed amounts of homework per day or week.

Public Relations: Demonstrate to the public that the school has rigorous standards for serious work, including homework. Also, productive interactions with the public may be designed as student-community homework assignments.

Punishment: Correct problems in conduct or productivity (not a defensible purpose).

All but one of the 10 purposes for homework are important, although most teachers say that the main reason they assign homework is to give students time to practice skills learned in class (see Becker and Epstein, 1982 [Reading 3.1]).

Homework for Practice and Preparation

Homework enables students to practice skills, increase the ease with which skills can be used, and increase understanding of how and when to use the skills. Garner (1978) studied 400 fifth-, eighth-, and tenth-grade students. He measured both class time and homework time for specific subjects to establish exposure or total time in and out of school allocated to specific subjects. He found greater variation in homework than in class time for math and language arts. For example, almost one-third of the fifth-grade students in his sample had approximately eight hours' more total exposure to language arts skills and activities than the rest of the students, or more than one extra day per week for learning and using language arts. Older students received more homework than did younger students. At the tenth-grade level, one-half hour of homework in math extended class time by 75 percent for more math learning. Even at the fifth-grade level, 25 minutes of math homework added half again the time of a typical math class period for learning, reviewing, or practicing math. In Garner's study, high-ability students were given more homework and class time, especially at the high school level. Garner's findings point to the potential value of well-planned use of homework time to extend learning time and to give time to practice skills.

Homework for Participation

Homework increases individual participation in lessons. In many classrooms, only a few children participate frequently and "carry the class," while other children passively absorb information or not. By contrast, homework requires each student to participate actively and continually by reading, thinking, and recording ideas and answers on paper and by making decisions about how to complete the work. Homework is a structured opportunity for students to take control of their learning and thinking. At home, students control the amount of time they need to learn something and the number of consultations with others (including parents and peers) to make discoveries or to receive support for academic work. Students make self-assessments on the quality of their work and may compare their self-assessments with their teachers' marks or grades on homework completed.

Homework for Personal Development

Some teachers assign homework to help students take responsibility for schoolwork. Students must record the assignment, create a schedule to do the work, finish it, store it in their notebooks, and bring it to school when it is due. Homework may be designed to help students build "study skills" and develop students' perseverance, ability to follow directions, neatness and completeness, and overall level of responsibility.

Homework for Parent-Child Relations and Parent-Teacher Communications

Sometimes homework is the only form of serious communication about school and learning between parents and school-aged children. Children may need help in following directions, remembering and interpreting what was learned in school, relearning information that was misunderstood or incompletely learned, and deciding whether their approach and presentation will be acceptable to the teacher. Homework provides a reason for parents and children to exchange information, facts, and attitudes about school. Maertens and Johnston (1972) found that students who had homework assignments and who received immediate or delayed feedback from parents had better mastery of math skills than did students who received no homework.

Homework provides a reasonable, feasible way for teachers to communicate regularly with all families about what their children are learning in school and how their children's skills are progressing. Parents see, via homework assignments, how their children write, think, and execute an assignment. Teachers sometimes assign homework so that parents will not be surprised by their children's report card grades that reflect the quality of classwork.

There are important questions for new studies to ask about parent involvement in learning activities at home. For example, do teachers advise all parents on how to monitor, check, and interact with children on homework? Do teachers ask parents to help when students have specific weaknesses and needs, or to more certainly "share the blame" for students' low achievement? Do parents who are guided in how to help at home have children who improve their achievement?

Homework for Peer Interactions

In addition to homework designed to encourage parent-child interactions, homework may be designed to encourage students to work with each other on assignments and projects. Students may check each other's math, listen to and edit stories, explore their community, and engage in other exchanges and activities to learn from and with one another. Assignments may enable pairs or small groups of students to combine their talents in art, music, writing, drama, and other skills.

Homework as School Policy

Homework may be assigned to comply with district or school directives that a certain amount of homework must be given to all students on a certain number of days each week. Surveys of parents indicate that they have time to interact with and help their children on weekends (see Epstein, 1986 [Reading 3.4]), but schools often assign homework only on weekdays. Homework policies should be reviewed from year to year, with input from teachers, parents, and students to ensure that homework is designed to meet various positive purposes, including family-friendly schedules for parent-child interactions.

Homework as Public Relations

Homework is sometimes assigned to fulfill public expectations for rigorous demands for high student achievement. If there is a belief that a "good school" is one that gives homework, then educators may assign homework to meet this standard for school organization.

Homework as Punishment

Homework may be assigned to punish students for lack of attention or for poor behavior in school. This includes the infamous assignments to write "I must not chew gum in school," or 500 words on appropriate behavior, or other reminders of school standards for behavior. Punishing assignments exercise the teacher's power to use up time at home that would otherwise be under the student's control. The assignments often center on behavior rather than academic skills and stress embarrassment rather than mastery. It is generally believed that punishment is an inappropriate purpose for homework, and there are no known studies of the effects of punishing assignments on students.

The 10 purposes of homework require different homework *designs*. It is clear that not all desired outcomes for students will result from just any assignment. That is, assigning minutes or more minutes of homework will not necessarily produce greater achievement, better study habits, more positive attitudes about school, or any other single desired outcome. Thus, the outcome or result measured in research should relate directly to the purpose of the homework. For example, if the stated purpose of the homework is public relations, then the outcome measured should concern the understanding and attitudes of parents or the public. If the purpose is improved basic skills, then the homework should focus on specific skills, and studies should measure how those skills are affected by doing or not doing homework.

If teachers, administrators, and parents define several purposes simultaneously, then multiple measures of results will be needed to determine whether any or all purposes are met. For some purposes, the *design* of homework—how it is structured, introduced, and followed up—may be as important as its topic or content. Keshock (1976) reported that when college science homework was graded and counted as part of the course grade, homework performance improved but test scores did not. Also, in a Los Angeles PUSH-EXCEL program, students were asked to work uninterrupted from 7:00 to 9:00 P.M. on home-learning activities. This requirement improved homework behaviors, but reports were not available on whether achievement was improved (Yeary, 1978).

Using data from the International Association for the Evaluation of Educational Achievement (IEA), Wolf (1979) reported that homework time was important for specific academic subjects. He reported significant correlations between homework in science and literature and achievement in those subjects at the school and individual student levels. However, in regression analyses that accounted for family background and instructional program (or curriculum track), variables were entered in blocks, making it impossible to pinpoint the independent effects on achievement of homework compared to other instructional variables. The results show only that good students do more homework than do poor students in science and literature. The important point from this research, however, is that homework in one subject may affect outcomes in that subject only and may not have a general effect on achievement test scores or on other student attitudes and behaviors.

DATA AND APPROACH

In this study, the following information about homework was collected from each source involved in the homework process.

Data from Teachers

Teacher data included homework policies of the school and district, the amount of homework assigned, subjects of homework, the purpose of homework, attitudes and policies about parental help with or corrections of homework, the policy of requiring parents to sign homework, estimates of students who complete homework, nominations of students who have problems with homework or who are homework "stars," and use of class time to check or correct homework.

Data from Principals

Principal data included district and school policies, procedures to check teachers' homework assignments, and attitudes about whether parents should help with homework.

Data from Parents

Parent information included reports of the amount of time the child spends on homework, teachers' policies on parental help on homework, evaluation of appropriate level of difficulty of the child's homework, the child's understanding and completion of homework, and communications with the teacher about homework.

Data from Students

Student information included the amount of homework assigned and completed, weekend homework, habits of doing homework, help at home on homework, parents' knowledge of homework assignments, problems and completion of homework, the appropriate level of challenge in homework, attitudes about homework, and written comments.

Surveys of teachers, principals, parents, and students in 16 Maryland school districts were conducted in 1980 and 1981. Approximately 3,700 first-, third-, and fifth-grade teachers and their principals in 600 schools were surveyed (see Becker and Epstein, 1982; Epstein and Becker, 1982 [Reading 3.2]). From the original sample, 36 teachers were identified who strongly emphasized parent involvement in learning activities at home. These "case" teachers were selected at random from a stratified sample of leaders in parent involvement to represent the three grade levels; the urban, suburban, and rural districts; the socioeconomic conditions of the communities in the state; and the teachers' education, experience, and teaching conditions. Forty-six "comparison" teachers were then matched to the case teachers on the same selection criteria, but these teachers were not leaders in their use of parent involvement in learning activities at home.

The case and comparison teachers and their principals were interviewed at length about instructional practices in general and parent involvement practices and leadership. The parents of the children in the 82 teachers' classrooms were surveyed about their attitudes toward and experiences with parent involvement. In all, 1,269 parents responded by mail to the survey, a response rate of 59 percent. Approximately 600 fifth-grade students were surveyed about their homework activities. This report uses data from parents and teachers to explore the correlates of homework activities and student achievements and behaviors in school.

EXPLORATORY ANALYSES

In this study, selected data from teachers, principals, students, and parents were explored to learn more about how homework assignments and home-school interactions were linked to student achievements and behaviors. Table 3.30 presents six sets of variables on homework and their zero-order correlations with reading and math achievements, homework performance, and classroom behavior. The six sets of selected variables and their scoring are described below.

Homework Time

Minutes spent per day is a 5-point score from no homework to one hour or more; minutes parent helps or could help per day is an 8-point score from no minutes to one hour or more.

Homework Quality

Appropriate amount and difficulty are 3-point scores from too easy to too difficult, and too little to too much; appropriate purpose is a 4-point score of parent disagreement that homework is just busy work (scored negatively).

Student Attitudes

Parent recognition that the child likes to talk about school and homework, and that the child is tense about homework (scored negatively), are 4-point scores from strongly agree to strongly disagree.

TABLE 3.30   Homework Variables as Correlates of Student Achievements and Behaviors[a, b]

	Achievements		Student Measures Behaviors			Mean/S.D.
	Reading	Math	Homework Star	Homework Problem	Discipline Problem	
1. Homework Time						
Minutes spent	−.108	−.052	.081	.000	−.011	3.00/1.25
Minutes parent helps	−.180	−.195	−.010	.070	.134	26.32/15.40
Minutes parent could help	−.042	−.077	.090	−.137	.045	43.84/17.34
2. Homework Quality						
Appropriate amount	.019	−.033	−.075	.030	.041	2.16/0.53
Appropriate difficulty	.032	.025	−.021	.012	.053	2.07/0.40
Appropriate purpose	.047	.025	.045	.009	.012	3.61/0.72
3. Student Attitudes						
Likes to talk about school and homework	.131	.117	.140	−.132	−.124	3.35/0.93
Not tense about Homework	.179	.141	.074	−.119	−.032	2.90/1.16
4. Teacher Practices						
Frequent requests for parent involvement	−.137	−.123	.054	.043	.020	3.98/3.36
Teacher thinks parents should help	−.187	−.172	−.025	.013	−.007	2.20/0.82
Parent receives ideas from teacher	−.061	−.077	.063	.019	−.042	2.44/1.17
Teacher talked to parent about:						
(a) Homework	−.087	−.137	−.070	.118	.012	0.18/0.38
(b) Parent help at home	−.132	−.110	.018	−.008	−.032	0.22/0.42
(c) Behavior	−.055	−.072	−.012	.061	.275	0.46/0.50
Parent rating of teacher quality	.060	.093	.105	−.026	−.077	3.76/1.19
Principal rating of teacher quality	.113	.093	−.044	−.085	.003	2.52/1.04
5. Parent Abilities and Resources						
Parent education	.196	.238	.027	−.100	−.057	2.60/1.23
Confidence in ability to help	.140	.166	.085	−.073	−.034	3.12/1.11
Educational items at home	.238	.262	.071	−.105	−.136	4.67/2.53
Number of books at home	.161	.192	.060	−.095	−.078	3.97/1.20
Regular place for Homework	−.043	−.056	−.053	.080	.019	1.09/0.29

(continues)

TABLE 3.30 *(continued)*

	Achievements			Student Measures Behaviors		Mean/S.D.
	Reading	Math	Homework Star	Homework Problem	Discipline Problem	
6. Other Student and and Family Factors						
Sex (Female)	.093	.033	.129	−.075	−.201	1.50/0.50
Race (White)	.083	.155	−.015	−.005	−.064	0.64/0.48
Residence (City)	−.043	−.146	.008	−.018	.034	0.35/0.48
Two–parent home	.057	.142	.085	−.066	−.056	1.76/0.43
Mother works	−.018	.021	.015	.027	−.019	0.61/0.49
Hours TV	−.053	−.082	.009	.003	.057	2.36/1.17
Parent expectations for education	.316	.308	.090	−.137	−.082	2.39/1.13
Grade level	−.002	.045	.033	.036	−.015	2.89/1.70

a N = 1,021 students whose parents participated in the survey for whom information on classroom achievements and behavior was provided by the teacher.

b Correlations of .08 or higher are significant at or beyond the .01 level.

Teacher Practices

Parents reported the frequency of use of 12 practices of parent involvement, including reading, discussion, informal activities, formal contracts, signing homework, tutoring, and drill and practice. Parents' reports that the teacher thinks parents should help, and reports that they receive many ideas from the teacher, are 4-point scores from strongly agree to strongly disagree. Parents agreed or disagreed that the teacher talked to them directly about their child's homework, need for parental help at home, or classroom behavior. Ratings by parents or principals on the overall quality of the teacher are 6-point scores from poor to outstanding.

Parent Abilities and Resources

Parent education is a 6-point score from less than high school to graduate school; confidence in ability is a 4-point score from strongly agree to strongly disagree that they have enough training to help the child in reading and math. Educational items is a checklist of 10 items that students may use at home for homework, including a ruler, dictionary, globe, and others. Number of books at home is a 5-point score ranging from fewer than 10 to more than 100 books. Regular place for homework is a single item of agreement or disagreement.

Other Student and Family Factors

Sex of student is scored female = 1, male = 0; race is scored white = 1, black = 0; residence is scored 1 = city, 0 = suburb/rural; family structure is scored 1 or 2 for one or two parents home, 1 or 0 for mother works or does not work outside the home, hours of TV per day ranging from none to 5 or more hours; parent expectations for child's education is a 4-point score from finish high school to finish graduate school; and grade level refers to the student's grade, 1, 3, or 5.

RESULTS: HOMEWORK PRACTICES AND STUDENT SKILLS AND BEHAVIOR

Homework Time

Section 1 of Table 3.30 shows how three measures of homework time correlate with student achievements and behaviors. The three measures are the average number of minutes spent by the child on homework per day; the average number of minutes the parent helps the child in response to teacher requests; and the number of minutes the parent could help if shown how to do so.

Time spent doing homework ranged from none (13 percent), to 15 minutes (21 percent), 30 minutes (36 percent), 45 minutes (13 percent), or one hour or more (17 percent). Parents helped on the average of 25 minutes per night when asked to do so by teachers but said they could help about 45 minutes per night if the teacher showed them how to help.

The relationships between homework time and parent help on student achievements in reading and math are negative. That is, students with lower achievement in reading and math spend more time on homework and get more help from parents. The negative relationships may indicate that teachers are reaching out to parents to obtain extra help for children who need additional learning time and/or that parents who recognize their children's weaknesses are trying to help on their own. This probability is supported by the fact that parents of children who are deemed homework and discipline "problems" spend more time helping their children than do other parents. Children who are doing well in school spend less time and need less help from parents than do weaker students.

The right side of the table in section 1 shows the associations of homework time and school-related behaviors. Teachers consider children who do more homework as homework "stars." Parents of homework stars say they *could* spend more time assisting their children. The parents of students who are homework and discipline "problems" already spend more time than do other parents assisting their children.

These data should not be interpreted to mean that if more time is spent on homework and more help is given, student achievement will decline. This is a good example of the inadequacy, indeed inappropriateness, of correlations to address questions of effects on students. These cross-sectional data simply tell what associations of variables exist, not whether one variable leads to or causes the other.

The patterns reported here are, however, indicative of some well-known facts about elementary school students and their homework. First, at the elementary school level, all students are likely to be assigned the same homework. The same assignment—such as learning 20 spelling words or completing 10 math problems—may take some students longer than others to complete. Students who have problems learning in school need to spend more time on an assignment to understand what other children master in class and complete quickly at home. Also, teachers may ask parents to see that their elementary school children finish their work, even if they do not ask the parents to help the child with needed skills. Thus, slower students may spend more time on homework, and parents will spend more time monitoring or helping students who need more time to learn or complete their work.

Homework Quality

Section 2 of Table 3.30 features three measures of parents' estimates of the appropriateness and value of the homework their children receive. There are no significant correlations of these measures with achievements or behaviors. One reason for this is the lack of variation in the parents' ratings. Approximately 92 percent of the parents agreed that homework was not busy work, 90 percent said that the child's homework was the appropriate level of difficulty, and 78 percent thought the child received the right amount of homework. Because parents of successful and unsuccessful students generally agreed about the value and appropriateness of homework, these variables do not explain student skills, homework completion, or classroom behavior.

Student Attitudes

Section 3 explores relationships of student attitudes toward homework with student achievement and behaviors. Children who like to talk about school and homework with a parent have higher reading and math skills and are more often considered homework stars. Children who do not like to talk about school and homework are more apt to be homework and discipline problems. Also, children who are not tense about homework are higher achievers and less likely to be identified as having homework problems.

In this sample, close to 20 percent of the elementary school students do not like to talk about school with their parents, and 35 percent say they are tense when working with their parents on homework. These attitudes and behaviors may be early warning signs of more serious problems of commitment to schoolwork. Teachers may be able to help parents learn how to help their children build confidence and positive attitudes about school and homework. Positive attitudes toward school are good indicators of day-to-day success in school, commitment to school goals, and the likelihood of staying in school, even if they do not directly relate to high achievement (see Reading 3.9). Here we see, however, that a very specific behavior—talking about school and homework at home—is correlated with reading and math achievement and with successful actions and behaviors.

Teacher Practices

Section 4 includes measures of teacher practices of parent involvement concerning homework. The correlations indicate that teachers make more requests of parents whose children achieve at lower levels. These results support the information reported in section 1 that parents spend more time with children who need more help, and suggest that parent time is given in response to requests from teachers.

The data indicate that homework and discipline problems are addressed through specific communications with parents. Teachers talk directly with parents about homework activities if the students are identified as having homework problems (r = .118), and teachers talk directly with parents about school behavior if students are identified as having discipline problems (r = .275). Teacher practices of parent involvement are more highly and consistently correlated with student achievement, showing clearly that teachers reach out especially when they need parents' help with students whose math and reading skills are low.

Parents say they receive more frequent requests, more messages that they should help, and more direct communications from teachers about how to help at home when their children are low in reading and math skills. Principals and parents, however, rate teachers higher in overall teaching quality when students are high in achievement, and parents give higher ratings to teachers if their children are homework stars.

Parent Abilities and Resources

Section 5 of the table examines five family resources that may aid student achievement and behavior. Four measures are significantly and positively correlated with reading and math skills: parent education, parental confidence about ability to help in reading and math, educational items in the home, and books in the home. When these resources are lacking at home, children are more likely to have homework problems.

Having a regular place for homework is not highly associated with achievement or behavior. Others have also reported that a regular place for homework is not as important as a regular habit of completion, regardless of where homework is done (McCutcheon, 1983). In these data, however, the lack of importance of the variable is probably due to the lack of variation in the responses, with about 91 percent of the families reporting that the children have a regular place for doing homework.

Other Student and Family Factors

Section 6 shows the association of other student and family factors that are believed to affect homework activities, achievements, and behaviors. There are strong correlations of race (white), location (noncity residence), and two parents at home with higher math skills, but not with reading skills. Female students tend to have higher reading scores and are more often viewed as homework stars, whereas males are more often labeled discipline problems.

Parental educational expectations for children are strongly associated with higher reading and math achievement, more homework stars, and fewer homework and discipline problems. Even more than socioeconomic status variables, parents' expectations are positively associated with student achievement. Parents' expectations are, in part, based on students' history of high achievement, good work, and good behavior. Thus, parents' expectations reported at one point in time reflect their children's prior tests, report card grades, homework assignments, and other parent-child and parent-teacher interactions. Parents have higher expectations for students who are achieving and behaving well in school.

Some family variables are less important than might be expected from popular opinion. Hours of TV watched per day are not highly correlated with reading or math skills and not at all correlated with being a homework star or having school-linked problems. There is no significant association of the mother working outside the home with reading or math achievements, homework completion, or classroom behavior. Student achievement and behavior are not significantly affected by grade level. There are high- and low-achieving students, and well- and poorly behaved students, at all grade levels.

SUMMARY AND DISCUSSION

Several intriguing patterns emerge from the six groups of variables reviewed in Table 3.30, to guide future studies.

Reading and Math Skills

Low achievement is associated with more time spent doing homework, more minutes of parent help, and more frequent requests from teachers for parent involvement in learning activities at home. The significant negative associations indicate that in the elementary school parents are asked to assist children who need more help. At this level of schooling, not much homework is assigned per night, and students who have trouble with the work can work a little longer to complete the assignment.

By the time students are in high school, much more homework is given, and more is given to brighter students. Poor students in high school tend not to work very long on what they do not understand and typically do not expect and may not want their parents' help. Most middle and high school teachers do not ask parents to help with or even monitor students' homework. These patterns are particularly interesting for what they might mean for improving homework designs, assignment, and connections with families.

Homework and Classroom Behavior

Parents report spending more time helping children that teachers say are discipline and homework problems. The parents of other children say they *could* spend more time helping their children at home, if they were shown how to do so. There is a supply of untapped parental assistance available to teachers that may be especially useful in improving the skills of average and below-average students who could do better with additional time and well-guided attention.

One important correlate of homework and discipline problems is the lack of educational trappings at home (e.g., books, rulers, globes, dictionaries, art supplies). Teachers who seek parental help in solving student homework and discipline problems may need to find ways (perhaps including connections to business partners) to make educational resources available for use at home.

Importance of Positive Attitudes and Exchanges about Schoolwork and Homework

Children who like to talk about school and homework with their parents and are less tense about their work tend to be good students, homework stars, and well behaved in class. Children who are tense when working with their parents on homework activities are more often homework problems. Yet children with achievement and discipline problems are those whose parents are spending more minutes helping at home. It is pretty clear that parents of children who have problems in school require guidance on *how to help* their children at home, or ineffective teaching at home could redouble the school problems.

Homework is a manipulable variable. Teachers and administrators control whether to assign homework and how much homework to assign. They design activities that encourage or prevent parental involvement in learning activities that students bring home.

Need for Full Analyses and Longitudinal Data

This study suggests that a simple association of homework time (assigned or spent) and student achievement is not enough to understand if or when homework is important for effective teaching and learning. The array of correlates makes it clear that future research must include multivariate analyses that take into account the variables from sections 5 and 6 of Table 3.30 of family resources and family and student factors that affect achievements and behaviors. The correlates are just a start for understanding the independent effects of homework time, quality, attitudes, and parent involvement on achievement and behavior.

The bottom line concerning homework is whether time spent pays off for improving and maintaining school achievement, homework completion, and other school attitudes and behaviors. This question is particularly important for students who need extra time and extra help to learn basic and advanced skills. Future studies will need longitudinal data to learn whether achievement and behavior improve when students put in time on homework and when they are monitored and assisted by their families. More broadly, new measurement models will be needed to study the complexities underlying homework design, assignment, completion, follow-up, and interactions with families.

The relationships of homework time, achievements, and behaviors at the elementary school level are important because they differ markedly from relationships noted for secondary school students. Younger students and their families are more responsive to school demands for mastering basic skills, and the children and their parents spend more time working on needed skills.

Somewhere between the elementary and middle grades, the philosophies and practices of teachers, students, and parents change. In the upper grades, brighter students tend to spend more time on homework, and many slower students stop doing homework altogether. In many cases, teachers in middle and high schools assign more homework to brighter students because they expect it will be done. Many parents in middle and high schools stop monitoring homework, especially if they are not given information about homework policies or how to work with their adolescents. There are many interesting questions for future research on the differences in the amount of time slower and brighter students spend on homework in the elementary and secondary grades, and why these patterns occur.

REFERENCES

Austin, J. D. (1978). Homework research in mathematics. *School Science and Mathematics* 78: 115–121.

Becker, H. J., and J. L. Epstein. (1982, November). Parent involvement: A study of teacher practices. *Elementary School Journal* 83: 85–102. (Reading 3.1).

Coleman, J. S., T. Hoffer, and S. Kilgore. (1982). *High school achievement.* New York: Basic Books.

Epstein, J. L. (1986). Parents' reactions to teacher practices of parent involvement. *Elementary School Journal* 86: 277–294. (Reading 3.4).

Epstein, J. L., and H. J. Becker. (1982, November). Teacher reported practices of parent involvement: Problems and possibilities. *Elementary School Journal* 83: 103–113. (Reading 3.2).

Garner, W. T. (1978). Linking school resources to educational outcomes: The role of homework. *Teachers College Research Bulletin* 19: 1–10.

Gray, R. F., and D. E. Allison. (1971). An experimental study of the relationship of homework to pupil success in computation with fractions. *School Science and Mathematics* 71: 339–346.

Keith, T. Z. (1982). Time spent on homework and high school grades: A large-sample path analysis. *Journal of Educational Psychology* 74: 248–253.

Keshock, E. G. (1976). The relative value of optional and mandatory homework. *Teaching Method News* 8: 3–32.

Maertens, N., and J. Johnston. (1972). Effects of arithmetic homework on the attitudes and achievements of fourth, fifth, and sixth grade pupils. *School Science and Mathematics* 72: 117–126.

McCutcheon, G. (1983). How does homework influence the curriculum? Paper presented at the annual meeting of the American Educational Research Association in Montreal.

Rutter, M., B. Maughan, P. Mortimer, and J. Ouston. (1979). *Fifteen thousand hours: Secondary schools and their effects on children.* Cambridge, MA: Harvard University Press.

Wolf, R. M. (1979). Achievement in the United States. Pages 313–330 in *Educational environments and effects,* edited by H. J. Walberg. Berkeley: McCutchan.

Yeary, E. E. (1978). What about homework? *Today's Education* (September–October): 80–82.

Student Reactions to Teachers' Practices of Parent Involvement*

Decades of studies indicate that home environments and family involvement in education are important for student success in school (Coleman et al., 1966; Epstein, 1984; Leichter, 1974; Marjoribanks, 1979; Mayeske, 1973; McDill and Rigsby, 1973). The evidence is clear that parental encouragement and involvement at school and at home boost children's achievement, even after student ability and family socioeconomic status are taken into account.

However, not all families get involved in school-related activities or show interest in their children's work (Lightfoot, 1978). It is important to learn what would happen if schools took steps to engage all parents, not just those who become involved on their own. Another crucial question is: What do students think about parent involvement? Ironically, although students are ultimately responsible for their own education, they are rarely consulted for ideas about how to improve their schools, or about how they, their teachers, and their families might best work together to enhance student success in school (Epstein, 1981). This study explores (1) what students know and say about home-school connections and (2) the results of students' experiences with family involvement on their school attitudes and behaviors.

STUDY BACKGROUND

Research shows that teachers vary in the extent to which they use different practices and strategies to involve parents in learning activities at home (see Becker and Epstein, 1982 [Reading 3.1]; Epstein and Becker, 1982 [Reading 3.2]). In a survey of 3,700 first-, third-, and fifth-grade teachers, some reported a high emphasis on parent involvement ("case" teachers), and some reported average or low emphasis on parent involvement ("comparison" teachers).

A sample of 30 case and 30 comparison teachers was matched on characteristics of their teaching situation, including grade level, city or county, district, socioeconomic status of the children taught, and type of teaching assignment. Additional data were collected in extended interviews with the case and comparison teachers and with their principals, surveys were administered to parents of these teachers' students, and surveys were obtained from fifth-grade students in case and comparison teachers' classes. The case and comparison teachers also provided data on their students' achievements, school behaviors, and homework

* By Joyce L. Epstein. An earlier version of this paper was presented at the annual meeting of the American Education Research Association in 1982. This research was supported by grants from the U.S. Department of Education/OERI. The results and opinions do not necessarily reflect the position or policy of OERI.

completion patterns. School records were culled for third- and fifth-grade students' achievement test scores. This study focuses on 390 fifth-grade students in the matched classrooms of nine case and nine comparison teachers.

Few previous studies of family involvement focus on upper elementary school-aged children. Several researchers and program developers report evidence from several completed studies and unpublished dissertations suggesting generally positive effects of the programs on parents and students (Comer, 1980; Gordon, 1979; Henderson, 1981; Rich, Van Dien, and Mattox, 1979). However, most studies are uneven and their measures of parent involvement are incomplete. One study of 764 sixth-grade students by Benson, Medrich, and Buckley (1980) is interesting even though it is not a study of teachers' practices of parent involvement on school-related activities. The researchers examined the natural variation in how parents spend time with their children at home in everyday interactions such as eating dinner together, in cultural enrichment activities, in participation at school, and in setting rules for their children. They looked at the relationship of parents' time and student achievement for students from low, middle, and high SES families. They found that family time in cultural and other activities positively influenced the achievement of students from all socioeconomic levels, but especially students from high and middle SES families. The results illustrate, again, how the self-initiated activities of some families are advantageous to their children.

In the present study, data from fifth-grade students are explored to determine if teachers' practices of parent involvement and reports of parents' assistance differ among students in case and comparison teachers' classes. The next sections give an overview of the data collected from students, principals, and teachers, and the results of analyses of the effects of multiple measures of parent involvement and support on student attitudes and school behaviors.

DATA

Surveys were collected from 390 fifth-grade students in case and comparison teachers' classrooms. The surveys asked students about their homework assignments, homework completion, parents' help at home, attitudes about school and homework, success in school, behavior, college plans, and open-ended comments about homework activities. In most classes the teachers administered the short, anonymous surveys and collected them in mailing envelopes that were returned directly to the researchers.

In one district, local regulations required students to obtain individual, signed parental permission slips to take surveys in class. The timing of the study in the spring of 1981 made it risky to wait for signed permission slips. Teachers did not have time to distribute and collect permission slips, then administer the surveys, when they were concluding tests and other end-of-year activities. In this set of classrooms, student surveys were included with the parents' surveys and were completed by the students at home and mailed back to the researchers.

In the school-administered settings, the response rate of students was from 90 to 100 percent, depending on number of children present the day of the survey. In the home-administered settings, the response rate averaged about 50 percent. The lower response rate of home-administered surveys reflects the parents' responses to the survey, parents' decisions to give the student survey to their children, and children's willingness to complete the survey at home. These obstacles highlight the benefits of conducting no-risk surveys of students as part of standard school and district evaluations of their own programs.

Independent Variables

Multiple Measures of Parent Involvement. Multiple measures of teachers' practices of parental involvement were collected from teachers, principals, and students. These included teachers' reports of their parental involvement practices; teachers' ratings of parents who are "helpful" to their children on school activities at home; principals' ratings of teachers' leadership in involving parents; students' estimates of the frequency of assignments from teachers that request parent involvement at home; and students' estimates of the extent of parental awareness and support of homework activities.

Because no single measure is perfect, multiple indicators of the construct of parent involvement were used to try to correct for measurement problems and check for consistent patterns of effects of parent involvement on students' achievements and behaviors. For example, teachers' reports of their parental involvement practices were collected one year before the survey of students was conducted. Principals may not be fully aware of how much and how well their teachers involved parents with students at home. Students' estimates of teachers' practices and parental support were obtained from a limited number of questions in a short survey. Teachers' estimates of parents who were helpful at home were based on different degrees of contact with the parents of the students in their classes.

Each of these measures, used alone, would raise doubts about the effects of parent involvement. By contrast, patterns of results from more than one measure should provide more credible and convincing information about positive, negative, or no effects of involvement on student achievements and behaviors.

Other Explanatory Variables. Student gender, race, location of school in city or suburb, student ability (i.e., ratings of low, average, and high ability provided by teachers), and the general quality of teachers' skills (i.e., quality of lessons, knowledge, creativity, and discipline) are used as statistical controls in regression analysis. These variables have been found to affect student outcomes and teaching effectiveness, and, therefore, must be taken into account in estimates of effects on students of teachers' practices of parent involvement.

Dependent Variables

Just as multiple measures of parent involvement were used to identify patterns of effects, this study incorporates a variety of dependent variables from the student surveys and teachers' reports to identify patterns of effects of involvement on indicators of student success or problems in school. The dependent variables include:

- two measures of student attitudes, including attitudes toward homework (two items: homework is a waste of time; I learn a lot from homework), and five items of student satisfaction with school (Epstein, 1981);
- one measure of home-school similarity (three items: my parent is a teacher; I learn important things at home; and school teaches what my family wants me to learn);
- one measure of extra schoolwork done at home (two items: I do weekend projects assigned by my teacher; I complete work on weekends on my own);
- one measure of teacher-family exchanges (two items: my teacher knows my family; if I am in trouble, my teacher lets my family know);
- one measure of student homework habits (two items: I do my homework at the same time; I do my homework in the same place);
- one measure of parent support (four items: my parent reminds me to do my homework; my parent knows when I need help with homework; my parent knows when my homework is finished; my parent knows when I have done a good job with homework); and
- teacher estimates of student behavior, including the identification of students who are homework stars, homework problems, and discipline problems.

RESULTS

Table 3.31 shows the background characteristics of students in the case and comparison teachers' classrooms, along with teachers' ratings of student and parent qualities and principals' ratings of teachers. In case teachers' classrooms, there were fewer males and more females, fewer white and more black students, and more students with average reading and math abilities. These characteristics are statistically controlled in all analyses of effects of teacher practices of parent involvement on the dependent variables.

Teachers were asked to nominate as many of their children as fit a set of descriptors: "homework star," "homework problem," and "discipline problem." The teachers also nominated families who were "helpful" or who typically provided "no follow-through" on homework and home-learning activities. More students in case teachers' classrooms were nominated as homework stars, and fewer

TABLE 3.31 Summary of Student Characteristics, Teacher Characteristics, and Student Opinions in Nine Case and Nine Control (Matched) Fifth-Grade Teachers' Classrooms

Student Background Characteristics	% Students in Case Teachers' Classrooms N = 199	% Students in Comparison Teachers' Classrooms N = 191
Male	41	56
Female	59	44
White	46	55
Black	54	45
Urban	53	52
Other	47	48
Reading ability		
Low	11	9
Middle	54	49
High	35	40
Math ability		
Low	14	26
Middle	48	34
High	35	40
Teachers' evaluations of student behaviors and family support for parent involvement		
Homework star	30	20
Homework problem	19	19
Discipline problem	11	18
Helpful parents	56	20
No follow–through by parent	12	17
Principals' estimates of teachers' qualities and excellent teaching skills (i.e., quality of lessons, knowledge, creativity, discipline)	51	45

were considered discipline problems, than in comparison teachers' classrooms. About equal numbers were homework problems. More students in case teachers' classrooms had parents whom teachers considered "helpful," and fewer parents showed "no follow-through," than in comparison teachers' classrooms. Overall, the raw data suggest that case teachers had more positive estimates of more of their students and families on homework and home-school connections than did the comparison teachers, reflecting and confirming the case teachers' emphasis on family involvement.

Student Attitudes and Behaviors

Table 3.32 summarizes the effects of the indicators of parent involvement and support on students' attitudes about school, homework, and home-school connections. Five measures of parent involvement and support derived from data from teachers, principals, and students are featured. The columns are labeled "Case/Comparison Teachers" (an indicator based on teachers' reports of the extent of practices of parental involvement), "Helpful Parents" (from a checklist from teachers of parents' helpfulness and follow-through); "Teacher Practices to Involve Parents at Home" (from principals' ratings); "Homework That Involves Parents"; and "Parent Awareness and Support" (two reports from students on the kind of homework they receive and their interactions with parents on homework).

Each dependent variable is regressed, separately, on each of the parent involvement measures along with student background characteristics (gender, race, reading and math abilities), school location (urban/suburban), and teacher quality. With these potentially important influences statistically controlled, we can look at the effects of parent involvement practices on student outcomes. Table 3.32 reports the standardized regression coefficient (ß) and, for significant associations, the test-statistic (F). The last column of the table lists other explanatory variables that significantly affect students' attitudes and behaviors.

Student Attitudes.   The first row shows that student attitudes toward school are positively and significantly influenced by four of the five parent involvement measures provided by teachers, principals, and students. Students have more positive attitudes about school if they report that their parents are aware of and are involved in helping with homework, if their teachers rate the parents as helpful, and if principals report that the teacher works to involve families at home. Student attitudes toward homework, in the second row of the table, also are significantly more positive when students say their teachers assign interactive homework and their parents are aware of and involved with them on homework.

Gender and race also influence attitudes toward school and homework. Female students and African American students have more positive attitudes than do other students, with all other background and ability measures statistically controlled. Interestingly, student reading and math abilities do not significantly influence student attitudes, echoing earlier evidence that achievement and attitudes about school are not necessarily highly related measures (Epstein, 1981).

Student Reports of Home-School Connections.   The middle three rows of Table 3.32 indicate that student interactions with parents at home about homework affect their beliefs that their home and school are similar and that their teacher knows their family. Student beliefs about strong home-school connections are explained by all five indicators of parent involvement from teachers, principals, and the students themselves.

Student ability and teacher quality also affect beliefs about home-school connections. Students with high reading and math abilities, and those with excellent teachers as rated by principals, also are more likely to see their home and school as more similar and their teachers and parents in closer communication.

Parent involvement indicators are less powerfully linked to student reports that their teacher would inform their family if they were in trouble in school, in part

TABLE 3.32 Summary of Analyses of Effects of Multiple Measures of Parent Involvement on Multiple Measures of Student Attitudes and Behavior*

Parent Involvement Measure:	Case/Comparison Teachers Surveys (Teachers) ß	(F)	Helpful Parents Checklist (Teachers) ß	(F)	Teacher Practices to Involve Parents Rating Scale (Principals) ß	(F)	Homework That Involves Parents at Home Survey (Students) ß	(F)	Parent Awareness and Support Survey (Students) ß	(F)	Which Other Variables Are Significant
Attitudes toward school	.028		.083	(4.19)	.151	(11.40)	.235	(33.31)	.139	(12.94)	Female, Black
R^2	.293		.301		.318		.364		.323		
Attitudes toward homework	.047		-.013		-.032		.218	(27.71)	.149	(14.58)	Female, Black
R^2	.266		.253		.255		.233		.293		
Home-school similarities	.040		-.044		.153	(11.01)	.198	(21.86)	.142	(12.68)	Not City, High Ability
R^2	.167		.177		.216		.251		.222		
Teacher knows family	.073	(3.21)	.219	(28.59)	.153	(11.05)	.158	(13.89)	.099	(6.10)	Not City, High Ability, Teacher Quality
R^2	.198		.280		.229		.238		.211		
Teacher informs family if trouble	.055		.092	(4.85)	.040	(3.82)	-.029		.079	(3.85)	Female, Black
R^2	.177		.180		.161		.159		.175		
Do homework at the same time	-.043		.024		.091		.142	(10.94)	.108	(7.22)	None
R^2	.110		.118		.140		.176		.158		
Do homework in the same place	.058		.015		.027		.139	(10.45)	.136	(11.40)	None
R^2	.110		.087		.091		.156		.161		
Assigned weekend homework	.143	(12.55)	.057		.018		.110	(6.74)	.033		White, City, High Ability
R^2	.251		.229		.223		.245		.225		
Do homework on weekend	.068		.059		.071		.157	(14.08)	.165	(18.03)	Female, Black, Not Urban
R^2	.263		.255		.256		.289		.298		

*Data from teachers, principals, and students, with gender, race, ability, location, and teacher quality controlled N = 390.

because there is less variation on this measure. Most students believe that their teachers would, indeed, contact their parents about trouble in school.

Homework Habits.   The last four rows of Table 3.32 reveal that students' knowledge and reports about their own experiences at home are the best predictors of their homework habits. Students are more likely to do their homework at the same time and in the same place if they frequently interact with parents and if parents are aware of their work. These homework habits are not explained by any of the other variables used in the equations, such as student gender, race, ability, and teacher quality.

Teachers' practices of parent involvement are, however, significantly linked to student reports that they are assigned homework on weekends. Teachers who frequently involve parents in learning activities at home are more likely to take advantage of available weekend time to encourage these interactions. Students say they *do* more homework on the weekend when their parents support their work.

Suburban students and those with high reading and math abilities are more likely than other students to see similarities between home and school, think the teacher knows their family, and have teachers who assign weekend homework, net of all other student and school characteristics. These analyses indicate, however, that *if* parent involvement is activated by teachers and experienced at home, students in any neighborhood and with low or high academic skills report strong family and school connections and do their homework whenever assigned, including weekends.

SUMMARY AND DISCUSSION

Overall, more than half (25) of the 45 tests of effects of the five measures of parental involvement on nine student behaviors and attitudes were significant. Many were not only significant, but also were strong and educationally important, even after other highly influential student ability, family background, and school and teacher characteristics were taken into account. Although gender, race, location, teacher quality, and student ability were sometimes important, these explanatory variables did not extinguish the positive effects of teachers' efforts to involve families and parent support at home on student attitudes and behaviors.

Two cross-cutting patterns in Table 3.32 are worthy of note. First, the most consistent positive effects on all nine measures of student attitudes and behaviors are linked to students' reports of having assignments that encourage interactions at home, and their recognition of parental awareness, support, and involvement. Second, the most consistent effect across the five measures of parent involvement from students, teachers, and principals is on student reports that the "teacher knows my family." Students are significantly more likely to say their teacher knows the family when their teachers report that they frequently involve parents; the teachers see parents as helpful; the principals recognize that teachers are working to involve families; and the students themselves say that their parents are aware of and engaged in homework activities.

The use of multiple measures of involvement, multiple reporters, and multiple measures of student attitudes and behaviors strengthens any single result reported in Table 3.32. Principals' views of teachers' skills in involving parents, teachers' reports of their practices of involvement, and their views of parents are important indicators of home-school connections. In this study, students' reports add significantly to an understanding of parent involvement. The data suggest that when their families are involved with them on school matters, students are significantly more likely to develop attitudes and conduct activities that will keep them in the students' role and on a successful path through school. At the same time, had only student reports been included, the self-reports might be considered distorted or inflated by self-interests. By including confirmatory reports from teachers and principals, the effects of parent involvement on student attitudes and homework habits are more clear and more credible than in the past.

Where do these results lead? Positive attitudes about school and homework and good homework habits are likely to help students stay in school, even if they are not the top or most academically successful students. Students are more likely to be successful in school if they see their parents as teachers, hear that their families want them to learn what their teachers teach at school, and say that the things they learn at home are important.

There is a growing consensus among educators that parents must play a more active role in their children's education. It is believed that parent involvement assists educators' efforts to help individual students attain basic skills and reach high academic standards. It is expected that if schools systematically and equitably informed and involved all parents, many more students would see that their families and teachers have similar goals for high achievement and good behavior in school and expectations for completing homework at home. This study suggests that parents' influence may be most powerful when they communicate directly with their children, so that students experience interactions, conversations, and activities at home that clearly translate parental interest in their work into students' positive attitudes and commitment to their work.

Studies of students at all grade levels are needed to check and confirm the results reported here. In particular, studies should explore the long-term results of family involvement and positive student attitudes, behaviors, and investments on student achievement and graduation from high school. Data on direct links among teacher practices, parent responses, student experiences, and ultimately, student grades and achievement test scores are needed to extend understanding of the benefits for students of well-organized and equitable home-school connections.

REFERENCES

Becker, H. J., and J. L. Epstein. (1982). Parent involvement: A study of teacher practices. *Elementary School Journal* 83: 85–102. (Reading 3.1).

Benson, C., E. Medrich and S. Buckley. (1980). A new view of school efficiency: Household time contributions to school achievement. In *School finance policy in the 1980's: A decade of conflict*, edited by J. Guthrie. Cambridge, MA: Ballinger.

Coleman, J. S., et al. (1966). *Equality of educational opportunity*. Washington, DC: U.S. Government Printing Office.

Comer, J. P. (1980). *School power*. New York: Free Press.

Epstein, J. L., ed. (1981). *The quality of school life*. Lexington, MA.: Lexington Books.

———. (1984). A longitudinal study of school and family effects on student development. Pages 381–397 in *Handbook of longitudinal research*, Vol. 1, edited by S. A. Mednick, M. Harway, and K. Finello. New York: Praeger.

Epstein, J. L., and H. J. Becker. (1982). Teacher practices of parent involvement: Problem and possibilities. *Elementary School Journal* 83: 103–113. (Reading 3.2).

Gordon, I. (1979). The effects of parent involvement in schooling. Pages 4–25 in *Partners: Parents and schools*, edited by R. S. Brandt. Alexandria, VA: Association for Supervision and Curriculum Development.

Henderson, A., ed. (1981). *Parent participation—student achievement: The evidence grows*. Columbia, MD: National Committee for Citizens in Education.

Leichter, H. J. (1974). *The family as educator*. New York: Teachers College Press.

Lightfoot, S. L. (1978). *Worlds apart: Relationships between families and schools*. New York: Basic Books.

Marjoribanks, K. (1979). *Families and their learning environments: An empirical analysis*. London: Routledge and Kegan Paul.

Mayeske, G. W. (1973). *A study of the achievement of our nation's students*. Washington, DC: U.S. Government Printing Office.

McDill, E. L., and L. Rigsby. (1973). *Structure and process in secondary schools: The academic impact of educational climates*. Baltimore: Johns Hopkins University Press.

Rich, D., J. Van Dien, and B. Mattox. (1979). Families as educators of their own children. Pages 26–40 in *Partners: Parents and schools*, edited by R. Brandt. Alexandria, VA: Association for Supervisors and Curriculum Development.

DISCUSSION AND ACTIVITIES

The comments in this section extend and update the content of the readings in this chapter. Main concepts and results are summarized and used to promote discussions and debates. Questions and activities are provided for class discussion and homework assignments. They may suggest other exercises, field activities, or research projects.

▣ MAIN CONCEPTS

Key Results

The results and issues reported in the readings in this chapter provide a base on which to build new research on school, family, and community partnerships and useful approaches in practice. Three important results, introduced in Chapter 2 and featured in this chapter, deserve particular attention because they changed the way we study and develop programs of partnership.

1. School and teacher programs and practices of partnership influence whether and which families become involved in their children's education and schools.
2. School programs and practices of partnership increase teachers' awareness and appreciation of family assistance and reduce teachers' stereotypes of nontraditional families as uncaring and uninvolved.
3. Subject-specific activities that involve families with their children in learning activities at home help to increase student achievement in specific subjects.

⌷⋮ COMMENT

School Practices Influence Family Involvement (Featured Result Number 1)

Baker and Stevenson (1986) reported interesting results about the connections of parents' knowledge or beliefs about involvement and their actions. Their data indicated that almost all parents (including those with more and less formal education) have similar knowledge about the importance of involvement in their children's education and about ways they might become involved. However, parents with more formal education were more likely to translate their knowledge into actions for and with their children.

This result looks, at first, like a simple story of social class differences. Parents with more formal education are better able to translate knowledge into action. However, the readings in this chapter cast Baker and Stevenson's results in a different light. Data from parents, teachers, and students show that schools' programs and practices help parents with less formal education to more successfully put their knowledge to work. Good information and guidance from school administrators, teachers, and other parents help all parents translate their knowledge about the importance of involvement into actions in working with the schools and with their children.

Although family background variables are important, they are not the only explanation for which parents influence their children's learning and development. The nature and quality of teachers' and administrators' practices to involve families are as or more important than family background variables such as race or ethnicity, social class, marital status, parental education, or mother's work status for determining whether and how parents become involved in their children's education. Family practices of involvement are also as or more important than family background variables for determining whether and how students progress and succeed in school.

Surveys of parents reveal that their activities and conversations about school with children at home are directly influenced by the types of practices that schools conduct to involve parents. That is, if schools invest in practices to involve families, most or all parents respond by taking part in those practices, including parents who might not have otherwise become involved on their own.

Surveys of teachers reveal a related result. Teachers' classroom practices to involve their students' families are strengthened when their schools' programs for involving families are strong. When teachers recognize that other teachers and administrators in their schools place high importance on involving families, they conduct more activities to involve their own students' families. Thus:

- Families do more when schools guide their involvement.
- Teachers do more when others in their schools share a commitment to practices of involvement.
- Family behavior (what families *do*) is as or more powerful than family characteristics (what families *are*) in influencing their children's school work and success.

These results should encourage educators to develop comprehensive, school-wide programs to reach out to inform and involve all families, including those who might not otherwise become involved on their own.

ACTIVITY

Classroom Debate and Discussion

A. Create a panel to debate the following resolution: *Resolved: What families do is more important than what families are.*
  1. Explain the distinction between family characteristics and family behaviors.
  2. Take one side of this debate. Prepare your main argument in a paragraph or two.
  3. Imagine your adversary in the debate. Prepare a paragraph or two taking that position.
  4. Discuss or debate this issue in class.
B. Why is it important for schools to develop programs and implement practices to involve families in different ways, rather than simply to expect or demand that families get more involved? Give at least one idea of why such programs and practices are important:
  1. for the school as a whole
  2. for an individual teacher, student, family, and for the community
C. Why is it important for *all families* to know *every year* that their schools and all teachers will:
  1. provide useful information about school programs and children's progress?

2. ask for and use information from them about their children?
3. create a climate of partnership as children progress through the grades?

D. Give one idea why C1, C2, and C3 are particularly important to one of the following: (a) a family with an excellent student, (b) a family with a failing student, or (c) a family of a student with special needs.

0: COMMENT

Teachers Who Involve Parents Rate Them More Positively and Are Less Likely to Stereotype Nontraditional Families (Featured Result Number 2)

Significantly, practices of partnership assist teachers as well as parents. For example, when they work to involve all parents, teachers gain greater understanding of parents' interests in and potential for assisting their children. Teachers who frequently involve families in their children's education rate single and married parents, low-income and middle-income parents, and more and less formally educated parents more positively and more equally in helpfulness and follow-through with their children at home. By contrast, teachers who do not frequently involve families give more stereotypic ratings to single parents, poor parents, and those with less formal education, marking them lower in helpfulness and follow-through than other parents.

QUESTIONS TO DISCUSS

1. A. Why do you think teachers who involve families more frequently give more positive ratings to all families?
   B. Why do you think teachers who do *not* involve families frequently are more likely to stereotype single parents, poor parents, or those with less formal education?
2. What other group(s) of families or students might these two types of teachers treat or rate differently? Explain your ideas.
3. Labels create stereotypes because they ignore important variations in family practices. That is, not all families *in any category* behave the same way. As stated in Reading 3.5, "Single parents are not a single group."
   A. How do labels such as "single parent," "working mom," "welfare family," and "less-educated parents" affect school, family, and community partnerships?
   B. How do labels such as "illegitimate child," "latchkey child," and "poor student" affect students in school and the roles the students play in school, family, and community partnerships?

C. How would you revise the labels listed in (A) and (B) to improve the wording of the descriptors and to correct any distortions that they create?

4. A. How are the following phrases defined statistically and colloquially?
   1. "nontraditional family"
   2. "traditionally uninvolved family"
   3. "traditionally underserved family"

   B. Justify or refute each of the above three terms as they relate to employed mothers, single parents, and parents with less formal education. Should these families be included in one or more of the categories listed above?

   C. How do you think the three phrases affect school, family, and community partnerships?

5. Reading 3.6 reports data from a sample of parents who, some educators and researchers believe, are *not* involved in their children's education. Re-examine the data reported in Reading 3.6.

   A. Select and identify two results that indicate whether parents in inner-city schools are involved or wish to be involved in their children's education.

   B. Explain why each of the two results you selected is important for understanding parents of elementary- and middle-grade students in inner-city schools.

ⓘ COMMENT

There Are Subject-Specific Links between Family Involvement and Student Achievement (Featured Result Number 3)

Practices to involve families at home in interactions with their children about a specific subject are likely to affect student achievement in that subject. In the study reported in Reading 3.7, data connected teacher practices, parent responses, and student achievement over one year. We learned that:

- Teachers' practices to involve parents in learning activities at home were mainly limited to reading, English, or related activities. Also, principals encouraged teachers to involve parents in reading and related skills.
- Parents reported more involvement in reading activities.
- Students improved reading scores more from fall to spring if their teachers frequently involved parents in reading-related learning activities at home, but the students' math scores were not affected.

The data indicate that when parents are involved in reading, students respond by focusing on and completing more reading activities at home. This may lead to greater attention, motivation, and success in reading in school.

The data from this study suggest that practices of partnership may be purposely designed to help boost student achievement in specific subjects. There also were some important related findings. Family involvement in one subject will not necessarily benefit the child in another subject. Family involvement in activities at home may not benefit students at all *unless* the activities are well designed, well implemented, and accompanied by excellent teaching every day in school.

◈ FIELD EXPERIENCE

Interview a Parent/Quick Survey

When the study in Reading 3.7 was conducted, most teachers in the elementary grades asked parents to become involved in reading more than other subjects. Find out whether this is still true.

A. Interview one parent of an elementary school student. Identify whether you are interviewing a mother or father and the grade level of the child. Note any other factors about the family or community that you think may influence responses. Ask:
   1. Does your child's teacher ask you to become involved with your child on homework?
   2. If YES, ask:
      A. In which subjects?
      B. If more than one subject is mentioned, check: In which subject are you most often asked to be involved?
   3. If NO, ask:
      A. Do you and your child work together on any subject or skills at home?
      B. If so, in what subject most of all?
B. Document your questions and responses. Write a paragraph summarizing what you learned from the parent you interviewed.
C. *Optional class activity:* Discuss the responses to these interviews in class. Do the results of your classmates' interviews suggest that there is more parent involvement in reading/English, as we found in the original study, or is there evidence of other patterns of subject-specific involvement?

▐: COMMENT

What Is and What Might Be

Research helps identify "what is" and "what might be" in school practices to involve families. An average score tells *what usually is*, whereas the variance helps point to *what might be*. Of course, variations in scores are higher and lower, better and worse than the average score. For example, many studies indicate that some teachers go far beyond average in conducting many activities to involve all students' families. Other teachers conduct far fewer involvement activities than the average.

The variation in practices of partnership is often more interesting than the average. Within a state, district, and even a school, teachers' and administrators' approaches to families vary. Some educators conduct many activities to inform and involve all families; others have not yet thought about how to integrate partnerships into their work as professional educators. The teachers and administrators who have already developed effective partnerships help researchers and other educators identify and study *what might be* possible in all schools. Those who avoid communicating with families help inform the field about problems that must be solved. Reading 3.2 presents ideas from both groups of teachers.

QUESTIONS TO DISCUSS

Select two challenges that teachers in Reading 3.2 described as barriers to parent involvement.

Example: One challenge discussed in Reading 3.2 is that *telephoning parents takes time*. To meet this challenge, you might think about organizing a schedule to guide teachers about whom to call, how often to call, how to mix positive messages with calls about problems, how to get help from volunteers in making certain kinds of calls, how to supplement phone calls with other communications, and other solutions. You may use this challenge as one barrier, or select two different challenges from Reading 3.2.

1. State the two challenges that you selected.
2. Outline at least two important issues that need to be resolved to meet each challenge.
3. List at least one activity that might be implemented to address the issues you outlined to meet each challenge.
4. Share the challenges, issues, and solutions in class. Examine the activities suggested for their feasibility, sensitivity to families' situations, and likely success.
5. *Optional class activity:* Collect the most promising ideas for a resource notebook or computerized idea file on school, family, and community partnerships for use in schools or for researchable topics.

❏⋮ COMMENT

Discrepancy Scores

Data in Reading 3.3 indicate that, on average, teachers are more likely to support the involvement of families if they think that *other* teachers and administrators in their schools have similar beliefs and goals about the importance of parent and community involvement. They also are more likely to conduct activities to involve their students' families if their school has a well-organized program of school, family, and community partnerships. By contrast, if they think that their colleagues do not support parent involvement, teachers are less likely to implement many practices themselves. In some schools, however, you will find *outliers:* teachers who are leaders in involving families, even if no other teachers do so.

◈ FIELD EXPERIENCE

Interview on Patterns of Collegial Support

A. Interview one school-based educator about his or her practices and school experiences to involve families and communities to see which model—the *group-support process* or the *individual-leader phenomenon*—seems to be working in the school. The educator may be a teacher, administrator, counselor, or other specialist at a preschool or elementary, middle, or high school. Identify the school level and position of the person you interview. Ask:
   1. At your school, does the power of the group influence practices to involve or avoid parents, or does each individual teacher decide whether and how to involve parents? Explain.
   2. Do most teachers conduct the same kinds of activities, or do individual leaders do more and better activities with parents than most other teachers? Explain.
   3. What is one example of a practice that all teachers in the school conduct with all or most families?
   4. What is one example of a particularly good practice that only one or two teachers conduct with the families of their students?
   5. Are formal plans written each year outlining all of the activities to involve parents and communities in the school at each grade level? If so, who writes these plans? If not, how are activities scheduled?
B. Add at least one question of your own about group or individual approaches to involve parents or communities.
C. Document your questions and the responses.
D. Write a paragraph summarizing what you learned or questions raised in this interview.

⚏ COMMENT

Diverse and Changing Families

For the past several decades, families have been changing structures and diversifying functions. There are more single parents, blended families, and other family forms than in the past. There are more families with two parents employed, single parents working outside the home, and, sometimes, parents who are unemployed. Some fathers are at home while mothers work outside the home. Some families are homeless or in temporary shelters or residences. Some families are highly mobile, moving frequently to new homes, schools, and communities.

Families will continue to vary in structure, composition, and situation. Nevertheless, just about all families send their children to school with high hopes for their success and happiness.

The results of the studies in Readings 3.4, 3.5, and 3.6 suggest that some parents (e.g., single parents, and parents with less formal education) are less involved in their children's education unless they receive good information and guidance from the schools.

QUESTIONS TO DISCUSS

Many parents—single and married—work full-time or part-time during the day, evening, or night. Employed mothers and fathers have limited time for meetings and events at the school building. These realities should affect the variety and schedule of activities to involve families at school or at home across the grades.

1. Describe two activities that would permit mothers or fathers who are employed during the school day to participate at the school building.
2. Describe two activities that would permit parents who are employed at night to participate at the school building.

◈ FIELD EXPERIENCE

Parent Interviews about Work and Family

A. Interview two single mothers (i.e., separated, divorced, widowed, or never married) *or* two married mothers who are employed full-time outside the home about the ways in which they are involved in the education of their school-aged children.
B. Before your interviews, write three questions that you will ask both interviewees about involvement in their children's education at home and at school and whether or how their children's schools welcome and guide their involvement.
C. Identify whether you are interviewing single or married mothers. Note the school and grade level of one child in the family and other factors that you think may influence responses to questions about parent involvement (e.g., parents' education; occupation; race/ethnicity; total number of children at home; urban, suburban, or rural community; or other factors).
D. List the questions you ask and the responses of each interviewee.

E. Summarize the results of the two interviews. Explain:
1. How are the two individuals you interviewed alike and different in their patterns of involvement at home and at school?
2. What do you think are some reasons for the similar or different patterns of involvement?
F. Is the information that you obtained representative or not representative of the views that would be obtained from a random sample of 100 single mothers or married and employed mothers? Explain.
G. *Optional class activity:* See how increasing the sample affects the results and conclusions of individual interviews. In class, combine and summarize the data from all interviews with single mothers. Then, combine and summarize the data from all interviews with married mothers. Discuss the full set of results:
1. In what ways are the combined data more useful than the individual reports? Which results might be important in school practice?
2. Which results raise questions that should be studied further?

⊓: COMMENT

Partnerships with Diverse and Changing Families

Families not only differ in form and function (see Reading 3.5), but they change from one year to the next. Single parents marry, married parents divorce, employed parents become unemployed, unemployed mothers start to work outside the home, and so forth. However they change, families still are responsible for their children and share responsibilities with schools for their children's education and development. Families that face stressful changes are more likely to remain partners with schools if administrators and teachers understand how to involve families who are in transition.

QUESTIONS TO DISCUSS

1. List two school, family, and community partnership activities that you believe are appropriate and important for all families to conduct, regardless of how families differ or how they change.
    A. Explain why these activities are important for all families to conduct.
    B. Explain one way in which schools could help families with each of the activities that you listed.
2. List one school, family, and community partnership activity that needs to be tailored for (a) single parents, (b) employed parents, and (c) parents who separate, divorce, or remarry to feel comfortable about participating.

Describe how and why you would tailor or adapt the activity you listed for these three groups.

ⓘ COMMENT

One-Parent Homes but Two-Parent Families

Some students live with one parent, and the other parent lives nearby. Many nonresident parents (usually fathers) would like to be more active in their children's education. Some nonresident parents have joint custody of their children and expect to be fully involved in their education, but the school may officially record the address of only one parent. Many nonresident parents would appreciate information and invitations from the school to become more involved. Studies suggest that children whose nonresident fathers are involved in their schooling are more likely to like school, do well in school, and participate in extracurricular activities than are children in one-parent homes whose nonresident fathers are uninvolved.

Some children have no contact with their nonresident parent. These students may be particularly sensitive to questions or school activities that refer to "your parents."

Depending on their situations, students may appreciate options to communicate with one or both parents or other relatives to involve important adults in their lives and in their school activities and experiences. These complex topics of how schools understand and interact with families that are differently structured require systematic study and innovative school and classroom practices.

◇ ACTIVITY

Review or Interview

A. Identify a level of schooling that interests you. Use your experience or interview a teacher or school administrator to address these questions:
   1. What is your school's policy about providing information or invitations to nonresident parents?
   2. What is your school's policy about vocabulary referring to *a parent* or *parents*:
      - in memos or other communications to the home?
      - in activities in class?
B. Write a short critique of the policies that are described. Is each one a good policy? Why or why not? If no policy exists, draft a short, workable policy statement on whether and how to provide information and invitations to nonresident parents.

C. *Optional follow-up activity:* Interview one nonresident parent of a school-aged child to learn if and how he or she is presently involved in a child's school and education. Identify whether this parent has joint custody of the youngster.

    1. Write at least five questions for your interview. Include one on the changes in school policies or practices concerning nonresident parents this individual would recommend.

    2. Record your questions and document the responses you obtain.

❏❘ COMMENT

Students Who Live with One Parent

In Reading 3.5, teachers' practices made a difference in whether single and married parents were productive partners with the schools in their children's education. This result reinforces the importance of measuring school and family practices *simultaneously* to understand what parents do and whether they are assisted to become involved by the programs and practices at their children's schools. Without this dual attention, many studies distort the desires and abilities of all families to be productively involved in their children's education.

    A study of midwestern youth in one- and two-parent homes concluded that, on average, kids do better in two-parent homes, but some students in single-parent families thrive, and some in two-parent homes do not. Family structure does not fully determine or explain children's and adolescents' well-being. What matters most, regardless of family structure, is what happens within the family (Benson, 1993). For example, adolescents in single-parent homes are much less at risk of failing or getting in trouble in school if they report that their families are involved in their schooling, provide social support, and monitor other aspects of their lives. Examine the following chart (Benson, 1993):

What Percent of Successful and Unsuccessful Students in One-Parent Homes Are Supported by Their Families in Different Ways?

Percent of students who report:

Students in one-parent homes	Family support for education	Parent involvement in schooling	Parental standards	Discipline at home
Of students who thrive:	64	29	85	60
Of students who do *not* thrive:	34	18	47	41

As shown in the chart, higher percentages of adolescents in single-parent families who "thrive" in school (i.e., achieve well, have high aspirations, do homework, stay out of trouble) report that they receive support and guidance from an involved parent at home, compared with students who do not thrive in school (i.e., have academic or behavior problems). Another way to say this is that more students from single-parent families who are successful in school report having strong parent support, standards, discipline, and involvement.

Saying that some single parents are involved in their children's education while others are not is important, but not surprising. Many studies conducted in the United States and other nations show that in all kinds of families, some parents are involved and others are not, and the children of involved parents are more likely to succeed in school in many different ways (see also Sanders and Epstein, 1998a, 1998b). Reading 3.5 adds the information that when teachers implement activities to involve all families, more single parents become involved in their children's education across the grades. Then, their children have a better chance of succeeding in school.

QUESTIONS TO DISCUSS

1. In the chart, which variable—family support, involvement, standards, or discipline—do you think presents the most important contrasting percentages for students in one-parent homes who thrive compared with those who do not?
   A. Identify the variable and percentages you are most interested in discussing.
   B. Explain why you think the percentages reported for that variable are important.
2. Write two questions that you would like to ask the students who were in Benson's study to better understand the family and school circumstances that contributed to the results in the chart. State your two questions and explain why each is important for understanding the variables in the chart.
3. Use at least two examples from Reading 3.5 to discuss this statement: *Family involvement and support in one-parent and two-parent homes is partly determined by school practices.*

▐▌ COMMENT

Who Is Hard to Reach?

Who are the hard-to-reach parents? In some ways, some of the time, every family is hard to reach. Parents who work outside the home may be hard to reach. Parents who are at a distance from the school may be hard to reach. Fathers may be hard to reach. Young parents, older parents, parents of older children, parents with less formal education, those who do not speak English, single parents, step-parents, foster parents, and parents of students who themselves are adolescent parents may be hard to reach. In some cases parents with advanced education or great wealth also may be hard to reach. Some families fit more than one of these descriptors, and may be particularly hard to reach.

Not all schools have the same hard-to-reach families. Some schools have figured out how to contact and involve families who seem unreachable at other schools.

◈ FIELD EXPERIENCE

Reaching Hard-to-Reach Parents

A. Interview one teacher or administrator from two different schools. Identify the positions of your interviewees, their school or grade levels, and important characteristics of their students, families, or communities. Ask:
1. Who are the hard-to-reach parents in your school?
2. Why are they hard to reach?
3. What strategies have been used at your school to try to reach one or more of the groups of families that you listed?
B. Add at least one question of your own.
C. List the questions you ask and the responses.
D. Write a paragraph on the similarities or differences in the responses of educators from the two schools, and possible reasons.
E. *Optional class activity:* Share and compare ideas with others in the class. Identify useful strategies for reaching hard-to-reach parents.

◧ COMMENT

Paired Data from Teachers and Parents

Readings 3.1 and 3.4 are "paired" with data from teachers and parents from the same schools, respectively, in a statewide sample of urban, suburban, and rural schools. Data in Readings 3.3 and 3.6 also are "paired" with data from teachers and parents from the same schools in a sample of urban elementary and middle schools. The data from these studies reveal common themes and important contrasts among teachers and parents. For example, most teachers think parents are *not* involved in their children's education, whereas most parents report they *are* involved—or try to be, often without guidance or assistance from the school or from their children's teachers.

As another example, almost all teachers (more than 90 percent) say they had conferences with parents, but 36 percent of the parents say they *never* had a conference with their child's teacher. These discrepancies must be discussed, explained, and addressed for parents and teachers to understand each other's work and their common interests in children.

QUESTIONS TO DISCUSS

1. How can the reports from 90 percent of teachers and 36 percent of parents about parent-teacher conferences *both* be true?
2. What are the implications of these contrasting results for improving the way in which parent-teacher conferences are organized, scheduled, and counted?
3. Read one pair of readings (3.1 and 3.4 or 3.3 and 3.6).
   A. Identify one set of results (not those discussed above) that indicate that parents and teachers, on average, view things similarly or differently.
   B. Explain how the similar or different results that you identified might affect school, family, and community partnerships.

❏⠿ COMMENT

Teachers as Parents

Despite the fact that most teachers are parents, data from many surveys show that teachers misunderstand what most parents try to do at home. Many teachers blame parents for their lack of involvement, despite the teachers' knowledge of how hard it is to stay informed and involved in their own children's education from year to year. It may be that teachers characterize all parents according to their worst experiences with families, rather than according to their best experiences. Determine if this is true through the following field experience.

◈ FIELD EXPERIENCE

Interview Teachers Who Are/Are Not Parents

A. Interview one teacher who is a parent of a school-aged child and one teacher who is not a parent. Write their responses to the following questions:
   1. What is your best experience with a parent?
   2. What is your worst experience with a parent?
   3. How would you describe the involvement of most parents?
B. Add a question of your own for these teachers.
C. Ask the teacher who IS a parent:
   1. In what grade level is your oldest school-aged child?

2. How easy or difficult is it for you to be involved at this child's school?
3. How easy or difficult is it for you to be involved with this child at home?
4. How much information or guidance do you get from this child's school and teacher to help you be productively involved?

D. Add a question of your own for this teacher.
E. Summarize what you learned from the two teachers you interviewed. Include the following reflections as well as other ideas:

1. From the first set of questions, how were the teachers' assessments of most parents influenced by their best and worst experiences?
2. From the second set of questions, how did the teacher's role as an educator affect interactions with his or her child's teacher(s)? How did the teacher's role as an educator affect interactions with the child at home?

⫶ COMMENT

Student Achievement and Family Involvement

Reading 3.7 uses *gain scores* to measure achievement (i.e., how much a student grows over one year), after accounting for initial skills. There are some typical or expected patterns in these data. For example, we find that students who start with lower scores make greater gains over one year.

There are statistical reasons for this result. One technical explanation is a general "regression to the mean," which suggests that, simply by chance and human nature, poor students will, on occasion, score higher than they did before. Similarly, good students will, on occasion, score lower than they did before. It may be more than chance or naturally occurring corrections, however, when measures are made after one year's time. For example, students who start out lower in skills have more room to grow, whereas students who start with high scores near the ceiling or top of a range of scores will not be able to show as much positive growth or change. They may be working hard simply to maintain their high scores.

There also are substantive reasons why students with low scores may gain more in one year than students with high scores. For example, schoolwork may be easier at the lower levels, making it possible for students to jump ahead more quickly from low starting points, once they are motivated to work. Or, schools may promote student learning with innovative and responsive curricula and instructional methods that enable slower students to make progress and brighter students to maintain their skills. These alternative, complex, statistical, and substantive issues need to be sorted out in research on the effects of family involvement on student achievement.

The data in Reading 3.7 suggest that gains in reading and math by students in urban elementary schools are influenced by different characteristics of parents, students, and teachers. Examine the following summary chart of results.

SUMMARY CHART

Factors Influencing Gains in Reading and Math in the Elementary Grades

Factors that affect gains in *reading*
- Initial reading scores— low-scoring reading students gain more
- Parent education *(Not significant in reading)*
- High quality rating of teacher *(Not significant in reading)*
- Teacher use of learning activities at home (in reading) *(Not significant in reading)*

Factors that affect gains in *math*
- Initial math scores— low-scoring math students gain more *(Not significant in math)*
- Younger grade levels *(Not significant in math)*
- Recency of teacher training *(Involvement in reading does not affect gains in math)*
- Parent reports of high-quality homework

QUESTIONS TO DISCUSS

1. Select one result in the summary chart that surprised you, and explain why.
2. Explain how the result you selected might affect school, family, and community partnerships.
3. If you were studying student progress in reading or math, what is one additional variable that you would measure to clarify the results in the summary chart? Explain why you think the variable you selected might be important.

▯: COMMENT

Giving Credit Where Credit Is Due

One intriguing result of the analyses of data from the study reported in Reading 3.8 is that teachers tend to evaluate parents based on their children's achievement. Parents of students who were homework "stars" were viewed more positively by teachers than were parents of students who had homework or discipline problems. Parents of homework stars were rated significantly more helpful than other parents. By contrast, parents of children who had trouble with homework or who behaved badly in school were rated significantly lower in helpfulness and follow-through than were other parents.

Student Ability/Behavior	Teachers' Ratings of Parents' Helpfulness and Follow–Through	
	ß	(F)
Homework star	.225	(35.76)
R^2	.4663	
Homework problem	–.146	(14.02)
R^2	.3763	
Discipline problem	–.110	(7.54)
R^2	.3348	

FIGURE 3.5   Teachers' Ratings of Helpfulness and Follow–Through

NOTE: This figure uses the same control variables as Table 3.32.

Parents make similar assessments of teachers. Table 3.30 shows that parents rate teachers higher in quality if their children are homework stars and if their children are doing well in math. Use these results and your experiences to answer the following questions.

QUESTIONS TO DISCUSS

1. Are students high achievers *because* their parents help them, or are parents helpful *because* their students are high achievers? Give one example of how each of these causal patterns could be true.
2. Do students have trouble in school *because* their parents are not involved, or do parents disengage *because* their children have trouble in school? Give one example of how each of these causal patterns could be true.
3. Are teachers more effective *because* their students are high achievers, or are children high achievers *because* they have better teachers? Give one example of how each of these causal patterns could be true.
4. *Optional:* Discuss these issues in class. What are the implications of the examples for research on the effects of family involvement on student achievement?

▯▮ COMMENT

Studying and Improving Homework

Homework is a strategy that can be designed to motivate students, increase learning, involve families, and improve teaching (Cooper and Valentine, in press). For too long, however, homework has been studied as an either/or, more/less variable. Many national and international studies still focus only on the number of minutes or hours of homework that are assigned or spent. The simple debates about minutes of homework miss important distinctions between assigning *more* homework and designing *better* homework. There is a difference between focusing on *time spent on homework* and the complex issues of the *purpose, content,* and *form* of homework.

After reviewing more than two dozen U.S. and international studies of homework and its effects on students, I developed a model for studying, understanding, discussing, and improving homework. This model (see Figure 3.6) specifies an extensive set of variables that should be measured to more fully study and understand the design and effects of homework on student learning, teacher effectiveness, and family understanding and involvement in children's education.

Variables in the Model

The chart on p. 281–283 shows examples of variables for each section of the conceptual model. These or related variables may be included in a measurement model to study the background, design, and effects of homework on students, teaching practice, and family practice.

1. Student and family background				8. Effects on student learning and development
2. Teacher background	4. Classroom organization and classwork	5. Homework assignments	6. Homework completion	7. Homework returns and follow–up
3. School organization and policy				9. Effects of teaching practice
				10. Effects on family practice

FIGURE 3.6 Reasearch Model for Studying Effects of Homework

NOTE: The variables at one point in time contribute to student, school, and family background in longitudinal designs, creating a conceptual and measurement "loop" for studying the effects of homework over time.

1. Student and Family Background
Gender
Race/ethnicity
Parent education
Other family socioeconomic status
(SES) indicators, e.g.:
- Occupation
- Income
- Family size

Student program/curriculum
track/ability group
Student personality variables affecting
homework completion, e.g.:
- Self-concept of ability
- Locus of control
- Diligence, persistence
- Neatness
- Creativity

Student prior or starting achievement
Student prior or starting attitudes
about school, homework
Peer/friendship group homework patterns
Student part-time work hours/schedule
Home conditions supporting learning,
e.g.:
- Place for homework
- Time for homework
- Supplies for homework
- Resources for learning (e.g.,
books, newspapers, art materials)

Climate and support for homework,
e.g.:
- Interruptions
- Competing responsibilities
- Interactions
- Final check

Parental knowledge about school and
classroom
Parental connections with school and
teachers
Community resources/library/museums

2. Teacher Background and Practice
Education
Teaching experience

Quality of teaching
Subject specialization
Attitudes toward students
Philosophy and attitudes about homework
Practices of family and community involvement

3. School Organization and Policy
Grade span
Program definition, e.g.:
- Magnet
- Charter
- Other special school program

Community characteristics
Aggregate student/family population
characteristics
District, school, and classroom homework policies
Standards for homework
Supervision of teachers' lessons and
homework
Articulation of feeder and receiver
schools

4. Classroom Organization and Classwork
Grade level
Subject
Teacher planning time
Interdisciplinary connections across
subjects
Classroom organization, e.g.:
- TARGET structures of task
- Authority
- Reward
- Grouping
- Evaluation
- Time to organize classwork

Plan for homework in instruction
Classroom behavior, discipline
External interruptions

5. Assigning Homework (by Teacher)
Amount and time expected
Frequency

Design/form/novelty/diversity/level of
  interest
Clarity
Coordination with curriculum
Coordination with student ability, e.g.:
  • Group/individual ability
  • Common/individualized assign-
    ments
Content:
  • Review
  • Remediation
  • Critical thinking
  • Creative thinking
  • Enrichment, extension of skills
  • Completion of classwork
Purpose
Practice and mastery of
  knowledge/skills
Preparation for new lesson
Participation, enjoyment of learning
Parent involvement:
  • Parent-child communication, in-
    teraction
  • Parent-teacher communications
Peer interactions
Public relations
Policy
Punishment
Alternative assignments, extra credit as-
  signments
Makeup assignments for absence
After-school activities
Parents' roles in identifying issues for
  homework assignments
Students' roles in identifying issues for
  homework assignments

**6. Completing Homework (by
  Student)**
Time spent:
  • On assigned homework
  • On unassigned homework
Location
  • In-school time for homework
  • After-school place for homework
Level of interest in subject, topic

Use of special skills or talents
Parent support, monitoring, assistance
Parent pressure, conflict, avoidance
Parent communications with teachers,
  e.g.:
  • Daily homework log
  • Computerized messages
  • Required signature
Competing activities for time at home,
  e.g.:
  • Chores
  • TV
  • Internet
  • Part-time work
  • Sports or talents
  • Other lessons
  • Responsibilities
Availability of peers for interactions,
  and extent of interactions of
  friends/classmates/siblings by tele-
  phone, in the neighborhood, and
  other ways

**7. Returning and Following up on
  Homework (by Teacher)**
Timing of return
Frequency of collection, checking
Feedback, e.g.:
  • Correction
  • Evaluation
  • Tally
  • Grade
  • Comment
Follow-up to redo/resubmit assignment
Role of parent after return
Rewards/penalties/consequences for stu-
  dent
Class time, other school time, after-
  school time to make up work
Homework part of report card grade
Extra homework assignments
Notification of parents

**8. Effects on Student Learning and
  Development**
Completion rate, quantity

Completion quality, accuracy, creativity

Improved learning:
- Readiness for next lesson
- Classroom subject tests
- Report card grades
- Achievement test scores

Improved behavior and attitudes toward:
- School
- Subjects
- Homework
- Learning
- Teachers

Attendance:
- Motivation to learn and to work as a student
- Willingness to work to improve
- Continued enrollment in school
- Selection of advanced courses
- Self-control/discipline
- Positive self-concept of ability

9. Effects on Teaching Practice

Organization of instructional time:
- Pace of lessons
- Homework as segment of instructional time

Introduction of homework, questions from students

Follow-up of homework, extension, enrichment

Design of homework and remedial instruction or assignments for individuals

Communications with parents and students

Attention to community and family conditions, interests, talents, and resources

10. Effects on Family Practice

Organization of home environment to support student homework

Frequency of interactions with child on homework

Content of interactions with child on homework

Quality of interactions with child on homework

Parent attitudes:
- About quality of school, teacher(s)
- About responsiveness of school and teacher(s) to child
- Importance of instructional program for preparing child for future
- Understanding of what child is learning in school

Quality of communications with teachers

Support for school program

◇ ACTIVITY

Variables That Affect Homework and Learning

Photocopy and complete the chart in Figure 3.7 or create it on your computer.

A. Select a grade level and a school subject that interests you.
B. In the chart in Figure 3.7, list one variable that interests you from each section of the model given above. For each variable, describe one problem that the variable may cause in the design, conduct, or results of homework, and how that problem might be solved to improve the homework process.

Grade level: _____
Subject: _____

Selected variables from homework model	One problem caused by the design, conduct, or results of homework	Possible solution to the problem that would improve the design, conduct, and results of homework
Example: School Organization and Policy—District, school, and classroom homework policies	**Example:** School or teacher homework policy is not clear to all students and parents	**Example:** Homework policy should be provided in written and other forms and discussed with all students and parents
1. Student and family background		
2. Teacher background, practice		
3. School organization and policy		
4. Classroom organization and class work		
5. Assigning homework		
6. Completing homework		
7. Returning and following up on homework		
8. Effects on student learning and development		
9. Effects on teaching practice		
10. Effects on family practice		

FIGURE 3.7 Variables That Affect Homework Design and Completion

An example for a "School Organization and Policy" variable is shown at the top of the chart.

QUESTIONS TO DISCUSS

Homework is not cost free. There are investments that students, teachers, and parents make for students to complete homework. For example, it "costs" teachers planning time to design homework that will be assigned to students. The investments in homework should yield benefits for students, teachers, and parents. Identify one cost and one benefit of homework for each group listed below. Include one reason why you think each of your listings is a cost or a benefit.

| | HOMEWORK | | HOMEWORK | |
	Cost	Reason	Benefit	Reason
Teachers				
Students				
Parents/Families				

 FIELD EXPERIENCE

Interview Students about Homework

Reading 3.8 uses data from teachers, principals, parents, and students to better understand homework and its links with student achievement and behavior.

A. Interview two students who are in different grade levels.
B. Tape-record or take notes on the students' responses to the following. Ask:
   1. What is the best homework assignment that you remember?
   2. What is the worst homework assignment that you remember?
C. For the best and worst examples, ask:
   1. Please describe the homework assignment you remember.
   2. Do you remember the purpose of this homework?
   3. About how long did this homework take you to complete?
   4. Did a lesson in class lead to the homework, or did the homework lead to a lesson later on? Or was this just a separate activity?
   5. Did you show this homework to a parent, friend, or someone else?
   6. What made the assignment especially good/especially bad?
D. Also check each student's age, gender, and grade level, and ask each student:
   1. General attitude about school: Do you like school a lot, a little, not much, or not at all?
   2. Average grades: Do you get mostly As, Bs, Cs, Ds, or Fs in school?

E. Summarize the students' responses. Write a reflective paragraph on whether the students' reactions to homework were thoughtful and what the students' reactions might mean for designing good homework. Do you see any connections between the students' experiences with and ideas about homework and age, grade level, gender, attitude about school, or report card grades?

F. *Optional class activity:* Combine the data collected by all students in the class. Analyze the basic connections of students report card grades, attitudes about school and homework, whether the students shared their best or worst assignments with a parent or friend, and other connections.

QUESTIONS TO DISCUSS

Most studies of homework indicate that, regardless of their starting skills, IF students do their homework, they are more likely to improve their skills and do better in school than similar students who do not do their homework. One interesting result discussed in Reading 3.8 is that in the elementary grades slower students spend more time than do brighter students completing their homework. By the middle and high school grades, data indicate that brighter students spend more time on homework.

1. Do you think it is possible to design homework that will encourage middle and high school students at all ability levels to spend the time they need to complete their homework? Give two ideas for YES and NO answers to the question.

2. *Optional class activity:* Discuss these ideas in class. Identify the most interesting ideas for improving the design and assignment of homework in middle and high schools to encourage all students to complete their assignments regardless of their ability levels.

◇ ACTIVITY

Reading to Understand Homework

A. Early and recent research on homework adds information to the data presented in Readings 3.8 and 3.9. Select an article, chapter, or book from the following list, or identify a recent publication on homework, and answer the questions below.

Balli, S. J. (1998). When mom and dad help: Student reflections on parent involvement with homework. *Journal of Research and Development in Education* 31: 142–146.
Chen, C., and H. W. Stevenson. (1989). Homework: A cross-cultural examination. *Child Development* 60: 551–561.
Cooper, H. (1989). *Homework*. White Plains, NY: Longman.

Cooper, H., J. Lindsay, B. Nye, and S. Greathouse. (1998). Relationships among attitudes about homework, amount of homework assigned and completed, and student achievement. *Journal of Educational Psychology* 90: 70–83.

Hoover-Dempsey, K. V., O. C. Bassler, and R. Burow. (1995) Parents' reported involvement in students' homework: Strategies and practices. *Elementary School Journal* 95, 435–450.

Keith, T. Z., and V. A. Cool. (1992). Testing models of school learning: Effects of quality of instruction, motivation, academic coursework, and homework on academic achievement. *School Psychology Quarterly* 7: 207–226.

Levin, I., R. Levy-Schiff, T. Appelbaum-Peled, I. Katz, M. Komar, and N. Meiran. (1997). Antecedents and consequences of material involvement in children's homework: A longitudinal analysis. *Journal of Applied Developmental Psychology* 18: 207–222.

MacBeath, J. (1998). The development of student study centres to improve homework and learning in Scotland. *Childhood Education* 74: 383–386.

Natriello, G., and E. L. McDill. (1986). Performance standards, student effort on homework, and academic achievement. *Sociology of Education* 59: 18–31.

Olympia, D. E., S. M. Sheridan, and W. Jenson. (1994). Homework: A natural means of home-school collaboration. *School Psychology Quarterly* 9: 60–80.

Paschal, R. A., T. Weinstein, and H. J. Walberg. (1984). The effects of homework on learning: A quantitative synthesis. *Journal of Educational Research* 78: 97–104.

Scott-Jones, D. (1995). Parent-child interactions and school achievement. Pages 75–107 in *The family-school connection: Theory, research, and practice*, edited by B. Ryan, G. Adams, T. Gullotta, R. Weissberg, and R. Hampton. Thousand Oaks, CA: Sage Publications.

Villas Boas, A. (1998). The effects of parental involvement in homework on student achievement in Portugal and Luxembourg. *Childhood Education* 74: 367–371.

Warton, P. M. (1997) Learning about responsibility: Lessons from homework. *British Journal of Educational Psychology* 67: 213–221.

Xu, J., and L. Corno. (1998). Case studies of families doing third grade homework. *Teachers College Record* 100: 402–436.

B. Answer the following questions about the article, chapter, or book that you selected:
1. List the title, author(s), date, and place of publication.
2. Identify three important variables that are discussed or analyzed in the publication you selected. Tell where you would place each of these variables in the 10 sections of Figure 3.6.
3. Identify one main result of the study you selected. Explain whether and how it is important for understanding the design and effects of homework.

❚⦂ COMMENT

Paired Data from Parents and Students on Homework

Reports from parents *and* students in Readings 3.8 and 3.9 suggest that weekends are underutilized as time for interactive homework. Parents overwhelmingly report that they have time on weekends to talk with their children about school and to help with homework. Students complete more homework and extra work on weekends if their teachers frequently involve their families in learning activities at home. Some schools give no homework on weekends as a matter of policy. Yet, weekends may provide family-friendly time for students to talk with someone at home about something interesting they are learning in class and about important decisions they must make about schoolwork and activities.

QUESTIONS TO DISCUSS

1. Identify a grade level that interests you.
2. Make a chart summarizing one pro and one con argument from the perspective of a teacher, parent, *and* student in the grade level you selected on the following:
   A. assigning homework to students on weekends
   B. assigning homework on weekends that requires students to talk with a parent or other family member about something interesting they are learning in class, or about a school-linked decision
3. Write a paragraph from your point of view about assigning homework on weekends in the grade level you selected.
4. An important result described in Reading 3.8 is that children who like to talk about school at home complete more homework and have higher academic skills than students who do not talk about school at home. This finding raises two "chicken or egg" questions:
   Which came first, doing well in school or talking about school at home?
   Which came first, doing poorly in school or not talking about school at home?

These questions require longitudinal studies to monitor changes in skills over time, but you can begin to explore these issues by discussing the following questions:

A. For the grade level you selected, describe two ways in which children show their distress or anxiety about homework.
B. For the grade level you selected, give one idea of how a teacher might:
   1. design homework assignments that minimize distress and anxiety.
   2. encourage children and parents to talk about schoolwork at home.
C. Which do you think comes first, doing well in school or talking about school at home? Discuss or write a paragraph about one activity that links home and school that might lead students on the positive path you selected.
D. Which do you think comes first, doing poorly in school or not talking about school at home? Discuss or write a paragraph about one activity that links home and school that might lead students on the negative path you selected.

Note: For more information on the design of interactive homework in practice, see Chapter 6.

CROSSCUTTING THEMES

Three quite different themes cut across the readings in this chapter: (1) changes in partnerships across grade levels; (2) partnerships as part of the school authority or decision-making structure; and (3) the use of multiple measures in studies of school, family, and community partnerships. The following comments and questions will help you explore these crosscutting themes.

0: COMMENT

Grade Level and Academic Subject Differences

The theory of overlapping spheres of influence assumes that school, family, and community responsibilities and activities will change over time across the grades, and from teacher to teacher. The readings in this chapter document that on average, elementary schools involve families more than do middle schools. In most middle schools, teachers give less information to parents, and parents report less involvement in their children's education than in the younger grades. Reading 3.6 reports, however, that parents of middle-grade students *want* to be as informed and involved as parents of younger children, although they may require different information and different interactions.

The data also reveal differences in practices among teachers of different subjects. Reading 3.1 shows that teachers were most comfortable in the early grades involving parents in reading and reading-related activities at home. Data in Reading 3.3 show that reading and English teachers involved families more than other teachers, even in the middle grades.

The data about *what is* typical in the elementary and middle grades raise many questions about *what might be* appropriate across the grades, and for teachers of different subjects.

QUESTIONS TO DISCUSS

1. Give examples from the readings and your experiences to address the following questions. (*Optional:* Interview a teacher, parent, or student about these questions. Identify your source, the grade level, and the responses.)
   A. How do school, family, and community partnerships presently change from one grade level to the next? Provide two examples.
   B. How do school, family, and community partnerships presently vary in different school subjects? Provide two examples.

C. How do partnership activities presently change from the beginning to the end of the same school year? Provide two examples.

D. How are communications from home to school affected when children move to a new school (e.g., in the middle of the year, at the start of a new school year, or when they graduate to the next level of schooling)? Provide two examples.

2. Use the results reported in the readings in this chapter and your own ideas to discuss:

A. Should the nature (design of practices, activities, subject matter) of involvement change as children move from the elementary to the middle grades? Provide two examples that support your view.

B. Should the extent (time, number of activities) of involvement change in the elementary and middle grades? Provide two examples that support your views.

▯⁞ COMMENT

Transitions to New Schools and New Grade Levels

Parents, teachers, and students must create new partnerships every year. Parents often are unsure about what is expected by their children's new teachers or how to help their children in new grade levels or new schools. Teachers are unfamiliar with most new students and families who enter their classes each year. Among many unknowns, students are unaware of whether and how their new teachers will keep families informed and involved about school programs and students' progress. For these and other reasons, commitments to school, family, and community partnerships must be renewed every year.

Data show dramatic declines in involvement after each transition to new levels of schooling (i.e., from preschool to elementary school, from elementary to middle school, and from middle to high school). Also, if students transfer to new schools during the school year, families are often uninformed about the school and how to become involved. Educators must have ways to welcome and connect with entering students and their families whenever they arrive at school.

Transitions are risky but important and exciting points of change and promise in students' lives. Appropriate and important school, family, and community partnerships should minimize problems and maximize success for students at points of transition.

QUESTIONS TO DISCUSS

1. Select a school transition that interests you (e.g., preschool to elementary school, elementary to middle school, middle to high school, or high school

to post-secondary education/training). Think about students and their families entering a new school at the transition point that you selected.

    A. Identify or design one activity that would help students and parents make a successful transition to the new level of schooling that you selected.

    B. Identify or design one activity that would give the teachers and administrators the information they need about the children and families who are making a transition to the new level of schooling that you selected.

2. Select a grade level that interests you. Think about students and their families entering a new grade level within their present school (not a transition to a new school).

    A. Identify or design one activity that could be implemented at the start of a new school year to give parents the information they need to help their children make a successful transition to the grade level that you selected.

    B. Identify or design one activity that could be implemented at the *start of a* new school year to give the teachers and administrators the information they need to make a good start with students and their families in the grade level you selected.

3. *Optional class activity:* Share and critique examples of activities to involve families at points of transition from school to school and from grade to grade. Add the most promising examples to a resource notebook or electronic idea file for use in practice or for research and development.

▯፧ COMMENT

Student Mobility

A study of the effects of family mobility indicates that elementary school students in two-parent homes who move up to seven times experience no more academic or behavioral problems than students who do not move. However, even one move increases the academic and behavioral problems of elementary school students in other family arrangements, such as mother-only, step, or blended families, and other family forms (Tucker, Marx, and Long, 1998). The researchers statistically accounted for many family characteristics (such as parent education, income, and recency and distance of moves) to explore the effects of diverse family arrangements and the number of family moves on students' success in school.

Two variables missing from the study should be included in new research. First, it is important to know whether the children had academic or behavior problems *before* they moved, to determine whether mobility and family arrangements are responsible for academic and behavioral problems. Second, it is important to know what schools do to welcome and orient new students and their families with useful information on school policies and parent involvement. Some school practices may reduce the stress of moving to a new community by integrating new students and families into the school community.

Research is needed on whether and how schools with comprehensive programs of school, family, and community partnerships intervene to reduce the risks of mobility to student success in school, especially in single-parent homes, step parent families, or blended families. A related study indicates that students in military families are not particularly affected when a parent is deployed as part of military duty (TDY—temporary duty assignments) (Thompson, 1998). In this study, one influential variable was parental satisfaction with the school's efforts to help students cope with the TDY. Some students are relatively resilient when their families move or when parents are temporarily absent, particularly if the school and community offer helpful information and support during turbulent times.

If schools are aware of stressful family situations and take action to assist students and their families, student achievement and behavior may not be as negatively affected as when families and students are left on their own to adjust to new schools and changes in family life.

QUESTIONS TO DISCUSS

1. In studies of effects of mobility on student success in school, why is it important for researchers to measure whether youngsters were good or poor students, well or poorly behaved *prior to* the move from one school to another?
2. In studies of effects of mobility on student success in school, why is it important to know whether schools conduct practices to welcome, inform, and involve families at school and at home?
3. Why might these partnership practices be particularly important to single parents in new neighborhoods and schools?

▯ COMMENT

The Authority Structure

School, family, and community partnerships are part of the authority structure of schools (see comment on authority and control in Chapter 2). The authority structure is defined, in part, by who participates in school decisions; how families are informed and involved in their children's education; and how often and why students, families, educators, and others in the community interact. The distribution and definition of *power* are altered by the way teachers, administrators, parents, and others in communities think about, talk about, and act to share responsibilities for education. Decisions about schools may be shared on any or all topics, including school organization; management; staffing; curriculum; student motivation; instructional methods; annual evaluations and recognition of teachers, administrators, and students; school climate; and specific policies and programs.

QUESTIONS TO DISCUSS

Use the articles and comments in this chapter to support your responses to the following questions:

1. *Teacher authority.* Is teacher and administrator authority more like a pie or an empire?
    A. How do you view a teacher's authority? Is it like a pie: If some authority is shared with families, there is less of the authority pie left, and the teacher loses power? Or is it like an empire: If some authority is shared and alliances are made with families, the teacher gains power, influence, and effectiveness? Or do you view the effects of partnerships on a teacher's authority in some other way?
    B. Explain your ideas.
    C. Discuss the above questions, substituting "administrator" for "teacher." Does the substitution affect your response? Why or why not?
2. *Family influence.* Is family influence on children weakened or enhanced when children go to school?
    A. How do you view the effects of school, family, and community partnerships on the influence families have to socialize, educate, motivate, and encourage their children? Do partnerships weaken and diffuse family authority and influence because teachers and others educate and socialize children? Or do partnerships strengthen and enhance family influence by providing parents with information and opportunities to interact with their children and educators about school decisions and school life? Or do you view the effects of partnerships on families' authority and influence in some other way?
    B. Explain your ideas.
3. *Student independence.* Is student independence boosted or delayed by school, family, and community partnerships?
    A. How do you view the effects of school, family, and community partnerships on student self-direction and independence? Do partnerships act as a catalyst through which parents, teachers, and others guide students toward greater independence? Or do partnerships act as an inhibitor, with collaborative activities delaying independence and keeping students dependent for too long on teachers, parents, or others? Or do you view the effects of partnerships on student independence in some other way?
    B. Explain your ideas.

Using Multiple Measures, Reporters, and Methods to Understand Family Involvement and Student Outcomes

Several readings in this chapter use multiple measures to study school, family, and community partnerships. The studies include (1) two or more measures from the same reporter, (2) two or more reporters on similar or related measures, or (3) multiple measures and multiple reporters. These techniques may produce consistent *or* inconsistent patterns of results that instantly confirm or dispute conclusions.

For example, in one study we identified teacher-leaders by using two measures, one from teachers' self-reports about their partnership practices and one from principals' ratings of the same teachers' practices. The principals' ratings confirmed or refuted teachers' self-reports on the extent to which they involved families of their students. The measures were cross-checked to identify concordant cases of teachers who were confirmed leaders who were particularly effective in their connections with families. The multiple measures created a better, more reliable independent variable of "teacher-leaders" than either measure could do alone.

As another example, in Reading 3.9, multiple measures were used to determine if reports about the level of family involvement from students, teachers, and principals produced consistent effects on students' attitudes, behaviors, and experiences. In this study, perspectives of different reporters at home and at school supported the conclusion that family involvement was linked to positive attitudes and higher student productivity.

QUESTIONS TO DISCUSS

1. Why might a researcher want to use two, three, or more measures of the same concept from the same reporter? Describe one problem that is solved and one problem that is created by this method of inquiry.
2. Why might a researcher want to obtain information from two or more reporters on the same concept? Describe one problem that is solved and one problem that is created by this method of inquiry.
3. Research on family and community involvement may be conducted using many different methods of data collection and analyses. There is no one right way to study partnerships. Various methods contribute different kinds of information to increase understanding and to raise new questions for future studies. For example, Readings 3.1 and 3.2 present quantitative analyses of survey data and qualitative analyses of teachers' comments, respectively.

A. What do quantitative analyses of survey research (Reading 3.1) contribute that cannot be learned only by observations or "testimonies" about programs?

B. What do the personal comments of teachers (Reading 3.2) contribute that cannot be learned from quantitative analyses of survey data?

▯፥ COMMENT

Effects of Partnerships on Students

Studies of effects on students of school, family, and community partnerships have increased and improved over time. Most early research did not control for students' prior skills when studying whether family involvement increased student achievement. When prior skills are omitted from such analyses, the results mainly indicate that high-achieving students have families who are involved or that families are involved when students are high achieving.

Also, most early research did not account for what schools do to involve families in various ways. When school programs and teacher practices are omitted from such analyses, results mainly indicate that some families become involved on their own, and that their children benefit from self-initiated family involvement.

Thus, information on students' prior skills and on the nature and quality of school programs and teacher practices of partnership is needed to fully answer questions about whether family involvement increases the achievement of students with initially different skill levels.

Analyses in Reading 3.7 statistically control for students' prior skills, teacher quality, and other variables that affect learning to identify the independent effects on students' standardized achievement test scores of teacher practices of involving families. The data link teachers' practices, parents' responses, and children's achievements.

If you see studies—old or new—that do not account for students' starting skills or behaviors, or for schools' practices to involve all families, you should be wary of claims that family involvement increases student achievement or other positive results. Such studies may be showing only that *good* students usually have parents who are more involved at school and at home.

Similarly, you should be wary of correlational results from cross-sectional or anecdotal data that show that family involvement links to poor achievement or problem behavior. This pattern—reported in Reading 3.8—may simply indicate that slower students require extra help at a particular point in time. The help they receive will vary in quality and may or may not have a positive impact on the problem at hand.

Researchers need well-specified measurement models and data that include students' starting skills to identify whether and how family involvement affects students' skills, achievement test scores, or behavior. Quantitative and qualitative studies must account for these complexities to address such questions as: Do school, family, and community partnerships lead to better achievement or other positive results for all students? If students need and receive help from school, home, and the community, do they improve their skills or attitudes?

◇ ACTIVITY

Hypothetical Study

Choose question A or B, according to your interests.

A. Students in Lincoln Elementary School start the fifth grade with very different reading and math skills and with different histories of family involvement. The fifth graders are placed in three classrooms with teachers who differ in how much and how well they involve parents in reading and math. Suppose Lincoln Elementary School has set goals that *all fifth graders will move on to middle school with at least sixth-grade reading and math skills.* Two of many possible research questions linked to school, family, and community partnerships are:
   - Do students have higher math and/or reading skills if their parents are involved in their education at school and at home?
   - Do more students graduate with at least sixth-grade math and/or reading skills if their teachers conduct activities to involve all families with their children in these subjects?
   How might you study these topics to help Lincoln Elementary School learn whether and how well it is reaching its reading and math goals?
   1. Select one of the bulleted questions above that interests you.
   2. There are many methods to use to address these questions. Outline how you might go about studying the question that you selected. How many teachers and students will be involved in your hypothetical study of Lincoln Elementary School? How many families will be included, and in what ways? How many months or years will your study take?
   3. List three major variables that you would include among others in your study, and explain why each variable is important.
B. Students enter Roosevelt High School in the ninth grade with very different reading, math, and other skills and with different histories of family involvement. Each ninth grader has several teachers who have not done much in the past to involve students' parents at school or in students' learning activities and school decisions at home. Suppose Roosevelt High School has set a goal that *at least 90 percent of all students who enter ninth grade will graduate from high school.* Two of many possible research questions linked to school, family, and community partnerships are:
   - Do entering students with similar backgrounds complete grade 12 and graduate from high school on time if their families are involved in their education at school and at home?

- If students fail one or more courses in grade 9, how are they helped by their school, family, and community to get back on the path to high school graduation? How successful are these students?

How might you study these topics to help Roosevelt High School learn whether or how well it is reaching its graduation goal?

1. Select one of the bulleted questions above that interests you.
2. There are many methods to use to address these questions. Outline how you might go about studying the question that you selected. How many teachers and students will be involved in your hypothetical study of Roosevelt High School? How many families will be included, and in what ways? How many months or years will your study take?
3. List three major variables that you would include among others in your study, and explain why each variable is important.

C. *Optional class activity:*
1. Share and discuss the designs of the hypothetical studies of Lincoln Elementary School and Roosevelt High School and the variables that students selected for their studies. Consider: Are the study procedures clear? Are the variables essential? If the proposed study were conducted, would the selected question be clearly addressed?
2. Discuss: Are the questions about fifth graders in Lincoln and high school students in Roosevelt equally easy to study? Explain your ideas.

❶ COMMENT

Importance of Reading Original Research

Although literature reviews, syntheses, annotated bibliographies, and other summaries (such as Reading 2.2) provide useful overviews of a field or topic, they do not replace original research. Syntheses of research ask you to accept the reviewers' interpretations of large numbers of studies. This is an efficient way to scan a field, but you also need to read original research to decide how an individual researcher reports a particular study. You may want to consider: Are the sample and data adequate? Are the methods credible? Do the results add new knowledge to the field? What debatable issues are raised? What new questions should be studied? By reading original research, you should be able to frame your own studies more successfully or judge and select the most promising approaches for educational practice.

◇ ACTIVITY

Reading Original Research

A. Select and read one original research publication (not a review or synthesis) on the effects of school, family, and community partnerships on students, teachers, administrators, or parents. You may choose one article, chapter, or book that is referenced in this chapter's readings, or in the following sources:

Booth, A., and J. Dunn, eds. (1995). *Family-school links: How do they affect educational outcomes*. Hillside, NJ: Lawrence Erlbaum Associates.

Chavkin, N., ed. (1993). *Families and schools in a pluralistic society*. Albany: State University of New York Press.

Christenson, S., and J. Conoley, eds. (1992). *Home and school collaborations: Enhancing children's academic and social competence*. Colesville, MD: National Association of School Psychologists (NASP).

Davies, D., and V. R. Johnson, eds. (1996). Crossing boundaries: Family, community, and school partnerships. *International Journal of Educational Research* 25(1): special issue.

Ryan, B. A., G. R. Adams, T. P. Gullotta, R. P. Weissberg, and R. L. Hampton, eds. (1995). *The family-school connection*. Thousand Oaks, CA: Sage.

Schneider, B., and J. S. Coleman, eds. (1993). *Parents, their children, and schools*. Boulder, CO: Westview Press.

Or you may choose one of the following journal articles:

Griffith, J. (1998). The relation of school structure and social environment to parent involvement in elementary schools. *Elementary School Journal* 99(1): 53–80.

Grolnick, W. S., C. Benjet, C. O. Kurowski, and N. H. Apostoleris. (1997). Predicators of parent involvement in children's schooling. *Journal of Educational Psychology* 89: 538–548.

Hoover-Dempsey, K., O. Bassler, and J. Brissie. (1992). Explorations in parent-school relations. *Journal of Educational Research* 85(5): 287–294.

Public Agenda. (1997). *Getting by: What American teenagers really think about their schools*. New York: Public Agenda.

Useem, E. L. (1992). Middle school and math groups: Parents' involvement in children's placement. *Sociology of Education* 65: 263–279.

Or you may identify a recent publication of original research that includes data from teachers, administrators, parents, and/or students about parental or community involvement in education.

Answer the following questions about the article, chapter, or book that you selected.

1. List the full reference of the publication that you selected.
2. In one or two paragraphs, summarize the questions and main results of the study.
3. Describe in a sentence or two:
    A. Were the sample and data adequate?
    B. Were the variables and measures clear?

C. Were the analyses and results convincing?
4. Identify two results from the publication you selected, and explain what each means for improving school, family, and community partnerships.
5. Write two questions that you think should be studied to follow up on the results of the publication that you reviewed.

REFERENCES

Baker, D. P., and D. L. Stevenson. (1986). Mothers' strategies for children's school achievement: Managing the transition to high school. *Sociology of Education* 59: 156–166.

Benson, P. (1993, June). The troubled journey, and youth in single parent families. *Source* (Search Institute) 9(2): 1–3.

Cooper, H. and Valentine, J. C. (in press). Special issue on homework. *Educational Psychologist.*

Sanders, M. G., and J. L. Epstein, guest eds. (1998a). School-family-community connections: International programs and perspectives. *Childhood Education* (Summer).

———. (1998b). School-family-community partnerships and educational change: International perspectives. Pages 482–502 in *International handbook of educational change,* edited by A. Hargreaves, A. Lieberman, M. Fullan, and D. Hopkins. Hingham, MA: Kluwer Academic Publishers.

Thompson, E. K. (1998). The effects of military deployment on children's adjustment at school. Ph.D. diss., University of Arizona, Tucson.

Tucker, C. J., J. Marx, and L. Long. (1998). Moving on: Residential mobility and children's school lives. *Sociology of Education* 71: 111–129.

PART TWO

Applying Research on School, Family, and Community Partnerships

4

Policy Implications

POLICIES AT THE FEDERAL, state, district, and school levels increasingly include goals for school, family, and community partnerships. Importantly, legislation and guidelines are beginning to go beyond broad objectives for "parent involvement" by including explicit commitments to assist states, districts, and schools to develop their partnership programs. The trend—too slow, but encouraging—is to provide leadership and finances at state, district, and school levels to enable every school to create stronger connections with families, businesses, community agencies, and other groups in ways that benefit students.

The trend is too slow because most state and district leaders have not had the information they need to establish and maintain comprehensive programs of partnership. Most have not assigned the staff and budgets that are needed to conduct state and district leadership activities that will enable all schools to plan and build their partnership programs.

At the state level, there have been too few incentives for action, and too few consequences for inaction, from state boards and state leaders to encourage all school districts and all schools to develop policies and programs of school, family, and community partnerships. Similarly, at the district level, neither incentives nor consequences from district superintendents and school boards are guiding school principals to establish and maintain programs of partnership.

These deficiencies in leadership and organization reflect a general lack of will to translate rhetoric on the importance of family and community involvement and policy statements into practices of partnership. The absence of incentives and consequences allows too many superintendents and principals to put partnership programs on the back burner, instead of placing school, family, and community connections front and center as an essential ingredient of school improvement.

The trend is encouraging, however, because over the past few years increasing numbers of states, districts, and schools have begun to develop and implement comprehensive partnership programs and pass legislation or guidelines on partnerships. The knowledge gained from these efforts should help other states, districts, and schools take similar actions to involve all families and communities in their children's education.

STATES

Some states are actively developing and improving their leadership and programs that support districts and schools in their work on partnerships. For example, several states joined the National Network of Partnership Schools at Johns Hopkins University to work on this agenda. In 2000 they were Alaska, California, Connecticut, Florida, Hawaii, Idaho, Illinois, Kentucky, Louisiana, Maryland, Missouri, New York, North Carolina, Ohio, Texas, Utah, Washington, and Wisconsin.

Leaders in these states are developing many ways to guide and reward districts and schools to improve their partnership programs. State leadership activities include writing state goals and policies, providing training in developing such programs, conducting conferences, making grants to districts and schools for improving partnerships, evaluating work and progress, and recognizing and rewarding excellent practices.

In Minnesota, an example of state leadership is found in legislation that requires employers to permit workers who are parents to use compensatory or flexible time to attend conferences or meetings at their children's schools. This kind of state policy promotes the development of school, family, and community partnerships in one clear way, and assists all schools and all families. This policy, however, does not take the place of state leadership that assists all districts and schools to build comprehensive partnership programs. Other examples of state leadership are discussed in the readings, comments, and activities in this chapter.

Too few of the 50 states have organized their work in ways that integrate family and community involvement activities across state departments or across branches of the state department of education. Too few have permanent offices with long-term plans for partnerships and line-item budgets for developing state-level expertise and excellence in partnership programs in all districts and schools. Too few have passed bold legislation that guides and advances partnerships throughout the state.

DISTRICTS

Some school districts in all states are implementing policies to help schools improve connections with students' families and communities. With or without state guidance and financial support, many districts are writing policies and goals for school, family, and community partnerships, and some are guiding and supporting the work of their schools. For example, in 2000 the National Network of Partnership Schools at Johns Hopkins included approximately 130 school districts that were committed to assisting schools to develop partnership programs. Their work should help other districts learn how to develop and maintain effective district-level leadership and school-level partnership programs.

Still, too few of about 15,000 school districts in the United States are engaged in systematic efforts to develop their programs of school, family, and community partnerships. Most school districts need to make clear commitments to support staff coordinators and facilitators for partnerships and to establish adequate budgets, clear structures, and feasible processes to help all elementary, middle, and high schools establish and continually improve their partnership programs. This includes providing targeted, ongoing staff development, guidance, school visits, and multischool sharing activities on partnerships. Even in very small school districts, superintendents and school boards can support the development of partnerships in many ways. Ultimately, every school must take the lead in planning, implementing, and continually improving its own partnership program.

SCHOOLS

Many elementary, middle, and high schools around the country are working to improve practices to inform and involve families and communities in their children's education across the grades. In 2000 over 1,300 schools located in about 30 states were members of the National Network of Partnership Schools at Johns Hopkins University to develop comprehensive partnership programs. The work of leading schools should help identify essential and effective components of partnership programs and encourage similar actions by other schools.

There are, however, approximately 88,000 public elementary and secondary schools in the country. Not enough presently have coherent and ongoing plans, budgets, and school-site action teams of teachers, parents, and administrators conducting comprehensive and results-oriented partnership programs.

FEDERAL LEADERSHIP

In the 1990s, the U.S. Department of Education and Secretary of Education Richard Riley shined a spotlight on school, family, and community partnerships. The department set a context, supported research and development, published reports, conducted traditional and satellite conferences, and contributed to a national conversation about improving the connections of home, school, and community.

For over 30 years, numerous federal policies have guided educators, families, businesses, and other community groups to understand the need for parental involvement in education. This includes focused guidelines since the 1960s in Head Start programs, and more recently in family leave policies, Title I regulations, Goals 2000 targets, and other legislation from the Departments of Labor, Health and Human Services, Commerce, and Education. Although leadership at the federal level has been influential, the products of federal offices are inevitably linked to the politics of education. The various legislated initiatives have been fragmented, disconnected across departments, dismissed by some states and districts, and too distant from schools and families to serve as the sole influence on the development of permanent programs of partnership in states, districts, and schools.

SUMMARY

Leadership and actions at all levels—federal, state, district, and school—are needed to increase the chances that all schools will improve communications with all families and communities in ways that benefit all students. The main work of school, family, and community partnerships occurs at the school level where principals, teachers, parents, and students meet daily. Federal, state, and district policies and support will be most valuable if they assist school principals, teachers, parents, students, and community members to work together to implement effective programs and practices that welcome, respect, inform, and involve all families.

Federal, state, and district policies and actions should be reviewed and revised periodically to ensure that they enable every school to build leadership skills and write and implement site-based plans for continuous progress in partnership programs. School policies must be judged on whether they enable teachers, families, and others in the community to work together effectively on behalf of the children they share (see Chapters 5 and 6).

This chapter includes a short reading outlining useful state policies and several examples of state and district policies that are consistent with the theory, research, and framework for school, family, and community partnerships presented in this volume. The examples show how educational leaders in the field are beginning to (1) correct vague goals for parent involvement by using the vocabulary of school, family, and community partnerships; (2) identify the six major types of involvement as the basis for policies and link practices of partnership to school improvement goals; (3) provide staff development to school action teams of administrators, teachers, parents, and others; and (4) offer incentives and recognition for innovative and effective programs and practices.

This chapter also includes a reading exploring policy-related questions that continue to be debated in the field: Should families be included in evaluating teachers? What perspectives do parents bring to these evaluations? The study shows that parents and principals have some similar and some different views of what makes a good teacher. The results suggest that parents contribute important perspectives as members of school improvement teams and committees on all topics, including the evaluation of teachers. The reading should promote discussions of other policy-related questions about the roles of school councils, parent associations, and community organizations in school and staffing decisions.

Taken together, the readings and activities in this chapter introduce you to policies for school, family, and community partnerships and to research on puzzling policy questions.

Parent Involvement:
State Education Agencies Should Lead the Way*

Words about the importance of parent involvement are meaningless without financial and technical support.

ABSTRACT

Parent involvement is on everyone's list of practices to make schools more effective, to help families create more positive learning environments, to reduce the risk of student failure, and to increase student success. State education agencies have offered mainly symbolic, verbal support for the importance of parent involvement, but little financial support for staff and programs needed to improve parent understanding, teacher practices, and family and school connections. This reading draws from research on school and family partnerships to outline actions needed at the state level to improve programs to involve families in every school.

OVERVIEW

One major finding from the research reported in Chapter 3 is that teacher leadership—not parent education or marital status—made the difference in whether parents improved their knowledge about the school and about helping their children, and whether the children improved their reading scores. Because teachers and administrators play the key roles in including or excluding parents from their children's education, state policies and actions should be directed to building teachers' and administrators' capabilities to conduct parent involvement practices that make a difference for student success in class.

STATE SUPPORT OF PARENT INVOLVEMENT

State policies, bylaws, guidelines, and funds for educational programs strongly influence or determine district and school leadership, teaching practice, and community support. These policies can either recognize or ignore the connections be-

---

* By Joyce L. Epstein. Excerpted from *Community Education Journal* 14(4) (1987): 4–10.

tween the simultaneous educational and socializing institutions in a child's life—the family and the school.

State programs that address the needs of all families for useful information and involvement in their children's education give something back to families and citizens for their education tax dollars. Parent involvement in a sequential, continuing program from kindergarten to grade 12 may be a key factor in preventing or reducing school failure. The quality of family and school connections all through school can dramatically affect the students' and families' futures and determine whether they become dependent on or contribute to the state. Programs through high schools that support parent involvement and parent-child interaction may be the most beneficial investments we can make at the state level to prevent more costly social and educational problems.

PARENT INVOLVEMENT AND CHOICE

The National Governors' Association Task Force on Parent Involvement and Choice focused a great deal of attention on the pros and cons of increasing parents' choices of the schools their children attend, especially choices among public schools with different programs. However, after the choice of schools is made (and even when there is no choice and children attend their neighborhood schools), parents and teachers must make choices about whether to emphasize parent involvement. Important family and school connections start with the choice of or assignment to schools and continue when the teachers, parents, and students interact on a regular basis.

Students must make many decisions each year. Their choices—of programs, courses, activities, opportunities, and special services—affect their futures. Parents need to be involved as knowledgeable partners in these decisions. They must understand how the school system works; the goals and programs of the schools their children attend; the options and consequences of decisions that concern their children each school year; the course objectives and requirements for passing; the ways teachers define and grade progress and success; the programs that are available to their children before and after school, on weekends, and on Saturdays; and how to become part of those programs.

Some parents have the information and experience they need to help their children through the elementary and secondary grades and into post-secondary schooling or work. Other parents—most parents—need and want information and guidance from teachers and administrators about how to help their children make key decisions and in learning activities. This is true in all schools—public or private, chosen or assigned—and at all levels of schooling—elementary, middle or junior high, and high school. There is much discussion about parent involvement in the choice of schools for their children but little about the importance of parent involvement after the choice of schools is made. This type of parent involvement requires special attention from state policy makers.

STATE LEADERSHIP FOR PARENT INVOLVEMENT

Research suggests that the following policies and actions at the state level will improve family-school connections and parent involvement programs.

1. Write a policy that outlines and discusses the state's commitment to parent involvement. An official written policy that specifies the state's perspectives, services, requirements, and expectations concerning parent involvement is the first step toward a viable parent involvement program. The state policy should recognize the importance of a comprehensive program of parent involvement—based on the six types of parent involvement—in every district and school to benefit all families and children. It is not enough to mandate only parent advisory councils, or only parent-teacher organizations, or only parent volunteers at the school building. These activities involve only a small proportion of the parents and have little impact on the abilities of all parents to help or monitor their children throughout the school years. Other types of involvement must be recognized, including effective conferences with teachers for all parents and parent involvement in learning activities at home. All children may benefit from parents who are knowledgeable about school programs and school decisions.

An official policy on parent involvement shows that the state will support activities in its districts and schools to improve the parent involvement practices of teachers, administrators, community educators, and others to help parents understand and exercise their role in their children's education.

2. Establish a clearinghouse, library, and dissemination office for parent involvement practices and research. This may be housed at the state department of education, one or more centrally located school districts, a cooperating college or university, a community agency, or in mobile units for use by teachers, parents, and others. Parent involvement programs, teachers' practices for involving parents, school surveys of parents, handbooks and other forms of communication with parents, child development information and activities, related research, community education programs, research studies, and other information and resources can be shared widely and easily only when there is a central location for collecting and disseminating the information.

Clearinghouse and dissemination services for parent involvement could help school districts and individual school staffs understand and build on the work of others to avoid duplication of invention and effort. Moreover, a great deal of time and money would be saved through the efficient collection and distribution of information to encourage program development in many districts, schools, and communities.

At least one full-time professional should be added or reassigned in each state to coordinate a clearinghouse and to provide leadership to school districts and schools. Additional full-time staff members in large school districts and part-time or full-time staff members in small districts are needed to increase the probability of success of parent involvement programs in all schools.

3. Support state requirements for teaching credentials to include credits for completing at least one comprehensive course in family and school connections

and the use of parent involvement in teaching. Currently, teachers in training are not required to demonstrate knowledge or expertise in understanding families or communities or ways to involve parents as partners with the schools in their children's education. Yet every teacher entering a classroom must work *every day* with children, their families, family conditions, and the connections between schools and homes. Teachers' abilities to master and use home and school connections are as critical to their success as their abilities to teach reading or manage classrooms. The state of Washington has already moved in this direction with specific credit requirements, and teacher educators in other states are pressing for similar policies at the state level.

4. Support state colleges and universities in the development of comprehensive preservice and inservice teacher and administrator training courses for improving practices of parent involvement. In addition to establishing requirements for credits, courses in parent involvement research and practice must be developed to provide the training needed by teachers. Only between 4 and 15 percent of the teachers in our and others' surveys had formal classes or courses in parent involvement. This means that between 85 and 96 percent of the teachers received no preparation to use parent involvement productively. Coherent courses need to be designed, or specific modules on different types of parent involvement and their effects need to be added to basic courses in teacher education, administrator training, effective school organization, community education, principal leadership centers, and teacher inservice programs.

Similarly, community educators need courses that would help them specialize in parent involvement and school, family, and community connections. Community educators need to understand schools, learning, and the potentials of parent assistance, just as they study community structures, decision making, and conflict resolution. The additional courses could prepare them to work with teachers, coordinate parent assistance with student need, and develop school and work connections with the business community.

Teachers and administrators need ongoing experiences that will help them understand and use parent involvement effectively. Districts could begin to develop and share useful, transferable inservice programs on different types of parent involvement, implementation strategies, evaluation procedures, and effects. Financial support in state and district budgets is needed for such inservice training for beginning and experienced teachers, administrators, community educators, and parents.

State grants and other awards for developing and offering courses and components of courses for undergraduate preservice, graduate, and inservice training could establish the leadership needed in state universities and colleges to advise and assist both beginning and experienced teachers and administrators.

5. Support master teacher, mentor or lead teacher, or other career ladder programs to build a cadre of specialists in the use of parent involvement. Many states are supporting or considering plans to improve the status of teachers. These programs for professional development often encourage and enable teachers to become subject matter specialists to assist other teachers. It would be appropriate and beneficial to promote teachers who are parent involvement specialists. At least one expert teacher is needed in each school to assist and train other teachers in the research, practices, materials development, and evaluation of parent involvement across the school grades. These master or lead teachers could also be important connections to community education specialists and through them to community agencies, businesses, and groups of citizens who can be important school resources.

Teacher specialists in parent involvement should receive financial compensation for extra responsibilities, perquisites such as extra planning time, or other recognition for their leadership. Parent involvement should be one of the recognized specialties to build leadership roles for teachers.

6. Establish funding and recognition programs, including small grants, for school districts and teacher-administrator-parent teams in individual schools to develop and evaluate comprehensive programs in parent involvement over several years. The most promising parent involvement programs will be developed at the school level. Teachers should be recognized and rewarded for working with other teachers, community educators, parents, and others to improve their practices to assist parents' knowledge and skills in ways that help teachers and students reach important school goals. A school-based management model is critical in the area of parent involvement, because schools start with different histories in programs that involve parents.

Along with state funding for some common programs and services across districts, funds are needed for small grants to local schools to encourage them to customize programs and practices for their local populations and to evaluate and improve their efforts. These funds could be used to provide teachers with planning periods, paid sabbaticals, and summer salaries to develop and adapt useful processes and materials for increasing and improving all types of parent involvement in their schools. Small grants can invigorate every school by supporting creative program development.

7. Support the development of programs for special populations of parents. Schools need additional financial assistance to develop their capabilities and to produce materials to involve all parents in their children's education, including those who require special services. Teenaged parents of infants and toddlers quickly become the young parents of school-aged children and may need especially clear and coordinated guidance and support in how to help their children in learning activities at home. Non-English-speaking *parents* need translators or translated communications of home-learning materials. Parents with low reading ability need differently designed communications and materials, so they can get the information they need to understand the schools and encourage their children. Parents of older children need special assistance to understand their continuing role in their children's education. Although the forms of communication and activities for parent involvement will change at different grade levels, all parents of children from pre-kindergarten through grade 12 need information and opportunities to build a repertoire of family skills, to understand their children's schools, and to assist with their children's skills and school decisions.

Each school may have different special groups, but some processes and practices can be shared to meet the needs of similar populations. State funding is required to reach these special populations—funding for program development, teacher training, community linkages, and parent involvement. Families in certain populations are at risk of misunderstanding school policies and programs. They have proportionately more children who are at risk of failing and dropping out. The parent involvement component for these groups is essential for creating positive support structures for students.

8. **Recognize and apply the work of community educators in programs to increase parent involvement in their children's education.** Community educators could play active, focused roles in improving parent and community involvement in students' education to assist teachers, parents, and students to improve K–12 programs. The state's support of community educators could promote a more focused set of activities for these potentially important "connectors" between schools and families. In the past, community education has been loosely defined to identify the limits and potentials of community educators to meet local needs. Now it may be important to focus on a few common problems to build a repertoire of skills among community educators that can be shared to strengthen communities across the state.

Two goals that would benefit from the leadership and energies of community educators are increasing parent involvement and reducing student failure. These topics are linked to each other and to several traditional interests of community educators, such as increasing adult literacy and using school facilities after the school day for academic and recreational activities. Community educators could help teachers make contact with hard-to-reach parents and children who are at risk of failing. This could be accomplished in coordination with the schools and teachers in the school and in other community locations before school, after school, on weekends, and during vacations all across the school grades.

9. **Encourage and recognize businesses that permit their employees to become involved in their children's education to strengthen the schools, the community, and the citizens and workers of the future.** The top education leaders in each state need to work with state legislatures to obtain tax incentives, tax credits, preferred status, or other types of recognition for businesses that:

- permit and encourage all parent employees to take up to a half day once or twice a year to attend parent-teacher conferences on company time, flex time, or other beneficial arrangements;
- permit and encourage parent employees and other employees to contribute time to volunteer in the schools;
- encourage parents to use business holidays that are different from school holidays to visit the schools;
- establish libraries at businesses and industries to provide information to parents about their children's development through childhood and adolescence, their continuing role in their children's education, and appropriate enrichment and learning activities for children at all grade levels;
- establish and support high-quality services at the workplace or under the auspices of the business to provide day care; after-school, holiday, and vacation programs; substitute parent care during children's minor illnesses; and other education programs for employees' children; and
- award small grants to schools and community agencies to improve parent involvement practices.

State education leaders need to develop incentives and recognition programs to encourage businesses to work with the schools, improve the parenting skills of employees, and improve the contributions of businesses to the success of students as an investment in the community.

10. **Support research and evaluation on parent involvement processes and effects in connection with pilot programs and small grants to schools.** Parent involvement and community education projects will remain "frills" unless there is clear accountability. Data need to be collected, analyzed, and reported clearly to show policy makers, citizens, and educators whether or not these programs are important to the parents, students, schools, and communities. Data on current conditions, including teachers' practices and levels of parent involvement, are needed to define the starting points and needed programs in each school. Information is needed on the success of implementation procedures of new approaches and on the expected and unexpected results of the programs and practices. Evaluations are needed to know whether to continue or change practices and whether programs can be used beneficially in other schools and districts. Each district—indeed, each school—needs to choose appropriate and useful ways to test and evaluate alternative practices of parent involvement to see which approaches work for that district and its populations of families, at which grade levels, and in which subjects. State departments of education can exercise leadership by requiring evaluation and allocating funds for it.

DISCUSSION

The policies and actions briefly outlined in this chapter require time, money, commitment, and leadership. State departments of education hold one important key to successful and lasting parent involvement: budget line-items that could be targeted to provide staff positions, teacher training, small grants, and evaluation studies in parent involvement. Funding for needed staff, training, and program development should be ensured for a reasonable period of time (at least five years) to develop useful practices and build the capabilities of teachers and administrators. Funds spent on parent involvement programs are likely to be returned to the state in the form of better-informed parents, more successful students, more effective teachers, fewer student failures, and fewer demands on other state and local resources for expensive social services when the students are adolescents and young adults.

Parent involvement is not the parents' responsibility alone. Nor is it the schools' or teachers' or community educators' responsibility alone. All groups need to work together for a sustained period of time to develop programs that will increase parents' understanding of the schools and their ability to assist their children and that will promote student success and reduce failure at every grade level.

Parent involvement is everybody's job but nobody's job until a structure is put in place to support it. Without financial and technical support from state education agencies, words about the importance of parent involvement are meaningless.

Sample State and District Policies on School, Family, and Community Partnerships

Three state policies from California, Connecticut, and Kentucky and four school district policies from Alexandria, Virginia; Montgomery County, Maryland; San Diego, California; and Syracuse, New York, are included in this chapter. The policies were selected because they are thoughtful, research-based, comprehensive, and include administrative commitments to help schools enact the policies. The words of these policies may help other states and districts develop their policies and enactments on school, family, and community partnerships.

Having a good policy is a good first step on the path to partnerships. This does not mean, however, that these states and districts have completed the work that the policies intend to support. Sometimes even well-conceived policies languish. Indeed, all of these states and districts have a great deal of work to do to help all schools develop and sustain comprehensive programs of school, family, and community partnerships.

STATE POLICIES: CALIFORNIA, CONNECTICUT, AND KENTUCKY

California State Board of Education Policy, Adopted: 1/14/89, 9/9/94

Subject: Parent Involvement in the Education of Their Children

Introduction

A critical dimension of effective schooling is parent involvement: Research has shown conclusively, that parent involvement at home in their children's education improves student achievement. Furthermore, when parents are involved at school, their children go farther in school and they go to better schools.

From research studies to date, we have learned the following important facts:

1. Families provide the primary educational environment.
2. Parent involvement in their children's education improves student achievement.

---

* The term *parent* refers to any caregiver who assumes responsibility for nurturing and caring for children, including parents, grandparents, aunts, uncles, foster parents, stepparents, etc. Many schools are now using the term *family involvement*.

3. Parent involvement is most effective when it is comprehensive, supportive, long-lasting and well-planned.

4. The benefits of parent involvement are not limited to early childhood or the elementary level; there are continuing positive effects through high school.

5. Involving parents in supporting their children's education at home is not enough. To ensure the quality of schools as institutions serving the community, parents must be involved at all levels in the schools.

6. Children from low-income and culturally and racially diverse families have the most to gain when schools involve parents. The extent of parent involvement in a child's education is more important to student success than family income or education.

7. We cannot look at the school and the home in isolation from one another; families and schools need to collaborate to help children adjust to the world of school. This is particularly critical for children from families with different cultural and language backgrounds.

Schools that undertake and support strong comprehensive parent involvement efforts, are more likely to produce students who perform better than identical schools that do not involve parents. Schools that have strong linkages with and respond to the needs of the communities they serve, have students that perform better than schools that don't. Children who have parents who help them at home and stay in touch with the school, do better academically than children of similar aptitude and family background whose parents are not involved. The inescapable fact is that consistently high levels of student success are more likely to occur with long-term comprehensive parent involvement in schools.

The California State Board of Education recognizes that a child's education is a responsibility shared by school and family during the entire period the child spends in school. Although parents come to the schools with diverse cultural backgrounds, primary languages, and needs, they overwhelmingly want their children to be successful in school. School districts and schools, in collaboration with parents, teachers, students and administrators, must establish and develop efforts that enhance parent involvement and reflect the needs of students and families in the communities which they serve.

To support the mission of California schools to educate all students effectively, schools and parents must work together as knowledgeable partners. All of the grade level reforms, Here they come: Ready or Not!, It's Elementary, Caught in the Middle, Second to None, and other major initiatives such as Healthy Start (SB 620) and School Restructuring (SB 1274), emphasize parent and community involvement in school restructuring. The reform efforts support school-based shared decision-making at the school site that includes all stakeholders, including teachers, administrators, students, parents and other community members.

The State Board of Education will continue to support, through the California Department of Education, assistance to school districts and schools in developing strong comprehensive parent involvement. Comprehensive means that parents are involved at all grade levels in a variety of roles. The efforts should be designed to:

1. Help parents develop parenting skills to meet the basic obligations of family life and foster conditions at home, which emphasize the importance of education and learning.
2. Promote two-way (school-to-home and home-to-school) communication about school programs and students' progress.
3. Involve parents, with appropriate training, in instructional and support roles at the school and in other locations that help the school and students reach stated goals, objectives and standards.
4. Provide parents with strategies and techniques for assisting their children with learning activities at home that support and extend the school's instructional program.
5. Prepare parents to actively participate in school decision making and develop their leadership skills in governance and advocacy.
6. Provide parents with skills to access community and support services that strengthen school programs, family practices, and student learning and development.

These six types of parent involvement roles require a coordinated school-wide effort that has the support of parents, teachers, students and administrators at each school site. Furthermore, research indicates that home-school collaboration is most likely to happen if schools take the initiative to encourage, guide and genuinely welcome parents into the partnership. Professional development for teachers and administrators on how to build such a partnership is essential.

The issue of parent involvement in the education of their children is much larger than improving student achievement. It is central to our democracy that parents and citizens participate in the governing of public institutions. Parent involvement is fundamental to a healthy system of public education.

Connecticut State Board of Education Adopts a Definition of School-Family-Community

Public Act 97-290, Section 14, requires each local and regional board of education to "develop, adopt, and implement written policies and procedures to encourage parent-teacher communication. These policies and procedures may include monthly newsletters, required regular contact with all parents, flexible parent-teacher conference, drop in hours for parents, home visits, and the use of technology such as homework hot lines to allow parents to check on their children's assignments and students to get assistance if needed." (The state laws went into effect September 1, 1998.)

The following is a copy of the *Position Statement of the Connecticut State Board of Education on School-Family-Community Partnerships*, adopted August 7, 1997.

The State Board of Education defines school-family-community partnerships as the continuous planning, support and participation of school personnel, families and community organizations in coordinated activities and efforts at home, in the school and in the community that directly and positively affect the success of all children's learning. Each partner is viewed as an equally contributing member, maintaining a certain independence while acknowledging shared responsibility. To succeed, the partnership must be flexible and based upon mutual trust and respect. Schools must take the lead in developing and sustaining effective partnerships.

The Connecticut State Board of Education recognizes that education is a shared responsibility throughout a student's entire educational career. Schools, families and communities all contribute to student success, and the best results come when all three work together. A comprehensive, well-planned partnership between family, school and community results in higher student achievement.

Research findings indicate school-family-community partnerships result in specific benefits for students, families and schools. Students in schools where there is a strong component of family involvement perform better than those in schools with less involvement. They have higher grades and test scores, better attendance, higher rates of homework completion and fewer placements in special education, and they stay in school longer. In fact, the most accurate predictor of a student's achievement in school is not income or social status, but the extent to which the student's family is involved in his or her education. Families also benefit; they develop a greater understanding of their role in their children's education, a sense of effectiveness, stronger social ties and a desire to continue their own education. Schools and communities benefit. Teachers report that their work becomes easier if they receive help from families, and families who are more involved have more positive views of teachers. Increased involvement also results in families feeling more ownership of their school and being more willing to support school and community initiatives.

An effective partnership offers a broad array of opportunities for schools, families and communities to interact. Not all school-family-community partnerships look the same. Successful partnerships exhibit as much variety as the local conditions that create them. Partnerships work best when they recognize and accommodate differences among families, communities and cultures.

The State Board of Education recognizes that schools must take the lead in developing and sustaining effective partnerships. In order to encourage comprehensive school-family-community partnerships, the Board recommends that schools develop programs related to the following six standards:

1. *parenting*—promote and support parenting skills and the family's primary role in encouraging children's learning at each age and grade level;
2. *communicating*—promote clear two-way communication between the school and families about school programs and children's progress;
3. *volunteering*—provide appropriate training and involve families in instructional and support areas both in and out of the school;

4. *learning at home*—involve families in learning activities at home, including interactive homework and other curriculum-linked or enrichment activities;
5. *decision making*—provide opportunities for all families to develop and strengthen their leadership role in school decisions; and
6. *collaborating with the community*—provide coordinated access to community resources for children and families, and serve as a resource to the community.

Each member of the school-family-community partnership plays a unique and important role in contributing to success for all students. Effective strategies for each partner, derived from current research, are described below.

A Role for Schools

Every school can develop effective strategies to involve all families in the education of their children. The State Board of Education believes that local schools and school districts should engage in specific actions to develop and sustain strong partnership programs: identify district-level goals for school-family-community partnerships; develop structures for systematically and comprehensively implementing the six standards of school-family-community partnerships; provide training and support for teachers, administrators, other staff members and parents in the areas of goals, practices and processes of partnership; monitor progress to learn which practices help schools produce the best results for students, parents, teachers, the school and community; make school facilities available for community and family activities; and contact local businesses, agencies and community organizations to develop collaborations that support school and district goals and programs.

A Role for Families

Families can make critical contributions to student achievement by providing a home environment conducive to lifelong learning. Families can take advantage of opportunities offered by the school to become involved in activities related to the six standards of school-family-community partnerships. Families can also let the school know how they would like to contribute. Families can use and contribute to community resources and help connect other families to the school and community.

A Role for Communities

Service organizations and agencies, religious groups, businesses and individuals can develop networks for communicating with schools and families about information and services that support family involvement in children's education. Community agencies can collaborate to provide integrated family support services that build upon existing community resources and linkages with public schools. Community members can serve as volunteers, role models and mentors, providing more individualized attention for students and demonstrating to both children and staff members that others in their community support education. Businesses can sponsor school-family-community partnership activities and encourage their employees to play an active role in education.

State Department of Education Leadership

The State Board of Education believes that the State Department of Education must provide leadership in developing and promoting comprehensive school-family-community partnership programs and activities that contribute to success for all students. The Department's leadership role includes supporting the standards for comprehensive school-family-community partnerships described above; promoting linkages among state- and local-level partners; and collecting and disseminating information about current research and best practice.

REFERENCES

Connecticut State Department of Education. (1998). *Policy action packet for school-family-community partnerships: A guide to developing partnership programs for student success*. Middletown, CT: Connecticut State Department of Education. Connecticut Association of Boards of Education, Parent Teacher Association of Connecticut, Special Education Research Center.

Schools & Families 1(1) Connecticut School-Family-Community Partnership Project newsletter. Hartford: Connecticut State Department of Education.

Kentucky Board of Education Policy Statement
Parent and Family Involvement Initiative

The Kentucky Board of Education recognizes that parent and family involvement is essential to educating our state's children to meet high academic expectations. Schools and families must partner together to develop strong programs and policies that meet the needs of each community. Educators must take the initiative in developing these vital collaboratives.

Kentucky's educational system includes numerous opportunities for active and *meaningful* parent and family involvement (e.g., school-based decision making, primary and preschool programs, family and youth services centers). The Kentucky Board of Education, in cooperation with the Kentucky Department of Education, will continue to support and assist schools and school districts in developing, implementing, and evaluating policies and programs that involve *all* parents and families. Successful programs will:

- Create welcoming atmospheres for parents and families.
- Support parents and families as advocates for lifelong learning and as decision-makers in school issues and programs.
- Promote clear, two-way communications between schools and families about school programs and students' progress.
- Assist parents, families, and guardians in acquiring techniques to support their children's learning.
- Involve parents and family members, wherever appropriate, in a variety of instructional and support roles both within and without the school.
- Provide access to and coordinate community and support services for children and families.
- Identify and reduce barriers to parent/family involvement.
- Provide professional development for teachers, and administrators, and staff on ways to effectively work with parents and families.
- Provide a written copy of the policy for each parent and/or family and post the policy in the school.

These forms of parent and family involvement require coordinated school-wide efforts and the support of parents, teachers, students, and administrators at each school site. The issue of parent and family involvement is much larger than improving student achievement. Effective parent and family involvement is fundamental to a healthy system of public education that expects all students to achieve at high levels.

SCHOOL DISTRICT POLICIES: ALEXANDRIA CITY (VA), MONTGOMERY COUNTY (MD), SAN DIEGO CITY (CA), AND SYRACUSE CITY (NY)

School Board of the Alexandria City Public Schools Policy on Parent/Family Involvement

The School Board of the Alexandria City Public Schools recognizes that parents, guardians, families, the schools and community share a collective responsibility for educating our students. The School Board acknowledges that parent/family involvement encompasses a variety of roles, opportunities and activities. The School Board believes that parents/families are the first and primary teachers of their children and that their participation is important to the success of students in attaining academic achievement and realizing personal goals. The School Board of the Alexandria City Public Schools is committed to working for participation of parents and families in full partnership with its schools throughout the student's entire school career.

Therefore, the Board directs the Superintendent take the necessary actions to:

1. Provide a welcoming, supportive climate in the schools that facilitates parent/family involvement as volunteers, audiences, joint problem solvers and especially supporters of children's learning.
2. Promote effective and on-going two-way communication with all parents/families while respecting their diversity and differing needs. Communication shall include, but not be limited to, information about school programs, policies, and student progress.
3. Work with parents/families in creating opportunities to support learning at home and at school.
4. Provide information about and access to school and community resources and services, as well as networking opportunities for parents/families.
5. Support parents/families as advocates, leaders and participants in decision-making opportunities within the school community.
6. Acknowledge the contributions made by parents/families to the school community as well as to their children's education.

The Superintendent shall:

- ensure that parent/family involvement is an integral component of each policy and program development effort of the school system and is incorporated in existing policies and programs and in each school's annual plan; and
- establish a baseline report on family involvement in each school with indicators to measure improvements over time. The baseline report shall be issued within six months of the enactment of this policy and thereafter a section of the Annual Report of the Alexandria City Public Schools will report on the state of family involvement using those improvement indicators.

The School Board shall:

- establish a committee made up of staff, parents/families to provide oversight on plans for increasing and evaluating parent involvement in the schools.

It is the Board's desire that the Alexandria City Public Schools be committed to working for full participation of families in partnership with administrators, teachers, and staff for the educational success of every child.

ADOPTED: 12/15/94
POLICY #1204

School Board Policy 1204 directs the Superintendent to take necessary actions to ensure that parent/family involvement is an integral part of the plans of each Alexandria public school. In order to implement the parent/family involvement policy each school shall:

1. Ensure that all its school employees have been trained in welcoming parents and prospective parents to the schools. This training shall include, but not be limited to, welcoming techniques, telephone manners, calls back to parents within a reasonable amount of time, ways to use parents effectively within the classroom and school, and other information as determined by the individual schools. It is expected that principals will monitor their staff on a regular basis and arrange for follow-up training where appropriate.

   The Superintendent and his/her designees shall conduct a minimum of two unannounced, on-site visits to each school. The purpose of these visits is to ensure that a supportive and welcoming climate exists in each school and to provide principals with feedback after each visit.

   Schools shall provide parents/families and visitors with inviting facilities. This is to include appropriate seating and reading materials for those waiting for appointments, work space for volunteer parents and other amenities as determined by each school's facilities and needs.

   Schools shall provide parents/families with general school information through regular publications, room parents/families, room representatives, newsletters and information bulletins. This information is to be sent home at least quarterly. Alternative methods for informing parents may include phone trees, the use of computerized phone messages or parents calling a hot line number. Whenever possible, translations into major languages within the school should be made.

   Schools shall also open two-way communications to provide parents and families with information regarding:

   A. Opportunities to serve as school classroom volunteers, audiences for children's programs, and as members of school-centered problem solving teams. Parents shall also be apprised of activities that they can participate in at home that will contribute to the school and their child's progress.

   B. Ways that parents/families can receive regular communication regarding their children's progress. This shall include, but not be limited to, interims, report cards, telephone calls, notes and regular reporting to parents/families on their children's progress. Information shall also be provided to parents/families regarding ways that they can ensure their children's success in school (how to help with homework, reading with the children, etc.).

 C. Ways that they can contribute and participate in the school community activities such as totaling grocery receipts, cutting out instructional materials, collating, filing, chaperoning, etc.

2. Schools shall also stress to the students their own importance and their responsibility as one of the essential links in all school/home communication efforts.

  Schools shall provide and document learning activities and workshops on topics that will support learning at home and at school. This is to be generated from local parent/family needs surveys. Schools should provide the most effective training based on the needs of parents/families.

  Opportunities for such learning may be provided at events such as family dinners, regular PTA meetings, and any other school events where parents/families are usually in attendance. Video tapes, mail, and cable productions are other ways to provide parents/families with learning opportunities.

  Schools shall also provide parents/families with learn-at-home opportunities such as take-home reading and mathematics materials and/or other curricular materials that require family discussion and/or activities.

  Schools shall also encourage parents'/families' awareness of homework requirements through the use of newsletters, course outlines, calendars, specific assignment sheets, books (agendas), homework hotlines, contracts and other methods found to be effective.

3. Schools shall provide information about access to community resources on at least a quarterly basis. This might be done through newsletters, announcements, taped messages, meetings or other ways parents are contacted.

  The information should include the community resources' addresses, phone numbers and hours/days of operation. This is to include, but not be limited to, such things as scout troop membership opportunities, local tutoring opportunities, child care, recreational services, free eye glasses, etc.

  Information on community resources will be collected and disseminated to the schools by the Parent/Family Involvement Coordinator. This will be updated on a yearly basis.

4. Schools shall provide information about and opportunities for parents/families to serve as advocates, participants and leaders in their respective schools. These opportunities (including dates, times, deadlines, if any, for nominations and applications) must be announced and advertised as far in advance as possible. Additionally, schools should keep these applications and all pertinent information in the school's main office and/or in the Parent Family Resource Room.

5. Schools shall establish ways that parents/families can be shown appreciation and recognition for all that they do for their children. This should be done in a way that will recognize the most parents/families. This should be done on at least a semi-annual basis, or more often where appropriate, in settings such as volunteer receptions, volunteer appreciation week, school assemblies, etc.

6. Each school plan shall include a parent/family involvement component. This component shall be based on identified school needs and data gathered from the previous year. Each school shall initiate and maintain a way to track parent participation in activities outlined in their school plan. This data should include, but not be limited to:
   * a survey of parents'/families' needs and/or interests
   * measurement by racial and ethnic categories
   * number of participants at various PTA meetings and school events
   * number of parent/family volunteers
   * number of parent/family members using the Parent/Family Resource Center
   * number of parents/families attending teacher/parent conferences
   * number of parents/families participating in various take-home activities
   * the number of parents/families providing oversight of their children's homework

7. The Superintendent shall direct the Central Office staff to support the School Board's established Parent/Family Involvement Committee in its efforts to provide oversight on the schools' parent/family involvement plans. Annually, a committee of parents/families shall be established in each school to provide constructive feedback based on the School Plan and these Regulations. Where appropriate, this information shall be used to revise next year's School Plan.

8. The Superintendent shall require a parent/family involvement component for any new programs or proposals.

9. The Superintendent shall direct that a review be conducted of existing programs and policies for the purpose of adding a parent/family involvement component.

Board of Education of Montgomery County (Maryland) Parental Involvement

Purpose

To reaffirm the Montgomery County public school system's strong commitment to the role of parents in their children's education and to promote effective, comprehensive parental involvement.

In this policy, "parent" is intended to include parents, guardians, and other family members involved in supervising the child's schooling.

Achievement of this purpose will be sought through a variety of efforts including:

1. Effective two-way communication between all parents and schools regarding school system policies and regulations, local school policies, and an individual child's progress.
2. Activities to encourage parental volunteer opportunities in schools both in the classroom and in other areas of the school including attendance at local school programs and events.
3. Information and programs for parents on how to establish a home environment to support learning and appropriate behavior.
4. Information and programs for parents about how they can assist their own children to learn.
5. Assistance to develop parental involvement in educational advocacy through PTAs and other organizations, including school system task forces and advisory committees.

Process and Content

While each division, office, and school must assess its role and plan of action to meet these goals, all MCPS employees are expected to convey a commitment to parental involvement.

1. Consistent with this commitment, local schools are expected to:
   A. Develop activities and materials that provide for effective two-way communication between parents and the school on local school policies and individual student progress
   B. Support and encourage parental volunteer opportunities
   C. Provide programs that assist parents in learning how they can help children learn, including activities that are connected to what children are learning in the classroom
   D. Work with PTA leadership to ensure parental input
2. In addition, appropriate staff in central and area offices are expected to support local school efforts and, where relevant:
   A. Communicate with parents on school system policies and regulations
   B. Provide for the development of parenting programs and materials, including the use of cable television, pamphlets, adult education courses, parent resource centers, and programs designed to orient new parents to MCPS
   C. Maintain and support with appropriate information and training parental volunteer opportunities countrywide

D. Assist in the development of parental leadership through PTAs and other recognized groups

E. Work with businesses, organizations, and other government agencies which by their policies and activities can provide support and assistance for parental involvement efforts

F. Provide appropriate teacher and staff training to support effective parental involvement; conduct staff and parent training in ways to communicate and work together including problem solving, conflict resolution skills, and outreach strategies

G. Identify and publicize promising programs and practices related to parental involvement

H. Work with colleges and universities that prepare teachers and administrators to support the inclusion of school and family connections in their training programs

I. Develop methods to accommodate and support parental involvement for all parents with special needs including those with limited English proficiency and those with physical handicaps

J. Develop mechanisms for local schools to use in order to assess the effectiveness of their parental involvement efforts

3. The superintendent will assess the status of parental involvement, review existing policies and procedures, and develop necessary regulations and procedures to support this policy, including a review of staff and budget support

4. The Board of Education will support parental involvement by seeking parental input on school system policies, including curriculum, facilities and funding issues.

Review and Reporting

This policy will be reviewed every three years in accordance with the Board of Education policy review process.

Policy History: Adopted by Resolution No. 669-90, November 13, 1990.

Montgomery County Public Schools
Administrative Regulation: Parent Involvement

Purpose

To establish guidelines for school, area, and central office staff for working with parents to ensure a strong home-school partnership and promote an environment that enhances the motivation, commitment, achievement, and self-worth of every student.

Rationale

Research has shown that involving parents in their children's education results in mutually supportive relationships among students, parents, and staff that win, guide, and enhance the intellectual and social development of students.

Guiding Principles

A. Parent involvement can be defined as efforts which enable parents and families to participate as partners in the educational process at home or in school. Parent involvement efforts should be aimed at developing a climate of open communication, trust, and mutual respect among all members of the school community.

B. Schools are responsible for developing effective parent/community involvement that is well planned, consistent, and comprehensive.

C. School personnel should recognize and value the role of parents as the child's first, most influential teacher, as well as recognizing parents' responsibilities: to meet the basic needs of their children, to stay in touch with school staff, to participate as they are able, in the school community, to expand on and support their children's school learning at home, and to inform themselves so that they can actively participate in decisions affecting the education of all children.

D. Communication with parents should be handled in a non-judgmental manner that recognizes the variety of parenting styles, family structures, and circumstances, as well as individual differences reflected in the values, cultures, and diversity of the MCPS population.

E. School personnel should keep in mind that they are sharing responsibility with parents, guardians and other family members who supervise the child's schooling.

F. School personnel should demonstrate sensitivity regarding requests and requirements made of families so as not to create an unreasonable burden.

Procedures for Schools

All MCPS employees are expected to convey a commitment to and demonstrate respect for parent involvement. As part of its management planning process, each school will assess its needs and develop its activities related to parent involvement. School staff should take the initiative to reach out to parents in a variety of ways to encourage parent participation. Each local school will:

A. Establish a parent involvement advisory committee that includes school staff, parents and students (where appropriate), and reflects the school/community diversity, to ensure continuous compliance with this regulation by:

1. Providing input for the management plan with regard to parent involvement
2. Assessing the degree of implementation by reviewing the documentation of activities, including:
   A. Communication
   B. Volunteer Opportunities
   C. Programs to help parents create a learning environment at home and assist their children to learn
   D. Support for parent advocacy
3. Making recommendations for positive change in these areas, as appropriate

B. In cooperation with parents and PTAs, develop and maintain a clear, consistent communication system that:

1. Provides information on local school and school system policies and regulations, programs, opportunities for collaboration, regular student progress reports, and parent-teacher conferences, through various means such as newsletters, school-parent orientation programs, and checklists
2. Solicits and considers parent comments and concerns and makes use of parent talents
3. Makes available information on such topics as the instructional program, student progress, assignments, testing schedules, etc.
4. Strives to ensure that staff are accessible for parent-teacher communications
5. Asks parents about needs for information
6. Asks parents about the effectiveness of parent outreach efforts (including content, processes, relevance, and usefulness)
7. Uses the resources of area and central offices

C. In accordance with regulation IRB-RA (Use of Volunteer Services), encourage parents to volunteer in the classroom, in other areas of the school, and/or at home by:

1. Providing training for staff in the development of jobs for volunteers
2. Designing activities and volunteer job descriptions to give all parents opportunities to participate in the school volunteer program
3. Eliminating barriers that may prevent parent volunteer participation
4. Providing orientation and training for parent volunteers, seeking support from area and central office personnel when appropriate
5. Assessing the effectiveness of the volunteer program, using such factors as:
   A. The number of parent participants
   B. The number and variety of programs served
   C. The benefits to staff, students, and parents
   D. The elimination of barriers to parent participation

6. Appointing a member of the school staff to work cooperatively with the PTA to encourage parent participation in the school volunteer program

D. In cooperation with the PTA and other parent groups, support programs for parents to learn how to create and sustain a home learning environment by:

    1. Sharing information, materials, and programs about how parents can:

        A. Recognize that they have an essential role to play in their children's education by supporting, encouraging, and assisting their children to learn

        B. Get information on "Parenting" topics such as nutrition, health, self-esteem, parent/child communication, motivation, discipline, child development, and other topics relevant to the specific population

        C. Foster their children's enthusiasm for learning at home as well as in school

    2. Providing space for parent training and parent materials, as feasible

    3. Ensuring that parenting information is provided to parents on a regular, systematic basis by using parenting sections in newsletters, discussion groups, conferences, etc.

E. Support parents' efforts to help their children learn by:

    1. Providing appropriate training for staff to work effectively with parents in order to support the concept of learning at home, including such topics as:

        A. How to share curriculum content with parents

        B. How to facilitate parent participation in children's learning at home

        C. How to reach out to all parents

    2. Providing materials on what their child is learning and how to expand on school learning at home, as well as suggestions about available resources

    3. Suggesting ways that parents can enrich and support the curriculum

    4. Using area and central office and PTA resources

F. Respect the right of parents to serve as advocates and support this advocacy by:

    1. Recognizing that advocacy requires that people understand issues, have information about the processes for addressing these issues, and have the skills to be focused "persuaders"

    2. Facilitating access to information about the local school, county programs, and educational issues

    3. Assisting parents to understand the processes of advocating for their children, for programs for children, and for all children

    4. Identifying channels for parents to build networks with others who have common concerns and interests

    5. Supporting leadership/advocacy training for parents

6. Encouraging strong PTAs that reach out within the school community, as well as participate in county, state and national PTA efforts for children and for education

Procedures for Central Area Offices

All MCPS employees are expected to convey a commitment to and demonstrate respect for parent involvement. To support this commitment and to ensure implementation of the parent involvement policy/regulation, appropriate staff in area and central offices will:

A. Communicate with parents about school system policies, regulations, and other general information;
B. Provide for the development of parenting programs and materials, including the use of cable television, pamphlets, adult education courses, parent resource centers and programs designed to orient new parents to MCPS by:
   1. Providing materials and resources to train staff and parents
   2. Developing and distributing curriculum-based learning materials designed for and by parents to be used for at-home learning
   3. In each area, helping parents with school-related issues, resolving problems, and finding resources
   4. Informing parents about the organization and function of the MCPS system
   5. Disseminating information about school and community resources to parents and staff
   6. Identifying and sharing successful parent involvement programs, plans, and activities for use by local schools;
C. Maintain and support countywide parent volunteer opportunities by providing information and training;
D. Assist in the development of parent leadership through PTAs and other recognized groups;
E. Work with businesses, organizations, and other government agencies to gain support and assistance for parent involvement efforts;
F. Through staff development units:
   1. Provide training opportunities for staff and parents to enable them to understand and support effective parent involvement
   2. Provide training opportunities for parents and staff to develop positive communication skills, including problem-solving, conflict resolution, and parent outreach strategies
   3. Include parent involvement rationale and strategies in A & S training, as well as new principal and new staff training;
G. Work with colleges and universities that prepare teachers and administrators to support the inclusion of school and family connections in their training programs;

H. Develop methods to accommodate and support parent involvement for all parents with special circumstances, including those with limited English proficiency and those with disabilities; and

I. Develop mechanisms for local schools to use in order to assess the effectiveness of their parent involvement efforts by:

1. Providing time lines for implementation of parent involvement
2. Monitoring local school action/management plans and the parent involvement advisory committees.

Administrative History: New Regulation, August 21, 1991.

Related Entries: ABA, ABA-RA, ABC, BMA, FAA, IEA, IEB, IED, IFB, IGP-FK, IRB-RA

Office: Deputy Superintendent for Instruction
    Area Associate Superintendents

San Diego City Schools Community Relations and Integration Services Division Parent Involvement Programs

Parent Involvement Policy Statement

The Board of Education recognizes the necessity and value of parent involvement to support student success and academic achievement. In order to assure collaborative partnerships between parents and schools, the board, working through the administration, is committed to:

A. involving parents as partners in school governance including shared decision making and advisory functions.

B. establishing effective two-way communication with all parents, respecting the diversity and differing needs of families.

C. developing strategies and programmatic structures at schools to enable parents to participate actively in their children's education.

D. providing support and coordination for school staff and parents to implement and sustain appropriate parent involvement from kindergarten through grade twelve.

E. utilizing schools to connect students and families with community resources that provide educational enrichment and support.

San Diego City Schools, 1989

Syracuse City School District
Partnership Policy

The Board of Education of the Syracuse City School District believes that education is the shared responsibility of the student, parents, family, school and community. Further, the Board recognizes that the academic achievement and success of our students depend on the strength of the partnerships developed among students, parents, families, schools and the community from preschool through graduation and beyond.

The Board of Education believes that strong partnerships can be developed through nurturing respect, sharing knowledge, supporting each partner's role, collaborating on matters of importance and by appreciating the contributions each partner makes to student achievement. Parents and families provide their children with values, supervision and assistance in goal setting. They offer knowledge of their children, unique histories, traditions, experiences, resources and challenges. Educators contribute professional dedication, caring and expertise. The community provides cultural and financial resources support services, collaboration and monitoring. Students, who are at the center of these partnerships, bring unique skills, talents and learning styles and ultimately, are responsible for their own academic achievement.

Therefore, the Board of Education encourages the development, implementation and evaluation of a comprehensive student, parent, family, school and community partnership initiative. The District, in its implementation plan, will provide a clear definition of the roles of the various partners.

The District, and each school, will develop plans that include all six of the following commitments:

Communication: We will communicate about curriculum, instruction, assessment, staff development, school programs and student progress through timely and effective school-to home, home-to-school and school-to-community methods. An emphasis will be made to communicate effectively with those parents who have limited proficiency in English or literacy challenges.

Parenting: We will provide opportunities for families to enrich their understanding of child and adolescent development, as well as their parenting and child-rearing skills, so they may strengthen the home conditions that support children at each age and grade level. We will assist personnel to work effectively with our diverse families.

Learning at Home: We will promote family involvement in learning activities at home including homework and other curriculum-related activities appropriate to the grade and development of the student.

Decision-making and Advocacy: We will include students, parents, families, schools and community members as partners in planning, governance and advocacy. We will encourage participation by parents and guardians in decisions that affect their child's educational experiences.

Volunteering: We will expand the recruitment, training, and recognition of family and community volunteers and provide opportunities for families and community members to contribute from home, the workplace, and other community-based sites.

Collaborating with Community: We will coordinate resources and services for students, families and schools with businesses, agencies, service organizations and other groups and provide services to the community through our volunteer efforts and community improvement projects.

In order to create the partnerships we envision, the Board of Education will provide the following resources:

- administrative leadership and vision,
- a budget allocation,
- a diverse workforce that reflects our community,
- staff development, and,
- aligned policies and practices.

The Board of Education directs the Superintendent of Schools to appoint a Partnership Task Force to monitor the implementation of this policy at both the school and District levels. The Task Force will report to the Board annually each October. The report will include information on:

- progress at both the school and district levels,
- compliance with all laws (including Title I), and regulations pertinent to family involvement,
- staff development activities conducted in support of this policy,
- resources utilized, and,
- resource gaps and organizational barriers which have hindered progress toward the attainment of a comprehensive and coordinated partnership model.

Syracuse City School District Cross-References
SCSD Strategic Plan 1991–1996
SCSD Synthesized Plan
Parent Partnership Program Site Based Plan, 1996–1999; 1997–2000.

A Question of Merit: Principals' and Parents' Evaluations of Teachers[*]

ABSTRACT

New financial incentive plans to restructure the rewards and professional development in teaching require fair and comprehensive evaluations to determine teacher quality. Some suggest that multiple judges are needed to help correct problems of shallow, partial evaluations. In this reading, principals' and parents' ratings of the same teachers are compared, and school, teacher, and family factors that may influence evaluations are examined. Results suggest that parents and principals emphasize different aspects of teaching when judging teachers' merits. Principals' ratings are influenced by situational factors and the extra work that establishes some teachers' leadership. Parents' ratings are influenced by the connections teachers make with families and the quality of classroom life their children experience. The ratings are not explained by teachers' education or years of experience, which are currently common criteria for annual salary increases. Although principals' judgments may be more central, parents can make important contributions in the evaluation of teachers.

INTRODUCTION

As a result of the intense debates about educational reform, many states and localities have begun to consider alternatives for evaluating and rewarding teachers. More than 40 merit, master, career ladder, incentive pay, or other financial incentive plans are in operation or under consideration in the United States (Changing course, 1985). Among the many difficult problems in designing and implementing these plans, the most difficult of all is the problem of evaluation (Cohn and Natriello, 1984; Johnson, 1984a; Jordan and Borkow, 1983). Teachers' acceptance of evaluation procedures will in large measure determine the success or failure of the new career development and compensation plans.

New ways to evaluate teachers also are needed for the regular, annual evaluations that affect teachers' salaries and promotions in school systems where incentive plans are not an issue. There is general dissatisfaction with the way evalua-

* By Joyce L. Epstein. This work was supported by a grant from the National Institute of Education, NIE-G-83-0002. The opinions expressed are those of the author and do not represent NIE policy. The author thanks John H. Hollifield, Dennis H. Holmes, and three anonymous reviewers for their helpful suggestions. An earlier version of this paper was presented at the 1984 annual meeting of the American Educational Research Association in New Orleans. Reprinted with permission from *Educational Researcher* 14(7) (1985): 3–10.

tions are conducted, what they measure, how they relate to the professional development and improved status of teachers, and how they contribute to the effective education of students (Darling-Hammond, Wise, and Pease, 1983; Millman, 1981). In contrast to mechanical counts of years of teaching experience or academic credits earned, judgments about teacher performance must be based on fair and comprehensive evaluation standards and procedures. This is true whether the evaluations are used to identify a few meritorious teachers or to assist many teachers to advance professionally.

Critics of current evaluation schemes complain that most are based on the principals' ratings of teachers that result from infrequent (sometimes just one) observations in teachers' classrooms; on cronyism, patronage, or other prejudicial decisions; or on seniority, credentials, and accumulated credits that do not involve the evaluation of teaching skills (Cramer, 1983; Johnson, 1984b; Jordan and Borkow, 1983; Natriello and Dornbusch, 1981; Stodolsky, 1984). Principals, also, dislike and distrust procedures that give them sole control over teachers' salary increases and advances (Burke, 1982; Johnson, 1984b). When principals' judgments are supplemented, it is usually by curriculum supervisors who also make infrequent visits to observe teachers. To paraphrase Scriven (1981), the principles and the principals are unclear in evaluations.

MULTIPLE JUDGES IN TEACHER EVALUATION

Instead of judgments by one individual on few occasions, some suggest that multiple judges could rate teachers on many teaching practices that are important to student learning and development (Darling-Hammond, Wise, and Pease, 1983; Educational Research Service, 1983). Different members of the school community undoubtedly have different views of good teaching, but few have attempted to determine empirically what multiple judges could contribute to the evaluation of teachers. Only with such information, however, will teachers know whether some types of judges or judgments help or hurt their chances for recognition of good teaching.

Principals and curriculum supervisors have long been recognized as appropriate evaluators of teachers, despite problems of partiality in ratings or infrequent and incomplete observations. Suggestions have been made to include teachers as participants in the design and conduct of self-evaluations and evaluations of their peers (Cohn and Natriello, 1984; Darling-Hammond, Wise, and Pease, 1983; Educational Research Service, 1983; Johnson, 1984b; Jordan and Borkow, 1983; Natriello and Dornbusch, 1981). A collegial model of school organization requires teachers and administrators to work cooperatively on all aspects of schooling, including staff evaluations (Iwanicki, 1981). Because teachers and their representatives must approve evaluation plans (Lipsky, Bacharach, and Shedd, 1984), teachers will need to be prominently involved in the development, implementation, and assessment of new evaluation systems.

Some proposals for educational reform have taken an even broader view of multiple judges. The Twentieth Century Fund Task Force (1983) suggests that school board members, school administrators, teachers, parents, and federal officials be included in identifying and selecting master teachers. Others point to the absence of parents and students from new plans to identify teachers for financial and career awards as if this were a deficit in design (Educational Research Service, 1983).

A broad definition of multiple judges that includes parents helps us extend recent discussions of theories of effective organizations and effective teaching that underlie designs for teacher evaluations (Darling-Hammond, Wise, and Pease, 1983). Parents, like principals or teachers, play a role in these two areas of research. Early organizational theories emphasized the incompatibility and separate responsibilities of families and schools (Parsons, 1959; Waller, 1932; Weber, 1947). Later theories of organizational effectiveness assume that connections and shared responsibilities are important between social institutions, and that schools and families will be more effective organizations if they work together to achieve common goals (Bronfenbrenner, 1979; Litwak and Meyer, 1974). Parents are members of the school community, well within the "secondary boundaries" of the school organization (Corwin and Wagenaar, 1976), with financial and personal investments in the schools. As "members," parents have an interest in the success, continuation, and improvement of school organizations and should participate, as do other members, in evaluating the organization and its components.

New Directions for Evaluating Teachers

Theories of teacher effectiveness concern the classroom management skills and instructional methods of teachers that have positive impact on student learning. In contrast to theories that assume that the teacher is solely responsible for instructing students, later theories and empirical studies suggest that teachers and parents share responsibility for the child's success in school and that parents can help teachers and students meet school goals (Epstein, 1984; Epstein, 1986 [Reading 3.4]; Seeley, 1981). When teachers involve parents in their children's education with learning activities at home, parents may be even more aware than principals of teachers' flexibility, creativity, and communication skills. They may be knowledgeable about how the teacher interacts with the child and the family, responds to the student's needs and skills, assigns appropriate challenges in books and in homework, and inspires the student to continue commitment to schoolwork at home—all indicators of effective teaching. With unique interests and investments in both teacher effectiveness and school organization effectiveness, parents may be legitimate and important contributors among multiple judges in the evaluation of teachers and school programs.

Because of the states' swift reactions to calls for educational reform, there has been little time for empirical research on alternate designs for teacher evaluations. This reading looks specifically at the potential contributions of parents in comprehensive evaluations of teachers. A large-scale survey of teacher practices of parent involvement (Becker and Epstein, 1982 [Reading 3.1]) offers data with which we can address three questions: How do parents and principals agree or differ in their ratings of the same teacher? What influences parents and principals to rate teachers highly? What do these two raters contribute to a fair and comprehensive evaluation system?

Data from Multiple Judges

Elementary school principals in 11 school districts in Maryland provided evaluations of 77 first-, third-, and fifth-grade teachers' general teaching skills. They used a six-point scale from poor to outstanding to compare the teacher to others in the school on four major teaching skills:

1. Classroom lessons: Prepares lessons well; uses class time effectively.
2. Knowledge of subjects: Understands the subject matter in all areas taught.
3. Discipline: Conducts well-run classes with few serious discipline problems.
4. Creativity: Makes learning exciting and important to the students; uses many novel ideas and approaches.

These categories are similar to those used in several merit/master teacher plans to evaluate teachers' planning, classroom management, instructional behavior, and school participation, and are similar to the kinds of checklists principals use to evaluate teachers in many traditional, annual evaluation systems.

Parents of 1,051 students in these teachers' classrooms provided evaluations of the overall teaching quality compared to other teachers on a six-point scale from poor to outstanding. Other data were collected on the teachers' training and experience, characteristics of the classroom population, teacher practices, family background, and family practices. The information from parents was aggregated to the classroom level and merged with data from principals and teachers. The linked data are unique, compared to previous studies of teacher evaluations, because they permit comparisons of principal and parent ratings of the same 77 teachers on overall teaching quality.

In this reading, the correlates of principal and parent ratings, variation in parent evaluations, and the determinants of principal and parent ratings are examined to learn more about which factors have independent and significant associations with principal and parent evaluations of teachers. Multiple regression analysis is used to identify and to compare the independent influences of student characteristics, school factors, and parent characteristics on principal and parent ratings. The analyses are conducted at the classroom level so that the principal's evaluation of one teacher is compared with the average rating of all the parents of the children in that teacher's class. This approach minimizes distortions that could result from unusually positive or negative personal relationships between a teacher and one or a few parents.

CORRELATES OF PRINCIPALS' AND PARENTS' EVALUATIONS OF TEACHERS

Table 4.1 presents the correlates of principals' and parents' ratings of teachers. The table includes measures of teacher background, teaching approaches, family background, parent involvement, and student characteristics that could contribute to high or low ratings of teachers. We need to know whether school and family characteristics and practices affect the evaluations parents make to understand whether problems are solved or created when parents are among the multiple judges of teachers.

Intercorrelation of ratings. The correlation of the principal and parent ratings is significant but modest (r = .274). There is some mutual recognition of strong and weak teachers, but also considerable disagreement in the ratings of the same teacher by parents and by principals.

Teacher background. Teacher education and years of experience are *not* significant correlates of either the principal or parent ratings. More experienced teachers or those with more credits earned beyond the bachelor's degree are not necessarily viewed as better teachers than less experienced teachers or those with fewer accumulated credit hours.

Teaching approaches. Teacher leadership in the use of parent involvement as recognized by the principal is associated with higher ratings of teachers by principals (r = .303) and by parents (r = .222). Teachers who report fewer discipline problems are given higher ratings by parents (r = −.233), but discipline problems are not significantly associated with principals' ratings of their teachers.

Family factors. Teachers are given higher ratings by principals if their classrooms are in city schools, include predominantly minority students, or include many children who live in one-parent homes. These factors of place, race, and parent marital status are not significantly related to parent ratings of teachers. The number of books in families' homes, the education of the parents, and the work status of the mother are not associated with higher ratings from principals or parents. There is no obvious connection, then, between the education of classroom parents and their ratings of teachers. Classrooms of better-educated parents are no more or less likely to overpraise or overcriticize teachers. Principals may give greater consideration than parents to demographic demands on teachers that require good teaching and classroom management.

Parent involvement. Parents' ratings of teachers are consistently and highly associated with whether the teacher frequently involves more of them (at the classroom level) in learning activities at home (r = .466), provides many ideas for them (r = .517), sends them many communications (r = .529), improves more parents' understanding of the school program (r = .495), and sends the message that parents should help at home (r = .332). Parent recognition that the teacher works hard to involve parents

TABLE 4.1   Correlates of Principals' and Parents' Ratings of Teachers*

	Principals' Ratings	Parents' Ratings
Teacher Background		
Years of teaching experience	−.138	.125
Highest degree	−.033	.044
Teaching Approaches		
Leader in parent involvement (rating by principal)	.303*	.222*
Teacher rates more children discipline problems	−.074	−.233*
Family Factors (Classroom Level)		
Race (white)	−.253*	−.059
City location	.280*	−.034
Parent education	−.012	−.010
Books in the home	−.057	−.079
Mother works	.085	−.182
Two-parent home	−.403*	−.110
Parent Involvement (Classroom Level)		
Parents active at the school	.013	.069
Parents believe teacher thinks they should help	.172	.332*
Parents report frequent requests from teachers	.329*	.466*
Parents know more about instructional program	.233*	.495*
Parents receive many ideas on how to help at home	.093	.517*
Parents receive many communications from teacher	.107	.529*
Parents report teacher works hard to interest and excite parents	.278*	.676*
Parents report positive interpersonal skills of teacher	.134	.719*
Student Status (Classroom Level)		
Grade level	−.006	−.238*
Classroom achievement	−.076	−.039

*Coefficients of .22 or more are significant at the .05 level; coefficients of .29 or more are significant at the .01 level.

N = 77

is highly associated with the parents' overall rating of teacher quality and ratings of teachers' interpersonal skills.

When more parents are involved in learning activities at home, principals hear about it from the teacher or from parents. Parent reports of high involvement, more knowledge about school, and recognition of teachers' hard work confirm or contribute to principals' high ratings of those teachers.

The number of classroom parents active at the school is not significantly associated with parent or principal ratings of teacher quality.

Student status. Although parent ratings of teachers were associated with the children's grade level, principal ratings were not. Parents give higher ratings to teachers of the younger grades. Neither principal nor parent ratings are associated with teachers' reports of average classroom achievement of students in reading and math.

Variations in Parent Evaluations of Teachers' Merit

One principal is usually responsible for evaluating each teacher in the school. The comparable measure from parents is the average rating of the parents of the children in the teacher's class. However, parent opinions about a teacher vary, just as ratings would vary if 20 administrators judged the same teacher. It is informative, then, to examine the factors that are associated with the variation in the parent ratings of teacher quality, as shown in Table 4.2.

High agreement by parents that the teacher works hard to interest or excite parents, and high agreement that parents know more as a result of the teacher's efforts, are related to significantly less variation in parents' evaluations of teacher quality. Teachers are rated higher by more parents in classrooms where parents recognize the teacher's efforts and effectiveness.

In contrast, grade level was related to greater variation in parents' estimates: the higher the grade level, the more variation in parents' estimates of teacher quality. Parents' reports about teachers may vary more in the upper grades for many reasons: Older students are more diverse in their needs, interests, and demands on teachers; parents of older students are more sophisticated about evaluation because they have more points for comparison with children's earlier teachers; and teachers of older students are more diverse in their teaching styles and practices and vary more in their approaches to parents. Some parents become increasingly discouraged about teachers, school, and their child's progress, whereas other parents remain or become more positive about upper grade teachers who are responsive to the needs and interests of their older children.

The more serious discipline problems there are in a classroom (reported by the teachers), the more variation there is in parents' estimates of teacher quality. Some teachers deal with discipline problems in ways that do not interfere with most students' learning. Other teachers' programs are disrupted by the number of disciplinary incidents or by the way the teacher deals with discipline problems. Parents may vary in their ratings of teachers according to their children's experiences in troubled classrooms.

Overall, the correlates in Table 4.2 suggest that parents achieve greater consensus about teachers' merits when the teachers are hard at work at parent involvement, when the parents know more about the ways schools and classrooms work, and when the teachers are responsive to more students.

Tables 4.1 and 4.2 show that certain variables are strongly associated with principals' or parents' ratings. Some of these may be especially important, independent determinants of principals' and parents' judgments of teachers' merits.

Influences on Principals' and Parents' Ratings

Table 4.3 presents the independent influences of family and student factors on principals' and parents' ratings. The first section examines the effects on principals' ratings of teachers. Principals give higher ratings to teachers who are in ur-

TABLE 4.2 Significant Correlates of Variation in Parents' Evaluations of Teachers

Classroom-Level Report	Correlation with Variation in Parents' Evaluations
Teacher works hard to involve parents	−.321
Parents know more about child's instructional program this year than in past	−.304
Grade level of child/teacher	+.274
Teacher reports more discipline problems in class	+.273

N = 77

ban schools, are recognized by the principal as leaders in parent involvement, and are rated highly by the parents in that classroom, with all other variables taken into account. Grade level; the number of discipline problems in the class; and traditional communications with parents such as notes, memos, or conferences do not independently influence principals' ratings of teacher quality. Principal ratings are especially sensitive to the conditions under which teachers teach and the extra work teachers add to their regular duties that establishes their leadership and distinguishes them from other teachers.

The second section shows the effects of school and family factors on parents' ratings of teachers. Parents give high marks to teachers who frequently request them to be involved in learning activities at home, frequently use traditional communications with families, have few classroom discipline problems, and are in suburban schools. Parent ratings are sensitive to the connections teachers make with families and to the qualities of calm and ordered classroom environments.

Each of the significant effects is independent of the other variables in the model. That is, after teacher practices that involve parents are taken into account, good classroom discipline influences parents to rate teachers higher in overall teaching quality. Parent involvement and communication with teachers are the most important determinants of parent ratings, contributing over 30 percent to the explained variance in parents' evaluations of teacher merits.

Although grade level initially has a significant effect on parents' ratings, the importance of grade level disappears after teacher practices are taken into account. Thus, the grade-level correlations reported in Tables 4.1 and 4.2 are attributed in Table 4.3 to differences in teachers' approaches to parent involvement.

The importance of school location becomes more prominent after teacher practices are accounted for. That is, teachers—both city and suburban—are given higher ratings if they use parent involvement techniques, but suburban teachers are rated higher by parents for other qualities, after accounting for parent involvement practices.

In other analyses, it was found that teachers' interpersonal skills were very important for the parent ratings of teacher quality. Teachers whose contacts with parents were high in cooperation, friendliness, respect, trust, and warmth, and low in conflict, misunderstanding, distance, lack of concern, and tenseness, were considered better teachers by parents (Epstein, 1986). The interpersonal qualities

TABLE 4.3   Factors That Influence Principals' and Parents' Ratings of Teachers

Principals' Ratings

Variables in Model	Urban Location	Discipline Problems	Grade Level	Observed Leadership in Parent Involvement	Traditional School-to-Home Communications	Parents' Evaluations	R^2
School/Class Factors	.294[a] (.649)	−.110 (1.020)	−.014 (−.009)				.091
Principal Observation	.268[a] (.592)	−.065 (−.603)	−.043 (−.027)	.277[a] (.250)			.164
Reports from Parents	.271[a] (.598)	−.013 (−.117)	.008 (.005)	.228[a] (.206)	−.030 (−.017)	.247a (.526)	.210
Zero-order Correlation	.280	−.074	−.006	.303	.107	.274	

Parents' Ratings

Variables in Model	Urban Location	Discipline Problems	Grade Level	Frequent Requests for Parent Involvement	Traditional School-to-Home Communications	Principals' Evaluations	R^2
School/Class Factors	.000 (.0003)	−.235[a] (−1.027)	−.241 (−.071)				.112
Parent Experiences	−.223a (−.232)	−.228 (−.996)	.030 (.009)	.439[a] (.119)	.347[a] (.092)		.441
Principals; Ratings	.250[a] (−.260)	−.213[a] (−.928)	.019 (.006)	.401[a] (.109)	.338[a] (−.090)	.160 (.075)	.463
Zero–order Correlation	−.034	−.233	−.238	.466	.529	.274	

NOTE: Standardized regression coefficients are shown first; unstandardized coefficients are in parentheses.

N = 77

a = Unstandardized coefficient is at least twice the standard error, or contributes more than 3% to explained variance.

of teachers that parents experienced did not influence principals' ratings, although principals' ratings were influenced by parent reports of teachers' hard work and overall teaching quality.

These data do not permit as detailed an analysis of the influences on principals' ratings as on the parents' ratings. The lower percent of variance explained by these measures for principals' evaluations of teachers is due, in part, to the absence of specific measures that underlie the principals' rating scheme. For example, we cannot tell how principals estimate the level of teachers' knowledge of subject matter or how they judge creativity. Other measures not included in this study—such as principals' personal friendship with the teachers, the principals' estimate of teacher-pupil relationships, or teachers' responsiveness to students' individual differences—will be important additions to new research. Despite the limitations of these data, we can conclude with conviction that the principals' ratings of teachers are not explained by teachers' advanced education or by years of teaching experience—indicators that are currently a common basis for teachers' yearly increases in pay. Others, too, have reported that excellence in teaching is curiously unrelated to years of teaching experience or accumulated credits (Corwin and Wagenaar, 1976; Rosenholtz and Smylie, 1984).

DISCUSSION

We need to know more about the interests, competencies, and biases of multiple judges and the contributions or problems they add to teacher evaluation. The conclusions we draw from this initial study may be useful in plans for practice and research on new forms of teacher evaluation.

1. **Parents and principals emphasize different aspects of teaching in judging teachers' merits.** Principals may know when teachers add extra duties to their teaching load, but may not be aware of more subtle changes in classroom teaching that affect individual students. Extra responsibilities that teachers undertake are often more visible and more dramatic than classroom teaching, or they directly assist the principal in administrative tasks. The findings suggest that teachers earn higher ratings from principals when they work under difficult school conditions or assume leadership roles.

Parents may know when teachers make special efforts to help children attain basic or advanced skills. Children's homework and talk of classroom activities provide a running commentary to parents about the subtle changes in teaching that affect children day by day. The data in this article indicate that teachers earn higher ratings from parents when they use parent involvement activities with more parents, send more communications home, and maintain good classroom discipline. Darling-Hammond, Wise, and Pease (1983) suggest that parents have a stake in the "bottom line" of teaching: the effects on student learning and development. This study shows that, when given an opportunity to evaluate teachers, parents relate teacher performance to the children's experiences in the classroom and to the resources and ideas that some teachers offer parents.

2. **The fairest evaluations may involve multiple judges rating those aspects of teaching for which they have proven competence and special interest.** Teacher performance can be judged in many ways, and no one way is likely to be wholly satisfactory. Principals' ratings alone are not necessarily the best or the only way of evaluating teachers' excellence. Achievement test scores are not the only way of judging teachers' talents and successes with children. Parents' ratings are not the only way to identify responsive teachers. Because there is no single set of skills that perfectly define effective teaching, measures of many aspects of teaching by multiple judges are likely to yield the fairest and most comprehensive evaluation of teachers.

Teachers are not opposed to fair evaluation by competent evaluators. Over 60 percent of teachers in one survey agreed that teacher evaluations should be based on how well they perform in class (Rist, 1983). But teachers are aware that serious problems occur when one judge rates teachers on the basis of few observations and on few teaching skills and practices (Darling-Hammond, Wise and

Pease, 1983; Natriello and Dornbusch, 1981; Shavelson and Dempsey-Atwood, 1976; Stodolsky, 1984). These problems will not be solved simply by using multiple judges, but they might be mitigated by thoughtful designs of different formats that make appropriate uses of multiple judges. If the teachers in our study were evaluated by principals and by parents using the data discussed here, more teachers would be recognized as good teachers for different skills and teaching abilities than if only principals rated the teachers.

Including all parents systematically in evaluation procedures may remove some of the bias in the reports principals typically receive from parents. Principals often hear from a small number of parents, those with complaints or the few parents who are very active at school. This survey shows that all parents can provide principals with assessments of teachers' efforts that principals may overlook.

Unfair evaluations result from the lack of stability and generalizability in ratings by individual judges who see few examples of each teacher's lessons and classroom management (Shavelson and Dempsey-Atwood, 1976; Stodolsky, 1984). When the reports from many parents in one classroom are aggregated, they provide one relatively stable rating of teachers. The grouped data from parents can balance the contributions of other, individual ratings. The variation in observations tells how consistent or generalizable the ratings are among parents.

3. Tests are needed of alternate forms of teacher evaluation that use multiple judges. We have no practical examples of how multiple judges, including parents, are involved systematically in the evaluations of teachers. Parents can be involved directly, as in periodic surveys along with other judges, or they can be involved indirectly, as in preliminary surveys that are used to help design the evaluations that principals or other educators will conduct. Tests are needed of direct and indirect evaluations by parents and their uses in programs for professional advancement and improvement. These exploratory tests could be conducted at experimental sites for merit, master, and other career development plans that states or localities have established.

Where they remain the sole evaluators of teachers, principals should supplement their broad-based, bureaucratic concerns with deeper examinations of the day-to-day instructional practices of teachers that are important to parents. But we suggest that principals should *not* remain the sole evaluators of teachers. Both principals' and parents' judgments may be needed in a comprehensive system of evaluation because these raters have interests in different educational processes and products, different competencies to judge particular aspects of teaching, and different cumulative experiences with teachers and students. For example, among multiple judges, parents may be well qualified to rate teachers on their responsiveness to individual students but poorly qualified to rate teachers on how they promote equality of opportunities and divide attention among all students in class.

This study begins to identify factors that influence principals' and parents' ratings of teachers. Other competent and appropriate judges of teachers are interested in other aspects of teaching that may be important for identifying good teaching or master teachers. We need studies on the factors that influence teacher self-evaluations, teacher peer review, supervisors' and school board members' evaluations, and students' ratings of teachers. Research on the components of teacher evaluation should help educators build practical systems of evaluation that fulfill two functions: to identify strong and weak teachers and to help all teachers improve specific teaching skills.

CONCLUSION

The next few years should see dramatic changes in the way teachers are recruited, motivated, evaluated, and rewarded. The recent surge of activity on career development plans in states and school systems across the country suggests strongly that neither the public nor the teaching profession will continue to support the lockstep salary schedules that pay the worst teachers as much as the best. In addition, competent individuals will not enter a profession that continues to limit challenge, compensation, and advancement. This study suggests that the fairest evaluations will result when teachers are rated by multiple judges, including parents, who have clear interests in effective teaching, and when teachers are judged on multiple criteria that are important for the education of students.

Principal and teacher-peer judgments will and should be more central and be given more weight than parents' ratings in the evaluation of teachers in merit pay, master status, and other pay and promotion plans. But parents' judgments may contribute importantly to more effective teaching and to more effective school organizations.

REFERENCES

Becker, H., and J. Epstein. (1982). Parent involvement: A study of teacher practices. *Elementary School Journal* 83: 85–102. (Reading 3.1).

Bronfenbrenner, U. (1979). *The ecology of human development.* Cambridge, MA: Harvard University Press.

Burke, B. T. (1982). Merit pay for teachers: Round Valley may have the answer. *Phi Delta Kappan* 64: 265–266.

Changing course: A 50-state survey of reform measures. (1985, February). *Education Week* 4(20): 11–30.

Cohn, M., and G. Natriello. (1984). Critical issues in the development of a merit pay system. Paper presented at the annual meeting of the American Educational Research Association, April, in New Orleans.

Corwin, R. G., and T. Wagenaar. (1976). Boundary interaction between service organizations and their problems: A study of teacher-parent relationships. *Social Forces* 55: 471–492.

Cramer, J. (1983). Yes—merit pay can be a horror, but a few school systems have done it right. *American School Board Journal* 170(9): 33–34.

Darling-Hammond, L., A. E. Wise, and S. R. Pease. (1983). Teacher evaluation in the organizational context: A review of the literature. *Review of Educational Research* 53: 285–328.

Educational Research Service. (1983). *Merit pay plans for teachers: Status and descriptions.* Arlington, VA

Epstein, J. L. (1984). Effects of teacher practices of parent involvement on change in student achievement in reading and math. Paper presented at the annual meeting of the American Educational Research Association, April, in New Orleans.

———. (1986). Parents' reactions to teacher practices of parent involvement. *Elementary School Journal* 86: 277–294. (Reading 3.4).

Iwanicki, E. F. (1981). Contract plans: A professional growth-oriented approach to evaluating teacher performance. Pages 203–228 in *Handbook of teacher evaluation*, edited by J. Millman. Beverly Hills: Sage.

Johnson, S. M. (1984a). Merit pay plans for teachers: A poor prescription for reform. *Harvard Educational Review* 54: 175–185.

———. (1984b). Merit pay plans: Effects on teachers and their work. Paper presented at the 1984 National Conference on Merit Pay for Teachers, American Center for Management Development, in Sarasota.

Jordan, K. F., and N. B. Borkow. (1983). *Merit pay for elementary and secondary school teachers: Background discussion and analysis of issues.* Washington, DC: Congressional Research Service, Library of Congress.

Lipsky, D. G., S. B. Bacharach, and J. G. Shedd. (1984). Merit pay and collective bargaining in public education. Paper presented at the National Conference on Merit Pay for Teachers in Washington, DC.

Litwak, E., and H. J. Meyer. (1974). *School, family, and neighborhood.* New York: Columbia University Press.

Millman, J., ed. (1981). *Handbook of teacher evaluation.* Beverly Hills: Sage.

Natriello, G., and S. M. Dornbusch. (1981). Pitfalls in the evaluation of teachers by principals. *Administrator's Notebook* 29: 1–4.

Parsons, T. (1959). The school class as a social system: Some of its functions in American society. *Harvard Educational Review* 29: 297–318.

Rist, M. (1983). Our nationwide poll: Most teachers endorse the merit pay concept. *The American School Board Journal* 170(9): 23–27.

Rosenholtz, S. J., and M. A. Smylie. (1984). Teacher compensation and career ladders. *Elementary School Journal* 85: 149–166.

Scriven, M. (1981). Summative teacher evaluation. In *Handbook of teacher evaluation*, edited by J. Millman. Beverly Hills: Sage.

Seeley, D. S. (1981). *Education through partnership: Mediating structures and education.* Cambridge, MA: Ballinger.

Shavelson, R., and N. Dempsey-Atwood. (1976). General theory of measures of teaching behavior. *Review of Educational Research* 46: 553–611.

Stodolsky, S. S. (1984). Teacher evaluation: The limits of looking. *Educational Researcher* 13: 11–18.

Twentieth Century Fund Task Force. (1983). *Making the grade.* New York: The Twentieth Century Fund.

Waller, W. (1932). *The sociology of teaching.* New York: Russell and Russell.

Weber, M. (1947). *The theory of social and economic organization.* New York: Oxford University Press.

DISCUSSION AND ACTIVITIES

The comments in this section extend and update the content of the readings in this chapter. Key concepts and results are summarized. Questions and activities are provided for class discussions, debates, and homework assignments. They may suggest other exercises, field activities, and research projects.

▣ KEY CONCEPTS

1. State, district, and school policies on school, family, and community partnerships must be clear, comprehensive, flexible, and responsive to the goals and needs of students, families, and schools.
2. State, district, and school policies on school, family, and community partnerships require enactments or other official commitments to ensure adequate staff, funding, training, dissemination, and other support needed to implement the policies.

❂ COMMENT

Policies and Enactments

Policies concerning school, family, and community partnerships must be clear and comprehensive, but also flexible. Such policies encourage state, district, and school programs to account for their starting points in partnerships and focus partnership practices on specific school and family goals for student success. Policies also should set high standards for excellent, ongoing programs of school, family, and community partnerships, and specify ways to measure how well programs are implemented and goals are met.

At the state and district levels, policies on partnerships should include explicit enactments such as funding, training, and other assistance that will enable schools to implement the policies. Policies without enactments are unfunded and unsupported, and will be unwelcome and ineffective.

State and district policies on partnerships must clearly outline how schools will be assisted to develop and evaluate partnership programs with training, funds, and other assistance, encouragement, and recognition from the state and district. The emphasis on assistance to schools is in contrast to top-down policies with rigid directives or prescribed activities that leave educators, parents, and students no flexibility to design programs or practices of partnership that they can call their own.

These seemingly simple guidelines for clear, comprehensive, flexible, funded, and facilitated policies are not as simple to implement as you might think. The discussions and activities in this chapter should help you to explore, critique, and consider policies for improving school, family, and community partnerships in states, districts, and schools.

◈ ACTIVITY

Comparing State and District Policies and Leadership

The state policy initiatives recommended in Reading 4.1 and other related policies that have been designed and implemented by states also may be important for school districts. State policies are written with the expectation that they will be implemented by districts and schools in different geographic locations and political contexts within a state. District policies are written with an understanding that they will be implemented in pre-, elementary, middle, and high schools, even though the schools, neighborhoods, students, and families may vary dramatically within a district. These differences may have implication for the design and implementation of state and district policies.

A. Photocopy Figure 4.1 on pages 349–350.
B. Write YES or NO to tell whether you think each policy is appropriate at the state and/or district levels.
   1. If YES for districts, explain one way in which the policy and resulting activities might differ in a district compared to a state.
   2. If NO for districts, explain one reason why the policy and resulting activities are not important or appropriate for districts to conduct.

ⅠⅠ COMMENT

The Power of Linked Policies and Practices

States can take actions that encourage partnership programs, whether or not they are guided by federal mandates or supported by federal funds. Districts can take actions that enable all schools to develop partnership programs, whether or not they are actively supported by their state departments of education. Schools can develop programs of school, family, and community partnerships, whether or not they are directly supported by their districts or states. Individual teachers can establish good partnerships with students' families and communities, whether or not they are guided or aided by their schools or by other policy levels and leaders. Efforts at any level may increase understanding and expertise in conducting partnership activities.

    Although each policy level may work on partnerships relatively independently, research and practical examples suggest that programs are stronger and of higher quality when federal, state, district, and school policies, funding, and technical assistance are linked. That is, programs are more effective in design and in results when federal policies support states, when state policies support districts and schools, and when district policies enable schools to establish good programs of partnership. The best links focus attention at the school level, where educators, families, and students interact on a daily basis to help students learn and grow.

QUESTIONS TO DISCUSS

1. *On the one hand.* Give two examples from readings in this or other chapters or from your experience that indicate why policies that are linked

Comparing State and District Policies

POLICIES AND ACTIVITIES	Is this an appropriate policy initiative for STATES? (Write YES or NO for each.)	DISTRICTS?	If YES for districts, tell one way the policy or resulting activities might differ in a district compared to a state. If NO for districts, give one reason why the policy is not appropriate.
A. Write a policy that supports comprehensive programs of family, school, and community partnership.	_____	_____	_____ _____ _____
B. Establish a single office with an expert leader and adequate staff to facilitate the development and continuous improvement of programs of partnership. This office provides staff development and technical assistance and coordinates partnerships across departments.	_____	_____	_____ _____ _____
C. Allocate a per-pupil expenditure or lump-sum budget for school, family, and community partnerships to cover staff and program costs.	_____	_____	_____ _____ _____
D. Establish small grants and other support for developing and implementing partnerships.	_____	_____	_____ _____ _____
E. Establish a clearinghouse to disseminate promising practices of partnership.	_____	_____	_____ _____ _____
F. Support requirements for teacher and administrator credentials on partnerships.	_____	_____	_____ _____ _____
G. Develop courses for preservice, advanced, and/or inservice education on partnerships	_____	_____	_____ _____

FIGURE 4.1 Policies and Activities

(continues)

FIGURE 4.1 *(continued)*

H. Support a master teacher, lead teacher, or professional coordinator in each school to assist with partnerships.

I. Develop partnership tools or products (e.g., brochures, lunch menus, templates for calendars, newletters, publications for all schools and families, guidelines for communicating with non-English-speaking families, and other examples in Reading 4.1.

J. Encourage business, industry, and other community connections to strengthen school, family, and community partnerships.

K. Establish an advisory committee for school, family, and community partnerships including educators, parents, and community members.

L. Institute an accountability system to monitor and evaluate progress; recognize and reward excellent work on partnerships.

M. Support evaluations of the effects of demonstration and ongoing partnership programs.

N. Conduct an annual conference for schools to share best practices with each other and to continue annual plans for improving partnership programs.

across state, district, and school levels create stronger and more effective programs to involve families and communities than do policies that are not linked or are issued at just one level.

2. *On the other hand.* Give two examples from the readings in this or other chapters or from your experience that indicate that individual teachers or administrators can create strong and effective programs and practices to involve families, even if their districts or states are *not* actively supporting such actions.

3. What advice would you give to a district leader who is considering whether to (1) develop district policies, guidelines, and assistance to help all schools in the district develop programs of school, family, and community partnerships, or (2) leave it up to each school to do this without district support? List two recommendations or guidelines you would give this leader and the reasons for your advice.

ⓄⓄ COMMENT

Federal Leadership and Federal Guidelines

At the federal level, some policies of the U.S. Departments of Education, Labor, Health and Human Services, and other departments concern connections among students, families, schools, and communities. Several programs have long histories of including family involvement among their required components.

Head Start, initiated in 1965, recognized that all families, including low-income families, are important in their children's education. Head Start legislated opportunities for low-income parents to have unrestricted access to program facilities, volunteer and work as paid aides, and serve on advisory committees to be involved in policy decisions that affect their own and other children. Head Start programs included home visits to help families with parenting skills and parent-child interactions, discuss children's progress, how to tutor at home, and where to obtain health and other services in the community.

Follow-Through, initiated in 1967, attempted to continue Head Start's emphasis on parental involvement in school programs and activities for children and families through the primary grades.

The Education of All Handicapped Children Act (Public Law 94-142), initiated in 1975, required teachers and parents to cooperate in setting annual educational and developmental goals for children.

Title I of the Elementary and Secondary Education Act (ESEA) of 1965, also called Chapter I for a while, included guidelines and mandates for school and family partnerships that are congruent with the theory and framework in this volume. Even in its current form, Title I recognizes the importance of family involvement in the education of children who, because of educational and economic difficulties, are not succeeding well or are at risk of failing in school. This ongoing federal policy requires districts to spend some Title I funds to develop positive and productive partnership programs to include families in their children's education in productive ways. Along with Title I, other programs in ESEA (Even Start, Title VI, Title VII, and the Individuals with Disabilities Education Act, IDEA) include guidelines for home-school-community connections to improve students' chances of success.

There have been two main problems in implementing federal guidelines and programs for home-school connections. First, educators in states, districts, and schools have not always understood the intent of the legislative language to establish coherent and important programs of partnership, and they faced no serious consequences for inaction. Second, in the past, the legislative guidelines led educators to separate Title I parents from other parents. The first problem stalled action and progress on partnerships in many locations; the second problem caused the separation and segregation of parents within schools, limiting the sense of community and contradicting the concept of partnerships.

◇ ACTIVITY

Finding and Critiquing Policies of Partnerships

Use the Internet to learn more about federal policies that include attention to parental involvement, community connections, or other aspects of school, family, and community partnerships.

A. Explore federal legislation, regulations, and other policy guidelines on *www.ed.gov,* the web site of the U.S. Department of Education. Or explore the web sites of the Departments of Labor, Commerce, and Health and Human Services for policies concerning connections among home, school, and community. Look for information on Title I, Title VI, Title VII, Goals 2000, Even Start, Head Start, Drug-Free Schools and Communities, and other policies and programs that concern the families of educationally disadvantaged children, children with special needs, and gifted and talented children.
B. Identify one policy that interests you.
C. Summarize and critique the policy you selected.
   1. What does the policy require or request of a state, district, school, family, or community concerning school, family, and community partnerships?
   2. Explain: Is the policy you selected clear? Flexible? Enabling?
   3. What is one positive *or* negative influence that the policy might have on the school, family, and community partnership practices of a school, school district, or state department of education?
   4. Describe one way that you would change and improve the policy that you selected.

Federally Funded Programs and Policies

Interview one educator who is associated with a Head Start, Even Start, Title I, or other federally funded program for children and families in a school or other location in your community.

A. Identify the program and the position of the person you are interviewing. Briefly summarize the goals of the program that you selected.

B. Ask:

    1. Does your program have a written policy and plan for school, family, and community partnerships?

        A. If YES, briefly summarize the policy.

        B. If NO, briefly summarize the program's approach to school, family, and community partnerships.

    2. Are *only* federal funds used in this program, or are other funds used to support the program and activities of school, family, and community partnerships?

    3. Describe one of the program's most effective and one of the program's least effective activities for family and community involvement.

    4. How effective is this program in informing and involving *all* of the families that are eligible for its services?

    5. What transitional activities help children and families move from this program to their next school?

    6. What is one way that you would like to improve the way this program works with families and communities in the future?

C. Add at least one question of your own about the federally funded program you selected.

D. Document your questions and responses.

E. Write a reflective paragraph on the information you obtained on the nature and quality of the program and the contributions of federal funds to its work.

▌▎ COMMENT

Top-Down, Bottom-Up, or Side-by-Side Policy

There is controversy about the differences, benefits, and disadvantages of "top-down" versus "bottom up" policies and directives. In this chapter, I suggest that the most important policies for school, family, and community partnership find expression at the school level. The readings and activities also suggest, however, that there are important state and district policies, activities, and support that enable schools to develop skills and programs of school, family, and community partnerships.

QUESTIONS TO DISCUSS

Use the information in this chapter or your experience to answer the following questions.

1. Do you think that a written federal, state, district, or school policy or mandate can *change* educators' and families' attitudes and behaviors about school, family, and community partnerships? Explain your YES or NO answer.
2. A. Give examples of one state policy or activity and one district policy or activity that might *not* find expression at the school level.
   B. Explain one purpose or goal of each of the policies you selected.
3. A. Give one example of a set of "linked" state, district, *and* school policies that illustrates how leadership, investments, and practices of partnership across levels affect the involvement of families and communities in their children's education at the school level.
   B. Explain one way your set of linked policies might improve or worsen the quality of a school's program of school, family, and community partnerships.

▯▮ COMMENT

The Ebb and Flow of Policy and Practice

In the real world of education, the ebb and flow of policy and practice sometimes prevent the development of permanent partnership programs. By ebb and flow, I mean that policies and actions may be halted long before the goals of the policies are achieved. In some states and districts, policies, goals, and activities for school, family, and community partnerships are started and then stopped, delayed, limited in scope, or redirected because of leadership and staff changes or budget cuts. In other states and districts, partnerships are maintained or expanded, despite changes in personnel. Following are a few of many examples of actions that retreated or advanced over time.

California's state policy, passed in 1989, was one of the first to specify in a short, clear form that all six major types of involvement identified in research (parenting, communicating, volunteering, learning at home, decision making, and collaborating with the community) are important in a comprehensive program of partnerships (Solomon, 1991). The policy included plans for state-sponsored staff development and assistance for district and school leaders and teams to maximize the chances that the state policy would be enacted. After a good start, progress was slowed by politics and budget cuts. Later, the state reestablished and strengthened initiatives on partnerships, building on its initial strong policy. (See more on California's leadership below, and see Reading 4.2.)

Similarly, Indianapolis's Parents in Touch office led the nation in district-level leadership during the 1980s. Progress was seriously affected by the retirements of key staff and changes in superintendents, common occurrences in school districts. Nevertheless, the school district's work was documented and provided many ideas for other districts (Warner, 1991). As it began to reconstruct district-level leadership on partnerships in the mid-1990s, Indianapolis was able to build on its earlier experiences.

It should be noted that progress on partnerships is not always halted by changes in personnel. For example, San Diego City and San Diego County school districts have maintained leadership in school, family, and community connections for over a decade across several school administrations. This was due, in part, to clearly written policies and to widespread expertise in school, family, and community partnerships, so that new leaders were ready and able to build on the work of those who left.

When its superintendent changed in the early 1990s, and then again, St. Paul, Minnesota's public schools maintained a clear vision about family involvement and increased efforts to improve home, school, and community connections in all schools. This was due, in part, to the decision by the new superintendents to expand the goals of their predecessors. Progress also was due to the growing knowledge of many school principals, teachers, and parents of the need to talk and work with each other. In St. Paul's within-district choice program, just about all schools' brochures and descriptions of their programs boasted that parents were welcome as partners in their children's education.

Personnel changes are guaranteed to occur in schools, districts, and state education agencies. Individuals move, are promoted, retire, or transfer to new assignments. Budgets are challenged as departments compete for limited funds. Even with these inevitable changes and challenges, however, state, district, and school investments in school, family, and community partnership programs can be protected and improved, just as reading, math, science, testing, and other programs continue despite the ups and downs of budgets and the comings and goings of leaders and staff.[2]

QUESTIONS TO DISCUSS

Think of the permanence and predictability of a reading, math, or testing program in schools, districts, *or* states. What might be done to organize ongoing programs of school, family, and community partnerships that will not disappear with staff or budget changes?

---

[2] See Zelma P. Solomon, California's policy on parent involvement: State leadership for local initiatives, *Phi Delta Kappan* 72(5) (1991): 335–362; Izona Warner, Parents in touch: District leadership for parent involvement, *Phi Delta Kappan* 72(5) (1991): 372–375.

1. Select and identify a policy level—state, district, or school—that interests you.
2. Describe two structures, processes, or activities that you think might help prevent setbacks in the progress of partnership programs due to staff or budgetary changes.
3. Explain why you think each idea might help stabilize or "institutionalize" a program of partnerships at the policy level that you selected.

0: COMMENT

What Are School, Family, and Community Partnerships Worth?

Programs of school, family, and community partnerships may be funded using a formula allocating a per-pupil expenditure or a lump-sum investment to support staff and program costs. Several years ago, I suggested a minimum per-pupil expenditure of $5, $10, and $25 at the state, district, and school levels, respectively, or minimum lump-sum investments of $100,000 per state, $50,000 per large district, and $15,000 per school to fund the leadership, development, training, implementation, evaluation, and continuous improvement of programs of partnership in states, districts, and schools (Epstein, 1991). Since that initial modest proposal, my colleagues and I have collected data from states, districts, and schools on the levels and sources of their investments in staff and activities to develop comprehensive partnership programs (Epstein, Sanders, Clark, and Van Voorhis, 1999). The following comments and activities draw from those data to address the question: What are school, family, and community partnerships worth?[3]

Exploring Funding Options: Per-Pupil Allocations

Imagine the following allocations for school, family, and community partnership programs at the state, district, and school levels:

- $0.25–$1 per student of state funds to be used *at that level* to fund salaries and benefits of a state director of partnerships and staff, state programs, and services for activities that assist districts and schools in their work on partnerships. State funds may support staff salaries and

---

[3] See J. L. Epstein, What we can learn from federal, state, district, and school initiatives, *Phi Delta Kappan* 72(5) (1991): 344–349, special section on *Paths to Partnership*; J. L. Epstein, M. G. Sanders, L. A. Clark, and F. Van Voorhis, (1999). Costs and benefits: School, district, and state funding for programs of school, family, and community partnerships (paper presented at the annual meeting of the American Sociological Association, Chicago).

benefits, grants to districts and schools, training and other inservice education, and other state leadership functions.

- $5–$10 per student of district funds to be used *at that level* to fund salaries and benefits of district coordinator(s) and facilitator(s), district programs, and services to assist all schools in the district to develop expertise and programs of school, family, and community partnerships. District funds may support training and other inservice education, grants to schools, the dissemination of effective practices, and other district leadership functions. The district's work should be coordinated with state policies and activities, when appropriate.

- $10–$15 per student of funds for use *at the school level* to support a program of activities planned each year by the school's Action Team for School, Family, and Community Partnerships. This includes activities conducted on the six types of involvement designed to inform and involve all students' families in their children's education at school and at home. Each school's program includes activities that are selected and tailored to meet important goals for student success and to meet the needs and interests of students and families. This may include a part-time, site-based coordinator, printed materials, refreshments, incentives, workshop presenters, web site development, and other specific involvement activities. The school policies, programs, and practices should be coordinated with state and district policies and activities, when appropriate.

For a few years in the early 1990s, Minnesota tested the feasibility of allocating $5 per child of state funds to districts or schools for parental involvement. Based on informal reports, the policy was successful in some locations but not in others. In fact, an allocation of $5 per student is not enough to fully fund state, district, *and* school leadership activities in comprehensive programs of partnership. By contrast, the funding levels proposed above range from about $15 to over $25 per pupil per year distributed across the state, district, and school levels to fully fund staff and program costs. Although Minnesota's policy was halted, it was an important exploration and recognition of the need to consider a funding formula for programs of school, family, and community partnerships.

Of course, any state, district, or school could justify investing more than the modest amounts suggested above, but few are presently making even these minimal investments. Different formulas could be used, for example, that increase district-level investments for large grants to all schools or to establish school-based facilitators or school-site health, recreation, after-school, and other educational programs and services for children and families.

Another way to determine a reasonable per-pupil investment is to assign 1 percent of the total per-pupil costs to educate youngsters to fund all state and district leadership, training, and support activities and all school-based programs of school, family, and community partnerships. For example, if it costs $4,000 per student per year for a full educational program, then $40 per student would be divided to fund the state, district, and school programs of partnership. This would closely approximate the minimum allocations suggested above for the state, district, and school levels.

Exploring Funding Options: Lump-Sum Allocations

Another funding alternative is based on the allocation of a lump sum for partnerships. States, districts, and schools may allocate new funds or reallocate and identify existing funds to support staff salaries and benefits, grants, training, and other activities to ensure the development and maintenance of comprehensive partnership programs. Table 4.4 summarizes the range of investments reported by schools, districts, and states in the National Network of Partnership Schools for the 1997–1998 school year. The reported average investments indicate that

- state leadership and support for programs of partnership averages about $160,000;
- district leadership and support for programs of partnership averages about $85,000 for districts of 15–30 schools, with proportionately more or less for larger and smaller districts; and
- school leadership and support for programs of partnership averages about $6,000 for schools with 400–800 students, and proportionately more or less in larger or smaller schools.

Table 4.4 suggests that by combining estimates of per-pupil expenditures at all policy levels, it is possible for all states, districts, and schools to begin to build comprehensive programs of school, family, and community partnerships for about $20 per student per year. This remarkably reasonable level of funding may be drawn from funds that are available in federal, state, and local programs that already are targeted to school, family, and community partnerships for student success. The estimates suggest that all states, districts, and schools can afford to develop programs that fulfill their goals for improving school, family, and community partnerships.

Table 4.4 shows that states, districts, and schools are using many sources of funds to invest in their programs of school, family, and community partnerships to increase student success in school. Some funds come from federal, state, and local programs that include requirements and recommendations for family and community involvement (e.g., Title I, Goals 2000, Title VI, Title VII, Safe and Drug Free Schools).

Title I requires the involvement of families in many ways; Goals 2000 calls for the development of strong partnership programs at all policy levels. Title VI funds may be applied creatively to improve curricular connections in school, family, and community partnerships, such as improving designs of homework, enriching the curriculum through volunteers, creating community-based career development and job shadowing programs, and other attention to school subjects. Title VII funds may be applied to programs that help students with limited English to increase school skills, including connections with families to motivate student learn-

TABLE 4.4 Levels and Sources of Funds for Schools, Districts, and States in the National Network of Partnership Schools

	Schools (N = 356)	Districts (N = 45)	States (N = 6)
Levels of Funding	Range: under $100–$88,500 Median = $2,000 Average = $5,722 Average per-pupil expenditure = $12.29	Range: under $100–$1.3 million Median = $20,000 Average = $83,871 Average per-pupil expenditure = $5.63	Range: $20,000–$410,000 Median = $125,000 Average = $163,333 Average per-pupil expenditure = $0.15
Major Sources of Funding	Bilingual Education Drug Prevention Even Start Foundation Grants General Funds Goals 2000 Principal's discretionary funds PTA/PTO Special Education State Compensatory Education Title I School-Wide Title I Targeted Assistance Title VI Title VII	Bilingual Education Drug Prevention Even Start Foundation Grants General Funds Goals 2000 School Board Special Education State Compensatory Education Superintendent's discretionary funds Title I School-Wide Title I Targeted Assistance Title VI Title VII	Drug Prevention Even Start Foundation Grants General Funds Goals 2000 Special Education Superintendent's discretionary funds Title I Title VI
Other Sources of Funding	American Legion Partnership Am South Grant (FL) At-risk funds Business Partnerships Center for the Revitalization of Urban Education (MI) Child First After School Program Commonwealth of Massachusetts Corporate sponsors Danforth Foundation District grants DoDEA extra duty compensation for teacher leaders (Department of Defense Schools) Eastern Michigan Univ. Grants (MI) FAST Grants (WI) Healthy Start Home and School funds (IL) Leona Group (MI) Parents as Partners Funds (MN) Partners in Education (WV) Ready to Learn Program Grant Savings from extended day funds School fund-raising activities School-generated funds Sight Impaired funds State grants Other local programs and in-kind donations	Business Partners/ Contributions CESA (WI) Community Education funds Department of Defense funds (DoD Schools) Department of Human Services (WI) District funds Family Preservation Grant (WI) Family Center Funding Jewish Education Center Lake County Education Association (Teacher's Union) BluePrint 2000 funds (FL) Law and Justice Grant Learning Readiness funds (MN) Maryland State grants Massachusetts Department of Education Massachusetts State Chapter 636 grant Mentors SB65 (CA) Private businesses in communities Rockefeller Foundation School Board funds (FL) Special Education Discretionary Grant State Academic Mentoring Grant (CA) State Compensatory Education Funds (MD) State DESEG Grant (MA) State of Michigan State grants United Way Youth Development	Adult Education and Literacy Community Education funds Federal Claude Pepper Act (CT) Goals 2000 Parent Resource Center Line item from legislature to Board of Education Martha Holden Jennings Foundation (OH) Serve America Youth Service Learning State funds Teacher Inservice funds (UT)

SOURCE: 1998 UPDATE survey of schools, districts, and states in the National Network of Partnership Schools.

Abbreviations in parentheses refer to grants and programs in specific states; L. A. Clark, J. L. Epstein, M. G. Sanders, and F. A. Van Voorhis (1999), Costs and benefits: School, district, and state funding for programs of school, family, and community partnerships (paper presented at the annual meeting of the American Sociological Association, Chicago).

ing. Safe and Drug Free Schools funds are used for prevention activities, including home, school, and community connections to improve and maintain good student attendance, behavior, and learning.

States, districts, and schools also use general funds, donations from parent associations, and grants and donations from businesses, foundations, community groups, and other sources. Funds from all sources are combined or blended to support state coordinators, district facilitators, activities planned by school Action Teams for School, Family, and Community Partnerships, and other personnel and program costs.

Exploring Funding Options: Other Factors

The number of districts in a state, the number of schools in a district, and the number of students and families in a school all may affect funding formulas. For example, a state with over 400 school districts with an average of 10 schools in each will need a different plan and funding formula than a state with under 50 districts with an average of 80 schools in each. Consider the following hypothetical states, each with about 4,000 schools:

State A has about 400 districts that average 10 schools per district
(ranging from 1 to 100 schools per district)
This state will need more staff and leadership activities at the state level to assist all districts and schools to organize and develop their expertise and programs of partnership. In small districts, with fewer than 15 schools, part-time coordinators may assist the schools. In very small districts (e.g., fewer than 5 schools) school leaders may work relatively independently, with state or regional support, as needed.
In State A, *state* leadership is more complex than in State B.

State B has about 50 districts that average 80 schools per district
(ranging from 10 to 200 schools per district)
This state will need only one or two full-time professional staff at the state level, adequate support staff, and a budget to assist districts and schools with their leadership and work on school, family, and community partnerships. Large districts in this state each will need a full-time facilitator to assist every 15–30 schools to develop and maintain their partnership programs.
In State B, *district* leadership is more complex than in State A.

Both hypothetical states will need a plan for organizing *state* leadership activities, including those discussed in Reading 4.1 and in the above comments and activities, and for developing within-state, cross-branch connections among programs that include attention to families and communities. Other organizations, intermediate staff development entities, and universities also may take leadership roles at the state and/or district levels to help districts and schools develop their knowledge, skills, and programs of partnership.

The schools in both hypothetical states will need adequate funding each year to support activities planned by their Action Teams for School, Family, and Community Partnerships. Support at the school level will depend on the size of the school, goals for students, student and family needs, the community context, and other factors.

Summary of Funding Options

There are many possible formulas for per-pupil or lump-sum allocations at the state, district, and school levels to support the real costs of developing and maintaining programs of school, family, and community partnerships in every school. Decisions will vary based on the conditions and needs in large and small states, districts, and schools. However derived, a reasonable plan for adequate funding is needed in every state, district, and school to ensure that all students' families are welcome in their children's schools and are informed about and active partners in their children's education at all grade levels. The examples of alternative funding plans force attention to such questions as:

- How much is it worth to develop and maintain productive school, family, and community partnerships so that all families are involved in their children's education across the grades?
- Where will the money come from, and how will it be spent?
- Who will decide?
- How will results of the investments be evaluated?

◈ ACTIVITY

Designing a Feasible Plan for Funding Partnerships

A. Select and identify one state, school district (local educational agency or LEA), or school that interests you. List its name, location, and size (e.g., number of districts, schools, and/or number of students served). This information may be obtained by phone, mail, the Internet, or in federal, state, or local directories, documents, or other sources. Or, use the following hypothetical information: NEW STATE has 100 school districts and approximately 1,600 schools. Every district, including NEW DISTRICT, has 10 elementary schools (grades K–5) with 300 students in each school; 4 middle schools (grades 6–8) with 750 students in each school; and 2 high schools (grades 9–12) with 1,500 students in each.

B. Working with the information in this chapter, create a realistic funding plan for school, family, and community partnerships for the state, district, or school that you selected.

1. Begin with a paragraph summarizing the philosophy or policy on which you will base your funding plan. Consider these requirements:
   A. The program you outline must enable educators, parents, and community members to work together in ways that support student success in school.
   B. The program and budget you describe must enable each school to build its capacity to plan, conduct, and maintain partnerships with all families, not just a few.
2. Outline the funding approach you will use (i.e., per-pupil expenditure or lump-sum allocation); at least five sample activities that you will fund at the state, district, or school level that you selected; and the level of funding you recommend for one year to support the activities you outlined. Give details on the allocations you recommend for staff salaries and benefits, training workshops, grants, and other activities in your comprehensive program of partnerships.

C. *Optional class activity:* In class, present and critique classmates' funding plans. Discuss:
1. Are the funding estimates realistic?
2. What would the plan permit, and what would it exclude in a full program of partnerships?
3. Do you think that the plan actually could be implemented in the school, district, or state you selected? Why or why not?

EXAMPLES OF STATE ACTIVITIES

The following section summarizes state-level leadership activities for school, family, and community partnerships in a few states. The activities are representative of work in other states and raise some questions about policies and actions to support partnerships.

Wisconsin

Wisconsin has an informative history of state leadership on school, family, and community partnerships. The Wisconsin Department of Public Instruction (DPI) proclaimed 1987–1988 the Year of the Family in Education, with a clear statement of purpose from the state superintendent and a large dissemination campaign. The DPI mailed monthly packets of materials on family involvement to over 400 district superintendents in the state. The packets included information on the importance of the family, home-school communications, family learning, family health, family work, family services, family and community, family play, learning, and other topics to help superintendents understand and develop good school, family, and community partnerships.

Wisconsin's Year of the Family in Education may have raised some superintendents' awareness of family involvement, but most did not take systematic steps to help their schools build programs of partnership. The ambitious initiative was just the beginning of a long line of state leadership activities that were needed to promote school, family, and community partnerships in districts and schools.

In 1993, the Wisconsin DPI took new steps and a different direction to assist districts and schools to develop partnership programs. The state superintendent and other leaders organized the Wisconsin DPI Family-Community-School Initiative, creating a logo for their program based on the framework of six types of involvement described in this volume. The program leaders developed a checklist to help schools identify current practices for the six types of involvement. They convened the first of a series of annual conferences to prepare Action Teams of School, Family, and Community Partnerships to plan and implement comprehensive school programs.

The state provided small grants or "seed money" to schools' action teams to help them pay for some activities planned in their school partnership programs. In 1994, for example, over $300,000 in federal and state funds was allocated for the program, including demonstration grants to learn more about which practices and processes work best for developing effective school, family, and community partnerships in Wisconsin. In addition to small grants, the DPI offered $2,000 competitive grants to support site-based Partnership Coordinators at the school level to improve the quality of partnerships. A state-sponsored "Share Sheet" enables Wisconsin schools and districts to disseminate ideas about how to improve their programs and practices of partnership. Over the years, Wisconsin's DPI has expanded its program and has supported several hundred schools in their efforts to improve their partnership programs.

In a related action, a DPI work group issued a report in 1997 outlining improvements needed in Wisconsin's teacher assessment and licensing requirements. Among the standards for educational excellence, the 10th standard states: "The teacher fosters relationships with school colleagues, parents, and agencies in the larger community to support students' learning and well being." The standards include knowledge, dispositions, and performances that educators are expected to meet, including establishing respectful and productive relationships and cooperative partnerships with parents and guardians from diverse home and community situations, consulting with parents, and identifying and using community resources. Underlying the standards are principles of collaboration, respect for diversity, and the need to develop communities of learning.[4]

California

The California State Department of Education approved a concise three-page policy in 1989 that outlined an overall goal for school, family, and community partnerships and explicit state commitments to help districts and schools develop their

---

[4] See Wisconsin Department of Public Instruction, *Restructuring teacher education and licensing in Wisconsin,* Bulletin 97306 (Madison: Division for Learning Support: Instructional Services, 1997).

programs to reach the goal (See Reading 4.2). Regional workshops were conducted to publicize the policy and to assist schools and districts with program development. Not long after, however, funds were cut, staff changes were made, and politics temporarily diverted attention away from partnerships.

California renewed its interest and intentions in school, family, and community partnerships and enhanced its policy in 1991 with Assembly Bill 322, which required schools to establish parent involvement programs if they received federal funds from Chapter I (now Title I) and state funds from Impact Aid and School Improvement. The legislation emphasized communicating with families, involving families with their children in learning at home, other practices for the six types of involvement, and an annual statement of program objectives.

In a related action in 1993, Assembly Bill 1264 required the California Commission on Teacher Credentialing to review and adopt standards to prepare educators to work as partners with diverse families to enhance student learning. Similarly, Senate Bill 1422 called for comprehensive changes to California's teacher training, including an emphasis on family involvement in children's education. In 1999 these recommendations were being reviewed for further action.

In the late 1990s, the California State Department of Education reinvigorated its plans to coordinate efforts across its branches or divisions to help districts and schools develop their programs of school, family, and community partnerships. The State Department of Education joined the National Network of Partnership Schools at Johns Hopkins to participate in discussions about state leadership on partnerships and to organize their leadership efforts.

The California Legislature continued its interest, with hearings conducted in 1998 by Senator Teresa P. Hughes in cooperation with the State Department of Education, the California State PTA, the California Teachers Association, the Association of California School Administrators, and the Los Angeles County of Education on ways to strengthen school, family, and community partnerships. The hearing also highlighted nearly 40 state house and senate bills that should support and improve family and community involvement in education. Even with its strong leadership activities, California still has a long way to go to turn policy statements and funded programs into universal practice in all districts and schools. California's initial written policy remains a useful example for states that are beginning to think about how to help districts help schools build partnerships with families and communities.[5]

Maryland

The Maryland State Department of Education (MSDE) has taken several steps over many years to encourage districts and schools to develop partnerships with families. In the 1980s, task forces on the improvement of high schools, middle

---

[5] See M. S. Ammon, *Preparing educators for partnership with families* (Report of the Advisory Task Force on Educator Preparation for Parent Involvement) (Sacramento: California Commission on Teaching Credentialing, 1997).

schools, and elementary schools all included clear recommendations for more and better connections with families. In 1990, a special report of the Parent/Community Involvement State Team of the Maryland School Performance Program, *Partners for Maryland's Future*, recognized the importance of school, family, and community partnerships for students' success. This report summarized research, including the six types of involvement, and introduced a State Policy on Parent/Community Involvement.

With the passage of its policy on parent involvement, MSDE awarded initial grants in the early 1990s to encourage districts and schools to plan and implement partnerships. Brochures and guidelines were written and given to all districts to help each one write a policy consistent with the state's policy. Districts also were asked to identify a key facilitator, establish a planning and management team, develop and implement plans at the school level, provide training for school staff and parents, and establish a district-level review committee to hold schools accountable for this agenda. Each district was encouraged to develop its own program. Some districts began their efforts well, others slowly, others poorly. MSDE convened several meetings and conferences to bring people together, share ideas, and increase understanding of the importance of the continuous development of partnerships.

In the 1996–1997 school year, MSDE initiated the Maryland School, Family, and Community Partnership Initiative, linked to the National Network of Partnership Schools at Johns Hopkins University. The state identified a department and staff to conduct state leadership activities to assist districts in helping their schools develop partnerships. The Family Involvement and Dropout Prevention Branch made small grants of $3,000–$5,000 to districts that voluntarily joined the initiative over several years. Initial incentive grants of $300–$500 were awarded to schools that voluntarily joined the Network and that wrote short proposals explaining how the funds would be used to pay for activities in program plans to involve "hard-to-reach" families. For three years, MSDE supported and recognized the work on partnerships of over 250 schools and over half of its 24 school systems.

Utah

Utah's Center for Families in Education is a cooperative project of the State Office of Education and the Utah PTA. For several years beginning in 1990, the Center exercised state leadership, awarded grants, and provided assistance to eight school districts for demonstration programs in selected schools based on the six types of involvement. The Center also conducted a number of other statewide activities, including parent-child activity calendars, newsletters, annual conferences for sharing good practices, and an information "hotline" in English and Spanish on more than 50 topics of interest to families and communities, such as state education tests and assessment issues, children's health, college opportunities, school laws, and family rights and responsibilities. The Center made several annual awards to recognize excellent projects throughout the state that advanced partnerships among schools, families, businesses, and community groups to benefit students. It also encouraged teacher education on the topic of school, family, and community partnerships and initiated other activities to promote better partnerships in all districts and schools throughout the state (Lloyd, 1996).

In the early 1990s, the Utah Center for Families in Education operated with a budget of over $300,000 per year, top administrative support, and a wide range of state partners. In the late 1990s, with a change in state superintendent, Center leader, and budget, Utah began to redesign and redirect its work. New leaders worked with a reduced budget to try to improve the way all schools—not just demonstration sites—developed partnership programs. The Utah Center continued to participate in the National Network of Partnership Schools.

In Utah's work, the flow of education policy on partnerships was demonstrated by an initial dramatic effort of large grants to a few locations, followed by a plan for broader support to all schools. One product designed and tested in Utah's early program is a process for organizing teacher-student-parent conferences. The Student Education Plan (SEP) and upper-grade Student Education and Occupation Plan (SEOP) now are used statewide to help teachers, students, and parents meet together to discuss, outline, and monitor goals and progress for students each year.[6]

Summary of Selected State Stories from Wisconsin, California, Maryland, and Utah

The ebb and flow of educational policy takes many forms and paths. In school, family, and community partnerships we see that some states' programs of partnership have moved from broad concepts to clear visions, or from selective demonstrations to broader, more inclusive programs. State leadership for improving partnerships has come from state departments of education, state legislature, task forces, state PTA, or combinations of these and other leaders.

QUESTIONS TO DISCUSS

1. Wisconsin, California, Maryland, and Utah have very different educational structures. For example, California includes about 1,000 local educational agencies (LEA) or school districts; Wisconsin has 426 LEAs; Utah has 40; and Maryland has 24 school systems. Give two ideas of how you think these four states' support for school, family, and community partnerships might be affected by their number of LEAs.
2. A. Select one of the states described above that interests you: Wisconsin, California, Maryland, or Utah.

---

[6] See G. Lloyd, Research and practical application for school, family, and community partnerships, in A. Booth and J. Dunn, eds., *Family-school links: How do they affect educational outcomes?* (Hillsdale, NJ: Lawrence Erlbaum Associates, 1996), pp. 255–264.

B. For the state you selected, identify one of its early stages of work on partnerships.
3. Give two reasons why the early effort alone was not enough to result in every district and every school developing comprehensive partnership programs.
4. A. For the state you selected, identify one of its later stages of work on partnerships.
   B. Do you think that the later stage of work that you identified will be enough to result in every district and every school developing comprehensive partnership programs? Give two reasons why or why not.

⬛ COMMENT

Laws to Assist Parents Who Work Outside the Home to Attend School Meetings

A 1990 law passed by the state legislature in Minnesota permitted workers who are parents to use up to 16 hours of accrued vacation time, sick leave, or other arranged time to attend parent-teacher conferences or other meetings related to their own children's education or to attend to their children's illnesses.

A similar bill in California (AB 2590, Chapter 1290 in the Statutes of 1994, expanded in 1997) specified that employers with 25 or more employees should allow each employee (parents, grandparents, or guardians) up to 40 hours of time to participate in their children's schools using vacation time, personal or sick leave, compensatory time, or leave without pay.

By contrast, Virginia's 1992 Policy 4.06 enables parents who are employees of the Commonwealth of Virginia to meet with teachers, attend functions, or volunteer at school. It provides paid leave of up to eight hours per year, credited to full-time employees each year, with proportional awards of leave time to part-time employees. This policy was designed to serve as a model for large businesses in the state to duplicate to demonstrate their commitment to families, children, and schools.

Reports from Minnesota and other states suggest that flexible leave policies promoted greater involvement of parents in their children's education, including more communication with their children's teachers, and more involvement of fathers. Research suggests why and how this happens.

An early study by Espinoza (1988) found that employers' typical short-term leave policies affected the involvement of employees who were parents. He studied a phone company where women in clerical jobs were not permitted to take less than a full day of unpaid leave when they wanted to attend parent-teacher conferences. In addition, nonmedical, unexcused absences worked against them when they were considered for transfers and promotions. Thus, the women were doubly disciplined by a loss of pay for more time off than they needed to attend conferences at their children's schools *and* by penalties for taking time off. They had to balance these factors with the personal and family benefits of attending the conferences to demonstrate good parenting, and to learn more about their children's progress and success in school.

Most parents in blue-collar jobs still face difficulties and penalties at work if they take time from work to attend parent-teacher conferences or to volunteer at their children's schools. Most white-collar workers have greater flexibility with compensatory time, flexible leave time, or other arrangements to attend conferences or other meetings and to volunteer, with no loss in pay and no penalties for their actions. Although mothers attend most of these activities, more fathers in white-collar jobs with flexible work conditions participate in school conferences and activities than do fathers in blue-collar jobs that impose more rigid work rules and penalties for absences.[7]

QUESTIONS TO DISCUSS

What changes in behavior, actions, or attitudes might result from the three state laws described above for Minnesota, California, and Virginia?

1. Describe one result that you would expect from each state.
2. Explain why you would expect the results you described.

 ACTIVITY

Exploring Employers' Support for Home-School Partnerships

Does your state *or* place of employment *or* a local company (with over 100 employees) have laws or guidelines that permit workers to take time to attend parent-teacher conferences or other meetings at their children's schools? Use your knowledge and experiences, reference materials, or interview a local employer about this.

A. Identify the employer you selected (e.g., state, business) and your method of inquiry.
B. If the employer you selected PERMITS parental leave for meetings at children's schools, report the following:
   1. Describe the formal or informal guidelines about parental leave.
   2. Are the guidelines used by employees? In what ways, or why not?
   3. Do you think the current guidelines are adequate and clear?

---

[7] See R. Espinoza, Working parents, employers, and schools, *Educational Horizons* 66 (1988): 62–65.

A. If so, how do the guidelines benefit the participating families, students, schools, communities, and the employer?
B. If not, how would you improve the guidelines or their applications?
C. If the state or business you selected does *not* permit parental leave:
  1. Write a hypothetical guideline that you think is clear, fair, and workable for the state or business you selected.
  2. Explain why the components you included are important for families, students, schools, communities, and the employer.
D. Whether or not guidelines about parental leave exist:
  1. Give one example of an activity that a school might conduct to adjust the schedule of conferences, meetings, and events to accommodate parents who work full-time or part-time during the day or evening.
  2. Give one example of an activity that a community organization or group (e.g., faith-based organization, neighborhood group) might conduct to assist working parents or single parents to maintain involvement in their children's schools.

WHAT'S HISTORY GOT TO DO WITH IT? STATES' ATTENTION TO PARTNERSHIPS FROM THE 1980S THROUGH THE 1990S

South Carolina

South Carolina's Education Improvement Act in 1984 was one of the first in the nation to mandate School Improvement Councils in every school. The councils, including parents, teachers, and administrators, were asked to create school improvement plans and to develop better home and school relations. The legislation also created a university-based School Council Assistance Project to help the schools move toward these goals. The Councils have been partly successful and partly not.

Research and development since 1984 indicates that School Councils are only one aspect of a school improvement initiative, and only one part of a comprehensive program of school, family, and community partnerships. Other structures and processes are needed to guide the work of councils, to help parent representatives link with other parents in two-way communications about school decisions, and to specify detailed plans for activities to inform and involve all parents in their children's education.

Indiana

A 1986 Task Force on Parent and Community Involvement in Indiana's Department of Education included representatives from many districts in the state. The resulting report, based on research and practical experience, recommended state, regional, district, and school building activities to improve family and community involvement in children's education.

Indiana's task force recommendations for *state-level leadership* included writing a policy, conducting a public relations campaign, creating a resource book, assisting districts with workshops for staff development, developing state pamphlets to assist parents, recognizing exemplary programs, providing lists of resources for parents, and funding these activities.

Indiana's task force recommendations for *district-level leadership* included establishing a district advisory committee; writing a district policy on family involvement consistent with the state policy, providing inservice education for teachers and administrators, collecting school-based plans and programs, identifying a district coordinator, recognizing exemplary programs, conducting annual conferences, working with community groups and adult education programs, developing guidelines for home visits and information for schools to give to parents to help them support their children each year, and linking to the state's efforts.

The task force's recommendations for *school-level leadership* included developing a comprehensive plan for partnerships; establishing a school-based advisory council; producing publications for parents at each grade level such as newsletters, handbooks, notes, and communications from teachers and the principal; developing community connections; and establishing a parent resource area in the school. The task force also listed many roles and responsibilities for parents to become involved at school and at home in their children's education.

In 1987, Indiana followed up the task force report with the A+ Program for Educational Excellence, including grants to schools to assist students who were at risk of failing in school and grants for demonstration programs for parent involvement. In the A+ Program, the state implemented several of the task force's recommendations, including a state conference, publicity, and pamphlets on school, family, and community partnerships, and use of the research-based framework of the major types of involvement.

Indiana's task force report and initial actions in the 1980s were forward thinking. The same recommendations have been and will continue to be made by any task force or leadership team that thinks about how to improve school, family, and community partnerships. After its first steps, however, Indiana did not build a lasting state leadership structure to continually conduct the proposed state-level activities or to help all districts and all schools develop comprehensive partnership programs.

Thoughtful reports, plans, and policies must be accompanied by expert staff, funds, and other structures and processes for states, districts, and schools to create, conduct, and continue comprehensive partnership programs. Most states fall short on the long-term commitment to carry out good plans.

Massachusetts

The Massachusetts State Department of Education initiated a competitive grants program called the Learning Together Project in 1992, with $200,000 for 19 awards for each of three years to learn more about how to build coalitions to address the complex problems of families, children, schools, and communities. The goal was to increase various types of involvement to improve students' attendance, achievement, and self-esteem and to integrate children with special needs and their families into the life of schools.

The Department also formed an interdivisional work group of staff from many units, including early childhood, adult education, Chapter I (now Title I), student development and health, language services, special education, community education, occupational education, educational equity, and others with responsibilities for children, families, schools, and communities. The goals were to increase the information each unit has about what the others are doing and to improve communications and activities among these units.

The initiatives were not unlike current efforts to improve school-community collaborations and cross-branch connections in many state departments of education. This missing link in Massachusetts in 1992, as in many other states, was a plan for how to use knowledge gained in demonstration projects to establish an ongoing plan and program for state, district, and school leadership and programs of school, family, and community partnerships.

Ohio

In the mid-1990s, Ohio's education leaders agreed with the intent of Goal 8 of the National Education Goals that every school should have a program of "partnerships that will increase parental involvement and participation in promoting the social, emotional, and academic growth of children." This goal-oriented approach to partnerships was supported by state superintendents and a local philanthropic foundation. The philosophy and funding established the Ohio Department of Education's (ODE) School, Family, and Community Partnership Initiative.

In cooperation with the National Network of Partnership Schools and many other partners, Ohio's leaders began to "scale up" the number and quality of school partnership programs. In the 1997 and 1998 school years, ODE leaders provided action team training and initial incentive grants of about $500 to more than 200 schools. The schools also joined the National Network for ongoing assistance and to connect with other schools across the country. Annually, Ohio's leaders have increased the number of school action teams that are trained and supported to develop productive partnership programs.

Whereas a change in leaders sometimes weakens initiatives established by the previous administration, a change in Ohio's state superintendent strengthened this effort with increased attention to linking school, family, and community partnerships to school improvement goals. Schools and districts are being guided to write annual plans for family and community involvement activities that will help improve reading, math, writing, or other school skills and achievements; behavior; attendance; attitudes; and other indicators of success in school. School, family, and community partnerships also are included on "local report cards" that document the progress of Ohio's schools and districts on key aspects of school improvement.

Ohio's leaders have worked to show what state leadership on school, family, and community partnerships looks like. The Ohio School, Family, and Community Partnership Initiative created a broad and strong state leadership team by developing interdepartmental and interagency connections and activities with the Ohio Family and Children First, Ohio Parent Information and Resource Center, State PTA, Title I office, Parent Advisory Council, and many others. Despite these strengths, Ohio's leadership on partnerships (and that of other states) is always threatened by the inevitable changes in leaders, funding, and collegial support.

Connecticut

The Connecticut State Board of Education adopted a definition of school, family, and community partnerships in August 1997:

> The State Board of Education defines school-family-community partnerships as the continuous planning, support, and participation of school personnel, families, and community organizations in coordinated activities and efforts at home, in the school and in the community that directly and positively affect the success of all children's learning. Each partner is viewed as an equally contributing member, maintaining a certain independence while acknowledging shared responsibility. To succeed, the partnership must be flexible, and based upon mutual trust and respect. Schools must take the lead in developing and sustaining effective partnerships.

In addition to defining school-family-community partnerships, the Connecticut State Board of Education adopted a set of standards based on the framework of six types of involvement outlined in this volume: parenting, communicating, volunteering, learning at home, decision making, and collaborating with the community. The position statement goes on to articulate the roles for schools, families, and communities in conducting these standards for involvement.

Along with its position statement, Connecticut's leaders produced a *Partnership Policy Action Packet* to help local boards and school administrators develop and implement policies and programs that support high-quality school, family, and community partnerships. This publication guides local and regional boards of education to fulfill state law (Public Act 97-290, Section 14, effective September 1998), which requires them to develop, adopt, and implement written policies and procedures that encourage parent-teacher communication.[8]

---

[8] See Connecticut State Department of Education, *Schools and Families* 1(1) (Spring 1998).

Policies Reflect Knowledge at the Time

Timing is important for policies and resulting actions. When South Carolina took innovative steps to mandate school councils in 1984, not much was known about how to organize the leadership, plans, and actions of councils, or the role of school councils in developing a comprehensive program of school, family, and community partnerships. Similarly, the forward-looking recommendations of Indiana's task force in 1986 were based on research that revealed "what" could and should be done, but not "how" to make things happen. The exploratory grants in Massachusetts in 1992 were important for learning new things about community collaborations, but they were not designed to contribute to an ongoing, organized partnership program. By the time that Ohio initiated its program of training and grants for schools in 1996 and Connecticut decided its state policy and approaches in 1997, much more was known about partnership programs, state leadership, and connections to districts and schools. Ohio's and Connecticut's efforts were purposely designed as steps on a path to state leadership on partnerships. All states now can catch up to new knowledge to implement their intended policies for productive school, family, and community partnerships.

QUESTIONS TO DISCUSS

Summarize what the states of South Carolina, Indiana, Massachusetts, Ohio, and Connecticut did to support partnerships. Make a chart with five sections, one for each state.

1. For each state, list one action that shows that state leaders were addressing WHAT should be done to advance school, family, and community partnerships.
2. For each state, list one idea about HOW each state might build on its initial actions.

Missouri

Parents As Teachers (P. A. T.) is Missouri's early education intervention program. It grew from a pilot program in 1981 to a nationally replicated model. Supported by the Early Childhood Development Act of Missouri, the program is designed to serve all families of infants and very young children, not just those with high-risk characteristics. P. A. T. trains parent educators who make five home visits per year to help participating families understand child development from birth to age three and to help all children become "ready to learn" successfully in school. Services include home visits, screening to monitor children's development and to identify and reduce risks to healthy development, parent education, group meetings for parents, and play experiences for children in a community center. One estimate of the cost of the pilot P. A. T. program was $210 per family, with $170 coming from the state and $40 from local funds.

Evaluations of P. A. T. in Missouri suggest positive effects on parents' attitudes and confidence, children's readiness skills and social development, fewer undetected hearing problems, and reduced effects of risk conditions on children's language development. Studies are in progress and more are needed on how the children in P. A. T. or similar programs proceed through their educational careers and whether and which families continue to be involved in their children's education after their children start elementary school.

P. A. T. is an example of a successful implementation of state leaders' visions of assisting families and their very young children. Although not yet fully funded to serve all families in Missouri, P. A. T. is a large, ongoing program in Missouri and is helping other states understand and implement early intervention programs.

A logical next step in Missouri is to implement programs that ensure the involvement of families in their children's education through the elementary and secondary grades. This would require a commitment from the legislature or State Department of Education to establish a plan and budget for state leadership to help all schools develop and maintain connections with all families and communities to increase student success in school.

QUESTIONS TO DISCUSS

1. Give two reasons why it is important for a state to focus on families of children from birth to age three, as is done in Missouri's P. A. T. and similar programs.
2. Give two reasons why it is not enough to focus on families of children from birth to age three in organizing home, school, and community partnerships.

▊▍ COMMENT

Other State Leadership Activities

Many other state departments of education have initiated activities for increasing school, family, and community partnerships in response to Title I mandates, Goals 2000, or state goals for involving families and communities to boost student success. Many states are participating in the National Network of Partnership Schools at Johns Hopkins University to gain and share information on developing their partnership programs.

Also, many state legislatures have standing committees on children and youth, or on children, youth, and families, to design and implement policies and practices that increase the quality of services, activities, and support for children to succeed in school and in life. Many states also have (or have had) commissions or task forces to address topics such as dropout prevention; adolescent parenting; at-risk youths; child welfare; early childhood education; special education; education for homeless children; and other topics concerning family responsibilities, parental involvement, and student success.

These initiatives suggest that state political leaders recognize the importance of partnerships and the need to improve the collaborative activities of various departments such as social services, welfare, public health, education, law enforcement, mental health, job training, and others. However, not all of the standing committees or plans for collaboration across departments have been adequately funded. Few legislative committees and projects have been productively connected to state education agencies, and even fewer to school systems, schools, and families. Few state leaders in any department have a detailed agenda for how they will advance the development of comprehensive programs of partnership in all schools. Many reports and recommendations on improving conditions for children, youth, and families ignore the fact that school, family, and community partnerships are needed for other recommendations for improving health, safety, or education to succeed.

At this time, then, most state initiatives for partnerships are in their initial stages and may be positively or negatively affected by changes in leaders, staff, budgets, and priorities from one administration to the next. Most state efforts on school, family, and community partnerships need to be stabilized to produce the goals expressed in state policies.

◇ ACTIVITY

The Organization of State Leadership on Partnerships

In most state education agencies, many divisions, departments, branches, or offices conduct activities for and with families and communities. These include elementary, middle, and secondary programs; compensatory education; special education vocational education; migrant education; bilingual education; adult education; community education; and others.

A. Select one state that interests you.
B. Find out whether the state education agency (SEA) of the state you selected has a single office that coordinates leadership for programs of school, family, and community partnerships, or whether such programs are located in different branches or divisions. Use the Internet. You can reach most state education agencies through the web site of the Council of Chief State School Officers: *www.ccsso.org*.

C. How many departments, divisions, branches, or units of the SEA that you selected refer to projects or programs that directly inform or involve families and communities in children's education?

D. From what you learned, how would you describe the organization of that state's leadership on school, family, and community partnerships?

◈ FIELD EXPERIENCE

State Policy Development Case Study

A. Select a state whose policies on school, family, and community partnerships interest you.

B. Identify a topic that interests you. For example, you may be interested in policies on family support that were considered and/or approved over the past three to five years; actions on partnerships over a defined period of time; funding decisions that affected children, families, schools, and/or communities; or evaluations of specific family, school, and/or community programs.

C. Identify a method of inquiry that you will use to study the state and topic you chose. You may conduct a phone interview, e-mail a set of questions to a cooperative leader, search records or documents, or use another method to obtain information on the history, progress, and status of proposed legislation, policies, and actions on school, family, and community partnerships, family support, business partnerships, or related topics.

D. Write five questions to guide your work.

E. Document your questions and the actions you take to study the topic you selected.

F. Summarize the results of your inquiry in a chart or short report.

G. From the information you gathered, discuss the extent and quality of the leadership on partnerships of the state you selected.

H. Write two or three recommendations for next steps on the topic you studied to help the state move forward in its leadership on school, family, and community partnerships.

EXAMPLES OF DISTRICT ACTIVITIES

Many school districts take important initial steps toward improving school, family, and community partnerships by writing policy statements that express the goal for teachers, parents, and others in the community to work collaboratively on behalf of children's learning and success. Many district policies are not accompanied by implementation plans, leadership, training, and other support needed to ensure that all schools develop the knowledge, skills, and programs they seek. Data from schools indicate, however, that written policies have little impact unless the district also facilitates and assists schools to develop high-quality partnership programs. That is, having a policy is one thing, but providing support and encouragement for partnerships is more important.

This section discusses a few examples of district-level leadership activities for school, family, and community partnerships. The activities are representative of work in other school systems and raise some questions to discuss about district policies and actions to support partnerships.

Cecil County, Maryland

For several years, the Home-N-School Program actively influenced partnerships in Cecil County, Maryland, a relatively small system in Maryland of about 30 public schools. The Home-N-School Program, developed by the Alliance of Students, Teachers, and Parents, awarded demonstration grants to elementary, middle, and high schools. Funded by the school system and local businesses, the small grants helped dozens of schools develop and implement scores of activities to assist, inform, and involve families in ways that would help students. In addition to the competitive grants program, the program conducted an annual fair where schools shared their projects and ideas with other educators, parents, and students. Parents and educators, including school district administrators, shared leadership for the program.

The district's 1989 mission statement specified: "[W]e will build partnerships with parents and the total community to utilize their resources and expertise to fulfill a shared responsibility for the child." With a good start from the Home-N-School program, the district recognized the need in the late 1990s to extend its efforts to help every school develop full and ongoing partnership programs.

Baltimore County, Maryland

The Baltimore County Board of Education in Maryland adopted a policy in 1991 on Community Relations: Family-Community Involvement. The research-based policy identified the major types of parental and community involvement, stated the need to connect family involvement to school reform, and recognized the need to publicize the policy so that all schools would understand and act on it. District leaders began providing staff development to school teams to help them develop their programs of school, family, and community partnerships. Some schools gave special attention to implementing interactive homework to encourage home-school connections on the curriculum. The policy and responsive leadership activities represented a good start for this large school district of over 150 schools.

In 1997, Baltimore County joined the National Network of Partnership Schools at Johns Hopkins University and the Maryland School, Family, and Community Partnerships Initiative. The growing school system established a leadership structure with district leaders and regional facilitators in five geographic areas in Family Resource Centers to assist all schools to develop and maintain programs of partnership. Incentive grants from the state of Maryland encouraged district and school actions. Even with a reasonable plan, however, this large countywide system has a long way to go to routinize its leadership, assist all schools, and evaluate progress on partnerships.

Montgomery County, Maryland

Montgomery County Public Schools passed Resolution 60-79, "A Shared Responsibility: The School and the Family/Community in the '90s." The policy recognized that it was the school system's and all schools' responsibility to involve families and the community in ways that promote positive expectations and results for minorities in academic achievement and participation and to promote interpersonal and intercultural communications with all students, families, and communities. (See Reading 4.2)

The large countywide school district of about 200 schools developed its parent involvement policies incrementally. In 1990, the school board passed a resolution specifying the six major types of involvement discussed in this volume, including a pledge that the district office would assist each school to implement a program based on the framework. Then a task force was formed to develop an "administrative regulation" to implement the policy. This group produced a thoughtful implementation plan nine months later.

The two steps, approving a policy and designing enactments, were necessary but not sufficient actions for ensuring that all schools develop excellent, permanent programs of partnership. Other steps also were required, including organizing leadership, allocating funds, and creating a districtwide plan to assist all schools with their work and progress. This large school system joined the Maryland School, Family, and Community Partnerships Initiative and the National Network of Partnership Schools to help organize its work. However, leaders still must connect the school system's policy statement with plans to assist all schools, and must meet the challenges of implementing these plans.

Baltimore City, Maryland

The School, Family, and Community Partnership Program of the Baltimore City Public School System (BCPSS) is a research-based approach that assists all elementary, middle, and high schools to develop and improve connections with students' families and communities. This program grew as a collaborative effort of BCPSS leaders, teachers, principals, families, and students; the Center on School, Family, and Community Partnerships at Johns Hopkins University; and the Fund for Educational Excellence, a community foundation.

The program began in BCPSS with 8 "pilot" schools in 1987, expanded to 15 "replication" sites in 1992, and then began work with the Area Executive Officers to extend the program to all elementary, middle, and high schools. By 1998, full-time Area Facilitators for School, Family, and Community Partnerships were working in all nine geographic areas of the school system. Each Facilitator helps about 20 elementary, middle, and high schools to plan, implement, evaluate, share ideas, and continually improve their connections with families and communities in ways that help reach school improvement goals.

Each school is assisted to form an Action Team for Partnerships that includes teachers, parents, and administrators. The Action Team writes a one-year action plan that includes activities for the six major types of involvement (parenting, communicating, volunteering, learning at home, decision making, and collaborating with the community) linked to school improvement goals and the needs and interests of students and families.

The program has demonstrated positive results for attendance, achievement, student behavior, school climate, and safety. For example, a study of 39 elementary schools indicated that schools with stronger partnership programs had better attendance, and more students scored at satisfactory or higher levels on the Maryland State Performance Assessment Program (MSPAP) reading, writing, and math tests, after accounting for prior attendance or test scores. After two years in the program, 12 schools in one area of the city met Maryland's satisfactory attendance standard of 94 percent or better, compared with only 3 schools previously.

Baltimore City Public Schools served as the "learning laboratory" for the National Network of Partnership Schools at Johns Hopkins University and contributed to the approaches described in Chapters 5, 6, and 7. The longtime collaboration of the schools, university researchers, and the community group was important for developing the knowledge that now assists thousands of schools, hundreds of districts, and many states across the country and in other nations.

Even with ongoing training workshops and in-school staff development, not all BCPSS schools have successfully organized their work to develop effective partnership programs, although almost all are trying to do so. The school system still has work to do at the district level to assist and coordinate the work of its Area Facilitators; encourage and recognize all schools to build their partnership programs; and oversee and integrate district-level leadership activities in public engagement, Title I parent involvement activities, family and community involvement for students with special needs, and other school, family, and community partnerships for student success.

◈ ACTIVITY

Charting Districts' Progress in Developing Partnership Programs

Districts often take the following steps on the path to partnerships:

1. Write a policy.
2. Build knowledge at the district level.

3. Implement district-level activities, such as a conference, fair, and handbook of ideas.
4. Assist schools on request.
5. Assist schools on a regular schedule, including ways to share ideas and approaches.
6. Evaluate the quality of district and school programs and effects of partnerships.

Most districts, however, start this work with steps 1 and 2, but never get to steps 5 and 6.

Review the above summaries of activities of Cecil, Baltimore County, Montgomery County, and Baltimore City. Using Figure 4.2, for each district list one activity that illustrates its highest step (from 1 to 6) on the path to partnerships, and one reason why more work is needed if strong partnership programs are to occur in all schools and at the district level.

Example District	Activity	Highest step (1–6 above) on the path to partnerships	One reason why more work is needed for all schools in the district to develop strong programs of partnerships
Cecil County			
Baltimore County			
Montgomery County			
Baltimore			

FIGURE 4.2   Partnership at District Level

Chicago, Illinois

The Illinois School Reform Bill of 1989, *P.A. 85-141—Local School Councils*, mandated local school councils consisting of six parents, two teachers, two community representatives, and one principal. The councils in 592 schools were to serve as management teams, practicing shared decision making; producing three-year improvement plans; and activating committees to improve curriculum and instruction, climate, discipline, staff development, security, parent development, and leadership development, among other topics. The parents, educators, and community members on each school's council were to work together on such responsibilities as evaluating the principal; renewing the principal's four-year performance-based contracts; allocating Title I funds; and other curriculum, staffing, and program decisions. In this way, parents and community voices are part of school decision making (Ryan, Bryk, Lopez, Williams, Hall, and Luppescu, 1998).

School councils (also called School Improvement Teams, Site-Based Management Teams, or other names) generally write, approve, or give advice on school improvement plans and goals that guide all other activities in a school. Schools vary in how well their councils work. They also vary in whether the councils plan and conduct other types of involvement to inform and involve all families in their children's education, not just the few who serve on the council.

Even after a decade, Chicago still must refine and improve the organization and effectiveness of school councils. The school councils also must refine and improve their actions for school improvement, including actions to implement comprehensive partnership programs that inform and involve all families in their children's education at all grade levels (McKenna and Willms, 1998).[9]

QUESTIONS TO DISCUSS

Review the list of responsibilities of Chicago's School Councils, summarized above.

1. Do you think that *any* school council can accomplish this list of responsibilities? Can *every* school council? Give one reason why or why not for each response.
2. What are two challenges that a school council might meet in conducting these responsibilities?
3. Discuss two reasons why a school council might benefit from an "action arm," team, or committee to design and implement a comprehensive program of school, family, and community partnerships.

Seattle, Washington

Seattle's public school system conducted an important test in the late 1980s of the feasibility and benefits of having full-time, school-based parent outreach coordinators in middle schools. Full-time equivalent (FTE) coordinators for two middle schools were hired using foundation grants to facilitate partnerships with families and the community, particularly for children at risk of failing their

---

[9] See S. Ryan, A.S. Bryk, G. Lopez, K. P. Williams, K. Hall, and S. Luppescu, *Charting reform: LSCs—Local Leadership at Work* (Chicago: Consortium on Chicago School Research, University of Chicago, 1998); M. McKenna and D. J. Willms, The challenge facing parent councils in Canada, *Childhood Education* 74 (1998): 378–382.

courses. The coordinators and their work with families were viewed positively by administrators, teachers, and parents in the schools, as well as by district leaders.

The superintendent reallocated funds in subsequent years to support parent outreach coordinators in a few more middle schools. His actions reinforced the fact that funding decisions for school improvement require making choices among competing priorities. Seattle's initiative illustrated how funds for family involvement can be "found" and how funding can directly assist individual schools to develop strong programs of partnership.

The forward-looking policy of supporting full-time school-based coordinators of family involvement in individual middle schools did not last, due to changes in leadership and budgets. Building on this and other history, in the late 1990s the state of Washington and several school districts and schools in the state began to develop more comprehensive approaches to partnerships with families and communities from children's birth through high school.

QUESTIONS TO DISCUSS

Seattle's support for full-time coordinators in several middle schools represented a relatively large investment in a full salary for an extra staff member at a school whose purpose was to build better partnerships with parents so that middle school students could succeed. By contrast, in some other districts, facilitators for school, family, and community partnerships each assist up to 30 schools. These facilitators visit each school, bring small groups of schools together for quarterly meetings, and train school-based Action Teams for Partnerships to plan and implement their programs and practices linked to their own school improvement goals. The investment per school in salaries and benefits is much less if one person helps 20 or 30 schools, compared to one person per school. In Wisconsin, the state department of education has made relatively small grants of $2,500 per school to fund a part-time facilitator on-site to help organize the Action Team meetings and to assist or coordinate activities as needed on-site throughout the year. Thus, there are several different ways to invest in leadership to help schools organize their partnership programs.

Similarly, we see differences in the size of grants for partnership projects. Previously, following a "demonstration project" approach, Utah, Massachusetts, New Jersey, and other states made large grants to a limited number of schools and/or districts to design and implement partnership programs or activities. More recently, in connection with their work with the National Network of Partnership Schools, Maryland, Wisconsin, Ohio, and other states have made small grants ($250–$500 on average) to many schools (often hundreds) to help them fund some activities within their full plan for partnerships.

1. What are two pros and two cons of making large grants to a few schools to support their programs of school, family, and community partnerships?

2. What are two pros and two cons of making small grants to many schools to support their programs of school, family, and community partnerships?

New York City, New York

The New York City Board of Education established an Office of Parent Involvement in 1989. This office developed handbooks and easy-to-read pamphlets for parents on district resources, policies for student suspension, school choice, transfers, school-based management, repeating a grade, uniforms, and other topics. The Office of Parent Involvement also supported a competitive grants program to fund innovative projects to improve involvement. The staff was responsible for assisting schools on request, training parent liaisons, establishing parent centers, advising parent organizations, helping schools reach out to more families, making presentations to parent groups, and conducting other districtwide partnership activities. The goals and initial activities were commendable, but the staff, budget, and plans were insufficient for sustaining the program in the large school system.

In 1998, New York City began a new initiative on family and community involvement with a policy and plan requiring all schools to have leadership councils with school, family, and community representatives. The school-based councils in New York City will have to learn the same lessons as those in Chicago and other locations about how educators, parents, and community members can work together to benefit students. New York City's councils will need to guide or support the development of comprehensive partnership programs that inform and involve all families in children's education in elementary, middle, and high school.

QUESTIONS TO DISCUSS

Chicago has had school councils for many years. New York City recently mandated leadership councils in all schools. These advisory and decision-making bodies include educators and parents working together to oversee and advise on school goals and continual improvements.

1. List two goals that you would set for a school council or other leadership group.
2. List two challenges a school council or school improvement team might face as it goes about its work.
3. Give one possible solution to each of the challenges you listed.
4. What are two district-level leadership activities that might help a school council succeed with its work?

Sacramento, California

For several years in the 1990s, Sacramento City Unified Schools supported a strong and innovative district leadership structure for family involvement. The Parent Community Partnership Center (PCPC) had a director and five staff assistants who were assigned to work with all schools in the district and with community organizations. PCPC provided services for parents (e.g., parenting classes, volunteer organization and training, resource materials), schools (e.g., leadership training, site-based assistance, facilitation of school Action Teams for School, Family, and Community Partnerships), and the community (e.g., community presentations, forums, resources). The stated mission of the PCPC was to "provide assistance and support by facilitating the continuous development of partnerships between families, schools, and communities, in their efforts to help children achieve academically and socially in school and throughout life."

Sacramento joined the National Network of Partnership Schools in 1996 to help schools organize their work on partnerships. Incremental progress was made over three years, as increasing numbers of schools were assisted by the PCPC staff to develop their school-based action teams and annual plans for partnerships. With changes in superintendents and the retirement of its director, the staff and functions of the PCPC were distributed among several departments. Time will tell whether the good start in over 30 schools continues and whether all schools in Sacramento will be assisted to develop high-quality partnership programs.

Summary: Selected Districts' Policies and Programs

The preceding examples illustrate many of the common steps that school districts take when they focus on partnerships. District leaders tend to write and pass policies, develop district plans, identify and prepare staff to work at the district level, and, finally, assist schools with their programs of partnership. In large districts, progress often is slow in assisting all schools with this work. Often, knowledge at the district level is not shared and dispersed in ways that help school teams develop skills and plans. Too often, changes in district leaders, staff, parents, priorities, and budgets halt or divert plans and progress on partnerships, leaving policies and intentions unfulfilled.

QUESTIONS TO DISCUSS

Several of the school districts described above illustrate the ebb and flow of program development that we discussed for states previously in this chapter. In some cases, initial start-up efforts in school districts were followed by focused plans and ever-improving programs. In other cases, ambitious beginnings were halted by the inevitable staff and budget changes that occur in education. Which districts summarized above illustrate these alternative patterns of program development?

1. Select one district discussed above that interests you.
2. From the short description, summarize one example of "flow," or progress, in the district you selected in developing school, family, and community partnerships.
3. From the short description, summarize one example of a delay or retreat in developing school, family, and community partnerships.
4. What are two next steps that you would recommend in the district that you selected to ensure that all schools in the district develop and maintain high-quality programs of school, family, and community partnerships?

⑊ COMMENT

Urban, Suburban, and Rural District Patterns of Partnership

In a study of 600 elementary schools in the state of Maryland (see Chapter 3), we found that schools in urban, suburban, and rural districts conducted some similar and some different practices for family involvement. For example:

- In urban districts, teachers involved parents in learning activities at home more frequently than did teachers in rural or suburban districts. They also conducted more workshops for parents at school.
- In suburban districts, teachers worked with parent volunteers more often than did teachers in other locations.
- In rural districts, teachers conducted more home visits with parents than did teachers in other locations.

It should be noted that in the early 1980s, when this survey was conducted, there were relatively few organized school programs to involve families at school or at home. The percent of teachers making home visits was lowest of all family involvement activities. Nevertheless, the urban, suburban, and rural districts in the same state differed from each other, on average, in the frequency with which the above activities were conducted.

QUESTIONS TO DISCUSS

1. What district, school, and/or family policies, conditions, or characteristics might explain the different involvement activities that were prominent in the urban, rural, and suburban schools? Give one example of a district, school, *or* family policy, condition, or characteristic to answer each of the following questions.
   A. Why might schools in urban districts have conducted more workshops for parents than did schools in suburban or rural locations?

B. Why might schools in urban districts have asked more parents to help their children with learning activities at home?

C. Why might schools in suburban districts have worked with more parent volunteers than did other schools?

D. Why might schools in rural areas have conducted more home visits than did other schools?

2. List one strategy that might help urban schools increase their use of volunteers or home visits.

3. List one strategy that would help suburban or rural schools guide children and parents in working on learning activities at home.

4. If practices of school, family, and community partnerships were measured today in urban, rural, and suburban schools, do you think researchers would find the same patterns of involvement that are described above? Explain why or why not.

◨ COMMENT

District Policies—Focus on Choice

Some states and districts have policies about school choice *and* about school, family, and community partnerships. School choice and partnerships are linked *and* separate policies. They are linked because choice involves families in major decisions about where their children will attend school or which program within a school a child will elect. They are separate because choice is a discrete event, which may or may not be followed by other opportunities for ongoing involvement.

Many states and districts are developing policies to permit, encourage, or require families to choose their public schools within or across school districts. Choices of magnet schools, charter schools, career academies, or other special schools or programs may be available at the elementary, middle, and high school levels. These options are designed to increase competition and the quality of school programs, build student talents and interests, respond to court orders for racially integrated schools, or meet other policy goals.

Policies for school choice may or may not be written to fully inform and involve all families about the choices they may make. This requires communications that are clearly written in languages that parents and students easily understand. Printed materials and oral presentations also must be clear about the options, rules for decisions about choices or assignments of schools or programs, consequences of different choices, support for transportation, and other topics to ensure that choices are offered within an equitable structure.

After the choice is made, schools of choice or programs within schools may or may not continue to involve all families in their children's education. Ongoing involvement requires a comprehensive program of school, family, and community partnerships every year as students proceed through school.

QUESTIONS TO DISCUSS

1. A. How might choosing a school increase the involvement of families?
   B. How might choosing a school decrease the involvement of families?
2. Select and identify the level of schooling (pre-, elementary, middle, or high school) that interests you. Suppose a family moved into a new community with a child who was entering the level of schooling you selected.
   A. Write three questions that you think a parent should ask in the new community if public school choice were an option. Note to whom each question should be addressed. Explain why each question is important to a parent.
   B. Write three questions that you think a parent should ask in the new community if all students were assigned to their schools and there were no options for school choice. Note to whom each question should be addressed. Explain why each question is important to a parent.
   C. *Optional class activity:* In class, collect the questions for each situation (choice versus assignment). Compare the main concerns that parents may have about their children's schools when they move to a new community. Discuss: Whose responsibility is it to address these issues in ways that are helpful and equitable to all parents?

◈ ACTIVITY

Reviewing State and District Policies

The sample policies (see Reading 4.2 in this chapter) are examples of actions taken by state and district boards of education to promote practices of school, family, and community partnerships. Some of the samples include enactments or plans that support actions to implement the policies. It is useful to compare, contrast, and critique the samples to identify sections, words, and investments that you think are particularly important for producing good programs of school, family, and community partnerships at the state, district, and school levels.

A. Select one state and one district sample policy in Reading 4.2 that interest you.
B. Does the state or district policy you selected:
   1. Include reference to all six types of involvement (parenting, communicating, volunteering, learning at home, decision making, and collaborating with the community) in any order or form? Explain.
   2. Refer to the involvement of parents at all grade levels?
   3. Confirm how the state or district will help all schools improve their partnership programs?

C. What *two* other features of the policy you selected do you think are particularly important? List the two features and explain why they are important.
D. Give your ideas of two ways to improve the policy you selected.
E. 1. How would you rate the policy you selected?
   "E" for excellent, enabling—likely to influence and assist all schools
   "S" for satisfactory—likely to influence some schools to develop their programs of partnership
   "N" for needs improvement, impact on schools questionable
   "F" for faulty, may be punishing, not likely to encourage every school to develop a comprehensive program
   2. Explain why you gave the policy this rating.

◇ ACTIVITY

Critiquing a State or District Policy on Partnerships

A. Select a state or district that interests you.
B. Does the state or district you selected have a written policy on parent involvement or school, family, and community partnerships?
   1. IF YES: Obtain and attach a copy of the policy to this assignment.
      A. What are the main components of the policy?
      B. Does the policy connect families and/or the community to student learning and to improving student success in school?
      C. Is the policy supported by a plan and budget for implementation? Describe.
      D. Compare the policy that you obtained to one of the sample policies in this chapter.
      E. Which policy is your comparison? Which do you think is more comprehensive and likely to affect practice? Explain why.
      F. Describe one way that you would improve or extend the policy that you selected.
   2. IF NO, should the state *or* district you selected write a policy on school, family, and community partnerships?
      A. If you think a policy SHOULD BE written, write a short rationale of why you think a policy is needed, and three recommendations for what the policy should include.
      B. If you think a policy SHOULD NOT BE written, explain why you think the state, district, or school does not need a written policy on partnerships.

States and districts are not the only leadership units that write policies and guidelines on school, family, and community partnerships. Some accrediting and professional organizations also are developing policy statements and recommendations to influence education and practice. Following are two examples.

For New Teachers: NCATE Standards for Teacher Credentials

The National Council for Accreditation of Teacher Education (NCATE, 1997) includes references to parent involvement among its standards for candidates for teaching. The standards aim to ensure that new teachers understand and are prepared to involve families in their children's education. NCATE's 1997 draft standards for elementary teachers include the following:

Standard for Professionalism: Positive collaborative relationships with families. Knowing the importance of establishing and maintaining a positive collaborative relationship with families to promote the academic, social, and emotional growth of children.

Supporting Explanation: Candidates for elementary teaching understand different family beliefs, traditions, values, and practices across cultures and within society and use their knowledge effectively. They involve families as partners in supporting the school both inside and outside the classroom. Candidates respect parents' choices and goals for their children and communicate effectively with parents about curriculum and children's progress. They involve families in assessing and planning for individual children, including children with disabilities, developmental delays, or special abilities.

NCATE also includes a standard on fostering relationships with colleagues and with the community to support students' learning and well-being.[10]

For Experienced Teachers: National Board for Professional Teaching Standards (NBPTS)

The NBPTS standards define what an experienced, exemplary teacher should know and be able to do. One standard specifies that excellent teachers should work actively as members of learning communities. For example, in the outline for the Early Adolescence/Generalist Certificate (NBPTS, 1996) the following standard and elaboration describe some of the ways that experienced teachers in

---

[10] See National Council for Accreditation of Teacher Education (NCATE), *Draft accreditation standards for candidates in elementary teacher programs* (Washington, DC: NCATE, 1997).

the middle grades should work with families and communities to help students succeed:

> *Proposed Standard X:* Highly accomplished generalists work with families to achieve common goals for the education of their children.
>
> *Elaboration:* The following are examples of practices that may be evaluated when a teacher applies for board certification: Build partnerships with parents; include parents in school activities; clarify mutual interests with parents; create a sense of community between school and home; learn about family background; seek common ground to solve difficulties in relationships; communicate about accomplishments; respond to family concerns; discuss students' work, report cards, test scores, course selection and consequences, planning for high school, how to help children with homework, studying, setting goals; share information on resources outside of school for health care, counseling; include parents in the development of curriculum and school improvement plans; and others.

As another example, the same standard for the Middle Childhood English/Language Arts certification states that teachers should take the initiative in forming alliances with parents, family, and community members on behalf of the literacy development of their students. The elaboration specifies practices such as understanding students' backgrounds and cultures; conducting two-way communications with families; engaging family support at school; discussing portfolios and report cards with families; enlisting family support for the completion of homework; and assisting families to become involved in the literacy development of children. Similar standards and elaborations are included in the guidelines for all NBPTS certificates in different subjects and grade-level specializations.[11]

QUESTIONS TO DISCUSS

Compare and contrast the NCATE guidelines for new teachers and the NBPTS guidelines for experienced teachers regarding practices to involve families and communities in children's education.

1. How might these guidelines encourage new and experienced teachers to develop and conduct activities to involve the families and communities of the students they teach? Give two ideas of how each of the guidelines might influence an individual teacher's practice.
2. How might these guidelines encourage teachers to contribute to their schools' programs of school, family, and community partnerships, beyond

---

[11] See National Board for Professional Teaching Standards, *Early Adolescent Generalist Certificate* (Washington, DC: NBPTS, 1996).

the work they do with students and families in their own classes? Give two ideas of how each of the guidelines might influence collaborative program development at a school.

3. How might each of these guidelines encourage teacher education programs to provide undergraduate courses for new teachers or advanced graduate courses for experienced teachers to develop knowledge and skills to involve families in their children's education? Give one idea of how each of the guidelines might affect teacher education.

◇ ACTIVITY

Exploring State Requirements for Teaching Credentials

A. Obtain a copy of the requirements for teacher or administrator or counselor credentials from a state that interests you. Do the requirements specify competencies in involving families and communities in children's education?
   1. If YES:
      A. List the requirements for competencies in partnerships.
      B. Are these requirements adequate for ensuring that the professional selected will be prepared to work productively with families? Explain why or why not. Make one change that you believe would improve the requirements.
   2. If NO:
      A. Create two hypothetical state requirements concerning school, family, and community partnerships that you believe would be important for the professional credential you selected.
      B. Explain why you think your recommendations are important and attainable.

B. Obtain a current catalog for your college or university.
   1. List the required *and* elective courses offered in education and in related social sciences that might help prospective professionals learn about school, family, and community connections or parent involvement.
   2. Review the course offerings. Do you think the available courses are adequate for preparing teachers, administrators, counselors, or other professionals to work with schools, students, families, and communities?
      A. If YES: Give two reasons why you think so.
      B. If NO: Suggest two additions, deletions, or other changes that you think would improve the courses and content on partnerships.

Should Parents Be Involved in Staff and Program Evaluations?

Some schools and school districts invite parents and others in the community to interview candidates for principals, teachers, or district superintendents and to provide input on other staffing decisions. When these activities are conducted as a matter of course, families and community members may be more likely to see that their opinions matter, and that educators recognize that parents and others have different, but important, views on the quality of educators for their children.

Some schools and districts give parents an annual survey and other opportunities to evaluate the quality of their children's schools and to make recommendations about improving programs, policies, and practices. When these activities are organized on a regular schedule (e.g., once a year or every other year), students, families, and community members may be more likely to view their schools as dynamic and ever-improving places, rather than as stagnant or rigid in design or development.

QUESTIONS TO DISCUSS

1. Reading 4.3 reports views of parents and principals about what a "good" teacher does.
   A. List one similarity and one difference in parents' and principals' ideas about good teachers.
   B. Based on Reading 4.3, how do you think *teachers* and parents would evaluate principals? List one similarity and one difference between teachers' and parents' criteria for a "good" principal.
   C. How do you think *principals* and *teachers* would evaluate parents' qualities and contributions? List one similarity and one difference between principals' and teachers' criteria for a "good" parent.
2. One set of linked results in Reading 4.3 indicates that:
   principals give higher ratings to teachers who frequently involve families in their children's education than they give to other teachers; and *parents* also give higher ratings to these teachers.
   A. How should teachers interpret these linked results?
   B. Why are these results important individually and together?
3. *Optional follow-up activity:* Discuss your lists from 1A, 1B, and 1C above with a parent, a principal, or a teacher to see if your ideas match theirs or whether they would alter or add to your lists. Identify the person you interview and the comments you obtain.

Reading Tables

Statistical tables provide information and spark ideas, but data tables must be interpreted to be useful. Table 4.2 (in Reading 4.3) reports correlations of classroom qualities with the variation in parents' evaluations of teachers. This statistic indicates whether and how much parents within classrooms agree or differ in their assessments of the teacher. For example, in Table 4.2 the correlation of +.274 indicates that the *higher* the grade level, the *greater* the variation in parents' evaluations of the same teacher.

QUESTIONS TO DISCUSS

1. Does the positive correlation of grade level with the variation in parents' assessments of the quality of their children's teachers surprise you? Why or why not?
2. When might a school or district leader want to narrow or decrease the variation in parents' evaluations of a teacher?
3. When might a school or district leader want to increase the variation in parents' reports about a teacher?
4. A. Select and identify two other correlations in Table 4.2 that interest you.
   B. Discuss what you think the two correlations you selected mean for school policies about school, family, and community partnerships.

FIELD EXPERIENCE

Panel Discussion

A. Invite a principal, teacher, and parent to discuss the following questions. A student may serve as panel moderator. Other questions may be added.
   1. Should parents be involved in decisions about hiring, promoting, and firing (a) teachers, (b) principals, and (c) district superintendents? Explain your reasons.
   2. Should parents be involved in evaluating (a) school policies, such as attendance, dress code, discipline, expulsion, grading policies; (b) curricula; and (c) practices to involve families? Explain your reasons.
      A. If YES:
         1. In what ways should parents be involved in these decisions?
         2. In what ways should they not be involved?
         3. What is one benefit you expect from the involvement of parents in these decisions?

4. What is one problem you expect from their involvement? How might this problem be solved?
B. If NO:
1. Why should parents be excluded from these decisions?
2. What is one major problem that you anticipate if parents were involved? Can this problem be solved?
3. What benefits might be missed if parents are excluded from these decisions? Can these benefits be gained in other ways?
B. After hearing the panelists' points of view, write a paragraph on your own position on each question, with reasons for your opinions.

OTHER POLICY ISSUES

In addition to questions about parental involvement in evaluating teachers and administrators, there are many other important and provocative policy-related questions that have emerged as the field of school, family, and community partnerships has grown. This section discusses a few policies and proposals that would affect state, district, and school policies on school, family, and community partnerships.

▐▌ COMMENT

Reaching the Hard to Reach

Some federal, state, and district policies call attention to the need to create positive partnerships with all families, including those who do not speak or read English well. For example, policies to improve the education of children who are limited in English proficiency need to be examined and applied to the *families* of these children. Policies also are needed when parents are limited in their proficiency with English, even if their children speak English well. In a modest proposal, I suggested that the *Lau vs. Nichols* (414 U.S. 563, 1974) decision, which affects education for children with limited English proficiency, should be reworded to reflect the results of research on school, family, and community partnerships, as follows:

> Where the inability of [parents of] school children to speak and understand the English language *excludes the children* from effective participation in the education program, *the school district* must take affirmative steps *to open its instructional program to these* [parents and their] children (emphasis added).

The proposed revision recognizes that language barriers between parents and teachers—like barriers between children and teachers—impede the equal participation of *children* in educational programs. If parents cannot understand their children's teachers, classroom programs, and communications from the school, then parents cannot effectively guide their children, monitor their work and progress, raise questions or concerns with teachers, or act as advocates for their children. Without clear and understandable communication, parents cannot effectively evaluate the quality of the schools or the education of their children.

Language barriers impede equal participation and eliminate some parents from school, family, and community partnerships. The *Lau vs. Nichols* decision focuses on the equal protection of children's educational opportunities, but it is clear that parents need to understand the school and classroom programs to effectively communicate with teachers, counselors, and administrators about their children. Thus, the needs of children and the needs of families are linked.

These comments about *Lau vs. Nichols* raise some general questions about the implications of other federal and state legislation on children and education for families. These include questions about the school's responsibility to ensure that appropriate communications are conducted with all parents, including those whose English is limited.

QUESTIONS TO DISCUSS

1. Do you think it is useful to reinterpret *Lau vs. Nichols* to ensure two-way communications with non-English-speaking parents and those whose English is limited? Give at least two reasons why or why not.
2. Whether or not the law was reinterpreted in this way, it is important to consider how to effectively involve all families in their children's education, including those who do not speak English. Give two examples of practical activities that you think would inform and involve families who do not speak or read English, or who do not speak or read it well.

▯⋮ COMMENT

Equity in Out-of-School Activities

Students gain knowledge and build cultural capital when they engage in and enjoy activities, events, and services in school and in their communities. Yet some families cannot afford transportation, admission fees, lessons, and dues that other families easily invest in their children's education outside of school. Federal, state, or local "vouchers" or certificates could be created for educational and cultural activities that support and enhance children's school learning and development. An "enrichment voucher"—a kind of "food-for-thought stamp"—could be distributed to families who cannot presently provide their children with supplementary learning and talent development activities. The subsidies could be funded and distributed to families whose children are eligible for free or reduced-price lunches to help families support their children's participation in educational experiences and activities in their communities.

The enrichment or talent development vouchers could cover payments for children's *and* parents' transportation and admissions to museums, zoos, science centers, and aquariums; dance, music, theater, and other performances; sports activities; and other community cultural activities, classes, and events. The mix of after-school, summer, weekend, and evening activities would supplement the school curriculum, promote students' success in school, and help develop students' special talents and skills. A well-designed enrichment program would provide care and enrichment for children while parents are at work and enable parents and children to attend some activities, events, and programs together as a family on evenings, weekends, holidays, and vacation periods.

Why Vouchers for Community Enrichment Activities Are Needed

Recognized Need by Parents.   In several surveys of families of elementary, middle, and high school students, the workshop topic of most interest to parents was: "How do I help my child develop his or her talents?" This was of particular interest to parents with low incomes who know that their children have special, sometimes hidden, talents that must be nourished, but who may not know where or how to gain access to community enrichment programs and services and may not be able to afford to do so.

Evidence of Long-Term Positive Effects.   Using national data from middle and high school students and families, Catsambis (1999) reported that student and family visits to museums during the middle grades have long-term effects on student success in high school, even after prior achievement scores are taken into account. The results suggest that cultural and educational activities may have lasting value for student success in school, but only some students have opportunities to benefit from these experiences.

Presently Unresponsive Community Schedules.   Some communities and schools create opportunities for families and children to participate in enriching educational and cultural community activities. These include free days at zoos or museums, community fairs, "first nights" for family New Year's Eve celebrations, and other special events and festivals on holidays and weekends throughout the year. Unfortunately, many poor families and those with limited English skills do not hear about these offers, do not have transportation to get to them, or do not feel welcome and comfortable at the events. The opportunities are often inaccessible to families, particularly those who may need them most. For example, free days at art, science, or history museums may be scheduled when children are in school or when parents are at work, making it impossible for most children and families to attend.

In sum, there are major inequities in opportunities for student learning outside of school. Some families lack access to all extra, enriching activities for their children. These youngsters lack opportunities to develop skills and talents that will help define who they are as individuals and as members of their communities.

Regardless of a family's ability to pay, children need access to enriching and educational events and opportunities in their communities. How shall such access be provided? The "modest proposal" for enrichment or talent development vouchers is one way. Alternatively, after-school programs can help organize these child and family enrichment activities, in cooperation with community partners.

Schools, families, and communities must think together in new ways to enrich and extend students' experiences after school, on weekends, and during summer and other vacations, including family cultural activities in their communities. In the absence of direct federal, state, or local subsidies to families for the educational and cultural enrichment of their children, federal, state, or local tax or other fiscal adjustments and incentives might be offered to community organizations, agencies, cultural groups, businesses, and others who organize such programs for children and their families.

QUESTIONS TO DISCUSS

1. Do you think communities should offer admission and transportation to enrichment activities to:
   A. Students who cannot afford these fees? Explain your views.
   B. Families who cannot afford these fees? Explain your views.
2. Make a pie chart illustrating your estimates of the proportion of influence of school, home, and community in student success in school.
   A. Label your chart. The sections of home, school, and community influence should total 100 percent.
   B. Write a summary explaining your estimates.

◈ FIELD EXPERIENCE

Toward Equal Access to Enriching Activities in Communities

A. Telephone two cultural organizations in your geographic area that routinely charge admission fees for children and adults. Ask:
   1. Do you have a "voucher" or "scholarship" system for children and families who cannot afford the price of admission to your location?
      A. If YES:
         1. Ask: How does the program work?
         2. Write a short critique of this program or activity in terms of its likely success in providing equal access for enrichment to economically disadvantaged children and families.

B. If NO:
    1. Ask: Could a voucher or scholarship system ever be arranged?
        A. If YES, how might that be done?
        B. If NO, why isn't this possible?
    2. Record the responses you are given.
B. Write a short critique of the information you obtained. Include your ideas
    on the feasibility of creating equal access to the program or activity.

◈ ACTIVITY

Reading More about State and District Policies on Partnerships

To increase your understanding of policies on partnerships, read at least one of the articles, chapters, or books listed below, or choose a recent, important publication on federal, state, district, or school policies of school, family, and community partnerships.

A. Identify one article, chapter, or book that addresses policies for school, family, and community partnerships at the federal, state, district, *or* school level, and give its complete bibliographic reference.
B. Write a summary of about one page in length of the selected publication. Include a brief overview of your selection, including the main topic(s) or question(s) that are raised in the publications, data (if any), and results or conclusions.
C. Write a critique of about one page in length of whether and how you think your selection might be useful to educators or policy leaders for improving programs of school, family, and community partnerships.
D. Write two questions that you think should be asked to extend the work that you read. Tell why you think each question is important for improving policies of partnerships.

Federal Policies

D'Angelo, D. A., and C. R. Adler. (1991). Chapter I: Catalyst for improving parent involvement. *Phi Delta Kappan* 72(5): 350–354.

Epstein, J. L., and J. H. Hollifield. (1996). Title I and school-family-community partnerships: Using research to realize the potential. *Journal of Education for Students Placed at Risk (JESPAR)* 1: 263–279.

Schneider, B. (1996). School, parent, and community involvement: The federal government invests in social capital. Pages 193–213 in *Implementing federal education legislation,* edited by K. Borman, P. Cookson, and A. Sadovnik. Norwood, NJ: Ablex.

Schorr, L. B. (1997) *Common purpose: Strengthening families and neighborhoods to rebuild America.* New York: Doubleday.

U.S. Department of Education. (1994). *Strong families, strong schools: Building community partnerships for learning.* Washington, DC: U.S. Department of Education.

U.S. Department of Education web site: www.ed.gov.

State Policies

Brittingham, Kenneth V. (1998). The characteristics of successful school, family, and community partnerships. Ph.D. diss., University of Wisconsin–Madison, Educational Administration.

Chapman, W. (1991). The Illinois experience: State grants to improve schools through parent involvement. *Phi Delta Kappan* 72(5): 355–358.

Connecticut State Department of Education. (1998/1999). *Schools and Families* 1(1–3).

Council of Chief State School Officers web site: www.ccsso.org.

David, J. L. (1994). School-based decision making: Kentucky's test of decentralization. *Phi Delta Kappan* 75: 706–712.

Nardine, F. E., and R. D. Morris. (1991). Parent involvement in the states: How firm is the commitment? *Phi Delta Kappan* 72(5): 363–366.

Solomon, Z. P. (1991). California's policy on parent involvement: State leadership for local initiatives. *Phi Delta Kappan* 72(5): 335–362.

Van Meter, E. J. (1994). Implementing school-based decision making in Kentucky. *NASSP Bulletin* 78: 61–70.

District Policies

Chavkin, N. F. (1995). Comprehensive districtwide reforms in parent and community involvement programs. Pages 77–106 in *Creating family/school partnerships,* edited by B. Rutherford. Columbus, OH: National Middle School Association.

Chrispeels, J. H. (1991). District leadership in parent involvement: Policies and actions in San Diego. *Phi Delta Kappan* 72(5): 367–371.

———. (1996). Evaluating teachers' relationships with families: A case study of one district. *Elementary School Journal* 97: 179–200.

Council of Great City Schools web site: www.cgcs.org.

Fullen, M., and A. Hargreaves. (1996). *What's worth fighting for in your school?* New York: Teachers College Press.

Warner, I. (1991). Parents in Touch: District leadership for parent involvement. *Phi Delta Kappan* 72(5): 372–375.

School Policies

Davies, D. (1991). Schools Reaching Out: Family, school and community partnerships for student success. *Phi Delta Kappan* 72(5): 350–354.

Funkhouser, J. E., and M. R. Gonzales. (1997). *Family involvement in children's education: Successful local approaches.* Washington, DC: U.S. Department of Education.

Haynes, N. M., and J. P. Comer. (1996). Integrating schools, families, and communities through successful school reform: The School Development Program. *School Psychology Review* 25(4): 501–556.

Lueder, D. C. (1998). *Creating partnerships with parents: An educator's guide.* Lancaster, PA: Technomic Publishing.

McDonald, L., and H. E. Frey. (1999). Families and Schools Together (FAST): Building relationships. *OJJDP: Juvenile Justice Bulletin* XX: 1–19.

McKenna, M., and J. D. Willms. (1998). The challenge facing parent councils in Canada. *Childhood Education* 74(6): 378–382.

Sanders, M. G. (1999). School membership in the National Network of Partnership Schools: Progress, challenges and next steps. *Journal of Educational Research* 92(4): 220–230.

Sanders, M. G., and J. L. Epstein. (2000). Building school-family and community partnerships in secondary schools: From theory to practice. Pages 339–362 in *Schooling students placed at risk: Research, policy and practice in the education of poor and minority adolescents,* edited by M. G. Sanders. Hillsdale, NJ: Lawrence Erlbaum Associates.

Cross-National Policies

Davies, D., and V. R. Johnson, eds. (1996). Crossing boundaries: Family, community, and school partnerships. *International Journal of Educational Research* 25(1): entire issue.

Sanders, M. G., and J. L. Epstein, eds. (1998). School-family-community connections: International programs and perspectives. *Childhood Education* 74(6): entire issue.

For other reports of state, district, and school policies for developing school, family, and community partnerships, see the "State Line," "District Record," and "School Report" columns in all issues of *Type 2*, the newsletter of the National Network of Partnership Schools, in the publications section of the Network's web site, *www.partnershipschools.org*. Also explore the web site of the Consortium for Policy Research in Education (CPRE), *www.upenn.edu/gse/cpre*, for reports on state and district education policies.

REFERENCES

Catsambis, S. (1999). Parents matter: Influences of parental involvement on adolescents' school-related behaviors, plans, and expectations. Paper presented at the annual meeting of the American Sociological Association in Chicago.

Epstein, J. L. (1991). What we can learn from federal, state, district, and school initiatives. *Phi Delta Kappan* 72(5): 344–349.

Espinoza, R. (1988). Working parents, employers, and schools. *Educational Horizons* 66: 62–65.

Lloyd, G. (1996). Research and practical application for school, family, and community partnerships. Pages 255–264 in *Family-school links: How do they affect educational outcomes?*, edited by A. Booth and J. Dunn. Hillsdale, NJ: Lawrence Erlbaum Associates.

McKenna, M., and D. J. Willms. (1998). The challenge facing parent councils in Canada. *Childhood Education* 74: 378–382.

National Board for Professional Teaching Standards (NBPTS). (1996). *Early Adolescent Generalist Certificate.* Washington, DC: NBPTS.

National Council for Accreditation of Teacher Education (NCATE). (1997). *Draft accreditation standards for candidates in elementary teacher programs.* Washington, DC: NCATE.

Ryan, S., A. S. Bryk, G. Lopez, K. P. Williams, K. Hall, and S. Luppescu. (1998). *Charting reform: LSCs—local leadership at work.* Chicago: Consortium on Chicago School Research, University of Chicago.

Solomon, Z. P. (1991). California's policy on parent involvement: State leadership for local initiatives. *Phi Delta Kappan* 72(5): 335–362.

Warner, I. (1991). Parents in touch: District leadership for parent involvement. *Phi Delta Kappan* 72(5): 372–375.

5

Framework for Developing Comprehensive Partnership Programs

T HIS CHAPTER TURNS FROM THEORY, research, and policy to practice. If theoretical concepts, research results, and policies are clear, then good practices of school, family, and community partnerships should follow. Reading 5.1 serves as a touchstone for Chapters 5, 6, and 7. It summarizes a research-based framework of six types of involvement, gives examples of practices for each type, describes challenges that must be met to conduct excellent activities, and reports expected results of well-designed and well-implemented activities. It also outlines the steps for organizing and maintaining strong partnership programs.

The comments, discussions, and activities in this chapter delve deeply into the six types of involvement. There are hundreds of activities that may be selected for each type of involvement. Here, we explore some that will help you understand how each type contributes to the work of all schools. The information in this chapter provides the background and understanding needed to resolve difficult challenges that arise for some types of involvement (also see Chapter 6) and for organizing comprehensive programs of school, family, and community partnerships (also see Chapter 7).

Based on research, development, and innovative practice, there are new ways to think about the six types of involvement, including new definitions and designs for workshops for parents, new structures for parent-teacher-student conferences and other communications, new locations for volunteers, new approaches to interactive homework, new responsibilities of parent organizations and leadership, and new goals for community-school collaborations. The basic and advanced activities explored in this chapter should help every teacher and principal connect with more families and community groups. By reviewing, discussing, and designing ideas for the six types of involvement, you will begin to see how activities for each type meet the needs of today's families and contribute to the attainment of school improvement goals for student success.

In education, you will be able to use the practical framework of six types of involvement to guide discussions and to customize plans and actions for programs of school, family, and community partnerships in the schools, districts, or states in which you work. In research, you will be able to use Reading 5.1 as a base on which to build new studies of the organization and results of specific types of involvement. Such studies will contribute to the field by extending, elaborating, confirming, or contradicting information on the challenges and results of different family and community involvement activities.

School, Family, and Community Partnerships— Caring for the Children We Share*

The way in which schools care about children is reflected in the way they care about the children's families. If educators view children simply as *students*, they are likely to see the family as separate from the school. That is, the family is expected to do its job and leave the education of children to the schools. If educators view students as *children*, they are likely to see both the family and the community as partners with the school in children's education and development. Partners recognize their shared interests in and responsibilities for children, and they work together to create better programs and opportunities for students.

There are many reasons for developing school, family, and community partnerships. They can improve school programs and school climate, provide family services and support, increase parents' skills and leadership, connect families with others in the school and in the community, and help teachers with their work. However, the main reason to create such partnerships is to help all youngsters succeed in school and in later life. When parents, teachers, students, and others view one another as partners in education, a caring community forms around students and begins its work.

What do successful partnership programs look like? How can practices be effectively designed and implemented? What are the results of better communications, interactions, and exchanges across these three important contexts? These questions have challenged research and practice, creating an interdisciplinary field of inquiry into school, family, and community partnerships with "caring" as a core concept.

The field has been strengthened by supporting federal, state, and local policies. For example, the Goals 2000 legislation sets partnerships as a voluntary national goal for all schools; Title I specifies and mandates programs and practices of partnership for schools to qualify for or maintain funding. Many states and districts have developed or are preparing policies to guide schools in creating more systematic connections with families and communities. These policies reflect research results and the prior successes of leading educators who have shown that these goals are attainable.

Underlying these policies and programs are a theory of how social organizations connect; a framework of the basic components of school, family, and community partnerships for children's learning; a growing literature on the positive

---

* By Joyce L. Epstein. Reprinted with permission from J. L. Epstein, School/family/community partnerships: Caring for the children we share, *Phi Delta Kappan* 76 (1995): 701–712. Reprinted/updated (Chapter 1) in J. L. Epstein, L. Coates, K. C. Salinas, M. G. Sanders, and B. S. Simon, *School, family, and community partnerships: Your handbook for action* (Thousand Oaks, CA: Corwin Press, 1997).

and negative results of these connections for students, families, and schools; and an understanding of how to organize good programs. In this reading I summarize the theory, framework, and guidelines that have assisted the schools in our research projects in building partnerships and that should help any elementary, middle, or high school to take similar steps.

OVERLAPPING SPHERES OF INFLUENCE: UNDERSTANDING THE THEORY

Schools make choices. They might conduct only a few communications and interactions with families and communities, keeping the three spheres of influence that directly affect student learning and development relatively separate. Or they might conduct many high-quality communications and interactions designed to bring all three spheres of influence closer together. With frequent interactions among schools, families, and communities, more students are more likely to receive common messages from various people about the importance of school, of working hard, of thinking creatively, of helping one another, and of staying in school.

The *external* model of overlapping spheres of influence recognizes that the three major contexts in which students learn and grow—the family, the school, and the community—may be drawn together or pushed apart. In this model, there are some practices that schools, families, and communities conduct separately and some that they conduct jointly to influence children's learning and development. The *internal* model of the interaction of the three spheres of influence shows where and how complex and essential interpersonal relations and patterns of influence occur between individuals at home, at school, and in the community. These social relationships may be enacted and studied at an *institutional* level (e.g., when a school invites all families to an event or sends the same communications to all families) and at an *individual* level (e.g., when a parent and a teacher meet in conference or talk by phone). Connections between schools or parents and community groups, agencies, and services can also be represented and studied within the model (Epstein, 1987 [Reading 2.1], 1992, 1994).

The model of school, family, and community partnerships locates the student at the center. The inarguable fact is that students are the main actors in their education, development, and success in school. School, family, and community partnerships cannot simply produce successful students. Rather, partnership activities may be designed to engage, guide, energize, and motivate students to produce their own successes. The assumption is that, if children feel cared for and encouraged to work hard in the role of student, they are more likely to do their best to learn to read, write, calculate, and learn other skills and talents and to remain in school.

Interestingly and somewhat ironically, studies indicate that students are also crucial for the success of school, family, and community partnerships. Students are often their parents' main source of information about school. In strong partnership programs, teachers help students understand and conduct traditional communications with families (e.g., delivering memos or report cards) and new communications (e.g., interacting with family members about homework or participating in parent-teacher-student conferences). As we gain more information about the role of students in partnerships, we are developing a more complete understanding of how schools, families, and communities must work with students to increase their chances for success.

HOW THE THEORY WORKS IN PRACTICE

In some schools there are still educators who say, "If the family would just do its job, we could do our job." And there are still families who say, "I raised this child; now it is your job to educate her." These words embody the theory of "separate spheres of influence." Other educators say, "I cannot do my job without the help of my students' families and the support of this community." And some parents say, "I really need to know what is happening in school in order to help my child." These phrases embody the theory of "overlapping spheres of influence."

In a partnership, teachers and administrators create more *family-like* schools. A family-like school recognizes each child's individuality and makes each child feel special and included. Family-like schools welcome all families, not just those that are easy to reach. In a partnership, parents create more *school-like* families. A school-like family recognizes that each child is also a student. Families reinforce the importance of school, homework, and activities that build student skills and feelings of success. Communities, including groups of parents working together, create school-like opportunities, events, and programs that reinforce, recognize, and reward students for good progress, creativity, contributions, and excellence. Communities also create family-like settings, services, and events to enable families to better support their children. Community-minded families and students help their neighborhoods and other families. The concept of a community school is reemerging. It refers to a place where programs and services for students, parents, and others are offered before, during, and after the regular school day.

Schools and communities talk about programs and services that are "family-friendly," meaning that they take into account the needs and realities of family life, are feasible to conduct, and are equitable toward all families. When all these concepts combine, children experience *learning communities* or *caring communities* (Brandt, 1989; Epstein, 1994; Viadero, 1994).

All these terms are consistent with the theory of overlapping spheres of influence, but they are not abstract concepts. You will find them daily in conversations, news stories, and celebrations of many kinds. In a family-like school, a teacher might say, "I know when a student is having a bad day and how to help him along." A student might slip and call a teacher "mom" or "dad" and then laugh with a mixture of embarrassment and glee. In a school-like family, a parent might say, "I make sure my daughter knows that homework comes first." A child might raise his hand to speak at the dinner table and then joke about acting as if he were still in school. When communities reach out to students and their families, youngsters might say, "This program really made my schoolwork make sense!" Parents or educators might comment, "This community really supports its schools."

Once people hear about such concepts as family-like schools or school-like families, they remember positive examples of schools, teachers, and places in the community that were "like a family" to them. They may remember how a teacher paid individual attention to them, recognized their uniqueness, or praised them for real progress, just as a parent might. They might recall things at home that were "just like school" and supported their work as a student, or they might remember community activities that made them feel smart or good about themselves and their families. They will recall that parents, siblings, and other family members engaged in and enjoyed educational activities and took pride in the good schoolwork or homework that they did, just as a teacher might.

HOW PARTNERSHIPS WORK IN PRACTICE

These terms and examples are evidence of the *potential* for schools, families, and communities to create caring educational environments. It is possible to have a school that is excellent academically but ignores families. However, that school will build barriers between teachers, parents, and children that affect school life and learning. It is possible to have a school that is ineffective academically but involves families in many good ways. With its weak academic program, that school will shortchange students' learning. Neither of these schools exemplifies a caring, educational environment that requires academic excellence; good communications; and productive interactions involving school, family, and community.

Some children succeed in school without much family involvement or despite family neglect or distress, particularly if the school has excellent academic and support programs. Teachers, relatives outside of the immediate family, other families, and members of the community can provide important guidance and encouragement to these students. As support from school, family, and community accumulates, significantly more students feel secure and cared for, understand the goals of education, work to achieve to their full potential, build positive attitudes and school behaviors, and stay in school. The shared interests and investments of schools, families, and communities create the conditions of caring that work to "overdetermine" the likelihood of student success (Boykin, 1994).

Any practice can be designed and implemented well or poorly. And even well-implemented partnership practices may not be useful to all families. In a caring school community, participants work continually to improve the nature and effects of partnerships. Although the interactions of educators, parents, students, and community members will not always be smooth or successful, partnership programs establish a base of respect and trust on which to build. Good partnerships withstand questions, conflicts, debates, and disagreements; provide structures and processes to solve problems; and are maintained—even strengthened—after differences have been resolved. Without this firm base, disagreements and problems that are sure to arise about schools and students will be harder to solve.

WHAT RESEARCH SAYS

In surveys and field studies involving teachers, parents, and students at the elementary, middle, and high school levels, some important patterns relating to partnerships have emerged:

- Partnerships tend to decline across the grades, *unless* schools and teachers work to develop and implement appropriate practices of partnership at each grade level.
- Affluent communities currently have more positive family involvement, on average, *unless* schools and teachers in economically distressed communities work to build positive partnerships with their students' families.
- Schools in more economically depressed communities make more contacts with families about the problems and difficulties their children are having, *unless* they work at developing balanced partnership programs that include contacts about positive accomplishments of students.
- Single parents, parents who are employed outside the home, parents who live far from the school, and fathers are less involved, on average, at the school building, *unless* the school organizes opportunities for families to volunteer at various times and in various places to support the school and their children.

Researchers (Ames, Khoju, and Watkins, 1993; Baker and Stevenson, 1986; Bauch, 1988; Becker and Epstein, 1982 [Reading 3.1]; Booth and Dunn, 1996; Clark, 1983; Dauber and Epstein, 1993 [Reading 3.6]; Dornbusch and Ritter, 1988; Eccles and Harold, 1996; Epstein, 1986 [Reading 3.4], 1990 [Reading 3.5]; Epstein and Lee, 1995; Lareau, 1989; and Scott-Jones, 1995) have also drawn the following conclusions:

- Just about all families care about their children, want them to succeed, and are eager to obtain better information from schools and communities so as to remain good partners in their children's education.
- Just about all teachers and administrators would like to involve families, but many do not know how to go about building positive and productive programs and are consequently fearful about trying. This creates a "rhetoric rut," in which educators are stuck, expressing support for partnerships without taking any action.
- Just about all students at all levels—elementary, middle, and high school—want their families to be more knowledgeable partners about schooling and are willing to take active roles in assisting communications between home and school. However, students need much better information and guidance than most now receive about how their schools view partnerships and about how they can conduct important exchanges with their families about school activities, homework, and school decisions.

The research results are important because they indicate that caring communities can be built intentionally; that they include families that might not become involved on their own; and that, by their own reports, just about all families, students, and teachers believe that partnerships are important for helping students succeed across the grades.

Good programs will look different at each site, as individual schools tailor their practices to meet the needs and interests, time and talents, ages and grade levels of students and their families. However, there are some commonalities across successful programs at all grade levels. These include a recognition of the overlapping spheres of influence on student development; attention to various types of involvement that promote a variety of opportunities for schools, families, and communities to work together; and an Action Team for Partnerships (ATP) to coordinate each school's work and progress.

SIX TYPES OF INVOLVEMENT— SIX TYPES OF CARING

A framework of six major types of involvement has evolved from many studies and from many years of work by educators and families in elementary, middle, and high schools. The framework (summarized in the accompanying tables) helps educators develop more comprehensive programs of school and family partnerships and also helps researchers locate their questions and results in ways that inform and improve practice (for other discussions of the types of involvement, practices, and challenges, see Connors and Epstein, 1995; Davies, Burch, and Johnson, 1992; Epstein, 1992; Epstein and Connors, 1994, 1995).

Each type of involvement includes many different *practices* of partnership (see Table 5.1). Each type presents particular *challenges* that must be met to involve all families and needed *redefinitions* of some basic principles of involvement (see Table 5.2). Finally, each type is likely to lead to different *results* for students, parents, teaching practice, and school climate (see Table 5.3). Thus, schools have choices about which practices will help achieve important goals. The tables provide examples of practices, challenges for successful implementation, redefinitions for up-to-date understanding, and results that have been documented and observed.

CHARTING THE COURSE

The entries in the tables are illustrative. The sample practices displayed in Table 5.1 are only a few of hundreds that may be selected or designed for each type of involvement. Although all schools may use the framework of six types as a guide, each school must chart its own course in choosing practices to meet the needs of its families and students.

The challenges shown (Table 5.2) are just a few of the many that relate to the examples. There are challenges—that is, problems—for every practice of partner-

TABLE 5.1   Epstein's Framework of Six Types of Involvement for Comprehensive Programs of Partnership, and Sample Practices

Type 1—Parenting	Type 2—Communicating	Type 3—Volunteering	Type 4—Learning at Home	Type 5—Decision Making	Type 6—Collaborating with the Community
Help all families establish home environment to support children as students.	Design effective forms of school-to-home and home-to-school communications about school programs and their children's progress.	Recruit and organize parent help and support.	Provide information and ideas to families about how to help students at home with homework and other curriculum-related activities, decisions, and planning.	Include parents in school decisions, developing parent leaders and representatives.	Identify and integrate resources and services from the community to strengthen school programs, family practices, and student learning and development.
Sample Practices	Sample Practices	Sample Practices	Sample Practices	Sample Practices	Sample Practices
Suggestions for home conditions that support learning at each grade level. Workshops, videotapes, and computerized phone messages on parenting and child rearing for each age and grade level. Parent education and other courses or training for parents (e.g., GED, college credit, family literacy).	Conferences with every parent at least once a year, with follow-ups as needed. Language translators assist families, as needed. Weekly or monthly folders of student work sent home for review and comments. Parent-student pickup of report cards, with conferences on improving grades.	School and classroom volunteer program to help teachers, administrators, students, and other parents. Parent room or family center for volunteer work, meetings, and resources for families. Annual postcard survey to identify all available talents, times, and locations of volunteers.	Information for families on skills required for students in all subjects at each grade. Information on homework policies and how to monitor and discuss schoolwork at home. Information on how to assist students to improve skills on various class and school assessments. Regular schedule of homework that requires	Active PTA/PTO or other parent organizations, advisory councils, or committees (e.g., curriculum, safety, personnel) for parent leadership and participation. Independent advocacy groups to lobby and work for school reform and improvements. District-level councils and committees for family and	Information for students and families on community health, cultural, recreational, social support, and other programs or services. Information on community activities that link to learning skills and talents, including summer programs for students. Service integration through partnerships involving school; civic, counseling, cultural, health,

(continues)

TABLE 5.1 *(continued)*

Sample Practices	Sample Practices	Sample Practices	Sample Practices	Sample Practices	Sample Practices
Family support programs to assist families with health, nutrition, and other services. Home visits at transition points to preschool, elementary, middle, and high school. Neighborhood meetings to help families understand schools and to help schools understand families.	Regular schedule of useful notices, memos, phone calls, newsletters, and other communications. Clear information on choosing schools or courses, programs, and activities within schools. Clear information on all school policies, programs, reforms, and transitions.	Class parent, telephone tree, or other structures to provide all families with needed information. Parent patrols or other activities to aid safety and operation of school programs.	students to discuss and interact with families on what they are learning in class. Calendars with activities for parents and students to do at home or in the community. Family math, science, and reading activities at school. Summer learning packets or activities. Family participation in setting student goals each year and in planning for college or work.	community involvement. Information on school or local elections for school representatives. Networks to link all families with parent representatives.	recreation, and other agencies and organizations; and businesses. Service to the community by students, families, and schools (e.g., recycling, art, music, drama, and other activities for seniors). Participation of alumni in school programs for students.

ship, and they must be resolved to reach and engage all families in the best ways. Often, when one challenge has been met, a new one will emerge.

The redefinitions (also in Table 5.2) redirect old notions so that involvement is not viewed solely as or measured only by "bodies in the building." As examples, the table calls for redefinitions of workshops, communication, volunteers, homework, decision making, and community. By redefining these familiar terms, it is possible for partnership programs to reach out in new ways to many more families.

The selected results (Table 5.3) should help correct the widespread misperception that any practice that involves families will raise children's achievement test scores. Instead, in the short term, certain practices are more likely than others to influence students' skills and scores, whereas other practices are more likely to af-

TABLE 5.2   Challenges and Redefinitions for the Successful Design and Implementation of the Six Types of Involvement

Type 1—Parenting	Type 2—Communicating	Type 3—Volunteering	Type 4—Learning at Home	Type 5—Decision Making	Type 6—Collaborating with the Community
Challenges	Challenges	Challenges	Challenges	Challenges	Challenges
Provide information to all families who want it or who need it, not just to the few who can attend workshops or meetings at the school building. Enable families to share information about culture, background, and children's talents and needs. Make sure that all information for families is clear, usable, and linked to children's success in school.	Review the readability, clarity, form, and frequency of all memos, notices, and other print and nonprint communications. Consider parents who do not speak English well, do not read well, or need large type. Review the quality of major communications (e.g., the schedule, content, and structure of conferences; newsletters; report cards). Establish clear two-way channels for communications from home to school and from school to home.	Recruit volunteers widely so that *all* families know that their time and talents are welcome. Make flexible schedules for volunteers, assemblies, and events to enable employed parents to participate. Organize volunteer work; provide training; match time and talent with school, teacher, and student needs; and recognize efforts so that participants are productive.	Design and organize a regular schedule of interactive homework (e.g., weekly or bimonthly) that gives students responsibility for discussing important things they are learning and helps families stay aware of the content of their children's classwork. Coordinate family-linked homework activities, if students have several teachers. Involve families with their children in all important curriculum-related decisions.	Include parent leaders from all racial, ethnic, socioeconomic, and other groups in the school. Offer training to enable leaders to serve as representatives of other families, with input from and return of information to all parents. Include students (along with parents) in decision-making groups.	Solve turf problems of responsibilities, funds, staff, and locations for collaborative activities. Inform families of community programs for students, such as mentoring, tutoring, and business partnerships. Ensure equity of opportunities for students and families to participate in community programs or to obtain services. Match community contributions with school goals; integrate child and family services with education.

(continues)

TABLE 5.2 *(continued)*

Type 1—Parenting	Type 2—Communicating	Type 3—Volunteering	Type 4—Learning at Home	Type 5—Decision Making	Type 6—Collaborating with the Community
Redefinitions	Redefinitions	Redefinitions	Redefinitions	Redefinitions	Redefinitions
Workshop to mean more than a meeting about a topic held at the school building at a particular time. *Workshop* also may mean making information about a topic available in a variety of forms that can be viewed, heard, or read anywhere, any-time.	*Communications about school programs and student progress* to mean two-way, three-way, and many-way channels of communication that connect schools, families, students, and the community.	*Volunteer* to mean anyone who supports school goals and children's learning or development in any way, at any place, and at any time, not just during the school day and at the school building.	*Homework* to mean not only work done alone but also interactive activities shared with others at home or in the community, linking schoolwork to real life. *Help* at home to mean encouraging, listening, reacting, praising, guiding, monitoring, and discussing, not "teaching" school subjects.	*Decision making* to mean a process of partnership, of shared views and actions toward shared goals, not just a power struggle between conflicting ideas. *Parent leader* to mean a real representative, with opportunities and support to hear from and communicate with other families.	*Community* to mean not only the neighborhoods where students' homes and schools are located but also any neighborhoods that influence their learning and development. *Community* rated not only by low or high social or economic qualities but also by strengths and talents to support students, families, and schools. *Community* means all who are interested in and affected by the quality of education, not just those with children in the schools.

fect attitudes and behaviors. Although students are the main focus of partnerships, the various types of involvement also promote various kinds of results for parents and teachers. For example, the expected results for parents include not only leadership in decision making, but also confidence about parenting, productive curriculum-related interactions with children, and many interactions with other parents and the school. The expected results for teachers include not only improved parent-teacher conferences or school-home communication, but also better understanding of families, new approaches to homework, and other connections with families and the community.

Most of the results noted in Table 5.3 have been measured in at least one research study and observed as schools conduct their work. The entries are listed in positive terms to indicate the results of well-designed and well-implemented practices. It should be fully understood, however, that results may be negative if poorly designed practices exclude families or create greater barriers to communication and exchange. Research is still needed on the results of specific practices of partnership in various schools, at various grade levels, and for diverse populations of students, families, and teachers. It will be important to confirm, extend, or correct the information on results listed in Table 5.3 if schools are to make purposeful choices among practices that foster various types of involvement.

The tables cannot show the connections that occur when one practice activates several types of involvement simultaneously. For example, volunteers may organize and conduct a food bank (Type 3) that allows parents to pay $15 for $30 worth of food for their families (Type 1). The food may be subsidized by community agencies (Type 6). The recipients might then serve as volunteers for the program or in the community (perpetuating Type 3 and Type 6 activities). Or consider another example. An after-school homework club run by volunteers and the community recreation department combines Type 3 and Type 6 practices. Yet it also serves as a Type 1 activity, because the after-school program assists families with the supervision of their children. This practice may also alter the way homework interactions are conducted between students and parents at home (Type 4). These and other connections are interesting, and research is needed to understand the combined effects of such activities.

The tables also simplify the complex longitudinal influences that produce various results over time. For example, a series of events might play out as follows. The involvement of families in reading at home leads students to give more attention to reading and to be more strongly motivated to read. This in turn may help students maintain or improve their daily reading skills and then their reading grades. With the accumulation over time of good classroom reading programs, continued home support, and increased skills and confidence in reading, students may significantly improve their reading achievement test scores. The time between reading aloud at home and increased reading test scores may vary greatly, depending on the quality and quantity of other reading activities in school and out.

Or consider another example. A study by Lee (1994), using longitudinal data and rigorous statistical controls on background and prior influences, found important benefits for high school students' attitudes and grades as a result of continuing several types of family involvement from the middle school into the high school. However, achievement test scores were not greatly affected by partnerships at the high school level. Longitudinal studies and practical experiences that are monitored over time are needed to increase our understanding of the complex patterns of results that can develop from various partnership activities (Epstein,

1991 [Reading 3.7], 1996 [Reading 2.2]; Epstein and Dauber, 1995; Epstein and Lee, 1993; Henderson and Berla, 1994).

The six types of involvement can guide the development of a balanced, comprehensive program of partnerships, including opportunities for family involvement at school and at home, with potentially important results for students, parents, and teachers. The results for students, parents, and teachers will depend on the particular types of involvement that are implemented, as well as on the quality of the implementation.

TABLE 5.3   Expected Results for Students, Parents, and Teachers of the Six Types of Involvement

Type 1— Parenting	Type 2— Communicating	Type 3— Volunteering	Type 4— Learning at Home	Type 5— Decision Making	Type 6— Collaborating with the Community
Results for Students	Results for Students	Results for Students	Results for Students	Results for Students	Results for Students
Awareness of family supervision; respect for parents. Positive personal qualities, habits, beliefs, and values, as taught by family. Balance between time spent on chores, on other activities, and on homework. Good or improved attendance. Awareness of importance of school.	Awareness of own progress and of actions needed to maintain or improve grades. Understanding of school policies on behavior, attendance, and other areas of student conduct. Informed decisions about courses and programs. Awareness of own role in partnerships, serving as courier and communicator.	Skill in communicating with adults. Increased learning of skills that receive tutoring or targeted attention from volunteers. Awareness of many skills, talents, occupations, and contributions of parents and other volunteers.	Gains in skills, abilities, and test scores linked to homework and classwork. Homework completion. Positive attitude toward schoolwork. View of parent as more similar to teacher and home as more similar to school. Self-concept of ability as learner.	Awareness of representation of families in school decisions. Understanding that student rights are protected. Specific benefits linked to policies enacted by parent organizations and experienced by students.	Increased skills and talents through enriched curricular and extracurricular experiences. Awareness of careers and options for future education and work. Specific benefits linked to programs, services, resources, and opportunities that connect students with community.

(continues)

ACTION TEAMS FOR SCHOOL, FAMILY, AND COMMUNITY PARTNERSHIPS

Who will work to create caring school communities that are based on the concepts of partnership? How will the necessary work on all six types of involvement get done? Although a principal or a teacher may be a leader in working with some families or with groups in the community, one person cannot create a lasting, comprehensive program that involves all families as their children progress through the grades.

TABLE 5.3   *(continued)*

Type 1—Parenting	Type 2—Communicating	Type 3—Volunteering	Type 4—Learning at Home	Type 5—Decision Making	Type 6—Collaborating with the Community
Results for Parents	**Results for Parents**	**Results for Parents**	**Results for Parents**	**Results for Parents**	**Results for Parents**
Understanding of and confidence about parenting, child and adolescent development, and changes in home conditions for learning as children proceed through school. Awareness of own and others' challenges in parenting. Feeling of support from school and other parents.	Understanding school programs and policies. Monitoring and awareness of child's progress. Responding effectively to students' problems. Interactions with teachers and ease of communications with school and teachers.	Understanding teacher's job, increased comfort in school, and carryover of school activities at home. Self-confidence about ability to work in school and with children or to take steps to improve own education. Awareness that families are welcome and valued at school. Gains in specific skills of volunteer work.	Knowledge of how to support, encourage, and help student at home each year. Discussions of school, classwork, and homework. Understanding of instructional program each year and of what child is learning in each subject. Appreciation of teaching skills. Awareness of child as a learner.	Input into policies that affect child's education. Feeling of ownership of school. Awareness of parents' voices in school decisions. Shared experiences and connections with other families. Awareness of school, district, and state policies.	Knowledge and use of local resources by family and child to increase skills and talents or to obtain needed services. Interactions with other families in community activities. Awareness of school's role in the community and of the community's contributions to the school.

From the hard work of many educators and families in many schools, we have learned that, along with clear policies and strong support from state and district leaders and from school principals, an ATP in each school is an essential structure. The action team guides the development of a comprehensive program of partnerships, including all six types of involvement, and the integration of all family and community connections within a single, unified plan and program. The trials and errors, efforts and insights of many schools in our projects have helped to identify five important steps that any school can take to develop more positive school-family-community connections (Burch and Palanki, 1994; Burch, Palanki, and Davies, 1995; Connors and Epstein, 1994; Davies, 1991; 1993; Davies, Palanki, and Burch, 1993; Epstein and Connors, 1994; Epstein and Dauber, 1991, [Reading 3.3]; Epstein, Herrick, and Coates, 1996; Johnson, 1994).

Step 1: Create an Action Team

A team approach is an appropriate way to build partnerships. The ATP can be the "action arm" of a school council, if one exists. The action team takes responsibility for assessing present practices, organizing options for new partnerships, implementing selected activities, evaluating next steps, and continuing to improve and coordinate practices for all six types of involvement. Although the members of the action team lead these activities, they are assisted by other teachers, parents, students, administrators, and community members.

The action team should include at least three teachers from different grade levels, three parents with children in different grade levels, and one administrator. Teams may also include at least one member from the community at large and, at the middle and high school levels, two students from different grade levels. Others who are central to the school's work with families may also be included as members, such as a cafeteria worker, a school social worker, a counselor, or a school psychologist. Such diverse membership ensures that partnership activities will take into account the various needs, interests, and talents of teachers, parents, the school, and students.

The leader of the action team may be any member who has the respect of the other members, as well as good communication skills and an understanding of the partnership approach. The leader or at least one member of the action team should also serve on the school council, school improvement team, or other such body, if one exists.

In addition to group planning, members of the action team elect (or are assigned to act as) the chair or cochair of one of six subcommittees for each type of involvement. A team with at least six members (and perhaps as many as 12) ensures that responsibilities for leadership can be delegated so that one person is not overburdened and so that the work of the action team will continue even if members move or change schools or positions. Members may serve renewable terms of two to three years, with replacement of any who leave in the interim. Other thoughtful variations in assignments and activities may be created by small or large schools using this process.

In the first phase of our work in 1987, projects were led by "project directors" (usually teachers) and were focused on one type of involvement at a time. Some schools succeeded in developing good partnerships over several years, but others were thwarted if the project director moved, if the principal changed, or if the project grew larger than one person could handle. Other schools took a team approach to work on many types of involvement simultaneously. Their efforts demonstrated how to structure the program for the next set of schools in our work. Starting in 1990, this second set of schools tested and improved on the structure and work of action teams. Now, all elementary, middle, and high schools in our research and development projects, and in other states and districts that are applying this work, are given assistance in taking the action team approach.

Step 2: Obtain Funds and Other Support

A modest budget is needed to guide and support the work and expenses of each school's action team. Funds for state coordinators to assist districts and schools and for district coordinators or facilitators to help each school may come from a number of sources. These include federal, state, and local programs that mandate, request, or support family involvement, such as Title I and other federal and state funding programs. (See discussions on funding in Chapter 4.) In addition to paying the state and district coordinators, funds from these sources may be applied in creative ways to support staff development in the area of school, family, and community partnerships; to pay for lead teachers at each school; to set up demonstration programs; and for other partnership expenses. In addition, local school-business partnerships, school discretionary funds, and separate fund-raising efforts targeted to the schools' partnership programs have been used to support the work of their action teams. At the very least, a school's action team requires a small stipend (at least $1,000 per year for three to five years, with summer supplements) for time and materials needed by each subcommittee to plan, implement, and revise practices of partnership that include all six types of involvement.

The action team must also be given sufficient time and social support to do its work. This requires explicit support from the principal and district leaders to allow time for team members to meet, plan, and conduct the activities that are selected for each type of involvement. Time during the summer is also valuable—and may be essential—for planning new approaches that will start in the new school year.

Step 3: Identify Starting Points

Most schools have some teachers who conduct some practices of partnership with some families some of the time. How can good practices be organized and extended so that they may be used by all teachers, at all grade levels, with all families? The action team works to improve and systematize the typically haphazard patterns of involvement. It starts by collecting information about the school's current practices of partnership, along with the views, experiences, and wishes of teachers, parents, administrators, and students.

Assessments of starting points may be made in a variety of ways, depending on available resources, time, and talents. For example, the action team might use formal questionnaires (Epstein, Connors, and Salinas, 1993) or telephone interviews to survey teachers, administrators, parents, and students (if resources exist to process, analyze, and report survey data). Or the action team might organize a panel of teachers, parents, and students to speak at a meeting of the parent-teacher organization or at some other school meeting as a way of initiating discussion about the goals and desired activities for partnership. Structured discussions may be conducted through a series of principal's breakfasts for representative groups of teachers, parents, students, and others; random sample phone calls may also be used to collect reactions and ideas; or formal focus groups may be convened to gather ideas about school, family, and community partnerships at the school.

What questions should be addressed? Regardless of how the information is gathered, some areas must be covered in any information gathering:

Present Strengths: Which practices of school, family, and community partnerships are now working well for the school as a whole? For individual grade levels? For which types of involvement?

Needed Changes: Ideally, how do we want school, family, and community partnerships to work at this school three years from now? Which present practices should continue, and which should change? To reach school goals, what new practices are needed for each of the major types of involvement?

Expectations: What do teachers expect of families? What do families expect of teachers and other school personnel? What do students expect their families to do to help them negotiate school life? What do students expect their teachers to do to keep their families informed and involved?

Sense of Community: Which families are we now reaching, and which are we not yet reaching? Who are the "hard-to-reach" families? What might be done to communicate with and engage these families in their children's education? Are current partnership practices coordinated to include all families as a school community? Or are families whose children receive special services (e.g., Title I, special education, bilingual education) separated from other families?

Links to Goals: How are students faring on such measures of academic achievement as report card grades, on measures of attitudes and attendance, and on other indicators of success? How might family and community connections assist the school in helping more students reach higher goals and achieve greater success? Which practices of school, family, and community partnerships would directly connect to particular goals?

Step 4: Develop a Three-Year Outline and One-Year Action Plan

From the ideas and goals for partnerships collected from teachers, parents, and students, the action team can develop a three-year outline of the specific steps that will help the school progress from its starting point on each type of involvement to where it wants to be in three years. This plan outlines how each subcommittee will work over three years to make important, incremental advances to reach more families each year on each type of involvement. The three-year outline also shows how all school-family-community connections will be integrated into one coherent program of partnerships. The full program should include activities that serve the whole school community, meet the special needs of children and families, address grade level differences, and link to district committees and councils.

In addition to the three-year outline of goals for each type of involvement, a detailed one-year action plan should be developed for the first year's work. It should include the specific activities that will be implemented, improved, or maintained for each type of involvement; a time line of monthly actions needed for each activity; identification of the subcommittee chair who will be responsible for each type of involvement; identification of the teachers, parents, students, or others (not necessarily action team members) who will assist with the implementation of each activity; indicators of how the implementation and results of each major activity will be assessed; and other details of importance to the action team.

The three-year outline and one-year detailed plan are shared with the school council and/or parent organization, with all teachers, and with the parents and students. Even if the action team makes only one good step forward each year on each of the six types of involvement, it will take 18 steps forward over three years to develop a more comprehensive and coordinated program of school, family, and community partnerships.

In short, based on the input from the parents, teachers, students, and others on the school's starting points and desired partnerships, the action team will address these issues:

Details: What will be done each year, for three years, to implement a program on all six types of involvement? What, specifically, will be accomplished in the first year on each type of involvement?

Responsibilities: Who will be responsible for developing and implementing practices of partnership for each type of involvement? Will staff development be needed? How will teachers, administrators, parents, and students be supported and recognized for their work?

Costs: What costs are associated with the improvement and maintenance of the planned activities? What sources will provide the needed funds? Will small grants or other special budgets be needed?

Evaluation: How will we know how well the practices have been implemented and what their effects are on students, teachers, and families? What indicators will we use that are closely linked to the practices implemented to determine their effects?

Step 5: Continue Planning and Working

The action team should schedule an annual presentation and celebration of progress at the school so that all teachers, families, and students will know about the work that has been done each year to build partnerships. Or the district coordinator for school, family, and community partnerships might arrange an annual conference for all schools in the district. At the annual school or district meeting, the action team presents and displays the highlights of accomplishments of each type of involvement. Problems are discussed and ideas are shared about improvements, additions, and continuations for the next year.

Each year, the action team updates the school's three-year outline and develops a detailed one-year action plan for the coming year's work. It is important for educators, families, students, and the community at large to be aware of annual progress, new plans, and how they can help.

In short, the action team addresses the following questions: How can it ensure that the program of school, family, and community partnerships will continue to improve its structure, processes, and practices to increase the number of families who are partners with the school in their children's education? What opportunities will teachers, parents, and students have to share information on successful practices and to strengthen and maintain their efforts?

CHARACTERISTICS OF SUCCESSFUL PROGRAMS

As schools have implemented partnership programs, their experience has helped to identify some important properties of successful partnerships.

Incremental Progress

Progress in partnerships is incremental, including more families each year in ways that benefit more students. Like reading or math programs, assessment programs, sports programs, or other school investments, partnership programs take time to develop, must be periodically reviewed, and should be continuously improved. The schools in our projects have shown that three years is the minimum time needed for an action team to complete a number of activities on each type of involvement and to establish its work as a productive and permanent structure in a school.

The development of a partnership is a process, not a single event. All teachers, families, students, and community groups do not engage in all activities on all types of involvement all at once. Not all activities implemented will succeed with all families. But with good planning, thoughtful implementation, well-designed activities, and pointed improvements, more and more families and teachers can learn to work with one another on behalf of the children whose interests they share. Similarly, not all students instantly improve their attitudes or achievements when their families become involved in their education. After all, student learning depends mainly on good curricula and instruction and on the work completed by students. However, with a well-implemented program of partnerships, more students will receive support from their families, and more will be motivated to work harder.

Connection to Curricular and Instructional Reform

A program of school, family, and community partnerships that focuses on children's learning and development is an important component of curricular and instructional reform. Aspects of partnerships that aim to help more students succeed in school can be supported by federal, state, and local funds that are targeted for curricular and instructional reform. Helping families understand, monitor, and interact with students on homework, for example, can be a clear and important extension of classroom instruction, as can volunteer programs that bolster and broaden student skills, talents, and interests. Improving the content and conduct of parent-teacher-student conferences and goal-setting activities can be an important step in curricular reform; family support and family understanding of child and adolescent development and school curricula are necessary elements to assist students as learners.

The connection of partnerships to curriculum and instruction in schools and the location of leadership for these partnership programs in district departments of curriculum and instruction are important changes that move partnerships from being peripheral public relations activities about parents to being central programs about student learning and development.

Redefining Staff Development

The action team approach to partnerships guides the work of educators by restructuring "staff development" to mean colleagues working together and with parents to develop, implement, evaluate, and continue to improve practices of partnership. This is less a "dose of inservice education" than it is an active form of developing staff talents and capacities. The teachers, administrators, and others on the action team become the "experts" on this topic for their school. Their work in this area can be supported by various federal, state, and local funding programs as a clear investment in staff development for overall school reform. Indeed, the action team approach as outlined can be applied to any or all important topics on a school improvement agenda. It need not be restricted to the pursuit of successful partnerships.

It is important to note that the development of partnership programs would be easier if educators came to their schools prepared to work productively with families and communities. Courses or classes are needed in preservice teacher education and in advanced degree programs for teachers and administrators to help them define their professional work in terms of partnerships. Today, most educators enter schools without an understanding of family backgrounds, concepts of caring, the framework of partnerships, or the other "basics" that are discussed here. Thus, most principals and district leaders are not prepared to guide and lead their staffs in developing strong school and classroom practices that inform and involve families. Most teachers and administrators also are not prepared to understand, design, implement, or evaluate good practices of partnership with the families of their students. Colleges and universities that prepare educators and others who work with children and families should identify where in their curricula the theory, research, policy, and practical ideas about partnerships are presented or where in their programs these can be added (Ammon, 1990; Chavkin and Williams, 1988; Hinz, Clark, and Nathan, 1992; and see Booth and Dunn, 1996; Christenson and Conoley, 1992; Fagnano and Werber, 1994; Fruchter, Galletta, and White, 1992; Rioux and Berla, 1993; Ryan et al., 1995; and Swap, 1993).

Even with improved preservice and advanced course work, however, each school's action team will have to tailor its menu of practices to the needs and wishes of the teachers, families, and students in the school. The framework and guidelines offered in this reading can be used by thoughtful educators to organize this work, school by school.

THE CORE OF CARING

One school in our Baltimore project named its partnerships the "I Care Program." It developed an I Care Parent Club that fostered fellowship and leadership of families, an *I Care Newsletter,* and many other events and activities. Other schools also gave catchy, positive names to their programs to indicate to families, students, teachers, and everyone else in the school community that there are important relationships and exchanges that must be developed to assist students.

Interestingly, synonyms for "caring" match the six types of involvement: Type 1—Parenting—supporting, nurturing, and raising; Type 2—Communicating—relating, reviewing, and overseeing; Type 3—Volunteering—supervising and Fostering; Type 4—Learning at Home—managing, recognizing, and rewarding; Type 5—Decision Making—contributing, considering, and judging; and Type 6, Collaborating with the Community—sharing and giving.

Underlying all six types of involvement are two defining synonyms of caring: trusting and respecting. Of course, the varied meanings are interconnected, but it is striking that language permits us to call forth various elements of caring associated with activities for the six types of involvement. If all six types of involvement are operating well in a school's program of partnerships, then all of these caring behaviors could be activated to assist children's learning and development.

Despite real progress in many states, districts, and schools over the past few years, there are still too many schools in which educators do not understand the families of their students; in which families do not understand their children's schools; and in which communities do not understand or assist the schools, families, or students. There are still too many states and districts without the policies, departments, leadership, staff, and fiscal support needed to enable all their schools to develop good programs of partnership. Yet relatively small financial investments that support and assist the work of action teams could yield significant returns for all schools, teachers, families, and students. Educators who have led the way with trials, errors, and successes provide evidence that any state, district, or school can create similar programs (Lloyd, 1996; Wisconsin Department of Public Instruction, 1994; and other examples at www.partnershipschools.org).

Schools have choices. There are two common approaches to involving families in schools and in their children's education. One approach emphasizes conflict and views the school as a battleground. The conditions and relationships in this kind of environment guarantee power struggles and disharmony. The other approach emphasizes partnership and views the school as a homeland. The conditions and relationships in this kind of environment invite power sharing and mutual respect and allow energies to be directed toward activities that foster student learning and development. Even when conflicts rage, however, peace must be restored sooner or later, and the partners in children's education must work together.

NEXT STEPS: STRENGTHENING PARTNERSHIPS

Collaborative work and thoughtful give-and-take among researchers, policy leaders, educators, and parents are responsible for the progress that has been made in understanding and developing school, family, and community partnerships. Similar collaborations will be important for future progress in this and other areas of school reform. To promote these approaches, the National Network of Partnership Schools at Johns Hopkins University was established. The Network provides state, district, and other leaders with research-based tools and guidelines to help their elementary, middle, and high schools plan, implement, and maintain comprehensive programs of partnership.

Partnership schools, districts, and states put the recommendations of this reading into practice in ways that are appropriate to their locations. Implementation includes applying the theory of overlapping spheres of influence, the framework of six types of involvement, and the action team approach. Researchers and staff members at Johns Hopkins University disseminate information and guidelines, send out newsletters, and hold annual workshops to help state and district coordinators learn new strategies and share successful ideas. Activities for leaders at the state and district levels are shared, along with school-level programs and successful partnership practices. The goal is to enable leaders in all states and districts to assist all schools in establishing and strengthening programs of school, family, and community partnership.

REFERENCES

Ames, C., M. Khoju, and T. Watkins. (1993). *Parents and schools: The impact of school-to-home communications on parents' beliefs and perceptions.* Report 15. Center on

Families, Communities, Schools and Children's Learning. Baltimore: Johns Hopkins University.

Ammon, M. S. (1990). University of California project on teacher preparation for parent involvement: Report 1, April 1989 Conference and Initial Follow-up. Berkeley: University of California. Mimeographed.

Baker, D. P., and D. L. Stevenson. (1986). Mothers' strategies for children's school achievement: Managing the transition to high school. *Sociology of Education* 59: 156–166.

Bauch, P. A. (1988). Is parent involvement different in private schools? *Educational Horizons* 66: 78–82.

Becker, H. J., and J. L. Epstein. (1982). Parent involvement: A study of teacher practices. *Elementary School Journal* 83: 85–102. (Reading 3.1).

Booth, A., and J. F. Dunn, eds. (1996). *Family-school links: How do they affect educational outcomes?* Mahwah, NJ: Lawrence Erlbaum Associates.

Boykin, A. W. (1994). Harvesting culture and talent: African American children and educational reform. Pages 116–139 in *Schools and students at risk,* edited by R. Rossi. New York: Teachers College Press.

Brandt, R. (1989). On parents and schools: A conversation with Joyce Epstein. *Educational Leadership* 47(2): 24–27.

Burch, P., and A. Palanki. (1994). Action research on family-school-community partnerships. *Journal of Emotional and Behavioral Problems* 1(4): 16–19.

Burch, P., A. Palanki, and D. Davies. (1995). *From clients to partners: Four case studies of collaboration and family involvement in the development of school-linked services.* Report 29. Center on Families, Communities, Schools and Children's Learning. Baltimore: Johns Hopkins University.

Chavkin, N., and D. Williams. (1988). Critical issues in teacher training for parent involvement. *Educational Horizons* 66: 87–89.

Christenson, S. L., and J. C. Conoley, eds. (1992). *Home-school collaboration: Enhancing children's academic competence.* Silver Spring, MD: National Association of School Psychologists.

Clark, R. M. (1983). *Family life and school achievement: Why poor Black children succeed or fail.* Chicago: University of Chicago Press.

Connors, L. J., and J. L. Epstein. (1994). *Taking stock: The views of teachers, parents, and students on school, family, and community partnerships in high schools.* Report 25. Center on Families, Communities, Schools and Children's Learning. Baltimore: Johns Hopkins University.

———. (1995). Parents and schools. Pages 437–458 in *Handbook of parenting,* edited by M. Bornstein. Hillsdale, NJ: Lawrence Erlbaum Associates.

Dauber, S. L., and J. L. Epstein. (1993). Parents' attitudes and practices of involvement in inner-city elementary and middle schools. Pages 53–71 in *Families and schools in a pluralistic society,* edited by N. Chavkin. Albany, NY: SUNY Press. (Reading 3.6).

Davies, D. (1991). Schools reaching out: Family, school and community partnerships for student success. *Phi Delta Kappan* 72: 376–382.

———. (1993). A more distant mirror: Progress report on a cross-national project to study family-school-community partnerships. *Equity and Choice* 19(1): 41–46.

Davies, D., P. Burch, and V. Johnson. (1992). *A portrait of schools reaching out: Report of a survey on practices and policies of family-community-school collaboration.* Report 1. Center on Families, Communities, Schools and Children's Learning. Baltimore: Johns Hopkins University.

Davies, D., A. Palanki, and P. Burch. (1993). *Getting started: Action research in family-school-community partnerships.* Report 17. Center on Families, Communities, Schools and Children's Learning. Baltimore: Johns Hopkins University.

Dornbusch, S. M., and P. L. Ritter. (1988). Parents of high school students: A neglected resource. *Educational Horizons* 66: 75–77.

Eccles, J. S., and R. D. Harold. (1996). Family involvement in children's and adolescents' schooling. Pages 3–34 in *Family-school links: How do they affect educational outcomes?* edited by A. Booth and J. F. Dunn. Mahwah, NJ: Lawrence Erlbaum Associates.

Epstein, J. L. (1986). Parents' reactions to teacher practices of parent involvement. *Elementary School Journal* 86: 277–294. (Reading 3.4).

————. (1987). Toward a theory of family-school connections: Teacher practices and parent involvement. Pages 121–136 in *Social intervention: Potential and constraints*, edited by K. Hurrelmann, F. Kaufmann, and F. Losel. New York: de Gruyter. (Reading 2.1).

————. (1990). Single parents and the schools: Effects of marital status on parent and teacher interactions. Pages 91–121 in *Change in societal institutions*, edited by M. T. Hallinan, D. M. Klein, and J. Glass. New York: Plenum. (Reading 3.5).

————. (1991). Effects on student achievement of teacher practices of parent involvement. Pages 261–276 in *Advances in reading/language research, Vol. 5: Literacy through family, community, and school interaction*, edited by S. Silvern. Greenwich CT: JAI. (Reading 3.7).

————. (1992). School and family partnerships. Pages 1139–1151 in *Encyclopedia of educational research, 6th ed.*, edited by M. Alkin. New York: Macmillan.

————. (1994). Theory to practice: School and family partnerships lead to school improvement and student success. Pages 39–52 in *School, family and community interaction: A view from the firing lines*, edited by C. L. Fagnano and B. Z. Werbe. Boulder, CO: Westview Press.

————. (1996). Perspectives and previews on research and policy for school, family, and community partnerships. Pages 209–246 in *Family-school links: How do they affect educational outcomes?* edited by A. Booth and J. F. Dunn. Mahwah, NJ: Lawrence Erlbaum Associates. (Reading 2.2).

Epstein, J. L., and L. J. Connors. (1994). *Trust fund: School, family, and community partnerships in high schools*. Report 24. Center on Families, Communities, Schools and Children's Learning. Baltimore: Johns Hopkins University.

————. (1995). School and family partnerships in the middle grades. Pages 137–166 in *Creating family-school partnerships*, edited by B. Rutherford. Columbus, OH: National Middle School Association.

Epstein, J. L., L. J. Connors, and K. C. Salinas. (1993). *High school and family partnerships: Surveys and summaries—Questionnaires for teachers, parents, and students, and How to summarize your high school's survey data*. Center on School, Family, and Community Partnerships. Baltimore: Johns Hopkins University.

Epstein, J. L., and S. L. Dauber. (1991). School programs and teacher practices of parent involvement in inner-city elementary and middle schools. *Elementary School Journal*, 91: 289–303. (Reading 3.3).

————. (1995). Effects on students of an interdisciplinary program linking social studies, art, and family volunteers in the middle grades. *Journal of Early Adolescence* 15: 237–266.

Epstein, J. L., S. C. Herrick, and L. Coates. (1996). Effects of summer home learning packets on student achievement in language arts in the middle grades. *School Effectiveness and School Improvement* 7: 383–410.

Epstein, J. L., and S. Lee. (1993). Effects of school practices to involve families on parents and students in the middle grades: A view from the schools. Paper presented at the annual meeting of the American Sociological Association, August, in Miami.

————. (1995). National patterns of school and family connections in the middle grades. Pages 108–154 in *The family-school connection: Theory, research and practice*, edited by B. A. Ryan, G. R. Adams, T. P. Gullotta, R. P. Weissberg, and R. L. Hampton. Newbury Park, CA: Sage.

Fagnano, C. L., and B. Z. Werber. (1994). *School, family, and community interaction: A view from the firing lines*. Boulder, CO: Westview Press.

Fruchter, N., A. Galletta, and J. L. White. (1992). *New directions in parent involvement.* Washington, DC: Academy for Educational Development.

Henderson, A. T., and N. Berla. (1994). *A new generation of evidence: The family is critical to student achievement.* Washington, DC: National Committee for Citizens in Education.

Hinz, L., J. Clarke, and J. Nathan. (1992). *A survey of parent involvement course offerings in Minnesota's undergraduate preparation programs.* Minneapolis: Center for School Change, Humphrey Institute of Public Affairs, University of Minnesota.

Johnson, V. R. (1994). *Parent centers in urban schools: Four case studies.* Report 23. Center on Families, Communities, Schools and Children's Learning. Baltimore: Johns Hopkins University.

Lareau, A. (1989). *Home advantage: Social class and parental intervention in elementary education.* Philadelphia: Falmer.

Lee, S. (1994). Family-school connections and students' education: Continuity and change of family involvement from the middle grades to high school. Ph.D. diss., Johns Hopkins University, Baltimore.

Lewis, C. C., E. Schaps, and M. Watson. (1995). Beyond the pendulum: Creating challenging and caring schools. *Phi Delta Kappan* 76: 547–554.

Lloyd, G. (1996). Research and practical application for school, family, and community partnerships. Pages 255–264 in *Family-school links: How do they affect educational outcomes?* edited by A. Booth and J. F. Dunn. Mahwah, NJ: Lawrence Erlbaum Associates.

Rioux, W., and N. Berla, eds. (1993). *Innovations in parent and family involvement.* Princeton Junction, NJ: Eye on Education.

Ryan, B. A, G. R. Adams, T. P. Gullotta, R. P. Weissberg, and R. L. Hampton, eds. (1995). *The family-school connection.* Thousand Oaks, CA: Sage.

Scott-Jones, D. (1995). Activities in the home that support school learning in the middle grades. Pages 161–181 in *Creating family/school partnerships,* edited by B. Rutherford. Columbus, OH: National Middle School Association.

Swap, S. M. (1993). *Developing home-school partnerships: From concepts to practice.* New York: Teachers College Press.

Viadero, D. (1994). Learning to care. *Education Week* (October 26): 31–33.

Wisconsin Department of Public Instruction. (1994, August/September). *Sharesheet: The DPI family-community school partnership newsletter* 3: 1–2.

DISCUSSION AND ACTIVITIES

The comments in this section extend and update the content of Reading 5.1. Key concepts and results are summarized. Questions and activities are provided for class discussions, debates, and homework assignments. They may suggest other exercises, field activities, and research projects.

▣ KEY CONCEPTS

1. **Six types of involvement.** A framework of six types of involvement *(parenting, communicating, volunteering, learning at home, decision making,* and *collaborating with the community)* grew from analyses of data collected from educa-

tors, parents, and students at the elementary, middle, and high school levels. The six types of involvement are demonstrably separable; include different practices; set different challenges for excellence; and lead to different results for students, families, schools, and communities.

2. Practices or activities. These terms are used interchangeably to describe specific implementations in schools. For district and state policies, practices, and activities, see Chapter 4.

3. Challenges. Challenges are problems that must be solved to improve the outreach or quality of school, family, and community partnerships. Some researchers, educators, and parents talk of "barriers" that prevent the involvement of some parents or community groups in children's education. However, every challenge that we identify has been solved by some educators, families, students, and community partners working together. Therefore, although every school will face challenges in designing and implementing activities for all types of involvement, the challenges can and must be met to sustain excellent partnership programs.

4. Results. The results of school, family, and community partnerships are complex because not every activity leads to all good things. Indeed, any activity to involve families or communities may be designed and conducted well or poorly and, thereby, may lead to positive or negative results. Moreover, there are two main patterns of effects. First, each type of involvement contributes to some unique results. For example, Type 5—Decision Making activities may increase parents' support for their children's schools, whereas Type 4—Learning at Home activities are likely to help students complete homework and gain skills in particular subject areas.

To complicate matters, some activities across types also may contribute to some of the same, targeted results. For example, activities for all six types of involvement may be designed to focus on improving students' reading skills. Educators, parents, and others must understand the potential and patterns of results of involvement to knowledgeably and purposely design or select activities that will help meet school improvement goals.

5. Resource notebook or idea file. The discussions and activities in Chapters 5, 6, and 7 focus on how to design and implement practical ideas to improve school, family, and community partnerships. Students who are preparing to be teachers or administrators may compile a resource notebook or computer file of ideas to use in practice teaching and in their work in schools or other professional leadership positions. Students who are preparing to conduct research may compile ideas and questions that need to be addressed or clarified in future studies.

▯▯ COMMENT

Why Six Types?

Over the years, a framework of six types of involvement grew from research, field studies with practicing educators and families, and emerging policies. The types of involvement—*parenting, communicating, volunteering, learning at home, deci-*

sion making, and *collaborating with the community*—were first identified in the elementary grades and became clearer with data from middle and high schools.

The types of involvement comprise activities conducted at school, at home, and in the community. Activities may be conducted by students, teachers, parents, administrators, and others to improve schools, strengthen families, and increase student success. This large and varied agenda could get lost if categories were too simple.

For example, if all involvement activities were labeled "at home" or "at school," important distinctions could not be made between assisting parents with parenting skills, which are used at home, by conducting workshops at school, and involving volunteers at home in ways that help the school. If categories were confounded, other distinctions would be lost. For example, some programs define parents as "supporters" or "learners," but these labels are confusing because families and educators are supporters and learners in all six types of involvement.

The framework of six types of involvement corrects the too simple and confounded labels. With this framework, it is possible to categorize all activities that involve families and community members; identify challenges; and link activities to short-term and long-term goals for students, parents, and the schools. There is general agreement about the usefulness of the framework, as it has been adopted by the National PTA (1998) and incorporated into the publications and training of the National Education Association (Dianda and McLaren, 1996) and American Federation of Teachers (1999). The framework has made it possible to move away from the task of "defining" involvement to the harder work of implementing comprehensive programs of school, family, and community partnerships.

The following comments and exercises will increase your understanding of the six types of involvement. I hope that familiarity will breed attempt! If you understand the framework and many ways to activate it in practice, you should be more likely to create and conduct comprehensive programs of school, family, and community partnerships. You may develop these programs with colleagues in the schools, districts, and state departments of education where you work as a professional educator, as an active parent, and as an involved member of the community.

Researchers, too, should be able to conduct studies that add information on and about the framework. New research on any or all of the six types of involvement should give educators and families more and better ideas about how to meet challenges to excellent partnerships, and improve information on the effects of different types of involvement on student achievement and other indicators of successful schools, students, and families. Details are needed on who benefits from specific partnership activities, how much, and at which grade levels. The summary charts in Reading 5.1 are extensive, but the entries are based on relatively few studies and fieldwork conducted over about 15 years—a short time in a new field of study. Many studies, using different methods, in diverse communities, and with students and families at all grade levels are needed to extend knowledge and strengthen all six types of involvement.

REFERENCES

American Federation of Teachers. (1999). *Parent and family involvement course, Educational Research and Dissemination Program*. Washington, DC: American Federation of Teachers.

Dianda, M., and A. McLaren. (1996). *Building partnerships for student learning*. Washington, DC: National Education Association.

National PTA. (1998). *National standards for parent/family involvement programs*. Chicago: National PTA.

◈ SUMMARY: TYPE 1—PARENTING ◈

Basic Responsibilities of Families

Type 1—Parenting activities help families fulfill their basic responsibilities of providing for children's nutrition, health, safety and protection, clothing, supervision, discipline, development of independence, and other attributes. Activities may include family support programs, parent education, workshops, and parent-to-parent connections that strengthen parents' understanding of child and adolescent development, parenting skills, and home conditions that support learning at each age and grade level. Type 1 activities also assist schools in understanding families' backgrounds, cultures, parenting styles, and goals for children.

Many schools address topics of parenting by conducting workshops for parents. One of the many Type 1 challenges is to get information from workshops to parents who cannot come to the school but want and need the information. Schools are meeting this challenge with old and new technologies to communicate information in written summaries, in video- and audiotapes, on computerized message systems, and with parent-to-parent networks. If Type 1—Parenting activities are well designed and well implemented, specific results can be expected. For example, student attendance and promptness should improve if parents are helped to understand the school's attendance policies, their responsibilities to get their children to school every day and on time, and the health and community services available to support student attendance.

Focus of Type 1 Activities

- Housing, health, nutrition, clothing, safety
- Parenting skills for all age levels
- Home conditions that support children as students at all grade levels
- Information and activities to help schools understand children and families

Challenges

- Provide information to all families who want it or who need it, not only to the few who attend workshops/meetings at the school building.

- Enable families to share information with schools about background, culture, talents, goals, and needs.

Redefinitions

- *Workshop* is not only a meeting on a topic held at the school building but also the content of that topic, which may be viewed, heard, or read at convenient times and varied locations.

Measurable Results for Students

- Balance of time spent on chores, other activities, and homework
- Regular attendance
- Awareness of family belief in the importance of school

Measurable Results for Parents

- Self-confidence about parenting as children proceed through school
- Knowledge of child and adolescent development

Measurable Results for Teachers and Schools

- Understanding of families' goals and concerns for children
- Respect for families' strengths and efforts

See Tables 5.1, 5.2, and 5.3 in Reading 5.1 for more on Type 1.

░ COMMENT

Understanding Type 1—Parenting

Parents have a continuous responsibility for raising their children, whereas most teachers have particular students for only one year, and most schools work with children for just a few years. To meet their children's needs, families say they want clear, understandable, ongoing information about child and adolescent development. Many families benefit from contacts with other parents about parenting skills, problems, and solutions at each age level. Others request or require professional, personal services for themselves and their children.

Just about all parents seek respect and appreciation from educators for their ongoing efforts at home to raise their children and for the support they provide to their children as students. Families want and need up-to-date information, conversations, and guidance to revise and adapt home activities and family discussions every year. With good information, many, most, or all parents would better understand their children and the expectations of teachers.

At the same time, teachers and administrators need information from families about their children and about family backgrounds, cultures, talents, goals, and expectations for students. Without such information, schools and teachers often operate on erroneous ideas about students and their families.

Most schools do not gather information from families about their children on a regular schedule. Most do not routinely give clear information to help all families remain knowledgeable partners in their children's education from year to year. It is not surprising, then, that many families feel unassisted and unappreciated by their children's schools. A good mix of Type 1 activities includes information *for* parents and *from* parents about children and families. This creates two main challenges that must be met for programs of partnership to effectively implement Type 1—Parenting.

Challenge Number 1: Provide Information to Families Who Cannot Always or Ever Come to Workshops at School

Many families cannot come to workshops on parenting, child and adolescent development, or other topics designed to help families understand their children. Most workshops, parent-to-parent meetings, and social activities with educators are attended only by a small number of the families served at a school. Even when a workshop is well attended, some families will not be there. An important challenge raised by Type 1 activities is: How shall schools get information to those who cannot come to the school building at a particular time?

The absentees are not bad parents. They may be busy with other children, work outside the home, live far from school, feel unwelcome or frightened by the school, or have other reasons for not attending a meeting at school on a particular day. The absentees may be just as caring, loving, and interested in their children as the parents who attend. Indeed, some absentees are parents who are teachers, administrators, or child care providers who are working with other people's children during the school day, and who cannot leave their schools to attend meetings at their own children's schools.

Challenge Number 2: Gather Information from Families to Help Schools Understand the Students and Their Families

In addition to increasing families' understanding of their children at each age and grade level, some Type 1 activities should increase educators' understanding of the students and their families, including their backgrounds, goals, strengths, and needs. As they become aware of and sensitive to the *strengths* of families, educators are better able to support all students and involve all families.

QUESTIONS TO DISCUSS

1. What information do you think families want and need every year from schools to understand child and adolescent development? List five items of information that you believe all families need to know every year from their children's schools.
2. What information do you think all schools want and need each year from families to understand the students and their families? List five items of information that you believe teachers, administrators, and/or counselors need to know every year from families.

 ACTIVITY

Linking Type 1 Challenges and Results

What results would you expect from Type 1—Parenting activities that were designed to meet the two challenges discussed above?

A. Select a grade level that interests you.
B. Copy the chart in Figure 5.1. Describe one Type 1—Parenting activity that you think would meet each of the listed challenges. You can use the list of ideas that you developed in the questions above or other ideas that you may have.
C. For each activity that you describe, give one short-term result that you would expect if the activity were well implemented.
D. Make clear whether the expected result will benefit students, parents, teachers, or others.
Which grade level did you select for this activity? _____

 FIELD EXPERIENCE

Parent Education Programs

Type 1 activities may be promoted through family support, parent education, and other programs that serve families. If these programs are well designed, responsive to families' needs, and well implemented, they should increase parents' confidence and the quality of their parenting.

Sample Challenges for Success with Type 1—Parenting	One activity that would meet this challenge	One short-term result the activity is likely to produce	Who will benefit?
Provide information *for* parents who cannot attend a workshop or meeting			
Obtain information *from* parents to help teachers understand their children and families			

FIGURE 5.1   Type 1 Challenges

A. Interview (or invite for a class interview) the director *and* a participant of a family support, family literacy, parent education, or other parenting program. Identify the interviewees and the program.
B. Discuss the goals of the program and how the impacts of the services, programs, or curricula are measured. Listen to the director's and participant's views. Prior to the interview, prepare at least five questions about the program on these topics:
   1. One question about the goals of the program and participants.
   2. One question about eligibility requirements or fees for services.
   3. One question about how the quality of the implementation of the program is measured.
   4. One question about the results of the program for participants and their families, and how results are monitored and measured.
   5. At least one more question that interests you about the program.
C. Document the questions and responses.
D. Summarize the similarities and/or differences in views of the director and participant.
E. Write two commendations on the program's successes and/or *two* recommendations for improving the program based on your interpretations of the interviewees' comments.

❏⋮ COMMENT

Looking Deeper into "Workshops"

Under the new definition of *workshop* stated above, the location, presenter, time, and technology of a workshop may vary:

Location: Workshops may be offered at the school building or at a location in the community. Some businesses or organizations host lunchtime or weekend workshops on school-related topics for their employees.

Presenter: Workshops may be offered by teachers, administrators, counselors, parents, other professionals, or members of the community. Some workshops for parents and teachers may be presented by students. Expertise is available in all communities on topics that are important to all families and students.

Time: Workshop information may be made available at various times, not just at one scheduled time, at the school or in the community, by using different forms of communication.

Technology: Workshops may be offered in traditional meetings and in other forms. Videotapes of workshops or commercially made videos on workshop topics may be viewed in the media center or parent room at school; borrowed to view at home; or made available at neighborhood libraries, businesses, family resource centers, health centers, or other locations. Audiotapes of workshops can be heard at school or community locations, borrowed for home use, or played on headsets or in automobiles. Workshop topics can be summarized in computerized phone messages, school or local newspapers, local cable TV or radio, on school or district web sites on the Internet, or in other forms. Follow-up discussions might include parent, educator, and student reactions, experiences, and suggestions. Print summaries of workshops may be available in the school's main office, family center, library, or other community locations.

Videos, audiotapes, printed summaries, or computerized files may be saved in school or public libraries, family resource centers, parent rooms, or other community locations, and may be accessed at any time. Different workshops may be scheduled each year to develop a "library" of important information for families on child development and other topics concerning education. The workshop products could then be shared among schools or districts.

Workshop topics should be thoughtfully selected with input from parents to meet their needs and interests in child and adolescent development. Each year, and across time, workshop topics should add up to something that helps parents understand their children and that helps schools understand families.

ACTIVITY

Workshop Topics

A. Select a grade level that interests you.

B. List one workshop topic about which educators have important information about children and schools that you think should be shared with parents at the grade level you selected.

C. Describe two ways in which the information could be shared with parents who were unable to attend the workshop.

D. Discuss one result that you would expect for
   - parents who attended the workshop
   - parents who received information in the ways you described in item C.

E. List one topic about which parents have important information about their children or families that you think should be shared with educators at the school.

F. Describe two ways to share the information you listed in item E. If the activity is conducted at school, include at least one idea of how families who cannot come to school might participate.

G. Discuss one result that you would expect from the activities you described in item F.

◇ ACTIVITY

Organize a Type 1—Parenting Activity

A. Select either item 1 or item 2 to organize a Type 1—Parenting activity.
   1. Workshop for parents:
      A. Select a grade level that interests you.
      B. List one topic that you believe parents want to know more about concerning their children's development at that grade level. You may use your ideas from the activity above or other ideas.
      C. Organize a "workshop" on the topic you selected. Use the new definition of *workshop* to ensure that all parents obtain good information on the topic you selected. Consider various locations, times, and technologies that would help convey information to all families. Write a complete plan outlining the content, facility, targeted audience, schedule, responsibilities for publicity, other organizational issues, and follow-up plans, if any.
   2. Family exchange and information for schools: In addition to workshops for parents, Type 1—Parenting activities help schools learn more about their students' families. For example, an annual Family Fair might help families share histories, talents, stories, customs, foods, crafts, and other specialties. Such activities could be photographed, collected in school albums, videotaped, and edited over time to establish a "family history" of the school that may be shared with each new class that enrolls.
      A. Select and identify a grade level that interests you.

B. Select one strategy that would encourage families to exchange important information with each other and with educators at the school.

C. Write a complete plan for organizing, conducting, and following up the activity you selected.

B. *Optional activity:* In class, critique the plans for the workshops and family exchange activities. Consider the importance of the topics, timing, technologies, strategies for providing information to non-attendees, and likely results. Save good ideas in your resource notebook or computer idea file.

◈ SUMMARY: TYPE 2—COMMUNICATING ◈

Basic Responsibilities of Schools

Type 2—Communicating activities help educators and families share information about school programs and student progress in varied, clear, and productive ways. Schools send information home in notes, newsletters, and report cards and share information in conferences and phone calls. Increasingly schools are using voice mail and web sites to communicate with families. Type 2 activities create two-way communication channels from school to home and from home to school so that families can easily communicate with teachers, administrators, counselors, and other families.

Most schools communicate in many ways with at least some parents about school programs and children's progress, but not all of the communications are understood by all families. One of the many Type 2 challenges is to use clear and understandable language in written and verbal exchanges to reach all families. Schools are meeting this challenge by translating written documents and providing interpreters for parents who speak different languages at meetings and conferences. Many schools are working to make their report cards and the criteria for grades clear to all students and parents. If Type 2 communications are well designed and well implemented, specific results can be expected. For example, if more families feel welcome and comfortable at parent-teacher-student conferences, they will be better able to follow up the conference with help for their children or with more questions for the teacher. If more parents understand criteria for report card grades, they may be better able to recognize and celebrate good work and progress at home and help their children maintain or improve their grades.

FOCUS OF TYPE 2 ACTIVITIES

School-to-Home Communications

- Memos, notices, report cards, conferences, newsletters, phone calls, computerized messages, web sites

- Information on school programs, tests, and children's progress
- Information needed to choose or change schools, courses, programs, activities

Home-to-School Communications

- Two-way channels of communication for questions, comments, and other interactions

Challenges

- Make all memos, notices, and other print and nonprint communications clear and understandable for *all* families.
- Obtain ideas from families to improve the design and content of communications such as newsletters, report cards, and conference schedules.

Redefinitions

- *Communications about school programs and student progress* are not only from school to home, but also from home to school, and with the community.

Measurable Results for Students

- Awareness of their own progress in subjects and skills
- Knowledge of actions needed to maintain or improve grades
- Awareness of their roles as courier and communicator in partnerships

Measurable Results for Parents

- Support for child's progress and responses to correct problems
- Ease of interactions and communications with school and teachers
- High rating of quality of the school

Measurable Results for Teachers and Schools

- Ability to communicate clearly with parents
- Use of a network of parents to communicate with all families

See Tables 5.1, 5.2, and 5.3 in Reading 5.1 for more on Type 2.

▯ COMMENT

Two-Way Communications between Home and School

One of the challenges for Type 2 activities is to establish easy-to-use, two-way communications between home and school about school programs and student progress. Teachers need to know when parents can be reached at home or at work and what numbers to call. Parents need to know when teachers, counselors, and principals can be reached at school or home and what numbers to call. Families may want to know how to connect with other helpful people such as the school nurse, social worker, officers of the parent organization, class parents, family center coordinator, and others. Some schools develop "telephone trees" or family directories each year for each grade level so that parents can easily contact each other.

Parents also need to be encouraged to ask questions and offer ideas that will help their children proceed successfully through the grades. Although this is a simple idea, many schools have not opened two-way communication channels so that information, questions, and conversations may flow easily from school to home and from home to school. This is a particular challenge when families speak many languages, have diverse reading skills, work different shifts or schedules, and have other circumstances that require thoughtful and responsive actions. Parents' requests for more and better information are indicators of family strengths, not weaknesses.

◈ FIELD EXPERIENCE

Interview about Type 2 Communications

A. Select a parent *or* educator (teacher, principal, or counselor) to discuss the two-way communications that he or she presently conducts and about needed improvements. Also identify the grade level of one school-aged child who links the home and school for the interviewee. Ask:
   1. What are two productive forms of school-to-home or home-to-school communications that you presently use?
   2. In your view, what two new or improved features would you add to your present practices or experiences to encourage two-way communi-

cations between parents and teachers or between parents and school administrators?

3. Some teachers give parents their home phone numbers. Others prefer not to do so. What are your feelings about this exchange of information?

B. Document the questions and responses.

C. What are two of the most difficult challenges to effective two-way communications that were identified in the interview? Explain why you think these challenges are formidable.

D. Share information in class to compare responses of educators and parents and how some have solved the challenges that others have not yet addressed.

⧉ COMMENT

The Role of Students in Type 2 Communications

Students are important for the success of *all* six types of involvement, including Type 2—Communicating. Communications from school to home and from home to school almost always involve students as couriers, commentators, observers, and targets of attention in both settings. From preschool through high school, students need guidance and recognition from teachers and administrators to effectively serve as home-school communicators and connectors.

Students and families need good information about the curriculum, tests and assessments, standards for success, report card marking systems, and other features and changes in school programs. Students and families should be involved in creating, reviewing, and improving all aspects of schooling that determine student success.

With good information and participation, families can assist educators in helping students adjust to new schools, new curricula, and other changes that affect their success in school. With good information and participation, students themselves can more successfully respond to changes that affect their work and progress.

QUESTIONS TO DISCUSS

1. What do families *and* students need to know about the following aspects of school programs, and what might families and students contribute to the success of these aspects of schooling?

	Families need to know	Students need to know	Families or students may contribute:
A. Curriculum, school subjects			

B. Tests and assessments

C. Report cards

D. Standards for students' work

E. Add one more topic: _____

2. A. Give two examples of how students might help conduct school-to-home or home-to school communications about school programs and student progress in learning and behavior.

B. Give two examples of how students might hinder school-to-home or home-to school communications about school programs and student progress in learning and behavior.

C. Give two examples of what teachers and/or parents could say or do to help students understand the importance of their roles in school-to-home-to-school communications.

▯⫶ COMMENT

Back-to-School Night

At the start of a school year, most elementary, middle, and high schools hold a Back-to-School Night or Open House to help families learn about school programs, meet their children's teachers, and hear about plans and requirements for specific subjects. These initial, annual gatherings are group meetings, not individual parent-teacher conferences. Some principals and teachers use the occasion to talk about their approaches to school, family, and community partnerships and to obtain information from parents about the families' goals for their children and their children's special talents.

◈ FIELD EXPERIENCE

Site Visit

The following activity may be completed alone, with a partner, or in cooperation with a teacher, administrator, or parent.

A. Visit a local school on Back-to-School Night. If that cannot be scheduled, interview a teacher, administrator, or parent who has attended a Back-to-School Night, or use your own experience. Indicate whether you made a visit, conducted an interview, or are relying on reflection.

B. Describe the type of school, location of the community, number of families attending the event, agenda and activities, and other observations or descriptions.

C. Evaluate the event for its strengths and weaknesses in welcoming parents; providing information about school programs and grade-level requirements; gathering information from parents; and establishing a climate for school, family, and community partnerships for the year.

◇ ACTIVITY

Letter Writing from School to Home

A. Identify a school level or grade level that interests you.
B. Write four letters that a teacher or administrator might send to families of students, including:
- an introductory letter to introduce yourself to all families at the start of the year, along with your ideas and plans for school, family, and community partnerships;
- a letter to set up a regular, individual conference with each parent at school or by phone at a time that is convenient for both of you;
- a "good-news" letter to share students' accomplishments with their families; and
- a letter to all families or to an individual family on another topic of your choice (e.g., a special conference to discuss an academic or behavior problem, a follow-up letter to report progress in solving a problem, or some other topic).

C. *Optional class activity:* In class, share the letters that were drafted. In small groups, pairs, or as a whole class, critique the letters for their form, vocabulary, readability for all families, awareness of family interests and needs, sensitivities to children's ages and grade levels, and other issues. Make changes to improve your letters. Collect examples as prototypes for future reference in your resource notebook or computer idea file.

◇ ACTIVITY

Newsletters

A. Collect one example of a school or classroom newsletter.
B. Identify the school level (preschool, elementary, middle, or high school) or grade level of the example.
C. Analyze the purpose(s) and content of the newsletter: Critique the format; readability; quality of information; participation of students, teachers, administrators, and parents; two-way communication strategies; and other qualities.

D. Give two suggestions of how you would improve the newsletter you reviewed.

E. Draw a diagram or layout to show what an excellent newsletter might look like for the school or grade level that you critiqued.

F. *Optional activity:* In class, share some of the sample newsletters and critiques.

◨ COMMENT

Contacts and Meetings with Parents— What Is Realistic?

Many educators say, "If we could just get the parents to the school, we would know they were involved." The fact is that most parents cannot come to school very often. Most work full-time or part-time during the school day. Others are too far from the school; have other family, faith, and neighborhood obligations; or have other reasons why it is not easy to come often to the school building.

Realistically, *how often each year* might a teacher or administrator contact every student's family individually? As a group? How might these contacts occur: in face-to-face meetings, in writing, by phone, or in other ways? What resources or support from the school or from the school district might be needed to encourage parents to come to school at certain times during the school year?

FOLLOWING ARE SOME WAYS IN WHICH INFORMATION MAY BE SHARED WITH *INDIVIDUAL* FAMILIES ABOUT THEIR OWN CHILDREN

- Parent-teacher conferences
- Parent-teacher-student conferences
- Student-parent interviews, conversations, or conferences at home
- Telephone conversations
- Informal meetings
- Notes, letters about individual students
- E-mail to individual parents or students
- Student report cards
- Weekly folders of students' work
- Interactive homework
- Add another example: _____

FOLLOWING ARE SOME WAYS IN WHICH INFORMATION MAY BE SHARED WITH *GROUPS* OF FAMILIES:

- Back-to-School Night or Open House
- School or class newsletters
- Grade-level meetings
- PTA or other parent organization meetings
- School and district policy statements
- School handbooks
- Web sites
- Add another example: _____

◈ ACTIVITY

Mapping Communications for a Year

A. Select and identify a grade level that interests you. For middle and high school grades, also select and identify a subject area. Estimate the number of students a teacher may teach at that grade level/subject.

B. Think of the time and resources needed for group meetings, individual parent-teacher conferences, home visits, phone calls, computerized messages, positive postcards, and the other communications listed above.

C. Create a calendar of the months and weeks of one school year (e.g., typically 180 days from September to June, or 36 full weeks, or in year-round schools, four 9-week sessions). If you wish, you may include vacation months. Outline a communication schedule that you believe is positive, realistic, and encourages two-way communication and problem-solving between a teacher and the families of students in the grade (and subject) you selected.

   1. Put an *I* next to the INDIVIDUAL communications with each student's family.
   2. Put a *G* next to GROUP communications that are the same for all families.
   3. Identify whether the communications would be conducted by the teacher-*T*, school administrators–*SA*, counselors-*C*, parents-*P*, students-*S*, or others-*O*.
   4. On your calendar, estimate the hours/minutes needed to plan, conduct, and complete the communications you listed.

D. *Optional activity:* Exchange and critique the calendars of communications in class. Are the activities realistic for teachers and for parents? Which activities ensure two-way channels of communication from school to home *and* from home to school? Discuss: Do the activities emphasize "bodies in the building," or is there a useful mix of communication strategies so that all parents are not asked always to come to the school building?

◈ FIELD EXPERIENCE

Parent-Teacher Conferences

Interview a teacher or parent about a parent-teacher conference in which he or she participated. Identify a few key characteristics of the interviewee and the grade level of the child who was the subject of the conference.

A. Ask the interviewee to think of one recent parent-teacher or parent-teacher-student conference and answer the following questions about that one conference:
1. What was the purpose of the conference? What was the content? How was it organized?
2. How would you describe the tone of the conference, feelings of the participants, and quality of the exchanges?
3. Was the student present?
   A. If YES, how did this affect the conference?
   B. If NO, how might that have affected the conference?
4. Give an example of whether (and how) you:
   A. Exchanged information about the student as a person, with interests, strengths, talents, concerns, and needs.
   B. Gained information about the student's progress on work in school in specific subjects, general knowledge, and social skills.
   C. Discussed important goals and strategies for reaching goals for progress in learning and success, including help needed to reach new goals.
   D. Celebrated the uniqueness and potential of the student as a part of the school, class, and community.
B. Add at least one question of your own about a parent-teacher conference, its schedule, content, follow-up, or other important topic.
C. Document your questions and responses.
D. Write a short critique of whether and why you think this was a good or poor conference.

◈ ACTIVITY

Role Play on Conferences and Meetings with Parents

A. With others in class, take the part of a parent, teacher, administrator, or student in one of the following school meetings:

1. Conference with a parent about a behavior problem
2. Conference with a parent about an academic problem
3. PTA meeting about a dress code or homework policy
4. Committee on the selection of textbooks
5. Meeting on special programs or services for children (e.g., library, guidance, summer school, after-school program, free breakfasts, student health issues, or a topic that you add)

B. List the topic, the roles, and the players.
C. The players should meet for at least 15 minutes to discuss the topic and plan a mock-interaction to perform for the class.
D. Conduct the interaction for the class. For each presentation, discuss:
1. What were the goals, fears, strengths, and needs of each participant?
2. If this were a real interaction of educators and family members, would all participants have felt that the exchange was positive and productive?
   A. If YES, explain why.
   B. If NO, explain what each participant might have done differently to produce a better result.

0⁞ COMMENT

Students in Conferences

One of the most common comments about parent involvement is that the best way to get parents to attend events at school is to have students involved. Student concerts, plays, sports activities, choruses, award assemblies, and, of course, graduation are just a few activities that parents attend happily. This common pattern alerts us to the need to consider when, why, and how students are included in school, family, and community partnerships. Increasingly, students are being given active roles in parent-teacher-student conferences.

A. Students may help prepare parents for parent-teacher conferences by:
   • describing and discussing the subjects they study;
   • drawing a map of the school to help parents find their teacher(s) and classroom(s);
   • providing a schedule of their classes, names of teachers, and room numbers; and
   • writing some questions for their parents to discuss with their teacher(s).
B. Students may participate in parent-teacher-student conferences by:
   • attending parent-teacher-student conferences; and
   • leading one part or all of the parent-teacher-student conferences.
C. Students may follow up conferences with needed actions by:

- discussing the results and recommendations of conferences they did not attend with their teachers and parents;
- setting goals and creating a work plan, as needed, to fulfill important recommendations; and
- following up at regular intervals to discuss with their teachers and parents how their work is continuing at high levels or improving.

To lead or conduct parent-teacher-student conferences, students need clear explanations and time with their teachers to prepare for the conference. Also, parents need to be prepared for the nontraditional format of a student-led conference. By conducting parent-teacher-student conferences, students demonstrate that they are the main actors in their education, and that they can plan and reflect on their work and progress.

QUESTIONS TO DISCUSS

1. A. Add one more example to list A (above) of how a student might prepare a parent for a parent-teacher conference.
   B. What are one benefit and one problem with any entry in list A?
2. A. Add one more example to list B (above) of how a student might actively participate in a parent-teacher-student conference.
   B. What are one benefit and one problem with any entry in list B?
3. A. Add one more example to list C (above) of how a student might follow up the results and recommendations of a parent-teacher conference.
   B. What are one benefit and one problem with any entry in list C?

◈ ACTIVITY

Inviting Parents to a Meeting at School

A. Select and identify a school level and grade level that interest you. Tell whether you will be thinking about this as a teacher or principal.
B. Select one of the following events that interests you: Back-to-School Night or parent-teacher-student conference.
C. Suppose you wanted *all* parents of your students to attend the event you selected.
   1. Describe one way that you would invite all parents to the event you selected.
   2. Some families in your class or school are difficult to reach and rarely come to such events. Select and identify one group of the following families who sometimes are hard to reach or reluctant to come to school events:

- Parents who disliked school when they were children
- Parents who do not speak English
- Parents who do not read English well
- Parents who work at night
- Parents who live at a distance
- Foster parents
- Noncustodial parents
- Other (please specify): _____

3. Describe two ways that you might try to reach the special group you selected to encourage them to attend the event.
4. Explain why you think your two communication strategies might work with the group you selected.

QUESTIONS TO DISCUSS

All students move through the grades and change schools at key points, such as from preschool to elementary, elementary to middle, and middle to high school. Even within schools with K–8, K–12, 7–12, or other broad grade spans, there are important within-school transitions from one school level to the next. How might students and their families be helped to make successful transitions from one school level to the next?

1. Select and identify one transition point in schooling that interests you.
2. If you were in the "feeder" school or grade, what is one piece of information about going to a new school that you would share with *all* students and families? How might you provide that information?
3. If you were the "receiving" school or grade, what is one piece of information about coming to a new school that you would share with *all* students and all families? How might you provide that information?
4. *Optional activity:* Critique the ideas in class and collect the most promising ones for a resource notebook.

◈ FIELD EXPERIENCE

Communicating with Families Who Are New to a School

What information is typically shared with families when they enroll their children in a new school, either because of a move to a new neighborhood or because of a change in school levels? Interview a principal, counselor, *or* teacher about his or her school's policies and practices of communicating with families who enroll children at or after the start of the school year. (Or invite all three for a class panel interview.)

A. Identify your interviewee's position and level of schooling. Ask:
   1. What formal connections are made with *all* families that are new to the school? What information is routinely provided to these families?
   2. What informal connections are made with *some* families that are new to the school?
   3. What is one improvement that you would make to better inform or assist families that are new to your school?
B. Add a question of your own.
C. Document your questions and responses. Summarize your opinion of how well new families are welcomed and included in this school.

 SUMMARY: TYPE 3—VOLUNTEERING

Involvement at and for the School

Type 3—Volunteering activities help educators and families work together to support the school program and children's work and activities. Type 3 activities include recruiting and training volunteers; arranging schedules, locations, and activities for volunteers; and recognizing parents who serve as audiences for students' events and performances as volunteers. Type 3 activities enable educators to work with regular and occasional volunteers who assist and support students in the school and in other locations. Type 3 activities enable parents and other family members to offer their time, talent, and ideas for productive activities for volunteers.

Many schools have at least a few volunteers, but often they are the same parents. One of the many Type 3 challenges to excellent volunteer programs is to recruit widely so that all families know they are valued as volunteers. Schools are meeting these challenges by enabling parents to volunteer their time and talent at convenient times in the evening, on weekends, and on vacation days. These decisions greatly increase the number of parents and others who can assist schools and students. If Type 3—Volunteering is well designed and well implemented, some or all students may gain or improve skills taught by or practiced with volunteer aides, lecturers, tutors, and mentors.

Focus of Type 3 Activities

- Volunteers *in* schools or classrooms—assist administrators, teachers, students, or parents as aides, tutors, coaches, lecturers, chaperones, and other leaders
- Volunteers *for* schools or classrooms—assist school programs and children's progress in any location and at any time

- Volunteers as members of audiences—attend assemblies, performances, sports events, recognition and award ceremonies, celebrations, and other events

Challenges

- Recruit widely, provide training, and create flexible schedules and locations for volunteers so that all families know that their time and talents are welcomed and valued.

Redefinitions

- *Volunteer* not only means those who come during the school day, but also those who support school goals and children's learning in any place and at anytime.

Measurable Results for Students

- Skills that are tutored or taught by volunteers
- Skills in communicating with adults

Measurable Results for Parents

- Understanding of the teacher's job
- Self-confidence about ability to work in school and with children
- Enrollment in programs to improve their own education and to prepare for jobs in education

Measurable Results for Teachers and Schools

- Readiness to involve all families in new ways, not only as volunteers
- More individual attention to students because of help from volunteers

See Tables 5.1, 5.2, and 5.3 in Reading 5.1 for more on Type 3. Also, see Chapter 6 for a special-challenge focus on Type 3.

QUESTIONS TO DISCUSS

1. The number of families who become volunteers at the school building may be increased if parents and other family members can volunteer to assist in

classrooms, in parent rooms, on the playground, in the lunchroom, and in other locations. Give one idea for how each of the following old ways of working with volunteers might be expanded or changed to enable more families to participate.

OLD way	NEW way
A. Volunteers must come to the school building.	
B. Volunteers must come during school hours.	
C. Volunteers must come during the school year.	
D. Volunteers must work with a specific teacher.	
E. Volunteers must have children in the school.	
F. Volunteers must not be involved in curriculum-related activities.	
G. Other idea: _____	

2. Suppose you notice, as the research shows, that working parents, single parents, or parents who live far from the school do not volunteer as much as other parents. What is one new approach to increase the number of each of the following groups of parents to volunteer in ways that help student learning and success?

One way to increase
participation as volunteers of:

A. working parents

B. single parents

C. parents who live far from the school

D. fathers

◇ ACTIVITY

Improving the Effectiveness of Volunteers

Not every task at school should be assigned to a volunteer. And not every volunteer is successful in what he or she is asked to do.

In Figure 5.2, give one idea of how a principal, teacher, or coordinator of volunteers might identify the problems shown and one idea of how to solve the problems should they occur.

QUESTIONS TO DISCUSS

Some parents cannot or do not volunteer at school. Many parents work full-time or part-time during the school day, when most volunteer activities are scheduled.

Potential Type 3 Problem	How to Identify Problem	Possible Solution
A. Ineffective volunteers who want to help but do not do well		
B. Underachieving volunteers whose talents are not well used		
C. Unsavory characters who should not be in school or working with children		
D. Add one other possible problem:		
_____ _____ _____		

FIGURE 5.2   Type 3 Problems

Those who work at night and those who are not employed still may not be able to volunteer during the school day. What if you redefined *volunteer,* as suggested above, to mean *any one who supports school goals and children's learning in any place and at any time.*

1. How would this definition enable more parents to become volunteers?
2. How would this definition assist a school, a teacher's classroom, families, and the community?
3. What is one problem with the new definition? What is one way to resolve that problem?
4. How far would you extend the new definition? Answer the following questions and explain your reasons:
   A. Should we consider parents and family members "volunteers" when they attend sports activities, drama productions, concerts, and other performances and assemblies? Why or why not?
   B. Should we consider parents "volunteers" when they come to school for parent-teacher conferences, for meetings on the Individual Education Plans (IEPs) for students with special needs, to readmit children who have been suspended, or for other required meetings? Why or why not?

COMMENT

Matching Volunteers' Talents and School Needs

One way that some schools begin to think about expanding Type 3—Volunteering, is to ask teachers, administrators, and school staff for a "wish list" of how volunteers' time and talents might be helpful. The activities on a wish list might be conducted by volunteers at school, in classrooms, on the way to and from school, in the community, or at home. The activities may be frequent and periodic, or occasional.

Another way that some schools begin to think about volunteers is to create a "talent pool" by asking parents, other family members, and even members of the community to indicate how they might like to help the school and students; what their talents, time, range of interests, or willingness to help are, and what a good location for their assistance would be.

 FIELD EXPERIENCE

Wish Lists or Talent Pools for Volunteers

A. Select one of the approaches above—a school's wish list or a parent talent pool—that interests you.
B. Design a tool that would help a school gather the information you selected. Try to make the form you design short, clear, and to the point, as well as easy to categorize and tally.
C. *Optional activity:* Invite a cooperating principal or teacher to work with your class.
   1. Ask a teacher, administrator, or counselor to critique one or more forms for collecting information about volunteers and give feedback on whether the forms are clear enough for teachers or parents.
   2. Ask the cooperating educator to share with you any similar approaches that are used as a wish list to identify needed volunteers or for creating a volunteer talent pool.
   3. If possible, ask the cooperating educator to use one or more of the forms you created to see if it produces useful information for the school about family volunteers.

◇ ACTIVITY

Creating Strong Volunteer Programs

Suppose you were working with a preschool, elementary, middle, or high school that wanted to organize and implement a useful volunteer program.

A. Identify the level of schooling that interests you (e.g., preschool, elementary, middle, or high school).

B. Identify whether you are thinking about the needs of the whole school or the needs of one teacher in a specific grade level or subject.

C. Include the following components in your plan for a successful volunteer program. List one example of how you will address each component.
- Recruit volunteers
- Match talents of volunteers with needs of teachers, students, others
- Train volunteers
- Schedule work for volunteers
- Evaluate volunteers
- Continue the program from year to year

D. Share the plans for organizing volunteers in class. For each idea, discuss:
1. Is the design feasible?
2. Would the proposed program reach out to all parents and other family and community members who would not typically become volunteers on their own?
3. Will the recruitment, training, and assignments of volunteers be easy to maintain from year to year?

Collect promising ideas for a resource notebook or computer idea file.

See Chapter 6 for a special-challenge focus on Type 3—Volunteering and additional questions and activities on volunteers.

 SUMMARY: TYPE 4—LEARNING AT HOME

Involvement in Academic Activities

Type 4—Learning at Home activities involve families with their children in homework, goal setting, and other curriculum-related activities and decisions. Information on homework policies, course choices, prerequisites, goal setting, and other academic decisions could help parents influence students' choices and learning in many different ways. Some schools encourage teachers to design homework that enables students to share and discuss interesting work and ideas with family members. These activities create two-way connections between home and school about the curriculum and academic learning.

Students in all schools learn many different subjects, but most parents are unaware of all that their children are learning or how to interact with their children on curricular matters. Most parents are uninvolved in important academic decisions that affect their children's and the family's future. One of many Type 4 challenges is for teachers to effectively and realistically assign students homework and guide parents in how to interact with students about their work at home. Schools are meeting this challenge with varied designs for interactive homework that enable students to conduct conversations with parents and demonstrate what they are learning in class. If Type 4—Learning at Home activities are well designed and well implemented, more students should complete their homework and improve the quality of their work, and more parents will be well informed about what students are learning in class. With family encouragement and input, students will be more actively involved in setting goals for success in school and in planning post-secondary educational pathways.

Focus of Type 4 Activities

- How to help at home with homework
- Skills required to pass each subject
- Curriculum-related decisions
- Students' goal setting for success in school and post-secondary planning
- Other skills and talents

Challenges

- Design and implement interactive homework in which students take responsibility to discuss important classwork and ideas with their families.
- Sequence information and activities that help students and families set ambitious goals and strategies for improving or maintaining success in school every year, and for post-secondary education, training, and work.

Redefinitions

- *Homework* not only means work that students do alone but also interactive activities that students share and discuss with others at home.
- *Help* at home means how families encourage and guide children, not how they "teach" school subjects.

Measurable Results for Students

- Skills, abilities, and test scores linked to classwork; homework completion
- Self-confidence in ability as learner; positive attitudes about school
- Viewing parent as more similar to teacher and home as in sync with school

Measurable Results for Parents

- Discussions with child about school, classwork, homework, future plans
- Understanding curriculum, what child is learning, and how to help at home

Measurable Results for Teachers and Schools

- Respect for family time; satisfaction with family involvement and support
- Recognition that single parents, dual-income families, economically disadvantaged families, and families that do not speak English can encourage and assist student learning

See Tables 5.1, 5.2, and 5.3 in Reading 5.1 for more on Type 4. Also, see Chapter 6 for a special-challenge focus on Type 4.

▯⋮ COMMENT

Understanding How Families Link to Homework

Many studies show that there are serious problems with the design, assignment, completion, and follow-up of homework in many elementary, middle, and high schools. School policies, teachers' designs of homework, student investments, and family activities *all* may need to be improved for students to benefit from their homework assignments.

Scott-Jones (1995a and 1995b) discusses four levels of involvement of parents and children in homework: valuing, monitoring, assisting, and doing. Families need good information each year to convey to their children that they value homework as an important task, they will monitor the completion of homework, and they want to assist students as best they can with their work. Everyone agrees that parents should *not* do their children's homework, and that homework is the students' responsibility. For example, the Teachers Involve Parents in Schoolwork (TIPS) interactive homework process (see Chapter 6) is designed to expedite the first three levels of valuing, monitoring, and assisting homework and to prevent the fourth, with directions to students to conduct the interactions with their families.[1]

---

[1] See S. J. Balli, The effects of differential prompts on family involvement with middle-grades homework (Ph.D. diss., University of Missouri, Columbia, 1995); S. J. Balli, When mom and dad help: Student reflections on parent involvement with homework, *Journal of Research and Development in Education* 31(3) (1998): 142–146.

See Chapter 3's readings and activities on homework.

REFERENCES

Scott-Jones, D. (1995a). Activities in the home that support school learning in the middle grades. Pages 161–181 in *Creating family/school partnerships,* edited by B. Rutherford. Columbus, OH: National Middle School Association.

———. (1995b). Parent-child interactions and school achievement. Pages 75–107 in *The family-school connection: Theory, research, and practice,* edited by B. A. Ryan, G. R. Adams, T. P. Gullota, R. P. Weissbert, and R. L. Hampton. Thousand Oaks, CA: Sage.

QUESTIONS TO DISCUSS

How does family valuing, monitoring, and assisting or interacting on homework change across the grades?

1. Select in ascending order three grade levels that interest you.
2. For each grade level, list one example of what you think parents might say or do to show their children that they (a) value homework, (b) monitor homework, and (c) will assist or interact with them on homework. What might parents say or do to show children that they:

Three Grade Levels:	(a) Value Homework	(b) Monitor Homework	(c) Assist or Interact with Homework
Grade __			
Grade __			
Grade __			

3. How do the messages you listed differ or remain the same across the grade levels you selected? Explain.
4. Select one grade level from your chart. How might a teacher help all parents to convey the messages you listed on how they value, monitor, and assist with student homework?

⊞ COMMENT

Homework Policies and Procedures

Parents help their children with homework, based on their own knowledge about school and school subjects. Most parents report that they need information every year to help their children do their best on homework. Over 70 percent of parents surveyed in elementary, middle, and high schools want to know: What is the school's homework policy? Over 90 percent want to know: How do I help my child at home this year? (See Chapter 3 for surveys of parents.)

QUESTIONS TO DISCUSS

1. How are parents affected if teachers DO or DO NOT provide the following information? List one result for parents that you would expect

	if teachers *do* provide information on . . .	if teachers *do not* provide information on . . .
A. homework policies each year		
B. requirements for passing each subject		
C. how to monitor students' homework		
D. how students can share something that they learned in class in interactive homework		
E. how to make choices of academic courses in math, science, foreign language, and electives in high school		

2. Select one result from your chart that you believe is particularly compelling. Describe one activity that might help teachers provide the information to all parents and that would produce the result that you expect.
3. Select one result from the chart that you believe is particularly troublesome. Describe one problem that could arise and an activity that would help solve that problem.

▯⦂ COMMENT

Innovative Designs for Interactive Homework

One way to redefine family involvement in homework or academic decisions is to place the *student* in charge of the interactions. This strategy acknowledges that parents are not and should not be expected to *teach* school subjects to their children every year. Rather, students are expected to share with families interesting things they are learning in class, or important decisions that must be made about academic courses, programs, or other opportunities. In addition to the special focus on Teachers Involve Parents in Schoolwork (TIPS) in Chapter 6, there are many ways to help families monitor their children's work and interact with them about ideas and academic decisions. The following comments and activities introduce a few interactive strategies for increasing conversations at home about students' skills in different subjects.

QUESTIONS TO DISCUSS

You often hear people say that students should do their homework on their own in a quiet place. Indeed, some homework should be completed independently to help students learn how to study on their own. But other homework should be interactive to enable students to share their work and to keep families informed about what their children are learning in school. Thus, homework may be either independent or interactive.

List in the chart below three purposes of independent and three purposes of interactive homework. What might each kind of homework accomplish for students and for families? What does each kind of homework accomplish?

Independent homework?	Interactive homework?
1. _____	1. _____
2. _____	2. _____
3. _____	3. _____

░ COMMENT

Student-Parent "Home Conference"

Ross Burkhardt, a talented middle-grade educator, taught children at Shoreham–Wading River Middle School, Long Island, New York, for many years. He designed a home conference on writing that students conduct at home. Students made formal appointments with a parent or family member to discuss their writing. Students provided their parents with a folder containing selected pieces of their writing or arranged to read the work aloud to their parents. Then, students conducted a structured interview that the class developed to gather parents' reactions to their work. Finally, students summarized their parents' reactions and wrote their own reactions to their parents' comments. They listed plans for improving or maintaining the quality of their writing.

This interaction enables each student to share writing samples with a parent; gather reactions, ideas, and suggestions from a parent; and write a reflective response to what he or she learned from the interactions. A student-parent home conference could be scheduled in any subject as an interactive homework assignment once or twice a year to keep families aware of students' work and to encourage curriculum-related conversations.

◇ ACTIVITY AND FIELD EXPERIENCE

Student-Parent "Home Conference"

A. Select a subject other than writing and a grade level that interest you.

B. Design a student-parent home conference for the subject and grade level that you selected. Include guidelines for students to:
- arrange an appointment with a parent;
- obtain a parent's reactions to the work;
- record the parent's reactions; and
- write their own reflections.

C. Add *one* more component that you believe should be part of a home conference in the subject and grade level you selected.

D. *Optional activity:*
1. Identify a cooperative teacher. Ask the teacher for feedback on the guidelines that you wrote for a home conference in item B above. Arrange for one class to conduct the student-parent home conference that you developed, or work with the teacher to design a set of guidelines for a home conference in writing or another subject. This will require the cooperating teacher to (a) use some class time to develop with students or explain the elements of a structured interview that all students will conduct with their parents; (b) develop with students or explain a recording form for students to report the parents' and their own reactions; (c) have students select a few pieces of their work in the selected subject for the home-conference folder; (d) assign the home conference as homework to the students and conduct the follow-up activity.
2. Collect and summarize the students' reactions to their parents' reviews. Write a paragraph to explain your views on whether or not the activity succeeded in increasing student-parent communications, parents' awareness of student work, and students' understanding of their own skills and goals.

⫶ COMMENT

"Home-Made Homework"
Designed by Students and Families

Another way to vary homework assignments is to periodically ask children and parents to design a family-related homework activity for the student to conduct. For example, students *or* parents may design activities for homework such as writing a story, poem, or speech; creating artwork; taking a photograph; planning a budget and activities for a special trip; making a list to complete an important family project; or other tasks that help students practice and demonstrate real-world applications of writing, speaking, math, science, social studies, and other school skills. The student and a parent or family member might create or select one assignment each month, such as:

- Write a letter to a grandparent, other relative, or family friend.
- Learn to play or sing a new song, practice it at home, and perform it in class on a traditional or created instrument.

- Write a critical summary or review of a movie, drama production, piece of music, restaurant, neighborhood location, or other family experience.
- Draw or paint a poster of a family holiday or celebration.
- Compose a speech on a topic of importance to the student or family.
- Describe an activity that the student conducted at home or in the community to help someone.
- Write a description or draw a portrait of a favorite relative or interesting person in the neighborhood.
- Write a story of something interesting that happened while conducting an ordinary activity at home (e.g., what happened when babysitting, lawn cutting, fixing a door, washing clothes, making dinner).
- Critique an interesting web site on a topic or hobby of interest to the student.
- Add one idea of your own of an activity a parent and child might choose or design for the child's homework.

◇ ACTIVITY AND FIELD EXPERIENCE

"Home-Made Homework"

Student- or family-designed homework assignments may be linked to different school subjects each month or on some other regular schedule.

A. Select a grade level of your choice.
B. Create a plan from October to May that would guide students and families to design or select a "home-made homework" assignment for the student to conduct. In elementary grades, vary the plan for different subjects or skills each month. In middle or high school grades, vary the plan for different skills or topics for the subject you selected.
C. *Optional activity:*
   1. Identify a cooperative teacher at the grade level you selected. Ask the teacher for feedback on your plan and an opportunity to test one of the activities with a class.
   2. Collect the assignment and review in writing the results of the home-made assignments.

⬙ COMMENT

Schoolwide Interactive Homework

A school may select a key theme or topic once a month or once a marking period and assign the same homework to everyone in a particular grade or to everyone in the school. This kind of assignment directs younger and older students to think about an issue or idea that is important to the school (What should a new playground for the school or community look like? How can we get more books for the library? How can we help our community or local senior citizens' center?). Alternatively, the assignment may help all students focus on a topic important for personal development (How can students be kind to each other? What does it mean to "study" for a test? What issues are important to me in the next election?). The assignment may focus all students on a matter of history or current events (What does this school think of the upcoming local or national election? How do we understand freedom and democracy?). Schoolwide or grade-level-wide homework assignments could be purposely interactive with sections for students to engage their families, friends, or members of the community, as in TIPS activities (see Chapter 6).

⬦ ACTIVITY AND FIELD EXPERIENCE

Schoolwide Homework

A. Schoolwide homework assignments may address different issues once a month, once a marking period, twice a year, or on some regular schedule.
B. Select a school level that interests you (i.e., preschool, elementary, middle, or high school).
C. Select a topic that you think is important for all students at all grade levels in the school to think and talk about.
D. Create a design for schoolwide interactive homework on the topic you selected. Outline how this work might be assigned to all students, noting (a) if adaptations are needed for younger and older students; (b) what the students will be asked to do; and (c) how they will be guided to conduct interactions with a family member, friend, or member of the community.
E. *Optional activity:* Identify a cooperative school.
   1. Ask the principal, master teacher, or department chairperson for reactions to your design for schoolwide homework.
   2. If possible, test the idea schoolwide or with more than one collaborating teacher.
   3. Collect the assignments and write a short critique of whether and how a common assignment worked with students in different grades or classes.

◈ SPECIAL-FOCUS FIELD EXPERIENCE

Homework Assignments in Practice Teaching

A. Select a subject that you are observing or assisting with as a practice teacher.
B. Identify the subject, grade level(s) of the students, and dates of at least two observations.

C. Summarize the main content of the classroom lessons, skills taught, and homework assigned on the dates of your observations.

D. For each observation, discuss whether you think the homework assigned was well designed or poorly designed for the students in the class. If the homework or some elements were well designed, explain why. If the homework or some elements were poorly designed, explain why, and design and explain one improvement.

E. Discuss your observations with your cooperating teacher and/or your practice teaching supervisor. Discuss the difficulties or ease with which homework is designed, assigned, and completed by students.

See Chapter 6 for a special-challenge focus on Type 4—Learning at Home, and additional questions and activities on interactive homework.

0⋮ COMMENT

Student Goal Setting

Another aspect of Type 4—Learning at Home focuses on parental involvement in discussions with students about goals and strategies for success in school. Every student should be guided to set goals for the school year and for the future. Some teachers outline goals for students, but it is more meaningful for students—the main actors in learning—to set at least some of their own goals and strategies to reach their goals. Often, parents are unaware that their children are setting academic and behavioral goals or how to help them reach their goals each year in school.

One high school devised an interesting way of bringing families into student goal-setting activities. First, during an English class, all students set goals for attendance, report card grades in all subjects, and a personal goal for increasing their skills and self-confidence. Second, at home, students shared their goals with a family partner and discussed various strategies for reaching their goals. Then, during another class in school, students reflected on their discussions with their families and their own ideas and wrote their final goals and strategies for the school year. The goals and strategies were kept in folders in their English classes. At the end of each marking period, students conducted another interactive homework assignment with a family partner to review and discuss their progress toward their goals and to make revisions in their goals and strategies for the next marking period.

◇ ACTIVITY

Helping Students Discuss Goals for Success at Home

A. Select a grade level that interests you. At the middle and high school levels, also select a school subject that interests you.

B. Using the description of a goal-setting strategy in the comment above, design the directions and forms that a teacher in the grade level/subject selected might use at the start of the school year to:
- guide students in school to set four important goals for success in school: attendance, achievement (in at least two subjects), homework completion, *and* behavior or one other important goal for the year;
- have students in school identify strategies that they will use to reach their goals;
- enable students to conduct an interactive homework assignment as a structured interview with a family partner at home to discuss their goals, strategies to reach their goals, and how parents or other family members may help the students with their goals and strategies; and
- guide students in school to write their final goals and strategies to reach their goals, after reflecting on their discussion with a family partner.

C. Share designs for goal-setting activities with a partner in class. Check whether the directions and processes are clear, well timed for students and families, and appropriate for the grade levels and subjects selected.

◈ SUMMARY: TYPE 5—DECISION MAKING ◈

Participation and Leadership

Type 5—Decision Making activities include families as participants in school decisions, governance, and advocacy activities through school councils or improvement teams, committees, PTA/PTO, and other school-based or independent parent organizations. Type 5 activities prepare parents for leadership roles and assist parent representatives to obtain information from and give information to the families that they represent.

Increasingly, schools are recognizing the importance of parent representatives on school councils, site-based management teams, committees, and other policy-advisory groups. One of the many Type 5 challenges is for parent representatives to reflect the diverse populations and neighborhoods served by the school. It also is important for parent representatives to communicate well with other parents to obtain input on school decisions and to report the results of school meetings. Schools are meeting this challenge by creating leadership positions for neighborhood representatives to reach out to traditionally underrepresented groups and ensure that all families have a voice in policy decisions. If Type 5—Decision Making activities are well designed and well implemented, more families should feel a strong attachment to their school. They may work for more effective state and district policies and funding to benefit their school and all students. Also, educators learn that parents' views improve and extend discussions that lead to more inclusive and responsive decisions.

Focus of Type 5 Activities

- PTA/PTO membership, participation, leadership, representation
- Advisory councils, school improvement teams, ATPs
- Title I councils, school-site management teams, other committees
- Independent school advisory groups

Challenges

- Include parent leaders from all racial, ethnic, socioeconomic, and other groups in the school.
- Offer training for parent representatives to develop leadership skills.
- Include student representatives along with parents in decision making.

Redefinitions

- *Decision making* means a process of partnership to share views and take action toward shared goals, not a power struggle.

Measurable Results for Students

- Awareness that families are represented in school decisions
- Specific benefits linked to policies enacted by parent organizations

Measurable Results for Parents

- Awareness of and input on policies that affect children's education
- Shared experiences and connections with other families

Measurable Results for Teachers and Schools

- Awareness of families' perspectives on policies and school decisions
- Acceptance of family representatives as equals on school committees

See Tables 5.1, 5.2, and 5.3 in Reading 5.1 for more on Type 5.

Type 5—Decision Making Partnerships, Not Power Splits

Type 5—Decision Making activities recognize and increase parents' abilities to express their opinions and contribute to school plans and policies. In Type 5 activities, parent representatives take leadership roles along with educators. Parent leaders help other parents understand and contribute ideas to issues and policies that affect the design and quality of school programs and opportunities for all children. Because parents and teachers share an interest in and responsibility for children's learning and development, parents' voices and ideas add important dimensions to school decisions about children's education.

To successfully implement Type 5—Decision Making, it is necessary for schools to address several challenges. One is to help parent leaders serve as true representatives of other families. This includes helping leaders obtain ideas from and return information to the families they represent about school decisions, programs, and activities.

In many schools, parents' opinions about school policies are not taken seriously. Some schools have no parent organization (e.g., PTA, PTO, PTSA). Some have no school council, site-management team, or committee structure that includes family representatives. Even when such groups include parents, only a few parents participate actively. When they do participate, few parent representatives collect information from other families or share the results of school meetings and decisions with other parents. Consequently, in most schools, only a few parents know what topics, issues, and decisions are discussed or enacted. Typically, only a few voices are heard from parent leaders who may or may not represent the views of other parents. These patterns and problems of selective participation are even more evident on district-level councils and committees.

Interestingly, most families do *not* want to serve on committees or in leadership roles, but most *do* want parents' voices represented in school decisions. In a study of high schools, for example, we found that only approximately 8 percent of parents wanted to serve on committees, but just about all others wanted parent representatives on councils and committees to have a say in school decisions.

For parent leaders to represent all parents on major committees, it is necessary to develop Type 5—Decision Making skills and strategies. For example:

- Parent leaders must be numerous, and be selected or elected in ways that give the parents of all groups of students (from different neighborhoods, racial and ethnic groups, special interests) representative voices in school decisions.
- Parent leaders must be assisted to effectively represent other parents by gathering their ideas on important issues and by reporting back to the families they represent. Because not every parent attends committee meetings, communication with parent leaders is evidence of all parents' participation.

- Similarly, administrators, teachers, students, or others from the community who serve on decision-making teams also must gather and give information to those they represent.
- New leaders must be continually prepared to serve as representatives and active participants in all schools. Processes must be organized and ongoing for selecting representatives and conducting decision-making activities because parent leaders move to other schools and to other neighborhoods as their children progress through the grades.

In comprehensive programs of school, family, and community partnerships, there must be adequate and effective representation of all parents' ideas by parent leaders.

QUESTIONS TO DISCUSS

Should parents' views be represented in *all* school decisions, or are there some decisions that should be made only by teachers and administrators?

1. Identify a level of schooling that interests you.
2. Divide a page in half.
   A. On one side, list arguments that support a response of YES to the above question for the level of schooling that you selected. Give at least two reasons why parents' views should be represented in all school decisions.
   B. On the other side, list arguments that support a response of NO to the above question for the level of schooling that you selected. Give at least two reasons why parents' views should not be represented in all school decisions, and give at least two examples of decisions that should be made only by teachers or administrators.
3. Share your ideas in a class discussion or debate.
4. After hearing others' ideas and considering your own arguments, write a policy statement about family representation in school decisions that you believe would work in a school or district. Discuss whether the policy statement would be feasible to implement.

See also Chapter 4 for a study, discussions, and other activities on parents' involvement in evaluating the quality of teachers.

◆ FIELD EXPERIENCE

Parent Participation in School Decisions

A. Interview a state, district, or school administrator *or* a teacher for ideas about how families *should be* and *could be* involved in school decisions and on policy-related committees. (This may be conducted as an individual assignment or class panel interview with one or more educators. One or two parents may be added to a class panel.)

B. Identify the policy level you selected and the job title of your interviewee. Ask:

1. Approximately how many students are served in your state/district/school?

2. In your work, which organizations, committees, or other formal policy-making groups presently include parent representatives?

3. If ANY, ask:

    A. This year, about how many parents serve on these decision-making or advisory bodies?

    B. What contributions do you think parents make to these groups?

    C. What leadership training is provided to parent leaders and to others on these committees?

4. If NONE, ask:

    A. What committees, task forces, or other groups or organizations do you think would benefit from parent representatives?

    B. What contributions do you think parents would make to these groups?

    C. What leadership training would be needed to prepare parent leaders and others on these committees?

C. What is *one* unusually successful example of family participation in school decisions that you have experienced or heard about?

D. What is *one* problem that you have experienced or heard about concerning family involvement in school decisions? What is *one* possible solution to this problem?

E. Add at least *one* question of your own about parent or community representation.

F. Document your questions and responses. From the information in this chapter and the answers from your interview:

1. Summarize your assessment of the quality of participation of families in Type 5—Decision Making in the state/district/school in your interview.

2. Include one recommendation that you would make to improve the quality of parent participation in Type 5—Decision Making in the program you discussed.

QUESTIONS TO DISCUSS

1. Suppose that your school or district served five different neighborhoods of white, African American, Latino, Asian American, and American Indian families, respectively. Your school has a PTA, a school improvement team, and an Action team for Partnerships (ATP). Your district has a parent advisory committee, a community development committee, and a business outreach committee. Right now, just about all of the parent representatives on these six school and district committees are from one of the five neighborhoods. Is this a problem that needs a solution?
   A. If YES, explain why, and provide one solution to the problem you defined.
   B. If NO, explain why this is not a problem.

2. Mr. Jones has been PTA president for nine years. His children have graduated from school, but he is still serving as PTA president of their prior elementary school. Is this a problem that needs a solution?
   A. If YES, explain why, and provide one solution to the problem you defined.
   B. If NO, explain why this is not a problem.

3. The monthly PTA meetings are poorly attended. Only the officers and a few regulars attend these meetings. Minutes are taken, but they are not distributed. Is this a problem that needs a solution?
   A. If YES, explain why, and provide one solution to the problem you defined.
   B. If NO, explain why this is not a problem.

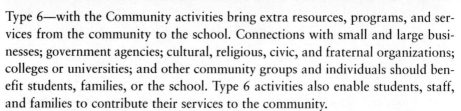

◆ SUMMARY: TYPE 6—COLLABORATING ◆ WITH THE COMMUNITY

Type 6—with the Community activities bring extra resources, programs, and services from the community to the school. Connections with small and large businesses; government agencies; cultural, religious, civic, and fraternal organizations; colleges or universities; and other community groups and individuals should benefit students, families, or the school. Type 6 activities also enable students, staff, and families to contribute their services to the community.

All schools are located in communities, but many schools are strangely isolated from their community businesses, agencies, senior citizens, cultural centers, and other potentially helpful groups and individuals. Students often live in one community, travel to the school community, attend religious services in another community, have after-school care somewhere else, and link to businesses in still other locations. Schools rarely tap the full set of resources from all communities that have ties to and interest in students. One primary Type 6 challenge is to identify the resources in the community that will advance school improvement goals, enrich school programs, and meet the needs of students and families. If Type 6 activities are well designed and well implemented, students and families will learn about and use the various community services and programs to improve health, increase skills, and develop the talents of all family members. Schools will enrich their curriculum and instruction and improve the school climate by collaborating with the community.

Focus of Type 6 Activities

- Community contributes to schools, students, and families
- Business partners, agencies, cultural groups, health services, recreation, and many other groups strengthen programs and classroom curricula
- Schools, students, and families contribute to community
- Service learning, encourage special projects to share talents, solve local problems

Challenges

- Solve problems of turf, responsibilities, funds, and goals to effectively organize school-community collaborations.
- Inform all families and students about community programs and services; ensure equal access and opportunities for participation.

Redefinitions

- *Community* includes not only families with children in the schools but also all who are interested in and affected by the quality of education.
- Communities are rated not only on economic qualities but also on the strengths and talents available to support students, families, and schools.

Measurable Results for Students

- Knowledge, skills, and talents from enriched curricular and extracurricular experiences, and from exploring careers in the community
- Self-confidence, feeling valued by and belonging to the community

Measurable Results for Parents

- Knowledge and use of local resources to improve health, increase skills, develop talents, and obtain needed services for family

- Interactions with other families and contributions to community

Measurable Results for Teachers and Schools

- Knowledge and use of community resources for curriculum and instruction

See Tables 5.1, 5.2, and 5.3 in Reading 5.1 for more on Type 6.

⬛ COMMENT

Getting to Know the "Community"

It is not easy for educators to know all the resources in their communities. Few teachers or principals live near their schools, as previously was the case. There are several reasons, however, why it may benefit students if educators and parents conduct Type 6 activities to learn more about their communities and to draw on available resources to help students succeed in school and in life.

One Type 6 challenge is to identify and mobilize community support of school goals for student learning. In some schools, contributions by business partners of equipment or volunteer time are unconnected to the goals of the school or to student learning. Ties with businesses and industries, organizations, agencies, and other groups and individuals in the community should be designed to support, enrich, and extend the school's agenda to promote success for more students (Mickelson, 1996; Sanders, 1999).

For example, one school's business partner (the local office of a national telephone company) placed phones in all teachers' classrooms, making it possible for teachers to communicate more easily with parents. Other business partners have funded small grants to schools to develop better school, family, and community partnerships on all types of involvement. Some community partners organize food banks with low-income families' assistance and participation, clothing for parents to attend school functions, eyeglasses for students, books for students or school libraries, Internet connections to scientists, mentors, job-shadowing programs for high school students, and other goal-oriented activities that are linked to student and family needs or interests and to school improvement plans. In this way, Type 6—Collaborating with the Community comes full circle to link with Type 1—Parenting to help families fulfill basic obligations to care for and guide their children.

A second challenge is for schools to view the term *community* broadly to build connections with many members and groups who have an interest in developing successful students and good citizens. These include the businesses, organizations, and other groups and individuals in and around the school, in neighborhoods where students live, in faith communities where students worship, in locations where parents work, and in other places that are important to students, families, and the school.

The "school community" includes all family and community members who care what happens to the school and to children, whether or not they have children in the school. Because children are the future citizens, workers, and families in communities, it is important to foster positive and productive connections with all who have a stake in good schools and student success.

REFERENCES

Mickelson, R. A. (1996). Opportunity and danger: Understanding the business contribution to public education reform. Pages 245–272 in *Implementing educational reform: Sociological perspectives on educational policy*, edited by K. M. Borman, P. W. Cookson, A. R. Sadovnik, and J. Z. Spade. Norwood, NJ: Ablex.

Sanders, M. G. (1999). Collaborating for student success: A study of the role of "community" in comprehensive school, family, and community partnership programs. Paper presented at the annual meeting of the American Educational Research Association (AERA), April, in Montreal. (In press in the *Elementary School Journal*.)

◇ ACTIVITY

Community Portraits

Many educators, families, and students are unaware of the resources in their communities. Indeed, many are unclear where the "community" begins and ends. The boundaries of a school community may be narrowly defined to include only the neighborhood around the school, broadly drawn to include the home communities of all who are served by the school, or even more inclusive of the whole town or city.

Students, teachers, and families can learn about available resources if they create a "community portrait" of the area around the school, home neighborhoods, and other locations where children, families, and teachers spend time and give or receive services (Family Resource Coalition, 1996; Goode, 1990). These include museums, zoos, libraries, shops, places for child care, places of worship, and other locations where students and families visit, work, give or obtain services, learn, or play. This activity asks you to think about *your* community, then consider how you might address the same questions in a school setting to help students and families think about *their* communities.

A. Divide a page in half with:

Side A: YOUR OWN community   Side B: OTHER communities

Answer the "a" questions on one side of the page and the "b" questions on the other side. Then, answer the summary questions.

1a. Where are the boundaries of *your* community?

1b. How might you guide students, teachers, and families to identify the geographic boundaries of what they consider their community?

2a. Who lives in *your* community?

2b. How might you guide students, teachers, and families to identify and report information on the various groups of people who live in their communities?

3a. What are the social and economic conditions in your community that identify its strengths and needs?

3b. How might you guide students, teachers, and families to collect information and report on the diverse social and economic conditions, strengths, and needs in their communities?

4a. What organizations, groups, programs, or special resources in your community are interested in schools, students, and families?

4b. How might you guide students, teachers, and families to collect information on groups that are interested in and have resources, services, programs, and opportunities for students and families in their communities?

B. Present the information on your community (from questions 1a, 2a, 3a, and 4a) in a "community portrait" as a report, chart, picture, or other form that you think might be useful for a particular audience of your choice (e.g., families, students, community group).

C. Present the outline and activity pages that you designed to guide teachers, students, and families in collecting and reporting the information in questions 1b, 2b, 3b, and 4b.

D. *Optional activity:* In practice teaching or with a cooperating teacher, review the guidelines for this kind of activity, improve them with the input of the cooperating teacher, and conduct an activity with the teacher in at least one class. Review the success or problems with the activity and improve the guidelines for creating community portraits.

REFERENCES

Family Resource Coalition. (1996). *Know your community.* Chicago: Family Resource Coalition.

Goode, D. A. (1990). The community portrait process: School community collaboration. *Equity and Choice* 6(3): 32–37.

▊ COMMENT

Finding Community

We need to define the *school community* to include all who have a stake in the quality of students' education. This includes families in the community with children in school *and* people in the community who have no children in school. The latter group is growing in size and is sometimes described as hostile to or uninterested in public schools.

Contrary to some beliefs, however, citizens with no children in school *are* connected to schools and to children in many ways. They have grandchildren, nieces, nephews, and other relatives or friends and neighbors in school. They hire students to work for them. They live next door to students and see them in the neighborhood. They follow school sports in the news, and are served by students and graduates in restaurants, stores, hospitals, and other locations in the community. Future policies, products, programs, services, and qualities of life in communities depend on the education, skills, and talents of the children they know *and* the children they do not know who are presently in schools.

◈ FIELD EXPERIENCE

Citizen Interview

A. Interview one citizen who has *no* children in the public schools. Identify this person's occupation, approximate age, and other characteristics that you think are important. Ask:
   1. How do you rate the public schools presently in your community: excellent, good, average, or poor? Explain.
   2. Did you attend public or private school in elementary school, middle grades, and high school? What was the quality of your educational program at each school level?
   3. Do you have any children?
      A. If YES, and they are *older* than school age: Did your children attend public or private school? Was it in this community? How would you rate the quality of the education they received at their schools: excellent, good, average, or poor?
      B. If YES, and they are *younger* than school age: Will your children attend public or private school in this community?
   4. Do you have any relatives whose children presently attend public schools in this or another community?
      A. About how many *in all*?
      B. About how many *in this community*?
   5. Do you have any friends whose children presently attend public schools in this or other communities?
      A. About how many *in all*?
      B. About how many *in this community*?
   6. Do you ever talk with children, adolescents, or graduates of the public schools in this community? If so, what is *one* example of an interaction you have had?
   7. How are you presently affected by the quality of education offered by the local public schools?

8. How do you think you will be affected in the future by the quality of the local public schools?
9. Add at least question of your own.
B. Document your questions and the responses.
C. Summarize your views of how this citizen is linked to the public schools. What are the implications of the responses that you obtained? How typical do you think this citizen is compared to others in the community?
D. Compare notes in class to learn about the variety of connections that citizens have with schools and students, whether or not their children are attending public schools.

⓪ COMMENT

Meetings with Parents at School and in the Community

Schools are the most common place for meetings with parents, but they are not the *only* possible sites. Meetings for parents and others in the community may be held in other locations that are open and accessible to all, including libraries, churches, community centers, apartment or community meeting rooms, and business or community auditoriums.

Some small meetings or "coffees" have been organized in volunteers' living rooms when large numbers of families live in or near a central location. Individual home visits also may be conducted to meet with parents.

Notices of school and community meetings may be posted in supermarkets, laundromats, and other neighborhood locations, and information on school programs, schedules, events, newsletters, and other announcements also may be distributed at these sites.

Although some meetings about school may be conducted in other settings, it is important for teachers and families to communicate easily with each other. Indeed, schools must make all families welcome and comfortable about coming to school for important meetings, conferences, celebrations, student presentations, and other school-linked activities.

QUESTIONS TO DISCUSS

1. Select one of the following activities: Back-to-School Night, parent-teacher conferences, meetings about a school policy, or a topic of your choice. Identify an activity and a grade level that interest you.
2. What are the pros and cons about conducting the activity you selected at school or in the community? Consider the location; the ease of access for all families; time, travel, and other conditions that are likely to affect attendance and participation of families; and the success of the activity. Create a chart that lists your ideas:

A. Which activity did you select? _____

B. Which grade level did you select? _____

	PROs *Two* reasons this IS a good location	CONs *Two* reasons this IS NOT a good location
AT SCHOOL	(1)	(1)
	(2)	(2)
IN THE COMMUNITY	(1)	(1)
In which location?	(2)	(2)

◫ COMMENT

Community Connections for Student Success

Students are either in school or out. When they are out of school, their families, peers, and communities either reinforce or redirect school goals for student learning and development. If the community *reinforces* school and family goals for student learning and success, the spheres of influence of home, school, and community "overlap" more in their messages to students about the importance of school and learning. If the community *redirects* students away from school or family goals, the spheres of influence are pushed apart. Thus, community groups, individuals, and programs may reward attitudes, behaviors, and knowledge that *help* or *hurt* students' chances for success in school and in life.

QUESTIONS TO DISCUSS

Example A. Some community groups recognize and reward students for excellence and improvement. For example, some community businesses participate in a "Gold Card" program to give middle or high school students discounts on purchases if they maintain high attendance or good grades or improve significantly over a marking period.

    A. Describe one other community recognition or support program for students that you know or have heard about.

    B. How might the Gold Card program or the program that you described help a student, family, school, and community?

Example B. Most students are assisted when schools, families, peers, and communities reinforce and enrich school, learning, and service. There are times, however, when this rule does not hold. For example, students who are *not* succeeding in school may be positively influenced by community programs and services that treat them better than they are treated in school. Nonschool contacts may give these students more respect and more rewarding messages than they receive in school. Nonschool contacts, including peers, families, employers, and other citizens, may appreciate students' ideas, assistance, special skills, and talents more than their teachers, administrators, and classmates do.

1. Describe one program or activity that you know or have heard about in which a student who is failing or having trouble in school is succeeding in an activity in the community.
2. How does the program or activity you described help the student, family, school, and/or community?
3. Discuss one way in which a student's success in community activities might be directly linked to schoolwork to increase the student's chances of success in school.

◈ FIELD EXPERIENCE

Interview with Community Organization Representative

How do community groups link to schools? Select a local community agency, cultural group, citizens' group, religious institution, government office, fraternal or other social organization, college or university public relations office, radio, TV, cable TV, newspaper community relations office, local foundation or philanthropic group, business, *or* other community location that has an interest in children and their success in school.

A. Identify the place and one contact person. Ask:
   1. In what way(s) is your organization interested in children, learning, schools, and families?
   2. In what way(s) does your organization presently assist children, schools, or families? What are your programs and their goals? How many participate? How long have the programs operated?
   3. What programs or activities would you like to add or improve in the future to link your organization to children, schools, and families? In your organization, how would decisions be made to implement these changes?
   4. Add at least one question of your own.
B. Document your questions and responses.
C. From the information you obtained, write a short summary on the quality and purposes of this organization's connections to students, families, and/or schools. Include one idea you would recommend for improving this organization's partnerships in the future.

▣ COMMENT

Part-Time Jobs in Communities

When they are in middle and high school, adolescents increase their connections with businesses, community groups, agencies, and others in the community. Students join clubs and organizations in their communities, shop, help neighbors with odd jobs, have part-time jobs, join summer programs, take lessons outside of school, volunteer to serve their community, and participate in many other community activities.

Many high school students and some middle school students work part-time during the school year. It is estimated that over 70 percent of students work part-time sometime during their high school years. Often, students' part-time or summer jobs or activities in the community are treated as if they were unrelated to the school program. Yet students gain academic and social skills on the job, meet and solve problems, and contribute to the community in their work and with their earnings.

There are important debates about whether students should work during high school, for how many hours, and in what kinds of jobs. Some early studies that concluded that students should not work too many hours during the school year were emotionally interpreted to mean that part-time work is bad for students. Recent studies based on national samples of students, longitudinal data, and more rigorous analyses indicate that most students are not adversely affected by their work experiences within the current range of hours worked, from a few hours to about 30 hours per week (Mortimer et al., 1994; Schoenhals, Tienda, and Schneider, 1998). Clearly, students need guidance about balancing school and work, and some need to be limited in their part-time work if their schoolwork is suffering. An equally important question is whether and how employers should require students to have or maintain excellent school attendance and report card grades to continue employment during the school year.

REFERENCES

Mortimer, J., M. Finch, K. Dennehy, C. Lee, and T. Beebe. (1994). Work experience in adolescence. *Journal of Vocational Education Research* 19: 39–70.

Schoenhals, M., M. Tienda, and B. Schneider. (1998). The educational and personal consequences of adolescent employment. *Social Forces* 77: 723–762.

◈ FIELD EXPERIENCE

Linking School and Part-Time Employment

How can students' part-time jobs during the school year and summer employment be more productively linked to their school programs? Interview an employer of a student, *or* a parent *or* teacher of an employed student, or a student with a part-time job. Or, invite one or more of these people for a class interview.

A. Identify the person you are interviewing: an employer, parent, teacher, or student. Ask:
   1. What are two things that an employer might do to help student employees place high priority on classwork, homework, studying, completing high school, and continuing their education?
   2. What are two things that families might do to ensure that their children do not fall behind in school as a result of part-time work?
   3. What are two things schools might do to link students' employment with required courses?
   4. What are two things students might do to demonstrate that they can successfully balance school, work, leisure, and family responsibilities?
   5. Give two ideas of how such school-family-community linkages might benefit students who work while they are in high school.
   6. Add at least one question of your own.
B. List your questions and the responses. Summarize your views on whether and which responses you received were feasible and important for connecting student jobs and student learning.

◇ ACTIVITY

Reading More about Community Partnerships

Many believe that if organizations and groups in communities worked with schools and families to combine resources on common goals for students' health, safety, learning, and talent development, then more students would succeed in school and, later, become more active in their communities. Similarly, if community groups worked with schools to offer integrated assistance to families on health, safety, job training, parent education, and family enrichment activities, more families would be continuously and successfully involved with their children and their children's schools.

Several researchers have studied and written about the many resources, skills, and talents that are available in all communities but that are often untapped by schools and families. "Funds of knowledge" (Moll, Amanti, Neff, and Gonzalez, 1992) are skills, talents, understandings, and commonsense ideas that are used in everyday activities at home or in the community. These include skills in home repair, gardening, butchering, cooking, sewing, using transportation, map reading, public speaking, chess, sports, music, dance, art, and many other skills and talents. Adults may share their skills, talents, and knowledge by coaching youngsters to help them develop their talents (Nettles, 1991). Other studies have focused on the role that communities could or should play in "full service schools" (Dryfoos,

1994) and in other community contributions to programs of school, family, and community partnerships (Sanders, 1999; Waddock, 1995).

Select one of the publications listed below, or identify one recently published article, chapter, or book that interests you on community connections with schools, families, and students. Give the full reference of the publication that you select. For the publication you selected:

A. In one or two paragraphs, summarize the author's main points about the connections of communities with schools, families, or students.
B. List one policy implication and one practical application that you draw.
C. Write one question that you would ask the author about the topic, methods, results, conclusion, or message.

Dryfoos, J. 1994. *Full service schools: A revolution in health and social services for children, youth, and families*. San Francisco: Jossey-Bass.

Mickelson, R. A. (1996). Opportunity and danger: Understanding the business contribution to public education reform. Pages 245–272 in *Implementing educational reform: Sociological perspectives on educational policy*, edited by K. M. Borman, P. W. Cookson, A. R. Sadovnik, and J. Z. Spade. Norwood, NJ: Ablex.

Moll, L. C., C. Amanti, D. Neff, and N. Gonzalez. (1992). Funds of knowledge for teaching: Using a qualitative approach to connect homes and classrooms. *Theory into Practice* 31(2): 132–141.

Nettles, S. M. (1991). Community involvement and disadvantaged students. *Review of Educational Research* 61: 379–406.

Sanders, M. G. (1999). Collaborating for student success: A study of the role of "community" in comprehensive school, family, and community partnership programs. Paper presented at the annual meeting of the American Educational Research Association (AERA), April, in Montreal. (In press in the *Elementary School Journal*.)

Waddock, S. A. (1995). *Not by schools alone: Sharing responsibility for America's education reform*. Westport, CT: Praeger.

REFERENCES

Dryfoos, J. 1994. *Full service schools: A revolution in health and social services for children, youth, and families*. San Francisco: Jossey-Bass.

Moll, L. C., C. Amanti, D. Neff, and N. Gonzalez. (1992). Funds of knowledge for teaching: Using a qualitative approach to connect homes and classrooms. *Theory into Practice* 31(2): 132–141.

Nettles, S. M. (1991). Community involvement and disadvantaged students. *Review of Educational Research* 61: 379–406.

Sanders, M. G. (1999). Collaborating for student success: A study of the role of "community" in comprehensive school, family, and community partnership programs. Paper presented at the annual meeting of the American Educational Research Association (AERA), April, in Montreal.

Waddock, S. A. (1995). *Not by schools alone: Sharing responsibility for America's education reform*. Westport, CT: Praeger.

To summarize, it is important to understand how the six types of involvement can be used to develop comprehensive programs of school, family, and community partnerships in all schools. We have learned that it is necessary to redefine parent involvement with new designs for school, family, and community partnerships. It also is imperative to meet the challenges that have prevented many families from becoming involved in their children's education. In this section, we explore how the six types of involvement are connected. This includes how basic and advanced activities both may contribute to a balanced program of partnerships, how one type of involvement promotes another, and how several types of involvement may strengthen the chances of reaching important results. The summary comments and activities should increase your understanding of the types of involvement, separately and in combination.

◆ SUMMARY: NEW DEFINITIONS FOR ◆
FAMILY AND COMMUNITY
INVOLVEMENT IN THE 21ST CENTURY

The framework of six types of involvement helps schools develop comprehensive programs of school, family, and community partnerships. Such programs include activities that are designed and implemented to involve all families in new ways at school, at home, and in the community. Data from many studies contributed to the following "redefinitions" of involvement that must be understood and activated for effective school, family, and community partnerships in the 21st century. (See Reading 5.1 and the summaries of the six types in this chapter for examples.)

QUESTIONS TO DISCUSS

1. Give one example of a school, family, and community partnership activity that would fulfill the spirit of each of the following redefinitions for selected activities for the six types of involvement.

Sample Redefinition—Type 1

Workshop is not only a meeting on a topic held at the school building but also the *content* of that meeting, which may be viewed, heard, or read at convenient times and varied locations.

    A. One activity that represents this new definition is:

Sample Redefinition—Type 2

Communications about school programs and student progress are not only from school to home but also from home to school and with the community.

B. One activity that represents this new definition is:

Sample Redefinition—Type 3

Volunteers are not only parents or others who come to help during the school day but also those who give their time to support school goals and children's learning in any location.

C. One activity that represents this new definition is:

Sample Redefinition—Type 4

Help at home does not mean that parents must know how to "teach" school subjects, but that families guide, encourage, and interact with their children on homework and school-related decisions.

D. One activity that represents this new definition is:

Sample Redefinition—Type 5

Decision making means exchanging views to plan and implement an effective, coordinated partnership program that will help students succeed in school, not a power struggle.

E. One activity that represents this new definition is:

Sample Redefinition—Type 6

Community includes not only families with children in school but also all citizens who are interested in and affected by the quality of education.

F. One activity that represents this new definition is:

---

2. Select one of the above redefinitions that interests you. Write a short paragraph on:
   A. One major difference between the "old" and "new" definitions of the term you selected.
   B. One way the new definition might affect how school, family, and community partnerships are conducted.

Meeting Challenges for Excellent Partnerships

Even if the redefinitions of involvement were applied, there still would be many challenges to meet in implementing high-quality partnership programs. By meeting key challenges, more or all parents will be informed and involved in their children's education. The exercise sentences in the following section start with a challenge for each of the six types of involvement that must be met with well-designed activities for elementary, middle, and high schools to reach out to all families.

QUESTIONS TO DISCUSS

Rewrite each of the following "challenge sentences" to give one idea of how schools might meet that challenge to try to involve *more* parents or *all* parents. An example is given for a Type 1 challenge.

Sample Type 1 Challenge

Challenge: Not all parents provide information to schools about their goals for their children.

    Rewrite: To meet this challenge, all schools could *conduct a short survey of all parents about their goals, dreams, and expectations for their children each year.*

Type 1 Challenge

Not all parents can attend workshops at school when they are scheduled.
    To meet this challenge, all schools could

_____

Type 2 Challenge

Not all parents feel comfortable asking teachers or principals questions about school programs and their children's progress or giving suggestions for improvements.
    To meet this challenge, all schools could

_____

Type 3 Challenge

Not all parents can volunteer to assist at the school building during the school day.
    To meet this challenge, all schools could

_____

Type 4 Challenge

Not all parents understand the teacher's homework policies or how to monitor and assist their children with homework.

To meet this challenge, all schools could

Type 5 Challenge

Not all parents want to serve on school committees or in other organized leadership roles, but they want parents' voices represented in school decisions.

To meet this challenge, all schools could

Type 6 Challenge

Not all parents have good information about the programs, resources, and services available to them and their children in their communities.

To meet this challenge, all schools could

⏸ COMMENT

Basic and Advanced Practices

Basic Activities

A common question about the types of involvement is: Which *basic* activities should we conduct to involve families? Are there some things that *all* schools should do with *all* families? Should some practices for each of the six types of involvement be implemented before other practices? There are no right answers to these questions. What is basic or essential in one school may be unnecessary in another. What is essential one year may not be needed the next year if the population of students and families changes or if school goals are changed or attained.

For example, if many families need help in obtaining food for their children, then a food bank may be a basic Type 1—Parenting activity at a school. If most families do not feel comfortable at school or knowledgeable about the school's programs, then a Family Fun and Learning Night (Type 2) may be basic for increasing parents' feelings of welcome and for initiating positive parent-teacher communications. If students are chronically absent, then family and community involvement focused on improving attendance is basic and essential for increasing student success. Schools with different goals or problems would select different *basic* activities to involve families and members of the community in important and useful ways.

Thus, it is the framework of six types of involvement that is *basic and prescribed* for an effective program of school, family, and community partnerships. Every school must thoughtfully select practices to create a balanced and productive partnership program that will meet its goals and the needs and interests of students, families, and teachers. Although every program will include some different practices, there are some common home, school, and community connections that are valued by parents and by educators in many or most schools.

For example, one very basic Type 2—Communicating activity is to create and maintain a welcoming environment for parents and the community so that everyone knows that the school is open to all and ready to discuss school programs and children's progress. Some schools need to hang welcome signs in many languages; some need to develop friendly sign-in procedures for parents and visitors who enter the building. Just about all schools need to organize ways to gather families' ideas for improving school programs from year to year.

Parent-teacher conferences also are basic Type 2 activities. These meetings may be designed as parent-teacher, parent-teacher-student, or student-led parent-teacher-student conferences. Such conferences may be individual, group, or grade-level meetings, using face-to-face, phone, or other communications. Whatever their format, conferences need to be scheduled so that all parents are able to attend.

Similarly, school or class newsletters are basic Type 2 practices in most schools. The newsletters may be more or less readable, long or short, with or without student work, on paper for all families and on the school's web site for those who prefer that format, and in English or multiple languages. Whatever their format, newsletters need to include two-way communication formats for families to respond with ideas, comments, or questions.

Preschool, elementary, middle, and high schools will select different basic activities for all six types of involvement to meet important needs and goals. At all school levels, however, all activities must be designed to meet key challenges to involve all families. That means, for example, that parent-teacher conferences should *not* be conducted *only* with parents of students who are having serious problems, nor *only* with the families of successful students. Newsletters should *not* be written using vocabulary that *only* some can read. Although basic communications will vary in design and quality, all excellent partnership programs will include some *basic* activities that are well planned, well implemented, and continually reviewed and improved.

Advanced Activities

In addition to basic or common activities to involve families and communities, there are *advanced, complex,* or *specially targeted* practices that may require more time and resources to design and conduct. For example, it takes considerable time and a large number of participants to plan and implement a multicultural fair, a monthly series of family workshops on curricular topics, a "turn-off-the-TV" series of events, weekly interactive homework assignments in particular subjects, a four-year sequence to help families and students plan for college or work, community improvement projects, and other large-scale projects.

Specially targeted advanced practices may be designed and implemented to meet the special needs of selected students and families. For example, some schools need to translate all print and nonprint communications with families into Spanish or other languages and to have translators at parent-teacher conferences and other meetings to assist some parents. By including these targeted activities, some families who would not be involved are included by design.

A comprehensive program of school, family, and community partnerships will include a reasonable mix of basic and advanced partnership activities that can be conducted and supported by educators, parents, and others working together (see Chapter 7 on an action team approach). The activities should be designed to meet major challenges to excellent involvement and contribute to the attainment of school improvement goals.

◇ ACTIVITY

Identifying Basic and Advanced Partnerships

What are some basic and advanced activities for each type of involvement?

A. Identify a level of schooling that interests you (preschool, elementary, middle, or high school).
B. Create a hypothetical school at the level you selected and give the school a name. List a few key features of your school, including its size (number of students), locale (urban, suburban, rural), and some features of the students and families served (e.g., racial and ethnic composition, family education background, and levels of student achievement).
C. Which family or community involvement activities might be basic at your school? Using Reading 5.1 and the summaries in this chapter, copy and fill in the chart below.
  1. List one basic activity for each of the six types of involvement that is common in most schools and that should be conducted in your hypothetical school.
  2. Give one reason why you think each basic activity is essential for your school.

Name of your hypothetical school: _____

Basic Partnership Activities

	One Basic Activity	Why Is It Important?
Type of Involvement		
Type 1—Parenting: To help parents understand child and adolescent development.		

	One Basic Activity	Why Is It Important?

Type 2—Communicating: To
help parents understand school
programs and children's progress.

Type 3—Volunteering: To support
the school and students.

*Type 4—Learning at
Home:* To help students and
families interact at home on
homework and the curriculum.

Type 5—Decision Making: To
develop parent leadership and
to encourage parent input on
school matters.

*Type 6—Collaborating with the
Community:* To connect people
and resources in ways that assist
students, families, and the school.

D. Which advanced or more complex activities are needed in your hypothetical school? Using Reading 5.1 and the summaries in this chapter, copy and
fill in the chart below.
1. List one advanced, complex, or specially targeted activity for each type
of involvement that would enrich your school's partnership program or
meet some unique needs and interests of students, families, and the
community.
2. Give one reason why you think each advanced activity would
strengthen, enrich, extend, or enliven your school's program of partnerships.

Advanced Partnership Activities

	One Advanced Activity	Why Is It Important?
Type of Involvement		
Type 1—Parenting:	_____	_____
Type 2—Communicating:	_____	_____
Type 3—Volunteering:	_____	_____
Type 4—Learning at Home:	_____	_____

Type 5—Decision
Making: _____   _____

Type 6—Collaborating
with the Community: _____   _____

⫼ COMMENT

Beyond "Bodies in the Building"

The framework of six types of involvement balances activities that are conducted at school, at home, and in the community so that parents who cannot easily come to the school building still can be productively involved in their children's education. This is important because some parents may feel guilty or frustrated if they cannot be at the school building often to volunteer or attend meetings. The framework also helps educators understand that parents who are not at school may be very much involved in their children's education.

Activities that require "bodies in the building" limit the involvement of many parents who cannot get to the building at a specific time. Thus, the "redefinitions" that we have discussed are particularly important for helping families become and remain involved in school and in other settings. Face-to-face communications will have to be supplemented by voice-to-voice, note-to-note, e-mail–to–e-mail, and other responsive technologies.

The fact is that some parents come to school regularly, whereas others come occasionally or rarely. What can you learn about whether, why, and when parents, other family members, or others in a community come to the school building?

◈ FIELD EXPERIENCE

What Kinds of Family and Community Involvement Can You See at School?

A. Visit a school for at least one hour to observe and record the family and/or community involvement that you see during a time of day that you select.
   1. Identify the name, location, and level of the school (i.e., elementary, middle, or high school).
   2. Identify the date and day of your observation.
   3. Identify the time of your observation (select one).

   _____ A. *at the start* of a typical school day, time: _____

   _____ B. *during selected hours* of a school day, time: _____

_____ C. *at the end* of a school day, time: _____

_____ D. at a scheduled *evening meeting,* time: _____

_____ E. other time (describe): _____

4. Identify where in the school you made your observations: _____

5. Describe whether, where, how many, and how parents or others from the community were involved at the school during your observation.

6. If parents are at the school, briefly interview two parents about:
   • why they are at school at the time you observed;
   • how often they come at this time;
   • how often they are involved with their children at home; and
   • at least one other question that you add.

   If no parents are at the school, briefly interview two teachers, administrators, or staff about:
   • why they think there are no parents present at the time you observed;
   • when most parents come to the school;
   • how much they believe parents are involved with their children at home; and
   • at least one other question that you add.

B. Record your questions and responses. Summarize your ideas about the nature and quality of family involvement that you observed. Are your observations sufficient for judging the involvement of parents and others at this school? Explain.

C. Compare observations in class to get a "big picture" from many observers of why and when parents are involved at the school building and in other locations.

◈ SUMMARY ◈
CONNECTING THE SIX TYPES OF INVOLVEMENT

The six types of involvement are labeled according to their main goals or purposes. The labels are designed to help schools classify and identify present practices, plan a results-oriented program of partnerships, monitor progress, and continually improve the quality of family and community involvement. As in all typologies, however, there are no "pure" types. Although some activities may represent just one type of involvement, others require or promote more than one type to produce particular results.

For example, school or classroom newsletters aim to inform families about school programs and events (Type 2—Communicating). Depending on their designs, however, newsletters may promote other types of involvement. A school or classroom newsletter may be produced by parent volunteers (increasing Type 3—Volunteering). In addition, students' academic work and home learning activities may appear in some newsletters for students to share their work and ideas with their parents (extending Type 4—Learning at Home), or community programs for children and families may be announced in newsletters (strengthening Type 6—Collaborating with the Community). Thus, all school or classroom newsletters have the goal of Type 2—Communicating, but some also may promote other types of involvement.

There are many such examples. A food cooperative or clothing swap-shop may be organized and conducted by parent volunteers (Type 3—Volunteering) to assist parents with their basic responsibilities to feed and clothe their children (Type 1—Parenting). The structure or organization of these activities may require one type of involvement to produce the intended results for another type of involvement.

QUESTIONS TO DISCUSS

How many types of involvement might be activated and combined to successfully organize and conduct:

1. A workshop to help parents understand their children's development at different grade levels (Type 1—Parenting)? List activities for at least three different types of involvement that might contribute to a successful Type 1—Parenting workshop.

   Type: Activities contributing to a successful workshop for parents:
   Type _____
   Type _____
   Type _____

2. A read-a-lot program that helps parents interact with their children who read at home for school or for pleasure (Type 4—Learning at Home). List activities for at least three different types of involvement that might be activated to guide families in encouraging and interacting with their children on reading at home.

   Type: Activities contributing to a successful read-a-lot at-home program:
   Type _____
   Type _____
   Type _____

◇ ACTIVITY

Charting Connections of Types of Involvement

The following chart depicts the connections of two types of involvement. A clothing swap-shop *aims* to produce results for Type 1—Parenting, but *is organized* to promote Type 3—Volunteering.

Chart A: Partnership Activities:
Clothing or Uniform Swap-Shop

Organization		Goal or Result
Volunteering (Type 3)	← promotes →	Parenting (Type 1)
Organize children's		Helps parents clothe
clothing/uniforms		their children at low cost.
for easy exchange		

Explanation: The two-way arrows indicate that one type of involvement ← promotes → another.

The arrow pointing to the right shows that a clothing/uniform swap-shop is run by volunteers (Type 3) to assist parents with their basic responsibilities to clothe their children (Type 1).

The arrow pointing to the left suggests that parents who use the swap-shop may meet other parents, become more comfortable at school, learn more about the school's need for their assistance, and become school volunteers.

Overall impact on partnerships: If well implemented and maintained, a swap-shop not only may have the intended effect of increasing the quality of parenting but also may build a sense of community at school *and* promote more volunteers.

A. Create Chart B to illustrate how one other partnership activity *aims* to produce results for one type of involvement, but *is organized* in ways that promote one or more other types of involvement. You may chart the examples discussed above (i.e., school newsletters, food bank, parenting workshop, reading at home) or identify an activity of your choice.

B. Complete the explanation of how the two-way arrows in your chart promote the kinds of involvement that you listed.

Chart B: Partnership Activity: _____

Organization		Goal or Result
_____ (Type __)	← promotes →	_____ (Type __)
Activity : _____		Result: _____

Explanation: The two-way arrows indicate that one type of involvement ← promotes → another.

The arrow pointing to the right indicates: _____

The arrow pointing to the left indicates: _____

Overall impact on partnerships: _____

⬛ COMMENT

Correlated Types of Involvement

The six types of involvement theoretically contribute to one broad concept of school, family, and community partnerships. Most schools, however, still do not conduct well-developed, comprehensive programs with all six types of involvement. They tend to emphasize one or a few types of involvement. Research reveals a few prominent patterns of how the types of involvement work independently or in combination.

For example, Type 2—Communicating activities are fairly well developed in most schools, even if other types of involvement are not implemented. Most schools try to communicate with families through memos, report cards, conferences, phone calls, and using other technologies, even though they still may need to improve the quality of their connections. These schools may not organize parent volunteers to work at the school (Type 3), invite parents to serve on decision-making committees (Type 5), or systematically involve families in other ways. Because most research on Type 2 simply tallies whether schools ever communicate with any families, there is little variation across schools on this type of involvement. Therefore, in many studies, Type 2 activities do not strongly correlate with or predict the use of other types of involvement.

By contrast, Type 4—Learning at Home activities are less prevalent in schools because they require every teacher to involve all families in children's learning activities at home in homework, decisions about courses, and other curricular-related activities. There is, then, considerable variation across schools in the use of Type 4 involvement. Type 4 activities tend to strongly predict the use of all other types of involvement. It may be that schools do not conduct Type 4 activities until they have successfully implemented all other, somewhat less complicated, types of involvement.

Other correlations between types of involvement also are interesting. Most studies indicate strong, positive correlations of Type 3—Volunteering and Type 5—Decision Making. These connections have been reported at the school level (i.e., when school programs and practices are measured) and at the individual parent level (i.e., when parents report their personal experiences). That is, schools with Type 3—Volunteering activities also tend to conduct Type 5—Decision Making activities with parents on school committees. In addition, parents who volunteer during the school day tend to be the same parents who participate in and lead the PTA/PTO or other parent association activities. In part, this may be because activities for both types of involvement typically require parents who can come to the school building, and both types require parents who feel welcome and confident at the school.

The size and direction of correlations of types of involvement are not fixed, but will change based on the design of activities, research samples, and measures. For example, if schools begin to define volunteers as parents who may assist in different ways at home, at school, *and* in the community, then parent volunteers (Type 3) may no longer be the same parents who are active leaders in the PTA or on decision-making committees (Type 5). By redefining volunteers, the previously strong correlations of Types 3 and 5 may be reduced in future studies.

Even if schools conducted comprehensive partnership programs with all six types of involvement, they would vary in which activities were selected, how well the activities were designed and implemented, and how results were measured. Most prior studies of involvement used relatively simple measures of a limited number of activities. With a better understanding of school, family, and community partnerships and with better measures of the quality and results of partnerships, future studies will be able to contribute new knowledge about the connections of the six types of involvement.

QUESTIONS TO DISCUSS

1. What is one reason why volunteers at a school might increase the likelihood that the school also will have an active PTA?
2. What is one reason why an active PTA at a school might increase the likelihood that the school also will have many volunteers?
3. Another prominent correlation in studies of involvement is reported between Type 5 (Decision Making) and Type 6 (Collaborating with the Community). Give two reasons why schools that include parents on decision-making committees or in an active PTA/PTO might also conduct activities that involve their communities.

⧉ COMMENT

Understanding Results of Involvement

Even if all of the challenges to excellent partnerships were met, there still would be questions about *which* activities should be implemented to produce the most successful partnership programs and to produce important results for students. To date, research suggests several important patterns that link family and community involvement to results for students, families, and schools.

1. Each type of involvement includes activities that produce different or unique results for students, families, and schools.

Table 5.3 in Reading 5.1 and the summaries on the six types of involvement in this chapter stress that each type of involvement may lead to some *unique* results as schools connect with families and communities in different ways. This emphasis is deliberate because too many people still believe that *any* activity for *any* type of involvement will increase student achievement test scores. This is not the case. For example, well-implemented Type 1—Parenting activities should help families understand child and adolescent development, whereas well-implemented Type 4—Learning at Home Activities should help families understand their children's school curricula, their children as "learners," and how to assist their children with homework and school decisions at each grade level.

2. Each type of involvement includes activities that may produce and strengthen the same results for students, families, and teachers.

It also is true that some activities for the six types of involvement may be combined to contribute to some of the *same* results, such as improving or maintaining good student attendance, school safety, and even student achievement. For example, national surveys and extensive fieldwork confirm that activities for several types of involvement help improve student attendance.

Type 1: Workshops and information for parents explain the family's role in getting children to school every day on time.

Type 2: Administrators clearly outline the school's attendance policies; all report cards communicate students' attendance and promptness to all families.

Type 3: Volunteers call parents of children who are absent to let families know that the school cares about student attendance and to remind parents and students about making up work that is missed.

Type 6: Businesses and community groups provide alarm clocks to families that need them; health services provide needed information and access to families and students.

As another example, schools have helped students improve their writing skills beyond expected levels by implementing activities for several types of family and community involvement that focus on writing. For example:

Type 2: Student writing is featured in school newsletters.

Type 4: Families are involved with students on weekly interactive homework assignments in writing.

Type 5: PTA/PTO sponsors annual "meet-the-authors" events for students, families, and the community.

Type 6: Community members come to the school on a regular schedule to show and share how writing is used in their various occupations.

There are many other examples of family and community involvement that may help improve student attendance, writing skills, or other results. The mix of activities across types of involvement creates a balanced partnership program by mobilizing family and community support at school, at home, and in other settings. The variety of activities makes it more likely that students will reach the stated goals than if only one activity for one type of involvement were conducted.

◈ ACTIVITY

Different Types Contribute to Same Results

A. Add one more activity to each list, above, for any type of family or community involvement that might help improve student attendance or writing skills.

1. One more family or community involvement activity to improve student attendance:
   Type _____ Activity: _____
2. One more family or community involvement activity to improve student writing:
   Type _____ Activity: _____

B. Identify a grade level that interests you.
   1. Select a goal for student success in a school subject (other than improving writing) that interests you. You may choose to focus on improving reading, math, science, social studies, foreign language, or another subject.
   2. List activities for at least three of the six types of family and community involvement that you think would help produce the goal you selected.
   3. Explain how each activity would help produce the desired results.

⊡ COMMENT

Steps from Family Involvement to Student Success

Not all family and community involvement activities will improve student learning, achievement test scores, or report card grades. Some activities produce other, different, and important results (see the summaries for the six types of involvement in this chapter). We are just beginning to learn which involvement activities will produce what results, for whom, in what amount of time, and with what inevitable challenges.

Following are two involvement activities that some people believe will increase student success in school. However, they differ in whether, how, and when they affect parents and students in the short term and in the long term.

Type 1—Parenting

A workshop for parents on child development may first increase parents' confidence about their interactions with their children. If parents attend the workshop or obtain information from the workshop in other ways, and if the information they receive from the school is understandable and important, then some parents might apply the information at home in their attitudes and actions. If parents implement the activities successfully, then some of their children may increase, improve, or maintain their motivation to learn in school, or other positive school behaviors. As children proceed through the grades, parents will need additional information to continue this chain of effects. If parents, students, or the school miss any of these or other intermediate steps, then the long and fragile chain of effects from workshops for parents to student learning will be broken. This chain of potential effects and some common "detours" or failures are shown in Figure 5.3.

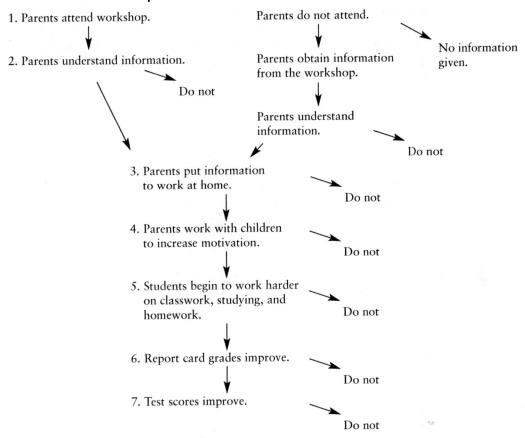

Workshop for Parents on Child/Adolescent Development

1. Parents attend workshop.

Parents do not attend.

No information given.

2. Parents understand information.

Do not

Parents obtain information from the workshop.

Parents understand information.

Do not

3. Parents put information to work at home.

Do not

4. Parents work with children to increase motivation.

Do not

5. Students begin to work harder on classwork, studying, and homework.

Do not

6. Report card grades improve.

Do not

7. Test scores improve.

Do not

FIGURE 5.3   Map 1: Selected Steps from Workshops for Parents to Student Learning

Type 4—Learning at Home

Homework is a key connector between school and home. Weekly interactive homework and other school-family-student connections about homework should help more students complete their assignments and talk about schoolwork at home. (See Chapter 6 for an example of how interactive homework can be organized.) Students who regularly complete their homework not only practice and strengthen their skills but also tend to be better prepared for the next day's class work. The completion of homework also should help students improve their report card grades, and may improve their performance on weekly tests. Over time, all of these improvements may affect achievement test scores. Interactive homework activities also help families remain aware of their children's curriculum, monitor their children's work, show interest in what their children are learning, and motivate their children to work in school.

If students attend school regularly, experience excellent teaching, participate in class, complete their homework, and are reinforced by their families, then students should improve their skills and success in school. The interactions at home in reading should contribute to improved reading skills, interactions in writing to improved writing skills, and so forth. It may be that *all* of these elements are needed for students to benefit from family involvement in learning activities at home. This chain of potential effects and some common "detours" or failures are shown in Figure 5.4.

In general, school-family-community connections are more likely to increase student learning if the activities directly engage students in interesting and important actions. These include family-school-community connections that require students to show and share their class work, complete and discuss homework, work with volunteers on specific skills and talents, or plan and take steps to reach specific goals. Because teachers are key in linking students with their families on curriculum-linked activities, it is possible for teachers to involve all or most students and their families in new ways at home.

Weekly Interactive Homework in Math for All Students to Share at Home

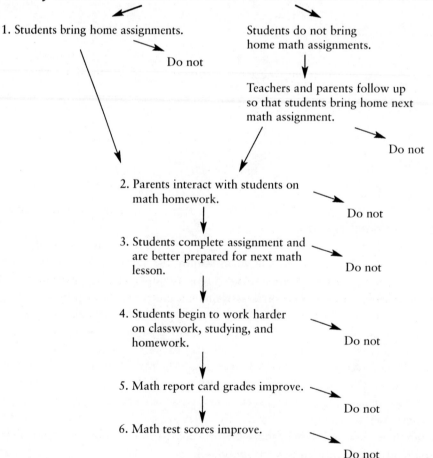

FIGURE 5.4   Map 2: Selected Steps from Weekly Interactive Homework in Math to Student Learning

School-family-community connections are less likely to increase student learning if the activities focus first on developing parents' attitudes and behaviors, without clear, immediate, and effective links to the students. Because most parents do not attend workshops, only a few may benefit from these activities. Even if workshop information is disseminated to all parents, many steps are needed to transfer new knowledge and new parenting behaviors to student learning.

QUESTIONS TO DISCUSS

Figure 5.3 (Map 1) shows some of the major steps that must be taken to transfer information from a workshop for parents on child development (Type 1, Parenting) to increased student learning. Figure 5.4 (Map 2) shows some typical steps needed to transfer weekly interactive homework in (Type 4, Learning at Home) to student learning and success in school.

1. Compare the two "maps."
   A. What are two or more factors that might make a difference in whether students are assisted positively by the involvement of a parent in Map 1 and Map 2?
   B. What are two or more factors that might make a difference in how many students in a school are assisted by the involvement of a parent in Map 1 and Map 2?
2. Each step (↓) along the path to partnerships takes time to implement and to produce results. Each step may lead to progress (i.e., the next step) or to failure. The timing, risks, and successes will, of course, vary from parent to parent and from student to student.
   A. Create a "time chart" for each of the maps.
   B. "Guesstimate" the time it would take a typical family and average student to complete each step (↓) from the parent involvement activity to student success.
   C. Show and label your time estimates for the seven steps in Map 1 and for the six steps in Map 2.
3. Draw two conclusions from your review of the two maps about the impact of family involvement on student achievement.

◇ ACTIVITY

Mapping Family Involvement to Student Success

Following are four more family involvement activities that some people believe should improve student success in school.

A. Select one of the following activities (or write a sequence of your own that describes how a family involvement activity may lead to student success).

1. **School or class newsletters (Type 2—Communicating).** School or classroom newsletters may *first* increase families' awareness of school and classroom programs and help parents talk with their children about school activities. If parents regularly discuss school activities with their children, then parents may reinforce the school's messages to students about the importance of their participation in school and in class. If students understand and accept that message and increase their participation in class, then students may improve their attitudes about school and, over time, increase their attention in class, work, and achievement.

2. **Parent Volunteers at School (Type 3—Volunteering).** Volunteers at school may lead *first* to more adult supervision of students, improve the safety in and around the school building, and improve the overall climate of the school. If volunteers are engaged in classrooms, then the closer adult supervision may improve student behavior in class. This may make it more likely that students who are in class will pay attention to their teachers and to their class work, which, in turn, may boost learning. If volunteers are well trained in assisting students with specific learning skills, then the students who are assisted should improve the skills on which they are assisted and, over time, other skills that build on what they learn.

3. **Parent Leaders (Type 5—Decision Making).** Inviting parents to contribute to school decisions as members of a school council or committee may *first* increase the parent leaders' support for the school. If the parent leaders communicate well, then other parents, too, may improve their understanding of and support for school programs. Over time, parents' input on school decisions may improve the quality of school programs, teaching conditions, curriculum and instructional advances, and how children succeed in school. Families with strong ties to the school may be more likely to understand and reinforce the school's messages to students about the importance of school and their work in school. Over time, parents' messages about school, vigilant monitoring, and continuous communications with their children may increase students' positive attitudes toward school, their attention in class, the quality of their class work and homework, and their learning.

4. **Before- and After-School Classes (Type 6—Collaborating with the Community).** Before-school and after-school programs conducted with community support and volunteers may help some students develop special talents and learn new skills. If students participate in these programs, then they should improve or learn skills in sports, music, dance, art, photography, computer use, chess, math, foreign languages, and other topics. Students who do not or cannot attend before- and after-school coaching and classes should not be expected to benefit in the same way as those who attend. The activities may affect student attendance, behavior, atti-

tudes about school, and other specific skills that are taught and, over time, may increase student learning and achievement test scores.

5. **An Activity You Select.** Write a sequence of steps from an involvement activity to student success.

B. Draw a "map" of major steps from the implementation of a family and community involvement activity to student achievement or success in school. Show the possible detours or failures of action along the way.

C. "Guesstimate" the time it may take for an average family and student to complete each step ($\downarrow$) on your map from involvement to student success.

D. Share and critique the maps and time lines in class. Discuss:

- whether the estimated time lines are realistic; and
- whether the family involvement activity is likely to improve student achievement for most students in a school.

0: COMMENT

Long-Term Results of Involvement

In the short term, the clearest or most dramatic effects of family and community involvement will be found for theoretically linked activities. That is, family involvement in reading should promote or improve students' reading skills, family and community involvement about attendance should improve student attendance, and so forth. (See Reading 5.1 and the summaries in this chapter for lists of activities and linked results.) Some short-term results may lead to long-term results because, as noted above, one type of involvement may promote other types, and because an early result of one type of involvement may lead to other results. (Activities for different types of involvement may create chains of action and chains of effects.)

For example, research and fieldwork show that family and community involvement activities focused on attendance can help improve student attendance in the short term. Over time, the involvement activities may lead to more and different family and community involvement as parents and other participants see that their efforts pay off. Also, students' good attendance may also promote other student successes. Students who were absent often, but who begin to attend school regularly because of increased family and community involvement about attendance, may improve their achievement by coming to class, experiencing excellent teaching, participating, and learning their lessons. Thus, over time, a complex chain of effects may be studied in research and in classrooms. Figure 5.5 shows one possible chain of actions and effects.

QUESTIONS TO DISCUSS

1. "Guesstimate" the time it may take to produce the actions and results described above.

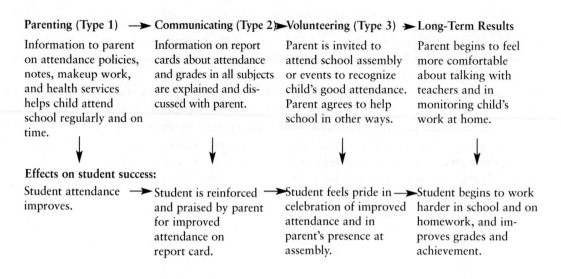

Parenting (Type 1) ⟶ Communicating (Type 2) ⟶ Volunteering (Type 3) ⟶ Long-Term Results

Information to parent on attendance policies, notes, makeup work, and health services helps child attend school regularly and on time.

Information on report cards about attendance and grades in all subjects are explained and discussed with parent.

Parent is invited to attend school assembly or events to recognize child's good attendance. Parent agrees to help school in other ways.

Parent begins to feel more comfortable about talking with teachers and in monitoring child's work at home.

Effects on student success:

Student attendance improves. ⟶ Student is reinforced and praised by parent for improved attendance on report card. ⟶ Student feels pride in celebration of improved attendance and in parent's presence at assembly. ⟶ Student begins to work harder in school and on homework, and improves grades and achievement.

FIGURE 5.5   Effects of Family Involvement of Types 1–3

A. Estimate the *shortest* time and the *longest* time (in days, weeks, months, or years) that you think it would take a typical *family* to take the steps toward increased involvement that are shown above.
B. What is one reason for the difference between your shortest and longest estimates for increasing family involvement?
C. Estimate the *shortest* time and the *longest* time (in days, weeks, months, or years) that you think it would take a typical *student* to move along the line of results that are shown above.
D. What is one reason for the difference between your shortest and longest estimates for results for students?
E. How would your estimates differ for a parent of a student entering kindergarten compared with a parent of a student entering high school?

2. Give two ideas about what your estimates of the connections of involvement and the production of results mean for schools that are working to improve their partnership programs.

⬚ COMMENT

Negative Correlations of Involvement and Achievement

Some connections between home and school are initiated by teachers or by parents when students are having academic or behavior problems. This fact causes some odd correlations in research studies and some unusual dynamics in practice.

For example, some measures of Type 2 activities are negatively correlated with measures of other types of parental involvement and with indicators of student success. If schools conduct parent-teacher conferences only or mainly with parents of students with academic or behavioral problems, then measures of parents' attendance at conferences with teachers will be negatively correlated with student achievement. That is, more parents of troubled or failing students attend more conferences than do parents of successful students.

This way of organizing parent-teacher conferences also affects other patterns of involvement. As they strive to help their children succeed, parents of troubled students may be *more* likely than other parents to monitor and assist their children on homework. Indeed, this may be part of the actions agreed upon in a parent-teacher conference. (See Readings 2.2 and 3.8 for other discussions about the meaning of negative correlations of involvement and student success.)

By contrast, parents of successful students may feel more welcome and comfortable at school. They may be more likely to volunteer (Type 3 activity) or take leadership roles in decision making (Type 5 activity). Thus, parents who report being involved in one way may be responding to their children's problems, whereas other parents are responding to their children's success in school.

These patterns of activities produce positive or negative correlations of involvement and student achievement, behavior, or other indicators of success in school. The correlations are not fixed, however, and will change as schools develop comprehensive programs of partnership. That is, if parent-teacher conferences are conducted with *all* parents, rather than only with parents whose children are in trouble, then the negative association of conferences with student achievement will diminish or disappear. There should be no significant correlation of attending a conference and student success. If teachers and principals communicate with families about good and bad behavior, then the negative correlations between phone calls and notes and student behavior will diminish or disappear.

These patterns are initially counterintuitive because we expect that frequent communications, parent-teacher conferences, and interactions about homework will have *positive* associations with student success in school. The negative correlations of involvement with achievement and behavior pose an important opportunity for studying the effects of interventions of targeted family involvement on *changes* in student achievement and behavior. That is, if students are having trouble in school, and parents and teachers meet, provide extra homework help, and conduct other corrective activities, then do students become less troubled and more successful over time? Do students succeed at higher levels if their teachers and parents communicate with each other and monitor the students' work and progress?

These crucial questions can be addressed in schools and classrooms with carefully monitored interventions and effects and in longitudinal research studies. It is important for educators and researchers to learn *which* school, family, and community partnerships make a difference in helping *which* troubled or failing students, at *which* grade levels, in *which* subjects or behaviors, and with what rate of success.

Negative Connections of Involvement and Achievement in Practice and Research

A. Invite an experienced researcher and an experienced educator to class to discuss their observations and understanding of some negative correlations of family involvement and student achievement or behavior, as discussed above.

B. Ask the educator:

1. Do you ever call parents of students in academic or behavioral trouble? Which parents do you tend to call more often?

2. If you counted the number of parent-teacher conferences you conduct, would you say:

   A. More conferences are conducted with parents of low-achieving students.

   B. More conferences are conducted with parents of high-achieving students.

   C. About the same number of conferences are conducted with parents of all students.

3. How might you monitor the results of parent-teacher conferences and other interventions and involvement that you conduct with parents of troubled or failing students?

4. How easy or difficult would it be to learn how much family involvement contributed to changes in students' skills or behavior? What else contributes to changes in students' skills or behavior?

C. Ask the researcher:

1. How might you (or other researchers) study the effects of parent-teacher conferences and other interventions and involvement on student achievement, in general, and on the achievement of troubled or failing students?

2. How easy or difficult would it be to learn how much family involvement contributed to changes in students' skills or behaviors?

D. From the panel reports and reactions, discuss: How do the educator and researcher think similarly and how do they think differently about these complex connections of family involvement and student success?

⫿⫶ COMMENT

Family Involvement in Successful School Programs

Successful schools understand and address the six types of involvement, their challenges, and connections to produce results. In a national search for effective academic curricula for the middle grades, family involvement was one common feature of the most promising programs in reading, math, writing, science, social studies, language arts, and thinking skills (Epstein and Salinas, 1992). In just about all of the better programs, connections were made to help parents (a) understand early adolescence and middle schools; (b) understand the curriculum; (c) become partners with teachers in encouraging children with their homework and schoolwork; (d) interact with their early adolescents at home about homework and school experiences; and (e) assist students with decisions about courses, school plans, and other programs and activities that affect their future.

Similarly, Blue Ribbon Schools selected by the U.S. Department of Education are expected to document their practices to involve families and communities. Other programs that recognize excellent elementary, middle, and high schools and exemplary teachers also include school, family, and community partnerships among the selection criteria.

National reports of successful students invariably point to the importance of family involvement with students on learning activities at home. For example, the National Assessment of Educational Progress (NAEP) (NCES, 1999) evaluates what students in grades 4, 8, and 12 know and do in various subjects. NAEP reading tests indicate that at all grade levels, students who discuss their school studies at home at least once or twice a week had higher reading scores than students who do so less frequently. The results were particularly noteworthy in grades 8 and 12 in middle and high schools. Similar analyses of students' writing, science, and math scores on NAEP tests reinforce the importance of curriculum-linked family involvement for successful schools and successful students.

◇ ACTIVITY

What's New?

When you read about excellent schools and successful students, parent or community involvement is usually mentioned as an important influence. When you read about school or student failures, the lack of family involvement often is noted. See if this is true in national or local news about education.

A. Collect at least two references to successful schools or students and two references to unsuccessful schools or students from newspapers, news magazines, or web sites about schools (e.g., for information on middle schools see www.middleweb.com/MGNews.html; for Blue Ribbon Schools see www.ed.gov/offices/OERI/BlueRibbonSchools).

B. Write a short summary of the articles or information that you found (including full citations). Include in your summary whether and how the reports about successful and unsuccessful schools refer to family and community involvement.

C. Share information in class to get a broader idea of whether and how school, family, and community partnerships are discussed in the media as a component of school and student success and failure.

◇ ACTIVITY

Resource Notebook

A resource notebook or computer file of ideas about school, family, and community partnerships may be as useful for practice and for research as a sketch pad is for an artist. You can collect the best and most useful activities and ideas that are shared in class in a hard-copy notebook or in a "virtual" computer file notebook. Your resource notebook also may include other promising, positive practices of school, family, and community partnerships for all six types of involvement that you collect from other readings, publications, practice teaching, observations, and other sources. Future teachers and administrators may draw from their resource notebooks when it is time to develop comprehensive programs of partnership in the particular schools and communities in which they work. Researchers may draw from their resource notebooks when it is time to identify questions for new projects and papers about family and community involvement.

A. Create a resource notebook with ideas about and examples of activities for the six types of involvement; how to meet challenges to excellence; and likely results of involvement for students, families, educators, and communities. Include the following sections:
- Type 1 ideas for workshops on child and/or adolescent development that may help parents understand their children's growth and development in the grade level(s) that interest you; other ideas on parenting, supervising children, and helping schools understand families.
- Type 2 examples of excellent communication strategies, including two-way school-to-home and home-to school communications. Include examples of age-appropriate activities for including students as partners in conducting school-to-home-to-school communications at each grade level. Include communication strategies using new technologies that will be common and important in schools of the future.
- Type 3 examples of various ways to organize volunteers to assist at school, in classrooms, at home, and in other locations.
- Type 4 ideas for involving families in discussions and interactions with students on curricular activities, academic choices and decisions, and homework assignments. Include student-led interactions designed by teachers that enable students to conduct conversations and activities with family partners.

- Type 5 ideas about how parent leaders and parents' opinions can be included on committees, councils, and school improvement teams at the school and district levels.
- Type 6 ideas about how to identify and obtain resources from the community and how to participate in the community.
- Other related topics that you select. See Chapters 6 and 7 for more ideas for your resource notebook on special topics of interactive homework, organizing productive volunteers, and using an action team approach to implement a comprehensive program of partnerships.

B. Periodically review the resource notebook and share particularly interesting ideas or innovative examples with others in class.

REFERENCES

Epstein, J. L., and K. C. Salinas. (1992). *Promising programs in the middle grades.* Reston, VA: National Association of Secondary School Principals.

National Center for Education Statistics. 1999. *The NAEP 1998 reading report card: National and state highlights.* Washington, DC: U.S. Department of Education/OERI. (NCES 1999-479).

Practical Applications: Linking Family and Community Involvement to Student Learning

TEACHERS INVOLVE PARENTS IN SCHOOLWORK (TIPS): INTERACTIVE HOMEWORK AND PRODUCTIVE VOLUNTEERS

Educators must understand all six major types of involvement (*parenting, communicating, volunteering, learning at home, decision making, and collaborating with the community*) to implement comprehensive programs of school, family, and community partnerships. Some types of involvement are implemented with familiar activities, such as workshops for parents in Type 1—Parenting, or parent-teacher conferences in Type 2—Communicating. Even common practices, however, pose challenges that must be met to involve all families in their children's education (see Chapter 5).

Some types of involvement are not so familiar, or have not been well organized. In this chapter, we examine two research-based approaches to involving families in their children's education in ways that are important to parents and students but that have not been well implemented in most schools. These applications were designed, developed, and tested to help educators systematically, equitably, and productively involve families at home and in school to improve student learning.

Reading 6.1 describes the Teachers Involve Parents in Schoolwork (TIPS) Interactive Homework process, which helps educators implement Type 4—Learning at Home Activities. This is a difficult component to sustain in a comprehensive program of partnerships because it requires *every teacher* to understand the connections between class lessons, student learners, and families as influential partners for children's learning. The TIPS Interactive Homework process helps teachers design and use homework assignments to connect home and school on curriculum-related activities. TIPS activities improve parents' understanding of what their children are learning; guide conversations at home; and, if well implemented, improve students' homework completion, subject-matter skills, and readiness for classwork.

Reading 6.2 describes the Teachers Involve Parents in Schoolwork (TIPS) Volunteers in Social Studies and Art process, which helps educators implement Type 3—Volunteering in the middle grades. This has been a particular challenge because teachers and administrators in middle schools typically have not identified productive roles and activities for parent and community volunteers. The TIPS approach solves this problem by training volunteers to present art-based interdisciplinary connections in social studies or other school subjects. If well implemented, the TIPS Volunteers program enriches and extends the curriculum and increases middle-grade students' knowledge and appreciation of art.

Both TIPS approaches focus on students. In TIPS interactive homework, students conduct conversations and other interactions with family partners, because homework is always the students' responsibility. Students' skills are evaluated to determine whether and how TIPS interactive homework contributes to learning. In TIPS Volunteers, students are the focus of the interdisciplinary lessons in social studies and art. Students' knowledge and attitudes about art are evaluated to determine if the volunteers' presentations are effective.

A common question is, "How does family and community involvement help students to succeed?" The question assumes a direct link between involvement and student learning. Research reveals, however, that not every type of involvement leads to higher student achievement (see related discussions in Chapters 2, 3, 5, and 7). The TIPS approaches illustrate two very different ways to link family and community involvement to student learning: by involving all families at home in supporting homework and by involving parents and other volunteers at school in activities that enrich the curriculum and extend students' experiences.

The TIPS research-based processes are not "canned" programs. Teachers cannot simply distribute someone else's homework assignments. Homework—including interactive homework—must be directly linked to class work and course objectives. Similarly, interdisciplinary art and social studies lessons must be linked to specific units of work. Thus, the "prototype" materials that have been developed for both approaches at Johns Hopkins University (referenced in Readings 6.1 and 6.2) must be reviewed, revised, and supplemented to match the school curriculum and other school, family, and student characteristics. The TIPS approaches require educators to work with families to design and produce materials, organize family-friendly schedules, conduct and improve activities, orient families and students to new approaches, conduct follow-up activities in class, evaluate results, and continue to improve the effectiveness of these programs.

By looking at two different processes for improving Type 3—Volunteering and Type 4—Learning at Home, you will see what it takes to organize productive partnerships linked to student learning. Other formal programs, like TIPS, may be designed to respond to particular challenges in implementing the six types of involvement.

The descriptions and examples of TIPS materials in this chapter may be particularly helpful in courses on curriculum and instruction, methods of teaching specific subjects, practice teaching seminars, and related instruction for future teachers and administrators. Principals, superintendents, curriculum leaders, and teachers of all subjects should know how to design and implement family and community connections that enhance student learning.

Teachers Involve Parents in Schoolwork (TIPS): Interactive Homework in Math, Science, and Language Arts*

LINKING FAMILY INVOLVEMENT WITH STUDENT ACHIEVEMENT

Although all six types of involvement mentioned above are important, not every type of family or community involvement will immediately increase student achievement and success in school. Type 4—Learning at Home is one type of involvement that may directly influence students' skills and achievements. Family interactions with children about schoolwork and homework may, if well designed and effectively implemented, increase students' completion of homework, improve students' attitudes toward school, boost students' readiness for the next class lesson, and improve students' performance on tests and report card grades.

Type 4—Learning at Home requires every teacher to understand the important connections between what is taught and learned in school and what is encouraged, practiced, discussed, and celebrated at home. It requires every teacher to inform and involve families about the work that their children do in class.

This could be a daunting, even impossible, task if it meant that teachers had to show every parent how to teach every skill in every subject. It would be equally unfair, even absurd, to expect all parents to know how to teach their children all school subjects every year. It is possible, however, to implement useful Type 4 activities to help students gain and strengthen skills, interact with parents or other family members about schoolwork at home, and keep parents informed about the skills their children are learning from week to week or month to month.

Most teachers and administrators report that they *want* parents to support their children's learning, help students practice important skills, and monitor homework. Most, however, have not organized ways to guide all parents in productive interactions with their children about homework or curriculum-related decisions. Some teachers and administrators worry that involving families with children in learning activities at home will diminish teachers' professional status. Studies indicate, however, that when teachers implement frequent, family-friendly practices of partnership, parents *increase* their respect for teachers and for the work that teachers do (see Reading 4.3).

Most parents do not want to teach school subjects to their children. Rather, parents want to know: "How can I *help* my child do well in school?" Many stud-

---

* By Joyce L. Epstein.

ies and interviews with thousands of parents about what they mean by "help" indicate that parents want to support, encourage, and motivate their children, monitor their work, celebrate progress, and conduct interactions that will help their children complete their homework and do well in school (Hoover-Dempsey and Sandler, 1995; see readings in Chapter 3). These preferences are expressed by parents of children at all grade levels, from preschool through high school, in diverse communities. Parents' requests require teachers to involve all families in new ways with their children in academic activities at home.

TIPS interactive homework was designed to fulfill this goal: Every teacher of every grade level and subject can select or design one homework assignment a week or every other week that requires students to talk to someone at home about something interesting they are learning in class. If such activities were well designed and assigned on a regular schedule, all families would be able to follow their children's progress in learning; all children would be able to share ideas and information at home; and all teachers would have a realistic strategy for communicating with families about students' curriculum, homework, and academic choices and decisions.

TIPS activities recognize the central role of students as the main actors in their own education. Students—not parents—must study, complete homework, take tests, and learn as much as possible. Students also are active participants in school, family, and community partnerships. They are couriers of all kinds of information from school to home and from home to school, including information on homework. Students are the natural leaders of and participants in conversations and interactions about schoolwork and homework, academic decisions such as course choices, and plans for the future.

RESEARCH LEADING TO TIPS

TIPS interactive homework processes grew from early research that revealed that when elementary school teachers frequently involved families in reading activities at home, more parents conducted these activities with their children, *and* more of these students improved their reading test scores from fall to spring of the school year. The study suggested an important subject-specific link between parent involvement in reading and gains in student achievement in reading (see Reading 3.1).

The same study revealed that although many teachers, particularly in the younger grades, asked parents to be involved with their children in reading, few teachers at any grade level asked parents to become involved in other subjects. Teachers did not have effective strategies to guide parental involvement in math, science, or other subjects and, therefore, did not feel comfortable about requesting involvement in these subjects. The research raised several questions:

- Could an interactive homework process be designed that would help teachers involve all families with their children at home in math, science, writing, and other subjects?

- Could interactive assignments be conducted successfully by students at different grade levels, with varying abilities, and in diverse communities?
- If teachers involved students in activities with family partners in math, science, or other subjects, would students increase their skills, improve attitudes, and complete more homework in these subjects?

To address these questions, my colleagues and I worked with educators, families, and students in the elementary and middle grades to design and study interactive homework and its effects (Epstein and Van Voorhis, in press). Initial work also has been conducted with high school educators, families, and students to learn how interactive homework might work in high schools.

TIPS prototype activities show teachers how to design research-based interactive homework assignments in math, science/health, and language arts. In TIPS activities, students may demonstrate their mastery of skills; conduct experiments; share ideas; obtain reactions and suggestions; conduct surveys or interviews; gather parents' memories of their own experiences as children, or memories of the students as young children; apply a skill to real life; or work with family members in other ways. The interactions are conducted by the students in ways that enable all parents to become involved in learning activities at home.

Different school subjects pose different challenges and require different designs for successful interactions. The next sections describe TIPS Math, TIPS Science, and TIPS Language Arts Interactive Homework. Sample interactive homework assignments are included at the end of this reading to illustrate TIPS Math, Science, and Language Arts for the elementary and middle grades, and there is a high school activity in social studies.

TIPS MATH

In studying interactive homework in math, we learned that teachers worried that parents did not know how their children were being taught math in school. Parents worried that they might confuse their children about math. And, children complained, cried, or argued, "You don't do it like my teacher does it."

The teachers knew that they could not teach all parents how to teach math, and that parents did not want to do this. Consequently, most families did not talk much about math with their children, and many did not approach math positively.

TIPS Math was designed to put parents, students, and teachers at ease in their interactions about math at home. TIPS Math:

- illustrates clearly how the teacher taught the skill in class;
- allows students to demonstrate, discuss, and celebrate their mastery of new math skills;
- enables parents to stay informed about their children's math work; and

- encourages parents to communicate with teachers about their observations, comments, or questions concerning their children's math homework and progress in math.

Math in the middle grades is more complex than is math in younger grades, making it even harder for most parents to monitor or assist their children. TIPS Math assignments in the middle grades guide early adolescents to review math skills and to talk with family partners about how each math skill is used in real-life situations.

Exploratory studies of TIPS Math in elementary schools in a low-income community in Illinois suggested that interactive homework was easily implemented, and that just about all parents were able to participate. Balli (1995) conducted a formal investigation of the TIPS Math process with sixth-grade students and their families in a suburban middle school. She compared the levels of family involvement and math achievement of students completing TIPS Math interactive assignments to students completing noninteractive math assignments (i.e., without directions for the student to involve a family member in the assignment). She found that parents appreciated the student-led interactions, students and parents reported more positive conversations about math, and most students believed that the interactions helped them be more prepared and successful in math class (Balli, 1998).

In Balli's study, all students had the same math teacher. On average, the students in all three classrooms improved their math achievement over time. However, those who were assigned TIPS Math interactive homework had significantly more student and parent interactions and more positive attitudes about math than did students who were assigned traditional math homework.

Links to Curriculum

TIPS Math interactive homework should be an integral part of the math curriculum. At each grade level, students can show family members that they are mastering major math skills. For example, TIPS Math prototype activities in grade 1 include more than 35 math skills, including counting from 1 to 100; writing numerals for sets of tens and ones; adding two-digit numbers without regrouping; and learning shapes, fractions, graphs, and other skills. TIPS Math in grade 5 includes more than 35 activities, such as estimating quotients, adding and subtracting mixed numerals, identifying line segments and rays, comparing unlike fractions, solving word problems requiring multiplication, creating graphs, and other skills. TIPS Math for the middle grades includes 20 prototype activities that help students review basic skills and focus on problem-solving and real-world applications.

From year to year, TIPS Math should help families see both that their children's math skills are increasing and how new skills build on earlier activities. For example, graphing is introduced in grade 1 or 2 when students share picture graphs with their family partners. By grade 5, students demonstrate how they construct their own bar graphs and line graphs. Graphs also are included in TIPS Science activities in the middle grades to help students observe and classify information systematically. Graphing is a good interactive homework assignment at all grade levels across the curriculum because children enjoy the challenge of creating and interpreting graphs, as well as sharing information with their families.

Format

TIPS Math enables students to show parents or other family members what they learn in math class and how they practice new skills and to discuss how to apply math skills in real-world problems. TIPS Math activities may include challenging games and problem-solving activities related to the specific skills in the assignments. TIPS Math enables teachers to obtain reactions from parents in home-to-school communications. Each interactive activity includes the following sections:

Look This Over shows an example of a skill that was taught in class, and allows the student to explain the skill to a parent or family partner. The answer to the example is given.

Now Try This presents another example for the student to demonstrate how to do the particular skill, with the answer on the back of the page.

Practice and *More Practice* are regular homework problems for the student to master the skill.

Let's Find Out or *In the Real World* may be added to help the student and family partner discover and discuss how the math skill is used at home or in common situations. Games or other interactions may be included to reinforce the math skill.

Home-to-School Communication invites the parent to record an observation, comment, or question for the math teacher about the skill the student demonstrated.

Parent Signature is requested on each activity.

Presentation and Schedule

Each activity must be prepared in readable type on two sides of one page and be printed on colored paper to stand out in students' notebooks. TIPS Math should be assigned on a regular schedule (e.g., once a week or twice a month) to help students and families talk about math at home and to help parents see what their children are learning in math. In one school, a parent wrote about TIPS Math: "When I see that yellow paper, I know that is important homework for my son to complete with me." Another noted: "Send more of these. I forgot how to do this. It was fun for us."

Materials Available

TIPS Math interactive homework includes over 200 prototype assignments for basic math skills from kindergarten through grade 5 and 20 prototype activities for functional math in the middle grades. There also are teacher manuals for implementing TIPS in the elementary and middle grades (Epstein and Salinas, 1995; Epstein, Salinas, and Jackson, 1995). Two examples of TIPS Math are included in the appendix to this reading:

Fractional Parts	Sample TIPS Math (elementary grades)
I Mean It!	Sample TIPS Math (middle grades)

TIPS SCIENCE

In studying interactive homework in science, we learned that most elementary school teachers did not have much time to teach science. After teaching math, reading, and language arts every day, many teachers had one block of time in which to fit social studies, science, art, music, physical education, and other subjects and activities. Because of the lack of class time and, in the 1980s, a lack of attention to science on standardized tests, few elementary teachers ever assigned science homework. Teachers almost never expected family involvement except on science fair projects, which often were isolated from the regular science program.

In the mid-1980s, the National Science Foundation called for at least 30 minutes of science instruction per day in the elementary grades, but few schools met that standard. This was confirmed in a national study that reported that only 25 percent of states and 40 percent of school districts in the nation required even minimum amounts of time for math or science in the elementary grades (Resnick and Resnick, 1985). Specific requirements for class time usually referred to math, not science.

It was clear from national assessments and international comparisons that elementary and middle-grade students in the United States were not getting enough science instruction and had few opportunities to work as scientists with hands-on activities. In the 1990s, one national education goal called for the country to be "first in the world" in math and science by the year 2000. To begin to work toward that goal, science was added to many national, state, and international lists of standards and assessments to make schools more accountable for science instruction.

Even now, few schools have organized programs to involve all families with their children in regularly scheduled interactive science homework. Most parents have no idea what their children are learning in science in the elementary grades and rarely talk with their children about science at home. In the middle grades, most students have daily science classes, but most students and families still do not converse about science at home.

TIPS Science addresses some of these issues. TIPS activities require students to work as scientists, involve a family "assistant," discuss conclusions, and interview family members about how science affects them in everyday life. TIPS Science:

- encourages teachers to introduce science topics in class and follow up with discussions or demonstrations, after the TIPS interactive homework assignments are completed;
- guides students to conduct, discuss, and enjoy science activities at home;
- enables parents to stay informed about their children's science work and progress; and
- encourages parents to communicate with teachers about their observations and questions concerning their children's science homework and progress in science.

Exploratory studies in TIPS Science in the middle grades indicated that parents and students enjoyed their conversations about science, and they strongly recommended that the school continue to use TIPS Science activities from year to year. Teachers who introduced and discussed the homework assignments in class, before students took them home, and who followed up the assignments with some discussion, had students with higher rates of homework completion than did teachers who did not follow these implementation strategies. Knowledge gained from several years of field observations, interviews, and surveys of teachers, parents, and students was incorporated in the TIPS manual for teachers (Epstein, Salinas, and Jackson, 1995).

New questions about the effects of TIPS Science homework in the middle grades were explored by Van Voorhis (2000). She conducted a quasi-experimental study of the TIPS Science process with 250 sixth- and eighth-grade science students in ten classes of four teachers in a suburban middle school. Students in six classes received weekly TIPS Science activities with specific guidelines for students to interact with family partners in science experiments and activities. Students in four classes received the same homework but with no guidelines for family involvement (ATIPS). Van Voorhis found that students who completed TIPS assignments reported significantly higher family involvement in science than did students in the ATIPS classes. TIPS students also had higher science report card grades, even after accounting for the strong influence of students' prior science abilities, parent education, and the amount of homework completed. Thus, over and above the effects of doing homework, TIPS Science added significantly and positively to students' report card grades. This study provides strong evidence that TIPS interactive homework is effective in increasing family involvement and in boosting the science achievement of students who involve family partners in homework.

Links to Curriculum

TIPS Science interactive homework should be an integral part of the science curriculum. TIPS Science hands-on activities help students build science skills such as observation, classification, hypothesizing, experimenting, graphing, recording data, interpreting data, drawing conclusions, and discussing ideas with others at home and in school. Prototype science activities emphasize writing across the curriculum as students record information and summarize results and conclusions from experiments and from interviews with family members.

Data collection in science becomes more complex across the grades. Simple charts or lists in the early elementary grades lead to longer systematic collections of data in the upper grades. Even young children, however, can keep track of data over time. For example, one TIPS activity asks third graders to draw the moon each night that it is visible for a month. An activity on osmosis asks seventh graders to chart changes in an egg that is set in vinegar over several days.

TIPS Science activities enable students to talk about science with family members at home and to see that science is all around us. For example, 12 prototype activities in grade 3 cover topics of living things, matter, and earth and space; and approximately 40 activities for grade 8 introduce topics in chemistry and physics. TIPS activities guide discussions on important issues as diverse as metric measures, pollution, digestion, and carbon dating to help students and families discuss and share opinions about the meaning of science in their lives at home and at school.

Some prototype science activities address health topics that require students to conduct conversations, gather reactions, or collect data from family members on good health and early adolescent development. Health may be covered in science, physical education, advisory periods, or separate health classes.

Regardless of their formal education, just about all parents have ideas to share about healthy development, such as good nutrition, the importance of exercise, or ideas for making good decisions. Sometimes, however, parents do not know how to begin to discuss sensitive topics with their children, such as adolescent sexual development, AIDS, or drug abuse prevention. TIPS interactive homework assignments on health topics give students opportunities and directions to start conversations with family members and exchange ideas and opinions on health issues. Prototype activities include such topics as physical changes in early adolescence; emotional development; personal strengths, weaknesses, plans, and values; and making tough decisions. Other sample activities include understanding sight/ blindness; hearing; drugs; and organ systems of the body, including the circulatory, respiratory, digestive, excretory, nervous, reproductive, and endocrine systems.

Format

TIPS Science guides students to conduct and discuss hands-on "lab" activities at home. All activities include a brief letter to parents explaining the topic and outline the learning objectives, materials needed, directions for data collection, discussion questions, conclusions, and home-to-school communications. Each interactive activity includes the following sections:

Letter to parent, guardian, or family partner explains briefly the topic and specific science skills involved in the activity. The student writes in the due date and signs the letter.

Objectives explain the learning goal(s) of the activity.

Materials are common, inexpensive, and immediately available at home or easily obtained. If they are not, the school should provide the materials.

Procedure guides the student, step by step. Each assignment includes hands-on actions that require the student to think and act like a scientist. Teachers may change, simplify, or increase the difficulty of activities to meet the special needs of students.

Lab report or *data chart* gives space for the student to report findings.

Conclusions guide the student to discuss results and real-world applications of science or health with family partners.

Home-to-school communication invites the parents to share comments and observations with science teachers about whether their child understood the homework, whether they all enjoyed the activity, and whether the parents gained information about the student's work in science and health.

Parent signature is requested on each activity.

Presentation and Schedule

TIPS Science/Health activities must be prepared in readable type, on two sides of one page, and be printed on colored paper to stand out in students' notebooks. TIPS Science interactive homework should be assigned on a regular schedule (e.g., once a week or twice a month) to help students discuss their work in science and health at home and to keep families aware of what their students are learning in science and health classes.

Typical comments from parents on TIPS Science include "His thought process was more mature than what I knew." And, "I think she could have done a better job with the consequences." Family partners' comments on health activities include "I am glad we discussed working with blind people." And, "This opened up an easier way of communicating."

Materials Available

TIPS Science prototypes are available for grade 3, and more than 100 examples are prepared for various science units in the middle grades (6–8). There also are teacher manuals for implementing TIPS Science in the elementary and middle grades (Epstein and Salinas, 1995; Epstein, Salinas, and Jackson, 1995). Examples of TIPS science activities for the elementary and middle grades are included in the appendix to this reading:

TIPS LANGUAGE ARTS

In studying TIPS Language Arts, we found that teachers in the middle grades were not as comfortable about guiding family involvement in reading, vocabulary, and writing as were teachers in the elementary grades. Middle school educators wanted assignments that went beyond asking parents to listen to their children read aloud or to give practice spelling tests. They wanted students to conduct conversations with family members about words, phrases, sentences, stories, speeches, and ideas.

Language arts is an excellent interactive subject because families like to listen to what their children write; help children practice a speech; or share ideas and memories that make good topics for stories, poems, and essays. Data from students in elementary, middle, and high schools show that students like to interview parents, gather ideas, demonstrate skills, and share their work. TIPS Language Arts:

- encourages teachers to design homework that builds students' skills in reading, writing, speaking, and listening through communications with family partners;
- guides students to conduct, discuss, and enjoy language arts activities at home;
- enables parents to stay informed about their children's language arts work and progress; and
- encourages parents to communicate with teachers about their observations and questions concerning their children's homework and progress in language arts.

Research was conducted to study the influence of TIPS Language Arts on students' writing skills, language arts report card grades, and completion of TIPS interactive homework assignments (Epstein, Simon, and Salinas, 1997). The study included 683 students in grades 6 and 8 in two urban schools where over 70 percent of the students qualified for free or reduced-price lunch. Students completed writing samples in the fall, winter, and spring of the school year and provided their reactions to TIPS. Parents also were surveyed on their attitudes toward TIPS and their participation with their children in TIPS activities. Analyses statistically controlled for family socioeconomic status, grade level, attendance, fall report card grades, and fall writing sample scores, to identify the effects of TIPS on students' skills in the winter and spring and student and family attitudes at the end of the school year.

As might be expected, students with higher writing scores in the fall had higher scores in the winter and spring. However, there also were some important homework-related results. The more homework assignments students completed, the higher were their language arts report card grades. The more parents participated, the better they liked TIPS interactive homework, and the higher were their students' writing scores in the winter and spring.

Nearly 100 percent of the families surveyed agreed that TIPS gave them information about what their children were learning in class. Over 80 percent of the students reported that TIPS gave them a way to show their parents what they were learning. Students said that they liked TIPS because they did not have to copy the homework from the board, because it was not boring, and because they learned something from or about their parents or families that they did not know before. Most teachers reported that more children complete TIPS than other homework. TIPS goals and the results of the study of the effects of TIPS Language Arts in the middle grades are shown in Table 6.1.

Links to Curriculum

TIPS Language Arts interactive homework should be an integral part of the language arts curriculum. TIPS Language Arts guides students to share a variety of skills in writing, reading, grammar, wordplay, and related language arts activities. The students do all of the reading and writing in the assignments, but students and family members may discuss, share, and exchange ideas. Parents or other family members may listen to students read their writing aloud; give reactions, ideas, memories, and experiences; and interact in other ways.

TIPS Language Arts interactive homework prototype assignments focus on skills such as writing descriptive sentences, letters, stories, tall tales, poems, and speeches; elaborating ideas and details; improving grammar; and studying words and meanings such as similes, homonyms, analogies, context clues, multiple meanings, and chronological order. TIPS sample writing activities show teachers how to design homework that guides students to plan their writing, discuss ideas, write a draft, read aloud, and edit and improve their work.

TIPS writing assignments should help students improve their skills from their own starting points. For example, the same assignment may help some students write a short paragraph while other students write a long essay. TIPS also helps students edit their work. When they read their writing aloud to someone at home, students are more likely to see and hear how their words and punctuation should be changed or corrected.

Format

TIPS Language Arts activities include the following sections:

Letter to parent, guardian, or family partner explains the purpose of the activity. The student writes in the due date and signs the letter.

TABLE 6.1   Linking the Goals of TIPS Interactive Homework to Results of a Study of TIPS Writing in the Middle Grades

Goals of Interactive Homework	Summary of Results
For families . . . To increase family awareness of their children's schoolwork To increase family involvement in children's learning activities at home linked to academic classes	**For families . . .** Nearly 100% of the parents agreed that TIPS gave them information about what their children were learning in class, and approximately 90% advised the school to continue TIPS next year. Over 80% of the families liked the TIPS process (44% a lot; 36% a little). Most were involved every week (40%) or every other week (23%). Parents who participated with their children in more TIPS activities liked TIPS better than did other parents, even after accounting for other parental monitoring of schoolwork.
For students . . . To increase students' ability to talk about schoolwork at home and the frequency of interactions with family members about homework To improve students' homework completion in specific subjects To improve students' skills in specific subjects	**For students . . .** About 60% of the students said TIPS activities are better than regular homework; 70% reported their parents liked TIPS; 82% believed TIPS "gives me a way to show my parent what I am learning in class"; and about 70% recommended that the school continue to use TIPS next year. Students' attitudes about TIPS were most influenced by their attitudes toward school and by their teachers' attitudes toward TIPS. Students' writing skills increased with more family involvement in TIPS, even after prior writing skills were taken into account. Students' language arts report card grades improved when more TIPS assignments were completed, even after prior report card grades and attendance were taken into account.
For teachers . . . To enable teachers to assign interactive homework designed to encourage students to share their ideas with family members To increase teachers' understanding of families' interest in their children's work	**For teachers . . .** Six of the eight teachers liked the TIPS process and reported that they could continue its use without assistance or supplies from the researchers. Seven of eight teachers agreed that TIPS "helps families see what their children are learning in class."

SOURCE: Epstein, Simon, and Salinas (1997).

Objectives explain the learning goal of the activity (if this is not clear from the title and letter).

Materials are listed if more than paper and pen are needed.

Writing activities include the following sections:

Prewriting gives the student space to plan a letter, essay, or story by outlining, brainstorming, listing, designing nets and webs, or other planning activities.

First draft gives the student space to write and edit. A student who needs more space may add paper. Some teachers ask the student to write a final copy on other paper at home or at school.

Interactions such as a family survey or interview guide students to interview someone for ideas or memories, read work aloud for reactions, edit their work based on responses, practice a speech, take turns with others in giving ideas, or other interactions.

Home-to-school communication invites the parents to share comments and observations with language arts teachers about whether their child understood the homework, whether they all enjoyed the activity, and whether the parents gained information about the student's work in language arts.

Parent signature is requested on each activity.

Presentation and Schedule

Each activity must be prepared in clear, readable type on two sides of one page and be printed on colored paper so that it stands out in the students' notebooks. TIPS Language Arts homework should be assigned on a regular schedule (e.g., once a week or every other week) to help students share their work and to keep families aware of what their children are learning in language arts or English classes. As one parent wrote in a home-to-school communication about TIPS Language Arts: "I can tell from Jenneaka relating the story to me that she really enjoyed reading it." Another wrote: "Very interesting assignment. I enjoyed this and it brought back good memories."

Materials Available

More than 100 TIPS Language Arts prototype assignments are available for the middle grades (6–8). There also are teacher manuals for implementing TIPS Language Arts in the middle grades (Epstein, Salinas, and Jackson, 1995). The process and activities can be adapted for use in other grades. Two examples of TIPS Language Arts are included in the appendix to this reading:

Hairy Tales	Sample TIPS Language Arts (elementary grades)
A Helping Hand	Sample TIPS Language Arts (middle grades)

GOALS OF TIPS INTERACTIVE HOMEWORK

The prototype activities in math, science, and language arts illustrate how the content and goals of different subjects require different designs for interactive homework. Nevertheless, TIPS activities in all subjects have some common goals for students, parents, and teachers. TIPS activities aim to:

- increase students' ability and willingness to talk about schoolwork at home and increase the frequency of these interactions;
- increase students' knowledge about real-world applications and the usefulness of skills learned in school;
- improve students' skills and homework completion in specific subjects;
- increase parents' awareness of their children's schoolwork;
- increase parents' confidence about talking with their children about schoolwork and homework;
- increase parents' involvement in their children's learning activities at home that are linked to class work;
- enable teachers to design homework that encourages students to share their work with family members;
- increase teachers' positive attitudes about families' interest in their children's work;
- increase positive attitudes of students, parents, and teachers about homework; and
- increase opportunities for students and parents to celebrate the mastery of skills and progress in learning.

HOW TO DEVELOP A TIPS INTERACTIVE HOMEWORK PROGRAM FOR ANY SUBJECT

Because TIPS interactive homework must match the curriculum that is taught in class, it is necessary to review, select, or design homework assignments that will be used throughout the school year in each school or school district. The following steps guide the development of TIPS interactive homework in any school, in any grade level, and in any subject (Epstein, 1993/1994).

1. Select the subject(s) for interactive homework. List or outline the major curriculum objectives, concepts, and skills that will be taught each week over one school year.

2. Select one skill for each week of the school year that would promote productive, family-friendly interactions. From the outline of learning objectives, identify one skill that will be taught or reviewed each week that lends itself well to an enjoyable and useful interaction between students and family members.

3. Select or design one interactive homework assignment for each of the weekly skills identified. Review the existing TIPS prototype activities to find those that match the selected skills or those that may be easily adapted. If appropriate prototype activities do not exist, design new interactive homework assignments to accompany the class lessons. Following are some helpful design elements:

- Keep the activities short and focused. TIPS assignments should fit on two sides of one page. They should ask students to involve family partners for up to 20 minutes, even if the students have more work to do on TIPS or other assignments.
- Require *only* inexpensive and readily available materials, or provide the students with the necessary materials.
- Include enjoyable and thoughtful student-family interactions in every activity.
- Draw on real-life experiences that are common to all families and that are not dependent on parents' formal education.
- Include a place for "home-to-school" communications on every activity so that parents may send a message back to the teacher about their interactions with their children on the assignment.
- Print the TIPS assignments on colored paper so they do not get lost in students' notebooks. Use the same color for all assignments in particular subjects so that students and families become familiar, for example, with yellow TIPS Math or blue TIPS Science activities.

4. Work with other teachers. Teachers who teach the same subjects at the same grade level can share the work of designing interactive homework. Teachers from the same school or school district may work together to plan, discuss, write, edit, test, and revise the TIPS assignments. Then, the resulting TIPS activities can be shared and used or adapted by all teachers who use the same or similar curricula.

5. Use the summer to plan, produce, or revise activities so that they will be ready for students and families for the next school year. Homework should be part of school plans for improving the curriculum, instruction, and family involvement. Federal, state, district, and school funds may be available for improving the curriculum, and therefore may be targeted to support teachers' time during the summer to design, develop, and organize TIPS interactive homework assignments for the next school year.

HOW TO IMPLEMENT TIPS INTERACTIVE HOMEWORK

Once the TIPS assignments are selected, adapted, or designed, plans and schedules are needed to effectively implement, evaluate, and maintain TIPS, beginning with the orientation of students and parents to the new approach to homework. Following are some key implementation guidelines.

Orient Parents and Students to TIPS

Students and parents need to be well prepared to conduct TIPS interactive homework successfully. Students need to know that they are responsible for all homework, and that they will conduct the interactions with family members in TIPS assignments. Students also need to hear frequently from the teacher that their families are important; that students are essential for the success of connections between school and home; and that students are expected to show and share their work, ideas, and progress at home. This information must be shared at the start of the school year and reinforced periodically throughout the year. Parents need to know the goals of TIPS assignments, their children's responsibilities to share their work, how parents should help, and the schedule for TIPS activities so that they can plan time for these interactions. Parents also need to hear frequently from the teacher that it is important for them to monitor their children's homework and to motivate and interact with their children.

To introduce parents to TIPS, teachers and principals may send a letter to all parents, announce the process in a newsletter, introduce and explain TIPS at parent-teacher meetings and conferences, and discuss the process with parents on other occasions. Teachers may conduct classroom or grade-level meetings to show parents examples of TIPS activities on an overhead projector and discuss with them how to proceed when their children bring TIPS activities home. Parents who cannot attend these meetings should be contacted by phone, paired with a "buddy" parent, or provided with easy-to-follow information from the orientation session.

Teachers must introduce each TIPS homework assignment in class and discuss each assignment with their students. By taking five minutes of class time to go over TIPS interactive homework, teachers will ensure that most or all students understand the sections that they will explain or share at home. Teachers should ask students if they have any questions about the directions or about their responsibilities for conducting interactions with family partners. This is the time for students to sign the short letter to parents in science or language arts assignments and to note when the assignment is due, so that they can plan when to complete the assignment when a parent or family member is available. This also is the time to reinforce the importance of students' interactions with family members at home. If teachers take five minutes to introduce and discuss the homework in class, all or most students will be able to conduct and complete the assignment at home.

Give Students Adequate Time to Complete Interactive Assignments

Some teachers give students two or more days to interact with family members and complete the homework. This ensures that even if parents are not available on one evening, they may be able to interact with students sometime the next day or evening. Some teachers assign TIPS homework over the weekend. In several studies, parents reported that they have time on the weekends to talk with their children about schoolwork.

Follow Up Each Assignment

Teachers should follow up the completed assignments with short, stimulating classroom discussions or demonstrations that reinforce or enrich the homework. Even a five-minute discussion reinforces the importance of completing homework on time and allows students to share some interactions they had with their families. Evaluations of TIPS indicate that teachers who regularly introduce and follow up the assignments have more students who complete their homework well.

Treat TIPS Assignments Like Other Homework

TIPS interactive homework should be collected, graded, and returned like other homework. For example, some teachers specify points for completing each section of the TIPS assignment, as they do for all other homework.

Answer Parents' Questions

The home-to-school communication section at the end of every TIPS assignment gives parents a place for comments or questions and encourages two-way communication between school and home. Teachers must follow up parents' questions by phone, notes, e-mail, or other communication on a regular schedule that is known to parents (e.g., once a week or once a month).

Recognize Good Work

Some teachers award Family-School Partnership Certificates of Merit (or other recognitions) after students complete a certain number of TIPS interactive homework activities with their families. This lets students and families know that the school recognizes and appreciates the time spent on interactive homework. This may be done once or twice a year or for each report card period.

Evaluate the Implementation and Effects of TIPS

There are two "built-in" evaluations in all TIPS assignments. First, students are expected to complete TIPS activities just as they do all homework assignments. Teachers should discuss, collect, grade, and return TIPS in the same way that they do other homework. Thus, students' homework completion and skills can be recorded for each assignment.

Second, every TIPS activity includes a section for home-to-school communications. In this section, parents report their observations of whether the child seemed to understand the assignment, whether it was enjoyable for everyone, and whether they have any questions about the assignment for the teacher. Teachers should monitor this section, record whether students shared their work with a family partner, and note whether they need to call or write to parents to respond to their questions. Parents' reactions to assignments should be noted to determine which activities should be edited or eliminated from year to year.

Educators should conduct a short, targeted assessment of whether students and parents understand the TIPS interactive homework process at the start of each school year when the first few activities are assigned. Teachers or counselors should call parents who are not involved to see if they understand the TIPS process and assure them that they do not have to "teach" their children school subjects but simply encourage the student to conduct the interactions. This implementation check will help maximize the number of students who are able to engage their family partners in guided conversations about schoolwork, as well as the number of parents who know how to encourage their children to take the lead in discussing the TIPS activities.

Formal evaluations of TIPS may be designed with school, district, or external researchers to determine the added value of homework to class lessons (Balli, 1995; Epstein, Simon, and Salinas, 1997; Van Voorhis, 2000).

For more information on what teachers, administrators, parents, and students do to successfully conduct interactive homework, see the TIPS implementation manuals (Epstein and Salinas, 1995; Epstein, Salinas, and Jackson, 1995) and guidelines and examples (www.partnershipschools.org; follow links to TIPS interactice homework). For research and references on homework see Reading 3.8; for other discussions of homework activities, see the Discussion and Activities section in this chapter.

REFERENCES

Balli, S. J. (1995). The effects of differential prompts on family involvement with middle-grades homework. Ph.D. diss., University of Missouri–Columbia.

——. (1998). When mom and dad help: Student reflections on parent involvement with homework. *Journal of Research and Development in Education* 31: 142–146.

Epstein, J. L. (1993/1994). Monthly columns for *Instructor Magazine* series on the Teachers Involve Parents in Schoolwork (TIPS) processes. September 1993 (TIPS Health), October 1993 (TIPS Math), November–December 1993 (TIPS Science), January 1994 (TIPS Language Arts), March 1994 (TIPS Health), April 1994 (TIPS Math), and May–June 1994 (Language Arts).

Epstein, J. L., and K. C. Salinas. (1995). *Manual for teachers and prototype activities: Teachers Involve Parents in Schoolwork (TIPS) Language Arts, Science/Health, and Math Interactive Homework in the elementary grades.* Baltimore: Center on School, Family, and Community Partnerships, Johns Hopkins University.

Epstein, J. L., K. C. Salinas, and V. E. Jackson. (1995) *Manual for teachers and prototype activities: Teachers Involve Parents in Schoolwork (TIPS) Language Arts, Science/Health, and Math Interactive Homework in the middle grades.* Baltimore: Center on School, Family, and Community Partnerships, Johns Hopkins University.

Epstein, J. L., B. S. Simon, and K. C. Salinas. (1997, September). Effects of Teachers Involve Parents in Schoolwork (TIPS) Language Arts Interactive Homework in the middle grades. *Research Bulletin* 18. Bloomington IN: Phi Delta Kappa, CEDR.

Epstein, J. L., and F. E. Van Voorhis. (in press). More than minutes: Teachers' roles in designing homework. *Educational Psychologist.*

Hoover-Dempsey, K. V., and H. M. Sandler. (1995). Parental involvement in children's education: Why does it make a difference? *Teachers College Record* 97: 310–331.

Resnick, D. P., and L. B. Resnick. (1985). Standards, curriculum, and performance: A historical and comparative perspective. *Educational Researcher* 14: 5–8.

Van Voorhis, F. E. (2000). The effects of interactive (TIPS) and non-interactive homework assignments on science achievement and family involvement of middle grade students. Ph.D. diss., University of Florida, Gainesville.

APPENDIX

Sample Teachers Involve Parents in Schoolwork (TIPS) Assignments in Math, Science, and Language Arts in the Elementary and Middle Grades, and High School Social Studies

Fractional Parts	Sample TIPS Math (elementary grades)
I Mean It!	Sample TIPS Math (middle grades)
Living Things—The Importance of Animals	Sample TIPS Science (elementary grades)
On Your Mark, Get Set, Go!	Sample TIPS Science (middle grades)
Hairy Tales	Sample TIPS Language Arts (elementary grades)
A Helping Hand	Sample TIPS Language Arts (middle grades)
Why Do We Need Government?	Sample TIPS Social Studies (high school)

TIPS: FRACTIONAL PARTS

Dear Family Partner,
My class is learning how to write fractions. This activity will let me show you what I know about fractions. We can talk about how we use fractions at home. This assignment is due_____.
Sincerely,

_____
Student's signature

I. LOOK THIS OVER: Explain this example to your family partner.

SAMPLE: What part of the shape is shaded?

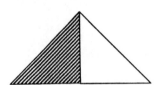

Count the parts: 2 parts

How many are shaded?: 1 part

1 part out of 2 parts =   1 part
                         — out of
                          2 parts

Answer: $\dfrac{1}{2}$ of the shape is shaded.

II. NOW, TRY THIS: Show your family partner how you do this example.

EXAMPLE: What part of the shape is shaded?

Count the parts:

How many are shaded?:

Answer: _____

If you need some help, ask your family partner to go over the example with you.
When you understand the work, explain what you did.

III. PRACTICE SECTION: Complete these examples on your own.
Explain one example to your family partner.

What part of the following shapes are shaded?

1.

Answer: _____

2.

Answer: _____

(continues)

What part of the following shapes are shaded?

3.

    Answer: _____

4.

    Answer: _____

5.

    Answer: _____

6. (Create a shape of your own)

    Answer: _____

DISCUSSION: 1) With a family partner, look over the examples you finished and tell what fractional parts are NOT SHADED

2) Ask a family partner: When do you use fractions at home?_____

ANSWER TO "NOW, TRY THIS":

Answer: $\dfrac{3}{8}$ is shaded

Count the parts: 8 parts

How many are shaded?: 3 parts

3 parts out of 8 parts = $\dfrac{3}{8}$ $\dfrac{\text{parts}}{\text{out of}}$ parts

IV. HOME TO SCHOOL COMMUNICATION:

Parent Observation: Please let me know your reactions to your child's work on this activity.

____ O.K. Child seems to understand this skill

____ PLEASE CHECK. Child needed some help on this, but seems to understand.

____ PLEASE HELP. Child still needs instruction on this skill.

____ PLEASE NOTE. (other comments)_____

Parent's signature: _____

Epstein, J.L., & Salinas, K.C. (revised 2000). Teachers Involve Parents in Schoolwork (TIPS) Interactive Homework for the Elementary Grades. Baltimore: Center on School, Family, and Community Partnerships, Johns Hopkins University.

Student's Name_____   Date_____

TIPS: I MEAN IT!

I. LOOK THIS OVER: Explain this example to your family partner.

Remember: To find the average (mean) for a set of data:
    1) add all of the data;
    2) divide by the number of pieces of data; and
    3) round to the nearest whole number if necessary.

DATA: 4, 9, 5, 6, 11
ADD: $4 + 9 + 5 + 6 + 11 = 35$
            5 pieces of data
DIVIDE by Number of Items in Set: $35 \div 5 = 7$
        AVERAGE (MEAN) = 7

II. NOW, TRY THIS: Show your family member how you do this example.

DATA: 7, 13, 23, 3, 17, 9, 12
ADD:
DIVIDE by Number of Items:
    AVERAGE (MEAN) =

III. PRACTICE SECTION: Complete these examples on your own. Show your work. Explain one example to your family partner.

1. List the ages of all your family and find the mean age.
    DATA:
    ADD:
    DIVIDE by Number of Items
    AVERAGE (MEAN) =   Is your age close to the mean?_____

2. Find the mean shoe size for all of your family (round half sizes up).
    DATA:
    ADD:
    DIVIDE by Number of Items
    AVERAGE (MEAN) =   Is your shoe size close to the mean?_____

3. Find the mean height (in inches) of all of your family.
    DATA:
    ADD:
    DIVIDE by Number of Items
    AVERAGE (MEAN) =   Is your height close to the mean?_____

(continues)

People use averages or means to report survey results. Poll four family members or friends. Include at least one family member.

ASK: How many hours each day do you <u>work</u> (at school, at a job, or at home)?
How many hours each night do you <u>sleep</u>? (Fill in the chart below with your data)

Names of people you surveyed	Number of hours of <u>work</u> each day (at school, at a job, or at home)	Number of hours of sleep each day
1.		
2.		
3.		
4.		
	AVERAGE (MEAN) =	AVERAGE (MEAN) =

Find the average (mean) amount of time the people you selected work and sleep each day.
WORK SPACE:

Explain your results to a family member. Discuss with your family member:
Would I find the same means if I surveyed only friends my own age? Why or why not?

_____

_____

ANSWER TO "NOW, TRY THIS":

ADD: 7 + 13 + 23 + 3 + 17 + 9 + 12 = 84
DIVIDE by Number of Items: 84 ÷ 7 = 12
AVERAGE (MEAN) = 12

IV. HOME TO SCHOOL COMMUNICATION:

Dear Parent/Family Partner,
Please give me your reactions to your child's work on this activity.
Write YES or NO for each statement.
_____My child understood the homework and was able to complete it.
_____My child and I enjoyed the activity.
_____This assignment helped me know what my child is learning in math.
Any other comments:_____
Parent's signature: _____

Epstein, J.L., Salinas, K.C., & Jackson, V. (revised 2000). Teachers Involve Parents in Schoolwork (TIPS) Interactive Homework for the Middle Grades. Baltimore: Center on School, Family, and Community Partnerships, Johns Hopkins University.

532

TIPS: LIVING THINGS—THE IMPORTANCE OF ANIMALS

Dear Family Partner,
We are learning to identify useful products that come from animals. This activity will help build science skills in observing, recording information, and drawing conclusions. I hope you enjoy this activity with me. The assignment is due _____.

Sincerely,

_____
Student's signature

OBJECTIVE: To identify useful products from animals and to draw conclusions about the importance of animals in our lives.

MATERIALS: Pen or pencil

PROCEDURE:

1. Discuss with your family partner different kinds of products that come from animals. Write a list of these products at the top of the Lab Report.

2. Observe objects in your living room, bedroom, and kitchen. In the kitchen, make sure to look in the refrigerator and cupboards for products that come from animals.

3. Record on the Lab Report the items that come from animals or animal products.

4. Next to each item on the Lab Report, write the animal the item is from.

5. Read your list of animal products to your family member. Add any other items that your family member suggests.

(continues)

DATA CHART:

Fill in the animal products you found and the animals the items come from:

ROOM	ITEMS FROM ANIMALS OR ANIMAL PRODUCTS	WHICH ANIMAL?
LIVING ROOM	1. 2. 3.	1. 2. 3.
BEDROOM	1. 2. 3.	1. 2. 3.
KITCHEN	1. 2. 3.	1. 2. 3.

CONCLUSIONS:

Discuss the following questions with your family member. Write complete sentences.

1. Which animal gave important food products to your home? _____
_____

2. Which animal gave important non-food items to your home? _____
_____

3. Which animal do you think is the most important to people? Why? _____
_____

HOME TO SCHOOL COMMUNICATION:

Dear Parent/Family Partner,
Please give me your reactions to your child's work on this activity.
Write YES or NO for each statement.
____My child understood the homework and was able to discuss it.
____My child and I enjoyed the activity.
____This assignment helped me know what my child is learning in science.
Any other comments: _____
Parent's Signature: _____

Epstein, J.L., & Salinas, K.C. (revised 2000). Teachers Involve Parents in Schoolwork (TIPS) Interactive Homework for the Elementary Grades. Baltimore: Center on School, Family, and Community Partnerships, Johns Hopkins University.

Student's Name_____   Date_____

TIPS: ON YOUR MARK, GET SET, GO!

Dear Family Partner,
In science we are studying the phases of matter. This activity focuses on liquids to help build skills in observing, recording, and drawing conclusions. I hope you enjoy this activity with me.
This activity is due_____.

Sincerely,

_____
Student's signature

OBJECTIVE: To understand <u>viscosity</u>—a liquid's resistance to <u>flow</u>

MATERIALS: ONE TEASPOON of 3-5 liquids that have different thicknesses—such as catsup, mustard, water, syrup, honey, milk, or others that your family partner will allow you to use.
Also, baking pan, teaspoon, clock with second hand or count seconds.

PROCEDURE:

1. Explain the following to a family partner to share what we are learning in class:
    Who is working with you? _____
    Some liquids are thicker and <u>more viscous</u> than others. They <u>flow slowly</u>.
    Some liquids are thinner and <u>less viscous</u> than others. They <u>flow quickly</u>.

2. With your family partner decide: Which 3-5 liquids will you test?

    a._____   d._____

    b._____   e._____

    c._____

3. Tilt the pan and prop it up against something like a phone book so that it is at an angle (between 45° - 60°). At about what angle is your pan tilted?_____

    One of you will put each liquid in the pan and identify the finish line. The other will serve as the timer. You can check each other to get an accurate observation.

    Start each teaspoon of a new liquid <u>at the same level at the top of the pan</u> at least one inch away from the previous liquid. Make sure the pan remains tilted at the same angle for each test. When you are ready with all of the materials, do these steps:

    a. Place one teaspoon of liquid at the top of your pan.
    b. <u>Time the seconds</u> it takes for the liquid to reach the "finish line" at the bottom of the pan.
    c. Record the information on the Data Chart.
    d. Continue until you have tested each teaspoon of liquid.

(continues)

DATA CHART

LIQUID	SECONDS TO "FINISH" LINE	OBSERVATION HOW VISCOUS IS IT?
_____	_____	_____
_____	_____	_____
_____	_____	_____
_____	_____	_____

CONCLUSIONS:

1. Which liquid finished
   first (fastest)   _____
   midway   _____
   last (slowest)   _____
2. Which liquid has high viscosity? _____
3. Which liquid has low viscosity? _____
4. Why was it important that your pan remained at the same angle for each test?
   _____

FAMILY SURVEY:

ASK: Can you think of any foods or other products that use viscosity (how fast or slow the flow) as part of the advertising to get you to buy it?

Family member's idea _____
My idea _____
Why is high viscosity (slow flow) a good feature (or a bad feature) of a product you use?
_____
_____

Why is low viscosity (quick flow) a good feature (or a bad feature) of a product you use?
_____
_____

HOME TO SCHOOL COMMUNICATION:

Dear Parent/Family Partner,
Please give me your reactions to your child's work on this activity.
Write YES or NO for each statement.
____My child understood the homework and was able to discuss it.
____My child and I enjoyed the activity.
____This assignment helped me know what my child is learning in science.

Any other comments: _____
Parent's signature: _____

Epstein, J.L., Salinas, K.C., & Jackson, V. (revised 2000). Teachers Involve Parents in Schoolwork (TIPS) Interactive Homework for the Middle Grades. Baltimore: Center on School, Family, and Community Partnerships, Johns Hopkins University.

Student's Name_____   Date_____

TIPS: Hairy Tales

Dear Family Partner,
In language arts I am working on using information gathered from others to write explanations. For this assignment, I am comparing today's hairstyles with those of the past. I hope that you enjoy this activity with me. This assignment is due _____.

Sincerely,

_____
Student's signature

Family Interview

FIND A FAMILY MEMBER TO INTERVIEW.

Who is it?_____
Ask:
1) In what decade were you born? (1960s, 1970s, etc.)_____

2) What is one hairstyle that was popular when you were my age?

For boys:_____

For girls:_____

3) What hairstyle did you have when you were my age?_____

4) Did your family agree with your choice of hairstyle?_____

5) What is your favorite current hairstyle and why?_____

6) What is your least favorite current hairstyle and why?_____

Ask your family member to show you a picture of a hairstyle from the past. Draw a picture of the hairstyle here.

First Draft
Use the information from your interview to write a paragraph about hairstyles.
Remember to:
- Give a paragraph a title.
- Be sure all of your sentences related to your topic.
- Use descriptive words to help explain the ideas.
- If you compare hairstyles, tell how they are alike and how they are different.

(continues)

Title:_____

_____

_____

_____

_____

_____

_____

_____

Read your paragraph aloud to your family partner. Revise or add sentences, as needed.

Extension Activity

Select another topic for comparison—for example, clothing styles, ways to have fun, or rules at home or school.   What topic did you choose? _____

Next to each "Q" line, write a question about your topic. Use your questions to interview a family member. Write the family member's answer next to each "A" line.

1. Q: _____
   A: _____
2. Q: _____
   A: _____
3. Q: _____
   A: _____

Home-to-School Connection

Dear Parent/Guardian,

Your comments about your child's work in this activity are important.

Please write YES or NO for each statement:

____My child understood the homework and was able to discuss it.

____My child and I enjoyed this activity.

____This assignment helps me understand what my child is learning in language arts.

Other comments: _____

Epstein, J.L., Salinas, K.C., & Jackson, V. (revised 2000). Teachers Involve Parents in Schoolwork (TIPS) Interactive Homework for the Middle Grades. Baltimore: Center on School, Family, and Community Partnerships, Johns Hopkins University. (Adapted for the elementary grades.)

TIPS: A HELPING HAND

Dear Family Partner,
We are writing narrative paragraphs that include the use of specific details. I hope you enjoy this activity with me. This assignment is due _____.
Sincerely,

_____
Student's signature

THINGS TO REMEMBER:

Narrative writing—
- Tells a story
- Includes a definite beginning, middle, and end
- Uses details to support the main ideas in a clear sequence of events

PROCEDURE:

1. Read the following prompt. You may discuss it with your family member.

PROMPT: A Helping Hand

Think of a time when you needed help and someone helped you. This person may have been a teacher, a neighbor, a classmate, a friend, or a family member. Write one paragraph or more to tell your teacher about a time when someone helped you.

Before you write, think about how the situation began. Think about who was involved and when and where it occurred. Think about what happened as it continued and how it ended. Think about your feelings toward the person who helped you.

2. Complete the pre-writing chart below.

Topic: _____   Purpose: _____
Audience: _____   Form: _____

QUESTIONS	ANSWERS	DETAILS
Who helped you?		
What happened first?		
Second?		
Next?		
Next?		
Last?		
Reactions?		

(continues)

3. Now, write the rough draft of your paragraph. Remember your title, topic sentence, and closing sentence.

Title: _____

_____
_____
_____
_____
_____
_____
_____
_____
_____
_____
_____

4. Read what you have written to your family member.
   Who is listening to you? _____
Add or delete details, or make other changes to improve your work.

FAMILY SURVEY—Ask: What experience do you remember when you were a teen and someone helped you? You write the example that your family partner shares. Use complete sentences.

_____
_____
_____
_____

HOME TO SCHOOL COMMUNICATION:

Dear Parent,
      Please give me your reactions to your child's work on this activity.
Write YES or NO for each statement.
____My child understood the homework and was able to discuss it.
____My child and I enjoyed this activity
____This assignment helped me know what my child is learning in language arts
Any other comments: _____
_____

Parent's Signature: _____

Epstein, J.L., Salinas, K.C., & Jackson, V. (revised 2000). Teachers Involve Parents in Schoolwork (TIPS) Interactive Homework for the Middle Grades. Baltimore: Center on School, Family, and Community Partnerships, Johns Hopkins University.

Student: _____   Class/Period: _____

Date Assigned: _____   Date Due: _____

TIPS: WHY DO WE NEED GOVERNMENT?
How have social conditions changed over time?

Interview a parent or other family partner who is at least 20 years older than you. Ask the following three questions. You record your family partner's opinions.

1. Compared to twenty years ago, have the following social conditions gotten better, stayed the same, or gotten worse? Please tell me in what way.

SOCIAL CONDITIONS	Got Better	Stayed the Same	Got Worse	IN WHAT WAY?
Education	___	___	___	_____
Environment	___	___	___	_____
Crime/violence	___	___	___	_____
Taxes	___	___	___	_____
Unemployment	___	___	___	_____
Poverty	___	___	___	_____
Health care	___	___	___	_____
Race relations	___	___	___	_____
Standard of living	___	___	___	_____
Individual freedom	___	___	___	_____
Family values	___	___	___	_____
Foreign Relations	___	___	___	_____

(continues)

2. Which TWO of the above topics do you think have been helped by governmental programs over the past 20 years, and IN WHAT WAY? You record your family partner's opinions .

TWO areas helped by government   IN WHAT WAY?

1. _____   _____

                                             _____

2. _____   _____

                                             _____

3. Which TWO of the above topics do you think could use MORE or LESS help from governmental programs over the next 5 or 10 years, and IN WHAT WAY? You record your family partner's opinions.

TWO areas that you think need
MORE OR LESS help from government   IN WHAT WAY?
(circle one)

MORE or LESS_____   _____

                                             _____

MORE or LESS_____   _____

                                             _____

STUDENT VIEW

Use a separate page to write your views, based on your interview of a family partner. Attach your work to this assignment.

      a. Write a short summary of your views on how social conditions have changed over the past 20 years.

      b. Choose TWO social conditions from the list on the first page. Discuss your views: Should there be more or less attention over the next 5-10 years from federal, state, or local government on the two social conditions you selected, and why?

Home-to-School Communication

Please ask your family partner for his/her views:

___Yes ___No   This assignment helped me know what my student is learning in Government/Social Studies.

Comments: _____

Family Partner's Signature: _____

Epstein, J.L. (2000). Teachers Involve Parents in Schoolwork (TIPS) Interactive Homework for High Schools. Baltimore: Center on School, Family, and Community Partnerships, Johns Hopkins University. (Assignment suggested by Chesapeake High School, Baltimore County.)

Organizing Productive Volunteers in the Middle Grades*

TEACHERS INVOLVE PARENTS IN SCHOOLWORK (TIPS) VOLUNTEERS IN SOCIAL STUDIES AND ART

Studies consistently show a dramatic decline in parent volunteers at the school building in the middle grades (see Readings 3.3 and 3.6). Middle-grade educators report that they do not seek volunteers because they believe that students do not want their parents at the school. Parents report that they do not volunteer in their children's middle schools, in part because many are working during the school day and in part because they are not invited to volunteer. There are few programs or guidelines available to help educators engage parents productively as volunteers in the middle grades. This chapter introduces one process that organizes volunteers in new ways to support student learning in the middle grades.

OVERVIEW

The Teachers Involve Parents in Schoolwork (TIPS) Volunteers in Social Studies and Art process integrates art appreciation into the social studies curriculum in the middle grades and increases the number of productive volunteers in middle schools. The volunteers present prints of important artwork to increase students' knowledge and appreciation of art and to demonstrate connections of art with history, geography, and social issues. Over three years of eight monthly presentations (e.g., in grades 6–8 or 7–9), students are introduced to the work of at least 24 artists from different eras with varied artistic styles. The artists and their artwork are linked to specific social studies curricular units.

GOALS OF TIPS VOLUNTEERS IN SOCIAL STUDIES AND ART

The TIPS Volunteers in Social Studies and Art process helps solve three common problems in the middle grades: a lack of easily implemented interdisciplinary curricula, a lack of productive family volunteers, and a lack of art appreciation education to develop students' cultural literacy (Jackson, 1987).

---

* By Joyce L. Epstein.

Creating an Integrated, Interdisciplinary Curriculum

Although most educators in the middle grades talk about the value of interdisciplinary curricula, schools have implemented relatively few such programs, in part because it is difficult to develop these connections. It requires teachers, administrators, and others to work together during common planning time to develop and test lessons and materials. In most middle schools, students still study most subjects separately, without much awareness of their connections. TIPS Volunteers in Social Studies and Art infuses major social studies units with related art prints, discussions and critiques, writing across the curriculum, and art activities for homework or classwork.

Improving Family Involvement in the Middle Grades

Although parent volunteers are visible in the elementary grades, they all but disappear in the middle grades. TIPS Volunteers in Social Studies and Art creates productive partnerships of social studies teachers and parents or other volunteers. Volunteers research the selected artist and prints and develop presentations and discussions that integrate art with the social studies curriculum. Once a month, the same or other volunteers present the art prints and conduct discussions with students in their social studies classes. The process provides new, substantive roles for volunteers without requiring a great deal of the parents' or teachers' time. Parents and other family members may volunteer in any classroom, not necessarily their own child's class; other community volunteers also may participate. The presentations of art "masterpieces" require a minimum of 20 minutes of volunteer time each month.

Increasing Art Appreciation Education in the Middle Grades

Art appreciation often is omitted from students' education in the middle grades. Required or elective art courses, if available at all, often are short-term, "exploratory" experiences in art techniques and media. These are necessary but insufficient experiences for students, because short courses do little to connect art with other subjects or to emphasize art history, criticism, and appreciation. The TIPS Volunteers in Social Studies and Art process organizes monthly presentations on artists and their work to extend all students' understanding about art in history and in the human experience.

Links with Curriculum

Forty prints were selected and prototype presentations were prepared that connect to three social studies units: American History, World Cultures, and Government and Citizen Participation (Epstein and Salinas, 1991). American History linkages are made in prototype presentations of prints of artwork by Frederic Remington, Currier and Ives, Edward Hicks, Horace Pippin, Georgia O'Keeffe, Romare Bearden, Robert Rauschenberg, Andy Warhol, and others representing a range of artists from different eras with diverse backgrounds and styles of painting. Similarly, prototype lessons for social studies units on World Cultures include presentations of work by artists from da Vinci to Picasso, and the lessons on Government and Citizen Participation include prints by artists from Vermeer to Mondrian.

EVALUATION

A case study evaluation of the effects on student learning about art was conducted in an urban middle school, serving approximately 80 percent African American students and 20 percent white students. At the time of the study, about 40 percent of the school's students were eligible for free or reduced-price lunch. The school scored higher in reading than most middle schools in the city, but did not meet the state's standards in math, writing, or student attendance. Approximately 400 students in grades 6 through 8 were included in the study of how students reacted to the TIPS Volunteers in Social Studies and Art program and what they learned (Epstein and Dauber, 1995).

Results indicated that students increased their awareness of art and developed attitudes and preferences for different styles of art. Approximately 80 percent of the students commented on an art print they liked, disliked, or would choose for their own living room. Students' comments reflected developmental changes from concrete to abstract thinking. The evaluation confirmed that the TIPS Volunteers process could be successfully implemented and that the results were notable for student learning about art and for helping students think critically about art.

Students recognized more artwork in the spring of the school year than they had the prior fall. It was easier for students to match paintings with their subjects or content than with their artists' names. Although students with higher report card grades knew more artists, students with Cs, Ds, and Fs also were able to recall paintings and their content. Report card grades did not influence whether students enjoyed the art presentations. Regardless of their school skills, students who enjoyed the art remembered more about the prints they saw. Students who had been in the program for at least two years also remembered more art prints. Most students preferred realistic art, but some, regardless of school grades, preferred abstract art. Their preferences may have reflected students' different stages of development of abstract thinking, including the early adolescent stage of bridging concrete and abstract concepts.

The study indicated that the TIPS Volunteers in Social Studies and Art process helps students begin to identify major artists and their work and describe and discuss art with greater insight and sophistication than they had done before. When time for art appreciation is limited and teachers trained in art education are scarce, it is difficult for schools to include art in all students' education. The TIPS

Volunteers in Social Studies and Art process is a useful tool for meeting the diverse goals of involving families, integrating subjects, and providing students with experiences in art awareness, appreciation, and criticism.

HOW TO DEVELOP AND IMPLEMENT TIPS VOLUNTEERS

The TIPS Volunteers in Social Studies and Art process links art prints to specific social studies units or topics. Therefore, it is necessary to review, select, and design prints and presentations that match the curriculum. It may be that the existing prototype presentations for units of American History, World Cultures, or Government and Citizenship Participation match some or all of the units taught in other schools. Or, new prints and new presentations will be needed for other social studies units.

The TIPS Volunteers Social Studies and Art process can be implemented in any school by following the steps described below.

1. Select a teacher coordinator. This may be the chair of the Social Studies Department, a team leader, or a social studies teacher who is committed to implementing an interdisciplinary program with parent volunteers.

2. Select a parent coordinator. This leader will help recruit and train the parent volunteers and coordinate their schedules. There should be an assistant or cocoordinator who will assume the job in the future. The coordinators may be PTA/PTO committee chairs; members of the school's Action Team for School, Family, and Community Partnerships (see Chapter 7); or other interested and responsible volunteers.

3. Select and order the art prints. The collection of art prints must be linked to the social studies curriculum for each grade level. Choices of art prints may include some or all of the prints for which there are prototype presentations, or new prints to match the content of the specific social studies units. Prints may be purchased for about $15 each from Shorewood Fine Art Reproductions (27 Glen Road, Sandy Hook, CT 06482, phone 800-494-3824, fax 203-426-0867, www.art.com) or from any museum or art catalog. The prints must be drymounted on heavy cardboard so that they will last for many years.

There should be enough prints to permit each social studies teacher to select a different print each month from October through May. A minimum of eight prints are needed per grade level. The maximum number of prints is determined by the number of teachers, their curricula, and the budget for the program. For example, *if* five sixth-grade social studies teachers present the same curricular units at different times during the school year, *then* a minimum of eight prints may be cycled over eight months to these sixth-grade classrooms. Multiple copies of prints would be needed if the five sixth-grade teachers taught the same topics in the same order. A maximum of 40 different prints (i.e., five teachers times eight prints) would be needed if the teachers taught completely different social studies units throughout the year.

Each art print remains on display in each classroom for one month, until the next presentation. Teacher and parent coordinators are urged to choose a variety of artists and styles of art for students to study each year. Teachers, students, and volunteers may select the prints together following guidelines for including diverse artists, styles, and topics.

4. **Recruit volunteers.** Some volunteers are needed to make classroom presentations. There should be a minimum of one volunteer for each teacher or a maximum of the same number of volunteers as social studies classes have. If there are not enough volunteers to cover all classes, then teachers or students must conduct the presentations in the classes without volunteers. The parents, other family members, or community volunteers who make classroom presentations need not be expert in art, but they must enjoy art and like talking with students in the middle grades.

If art prints are selected that are not among the prototypes, some volunteers will be needed to conduct research and prepare the presentations, following the style, content, and format of the prototypes. (Some helpful information can be found on the web site artsednet@getty.edu.) The research volunteers may or may not choose to present the prints in class. Sometimes parents who cannot come to school during the school day are happy to develop the presentations because they can do that work on their own schedule.

5. **Orient and train the volunteers.** Volunteers must be prepared to make their monthly presentations. Orientation and training sessions may be conducted in one to two hours at the start of the school year. Duplicate training sessions should be offered during the day and in the evening, if needed, to meet the varied schedules of the volunteers. At the training workshop, the parent coordinators describe the program, schedule, and volunteers' responsibilities and demonstrate how to conduct a successful presentation with students in the middle grades.

If volunteers are employed during the school day, letters may be sent to employers requesting permission for the volunteers to assist the school for one hour once a month. Cooperating employers should be recognized as school business partners.

6. **Implement the Social Studies and Art program.** Once volunteers have been prepared, the following basic steps must be followed to conduct the program:

A. **Schedule monthly presentations.** Art prints are scheduled according to the topics that will be covered in social studies from month to month. Presentations are scheduled at times that are mutually convenient for the volunteers and the teachers. Volunteers meet with the same classes each month. They may visit one class for 20 minutes, or, if time permits, two consecutive classes by scheduling presentations for the last 20 minutes of one class and the first 20 minutes of the next class. Volunteers and teachers agree on the day and date (e.g., the second Thursday of each month) and the time (e.g., the first period and second period classes). Teachers remain in the classroom during the volunteers' presentations.

In a typical 20-minute presentation, the volunteer introduces the artist and something about the artist's life (2–4 minutes), discusses the technique and type of painting (2–4 minutes), gives the story behind the particular print (4–6 minutes), and connects the print to social studies (2–4 minutes). Then, the volunteer conducts an active discussion with the students about what they see in the print, how they react to it, and why (5–8 minutes).

The print remains on display in the classroom for one month, until the next presentation. Students are asked to examine the print while it is in the classroom and form their own opinions about the art. Teachers may use optional follow-up activities that are included in the manual or devise their own classroom or homework activities.

B. Assist volunteers. Parent coordinators check in with volunteers and with the teacher coordinator after the first presentations, and periodically throughout the year, to ensure that the program is proceeding as planned. Parent coordinators remind volunteers about their schedules from month to month, obtain or serve as substitutes, as needed, and address any questions that may arise as volunteers prepare their presentations.

C. Evaluate the program and results. Teachers evaluate students to determine whether the program increases students' appreciation and knowledge about the artists and artwork. Parent and teacher coordinators may conduct other annual or periodic evaluations of volunteers, teachers, and students to gather reactions to the program and suggestions for improvements. Sample tests of students' skills and sample surveys of participants' attitudes about the program are included in the manual.

ADAPTING AND EXTENDING TIPS VOLUNTEERS

The guidelines for implementing TIPS Volunteers in Social Studies and Art may be used to develop other productive work by volunteers, such as interdisciplinary connections of art or music with English or science. The TIPS Volunteers process was designed for the middle grades, but it may be adapted for younger or older students. Indeed, TIPS Volunteers grew from an art appreciation activity called "Picture Parents" in the elementary grades. In that program, parent volunteers discussed artwork in elementary classes from kindergarten through grade 5, but did not link the art to social studies or other subjects. At the high school level, TIPS Volunteers might include parent or family volunteers; community volunteers such as museum staff, docents, or visiting artists; student leaders paired with volunteers; or other volunteers, and might focus on art and history or other interdisciplinary connections.

MATERIALS AVAILABLE AND PROGRAM COSTS

Prototype presentations, designed by researchers and volunteers and tested in grades 6, 7, and 8, are available for approximately 40 art prints linked to social studies units on American History, World Cultures, and Government and Citizenship Participation. Each presentation includes information on the artist's life, technique, and specific artwork; connections to social studies; connections to other school subjects; connections among two or more artists and prints; where to see original work by the artist; and topics for class discussions. The prototype assignments can be adapted to other social studies units, other grade levels, or other interdisciplinary combinations (e.g., art and English, music and social studies).

An implementation manual for TIPS Volunteers in Social Studies and Art includes ideas for written assignments and art activities that teachers may use as classwork or homework to extend the volunteers' presentations. Also included in the manual are prototype guidelines for field trips to art museums; questionnaires to assess reactions to the program by teachers, students, and volunteers; and sample quizzes to assess students' knowledge and reactions to the program.

The total cost of the art prints, implementation manuals, prototype presentations, training of volunteers, mailing reminders, recognition or celebration events at the end of the year, and other program costs should be under $2,000 in the first year, and approximately $500–$700 in subsequent years, depending on the size of the school and the need for replacement materials. Schools may decide to invest additional funds in art materials, trips to museums, and other enrichment activities.[1]

REFERENCES

Epstein, J. L., and S. L. Dauber. (1995). Effects on students of an interdisciplinary program linking social studies, art, and family volunteers in the middle grades. *Journal of Early Adolescence* 15: 114–144.

Epstein, J. L., and K. C. Salinas. (1991). *TIPS social studies and art manual and prototype presentations*. Baltimore: Center on Families, Communities, Schools and Children's Learning, Johns Hopkins University.

Jackson, P. W. (1987). Mainstreaming art: An essay on discipline-based art education. *Educational Researcher* 16(6): 39–43.

DISCUSSION AND ACTIVITIES

The comments in this section extend and update the content of the readings in this chapter. Key concepts are summarized. Questions and activities are provided for class discussions, debates, and homework assignments. They may suggest other exercises, field activities, and research projects.

▣ KEY CONCEPTS

Interactive Homework. Interactive homework is a method of designing homework assignments that enables students to share interesting things they are learning in class with family members, friends and peers, or

---

[1] For more information, guidelines, and examples, see the TIPS *Social studies and art manual and prototype presentations* (Epstein and Salinas, 1991); examples at www.partnershipschools.org (follow the links to TIPS Social Studies and Art Volunteers).

members of the community. This kind of homework requires students to share ideas, gather information, or interact with someone in other ways to complete the assignments.

Teachers Involve Parents in Schoolwork (TIPS) Interactive Homework. TIPS is one approach for designing and implementing interactive homework. Used on a regular schedule, TIPS activities help parents remain aware of what their children are learning in school subjects. The activities encourage students and family members to engage in positive conversations about homework.

Teachers Involve Parents in Schoolwork (TIPS) Volunteers in Social Studies and Art. This process is one approach for organizing productive volunteers in the middle grades. Volunteers present and discuss art prints to increase students' art appreciation and awareness of interdisciplinary connections between art and history.

❐⦂ COMMENT

Key Components of Interactive Homework

Interactive homework is more interesting and effective when the following four features are built into the design.

Student-directed interactions. Students—not parents—must do the work of conducting interviews, gathering reactions, and completing the homework. Parents should not be required to teach school subjects, nor read or write for students. Homework is always the students' work.

Family input. Family members should be asked by students to share ideas, listen and react to something that the student reads aloud, recall experiences or memories, and participate in other kinds of conversations. The guided interactions should not depend on family members' formal education but rather on their care for and interest in their children.

Completed homework returned to class on time. Students and family members must do more than talk. Students must record something of the interactions in writing or in other forms. The activity sheet, data chart, or other papers or products must be completed and returned to class as regular homework. Interactive homework should be collected, reviewed, graded, discussed, or treated in the same way as other daily homework. If a parent cannot participate in a particular assignment, then another family member, neighbor, or peer may "substitute" for a parent to ensure that each student talks with someone about the work.

Positive, thoughtful, and enjoyable exchanges. Students and family partners should enjoy the interactive homework assignments. The activities should be important (linked to the class curriculum), challenging (not too hard or too easy for students to conduct), and enjoyable for students and parents.

Two-way communications. Interactive homework should include two-way communications. The assignment comes from school to home, but observations, questions, and reactions may come from home to school. Activities should include an easy-to-read checklist for parents' reactions, a place for a signature, and space for optional notes or questions.

QUESTIONS TO DISCUSS

The five features outlined above emerged from data collected from parents about their children's homework.

1. From Reading 6.1, add one feature to the above list that you think is another key element for successful interactive homework.
2. Give one reason why you think each of the six features of interactive homework (the five listed above and the one that you added) is important to each of the following:
   A. parents
   B. students
   C. teachers
3. Review the TIPS Math, TIPS Science, and TIPS Language Arts approaches in Reading 6.1.
   A. Identify two *similarities* in the approaches for interactive homework in different subjects and explain why the similarities are important.
   B. What are one challenge that may arise in implementing the similar aspects of TIPS interactive homework and one potential solution to that challenge?
4. A. Identify two *differences* in the approaches for interactive homework in different subjects and explain why these differences are important.
   B. What are one challenge that may arise in implementing the different aspects of TIPS interactive homework and one potential solution to that challenge?
5. TIPS interactive homework activities are designed to be distributed once a week, twice a month, or on some other regular schedule in conjunction with particular class lessons. Some teachers have revised this approach and put many assignments together in a "homework packet" for students to take back and forth over the course of a unit of work or marking period. Controlled studies are needed on alternative formats, but field experience suggests that packets of assignments are less successful in encouraging all families to become involved with their children than are individual weekly activities.
   A. Identify a grade level and subject that interest you.
   B. Create a chart of pros and cons for the two TIPS formats: TIPS distributed as weekly activities or as packets of assignments. For the grade

level and subject you selected, give two pros and two cons for each of the two formats: TIPS one-page (two-sided) assignments distributed once a week versus a packet of many TIPS activities for a unit or marking period.

C. Discuss the pros and cons in class to hear others' ideas about these options.

◈ ACTIVITY

How Many Ways Can Homework Be Interactive?

Using the information in Readings 6.1, 3.8, and your own ideas, list as many ways as you can of how students and parents may converse and interact around homework.

A. Identify a grade level and two subjects that interest you.
B. Label three columns: (1) *Interactions,* (2) *What the Student Does,* (3) *What the Family Partner Does.* For each subject:
  1. In the first column, list at least eight different kinds of interactions that students might conduct with family partners (e.g., show-and-tell, interviews).
  2. In the second column, briefly explain what a student might do to engage a family partner in each kind of interaction (e.g., student reads sentences aloud; student demonstrates math skill).
  3. In the third column, briefly explain what a family partner might do to assist or respond to the student (e.g., family partner shares ideas, listens to student).
  4. In the third column, put an X next to any interaction that requires a parent or family partner to read or write on the student's homework (other than for a home-to-school communication and parent signature). For each X that you marked, explain whether all families could conduct the activity or which families would not be able to participate in that interaction.
  5. Examine the interactions that you listed for the *two* subjects that you selected. Write a short summary of the similarities or differences in your lists due to the nature or demands of the different subjects.

⑪ COMMENT

Helping All Parents Do What a Few Do on Their Own

Although some parents know how to help their children with homework because of their own school experiences, most parents say they do not know how to approach school subjects and topics across the grades. In the past, many teachers believed they should *not* try to involve parents in learning activities at home, because there always were a few parents who could not or would not become involved. Studies indicate that about 20 percent of parents become involved with their children and the schools on their own, but over 70 percent of parents say they want to become involved and would if they were guided in how to do so. TIPS interactive homework may help because it is assigned to *students* and asks them to show their skills and discuss ideas with a parent or other family partner. With well-designed interactive assignments for students from kindergarten or first grade on, just about all parents should be able to continually monitor their children's work and progress and discuss ideas with their children.

QUESTIONS TO DISCUSS

1. Select a grade level and subject that interest you.
2. List two reasons why the TIPS approach might help students and families conduct conversations about student work in the grade and subject you selected.
3. List two problems that might occur with interactive homework for students or for parents in the grade and subject you selected and a potential solution to each problem you listed.
4. If about 20 percent of parents already are involved with their children in learning activities at home, and if about 70 percent would like to be so, which is more important:
   A. Guiding all parents' involvement, even if a few cannot become involved?
   B. Leaving involvement up to parents to figure out on their own?
   C. Give two reasons in support of item A or item B and explain why you think this approach is the better one.

◻⦂ COMMENT

Common Questions about TIPS

Following are several common questions that teachers raise about TIPS.

1. **What if a parent is not able to interact with the student about math (or any subject) on a particular night?** It is highly recommended, based on data from parents, that teachers assign TIPS interactive homework over two or three days (e.g., assigned Tuesday, due Thursday or Friday, or assigned over the weekend). Research shows consistently that most parents (over 90 percent on several surveys) say they can find time over the weekend to talk and work with their children on homework. This is the very time that some schools do not give homework.

Students should be guided to share their work with other family partners if a parent is not available. This includes older siblings, grandparents, other relatives, child care providers, or even a neighbor or friend. Most parents or other family members are available in the evening, morning, or on the weekend. Teachers' schedules for TIPS assignments should take into account when their students' parents are available for interactions. An orientation for parents and follow-up calls should help all parents understand the TIPS process and their roles in encouraging their children to complete their homework and in motivating their children's interest in school.

2. What if a family does not have the materials needed for a science activity on a given night? TIPS Science materials must be common, inexpensive, and readily available at home. Unusual or costly items should be provided by the school. Students whose families cannot afford any extra expenses should be provided with the materials needed for each science activity. If the TIPS schedule is family-friendly, students and families will be able to find time and the common materials for TIPS Science activities.

3. What if a parent does not read English well? All homework is the student's responsibility. Parents do not have to read or write English well to talk with their children or to listen to their children talk about schoolwork. The student must understand that TIPS, like all homework, must be completed, and that all of their families can be involved. For example, teachers must reinforce that students should read their work aloud, translating or interpreting the information into their home language, just as they would other memos or notices from school. Some schools translate the letter to parents and the home-to-school-communication section of TIPS activities into other languages. The sections of student work, however, are in English.

One interesting application of TIPS was in a Japanese foreign language class for English-speaking students. The teacher knew that the students' parents did not know Japanese and could not "help" their children with their homework. She knew, however, that the children could show and share the new words and skills that they were learning in Japanese because TIPS guided students to conduct these interactions. The same would be true for students in homes where parents speak languages other than English. Students could still demonstrate their skills and share ideas in the language that they speak with parents at home and complete their TIPS interactive homework.

4. Can you give the same TIPS activity to students who are slower learners and to those who have advanced skills? Like other homework, TIPS activities must match students' levels of ability. If homework is too hard, it will be frustrating and will not be completed. If homework is too easy, it will be boring and students may disengage. TIPS activities should be written at an appropriate reading level for all students in a group or class. Teachers may assign slower students some parts or sections of the assignments. Other sections may be assigned for extra credit and include specific challenges for advanced students. Or, groups within classes may be assigned different TIPS activities, if they are assigned different homework on other days.

QUESTIONS TO DISCUSS

All four of the topics discussed above are about equity.

1. What is the equity issue that underlies each of the four questions about TIPS homework?
2. Explain how the TIPS interactive homework process addresses each issue.

◇ ACTIVITY

Design an Interactive Homework Assignment

A. Identify a grade level, subject, and specific skill in that subject that interest you.
B. Design one interactive homework activity using the TIPS format that requires children to talk with a family member to complete the assignment. Use your computer to store the assignment to permit easy editing in item C below.
  1. For useful formats, see the samples of TIPS Math, Science/Health, and Language Arts in this chapter. For social studies, foreign language, family life, or other subjects, adapt one of the existing TIPS formats to fit the subject and skill that you selected.
  2. Include a short and clear introductory letter to parents about the assignment. The letter should be signed by the student.
  3. End the assignment with a section for a home-to-school communication and for a parent's signature.
C. *Class activity:*
  1. Share the draft designs of TIPS interactive homework in class. Work with a partner, taking the roles of student and family partner conducting the interactive assignment at home.
  2. Exchange design and editing suggestions about how to make the assignments clear, family-friendly, and feasible for students to conduct at the grade levels selected for each design.
  3. Edit the homework design to take into account your classmates' suggestions. Polish the assignment so that it is attractive, well spaced, and includes graphics, as needed.
  4. Collect examples of good activities for a resource notebook.

◈ FIELD EXPERIENCE

Test of a TIPS Assignment

A. Arrange with a cooperating teacher to assign one TIPS interactive homework item that resulted from the above activity, design a new TIPS interactive homework task with the cooperating teacher to match a specific class lesson, or use an existing TIPS prototype activity that matches a specific class lesson.

B. Review with the cooperating teacher the steps needed to use a TIPS activity:

1. Provide more than one night to allow students and families to find time for their interactions.

2. Orient the students to the work they will do on the assignment at home. (Because this field experience involves just one class and one experimental assignment, it should not be necessary to conduct the full orientation process with parents that is needed when TIPS is used as a regularly scheduled approach to homework.)

C. The cooperating teacher will assign the TIPS activity to students in at least one class, after taking time to explain the sections where they will conduct conversations, demonstrations, or activities with a family partner.

D. The cooperating teacher will collect the TIPS interactive homework assignments when they are due.

E. Review the students' work with the cooperating teacher. Write a summary of your reactions to:

- the rate and quality of students' completion of the homework;
- evidence of participation by family partners;
- parents' home-to-school communications and comments; and
- other observations that you have about the clarity of the assignment, the student-family interactions, the teachers' views of the sample activity, and other issues.

🛈 COMMENT

Linking Communities to the School Curriculum

In addition to interactions with family partners, some schools are encouraging more productive interactions of students with members of their school, home, and work communities. Beginning in the elementary grades, there is increasing interest in "service learning" activities that help students contribute to their communities by conducting helpful, voluntary, or negotiated good deeds and problem-solving. At all grade levels, mentoring programs connect individuals from the community, business, industry, government, and civic institutions with individual students, small groups, and whole classes. Mentors share wisdom and demonstrate that the community cares for students. Also, as noted in Chapter 5, early adolescents and teens in middle and high schools begin to extend their interactions with people in the various places where they live, go to school, attend faith-based organizations, have part-time jobs, participate in sports, and other activities.

Many students, then, at all grade levels are involved in activities and events in their communities, but they may not connect these activities with their school experiences or the specific subjects they learn in school. Many other students are not linked to mentors, service learning, or various activities in their communities, and have little or no contact with other adults or organizations beyond home and school.

Community-based TIPS interactive homework is one way to design purposeful, curriculum-linked connections that all students can conduct with various individuals or groups in the community. This variation of TIPS may be assigned once or twice a year, once per marking period, or on some other regular schedule to help students see connections between what they are learning in class and the work and ideas of people in the community. Community-based TIPS activities also should permit students to share their community experiences and knowledge with their family members. In this way, the students, families, schools, and communities connect and support students' learning.

◇ ACTIVITY

Designing Community-Based Interactive Homework

A. Identify a grade level, subject, and specific skill in a subject that interest you.
  1. Design one community-based interactive homework assignment using a TIPS format that requires children to talk with someone in the neighborhood or community (not only a family member) to complete the assignment. Consider the neighborhoods where students might conduct their interactions; the amount of time needed to complete the activity; whether a student would work with another student or family member; and other factors to ensure that the assignment is safe, well timed, appropriate for the grade level, and important for learning.
  2. Select a TIPS format that fits the grade level and subject matter you chose.
  3. Start with a short, clear introductory letter to the community partner about the topic and purpose of the activity. Include the due date and the signature of the student.
  4. Include one interaction that enables the student to share information from the community with a family partner.
  5. End the assignment with a section that enables the community member and a family member to communicate with the teacher.
B. *Class activity:*
  1. Share the draft designs of community-based TIPS interactive homework in class. Work with a partner, taking the roles of student and community contact conducting the interactive assignment.
  2. Exchange design and editing suggestions about how to make the assignments clear, community-friendly, and feasible for students to conduct at the grade levels selected for each design.

3. Edit the homework design to take into account classmates' suggestions. Polish the assignment so that it is attractive, well spaced, and includes graphics, as needed.

4. Collect examples or files of good activities for a resource notebook.

5. *Optional activity:* See the field experience with a cooperating teacher in the section on TIPS, above. Conduct a similar activity with a cooperating teacher for the community-based interactive homework assignment.

For other information on homework, including various interactive homework designs, see the comments and activities on Type 4—Learning at Home in Chapter 5.

▯: COMMENT

Creating a Leadership Structure for Volunteers

To implement the TIPS Volunteers in Social Studies and Art process, one school created the position of Parent Coordinator for Volunteers as one of its standing committees of its parent-teacher organization (PTO). Other schools with an Action Team for Partnerships have a Type 3—Volunteering committee chair or cochairs to organize productive volunteers for the school (see Chapter 7). These organizational approaches solve the problem of having to scramble to identify a parent coordinator for the TIPS Volunteers in Social Studies and Art program each year. An assistant or cocoordinator also could be selected each year from among the volunteers who have at least one year of experience in the program. The parent leaders work together, and the assistant may become the coordinator over time. With ongoing and backup leadership, there is greater likelihood that the TIPS Volunteers in Social Studies and Art program will continue from year to year.

By creating a PTA/PTO committee for TIPS Volunteers in Social Studies and Art, a school also solves the problem of publicizing the program. The designated coordinator has various opportunities to share information at organizational meetings, in newsletters, and in other communications, and is able to recruit volunteers for the program. This strategy also encourages the parent association to contribute funds to purchase new or replacement art prints and other supplies or materials needed by the volunteers for their presentation or by teachers for following up the discussions with related art activities. Similarly, a Type 3, Volunteering committee of an Action Team for Partnerships strengthens and stabilizes school volunteer programs, while other committees organize and conduct activities for the other types of involvement.

QUESTIONS TO DISCUSS

1. Imagine that a school principal or curriculum leader asks you for advice about organizing a TIPS Volunteers in Social Studies and Art program. Se-

lect a school level that interests you (e.g., preschool, elementary, middle, or high school).

2. Identify a grade level that interests you and the number of social studies teachers for that grade level.

3. Review the program components for TIPS Volunteers in Social Studies and Art in Reading 6.2. List one idea that will guide the school and the selected grade level in how to organize each of the following activities so the TIPS Volunteers in Social Studies and Art program will easily continue from year to year.

HOW TO:	ONE IDEA:
A. Select a coordinator and assistant	
B. Recruit parent and other volunteers	
C. Train volunteers in how to present art prints to students' classes	
D. Schedule volunteers for each teacher's room	
E. Monitor the work of the volunteers	
F. Extend the program to other grade levels in the school	

❏⦂ COMMENT

Reactions to TIPS Volunteers in Social Studies and Art

When we first started to develop TIPS Volunteers in Social Studies and Art, some teachers worried that middle school students would not want their parents to participate. Our studies indicated that middle-grade students did not want their parents to work with them and their teachers in the same ways as in elementary school. In the middle grades, parents were not supposed to talk with their own children and were not supposed to hug anyone! However, middle-grade students were positive in their evaluations of TIPS Volunteers in Social Studies and Art (Epstein and Dauber, 1995; see Reading 6.2). They appreciated the mothers, fathers, grandparents, aunts, and other volunteers who brought art to their social studies classes, and they liked viewing art prints and deciding their likes and dislikes.

Volunteers in the middle grades did not typically work in their own child's classroom. Although some selected their child's class or teacher, most worked with any teacher who needed a volunteer. Initial evaluations revealed no systematic differences in the success of the program based on whether parents were in their own children's or other classrooms. Teachers appreciated the parents' contributions to the program. The parent volunteers were particularly enthusiastic, with some obtaining permission from their employers to participate once a month and others taking personal time off from work to participate.

◈ ACTIVITY AND FIELD EXPERIENCE

Ideas and Interview about Volunteers in the Middle Grades

A. Should educators in the middle grades base their family involvement policies and practices on the belief that "students do not want their parents at school"? Explain your ideas.

B. Give two examples of how parents might be helpful volunteers in the middle grades.

C. 1. Identify two concerns that teachers or principals might have about volunteers who are asked to visit the same social studies class each month to share a new art print.

    2. List one idea to address each question or concern to maximize the success of the volunteers and benefits to students.

D. 1. Identify two concerns that parents or other volunteers might have about visiting the same social studies class each month to share a new art print.

    2. List one idea to address each question or concern to maximize the success of the volunteers and benefits to students.

E. Check your examples and concerns with a middle school teacher, parent, *or* student.

    1. Identify your source and report whether he or she believes your examples (in item B) are realistic.

    2. Ask your source for two more examples of how parents may be helpful and productive volunteers in the middle grades.

    3. Ask your source if the concerns in items C1 and D1 are serious, and why.

    4. Ask your source if the solutions in items C2 and D2 are realistic, and why.

    5. Record your questions and the responses you obtained.

◈ ACTIVITY

Designing Other Interdisciplinary Connections for Volunteers

The TIPS Volunteers in Social Studies and Art process was designed to integrate art appreciation in social studies classes, but other interdisciplinary linkages may be made. How might volunteers be organized to link art, music, performing arts, architecture, or other enrichments with English, a foreign language, science, or other subjects? Note that the interdisciplinary connections include art, music, crafts, technology, or some other extensions that are likely to be among the skills and talents of many parents or other volunteers.

A. Identify a grade level that interests you.
B. Identify an interdisciplinary connection (*not* art and social studies) that might productively use volunteers to help teachers enrich students' understanding and experiences in the grade level that you selected.
C. Give two reasons for developing the interdisciplinary connections you selected.
D. Design one activity that a volunteer might conduct (a presentation, lesson, discussion) to make the interdisciplinary connection that you identified in the grade level you selected. Check the components of the TIPS Volunteers in Social Studies and Art process to guide your design. For example, the activity might be conducted monthly for about 20 minutes of class time with students at the grade level you selected. Include a suggestion for how the teacher can follow up and build on the volunteer's activity with a class discussion or homework assignment. The activity should develop or extend students' awareness, knowledge, and experiences about an important topic.
E. Share and critique the draft designs for interdisciplinary volunteer activities. For each one, consider:
1. Is the interdisciplinary connection important?
2. Is the topic of the activity compelling and appropriate for the grade level selected?
3. Would the activity engage the students at the grade level selected?
4. Is the activity using the time and talents of volunteers well?
5. Collect some of the best examples for a resource notebook.

❖ FIELD EXPERIENCE

Test of TIPS Assignment

A. Arrange with a cooperating teacher to test the interdisciplinary connection for volunteers that you or a classmate designed in the preceding activity. You may serve as the "volunteer" in this test case.
1. Review the design with the cooperating teacher at the grade level for which the activity was designed. Make the necessary changes to fit the class curriculum and students' characteristics. (Or, with a cooperating teacher, test one of the prototypes in the TIPS Volunteers in Social Studies and Art program.)
2. As the "volunteer," you conduct the interdisciplinary activity that you designed or developed with the cooperating teacher. Work with the cooperating teacher on the steps needed to test a TIPS Volunteers activity:

A. Review the goals, content, and timing of the presentation or activity.
B. Schedule time to conduct and complete the activity.
C. Check the students' reactions to the activity.
D. Conduct one follow-up class or homework activity.

B. Interview the cooperating teacher for his or her reactions to the presentation, the follow-up activity, and the process for enlisting volunteers to increase interdisciplinary connections in the selected grade level and subject.

C. Summarize what you learned from the cooperating teacher and students in your test of the activity. Describe how the activity was successful and how it might be improved to increase the effectiveness of a volunteer and the benefits to students.

For other information about volunteers, see comments and activities on Type 3—Volunteering in Chapter 5.

REFERENCES

Epstein, J. L., and S. L. Dauber. (1995). Effects on students of an interdisciplinary program linking social studies, art, and family volunteers in the middle grades. *Journal of Early Adolescence* 15: 114–144.

7

Strategies for Action in Practice, Policy, and Research

THIS CHAPTER SERVES AS A SUMMARY and as a starting point. What have we learned about school, family, and community partnerships? What can we do with what we have learned? How should educators in schools, districts, and states develop policies and programs of partnership that improve schools, strengthen families, and help more students succeed? How might new teachers, principals, counselors, and others who work in schools and with families be prepared to conduct effective partnership practices? How could researchers contribute new knowledge that will help policy leaders and practitioners with their work?

One important question raised by all of the research and applications in this volume is: *Who* is responsible for developing and maintaining school, family, and community partnerships? The answer, of course, is that everyone with an interest or investment in children is responsible for producing and maintaining good schools, productive partnerships, and successful students. This includes state and district leaders whose policies and assistance support the development of excellent schools. It includes teachers, administrators, parents, and students who work together in each school to help students develop and learn. It includes members of the broader community, whose lives tomorrow depend on the skills of students today. And it includes researchers who conduct studies that contribute to wise policies and to research-based practices for excellent schools.

It is abundantly clear that one principal, teacher, or parent working alone cannot create a comprehensive and lasting program of partnership. Many partners in states, districts, schools, homes, communities, and research settings must work together to improve knowledge, policies, plans, and programs. It also is well known that if *everyone* is in charge of something, then *no one* is really responsible.

A crucial question, then, is: *How* are partnership programs organized and sustained? Over the years, our work with educators and families in many communities has shown that state and district Leadership Teams for Partnerships and school Action Teams for Partnerships are needed to develop and sustain successful programs. Team leaders must be identified; team structures must be set; team processes must be selected; budgets must be allocated; annual action plans must be written; and evaluations must be conducted to implement and continually improve programs of school, family, and community partnerships in schools, districts, and states.

Leadership, teamwork, written plans, funding, internal and external support, implementation, evaluations, and continuous improvement make a difference in whether, which, when, why, and how families and communities become involved in children's education. These organizational components have emerged from data from hundreds of schools, scores of districts, and several state departments of education in the National Network of Partnership Schools whose actions have been evaluated to learn what it takes to establish and maintain programs of school, family, and community partnership. When these components are well organized, educators and families develop the capacity and expertise to implement partnership programs as part of regular school practice.

This chapter builds on Reading 5.1 with a detailed discussion of the structure and activities of school-based Action Teams for Partnerships (ATP). The ATP is the "action arm" or "work group" of a school improvement team or school council. The members of an ATP—educators, parents, and others—work together to implement, monitor, and improve school, family, and community partnership practices that will help reach school and classroom goals. The ATP turns partnership plans into actions and partnership goals into results.

Without an ATP, this teacher or that leader may conduct selected partnership projects or activities with some parents. With an ATP, every elementary, middle, and high school and all teachers will have a full and feasible plan for involving all families in their children's education at all grade levels. With well-functioning ATPs, programs of school, family, and community partnership should be as regular as reading, as expected as English, as methodical as math, and as standard as science or other subjects. Along with the school's curriculum, instruction, and assessments, a program of partnership should be viewed as an essential aspect of school organization, a regular part of school life.

This chapter also summarizes the central themes and major conclusions about school, family, and community partnerships that have been presented in the readings, discussions, and activities throughout the volume. Having a school action team or a district or state leadership team to organize a partnership program is a structural matter. Program plans and practices must be based on key principles that get to the heart of the matter.

All of the studies, comments, and activities in this volume point to the need for mutual trust and respect by educators and parents for partnerships to succeed, the need for equity in partnership programs so that all families are informed and involved in their children's education, and the simultaneous need for diversity in partnership programs to address the different situations and requirements of some families. Here, we explore these central themes. Finally, eight crosscutting conclusions not only summarize what has been learned from many studies but also raise new questions about how to effectively involve all families in their children's schools and education.

If you are a researcher, you are encouraged to establish connections with school, district, and state partners to bring research-based approaches to school, family, and community partnerships into education policy and practice and to study the results of these efforts. If you are an educator, this chapter should lead you from an understanding of the theory, research, and policies of partnership to the application of useful strategies in the real world. The fact is, all that you have learned about partnerships must be tailored to the goals and conditions of the specific schools and classrooms, districts, and states in which you work. Thus, for researchers and for practitioners, the readings, discussions, debates, and projects in this volume are just the beginning of your work on school, family, and community partnerships.

DISCUSSION AND ACTIVITIES

The comments in this section extend and update the second half of Reading 5.1 to focus on the actions needed to organize programs of partnership in schools. The comments also review the central themes and crosscutting conclusions from all readings and activities in this volume. Key concepts are summarized. Questions and activities are provided for class discussions, debates, and homework assignments. They may suggest other exercises, field activities, and research projects.

KEY CONCEPTS

1. **Comprehensive program of school, family, and community partnerships.** A full program of partnerships includes activities for all six types of involvement so that families and community members may be involved at home, at school, and in other locations. Partnership activities are selected and designed to focus on specific goals; meet key challenges; and produce results for students, families, teachers, schools, and the community. Comprehensive programs are ongoing. Leaders in schools, districts, and state departments of education plan and implement comprehensive programs of school, family, and community partnership as a regular part of their work every year.

2. **Action Team for Partnerships (ATP).** The Action Team for Partnerships is the basic school structure for implementing an ongoing, comprehensive partnership program tailored to school improvement goals. The ATP, including teachers, parents, administrators, and others, is the "action arm" of a school improvement team. The ATP is responsible for turning general plans for involving families and communities in children's education into detailed plans, implemented actions, and evaluated practices in a comprehensive program of school, family, and community partnerships.

3. Leadership Team for Partnerships (LTP). The Leadership Team for Partnerships is the basic structure for developing comprehensive programs of partnership at the state and district levels. Members of LTPs include interdepartmental colleagues who are responsible for federal, state, and local programs to involve families and communities in children's education. State-level LTPs develop and implement coherent policies and actions that apply across districts and schools. District-level LTPs conduct activities that assist all elementary, middle, and high schools in creating and maintaining their programs of school, family, and community partnerships. This includes helping educators, parents, and others in every school gain the knowledge and skills they need to work together to plan and implement partnership programs to meet school goals. (See Chapter 4 on state and district activities.)

4. Action plans. One-year action plans for school, family, and community partnerships, and multiyear missions or vision statements for improving partnerships, are essential for making progress in involving families and communities in children's education. One-year action plans for partnerships include activities for all six types of involvement that are linked to important academic, behavioral, and school-climate goals, as specified in school improvement plans. Action plans provide the detailed schedules and responsibilities for all partnership activities to ensure that what is planned will be successfully implemented.

5. Central themes. There are several crosscutting characteristics of strong programs of school, family, and community partnerships. High-quality partnership programs build trust and mutual respect among partners in children's education, attend to issues of equity, and celebrate diversity. When partnership programs are equitable they inform and involve all families, not just a few. When programs are responsive to all families, they recognize *and* meet special needs of diverse families and students. The simultaneous, seemingly contradictory, goals of ensuring equity and responding to diversity can be met only if educators, parents, and community partners develop mutual respect for their individual and collaborative work with children. Thus, in addition to the instrumental structure of ATPs and detailed procedures of one-year action plans, the expressive and humane qualities of trust, respect, equity, and diversity are at the heart of school, family, and community partnerships.

❶❸ COMMENT

Program Versus Activities of School, Family, and Community Partnerships

What is a *program* of partnership? How does it differ from the parent involvement activities that most schools or individual teachers already conduct? Most principals and teachers communicate with families occasionally, not regularly; and in isolation from one another, not as part of a coherent and continuing schoolwide program. Typically, involvement activities are conducted by one teacher or a few, with some families but not with all.

By contrast, a comprehensive program of partnership is based on a long-term vision and annual, detailed plans and schedules of activities for all six types of involvement that are linked to school improvement goals. In comprehensive programs of school, family, and community partnerships, each of the six types of involvement is represented by several activities, not just one. As programs develop, there should be many ways for parents, other family members, community groups, and other citizens to gain and share information about parenting (Type 1); communicate with educators and each other about school programs and children's progress (Type 2); volunteer at school, at home, or in the community (Type 3); interact with children in class work, homework, and academic decisions such as course choices (Type 4); become informed about and involved in school decisions (Type 5); and connect with organizations, services, and other opportunities in the community (Type 6). In a comprehensive partnership program, the quality of activities is reviewed and improved from year to year to involve all families of students at all grade levels and to incorporate community connections that promote student success in school.

QUESTIONS TO DISCUSS

1. What difference might a program of school, family, and community partnerships make to parents? In the chart in Figure 7.1, list two ways in which a typical parent might be differently informed or involved by a school *with* and *without* a comprehensive partnership program. Consider, as examples, a parent whose child is (a) entering kindergarten and (b) progressing from middle to high school.
2. Think of the four hypothetical students (A, B, C, and D) that are represented in the four sections of Figure 7.1. Give each student a name, and explain how each student may be affected by the kinds of family-school connections that you listed.

❒ COMMENT

Understanding Action Teams for Partnerships (ATP)

Many schools have school councils, school improvement teams, or other site-based governance or management committees that advise on and oversee the progress of school improvement plans and goals. School councils usually identify changes that are needed in the curriculum, instruction, staffing, management, family involvement, community connections, and other areas of school and classroom organization. These decision-making or advisory bodies often set ambitious

	What might a typical parent expect from:	
When:	A school *with* a comprehensive program of partnerships?	A school *without* a planned program of partnerships?
Child is being enrolled in kindergarten	A (1) (2)	B (1) (2)
Student is progressing from middle to high school	C (1) (2)	D (1) (2)

FIGURE 7.1   Parent Expectations

goals and write broad plans for school improvement, but do not often organize clear structures, processes, schedules, and responsibilities for turning plans into action.

In working with schools over many years, my colleagues and I have found that school councils, improvement teams, or other planning and advisory committees need "action arms" to ensure that activities planned are implemented from year to year. These are action teams, work groups, or committees of teachers, parents, administrators, and others in the community who focus explicitly, as partners, on implementing activities to meet the major goals of a school improvement agenda. For example, if a school aims to improve or maintain the involvement of families and communities, then an ATP will see that involvement activities are selected, scheduled, implemented, evaluated, improved, and sustained. Similarly, if a school aims to help students improve their math skills and math test scores, then an Action Team for Math (ATM) needs to take appropriate actions to reach that goal. Action teams are needed to turn plans into actions that will help students reach major school improvement goals.

QUESTIONS TO DISCUSS

1. Give two reasons why a school improvement team or school council might need an "action arm" or committee to take responsibility for implementing specific activities that support the goals of a school improvement plan.

2. Why must an ATP include educators *and* parents, not only teachers and administrators?

3. List and explain three activities that are the responsibility of a school improvement team or council but should not be conducted by the action arm or committee that focuses on school, family, and community partnerships.

▯▮ COMMENT

ATP Organization and Committee Structure

There are two main ways in which to organize the work of an ATP. The *process-oriented approach* organizes plans and committees to conduct activities for the six types of involvement. The *goal-oriented approach* organizes plans and committees to conduct and improve involvement activities that are directly linked to school improvement goals.

Focus on the Six Types of Involvement

The process-oriented approach to school, family, and community partnerships creates ATPs dedicated to understanding, organizing, and enacting the framework of six types of involvement (parenting, communicating, volunteering, learning at home, decision making, and collaborating with the community). In this approach, each member of the ATP becomes a chair, cochair, and resident expert for one of the six types of involvement.

For example, in a well-functioning, process-oriented ATP, one or two members will be the school's experts in Type 1—Parenting. These Type 1 co-chairs will plan, organize, or delegate leadership for parent workshops on child development, parent-to-parent connections, activities for families to inform the school about their children's needs or family goals, and other Type 1 activities. Other members of the ATP will become experts in Type 2—Communicating. The Type 2 cochairs will plan, organize, monitor, or delegate leadership for activities that improve the clarity of communications, create two-way channels of communication, secure translators needed at parent-teacher conferences, develop new technologies for communicating, and other Type 2 activities. Still other ATP members will become the experts in organizing and assisting volunteers (Type 3 cochairs), teachers' designs of interactive homework and curriculum-related involvement activities (Type 4 cochairs), training parent representatives for committees and councils (Type 5 cochairs), and identifying resources in the community (Type 6 cochairs).

The process-oriented ATP evaluates its progress based on whether and how well activities for the six types of involvement effectively involve all families; whether the program is balanced with activities that are conducted at home, at school, and in the community; and whether various activities contribute to student success and other school goals.

In the process-oriented approach, the quality and results of activities for all six types of involvement should improve from year to year, along with the quality of ATP members' expertise and teamwork. As the chairs or cochairs for each type of involvement build their competencies, they should be increasingly able to select and implement activities that link to school improvement goals.

Focus on the School Improvement Goals

The goal-oriented approach to school, family, and community partnerships creates ATPs dedicated to understanding, organizing, and conducting involvement activities that are directly linked to school improvement goals. In this approach, each member of the ATP becomes a chair, cochair, and resident expert in linking family and community involvement to one major school improvement goal for student success. This ensures that the school's partnership program will focus each year on involving families and the community in improving math, reading, writing, attendance, behavior, or other major goals in the school improvement plan.

Each ATP member may select whether to focus on family and community involvement that helps improve students' reading skills, attendance, the school climate for partnerships, or another goal from the school improvement plan that is detailed in the one-year action plan for partnerships. For example, the goal-oriented ATP's committee for improving attendance might include activities for some or all six types of involvement to reduce unexcused absences or improve on-time arrivals. Activities would be selected and scheduled to increase families' understanding of their roles and actions in getting children to school on time every day, clarify report card statistics on attendance, train volunteers to telephone absent students' families, help families pick up homework for students who are absent, and other activities that focus on improving student attendance and success.

The ATP will include activities that involve families and communities in all six types of involvement across the targeted school improvement goal. The school's improvement goals organize the action plans for partnerships, and the program is evaluated on whether progress is made toward those goals.

The two approaches for organizing the work of ATPs are not mutually exclusive. Indeed, a process-oriented ATP that focuses on the six types of involvement still will choose activities that help reach important school goals. A goal-oriented ATP that focuses on involvement linked to school improvement goals still will select activities that cover the six types of involvement. The main differences between the process-oriented and goal-oriented approaches are in how the ATP's plans are written and evaluated each year and how the ATP members select their areas of expertise and describe how their work is linked to the overall school improvement plan. Tools for implementing the two approaches are included in an implementation guidebook (Epstein, Coates, Salinas, Sanders, and Simon, 1997).

REFERENCES

Epstein, J. L., L. Coates, K. C. Salinas, M. G. Sanders, and B. Simon. (1997). *School, family, and community partnerships: Your handbook for action.* Thousand Oaks, CA: Corwin.

◇ ACTIVITY

How Family and Community Involvement Helps Reach School Improvement Goals

Whether a school uses a process-oriented or goal-oriented approach, the activities to involve families and the community should contribute to the attainment of important school goals.

Suppose a school was working to meet the following goals:

- improve attendance
- improve math skills
- improve attitudes toward science
- improve student behavior
- improve the school climate for partnerships
- add one common, important goal: _____

In the chart below:

A. List one family or community involvement activity that you think would directly contribute to reaching these goals.
B. Give one reason why you think there is a direct connection between the activity and the desired result.

Goal	Family or community involvement activity	Type of involvement?	Why would the activity help produce this goal?
1. Improve attendance			
2. Improve math skills			
3. Improve attitudes toward science			
4. Improve student behavior			
5. Improve the school climate for partnerships			
6. Another goal that you select:			

Action Team Members and Leaders

Effective partnership programs cannot be developed by just one person or by an elite group. Every year, some school principals and teachers move, are promoted, or retire. Many active parents move or "graduate" with their children to new schools. Programs and practices that depend on just one leader may disappear completely if that person leaves the school. A small group of a few active parents may be viewed as a clique that makes other parents or teachers feel unwelcome, uncomfortable, and unlikely to participate in school activities. Sometimes programs that depend on one person or the same few leaders are viewed as *somebody's* program, and not as the *school's* program of partnerships.

Action Team Members

An ATP should have six to twelve members. Members include at least two teachers, at least two parents, an administrator, and other school and family leaders who have important connections with families and students (e.g., the nurse, social worker, Title I parent liaison, a PTA/PTO officer or representative, special education leader, or others). The ATP also may include representatives from the community. High school ATPs must include one or two students. The diverse members contribute many points of view to plans and activities for school, family, and community partnerships.

Very small schools may adapt these guidelines to create smaller ATPs. Very large middle and high schools may adapt these guidelines to create multiple ATPs for schools-within-the-school, grade levels, houses, career academies, or other large subdivisions. Indeed, other appropriate structural and procedural adaptations will be needed to accommodate the characteristics and constraints in diverse schools.

The ATP provides a stable structure that should endure even if some team members leave each year. New team members are selected to replace those who leave, then are oriented to the work of the ATP. Thus, teachers who leave the team are replaced by teachers, parents by parents, and so on.

Action Team Leaders

Many people may play important leadership roles in organizing an ATP, implementing plans, conducting activities, and evaluating results of partnership programs.

The *principal* plays an essential role in supporting and maintaining the work of an ATP and in guiding the ATP's connections to the school improvement team or council. Ideally, the principal should not be the chair of the ATP, but should be an active member and strong supporter of the action team. For example, principals should call all teachers' attention to the importance of planning and conducting school, family, and community partnerships with their students' families. Principals also should stress the importance of the participation of educators and families in schoolwide activities that help develop a welcoming school climate. The principal should evaluate each teacher's activities to involve families as part of the teacher's annual or periodic professional reviews of work and progress. Principals and other administrators also should recognize the various leaders, participants, and successful involvement activities that are conducted throughout the school year.

Guidance counselors, school psychologists, school social workers, assistant principals, or other *social service professionals* may be members of an ATP and may serve as team chairs or cochairs. Guidance counselors and assistant principals are particularly helpful team leaders or coleaders in middle and high schools because their professional agendas link directly to students, families, and communities. These school professionals may have more time than others to schedule team meetings. They also may have more training and experience in guiding teachers, parents, students, and community members to work together on plans and activities for the school. Even if other administrators and counselors are on the ATP, the principal's leadership and support still are essential.

Master teachers, lead teachers, and department chairs must be members of an ATP and may serve as team chairs or cochairs. At least two or three classroom teachers should be members of the ATP. The teachers on the ATP may work with all teachers in the school to reinforce the importance of their connections with students' families at all grade levels and to encourage teachers' participation in schoolwide partnership activities and events. In some schools, one teacher from each grade level serves on the ATP to ensure that family involvement activities are planned, implemented, and shared across the grades.

Parents and community members must be members of the ATP and may serve as cochairs of the team, along with an educator. They also may serve as chairs or cochairs of ATP committees on the six types of involvement or specific school goals.

Students in high schools are essential members of an ATP. They may serve as cochairs of ATP committees on the six types of involvement or specific school goals.

The principal, other administrators, counselors, lead and classroom teachers, parents, and others form the school-based ATP. There are important supportive roles that district and state leaders play to ensure that the school teams are successful.

District leaders play important roles in facilitating and reinforcing the work of schools' ATPs. Superintendents and school boards may officially evaluate progress on school, family, and community partnerships as part of principals' and teachers' annual or periodic professional reviews. This policy links the district's mission statements about the importance of partnerships with a high-stakes evaluation and encourages school leaders to work diligently on improving and maintaining their partnership programs.

In large school districts, district-level facilitators for school, family, and community partnerships are needed to help from 15 to 30 elementary, middle, and high schools organize their ATPs. The facilitators guide and assist all ATPs to develop their expertise in planning, implementing, and maintaining comprehensive programs of partnership. They also help their schools share ideas with each other, evaluate their work, and continue to improve their programs from year to year. Facilitators' salaries may be supported by compensatory education funds, Title I, and other federal, state, and local funding sources. In small districts, part-time facilitators may work with fewer than 15 schools to help them develop and maintain their programs of school, family, and community partnerships.

State leaders also have important leadership roles in ensuring successful partnership programs in districts and in schools. State superintendents; state boards of education; and leaders of many departments, divisions, and programs that concern families and communities need to conduct activities that support schools and districts in understanding and developing partnership programs.

At the district and state levels, Leadership Teams for Partnerships (LTPs) develop and implement policies and activities that support and advance school, family, and community connections. This includes two types of actions. LTPs conduct and coordinate state-level or district-level policies and programs that affect all schools, such as staff development workshops; state, regional, or districtwide conferences; team training on school, family, and community partnerships; competitions for small grants to support partnership practices; dissemination of best practices; and other activities. LTPs also may assist or facilitate individual schools with partnership plans and programs. (See Chapter 4 on state and district leadership and activities.)

Other organizations also have roles to play in leading and participating in school, family, and community partnership programs. For example, state and local PTAs, community organizations, teacher or administrator unions, Chambers of Commerce, business and labor leaders, and others may be part of leadership and action teams at the state, district, and school levels to improve programs of school, family, and community partnerships.

Chair or Cochairs of the ATP

At the school level, there must be a chair or cochairs of the ATP. The chair must be someone whose leadership is recognized and accepted by all members and who communicates well with educators, parents, and community members. Most often, this is a teacher, counselor, or assistant principal who understands the importance of family involvement in children's education.

Some schools select an educator *and* a parent to serve as cochairs of the ATP. Chairs and cochairs also must be selected to lead the various ATP committees that conduct specific activities on the types of involvement or goals for involvement that are scheduled in the one-year action plans for partnerships. Having educators and parents as cochairs or coleaders of the ATP and its committees sends an important message to everyone in the school community about teamwork. The cochair structure also gives greater stability to the ATP in the event that one leader leaves the school. The chair or cochairs of the ATP also may serve as "linking members" on the school council or school improvement team.

Linking ATP Members with the School Improvement Team

A common question about organizing partnerships is whether the school improvement team should also *be* the ATP. If the school improvement team (or council) is very large, it may *be* subdivided into "action teams," "work groups," or committees to write the detailed plans and to implement activities for the goals for school improvement (e.g., improving attendance; improving science instruction; increasing reading or math scores; improving writing skills; improving school, family, and community partnerships). In most schools, however, the school improvement team is the main policy or advisory group that oversees all areas of the school's program and progress. Because educators and parents who serve on the school council or improvement team have limited time for meetings, it helps to recruit other teachers, parents, and community members to serve on the ATPs, the action arm of the school improvement team. With different people on the policy and action teams, a school will ensure that the same leaders are not trying to do too many things, and that leadership skills are developed by many teachers, administrators, parents, and community partners. One "linking" member in addition to the principal may serve on both the school council and ATP to ensure the ongoing exchange of information between the policy group and its "action arm."

QUESTIONS TO DISCUSS

1. Select a policy level that interests you (i.e., school, district, or state level).
2. Identify two job titles at the level you selected that you believe are typically represented by people who could take leadership roles for improving school, family, and community partnerships.
3. Next to each job title that you listed, note (a) the professional training, (b) goals, (c) interpersonal skills, and (d) one other characteristic that people in these positions typically have that would help them facilitate and support the work of teachers, parents, and administrators in developing programs of school, family, and community partnerships.

◇ ACTIVITY

Ideal Members of an Action Team for Partnerships

Suppose that you are in a school that wants to create an ATP whose members will work together on all types of family and community involvement. Let us say that

| Team Members' Names | Team Members' Positions | Team Members' Special Talents or Interests | Check ✔ column A OR B to tell if the ATP is organized by: ❑ A. Six Types *or* ❑ B. School Goals | |
			A. Six Types — Team members will become experts on which types of involvement	B. School Goals — Team members will become experts in involvement for which school goals
1. (YOU)				
2.				
3.				
4.				
5.				
6.				

FIGURE 7.2   ATP Member Chart

you are one member of a six to twelve-person team. Who else would you want on an ideal ATP? How might the ATP divide responsibilities to develop expertise in partnerships among its teachers, parents, and administrator?

A. Select the level of schooling that interests you (preschool, elementary, middle, or high school).
B. Give your hypothetical school a name.
C. Give the ATP a name that sends a message of partnerships.
D. In Figure 7.2, identify:
    1. Your own position on the ATP (e.g., teacher, principal, counselor, parent, or some other position).
    2. The other members of the ATP. Include at least two or three teachers, two or three parents, and an administrator. Give all members hypothetical names and list their positions.
Then:
    3. For each team member, note one of his or her special talents or interests that may contribute to the work of the ATP.
    4. Check (√) whether the school is organizing its work using the process-oriented approach that focuses on the six types of involvement or the

goals-oriented approach that links involvement directly to school improvement goals.

5. Assign each team member as chair or cochair of one of the types of involvement or school goal, using his or her talents or interests to guide the assignments.

E. **Note:** You may extend the table to include more than six members of your ideal ATP and consider cochairs for committees on the six types of involvement or on partnerships to reach school goals.

F. List three challenges that could prevent these team members from working well together to write and implement plans and activities for school, family, and community partnerships. For each challenge, provide one solution that might help the team succeed with its work on partnerships.

▯ COMMENT

Action Team Responsibilities

In elementary, middle, and high schools, the ATP plans, implements, coordinates, and oversees action; monitors progress; solves problems; presents reports; and designs new directions for positive connections with families and communities to increase student success. Members of the ATP do not work alone on the planned activities; they work with other faculty, parents, community members, and the school council or improvement team (if one exists). The ATP gathers input and presents ideas to the full faculty, school improvement team, and parent association for the school's one-year action plan. The ATP also recruits other teachers, parents, students, administrators, and community members, or delegates leadership to help design, conduct, and evaluate family and community activities for each type of involvement or for each major school goal.

Whether it uses the process-oriented or goal-oriented approach to organize involvement activities, the ATP conducts the following leadership activities at each school:

- Documents present and new practices of partnership so that everyone knows how individual teachers and the school as a whole communicate and work with families.
- Develops a detailed one-year action plan for improving partnerships linked to school improvement plans, including activities for all six types of involvement that involve families in ways that help students reach school goals.
- Reports its work and progress semiannually (or on a regular schedule) to the school council, school improvement team, parent organization, faculty, and/or broader community.

- Recognizes excellent participation from parents, other family members, students, and others in the community who contribute to the success of the planned partnership activities.
- Gathers ideas for new activities and solves problems that impede progress.
- Evaluates progress in improving the quality of implemented activities and the results of various involvement activities. This includes results for the school and teachers, results for parents and other family members, and results for students.
- Writes a new one-year action plan each year to ensure an ongoing program of partnerships in the life and work of the school.
- Replaces teachers, parents, administrators, or other members who leave the ATP with new members so that a full team is always ready to conduct a planned program of partnerships at the school.
- Integrates new projects, grants, and activities for home, school, and community connections into a unified program of partnerships. Many activities that enrich and extend partnerships of home, school, and community come and go each year. These activities should be viewed as part of, not separate from, the school's ongoing, dynamic, comprehensive program of partnerships.

If the ATP conducts its leadership activities well, then everyone in the school should know that the school has an active program of school, family, and community partnerships. All teachers, parents, school staff, community members, and students should know how they might help design, conduct, and evaluate partnership activities. From year to year, the number and quality of activities in each one-year action plan should improve, along with positive results of the activities.

QUESTIONS TO DISCUSS

1. Which of the ATP actions listed above do you think is:
   A. easiest to accomplish, and why?
   B. most difficult to accomplish, and why?
2. Select three of the leadership actions of the ATP listed above that you believe are most important for a high-quality program of partnerships. Explain how each of the actions you selected would help make a school's program of school, family, and community partnerships *permanent* and a regular part of school life.

▯▯ COMMENT

Using Tools to Take Action

To fulfill the responsibilities listed above and to develop and strengthen its program of partnerships from year to year, an ATP must address the following questions:

1. Where is this school starting from in its present practices at each grade level on each of the six major types of involvement? What do teachers do individually, and what does the school do as a whole, to involve families and communities?
2. What are this school's major goals for improving or maintaining student success?
3. What should this school's program of family, school, and community partnerships look like three years from now?
4. Which partnership practices that are currently being conducted should be maintained or improved?
5. Which new practices should be added for each type of involvement? To reach more families? To contribute to specific goals for students? To reach other school goals?
6. How is this school progressing? What indicators are used to measure the quality of partnerships and progress toward goals for student success? What activities should be monitored, documented, and formally evaluated to learn about the effects of school, family, and community partnerships?
7. How will the results of the assessments and evaluations be used to improve the next one-year action plan for partnerships?

Educators and researchers working together have developed several tools to help ATPs address these basic questions. The following tools are discussed in the implementation guidebook *School, Family, and Community Partnerships: Your Handbook for Action* (Epstein, Coates, Salinas, Sanders, and Simon, 1997).

A. *Starting points:* An inventory of present practices for the six types of involvement, accounting for the grade levels in which activities are presently implemented.
B. *Three-year outline:* A long-term vision statement of how the school will develop and improve school, family, and community partnerships over time, with realistic goals to involve all families in ways that help students reach important goals.
C. *One-year action plan:* An annual, detailed plan with a month-by-month schedule and specific responsibilities for members of the ATP and others to implement current or new activities linked to school goals for the six types of involvement throughout the school year. Options include a process-oriented or goal-oriented action plan.
D. *End-of-year evaluation:* A reflective assessment of progress and challenges to address in the next one-year action plan, with attention to accomplish-

ments on each type of involvement (process-oriented evaluation) or on how involvement addressed major goals (goal-oriented evaluation).

E. *A measure of school, family, and community partnerships* (Salinas, Epstein, Sanders, Davis, and Aldersebaes, 1999): Extends starting points to help action teams annually assess how well they are implementing partnership practices and how well they are meeting key challenges for involving all families in their children's education.

REFERENCES

Salinas, K. C., J. L. Epstein, M. H. Sanders, D. Davis, and I. Aldersebaes. (1999). *Measure of school, family, and community partnerships*. Baltimore: Center on School, Family, and Community Partnerships, Johns Hopkins University.

 **ACTIVITY**

Matching Tools to Tasks

The set of tools outlined above might help ATPs address major questions that underlie plans for good partnerships. Other information (e.g., the school improvement plan) also may be needed or helpful to address the questions and to tailor partnership programs to particular schools. Which of the tools in the list above (A, B, C, D, or E) do you think might help an ATP address the seven major questions listed above? Whether or not the tools look useful, what other kinds of information might help an ATP address the questions?

A. In Figure 7.3, fill in A, B, C, D, or E to indicate which of the above tools may help an ATP address each of the major questions (Tools may be used more than once.)
B. Fill in other school information that might be needed or helpful, with or without the use of the tools.

COMMENT

Scheduling Meetings—Not Too Many, Not Too Few

In its one-year action plan, an ATP must create a realistic schedule for full-team meetings, committee meetings, and periodic reports to other school groups so that all teachers, parents, students, and members of the community will know about the school's plans and activities for partnerships. This schedule includes the following team meetings and reports:

Question	Which tool might help? (A, B, C, D, or E)	What other information might be needed?
1. Where is this school starting from in its present practices on the six types of involvement?		
2. What are this school's major goals for improving or maintaining student success?		
3. What should this school's program of family, school, and community partnerships look like in three years?		
4. Which partnership practices that are currently conducted maintained or improved this year?		
5. Which new practices should be added for each type of involvement to reach more families or to promote school goals this year?		
6. How is this school progressing in the quality of school, family, and community partnerships?		
7. What should be included in the next one-year action plan for partnerships?		

FIGURE 7.3   Matching Tools to Tasks

- The full ATP should meet on a regular, realistic schedule (at least monthly for at least one hour) to plan and schedule activities, coordinate actions, conduct events, evaluate results, identify problems, and celebrate progress. The meetings should be designed and conducted to keep the planned program moving forward.
- ATP committees should meet as needed to implement specific activities in the one-year action plan for which they are responsible. For teams using the process-oriented approach, six ATP committees on the six types of involvement will meet, as needed, throughout the year to implement their planned activities. For teams using the goal-oriented ap-

proach, ATP committees will meet to implement the activities planned on their specific goals.

- The chair, cochairs, or designated members of the ATP should report regularly (at least twice a year) to the school council or school improvement team, the full faculty, and the parent association on plans for and progress on school, family, and community partnerships. These also are occasions to gather information and ideas for needed changes and improvements and to recruit leaders and participants for various activities.

- The chair, cochairs, or designated members also should report the ATP's plans, activities, and progress to all families, students, and the community in school or community newsletters and in other forums where the work, plans, and goals of the school are discussed.

◇ ACTIVITY

How Many Meetings?

A. Interview a teacher or administrator to discuss some of the challenges educators and parents face in finding time to meet and work together on an ATP and some workable options. This activity may be conducted individually, or invite an educator to discuss these issues with the class. First set the stage or scenario:

Suppose that the teachers, administrators, and parents in your school had learned about the importance of school, family, and community partnerships, and formed an ATP to guide progress in this area of school improvement. The ATP has written a one-year action plan to begin its efforts with activities linked to school improvement goals. Now, the principal, school improvement team, and ATP members are meeting to discuss and determine a reasonable schedule for the kinds of meetings and reports that are needed to implement their plans and sustain their partnership program. They want to have just enough meetings—not too many, and not too few—to ensure that their work is well organized. Given the realities of school life in your school, what would your recommendations be on the following requirements for a well-functioning ATP?

Team Meetings: If your school had an ATP that included teachers, parents, and an administrator, how often should the whole team meet to plan, conduct, and monitor their work and progress? What should be the schedule, time, and place for these meetings?

Committee Meetings: If your ATP had committees to conduct activities on the six major types of involvement or to reach specific school goals (e.g., improving attendance, improving math achievement), how often should each committee meet to plan, conduct, and monitor their specific activities? What should be the schedule, time, and place for these meetings?

Reports on Partnerships: If your school had an ATP, how often should reports about partnership plans and progress be made to the following groups? What form should those reports take: oral report, computerized phone message, written summary, detailed written report, or some other form?

Action Team for Partnerships should report to:	How Often?	In What Form?
(1) the school improvement team or council?		
(2) the PTA or parent organization?		
(3) all parents in the school?		
(4) the full faculty?		
(5) students?		
(6) community members?		
(7) any others?		

Assessments and New Plans: If your school had an ATP, how much time should be spent evaluating its work and writing new one-year action plans for the next school year? What should be the schedule, time, and place for these activities?

B. Summarize the questions and responses.

C. From the responses to the interview questions, and from your readings in this chapter on the composition and activities of an ATP, create and label a realistic meeting schedule over 12–18 months for ATP meetings and reports. Include in the calendar time for the ATP to:

- orient new members of the team;
- write a one-year action plan;
- meet as a whole and as committees on the six types or school goals;
- report their work and progress to major stakeholder groups;
- evaluate their work and progress;
- write plans for the next school year; and
- conduct other meetings and major responsibilities.

▯⦂ COMMENT

Establishing Permanent Partnership Programs—As Regular as Reading!

A school's partnership program should be organized to operate as surely as a school's reading, math, science, other curricula, and testing programs. For example, a school's reading program accounts for all of the reading and literacy activities that are conducted with students at all grade levels. Reading skills are planned, taught, tested, reported, and continually improved. Every principal, teacher, student, and parent knows that the school has a reading program that students experience daily. If new reading activities or opportunities come along (such as a grant for improving reading instruction, for purchasing new books, or for teachers' professional development in linking reading and writing), the additions are woven into the fabric of the school's reading program.

Similarly, a well-organized, comprehensive program of school, family, and community partnerships accounts for all home-school-community connections that are planned and conducted with students and families. Some activities are conducted by classroom teachers, some as grade-level events, and others are schoolwide. Some are individual connections between a parent and teacher, administrator, or counselor; others are group activities; and still others involve all students, families, educators, and the community.

Like reading, partnership programs and practices must be planned, reviewed, and improved each year. If new partnership projects, grants, and activities are initiated, they should be integrated into the school's ongoing partnership program. This simple analogy—partnership programs must be planned and conducted "like reading"—is key to sustaining school, family, and community partnerships that inform and involve all families in their children's education every year.

◇ ACTIVITY

How Are Partnerships Like and Unlike Reading?

A. Invite a school principal, or teacher, or school district or state education leader to discuss how one "regular" or "permanent" program (such as reading, math, science, other subject, testing, *or* counseling) is organized to ensure that it continues and improves from year to year. Fill in the chart below to summarize the information about the selected, permanent program. Ask:

1. What is one program in your school(s) that is permanent, regular, and expected from year to year?
2. How do the following organizational features help make the selected program permanent? (Fill in column 1.)
3. Do the same organizational features contribute to the development of a program of school, family, and community partnerships in your school(s)? If YES, how does each feature apply? If NO, why not? (Fill in column 2.)

One permanent program is: _____

1. How does each feature help to make the selected program permanent?

   Organizational feature:

   a. Policies:
   b. Plans:
   c. Funding:
   d. Leadership/Supervision:
   e. Teamwork
   f. Materials, equipment:
   g. Orientation of new participants:
   h. Evaluations:
   i. Any other feature?

2. How does each feature apply to programs of school, family, and community partnerships?

B. From what you learned in the interview, how permanent do you think the selected program is, and how permanent do you think school, family, and community partnerships in this educator's school(s) are? Explain.

ⓘ COMMENT

What's in a Name?

A school may call its team the (School Name) Action Team for Partnerships; or the (School Name) School, Family, and Community Partnership Team; or the Home, School, Community Partnership Team. Or, a school may choose a unique name for its team, such as the Parent-Educator Network (PEN), Teachers Getting Involved with Families (TGIF), Partners in Education (PIE), Partners for Student Success (PASS), Partners in Progress, or Teachers and Parents for Students (TAPS).

School districts and state departments of education often call their LTPs the (District/State Name) School, Family, and Community Partnership Program; or Family-School-Community Partnerships; or a variation of these terms. Others give their program unique names, such as Building Educational Success Together (BEST). Others see their schools as a "network" with the name (District or State Name) Network of Partnership Schools, which then links to the National Network of Partnership Schools.

QUESTIONS TO DISCUSS

1. Give two reasons why a school, district, *or* state might want to give its ATP a unique name.
2. Why are the above names for ATPs and LTPs better than names that focus only on parents (such as Parent Network, Family Focus Group, or Parents Involved in Education), or that focus only on community connections

(such as Community Education Committee)? Give two reasons why ATPs and LTPs should have a "partnership" focus.

⊡ COMMENT

Organizing Action Teams for Comprehensive School Reform

In the preceding sections we discussed how an ATP may be organized to plan and conduct activities to strengthen the six types of involvement or to use family and community involvement to help reach specific school improvement goals. Schools with ambitious goals to improve student academic success, behavior, or school climate may go farther with the goal-oriented approach by organizing comprehensive school reform (CSR). In the Partnership Schools–CSR model, *several* action teams are organized to ensure that plans are written and implemented to attain all major school improvement goals.

Number of Teams in CSR

How many goals and action teams should there be in the Partnership Schools–CSR model? In field studies, we find that most schools can begin to address three to five major goals in one school year. For example, a school may have two or three achievement-related goals (such as improving reading, writing, and math), one noncurricular goal (such as improving attendance or behavior), and one goal for improving the overall school climate and partnerships with families and the community. In the Partnership Schools–CSR model, that school would need five action teams, one for each of the main improvement goals

Members of Teams in CSR

In the Partnership Schools–CSR model, *every* member of the faculty and school staff joins *one and only one* action team to build expertise in one area that is important to the school. Parent and community representatives also serve on all action teams to ensure that key stakeholders in student success have input into and communicate about major school improvements. Students are members of all high school action teams and may serve on middle school committees. The principal is an ex-officio or active member of all teams. All action teams (like ATPs) will have six to twelve members, including at least two or three teachers, two or three parents, the administrator, and others who may be added to each team.

Responsibilities of Teams in CSR

In a Partnership Schools–CSR model, each action team reviews its specific goal, writes detailed plans, and implements and oversees actions that will lead to the attainment of the goal. In the Partnership Schools–CSR model, all action teams contribute to the school's three-year outline or long-term mission and goals for improvement. All action teams write detailed one-year action plans for their specific goals. Each action team may select and schedule activities to review and continually improve the curriculum, instructional approaches and materials, management, assessments, policies, *and* family and community partnerships.

For curriculum-related goals (e.g., improving student reading or math skills and scores), activities may focus on improving the content of the curriculum, how instruction is offered, how students receive extra help for learning, other in-school academic and social activities, *and* family and community involvement that will help reach these goals. Teams may recommend the adoption of textbooks or national reforms in reading, math, science, and social studies and present ideas about the pros and cons of alternative approaches for attaining each goal.

For noncurriculum-related goals (e.g., improving student behavior or attendance), activities may focus on improving school policies, responsibilities, responsive activities and incentives to engage students in school programs and to recognize excellence and progress, *and* family and community involvement that will help reach these goals.

All action teams report their plans and progress in implementing planned activities on a regular schedule to the school improvement team or school council and to other school groups such as the full faculty, the parent association, or the school board. All action teams evaluate the progress that is made toward their goals each year. Thus, all teams in the Partnership Schools–CSR model fulfill the same responsibilities and address the same kinds of questions as outlined above for the ATPs. In short, the Partnership Schools–CSR model extends the goal-oriented approach to partnerships by using an action team approach and partnerships to address all important school goals.

Example: How Does the Partnership Schools–CSR Model Work?

Action teams review and attend to school improvements in curriculum, instruction, management, tests and assessments, and family and community involvement activities to address their targeted goals. For example, in the Partnership Schools–CSR model, one team of teachers, administrators, parents, paraprofessionals, and community members may focus on improving students' math experiences and math test scores. As the school's experts or guides in math, the Action Team for Math (ATM) plans and oversees activities to improve all aspects of math teaching and learning to help the school reach its math goals. The ATM calls on all math teachers and others inside and outside of school to design, select, conduct, evaluate, and continue activities in a one-year action plan for math.

ATM members work together to review the math curriculum; select new math texts and materials, as needed; discuss and improve math instruction; review and prepare for new math tests and assessments; consider how math report card grades are determined; and design and implement family and community involvement activities that focus on math (e.g., TIPS–Math interactive homework, Family Math Nights, and community connections about math). The ATM also monitors changes in students' math skills, test scores, attitudes toward math, extra help needed, and other math-related results.

Similarly, the Action Team for Reading (ATR) will create committees that focus attention on all aspects of reading: curriculum, instruction, assessments, partnerships, and other components of excellent reading programs. The Action Team for Behavior (ATB) would plan, implement, and oversee the year's activities to reach their goal of improving school discipline and related student behaviors. The Action Team for Partnerships (ATP) would focus on *other* connections with families and communities for the six types of involvement that establish a welcoming climate and that create a true "partnership school." Activities planned by the ATP might include workshops for parents on child development, a back-to-school night, a school newsletter, volunteers, and other activities for the six types of involvement.

In all, then, this hypothetical school using the Partnership Schools–CSR model would have four action teams—on math (ATM), reading (ATR), behavior (ATB), and general partnerships (ATP)—to reach these four major school improvement goals.

◇ ACTIVITY

How Effective Are School Improvement Committees?

A. Select a school level that interests you (i.e., preschool, elementary, middle, *or* high school).
B. Interview a teacher or administrator about the *current* and *ideal* committee structures in that person's school. Ask:
   1. About how many students are in this school?
   2. About how many teachers and administrators are in this school?
   3. What are four major goals or objectives that this school has for improving or maintaining student success and the quality of the school's program?
   Goal 1: _____
   Goal 2: _____
   Goal 3: _____
   Goal 4: _____
C. Create a chart like the one below that outlines the interviewee's responses to the questions in this chart.

School conditions and committee structure	What is the CURRENT situation?	What is IDEAL for this school?
1. What advisory school or grade-level committees regularly meet with the principal?		
Who serves on these committees?		
2. What decision-making committees meet regularly?		
Who serves on these committees?		
3. What action-oriented committees are there that implement planned activities?		
Who serves on these committees?		
4. How effective are the various committees?		
5. How well do the committees link their work to the four goals or objectives listed in question B, above?		

D. Look over the information from the interview. How would you describe the school's *current* committee structure and the representation of teachers, parents, and community members? Is there evidence of teamwork? Of broad representation of teachers, parents, other staff, community members?

E. Do you agree with the interviewee's ideas for the *ideal* committee structure for the school? Explain.

F. List two actions that you would recommend to help this school improve its committee structure and representation. Give one reason for each of your recommendations.

CENTRAL THEMES

The readings and discussions in this volume provide an understanding of the theory, research, and implementation of programs and practices of school, family, and community partnerships. The next sections review the central themes and major conclusions that crosscut the readings and activities.

Central Theme Number 1: Building Mutual Trust and Respect of Teachers and Parents

Everyone agrees that mutual trust and mutual respect between parents and teachers are basic and required qualities of good partnerships. Programs of school, family, and community partnerships will not be sustained unless teachers, administrators, parents, and others who share an interest in children understand each other; respect the hard work they each do for children; convey their mutual respect to each other; and demonstrate their mutual trust in the way that they design and conduct programs of school, family, and community partnerships.

Trust and respect are not just words; they are required actions for successful partnerships. These qualities cannot be legislated or mandated but must be developed over time within school communities. These attitudes are represented by the theory of overlapping spheres of influence of home, school, and community, and supported by policies and activities that help teachers, parents, and others work together in productive ways on behalf of children.

QUESTIONS TO DISCUSS

1. Discuss one way in which the mutual respect and trust between parents and teachers are *prerequisites* for some practices of partnership.
2. Discuss one way that mutual respect and trust between parents and teachers *facilitate* good partnerships.
3. Discuss one way that mutual respect and trust between parents and teachers are the *results* of good practices of partnership.
4. Suppose that a school or district wanted its program of school, family, and community partnerships to increase parents' and teachers' mutual trust and respect for each other.
   A. Select a level of schooling that interests you (e.g., preschool, elementary, middle, or high school).
   B. Select one type of involvement that interests you.
   C. Describe one activity for the type of involvement you selected that you think would help build mutual respect and trust between parents and teachers at the school level you selected.
   D. Explain why you think this activity would produce trust and mutual respect between teachers and parents.
   E. Analyze the following features of the activity you described at the school level you selected:
      1. Would all families benefit from this activity, even if parents work during the school day or cannot come to the school building for other reasons?
      If YES, describe how the activity involves all parents.
      If NO, add one idea about how to inform and include families, even if they were not able to participate.

2. What is one way that the activity you described might involve or affect students, in addition to parents?

◐ COMMENT

Resolving Conflicts and Concerns

Activities to inform and involve families in children's education at school and at home are not always successful on the first try. Some teachers and principals need practice in relating to and cooperating with parents. Some parents may not see eye to eye with their children's teachers. Sometimes good partners have honest disagreements and must work out their differences.

Parents may have different opinions from teachers and from each other about homework (e.g., too much or too little), student placements (e.g., the group or special program in which the child should be placed), improvements needed in school subjects and programs, and other topics. Some differences in opinions occur when educators are not aware of parents' views or when teachers or administrators are inflexible about responding to requests from families. Differences in opinions may occur if parents are not well informed and included in decisions about their children's education from preschool on. Without information and involvement every year that children are in school, gaps are created in parents' and educators' knowledge of and comfort with each other. Such gaps, if not addressed, become increasingly hard to bridge.

Even when parents and teachers share mutual respect and trust, problems still may arise, but solutions should be easier to achieve. For example, by knowing and respecting the families of their students, many schools have redesigned winter holiday concerts and celebrations to prevent offending or excluding students of different cultures or religions. Others have "detracked" courses to offer challenging programs to all students, not just to a few who are labeled "gifted." One school in a large urban area served many families who, because of their religious beliefs, objected to some curricular topics. Instead of ignoring or criticizing the parents, teachers created alternative learning activities for students to select to develop the same important skills in reading, writing, or social studies. Schools in many communities now give parents and students choices of whether or not to attend classes or activities that counter family beliefs.

A well-functioning action team will have designed ways to review and discuss parents' concerns and opinions. Indeed, good communications help build an important base of trust and respect needed to address questions and resolve differences.

QUESTIONS TO DISCUSS

A. How might an ATP respond to the following parental concerns? Give one possible solution to each of the following issues:

Parental concern	*One* strategy that may address the issue:
1. Parent complains that the family's religious beliefs are contradicted by school program or policy (a Type 1 concern)	_____
2. Parent wants to meet with the child's teacher, but does not speak English (a Type 2 concern)	_____
3. Parent feels unwelcome by other volunteers (a Type 3 concern)	_____
4. Parent says that the child is being given too little homework (a Type 4 concern)	_____
5. Parent thinks that children in the afternoon kindergarten have fewer hours of school than do children in the morning session (a Type 5 concern)	_____
6. Parent is worried that children are unsafe walking to and from school (a Type 6 concern)	_____

B. Not all strategies will fully address parental concerns. Some may help a concerned parent understand and accept the school's point of view; some may help the school understand and accept the parent's point of view. Discuss the suggested strategies in class: Are the actions realistic? What is the likely result if the suggested strategy were enacted? Will the exchange build trust or distrust between parents and educators?

Central Theme Number 2: Recognizing the Diversity of Families

1. The diversity of family cultures and languages will continue in the nation's schools. Students come to school from families with diverse cultural and linguistic backgrounds, religions, customs, talents, and experiences. Cultural and linguistic diversity will increase as the nation welcomes new groups of immigrants and as generations of immigrant children and families assimilate into their new country but maintain pride in their heritage.

2. The diversity of family structures will continue in the nation's schools. Students come to school each day from one-parent and two-parent homes, blended, extended, gay, and foster families, and other family arrangements. Some children are from large families, others from small families. Some have grandparents nearby, others do not. Families have diverse forms and members.

3. The diversity of family work experiences will continue in the nation's schools. In most families, one or both parents work full-time or part-time outside the home. Some parents are or may become unemployed, are on or off welfare, are in training for new jobs, or are moving to new locations. Families have diverse work schedules and experiences.

4. The diversity of family economic situations will continue in the nation's schools. Some parents are wealthy, most are middle class, others are poor. Some children have many economic advantages that facilitate educational experiences. Other children and their families need various kinds of assistance to participate fully in educational programs. Families have diverse resources, even in seemingly homogeneous communities.

5. Diverse families also are similar in many ways. Despite many important cultural, structural, and economic differences, families are *similar* in profound ways. All (or just about all) families care about their children and want them to succeed in schools with excellent educational programs. All families want to feel welcome at their children's schools, respected by their children's teachers, and safe in their communities. All students are eager to succeed, want their families to be appreciated by their schools, and want their families as knowledgeable partners in their education.

QUESTIONS TO DISCUSS

1. Add to the list above one more way in which you believe families within a school are different from one another, and explain.
2. Add to the list above one more way in which you believe families within a school are similar to one another, and explain.
3. Identify one of the features of diversity from the list that interests you.
   A. Identify one type of family involvement and one grade level that interest you.
   B. Describe one activity for school, family, and community partnerships for the type of involvement and grade level you selected that you believe would
      - help diverse families and students appreciate their differences;
      - help diverse families and students appreciate their similarities; and
      - help teachers or principals learn more about the strengths, interests, needs, or goals of diverse families.

◈ FIELD EXPERIENCE

How Do Communities Address Diversity?

A. Identify a community that interests you.
B. Select a parent, educator, *or* citizen in that community to interview about

whether and how the community recognizes similarities and differences of families and students. Ask:

1. How diverse is this community's population, and in what ways?
2. Are the local schools more or less diverse than the surrounding community, or about the same? Explain.
3. Are similarities, common goals, and interests of families in this community discussed and celebrated? If so, give one example of how this is done. If not, give one reason why this is not done.
4. Are differences between goals and interests of families in the community discussed and celebrated? If so, give one example of how this is done. If not, give one reason why this is not done.

C. Write at least one more question to ask the parent, educator, *or* citizen about similarities or differences in the community.
D. Summarize the questions and responses. From this interview, how would you describe the "sense of community" in this location? Provide one idea that you think would strengthen this community's understanding of its families.

◇ ACTIVITY

Appreciating Family Diversity

Family histories, cultures, talents, values, and religions are rarely discussed in school. These topics are important, however, for increasing students' understanding and appreciation of others who are different from themselves. Comprehensive partnership programs include activities that illuminate family backgrounds and strengths to help students, families, and educators understand and appreciate each other's similarities and differences.

A. Identify a grade level that interests you.
B. Design a bulletin board for a classroom, school hallway, or community location for the grade level you selected that focuses attention on the strengths, similarities, or diversities of families. For example, consider displaying student drawings, stories, or photographs about aspects of family life that students may enjoy sharing (e.g., favorite foods, sports, holidays, sayings, histories, hopes and dreams, talents, hobbies and interests, stories of coming to America, or other topics of interest).
   1. Show a diagram of how you think the display will look.
   2. Explain the purpose and content of your design.
   3. Design one classroom or homework activity for students to plan, create, or react to the bulletin board.
C. "Bulletin boards may celebrate the diversity of families in a school, but they are not enough to help students develop an understanding and appreciation of their similarities and differences."
   1. Do you agree or disagree with the above statement?

2. Write or discuss at least two arguments to support or refute this statement for the grade level you selected.
3. In addition to a bulletin board, what is one activity that might strengthen a school's focus on the similarities and differences of its students and families?

▯┇ COMMENT

Choices That Respond to Diverse Students' Needs

From preschool on, decisions are made for, about, and with students and their families that affect students' experiences in school. Some states, districts, and schools offer families and students options in their education, including choice of:

- schools
- courses
- teachers
- special programs in schools
- activities in programs
- after-school activities
- summer school or enrichment programs
- ways to make up a failing grade
- add one more choice that may be made: _____

To make wise choices, families and students need good information in useful forms and understandable language. For example, some families prefer information in print form, while others prefer to talk with other parents, educators, or others in the community. Or, a combination of verbal and written exchanges might be needed.

QUESTIONS TO DISCUSS

1. Identify one of the choices that interests you from the bulleted list above.
2. For the choice you selected:
   A. What do parents need to know to make an informed choice?
   B. Discuss at least one equity issue associated with this choice that determines whether all families or some families exercise their options.
   C. Describe two strategies that schools might use to provide the kinds of information that all families need to make good decisions for this choice. Describe each strategy and the results you anticipate.

Central Theme Number 3: Equity in School, Family, and Community Partnerships

Can family involvement at home ever be equal for all children and families?

- Some parents have more formal schooling than other parents.
- Families have different skills to share, such as music, sports, arts, cooking, carpentry, car repair, sewing, and child care.
- Some parents have more time to spend with their children than others.
- Some families have more money to spend on tutoring, lessons, and summer experiences.
- Some communities have more free activities for families and for children than do other communities.
- Some families have older children who can help the younger ones with schoolwork.
- Some families have only one child, who receives all of the parents' attention.
- Add one or two other inevitable inequalities that exist for children and families at home that you believe have an impact on student success in school: _____

The inequalities listed above are not all associated with wealth or formal education. For example, some parents, though economically strapped, may spend more time with children than do other families. Some communities in distressed neighborhoods help students and families participate in enriching activities. All families, regardless of socioeconomic status, have useful skills and knowledge to share with children.

QUESTIONS TO DISCUSS

Almost all families want to do the best they can for and with their children, but many conditions and resources are different and unequal. What do these inequalities mean for producing greater equity in school, family, and community partnerships?

1. Select one of the inequalities in the list above.
2. Discuss the importance of the factor you selected for children's success in school.
3. Describe one activity in a program of school, family, and community partnerships that might help to increase equality on the factor you selected.

Luck Versus Equity in Partnerships

Parents speak of involvement in their children's education in terms of "luck." A parent may say: "I'm really lucky this year. Paul's teacher is so open and encouraging. I can call with my questions, and I know she will return the call." Or, "We are so lucky. Molly's teacher is so helpful. He keeps us informed about how she is doing and how to help at home." These parents may not feel so lucky the next school year.

Families also talk about their children's schools in the same way. Parents may say: "We are so lucky that our school welcomes ideas from parents. In the last school our children attended, the principal was not interested in what we had to say." Families feel *lucky* if they are welcomed, informed, and involved.

Teachers also speak of luck. A teacher says: "I am so lucky this year. My students' parents are so easy to reach. They are eager to help me and my class at school, and they work with their children at home." Teachers appreciate parents' help. They talk about being lucky if they have good relationships with their students and families.

This volume suggests that it is possible to take school, family, and community partnerships out of the realm of luck and put them into regular teaching practice. This can be done by planning and implementing a comprehensive, permanent program of partnerships that involves all teachers, all families, and the community every year that students are in school.

 FIELD EXPERIENCE

Do Parents Feel Lucky or Sure about Partnerships?

A. Select a parent whose child has been in the same school for more than one year. Identify the child's grade level, and whether the school is public or private. Ask:
   1. This year, how does your child's school and teacher(s) inform and involve you in your child's education?
   2. How do you feel about the information and opportunities you receive?
   3. How did you feel last year about the information and opportunities for involvement that you received from the school or your child's teacher(s)?
B. Add one question of your own.
C. Record the questions and responses.
D. Summarize the parent's reports about contacts with the school to tell:
   1. Were the parent's experiences consistent or different from one year to the next?

2. Were parents expecting information and opportunities for involvement, or did they feel "lucky" this year or last year?

E. Add other reflections.

▯ COMMENT

Real or Imagined Families

We need to design and implement family involvement activities that meet the needs of today's families, not real or imagined families of the past. This means understanding families' conditions and constraints. Not all families can come to all workshops, meetings, or events on the school's schedule. Not all who are employed can leave work to come to parent-teacher conferences. Not all parents can volunteer at school during the day. Not all parents can help with homework on a specific evening. Not all parents want to serve on school committees. Not all parents can work in their communities at specifically scheduled times.

These are not new problems. There always were diverse situations and constraints on time that restricted family involvement. There always were one-parent and two-parent homes where parents were employed during the school day, or in one, two, or more jobs, who could not come often or easily to the school building. There always were immigrant parents and others who did not feel welcome at school. Most parents had very limited knowledge of their children's schooling across the grades, and most had limited information about how to work with their children's schools to maximize student success.

The imagined "golden years" of parent involvement never existed in all schools for all families, or in most schools for most families. Most parents have always needed more and better information than they were given, and more and different opportunities for involvement at school and at home. Because of advances in research, policy, and practice, we know more now than in the past about the organization of programs and practices that enable all families to be involved in their children's education across the grades.

◇ ACTIVITY

Meeting the Needs of 21st-Century Families

A. Figure 7.4 shows just six of many crucial challenges to excellent progress on the six types of involvement. Give one example of an activity that would help meet each of the following challenges so that more of today's families might become more involved in their children's education.

Selected Challenges to Excellent Partnerships	One Strategy or Activity That Schools Could Use to Meet Each Challenge to Involve All Families
Type 1 challenge: To provide information to families who cannot come to a meeting at school.	
Type 2 challenge: To schedule conferences so that employed parents can attend.	
Type 3 challenge: To organize volunteer work that can be done at home or in the community.	
Type 4 challenge: To keep families informed about what their children are required to learn to pass each subject and what students are learning from month to month, without requiring parents to "teach" school subjects.	
Type 5 challenge: To organize committees so that parent leaders from the major racial, ethnic, socioeconomic, and other groups in the school are involved.	
Type 6 challenge: To organize business and other community partnerships so that attention and resources focus on school improvement goals for student success.	

FIGURE 7.4   Challenges to Partnerships

B. Discuss ideas about the strategies listed in class. How would each suggestion address the simultaneous challenges of equity in partnerships to involve all families and meeting the needs of diverse families?

▯: COMMENT

Conclusions and Looking Ahead

This volume has taken readers on a journey from theory to research, to policy, and to the development of school, family, and community partnership programs in practice. From the collection of readings, activities, and other research, we draw eight conclusions to help you think about, talk about, and take action on school, family, and community partnerships as you proceed to use and build on what you have learned.

1. School, family, and community partnerships are about children and their success as students in school. Teachers, parents, administrators, and community members care about their children, and want them to succeed in school and in life. Indeed, *children* are the reason these partners communicate and work together. Research suggests that children who have multiple sources of support at home, at school, and in the community are more likely to succeed in school, graduate from high school, and make post-secondary plans for the future. Well-designed partnerships should help all of the people who care about children to organize their interactions and mobilize their resources in ways that help youngsters define themselves and work as "students." Some partnership activities also may benefit parents, educators, and others, but these results are the means to the main goal of promoting students' learning, development, and success.

2. School, family, and community partnerships are for all families. Partnerships are not just for families who are formally educated, easy to reach, or able to come often to school. Not just for families whose children are doing well in school, and not just for those whose children are in trouble. Not just for families who live close to the school, or only those who have telephones and computers with Internet access. Not just for those who speak English or read it well. Not just for families who always agree with school policies. Comprehensive programs of school, family, and community partnerships are designed to inform and involve families of all races, cultures, structures, and educational backgrounds. Schools with excellent partnership programs reach out to mothers and fathers, foster parents and guardians, grandparents, and others who are raising children in all families.

When comprehensive programs of partnership are conducted, schools send powerful messages to students:

Your school respects all families. Your school will communicate and collaborate with your family to help you succeed.

Partnership programs say to teachers:

Involving families in children's education is part of educators' professional work. This school does not stereotype or dismiss any families as irrelevant to their children's learning and development.

Crucial messages also are sent to families:

All students and all families are important in this school. We communicate with families, and we encourage families to communicate with educators to help students succeed.

3. School, family, and community partnerships are important at all grade levels, from preschool through high school. Families are important in their children's lives every year, not just in preschool and the primary grades. Community services and programs assist families and their children from infancy on, not just in the upper grades.

Of course, practices of partnership change each year as children mature and assume more responsibilities for their own learning; school programs become more complex; and families accumulate information about their children's education, talents, and interests. Partnerships are particularly important at times of transition when children and their families move to new schools or are promoted from one grade level to the next. To do their best for their children, families need good information about their children's development, school programs, community services, and how to help at home at every grade level.

4. **Students are key to the success of school, family, and community partnerships.** Not only are students the reason for partnerships, they also are essential partners. Students are important couriers, messengers, interpreters, negotiators, interviewers, decision makers, and discussants in school, family, and community partnership activities for all six types of involvement. Students help teachers, counselors, and administrators reach their families, and they help their families communicate with their schools. They often are the main source of information for families about school and community programs. Without students' participation in communications between school and home, there will be few successful partnerships of any type at any grade level. Most important, students are the main actors in their own education and, ultimately, in charge of their own success in school. Still, teachers, parents, and others in the community must work with students and with each other to help students succeed.

5. **The community is important for the success of partnership programs.** *Community* extends from the family to the school, to the neighborhood, city, and all of society. The vastness of the term means that every school, district, or state must identify its community and design productive connections that will strengthen the school programs, assist families and students, and advance the interests of the community.

Community resources include people, programs, policies, facilities, finances, and other less tangible norms, beliefs, and attitudes that can be targeted to help students succeed. Business partners; cultural, civic, religious, and educational groups; the media; and others in the community may contribute to comprehensive partnership programs in ways that help prevent students' academic and behavioral problems and that promote student success. All communities, not just wealthy ones, have traditions, talents, and opportunities that can be organized to enrich the lives of children.

Community also is an attitude and a feeling of connectedness. When educators, parents, other citizens, and organizations work together to help students succeed, they strengthen the sense of community in and beyond the school.

6. **Developing and implementing programs and practices of school, family, and community partnerships are processes, not events.** Programs of partnership are developed over time, not overnight. It takes time to plan, implement, evaluate, and improve school-level partnership programs. It takes time to develop insightful and facilitative district and state policies, organize staff, implement inservice education, award grants, and conduct conferences and other leadership activities

that support and assist all schools. Planned programs make the difference in whether, which, and how families and communities become involved in children's education. About three to five years are needed for schools, districts, and states to establish strong leadership and effective processes for school, family, and community partnerships. After that, annual plans and continuous attention are needed to sustain excellent programs of partnership.

7. **School, family, and community partnerships** *focus on results* **to help students succeed in school.** After establishing a welcoming school environment that sends messages of trust, respect, and welcome to all families, schools' programs of partnership must focus on results for student success in school. Annual plans for school, family, and community partnerships must include activities that involve families and communities in productive ways to help promote, improve, or maintain school goals and high standards for student success. It is no longer enough to count "bodies in the school building" to measure family involvement. Involvement activities must be balanced to include some conducted at school, at home through homework, and in community settings. Involvement activities may be designed to help students increase skills in reading, math, writing, or other subjects. Or, productive partnerships may focus on improving student attendance, behavior, or attitudes toward school and learning so that students are in school, on time, and motivated to learn and do their best.

A focus on results requires schools, districts, and state departments of education to monitor the quality of partnership programs and to measure the impact of family and community involvement on student success. Clear measures are needed, first, of the quality of involvement activities to learn whether planned activities are implemented, who is involved and who is excluded, and how well the activities are conducted. Next, clear measures of results are needed to learn whether there are added benefits for all or some students or others as a result of participating in the activities that are implemented. This "two-step" approach to evaluation ensures that results will not be expected unless activities are effectively implemented. A focus on results affirms that involvement activities will be periodically reviewed and continually improved.

8. **School, family, and community partnerships** *do not* **substitute for other school improvements and innovations that are needed to increase student learning and success.** The best way to ensure student success and high achievement is for all students to have excellent teachers every day, every year, in every subject. Schools must provide *all* students with talented teachers; challenging curriculum; effective instruction; up-to-date technology; equal opportunities to learn; responsive assessments; enriching educational resources and activities; *and* excellent school, family, and community partnerships.

In sum, school, family, and community partnerships are about children, include all families, at all grade levels, give key roles to students, involve the community, are planned and ongoing, and are evaluated for their quality and results. *Along with* all other aspects of excellent schools and excellent teaching, school, family, and community partnerships are necessary for increasing students' test scores, reducing dropout rates, improving attendance, or increasing other indicators of student success. The eight conclusions lead, full circle, back to the first chapter's list of facts and call for action for better professional preparation of educators about school, family, and community partnerships.

QUESTIONS TO DISCUSS

1. Based on the eight conclusions listed above and your other readings, in the chart below list one reason why each of the following *IS* important in a comprehensive program of partnership. Then, list one reason why each focus *IS NOT enough* for ensuring trust, respect, equity, and diversity in programs of partnership.

Focus	Why is this important?	Why is it not enough for a comprehensive partnership program?
a. Involve parents of young children		
b. Involve families in workshops on parenting		
c. Involve well-educated families who understand schools		
d. Involve families when students are in trouble		
e. Involve families and the community in one big event at school each year		
f. Involve families and the community to improve public relations		
g. Involve teachers in decisions about new curriculum, new instruction, and new tests		

2. Discuss classmates' ideas of why each focus is necessary but not sufficient in excellent programs of partnership.

▯┋ COMMENT

20/20 Vision of School, Family, and Community Partnerships

Today's students are tomorrow's parents. They are witnessing and experiencing how their schools treat their families and how their families treat the schools. They are learning by example how parents are involved at school and at home in their children's education.

In 10 years, some elementary school students (now 6–10 years old), more middle-grade students (now 11–14 years old), and many high school students (now 15–18 years old) will be parents. By 2020, many of their children will be in daycare, preschool, and elementary school. Will tomorrow's parents be good partners with their children's schools? Will the schools be good partners with tomorrow's parents?

QUESTIONS TO DISCUSS

Based on the articles that you read and the discussions and activities that you conducted, how do you think school, family, and community partnerships *should be* conducted in the future?

1. Identify a school level that interests you (i.e., preschool, elementary, middle, or high).
2. For the school level you selected, address this theme: *In the year 2020, how should schools connect with families and communities? How should parents connect with their children's schools, interact with educators, and influence their children's education?*
   A. Write an essay on your vision of ideal school, family, and community partnerships in 2020.
   B. Include ideas about the policies and actions that will be needed to realize your vision. These may include school, district, state, and/or federal policies; educators' preparation; family factors and approaches; and other requirements.
   C. How likely is it that your vision of school, family, and community partnerships will be fulfilled by 2020? Explain.

▯⁝ COMMENT

Shaping the Future

We cannot change past patterns of school, family, and community partnerships, but we can shape the future. This includes improving preservice, advanced, and inservice education so that all teachers and administrators understand school, family, and community partnerships and can apply what they know.

From all of the studies, fieldwork, discussions, and activities discussed in this volume, one thing is very clear. It is unreasonable to expect parents, on their own, to create the knowledge needed every year to interact productively with their children as students or to connect with their children's schools and teachers. By contrast, it *is* reasonable to expect all schools, districts, and state departments of education to organize ongoing programs of school, family, and community partnerships so that all parents are well informed and productively involved every year with their children and schools.

This volume for preparing educators to understand school, family, and community partnerships takes readers one step toward improving policies and practices of involvement. When well-prepared teachers, administrators, counselors, and other professionals take positions in schools, districts, and state departments of education, the real work to organize, implement, and sustain programs of partnership begins.

Index

Spock, Benjamin, 25
Standards
    for teacher credentials, 389–391
    personal and universal, 31–33
Standards Revisions Teacher Education
        and Certification (Ohio), 8
State leadership and policy
    action teams and, 574
    diverse state policies, 314–320
    funding options for programs, 358
    linking policy and practice, 347–351,
        354
    organization of leadership, 375–376
    partnership activities, 362–367,
        374–375
    policy and programs, 304, 309–314
    readings, 398
    review of, 387–389
    role in partnerships, 319
    school improvement plans, 369–375
    support of parent involvement, 307–308
    teaching credential standards, 391
Stereotypes, 45
    of parents, 114–117
    teacher practices and, 265
Strengths model, of family functioning,
        178–179
Student-parent-teacher conferences, 436,
        444–446, 458–459
Students
    action teams and, 573
    adults' perception of partnerships, 100
    attitudes toward parent involvement,
        253–261
    characteristics affecting family
        involvement, 142–143, 143(table),
        212
    communications, 439–440
    community employment, 477–478
    community groups, 475–476
    developing responsibility, 127–128
    effects of partnerships on, 295–297
    evaluation of teacher practices,
        257(table), 340
    expected results of involvement,
        414–415(table)
    factors affecting achievement, 221–233,
        225(table), 227(table), 229(table),
        231(table)

families' obligations to, 135–137
from partnerships to success, 494–505
funding allocations for partnership
    programs, 356–362, 359(table)
goal setting, 462–463
grade level and parent involvement,
    113–114
homework attitude, 247–248
homework time, 214–217, 216(table)
language as barrier to learning,
    394–395, 554
mapping success, 498–499
mutual respect, 86
of single-parent homes, 178–179
overlapping spheres, 83–84
partnership role, 60–62, 66–67, 93, 601
perception of, 403–405
student mobility, 291–292
student-parent-teacher conferences, 436,
    444–446, 458–459
subject specificity and achievement,
    266–267
teacher evaluation of homework,
    191–195, 193(table), 194(table)
time for family involvement,
    122–123
TIPS program goals, 521(table)
See also Families; Homework; Single-
    parent homes; Teacher practices
Subject areas, 523–527
    effect on parent programs, 148
    family involvement education, 11–12
    grade level and, 289–290
    home involvement, 11–12, 93–94,
        117–118
    impact of homework, 241
    improving definition of knowledge of,
        52–53
    research across academic disciplines,
        41–42
    responsibility of teaching, 87–89
    specificity of family involvement, 45–46
    subject specific achievement, 266–267,
        511–512
    teachers' involvement practices,
        144–145
    See also Art; Language arts; Math;
        Science; Social studies
Suburban schools, 385–386